新航道 NEW CHANNEL

MW01688468

新托福

词汇精选

TOEFL® iBT

■胡 敏 编著

CTPC 中国出版集团
中国对外翻译出版公司

图书在版编目(CIP)数据

新托福词汇精选/胡敏编著.—北京:中国对外翻译出版公司,2008.4

ISBN 978-7-5001-1937-1

Ⅰ.新... Ⅱ.胡... Ⅲ.英语—词汇—高等教育—自学参考资料

Ⅳ.H313

中国版本图书馆CIP数据核字(2008)第043041号

出版发行/中国对外翻译出版公司

地　　址/北京市西城区车公庄大街甲4号物华大厦六层

电　　话/(010)68359376　68359303　68359101　68357937

邮　　编/100044

传　　真/(010)68357870

电子邮箱/book@ctpc.com.cn

网　　址/http://www.ctpc.com.cn

责任编辑/韦　莉　刘　琦

责任校对/李　鲜

印　　刷/保定华泰印刷有限公司印刷

经　　销/新华书店

规　　格/787×1092毫米　1/16

印　　张/36

版　　次/2008年4月第1版

印　　次/2008年8月第2次

ISBN 978-7-5001-1937-1　　定价:45.00元

中国对外翻译出版公司

给你一双隐形的翅膀（代序）

前不久在新航道学校的联欢会上偶然听到同事们唱起张韶涵的这首流行歌曲时，我被深深地感动了。我相信所有参加托福考试的考生都有自己“恒久比天长”的梦想，也都会经历徘徊和孤单，但是只要你坚信自己有一双隐形的翅膀，总有一天你会飞翔！

对于备考新托福的人来说，词汇仍然是大家需要过的第一关。许多人经常是在这第一关徘徊、绝望。我们今年推出的这本新托福词汇书将会帮助大家走出绝望。

本书的特点

一、词条的选择新颖而全面

本书收录的大约3500个词条是根据编者对新托福考试真题的研究，并大量参考国内外的同类词汇书，精心选择的。加上同义词、反义词和派生词，词汇总量在9000个左右，可以完全覆盖新托福考试的各个部分。由于社会生活的变化和语言的发展，一些旧词添新义，也是值得广大考生特别注意的地方，所以本书还特别添加了一些常用词的新的义项。比如equity，以前的托福词汇书的释义都只有“公平，公正”这一个解释，但是这个词现在用得更广的意思是“证券”，只要在google里面一搜索，绝大部分的与equity相关的链接，比如equity market（证券市场）和private equity（私募股权投资）等都是和证券有关的。

二、例句的选择独立而易记

新托福是从听、说、读、写四个方面来考察学生综合应用英语的能力。就词汇方面来看，既要求考生有一定的词汇量，又要求熟练掌握一些核心词的用法，所以使用单词的语境更重要。记单词要在语境里面记，所以我们从权威的词典（主要是《牛津高阶英汉双解词典》和《朗文当代高级英语辞典》）精选出了可以在独立的小语境下理解的句子，并且例句尽可能地短小，来帮助大家记住单词的运用环境，如果某个单词有几个义项，就有不同的例句对应不同的义项。每个例句都有中文翻译，这样更符合中国人学英语的习惯。

三、词根词缀的记忆科学而权威

除了一些单音节词，本书的绝大部分单词都有科学可靠的词根和词缀记忆方法。编者大量翻阅权威的词根词缀专业书，查找国内外官方词典网站，力求每一个词根词缀都有它有据可考的出处。这是目前为止在词根词缀记忆方面做得最好的一本托福词汇书。它不仅可以帮助你轻松记忆词条上的主词，还能够让你对英语单词的构成有一个系统的认识，而不是随便联想。通过对一些主要的词根词缀的记忆，可以让你触类旁通，即使以后遇到不认识的生词，也能够举一反三，科学猜词。

四、同义词、反义词和派生词丰富而不生僻

单词不能孤立地记，因为单词不能孤立地存在，它总是会和其他的词发生关系，如同义关系、反义关系和派生关系等。所以本书特别添加了同义词、反义词和派生词和核心主词一起记忆，这样不仅可以记住核心的主词，还能同时迅速扩大词汇量，可以起到事半功倍的效果。本书的同义词、反义词和派生词虽然丰富，但是根据我们对托福真题的研究，所选的同义词和反义词都力求在托福的考察范围之内，决不生僻。同义词、反义词主要选自《牛津英语同义词词典》和 *the Merriam-Webster Dictionary of Synonyms and Antonyms*，派生词主要选自《英汉大词典》。

五、附录的分类词汇表全面而实用

本书后面的附录词汇表是按照不同的领域进行分类总结的，涉及了托福考试各个部分的各个领域，释义准确而简单。但是因为专业性较强，不必花时间记忆，只是为了便于大家在需要的时候查找使用。

本书在编写过程中参考了大量国内外相关的词典、书籍和网站，无法一一注明，在此谨表示感谢！虽然已经过编、译、审、校，多次修改，力求审慎，但恐仍有疏漏之处，恳请读者予以赐正。

我在歌曲优美的旋律中完成了这篇序言，真诚地希望本书能成为你隐形的翅膀，帮你飞过绝望，让所有梦想都开花结果。

北京新航道学校校长

目录

Contents

A

abandon [ə'bændən] *v*. 放弃，遗弃

【记】 a(= ad，不) + bandon(控制)→不再控制→放弃

【例】 When the fire got out of control，the captain told the sailors to *abandon* the ship. 当火势已无法控制时，船长吩咐水手们弃船逃生。

【同】 desert，forsake，give up

【反】 maintain，reclaim

abash [ə'bæʃ] *v*. 使羞愧，使窘迫

【记】 a(= ex，向外) + bash(惊呆)→使惊呆→使窘迫

【例】 His boss's criticism left him feeling rather *abashed*. 老板批评了他，他感到有些难为情。

【同】 embarrass，shame

【反】 ease

【派】 abashed *adj*. 羞愧的，局促不安的

abate [ə'beɪt] *v*. (数量、程度等)减少，减轻，缓解

【记】 a(= to) + bate(打击)→进行打击→减少，减轻

【例】 People are campaigning to *abate* the noise in our cities. 大家正在进行一场减少城市噪音的运动。

【同】 decrease，lessen，diminish

【反】 add，raise

【派】 abatement *n*. 消除

abbreviate [ə'bri:vɪeɪt] *v*. 缩短，缩写

【记】 ab(= to) + brevi(短) + ate(动词词尾)→使变短→缩略

【例】 The United States of America is commonly *abbreviated* to the USA . 美利坚合众国常被缩略为 USA。

【同】 shorten，abridge

【反】 lengthen，amplify

【派】 abbreviation *n*. 缩略，缩写词

abdicate ['æbdɪkeɪt] *v*. 1. 让位，辞职；2. 放弃(权利或责任)

【记】 ab(离开) + dict(说) + ate(动词词尾)→宣布离开 →辞职

【例】 1. King Edward VIII *abdicated* in 1936. 英王爱德华八世于 1936 年退位。

2. He's *abdicated* all responsibility in the affair. 他已经放弃了这件事中的一切职责。

【同】 resign；relinquish，renounce，abandon

【派】 abdication *n*. 退位，让位；弃权

abduct [æb'dʌkt] *v*. 绑架，拐走

【记】 ab(离开)＋duct(引领，带领)→带走→拐走

【例】 The police think the boy has been *abducted*. 警察认为那个孩子已被绑架了。

【同】 kidnap

【派】 abduction *n*. 诱拐，绑架

abet [ə'bet] *v*. (-tted；-tting)1. 教唆，唆使；2. 帮助，支持

【记】 a(= to)＋bet(诱饵)→给以诱饵→教唆

【例】 1. He was *abetted* in these illegal activities by his wife. 他受妻子怂恿进行这些非法活动。

2. The police say he aided and *abetted* the robber in robbing the bank. 警方说他伙同该匪徒抢劫银行。

【同】 advocate，encourage；assist

【派】 abetment *n*. 教唆，煽动；帮助，支持

abide [ə'baɪd] *v*. (-d，-d；或 abode，abode)1. 容忍，经受住；2. 遵守，服从

【记】 a(加强语气)＋bide(忍受)→容忍

【例】 1. How could you *abide* such conditions? 这种环境你怎么受得了呢？

2. If you join the club you must *abide* by its rules. 如果你参加俱乐部，就必须遵守它的规章制度。

【同】 endure，tolerate；accept，obey

【派】 abidance *n*. 遵守，持续

abiding *adj*. 持久不变的，永久的

abnormal [æb'nɔːməl] *adj*. 反常的，非常态的

【记】 ab(离开)＋norm(标准)＋al(形容词词尾)→离开标准的→反常的

【例】 We do not think such an *abnormal* phenomenon will last long. 我们认为这样的反常现象不会持续很久。

【同】 aberrant，weird

【反】 normal

【派】 abnormality *n*. 反常，变态，畸形

aboard [ə'bɔːd] *adv*./*prep*. 在船(飞机、车)上

【记】 a(= on，…上)＋board(甲板)→在甲板上→在船上

【例】 The plane crashed，killing all 200 people *aboard*. 飞机坠毁了，机上 200 人全部遇难。

【同】 onboard

【反】 ashore

abolish [ə'bɒlɪʃ] *v*. 废除，取消

【记】 ab(离开)＋ol(长大)＋ish(动词词尾)→使不再长大→废除

【例】 Should the death penalty be *abolished*? 应该废除死刑吗？

【同】 annul，exterminate，do away with

【反】 create，establish

【派】 abolition *n*. 废除，废止

aboriginal [ˌæbəˈrɪdʒənəl] *adj*. 土著的，土著居民的；*n*. 土著居民，土生动物(或植物)

【记】 ab(来自)+origin(起源，出身)+al(形容词词尾)→始于最初的的→土著的

【例】 This book describes the creativity of *aboriginal* people living in the driest parts of Australia. 这本书描述了居住于澳大利亚最干旱地区的土著居民的创造力。

【同】 native，indigenous

【反】 alien(外国的)

abort [əˈbɔːt] *v*. 1. 流产，堕胎；2. 中途失败，夭折

【记】 ab(离开)+ort(开始，生长)→离开生长→不再发育→流产

【例】 1. The doctor had to *abort* the baby. 医生不得不打掉胎儿。

2. The space flight had to be *aborted* because of difficulties of the computer. 由于电脑方面的故障，这次太空飞行不得不中止。

【派】 abortion *n*. 流产，夭折；失败，中止

abortive *adj*. 早产的；失败的，无结果的

abound [əˈbaʊnd] *v*. 充满，富于

【记】 ab(离开)+o+und(波浪)→像波浪一样铺开去→充满

【例】 Oranges *abound* here all the year round. 这儿一年到头都有很多橙子。

【派】 abounding *adj*. 丰富的，大量的

abrade [əˈbreɪd] *v*. 磨损，刮擦

【记】 ab(去掉)+ras(刮，擦)+ion(名词词尾)→擦掉→磨损

【例】 Sharp edges might *abrade* string and cause the string to eventually break. 锋利的边缘可能会磨损线，最后会把绳子弄断了。

【同】 abrase，wear away

【派】 abrasion *n*. 磨损；磨损处，擦伤处

abrasive *adj*. 研磨的；*n*. 研磨剂

abridge [əˈbrɪdʒ] *v*. 缩短，删节

【记】 a(=to)+bridg(短的)+e→使变短→缩短

【例】 It was *abridged* from the original work. 这是根据原著缩节而成的。

【同】 abbreviate，foreshorten

【反】 extend

【派】 abridgement *n*. 删节，删节本

abroad [əˈbrɔːd] *adv*. 往国外，海外

【记】 a(=on，…上)+broad(宽阔的)→在更宽阔的地方→海外

【例】 Are you going *abroad* for your holidays? 你打算去国外度假吗？

【同】 overseas，internationally

【反】 home

abrupt [əˈbrʌpt] *adj*. 突然的，陡峭的

【记】 ab(离)+rupt(打破)→打破掉的→突然的

【例】 The meeting came to an *abrupt* end. 会议突然结束了。

【同】 sudden, unexpected

absenteeism [æbsən'tiːɪzəm] *n*. 旷课，旷工

【记】 ab(离开) + sent(存在) + ee(人) + ism(名词词尾，表特性)→不在的人的特性→旷课，旷工

【例】 The non-financial incentive scheme did appear to assist in controlling *absenteeism* in the short term. 非金钱激励方案确实使用过，来帮助控制短期旷工(的情况)。

【派】 (逆构)absent *adj*. 不在的，缺席的

absentee *n*. 缺席者，未上班者

absolve [əb'zɒlv] *v*. 1.(宗教上的)宽恕；2.赦免(罪行、过失等)，解除(责任等)

【记】 ab(离开) + solve(松开)→完全松开→宽恕

【例】 The court *absolved* the accused man from all responsibility for her death. 法官判决被告对她的死亡不必负任何责任。

【同】 discharge, excuse

【反】 accuse, blame

【派】 absolvent *adj*. 赦免的

absorb [əb'sɔːb] *v*. 吸收(液体、知识等)

【记】 ab(去掉) + sorb(吸收)→吸收掉→吸收

【例】 Clever children *absorb* knowledge easily. 聪明孩子容易吸收知识。

【同】 assimilate, suck up

【派】 absorption *n*. 吸收

absorbing *adj*. 极有趣的，吸引人的

absorber *n*. 消音装置，隔音设备

abstain [əb'steɪn] *v*. 1.自制，戒绝；2.弃权

【记】 abs(离开) + tain(保持)→不再保持→戒绝

【例】 1. She *abstained* from smoking and drinking for a month. 她有一个月时间烟酒不沾。

2. Five members voted for the proposal, twelve voted against, and three *abstained*. 对于这项建议，5人投票赞成，12人反对，3人弃权。

【同】 refrain

【反】 indulge

【派】 abstinence *n*. 自制，节制(禁欲、戒酒)

abstention *n*. 弃权

abstract ['æbstrækt] *adj*. 1.抽象的；2.难解的，深奥的；*n*. 摘要，梗概

【记】 abs(从) + tract(拉，抽出)→从…抽出的→抽象的

【例】 1. We may talk of beautiful things, but beauty itself is *abstract*. 我们尽可谈论美的事物，然而美本身却是抽象的。

2. Astronomy is an *abstract* subject. 天文学是一门深奥的学科。

3. No *abstract* is available now. 现在还拿不到摘要。

【同】 metaphysical; abstruse, complex

【反】 concrete; easy, obvious

【派】 abstraction *n*. 抽象，抽象概念

abstruse [æb'struːs] *adj*. 难懂的，深奥的

【记】 abs(离开) + trus(推开) + e→推开的→难懂的

【例】 Philosophical semantics is too *abstruse* to understand. 哲学语义学派玄而又玄，无法读懂。

【同】 abstract, profound

【反】 easy, obvious

【派】 abstrusity *n*. 难解，深奥

absurd [əb'sɜːd] *adj*. 荒谬的，可笑的

【记】 ab(离开) + surd(聋)→因听不见而产生荒谬的事件→可笑的

【例】 It was *absurd* of you to suggest such a thing. 你竟提出这种事，真是荒唐。

【同】 ridiculous, ludicrous

【反】 rational, reasonable, sensible

【派】 absurdity *n*. 荒谬，谬论

abundant [ə'bʌndənt] *adj*. 丰富的，充足的，大量的

【记】 ab(加强语气) + und(波动) + ant(形容词词尾)→多得像波浪一样→丰富的

【例】 The country has *abundant* supplies of oil and gas. 这个国家的石油和天然气供应非常充足。

【同】 affluent, rich

【反】 lacking, scarce

【派】 abundance *n*. 丰富，充足

abuse [ə'bjuːz] *v*./*n*. 1.滥用，妄用；2.虐待，伤害；3.辱骂

【记】 ab(离开) + use(使用)→离开正确用法→滥用

【例】 1. Politicians should beware of the *abuse* of power. 从政的人应该警惕，不得滥用权力。

2. Child *abuse* was virtually eliminated. 虐待儿童的现象几乎杜绝了。

3. She *abused* him roundly for his neglect. 他因疏忽而被她痛骂了一顿。

【同】 misuse; ill-treat, maltreat; curse

【派】 abusive *adj*. 辱骂的，毁谤的；虐待的

abut [ə'bʌt] *v*. (-tted; -tting)邻接，毗邻

【记】 a(= to) + but(终端)→使终端在一起→毗邻

【例】 His land *abuts* on the motorway. 他的土地和高速公路毗连。

【同】 border

abyss [ə'bɪs] *n*. 深渊，深坑

【记】 a(没有，无) + byss(底)→没有底的→深渊

【例】 He has been in the *abyss* of despair. 他已陷入绝望的深渊。

【同】 gap, pit

【派】 abyssal *adj*. 深渊的；极度悲惨(恶劣，卑下)的

academic [ˌækə'demɪk] *adj*. 1.学院的，学术的；2.理论的

【记】 academ(学院) + ic(形容词词尾)→学院的

【例】 1. In Britain the *academic* year runs from October to July. 英国的学年是从十月到七月。

2. Where we ought to go for our holidays is a purely *academic* question because we can't afford a holiday at all! 我们应该到何处去度假纯粹是个理论上的问题，因为我们根本没钱度假。

【同】 educational；theoretical

【反】 practical

【派】 academia *n*. 学术界；学术生涯

academy *n*. 学院

academician *n*. 学会会员；院士；学者

accelerate [æk'seləreɪt] *v*. 1. 加快，加速；2. 促进，促使…早日发生

【记】 ac(= ad, to) + celer(快速的) + ate(动词词尾)→使快速→加快

【例】 1. The car *accelerated* as it overtook me. 那辆汽车一加速就超越了我。

2. The factory must *accelerate* production. 工厂必须促进生产。

【同】 hasten, quicken, speed up; promote, stimulate

【反】 decelerate, retard

【派】 acceleration *n*. 加速，加速度；促进

accelerator *n*. 加速者，加速器

accentuate [æk'sentjʊeɪt] *v*. 1. 突出(某事物)；2. 强调

【记】 ac(= ad, to) + cent(唱) + u + ate(动词词尾)→把…唱出来→突出

【例】 1. Her black hair *accentuated* the whiteness of her skin. 她的黑头发更显出皮肤的白皙。

2. Try to *accentuate* the positve aspects. 努力强调那些积极的方面。

【同】 emphasize, stress, highlight

【派】 accentuation *n*. 强调，加强

access ['ækses] *n*. 1. 入口，进入；2. 接近(或进入)的机会

【记】 ac(= ad, to) + cess(去)→向…去→接近

【例】 1. The only *access* to the farmhouse is across the fields. 要到那农舍去唯有穿过田地。

2. Citizens may have free *access* to the library. 市民可以自由使用图书馆。

【同】 entrance, entry

【派】 accessible *adj*. 易接近的，能进入的

accessory *adj*. 附加的，补充的；*n*. 附件，零件；帮凶，从犯

accessibility *n*. 易接近；可到达

accidental [ˌæksɪ'dentl] *adj*. 意外的，偶然的

【记】 ac(= ad, to) + cid(落下) + ent(事) + al(形容词词尾)→落到头上的事→意外的

【例】 Their marriage was quite *accidental*. 他们的结合是很偶然的。

【同】 fortuitous, incidental, adventitious

【反】 intentional, planned

acclaim [ə'kleɪm] *v*. 欢呼，喝彩；*n*. 赞誉，赞许

【记】 ac(= ad, to) + claim(大叫)→大叫出来→欢呼

【例】 1. The new drug has been *acclaimed* as the most important discovery for years. 这种新药很受欢迎，被认为是近年来最重要的发明。

2. The book received great critical *acclaim*. 这本书大获评论界的赞扬。

【同】 applaud, approve

【派】 acclamation *n*. 欢呼(声)，喝彩(声)

acclamatory *adj*. 欢呼的，称赞的

acclaimed *adj*. 受赞誉的

accommodate [əˈkɒmədeɪt] *v*. 1. 容纳，供应(住宿)；2. 使适应，迁就

【记】 ac(= ad, to) + com(共同) + mod(方法) + ate(动词词尾)→使…用共同的方法→使…适应

【例】 1. This hotel can *accommodate* up to 500 guests. 这旅馆可供 500 位来宾住宿。

2. I will *accommodate* my plans to yours. 我修改一下计划以便和你的计划相适应。

【同】 adapt

【派】 accommodation *n*. 住处，膳宿

accommodating *adj*. 与人方便的，肯通融的

accompany [əˈkʌmpənɪ] *v*. 1. 陪伴，陪同；2. 伴奏；3. 和…一起发生(或存在)

【记】 ac(= ad, to) + com(共同) + pan(面包) + y→共同吃面包→陪伴

【例】 1. I must ask you to *accompany* me to the police station. 我得要求你陪我去一趟警察局。

2. Mary sang and I *accompanied* her on the piano. 玛丽唱歌，我弹琴给她伴奏。

3. Each application should be *accompanied* by a stamped addressed envelop. 每份申请书均须附回邮信封，贴上邮票，写好地址。

【同】 attend

【派】 accompaniment *n*. 伴随发生的事物；伴奏，伴唱

accomplice [əˈkɒmplɪs] *n*. 同谋者，帮凶

【记】 ac(= ad, to) + com(一起) + plic(折叠) + e→一起折叠的人→共同做事的人→帮凶

【例】 The police arrested him and his two *accomplices*. 警方逮捕了他和他的两个同谋。

【同】 accessory

accomplish [əˈkɒmplɪʃ] *v*. 1. 完成(任务等)；2. 达到(目的)，做到

【记】 ac(= ad, to) + com(共同) + pl(i)(充满) + ish(动词词尾)→来共同充满→完成

【例】 1. You should *accomplish* the task within the allotted time. 你们必须在规定时间内完成这项任务。

2. I don't feel our visit really has *accomplished* anything. 我觉得我们的访问什么成效也没有。

【同】 achieve, complete, fulfill, finish

【派】 accomplishment *n*. 成就

accomplishable *adj*. 可完成的，可达成的

accomplished *adj*. 完成了的，已实现的；有才艺的

accost [əˈkɒst] *v*. 向人搭话

【记】 ac(= ad, to) + cost(= rib, 肋骨，侧面)→走向某人→搭讪

【例】 She was *accosted* by a complete stranger. 有一个她完全不认识的人过来跟她搭讪。

account [əˈkaʊnt] *n*. 1. 讲述，描述，说明；2. 账户，账单；3. 理由，根据
v. 1. 解释，说明；2. 占(比例)

【记】 ac(= ad, to) + count(计算)→ 把…数进去→账

【例】 1. She gave the police a full *account* of the incident. 她把事件向警方作了详细叙述。

2. My salary is paid directly into my bank *account*. 付给我的工资直接存入我的银行账户。

3. We delayed our departure on *account* of the bad weather. 由于天气不好，我们将启程的时间推迟了。

4. How do you *account* for losing five games in a row? 你怎么解释一连输了五场比赛呢?

5. Coal is expected to continue to *account* for almost 27 per cent of the world's energy needs. 预计煤炭将继续在全世界的能量需求里占约 27%的比例。

【同】 description；list，sum；explain

【派】 accountancy *n*. 会计工作，会计职务
accountant *n*. 会计人员，会计师
accountable *adj*. 应作解释的，负有责任的

accredit [əˈkredɪt] *v*. 1. 授权，委派；2. 鉴定…为合格，确认…达到标准；3. 归功(某事)于(某人)，把…归于

【记】 ac(= ad, to) + credit(相信)→对…相信→委派

【例】 1. He was *accredited* to/at Madrid. 他被委任为驻马德里的大使。

2. The school was *accredited* and allied with another college. 那所学校经鉴定合格，同另一所学院挂了钩。

3. He is *accredited* with having first introduced this word into the language. 是他在这个语言中首先使用这个词的。

【同】 appoint；certify；ascribe，attribute

【派】 accreditation *n*. 委托，任命；资格鉴定，认证
accredited *adj*. 可信任的，官方认可的

accrue [əˈkruː] *v*. 自然增长或利益增加，积累

【记】 ac(= ad, to) + crue(生长)→增长

【例】 Interest will *accrue* if you keep your money in a savings account. 把钱存在储蓄账户里就会生息。

【同】 grow，accumulate

【反】 fall

【派】 accrual *n*. 自然增长；获利

accumulate [əˈkjuːmjʊleɪt] *v*. 堆积，积累

【记】 ac(= ad, to) + cumulate(= heap up, 堆积)→积累

【例】 By investing wisely she *accumulated* a fortune. 她由于投资精明而积蓄了一笔财产。

【同】 gather, collect, assemble

【反】 dissipate, waste

【派】 accumulation *n*. 堆积，积累，积聚

accumulative *adj*. 积累而成的，累积(性)的

accurate [ˈækjʊrɪt] *adj*. 准确的，精确的

【记】 ac(= ad, to) + cur(注意，留心)→非常小心的→准确的

【例】 Her report of what happened was *accurate* in every detail. 她对发生的情况所作的报告，其全部细节都是准确的。

【同】 correct, perfect

【反】 inaccurate, incorrect

【派】 accuracy *n*. 准确(性)，精确(性)

accuse [əˈkjuːz] *v*. 1.指控控告；2.指责，归咎

【记】 ac(= ad, to) + cuse(案子)→提交案子→指控

【例】 1. He was *accused* of murder. 他被控犯了谋杀罪。

2. The report *accused* the government of shirking its responsibilities. 这份报告指责政府推卸责任。

【同】 charge, blame

【派】 accusation *n*. 控告，谴责

accused *adj*. 被控告的；*n*. 被告

accustom [əˈkʌstəm] *v*. 使习惯于…

【记】 ac(= ad, to) + custom(习惯)→使习惯于

【例】 He quickly *accustomed* himself to this new way of life. 他很快就习惯了这种新的生活方式。

【同】 adapt, adjust, get used to

【派】 accustomed *adj*. 习惯的，通常的

acid [ˈæsɪd] *n*. 酸，酸味物质；*adj*. 1.酸的；2.尖酸的，刻薄的

【例】 1. Some *acids* burn holes in wood. 有些酸能把木头烧成洞。

2. Lemons taste *acid*. 柠檬的味道是酸的。

3. She has an *acid* tongue. 她的嘴巴很刻薄。

【同】 sour, vinegary; sharp

acknowledge [əkˈnɒlɪdʒ] *v*. 1.承认；2.就…表示谢忱，报偿

【记】 ac(= ad, to) + know(知道) + ledge(名词词尾)→使…知道→承认

【例】 1. Joe is *acknowledged* as the best basketball player of the year. 乔被公认为是今年最佳篮球选手。

2. His services to the country were never officially *acknowledged*. 他对国家所做的贡献从未受到过正式的表彰。

【同】 recognize, admit; grant

【反】 deny, disregard

【派】 acknowledg(e)ment *n*. 承认；(作者的)致谢

acquaint [əˈkweɪnt] *v*. 使认识，使了解

【记】 ac(= ad, to) + quaint(知道)→使知道→使认识

【例】 The lawyer *acquainted* himself with the details of his client's business affairs. 那位律师了解委托人生意上的详情。

【同】 inform

【派】 acquaintance *n*. 认识，了解；熟人

acquiesce [ˌækwɪˈes] *v*. 默认，默许，顺从

【记】 ac(= ad, to) + qui(安静) + esce(拉丁文动词词尾)→向…沉默→默许

【例】 Her parents will never *acquiesce* in such an unsuitable marriage. 她的父母决不会答应这门不相宜的婚事。

【同】 consent, assent, accede

【反】 object, dissent

【派】 acquiescence *n*. 默认，默许，顺从

acquiescent *adj*. 默认的，默许的，顺从的

acquire [əˈkwaɪə] *v*. 取得，获得，学到(知识等)

【记】 ac(= ad, to) + quire(追求)→去求得→取得

【例】 The company has recently *acquired* new offices in central London. 公司最近在伦敦市中心弄到了新的办公室。

【同】 get, gain, obtain

【反】 lose, miss

【派】 acquisition *n*. 获得，获得物；收购

acquisitive *adj*. (对知识、财富等)渴望得到的；贪婪的

acquit [əˈkwɪt] *v*. 宣告无罪

【记】 ac(= ad, to) + quit(自由)→使…自由→宣告无罪

【例】 The jury *acquitted* him of murder. 陪审团宣告他谋杀罪不成立。

【同】 absolve, discharge

【反】 convict

【派】 acquittal *n*. 宣判无罪

acrobatic [ˌækrəʊˈbætɪk] *adj*. 杂技的，杂技演员的

【记】 acro(高) + bat(走) + ic(形容词词尾)→在高处走的→杂技的

【例】 There are no animals—just very talented clowning and *acrobatic* routines. 这里没有动物——只是一些很有才华的小丑表演和一般的杂技表演。

【派】 acrobatics *n*. 杂技

activate [ˈæktɪveɪt] *v*. 激活，使活动

【记】 act(行动) + i + ate(动词词尾)→使行动起来→激活

【例】 Such behavior *activates* many different parts of the brain. 这些行为激活大脑许多不同的部分。

【同】 excite, actuate, trigger

【派】 activation *n*. 活化，激活

activator *n*. 触媒，催化剂

actuate [ˈæktjʊeɪt] *v*. 使(某人)行动，促使

【记】 act(行动) + u + ate(动词词尾)→使…行动→开动，行动

【例】 He was *actuated* solely by greed. 他完全是受了贪欲的驱使。

【同】 activate, trigger

acumen [əˈkjuːmən] *n*. 敏锐，聪明，才智

【记】 acu(尖的) + men(名词词尾)→尖的东西→敏锐，聪明

【例】 Her business *acumen* has made her very successful. 她灵活的经商头脑使她的生意十分兴隆。

【同】 intelligence, insightfulness

acute [əˈkjuːt] *adj*. 1. 尖锐的，敏锐的；2.(疾病等)急性的，剧烈的

【记】 acu(尖的) + te(形容词词尾)→有尖的→尖锐的

【例】 1. She still has very *acute* hearing, though she is eighty years old. 尽管她已经 80 岁了，但她的听觉仍然很灵敏。

2. The old and ill are the most vulnerable to the *acute* effects of heavily polluted stagnant air. 当重度污染且滞留不去的空气造成严重影响时，老人和病人最容易受到伤害。

【同】 keen, sharp; fierce, severe

【反】 dull, blunt; chronic

adage [ˈædɪdʒ] *n*. 谚语，格言

【记】 ad(to) + age(说)→说的话→格言，谚语

【例】 'The athlete must choose his parents carefully.' says Jesus Dapena, invoking an oft-cited *adage*. "运动员必须慎重选择自己的父母。"杰瑟斯·达皮纳说，他援引了一句常引用的格言。

【同】 proverb

adamant [ˈædəmənt] *adj*. 倔强的，坚定不移的

【记】 a(= not, 不) + dam(屈从) + ant(形容词词尾)→不屈从的→坚定不移的

【例】 He was *adamant* in his determination to punish the corrupt officials. 他下了决心，坚决惩治那些贪官污吏。

【同】 inflexible, persistent

【反】 yielding

adapt [əˈdæpt] *v*. 1. 使适应，使适合；2. 改编，改写

【记】 ad(to) + apt(适当)→使适当→使适应

【例】 1. This machine has been specially *adapted* for use underwater. 这机器是为水下使用而特别改装的。

2. This novel has been *adapted* for radio from the Russian original. 这部小说已由俄文原著改编成无线电广播节目。

【同】 adjust, conform; rewrite

【派】 adaptability *n*. 适应性，顺应性

adaptable *adj*. 能适应新环境的，适应性强的；可改编的

adaptation *n*. 适应，改编

adaptive *adj*. 适应的

addict [ə'dɪkt] *v*. 使沉溺，使成瘾

【记】 ad(to) + dict(说)→说了还说→沉溺

【例】 My children are hopelessly *addicted* to television. 我的孩子们都成了电视迷，简直是不可救药了。

【派】 addiction *n*. 上瘾

addicted *adj*. 入了迷的，上瘾的

addictive *adj*. 使人入迷的，使人上瘾的

adept ['ædept,ə'dept] *adj*. 擅长的，熟练的，内行的

【记】 ad(to) + ept(达到)→能够达到的→擅长的

【例】 He was very *adept* at making up excuses for his lateness. 他非常擅长为自己的迟到编造借口。

【同】 skillful, proficient, skilled

【反】 unskillful, inept

adequate ['ædɪkwɪt] *adj*. 足够的，适当的

【记】 ad(to) + equ(相等的) + ate(形容词词尾)→使达到相等的→足够的

【例】 Our accommodation is barely *adequate*. 我们的住房不太够用。

【同】 enough, sufficient, plenty

【反】 inadequate, insufficient

【派】 adequency *n*. 足够；适应

adhere [əd'hɪə] *v*. 1. 粘附；2. 坚持，遵守

【记】 ad(to) + here(粘着)→粘在一起→粘附

【例】 1. Paste is used to make one surface *adhere* to another. 糨糊是用于使一个接触面粘住另一个接触面的。

2. They failed to *adhere* to our original agreement. 他们未能遵守我们原定的协议。

【同】 cling, stick

【派】 adherence *n*. 坚持；信奉

adherent *adj*. 粘着的，附着的；*n*. 信徒，拥护者

adhesive *adj*. 黏的，粘着的；*n*. 粘合剂

adjacent [ə'dʒeɪsənt] *adj*. 附近的，毗邻的

【记】 ad(to) + jac(投掷) + ent(形容词词尾)→能投掷的范围→附近的

【例】 The council offices are *adjacent* to the library. 市政会各办公室就在图书馆旁边。

【同】 adjoining, near

【派】 adjacency *n*. 邻近的地方，四周

adjoin [ə'dʒɔɪn] *v*. 相邻，临近

【记】 ad(to) + join(连接)→连接

【例】 The playing-field *adjoins* the school. 运动场紧靠着学校。

【同】 border, connect

【派】 adjoining *adj*. 毗邻的

adjourn [ə'dʒɜːn] *v*. 延期，休会

【记】 ad(= to) + journ(日)→给些日子→推迟日期→延期

【例】 The trial was *adjourned* until the following week. 审讯暂停，下星期继续进行。

【同】 postpone, recess

【派】 adjournment *n*. 休会，延期

adjunct [ˈædʒʌŋkt] *n*. 附件，附属，附属物

【记】 ad(= to) + junct(连接)→连接上的东西→附件

【例】 The American Civil War was the first to see railways used as an *adjunct* to military operations. 在美国南北战争中，铁路被首次用来辅助军事行动。

【同】 accessory, auxiliary, subsidiary

【派】 adjunctive *adj*. 附属的，附加的

adjust [əˈdʒʌst] *v*. 调整，改变…以适应

【记】 ad(to) + just(公正)→使公正→调节

【例】 He *adjusted* himself very quickly to the heat of the country. 他很快就使自己适应了这个国家的炎热气候。

【同】 adapt, alter, conform

【派】 adjustment *n*. 调节，校正

administer [ədˈmɪnɪstə] *v*. 1. 管理，执行；2. 施给，给予

【记】 ad(to) + minister(大臣)→克尽大臣职守→管理

【例】 1. The company's finances have been badly *administered*. 公司财务管理不善。
2. The priest *administered* the last rites to a dying man. 神父为临死的人主持临终圣礼。

【同】 administrate, direct, govern; contribute

【派】 administration *n*. 管理；行政机关，管理部门
administrative *adj*. 管理的，行政的
administrator *n*. 管理人，行政官员

admire [ədˈmaɪə] *v*. 钦佩，赞赏

【记】 ad(to) + mire(惊奇)→对…表示惊奇→钦佩

【例】 You may not like him, but you have got to *admire* his persistence. 你可以不喜欢他，但你不得不佩服他那种坚忍不拔的精神。

【同】 respect, esteem

【反】 abhor, despise

【派】 admirable *adj*. 令人钦佩的，极好的
admiration *n*. 钦佩，羡慕；受人钦佩的人(或物)

admission [ədˈmɪʃən] *n*. 1. 准许进入，入场券；2. 承认，供认

【记】 ad(朝向) + miss(送) + ion(名词词尾)→向…送入的行为→准许进入

【例】 1. *Admission* to British universities depends on examination results. 英国大学入学以考试成绩为准。
2. His *admission* that he was the thief surprised everyone. 他承认那是他偷的，这使大家很惊讶。

【同】 admittance, entry, access; acknowledgement, confession

【反】 prohibition

admittedly [əd'mɪtɪdlɪ] *adv*. (尤用于句首)无可否认地，诚然

【记】 admit(承认) + (t)ed(分词词尾) + ly(副词词尾)→承认地→无可否认地

【例】 *Admittedly*, he works slowly, but his essays are always excellent. 应该承认，他干得很慢，但他的论文总是写得非常出色。

【派】 (逆构)admit *v*. (-tted; -tting)容许，承认

admitted *adj*. 被承认的，被确认无疑的

admonish [əd'mɒnɪʃ] *v*. 劝告，告诫

【记】 ad(= to) + mon(劝告) + ish(动词词尾)→提出劝告→告诫

【例】 The witness was *admonished* by the judge for failing to answer the question. 证人因不回答问题而受到法官的告诫。

【同】 warn, advise

【派】 admonition *n*. 警告，劝告

adolescence [ædəʊ'lesəns] *n*. 青春，青春期

【记】 ad(to) + olesc(生长) + ence(名词词尾)→正在生长的时候→青春期

【例】 It has been calculated that 17 per cent of cases of lung cancer can be attributed to high levels of exposure to second-hand tobacco smoke during childhood and *adolescence*. 据计算，有17%的肺癌病例可归咎于以下事实，即病人在其童年及青少年时期曾深受二手烟雾的侵袭。

【同】 youth

【派】 adolescent *adj*. 青春期的，青少年的；*n*. 青少年

adopt [ə'dɒpt] *v*. 1.采取，接受；2.继承，收养

【记】 ad(to) + opt(选择)→做出选择→采取

【例】 1. England was one of the first countries where scientists *adopted* and publicized Copernican ideas with enthusiasm. 科学家们接受并热情宣传哥白尼的思想，英格兰是最早的几个国家之一。

2. Having no children of their own, they decided to *adopt* an orphan. 他们因为没有亲生儿女，所以决定领养一个孤儿。

【同】 accept, espouse; foster

【反】 reject

【派】 adoptive *adj*. 采取的；收养的

adoption *n*. 采取，正式通过；收养

adore [ə'dɔː] *v*. (无进行式)热爱，崇拜

【记】 ad(to) + ore(说)→一直说→崇拜

【例】 He *adores* his wife and children. 他深爱妻儿。

【同】 love, worship

【反】 abhor, hate

【派】 adoring *adj*. 崇拜的，敬慕的

adorer *n*. 崇拜者，爱慕者

adornment [ə'dɔːnmənt] *n*. 装饰，装饰品

【记】 ad(to) + orn(装饰) + ment(名词词尾)→装饰

【例】 Many *adornments* were carved on the temple walls. 寺院的墙壁上刻着很多装饰(花纹)。

【同】 decoration, ornament

【派】 (逆构)adorn *v*. 装饰

adroit [ə'drɔɪt] *adj*. 熟练的，灵巧的

【记】 ad(to) + (d)roit(= right, 右的)→用右手的→熟练的

【例】 He soon became *adroit* at steering the boat. 他很快就熟练掌握了驾船技术。

【同】 dexterous, skillful

【反】 maladroit, unskillful

advent ['ædvənt] *n*. (尤指不寻常的人或事)出现，到来

【记】 ad(to) + vent(来到，降临)→降临，出现

【例】 People are much better informed since the *advent* of television. 自从有了电视，人们消息灵通多了。

【同】 arrival

adventure [əd'ventʃə] *n*. 冒险经历，奇遇

【记】 advent(降临) + ure(名词词尾)→降临的事情→奇遇

【例】 All the children listened to his *adventures* with eager attention. 孩子们注意力十分集中地听他讲他的冒险经历。

【同】 exploit, incident

【派】 adventurous *adj*. 喜欢冒险的，敢做敢为的

adverse [æd'vɜːs;'ædvɜːs] *adj*. 逆的，不利的，敌对的

【记】 ad(to) + verse(转移，转向)→转过去的→敌对的

【例】 The proposal has attracted a lot of *adverse* comment. 这个建议招来很多非难。

【同】 opposite, contrary, unfavorable

【反】 favorable

【派】 adversity *n*. 厄运，逆境；(常用复数)灾祸，苦难

advertise ['ædvətaɪz] *v*. 1. 做广告，登广告；2. 使(某事物)尽人皆知，公布

【记】 ad(to) + vert(转移，转向) + ise(动词词尾)→使人的注意力转向…→做广告

【例】 1. Are lawyers allowed to *advertise* their services? 准许律师为他们的业务做广告吗？
2. It may be safer not to *advertise* your presence. 不把你出席的事声张出去也许更为安全。

【派】 advertisement *n*. (缩写为 ad.)广告
advertising *n*. 广告业，广告总称

advisable [əd'vaɪzəbl] *adj*. 可取的，明智的

【记】 advis(e)(建议) + able(形容词词尾)→值得建议的→可取的

【例】 It is *advisable* always to wear a safety belt when you're driving. 开车的时候最好总是系着安全带。

【同】 wise, sensible

【反】 inadvisable

【派】 (逆构)advise *v*. 建议，劝告
adviser *n*. 导师，辅导人员
advisory *adj*. 顾问的，劝告的

advocate ['ædvəkəɪt;'ædvəkɪt] *v*. 提倡，鼓吹；*n*. 提倡者，主张者
【记】 ad(to)+voc(喊叫)+ate(动词词尾)→为…大声喊叫→提倡
【例】 1. Do you *advocate* banning cars in the city center? 你支持禁止汽车在市中心通行这一主张吗?
2. He is a lifelong *advocate* of disarmament. 他是一个为裁军奋斗终生的人。
【同】 support，uphold
【反】 impugn
【派】 advocacy *n*. 拥护，提倡

aerate ['eɪəreɪt] *v*. 充气，让空气进入，(水、饮料等)加气
【记】 aer(空气)+ate(动词词尾)→加空气于→充气
【例】 The potatoes were set outside to *aerate*. 马铃薯被放到外面通风。
【同】 ventilate
【派】 aeration *n*. 暴露于空气中，通气

aerobics [ˌeə'rəʊbɪks] *n*. 有氧运动
【记】 aero(空气的)+bic(=bio，生命)+s(名词词尾)→在空气中有生命的→有氧运动
【例】 We offer a range of sporting activities including badminton，basketball，table tennis，volleyball and *aerobics*. 我们提供各种体育运动，包括:羽毛球、篮球、乒乓球、排球和有氧运动。
【派】 (逆构)aerobic *adj*. 生存于氧气中的，增氧健身法的

aesthetic [iːs'θetɪk] *adj*. 美学的，审美的
【记】 aesthet(感觉)+ic(形容词词尾)→对…有感觉的→审美的
【例】 The building is *aesthetic* but not very practical. 这幢建筑物具有美学价值，但不太实用。
【同】 artistic
【派】 aesthetics *n*. 美学，美学理论

affable ['æfəbl] *adj*. 和蔼可亲的，亲切友善的
【记】 af(=ad，to)+fa(说)+ble(形容词 词尾)→可以交谈的→和蔼可亲的
【例】 He found her parents very *affable*. 他觉得她父母很好说话。
【同】 amiable，friendly，genial
【反】 unfriendly
【派】 affability *n*. 和蔼，亲切

affection [ə'fekʃən] *n*. 友爱，挚爱，情爱
【记】 af(=ad，to)+fect(做)+ion(名词词尾)→做出来的东西→展示出来的东西→爱
【例】 The old king was held in great *affection*. 年老的国王极受爱戴。
【同】 fondness，love
【派】 affectionate *adj*. 亲爱的，挚爱的

affiliate [ə'fɪlɪeɪt] *v*. 使紧密联系，使隶属

【记】 af(= ad, to) + fili(儿子) + ate(动词词尾)→使成为…儿子→使隶属于

【例】 The College is *affiliated* to the University. 这个学院附属于这所大学。

【同】 attach, associate

【派】 affiliation *n*. 联系，从属关系

affinity [ə'fɪnɪtɪ] *n*. 1. 特点相近，类似；2. (尤指姻亲)关系，密切关系；3. 吸引，喜爱

【记】 af(= ad, to) + fin(范围) + ity(名词词尾)→能进入同一个范围的→类似

【例】 1. There is (a) close *affinity* between Italian and Spanish. 意大利语和西班牙语很近似。

2. He was not an impartial witness because of his *affinity* with the accused. 他不是公正的见证人，因为他与被告有姻亲关系。

3. She has a strong *affinity* for Beethoven. 她酷爱贝多芬的乐曲。

【同】 similarity; kinship; sympathy

【反】 consanguinity

affirm [ə'fɜːm] *v*. 证实，断言

【记】 af(= ad, to) + firm(坚固的)→使坚固→证实

【例】 He *affirmed* that he was responsible. 他肯定是他负责。

【同】 declare, state, confirm

【反】 deny

【派】 affirmative *adj*. 肯定的，积极的

affirmation *n*. 断言，肯定

afflict [ə'flɪkt] *v*. 使苦恼，折磨

【记】 af(= ad, to) + flict(打击)→打倒→使痛苦→使苦恼

【例】 Severe drought has *afflicted* the countryside. 严重的干旱使乡村深受其害。

【同】 torment, torture

【反】 comfort

【派】 affliction *n*. 痛苦，不幸

affluent ['æfluənt] *adj*. 1. 富裕的，富足的；2. 丰富的，大量的

【记】 af(= ad, to) + flu(流动) + ent(形容词词尾)→使大量流入→丰富的

【例】 1. *Affluent* he may be, but he is by no means sure what to tip the doorman. 尽管他可能是富裕的，但他一点不知道该付多少小费给看门人。

2. The new magazine will be directed at a more *affluent* circulation. 新的杂志将争取更大的发行量。

【同】 rich, wealthy; abundant, plentiful

【反】 poor, impoverished; insufficient

【派】 affluence *n*. 富裕，丰富

afford [ə'fɔːd] *v*. 1. 买得起，担负得起；2. 提供

【记】 af(= ad, to) + ford(拿出)→能拿得出(钱)→买得起

【例】 1. They walked because they couldn't *afford* (to take) a taxi. 他们因为坐不起计程车而步行。

2. Television *affords* pleasure to many people. 电视给很多人带来乐趣。

【同】 spare; supply, provide

【派】 affordable *adj*. 买得起的

agency ['eɪdʒənsɪ] *n*. 1. 代理行，经办处；2. 专业行政部门，公众服务机构

【记】 ag(= act, 做) + ency(名词词尾)→做事情的地方→行政部门

【例】 1. Our company has *agencies* all over the world. 本公司在全世界都设有代办处。

2. By and large the work of the news *agency* is appreciative. 一般而论这家新闻社的工作是让人感激的。

【同】 bureau, office

【派】 agent *n*. 代理人，代理商

agenda [ə'dʒendə] *n*. 议事日程，待议诸事项(一览表)

【记】 ag(= act, 做) + enda(拉丁语名词词尾)→做的事情→议程

【例】 The question of salary increases is high on the *agenda*. 增加薪金问题是要讨论的摘要议程。

【同】 schedule, plan

aggravate ['ægrəveɪt] *v*. 加重，加剧，使恶化

【记】 ag(= ad, to) + grav(重) + ate(动词词尾)→使…重→加重

【例】 He *aggravated* his condition by leaving hospital too soon. 他因过早出院而使病情恶化。

【同】 worsen

【反】 alleviate

【派】 aggravation *n*. (病情，负担)加重，恶化

aggravating *adj*. 恼人的，讨厌的

aggregate ['ægrɪˌget; 'ægrɪgeɪt] *n*./*v*. 总数，合计

【记】 ag(= ad, to) + gregat(收集) + e→收集在一起→总数

【例】 1. Her earnings from all sources *aggregated* £100, 000. 她的各项收入总计达10万英镑。

2. What were your *aggregate* wages last year? 去年你的工资一共是多少?

【同】 total, amount

【派】 aggregation *n*. 集合，聚集物

aggression [ə'greʃən] *n*. 侵犯，侵略

【记】 ag(= ad, to) + gress(行走) + ion(名词词尾)→向…走去→侵略

【例】 The military exercise was condemned as an act of *aggression*. 这次军事演习被谴责为一次挑衅行为。

【同】 intrusion, invasion

【派】 aggressive *adj*. 侵略的，挑衅的；积极进取的

aggressor *n*. 侵略者，挑衅者

aghast [ə'gɑːst] *adj*. 惊骇的，吓呆的

【记】 a(加强语气) + ghast(= ghost, 鬼)→像看到鬼一样→惊骇的

【例】 He stood *aghast* at the terrible sight. 他被那可怕的景象吓呆了。

【同】 appalled, shocked

agile [ˈædʒaɪl] *adj*. 敏捷的，活泼轻快的

【记】 ag(行动，活动)+ile(形容词词尾)→活动的→敏捷的

【例】 The boy escaped with an *agile* leap. 这男孩灵敏地一跳，脱逃了。

【同】 nimble

【反】 dull, slow

【派】 agility *n*. 敏捷，活泼

agitate [ˈædʒɪteɪt] *v*. 1.鼓吹，煽动；2.使激动，使恼怒，使焦虑

【记】 ag(行动)+it+ate(动词词尾)→使…动起来→煽动

【例】 1. The fiery speech *agitated* the crowd. 充满激情的演说使人们狂热不已。

2. He became quite *agitated* when he was asked about his criminal past. 当问到他过去的犯罪历史时，他变得十分焦虑不安。

【同】 disturb, rouse, stir

【反】 calm

【派】 agitation *n*. 1.公开辩论，大辩论；2.焦虑，不安

agonize [ˈægənaɪz] *v*. 使极度痛苦，折磨

【记】 agon(y)(痛苦)+ize(动词词尾)→使痛苦

【例】 We *agonized* for hours about which wallpaper to buy. 对买哪种壁纸，我们伤了几小时的脑筋。

【同】 afflict

【反】 comfort, relieve

agony [ˈægənɪ] *n*. 痛苦，创痛

【记】 agon(挣扎，斗争)+y(名词词尾)→斗争→痛苦

【例】 She was in an *agony* of indecision. 她陷于犹豫不决的痛苦之中。

【同】 torment, torture, pain

【反】 rlief, comfort

agreeable [əˈgrɪəbl] *adj*. 1.(指计划等)使人愉快的，合意的；2.容易相处的

【记】 agree(同意)+able(形容词词尾)→能够使人同意的→使人愉快的

【例】 1. If you're *agreeable* to our proposal, we'll go ahead. 如果你同意我们的建议，我们就进行了。

2. I found him most *agreeable*. 我觉得他极易相处。

【同】 consonant; congenial

【反】 disagreeable

ailment [ˈeɪlmənt] *n*. 疾病(尤指微恙)

【记】 ail(痛的)+ment(名词词尾)→痛苦的状况→疾病

【例】 He's prone to minor *ailments*. 他动不动就生点儿病。

【同】 illness

【派】 (逆构)ail *v*. 有病，生病

airborne [ˈeəbɔːn] *adj*. 1.空气传播的；2.空运的，空降的

【记】 air(空气)+borne(bear 的过去分词，带有)→在空中的

【例】 1. She has an allergic reaction to *airborne* pollen. 她对空气中的花粉有过敏性

反应。

2. Smoking is forbidden until the plane is *airborne*. 飞机升空时禁止吸烟。

aisle [aɪl] *n*. 过道，走廊

【例】 Products placed at the beginning of *aisles* don't sell well. 放在过道顶端的商品销售情况不是很好。

【同】 gangway, passageway

ajar [əˈdʒɑː] *adj*. (门、窗等)微开的

【例】 The door was *ajar*. 那扇门半开着。

【同】 open

【反】 fastened

akin [əˈkɪn] *adj*. 同类的，有密切关系的

【记】 a(= into, 进入) + kin(亲戚)→是亲戚的→有密切关系的

【例】 He felt something *akin* to pity. 他感到有一种近于怜悯的感情。

【同】 alike, associated

【反】 alien

alert [əˈlɜːt] *adj*. 机敏的；*v*. 警戒，戒备；*n*. 警戒，警报

【记】 al(= ad, to) + ert(= erect, 直)→站直了看→警觉的

【例】 1. Although he's over eighty his mind is still remarkably *alert*. 他虽已年过80，但头脑仍然十分机敏。

2. Why weren't the police *alerted*? 为什么警方没戒备起来?

3. Sirens sounded the *alert* for an air raid. 空袭警报的警笛响起。

【同】 watchful, attentive; alarm

【反】 dull, slow

alien [ˈeɪljən] *adj*. 1. 外国的，陌生的；2. 相异的，不相容的；*n*. 外国人，外侨

【记】 ali(其他的) + en(形容词词尾)→其他的→陌生的

【例】 1. Their ideas are quite *alien* to our own. 他们的想法跟我们的截然不同。

2. After being away for so long, he feels like an *alien* in his own country now. 背井离乡这么久，现在在他自己的国家，他觉得自己像个外人。

【同】 foreign, strange; foreigner

【反】 civil, national

alienate [ˈeɪljəneɪt] *v*. 使疏远，离间

【记】 ali(其他的) + en(形容词词尾) + ate(动词词尾)→使成为其他的→使疏远

【例】 By adopting this policy, they risk *alienating* many of their supporters. 他们采取这个政策，就要冒同许多支持者疏远的风险。

【同】 disaffect, estrange

【反】 align, ally

【派】 alienation *n*. 疏远，离间

align [əˈlaɪn] *v*. 1. 使成一行；2. 使结盟

【记】 a(= ad, to) + lign(= line, 行，线)→使成一行

【例】 1. Could you *align* this table with those? 你能把这张桌子同那些桌子排成一行吗?

2. They are closely *aligned* with the opponents of the government. 他们和反政府派密切合作。

【同】 aline, array; ally

【反】 alienate

【派】 alignment *n*. 调整；结盟

allege [ə'ledʒ] *v*. 断言，宣称

【记】 al(= ad, to) + leg(说，发出) + e→说出来→宣称

【例】 The prisoner *alleges* that he was at home on the night of the crime. 囚犯辩称案发当晚他在家中。

【同】 declare, state

【派】 alleged *adj*. (未经证实而)陈述的

allegation *n*. 陈述，辩解

allegiance *n*. 拥护，忠诚

allergy ['ælədʒɪ] *n*. 变态反应，过敏性

【记】 all(= ali, 其他的) + ergy(行为，作用)→其他的作用→变态反应

【例】 This climatic phenomenon was accused of wrecking tourism, causing *allergies* and melting the ski-slopes. 这种气候现象被指责为旅游业滑坡、过敏症发作、滑雪坡融化的罪魁祸首。

【派】 allergic *adj*. 过敏的

alleviate [ə'liːvɪeɪt] *v*. 减轻(痛苦等)，缓解

【记】 al(= ad, to) + levi(变轻) + ate(动词词尾)→使变轻松→减轻

【例】 The doctor gave her an injection to *alleviate* the pain. 医生给她打了一针，以减轻她的痛苦。

【同】 lessen, reduce, relieve

【反】 aggravate

【派】 alleviation *n*. 减轻，缓和

alleviative *adj*. 起缓解作用的，减轻的；*n*. 缓和剂，解痛物

alliance [ə'laɪəns] *n*. 联盟，联合

【记】 al(= ad, to) + li(= lig, 绑) + ance(名词词尾)→绑在一起→联盟

【例】 States seek to become stronger through *alliance* 各国力求通过结盟而更加强大。

【同】 alignment, confederation

【反】 alienation

alliteration [əˌlɪtə'reɪʃən] *n*. 头韵

【记】 al(= ad, to) + liter(文字，字母) + ation(名词词尾)→使字母一致→头韵

【例】 'Round the rocks runs the river' is an example of *alliteration* "河水绕过石头流去"就是一个头韵的例子。

【同】 rhyme

allocate ['æləʊkeɪt] *v*. 1. 拨给，划拨；2. 分配，配置

【记】 al(= ad, to) + loc(场所) + ate(动词词尾)→指定场所→分配

【例】 1. The governmenthas *allocated* over 100 million dollars to the job creation program. 政府已拨出一亿多美元用于一项创造就业机会的计划。

2. Each of the refugees has been *allocated* accommodation. 每个难民都分到了住处。

【同】 allot; distribute, apportion

【反】 withhold

【派】 allocation *n*. 分配，配给，拨款

allot [ə'lɒt] *v*. (-tted; -tting) (按份额)分配，拨给；2. 摊派(时间，钱，任务等)

【记】 al(= ad, to) + lot(分享)→使…分享→分配

【例】 1. How much cash has been *allotted*? 拨给多少现款？

2. We were unable to finish it in the *allotted* time. 我们无法在规定的时间内完成这项工作。

【同】 allocate, apportion, distribute; assign

【反】 withhold

【派】 allotment *n*. 分配，分派

allowance [ə'lauəns] *n*. 1. 允许，承认；2. 津贴，补贴

【记】 allow(允许) + ance(名词词尾)→允许，承认

【例】 1. I'm afraid the lecturers will make no *allowance* for the presence of non-native speakers in the audience. 我恐怕老师是不会允许不会说本地语言的学生来听课的。

2. The scholarship includes an *allowance* for books. 奖学金包括书籍补贴费。

【同】 admission; allotment, grant

【派】 (逆构)allow *v*. 允许，承认

alloy ['ælɔɪ] *n*. 合金

【记】 al(= ad, to) + loy(绑)→绑在一起→合金

【例】 Brass is an *alloy* of copper and zinc. 黄铜是铜和锌的合金。

【同】 mixture; mix

allude [ə'ljuːd] *v*. 提及，暗指

【记】 al(= ad, to) + lude(玩)→玩耍→展示→提及

【例】 You *alluded* to certain developments in your speech—what exactly did you mean? 你在讲话中提到某些发展——确切的意思是什么呢？

【同】 imply, refer

【派】 allusion *n*. 提及，暗示

allure [ə'ljuə] *v*. /*n*. 引诱，吸引

【记】 al(= ad, to) + lure(诱惑)→引诱

【例】 Many settlers were *allured* by promises of easy wealth. 很多安家落户的人都是受了诱惑，以为很容易就能发财。

【同】 attract, tempt

【派】 alluring *adj*. 迷人的，吸引人的，诱惑的

allurement *n*. 诱惑物，魅力

ally [æ'laɪ; ə'laɪ] *v*. 结盟；*n*. 联盟，同盟者

【记】 al(=ad, to)+ly(绑)→绑在一起→结盟

【例】 1. Italy *allied* itself with Germany during World War II. 在第二次世界大战期间意大利和德国结成同盟国。

2. France and England were *allies* in the war. 法国和英国在这次战争中是同盟国。

【同】 alliance, confederate; align, filiate

【反】 enemy, rival

aloof [ə'luːf] *adj*. 冷淡的，漠不关心的

【记】 a(=in, 在…中)+loof(=luff, 船向上风行驶)→远离的→冷淡的

【例】 Throughout the conversation he remained silent and *aloof*. 在谈话过程中他始终一言不发，无动于衷。

【同】 distant, reserved

【反】 approachable

alphabet ['ælfəbɪt] *n*. 字母表

【记】 alpha(希腊语中第一个字母)+bet(=beta, 希腊语中第二个字母)→字母表

【例】 There are 26 letters in the English *alphabet*. 英语字母表中有26个字母。

【同】 characters, letters

【派】 alphabetical *adj*. 按字母顺序的

alter ['ɔːltə] *v*. 改变，更改

【记】 alter本意为"其他的"→成为其他的→改变

【例】 She had to *alter* her clothes after losing weight. 她瘦了以后，衣服也得修改了。

【同】 change, modify

【反】 preserve, conserve

【派】 alteration *n*. 改变，更改

alternate [ɔːl'təːnɪt] *v*. 交替，轮流；*adj*. 交替的，轮流的，供替换的

【记】 alter(其他的)+n+ate(动词词尾)→变成其他的→交替

【例】 1. The weather *alternated* between rain and sunshine. 时而下雨，时而放晴。

2. Meetings are held on *alternate* Thursdays. 每隔一个星期的星期四举行一次会议。

【同】 interchange, rotate; alternative

【反】 consecutive, successive

【派】 alternation *n*. 交替，轮流

alternative [ɔːl'təːnətɪv] *adj*. (两种或以上的)另一可选用的，另外的；*n*. 可选事物，另一种选择

【记】 alter(其他的)+n+ative(形容词词尾)→其他的→另外的

【例】 1. We retured by the *alternative* road. 我们从另外一条路返回。

2. There was no other *alternative* but to fight till the victory. 除了战斗直到胜利，别无选择。

【同】 alternate; choice, option

【派】 alternatively *adv*. 非此即彼，二者择一地

altitude ['æltɪtjuːd] *n*. 海拔，高(度)

【记】 alt(高的)+itude(抽象名词词尾)→高度→海拔

【例】 What is the *altitude* of this village? 这个村子海拔多少？

【同】 height

【反】 depth

altruism ['æltruɪzəm] *n*. 利他主义，无私

【记】 altru(=alter，其他的)+ism(名词词尾)→为他人的→利他主义

【例】 Do you think *altruism* is the foundation of the modern society? 你认为利他主义是现代社会的基础吗？

【同】 selflessness

【反】 egoism

【派】 altruistic *adj*. 利他主义的，无私的

altruist *n*. 利他主义者，无私的人

alumna [ə'lʌmnə] *n*. (复数 alumnae)女毕业生，女校友

【记】 alum(滋养，培养)+n+a(拉丁语名词词尾，表阴性)→被培养的女性学生→女毕业生

【例】 There will soon be an assembly for all *alumnae* of the University of Manchester. 曼彻斯特大学的女校友很快要组织一次聚会。

【同】 alum，graduate

alumnus [ə'lʌmnəs] *n*. (复数 alumni)男毕业生，男校友

【记】 alum(滋养，培养)+n+us(拉丁语名词词尾，表阳性)→被培养的男性学生→男毕业生

【例】 He was an *alumnus* of Peking University of the class of 1984. 他是北京大学 1984 届的毕业生。

【同】 alum，graduate

amalgamate [ə'mælgəmeɪt] *v*. 混合，合并

【记】 amalgam(汞合金)+ate(动词词尾)→使变成汞合金→混合

【例】 The boys' and girls' schools have (been) *amalgamated* to form a new comprehensive. 男校和女校联合而组成了一所新的综合中学。

【同】 combine，unify，incorporate

【派】 amalgamation *n*. 融合，合并

amass [ə'mæs] *v*. 把…聚成堆，积累

【记】 a(=to)+mass(团)→使成为一团→把…聚成堆

【例】 They *amassed* enough evidence to convict him on six charges. 他们搜集了足够的证据，宣判他有六条罪状。

【同】 gather，collect

amateur ['æmətɜː，'æmətjʊə] *n*. 业余爱好者，业余运动员；*adj*. (贬义)业余的，外行的

【记】 amat(爱)+eur(表示"人"的名词词尾)→爱上…的人→业余爱好者

【例】 1. Although he's only an *amateur* he's a first-class player. 虽然他只是个业余爱好者，但却是一流的高手。

2. We made a rather *amateur* job of paiting the house. 我们把房子油漆了一遍，但

漆得很不在行。

【同】 nonprofessional，inexpert

【反】 professional，expert

【派】 amateurish *adj*. 业余的，不熟练的

amazing [ə'meɪzɪŋ] *adj*. 令人惊奇的，惊人的

【记】 a(加强语气) + maz(e)(迷宫，迷惑) + ing(形容词词尾)→使人困惑的→令人惊奇的

【例】 The new car goes at an *amazing* speed. 这辆新车开起来速度惊人。

【同】 astonishing，surprising，shocking

【派】 (逆构)amaze *v*. 使惊讶

amazement *n*. 惊奇，吃惊

ambassador [æm'bæsədə] *n*. 大使，使节

【记】 ambassa(使命) + (d)or(名词词尾)→完成使命的人→使节

【例】 He was appointed *ambassador* to the United States. 他被任命为驻美国大使。

【同】 envoy

【派】 ambassadorial *adj*. 大使的，使节的

ambassadress *n*. 大使夫人，女大使

ambience ['æmbɪəns] *n*. 周围环境，气氛

【记】 ambi(周围的) + ence(名词词尾)→周围的东西→环境

【例】 This little restaurant has a pleasant *ambience*. 这家小饭店的环境幽雅宜人。

【同】 atmosphere

【派】 ambient *adj*. 周围的

ambiguous [ˌæm'bɪgjuəs] *adj*. 含糊不清的，不明确的，模棱两可的

【记】 ambi(两边的) + (i)gu(驱使，驱赶) + ous(形容词词尾)→朝两个方向驱赶→模棱两可的

【例】 Frustrated by *ambiguous* instructions, the parents were never able to assemble the new toy. 对于含糊不清的说明，这对父母感到很沮丧，因为根本不可能把新玩具组装好。

【同】 vague，obscure

【反】 clear，distinct，definite

【派】 ambiguity *n*. 含糊不清，歧义，模棱两可

ambition [æm'bɪʃən] *n*. 雄心，野心

【记】 amb(= ambi，周围) + it(走动) + (t)ion(名词词尾)→以前这个词只用于政客，指想求取官位的人，总是穿着白衣，到处奔走演说，以求多得选票。因此"到处走动"就代表"渴望权势"。→雄心，野心

【例】 One of his *ambitions* is to become the President of the Motor General. 他的抱负之一是当通用汽车公司的总裁。

【同】 desire，enthusiasm

【派】 ambitious *adj*. 有雄心的，有抱负的；有野心的

ambivalent [æm'bɪvələnt] *adj*. 有矛盾情绪的

A

【记】 ambi(两个的) + val(强壮的) + ent(形容词词尾)→有两种强烈(情绪)的→有矛盾情绪的

【例】 His *ambivalent* reply means I still don't know what he wants. 他自相矛盾的答复叫我仍旧不明白他要什么。

【同】 ambiguous, confusing

【派】 ambivalence *n*. 正反感情并存，矛盾心理

amble [ˈæmbl] *v*. /*n*. 漫步，缓行

【例】 He came *ambling* down the road. 他沿路溜溜达达地来了。

【同】 saunter, stroll, walk

ambulance [ˈæmbjuləns] *n*. 救护车，流动医院

【记】 ambul(行走) + ance(名词词尾)→走的东西→救护车

【例】 The injured man was fairly far gone by the time the *ambulance* arrived. 救护车赶到时那伤者已生命垂危。

amenable [əˈmiːnəbl] *adj*. 1. 经得起检验的；2. 顺从的，应服从的

【记】 a(= ad, to) + men(引导) + able(形容词词尾)→能够引导的→顺从的

【例】 1. This case is not *amenable* to the normal rules. 这件事经不起常规的检验。

2. I'm sure she'll be *amenable* to any sensible suggestions. 我相信任何合情合理的建议她都会接受的。

【同】 compliant, willing

【反】 obstinate

amend [əˈmend] *v*. 修改，修订

【记】 a(出来) + mend(缺点)→把缺点挑出来→修改

【例】 The new government *amended* the law. 新政府修订了法律。

【同】 improve, rectify, mend

【派】 amendment *n*. 修改，修订

amenity [əˈmiːnɪtɪ] *n*. (常用复数)生活设施，便利设施

【记】 amen(愉快) + ity(名词词尾)→使人愉快的东西→便利设施

【例】 Parks and a theatre are just some of the town's local *amenities*. 公园和剧院只是市镇娱乐设施的一部分。

【同】 facility

amiable [ˈeɪmjəbl] *adj*. 亲切的，和蔼可亲的

【记】 ami(爱) + able(形容词词尾)→有爱心的→和蔼可亲的(强调自身具备的性格)

【例】 My father is an *amiable* man. 我父亲是一位和蔼可亲的人。

【同】 affable, friendly, genial

【反】 abominable, detestable, ill-natured

【派】 amiability *n*. 和蔼可亲，亲切

amicable [ˈæmɪkəbl] *adj*. 友善的，和平的，和睦的

【记】 ami(爱) + (i)c(形容词词尾) + able(形容词词尾)→显示爱的→友善的(强调对外界友好的态度)

【例】 We had pleasant discussion and soon reached an *amicable* agreement. 我们进行了

愉快交谈，并且很快达成了一项友好协议。

【同】 friendly, peaceful

【反】 hostile

【派】 amicability *n*. 友善，亲善

ammunition [ˌæmjuˈnɪʃən] *n*. 军火，弹药

【记】 a(是法语 la 的转用)m + muni(防御) + tion(名词词尾)→防御用的东西→军火，弹药

【例】 They had to meet the attack with very little *ammunition*. 他们不得不以极少的弹药应战。

【同】 powder, bullet

amnesia [æmˈniːzjə] *n*. 记忆缺失症，健忘症

【记】 a(表否定，无) + mne(记忆) + (s)ia(名词词尾)→没有记忆→健忘症

【例】 She suffered *amnesia* after the car crash. 出了车祸之后，她得了记忆缺失症。

【同】 forgetfulness

amount [əˈmaʊnt] *n*. 总数，数量；*v*. 合计，共计

【记】 a(= ad, to) + mount(= mountain, 山)→登山→上升→总数达到

【例】 1. Large *amounts* of money were spent on the bridge. 那座桥花费了大量金钱。

2. His debts *amount* to over 3000 dollars. 他的欠债总数已达 3000 多美元。

【同】 sum, total, quantity

ample [ˈæmpl] *adj*. 大量的，足够的

【记】 am(= amb, 周围) + ple(充满)→充满周围的→大量的

【例】 We have *ample* money for the journey. 我们有足够的钱去旅游。

【同】 abundant, sufficient

【反】 scanty

amplify [ˈæmplɪfaɪ] *v*. 1. 放大，增强；2. 补充叙述，详述

【记】 am(= amb, 周围) + pli(充满) + fy(动词词尾)→使充满周围→放大

【例】 1. The sounds of the guitar are then *amplified* and sent through the speakers. 吉他的声音因此被扩大，然后通过扬声器放出。

2. We must ask you to *amplify* your statement. 我们得请你对你的说法作进一步的说明。

【同】 magnify, expand; exaggerate

【派】 amplification *n*. 扩大，详述

analogy [əˈnælədʒɪ] *n*. 类比，类推

【记】 ana(根据) + log(说) + y(名词词尾)→根据…说→类比

【例】 The author draws an *analogy* between the way water moves in waves and the way light travels. 作者用水的波动作比喻，来说明光的运行方式。

【同】 simulation, comparison

【派】 analogous *adj*. 相似的，类似的

analyze [ˈænəlaɪz] *v*. 分析，研究

【记】 ana(回去) + lyze(放松，松开)→松开回到原处→分析

【例】 He *analyzed* the food and found it contained poison. 他对这种食物作了化验分析，发现有毒。

【派】 analysis *n*. (复数-ses)分析，分解

analyst *n*. 分析者

anarchy ['ænəkɪ] *n*. 无政府，混乱

【记】 an(没有) + arch(统治者) + y(名词词尾)→没有统治者的状态→无政府

【例】 The overthrow of the regime was followed by a period of *anarchy*. 那政权被推翻以后，有一段时期是无政府状态。

【同】 disorder

【派】 anarchist *n*. 无政府主义者

anatomy [ə'nætəmɪ] *n*. 解剖，解剖学

【记】 ana(分离) + tom(切割) + y(名词词尾)→把…切割开→解剖

【例】 We have to do *anatomy* next term. 我们下学期得学解剖学了。

【派】 anatomical *adj*. 解剖的，解剖学上的；结构(上)的

ancestor ['ænsɪstə] *n*. 祖宗，祖先

【记】 an(= ante，前面) + ces(走) + tor(名词词尾)→走在前面的人→祖先

【例】 His *ancestors* had come to England as refugees. 他的祖先来到英国的时候是难民。

【同】 ascendant，forebear

【反】 descendant，offspring

【派】 ancestral *adj*. 祖先的，祖先传下的

anecdote ['ænɪkdəʊt] *n*. 轶事，奇闻

【记】 an(不) + ec(= ex，外面) + dot(给予) + e→没有被传到外面的事→轶事

【例】 In Britain，for example，there are plenty of *anecdotes* describing how glow-worms have been used to read by or used as emergency bicycle lamps. 比如在英国，有很多奇闻轶事记述了萤火虫是如何被用做读书的灯光，或者自行车的备用车灯。

【同】 story，tale

【派】 anecdotal *adj*. 轶事的，趣闻的

anesthesia [ˌænɪs'θiːzjə] *n*. 麻醉

【记】 an(不) + esth(感觉) + esia(名词词尾)→使没有感觉→麻醉

【例】 *Anesthesia* can alleviate a patient's pain during the surgery. 麻醉可以减轻病人在手术时的疼痛。

【派】 anesthetic *n*. 麻醉剂，麻药

anguish ['æŋgwɪʃ] *n*. 极度的痛苦，苦闷

【记】 ang(窒息) + u + ish(形容词词尾，转用做名词)→令人窒息的→极度的痛苦

【例】 She was in *anguish* over her missing child. 孩子失踪了，她心里极度悲痛。

【同】 agony，grief，torment

【派】 anguished *adj*. 痛苦的，苦恼的

animate ['ænɪmeɪt] *v*. 赋以生命，绘制动画片；*adj*. 动画的，动画片的

【记】 anim(呼吸，气息) + ate(动词词尾)→使…能呼吸→赋以生命

【例】 1. Early cinema programmes were a mixture of items，combining comic sketches， free-standing narratives, serial episodes and *animated* film. 早期的电影形式是个大杂烩，包括喜剧短剧、独立故事片、系列剧和动画片。

2. The dog lay so still it scarcely seemed *animate*. 那条狗卧着一动也不动，简直不像活的。

【同】 enliven

【反】 deaden

【派】 animated *adj*. 活跃的，活泼的；看起来活动的

animation *n*. 活泼，激励；动画片

annex [ə'neks] *v*. 1. 兼并，并吞(土地等)；2. 附加

【记】 an(= ad, to) + nex(绑)→把…绑在一起→兼并

【例】 1. The powerful nation *annexed* the small islands near its coast. 那个强国吞并了靠近其海岸的几个小岛。

2. A new wing has been *annexed* to the hospital. 医院已经增建了一个新侧楼。

【同】 append, attach

【派】 annexation *n*. 并吞，附加；附加物

annihilate [ə'naɪəleɪt] *v*. 1. 消灭，歼灭；2. 取消，废弃

【记】 an(= ad, to) + nihil(无) + ate(动词词尾)→使…变成无→消灭

【例】 1. The enemy was *annihilated*. 敌人被歼灭了。

2. Radio communication has *annihilated* space. 无线电通讯已消除了空间的阻隔。

【同】 eliminate, eradicate; abolish

【派】 annihilation *n*. 全部毁灭，灭绝

anniversary [ˌænɪ'vɜːsərɪ] *n*. 周年纪念，周年纪念日

【记】 anni(年) + vers(转向) + ary(名词词尾)→一年转到一次→周年纪念日

【例】 She reproached her husband for having forgotten their wedding *anniversary*. 她责怪丈夫忘了他们的结婚周年纪念日。

annotate ['ænəʊteɪt] *v*. 注解，注释

【记】 an(= ad, to) + not(记号，标记) + ate(动词词尾)→加以标明→注解

【例】 Some people *annotate* as they read. 有的人一面读书一面做注解。

【同】 footnote

【派】 annotation *n*. 注解，注释

announce [ə'naʊns] *v*. 宣布，声称

【记】 an(= ad, to) + nounce(通知)→发出通知→宣布

【例】 They *announced* their engagement to the family. 他们向家里宣布他们已经订婚了。

【同】 declare, proclaim, notify

【派】 announcement *n*. 宣布，通知

annoy [ə'nɔɪ] *v*. 使恼怒，打搅

【记】 an(= in, 在…里) + n + oy(憎恨)→使处于愤恨→使恼怒

【例】 The sound of footsteps on the bare floor *annoyed* the downstairs neighbors. 楼上光地板上的脚步声吵得楼下住户心烦。

【同】 irritate，bother，vex，rile

【派】 annoyance *n*. 恼怒，烦恼；讨厌的东西(或人)

annual [ˈænjʊəl] *adj*. 每年的，一年的

【记】 ann(年)+ual(形容词词尾)→每年的

【例】 The *annual* value of these subsidies is immense. 这些补贴每年支出的价值总额是巨大的。

【同】 one-year，yearly

【派】 annually *adv*. 年度，每年

annul [əˈnʌl] *v*. (-lled；-lling)废除，取消

【记】 an(= ad，to)+nul(无)→使…变成无→废除

【例】 I am afraid that his family will try to have the marriage *annulled*. 恐怕他的家庭想要宣告他的婚姻无效。

【同】 abolish，nullify，invalidate

anomaly [əˈnɒməlɪ] *n*. 1. 异常的人或物，畸形；2. 异常，不规则

【记】 a(表示否定，没有)+nom(规律)+(a)ly(名词词尾)→离开规律的东西→异常

【例】 1. A cat with no tail is an *anomaly*. 没有尾巴的猫是只畸形猫。

2. The *anomaly* of his position is that he is the chairman of the committee but isn't allowed to vote. 他的地位很怪，虽然是委员会主席，可是没有投票表决权。

【同】 abnormality；exception

【反】 normality

【派】 anomalous *adj*. 异常的，反常的，不规则的

anonymous [əˈnɒnɪməs] *adj*. 匿名的

【记】 an(无，没有)+onym(名字)+ous(形容词词尾)→没有名字的→匿名的

【例】 The author wishes to remain *anonymous*. 作者希望姓名不公开。

【同】 nameless

【反】 onymous

【派】 (逆构)anonym *n*. 假名，匿名者

antagonism [ænˈtægənɪzəm] *n*. 对抗，敌对

【记】 ant(= anti，反的)+agon(y)(斗争)+ism(名词词尾)→站在反面与之做斗争→对抗

【例】 The *antagonism* he felt towards his old enemy was still very strong. 他对旧冤家的敌对情绪仍然很大。

【同】 hostility，enmity

【反】 harmony，comity

【派】 antagonistic *adj*. 对抗的，敌对的

antagonist *n*. 对抗者，敌手

antagonize *v*. 敌对，对抗

anthem [ˈænθəm] *n*. 圣歌，赞美歌

【例】 *Anthems* are often with words taken from the *Bible*. 圣歌的歌词多取自于《圣经》。

【同】 hymn，chant

anthology [æn'θɒlədʒɪ] *n*. 诗集，文选

【记】 antho(花) + log(收集) + y(名词词尾)→把花收集起来→把诗歌收集起来→诗集

【例】 This is an *anthology* of 20th-century American poetry. 这是一本20世纪美国诗歌选集。

【同】 collection, selection

【派】 anthologist *n*. 选集的编者

anthropology [ˌænθrə'pɒlədʒɪ] *n*. 人类学

【记】 anthrop(人类) + ology(…学)→研究人类的学科→人类学

【例】 How does archaeology relate to disciplines such as *anthropology* and history that are also concerned with the human story? 考古学与人类学、历史学之类同样和人类历史有关的学科有什么联系呢?

【派】 anthropological *adj*. 人类学的，人类学上的
anthropologist *n*. 人类学者，人类学家

antibiotic [ˌæntɪbaɪ'ɒtɪk] *adj*. 抗菌的，抗生的；*n*. 抗生素

【记】 anti(反，抗) + bio(生命) + tic(形容词词尾)→抗生的

【例】 The *antibiotic* medicine can be used against infection. 抗生素类药物可以用来防止感染。

anticipate [æn'tɪsɪpeɪt] *v*. 预期，期望，预料

【记】 anti(前) + cip(拿，取) + ate(动词词尾)→提前取→预期

【例】 We *anticipate* that demand is likely to increase. 我们预料需求可能增加。

【同】 expect, foresee, predict

【派】 anticipation *n*. 预期，期望，预料

antipathy [æn'tɪpəθɪ] *n*. 反感

【记】 anti(反) + path(感情) + y(名词词尾)→反感

【例】 She felt no *antipathy* towards younger women. 她对比她年轻的妇女没有反感。

【同】 aversion, distaste

【派】 antipathetic *adj*. 讨厌的，反感的，格格不入的

antiquated ['æntɪkweɪtɪd] *adj*. 古老的，陈旧的，过时的

【记】 anti(前) + (i)qu(e)(形容词词尾，表示…的风格) + at(e)(动词词尾) + ed(形容词词尾)→具有以前的风格的→过时的

【例】 We have replaced our *antiquated* computer system. 我们更换了过时的计算机系统。

【同】 antique, old, outdated

antique [æn'tiːk] *adj*. 古代的，古老的，陈旧的；*n*. 古物，古董

【记】 anti(前) + (i)que(形容词词尾，表示"…风格的")→具有以前的风格的→古代的

【例】 1. The *antique* furniture was made in 1700. 这件古老的家具是1700年制造的。
2. The *antique* is a fake. 这件古董是一件赝品。

【同】 old, ancient, antiquated

【反】 modern, current

【派】 antiquity *n*. 古老，古代遗物

antiseptic [ˌæntɪˈseptɪk] *n*. 杀菌剂，防腐剂；*adj*. 消过毒的，无菌的

【记】 anti(反，抗) + sept(腐烂的) + ic(形容词兼名词词尾)→抗腐烂的东西→杀菌剂

【例】 1. The doctor put *antiseptic* on the wound. 医生把消毒液涂在伤口上。

2. The surgical instruments are *antiseptic*. 这些外科医疗器械是消过毒的。

【同】 aseptic，disinfectant；sterilized

apathy [ˈæpəθɪ] *n*. 冷淡，无动于衷

【记】 a(无) + path(感觉) + y(名词词尾)→没有感觉→无动于衷

【例】 He was sunk in *apathy* after his failure. 他失败后心灰意懒。

【同】 indifference

【反】 passion，enthusiasm

【派】 apathetic *adj*. 无兴趣的，冷淡的，无动于衷的

aperture [ˈæpətjʊə] *n*. 1. 开口，孔；2. (照相机等的)孔径，光圈

【记】 aper(开) + ture(名词词尾)→开的地方→孔

【例】 1. The *aperture* in the door is so wide. 门上的孔隙太大了。

2. What *aperture* are you using? 你使用多大的光圈?

【同】 hole，pore

apex [ˈeɪpeks] *n*. (复数 apexes 或 apices)顶点，最高点

【例】 At 41 he'd reached the *apex* of his career. 他 41 岁时到达事业的顶峰。

【同】 peak，summit，tip，top

【反】 bottom

aphorism [ˈæfərɪzm] *n*. 警句，格言

【记】 ap(= apo，离开) + hor(边界，界限) + ism(抽象名词词尾)→没有边界的，到处都适用的→警句，格言

【例】 'Art is long, and life is short' is an *aphorism*. "艺术长存，生命短暂"是一句格言。

【同】 saying，adage

【派】 aphoristic *adj*. 警句(似)的，格言(似)的

apologize [əˈpɒlədʒaɪz] *v*. 道歉，谢罪

【记】 apo(过错) + log(说话) + ize(动词词尾)→因为过错而说话→道歉

【例】 I *apologized* to the chairman for being late. 我因迟到向会议主席道歉。

【同】 repent，say sorry

【派】 (逆构)apology *n*. 道歉，歉意

appall [əˈpɔːl] *v*. 使惊骇，使充满恐惧

【记】 ap(= ad，to) + pall(= pale，苍白)→使(脸)变得苍白→使惊骇

【例】 The prospect of another war *appalled* us. 想到有可能发生另一场战争，我们不寒而栗。

【同】 horrify，shock

【反】 hearten，inspire

【派】 appalling *adj*. 骇人的，可怕的，令人震惊的

apparatus [ˌæpəˈreɪtəs] *n*. (复数-ses 或原形不变)器械，仪器，设备

【记】 ap(= ad，to) + par(准备) + atus(名词词尾)→准备好要用的东西→器械

【例】 Firemen needed breathing *apparatus* to enter the burning house. 消防队员需用呼吸器械才能进入燃烧着的房屋。

【同】 equipment, appliance, device

apparent [ə'pærənt] *adj*. 1.清晰可见的，明显的；2.表面上的，假的

【记】 ap(= ad, to) + par(出现) + ent(形容词词尾)→出现的→清晰可见的

【例】 1. It was *apparent* to all that he was guilty. 众所周知，他是有罪的。

2. Her *apparent* indifference made him even more nervous. 她表面上若无其事反而使他更加紧张。

【同】 distinct, obvious, evident; seeming, superficial

【反】 obscure; concealed

appeal [ə'piːl] *v*. /*n*. 1.有吸引力，有感染力；2.呼吁，恳求；3.上诉

【记】 ap(= ad, to) + peal(驱使)→向…驱使→有吸引力

【例】 1. Does jazz hold any *appeal* for you? 你对爵士乐有兴趣吗？

2. I am *appealing* on behalf of the famine victims. 我代表饥民恳求援助。

3. She *appealed* to the high court against her sentence. 她不服判决而向高等法院上诉。

【同】 ask, request, plead

【派】 appealing *adj*. 吸引人的；令人同情的

appease [ə'piːz] *v*. 安抚，平息

【记】 ap(= ad, to) + pease(= peace, 和平)→使平静下来→安抚

【例】 I tried to *appease* them by offering to replace the car with a brand-new one. 我提议用一辆崭新的车子取代这辆车，以平息他们的不满。

【同】 calm, pacification

【派】 appeasement *n*. 安抚，平息的行动或政策

appetite ['æpɪtaɪt] *n*. 1.胃口，食欲；2.爱好，兴趣

【记】 ap(= ad, to) + pet(追求) + ite(名词词尾)→追求的情绪→食欲

【例】 1. When I was ill I completely lost my *appetite*. 我生病时完全没有食欲。

2. He has an amazing *appetite* for hard work. 他出奇地喜爱艰巨的工作。

【派】 appetiser *n*. 开胃品

applaud [ə'plɔːd] *v*. 鼓掌欢迎，赞成

【记】 ap(= ad, to) + plaud(拍打)→一起拍手→鼓掌

【例】 The crowd *applauded* the performance for five minutes. 群众为演出鼓掌5分钟。

【同】 clap, acclaim, approve

【反】 disapprove, criticize

【派】 applause *n*. 鼓掌，称赞

appliance [ə'plaɪəns] *n*. 器具，器械，装置

【记】 appli(= apply, 应用) + ance(名词词尾)→应用的东西→器具

【例】 The kitchen is equipped with modern *appliances*. 厨房里备有各种现代厨具。

【同】 equipment, device, instrument, utensil

apply [ə'plaɪ] *v*. 1.应用，运用；2.申请，请求；3.涂，敷，抹

【记】 ap(= ad, to) + ply(折叠)→去折叠→去做→应用

【例】 1. The principle of diligence and frugality *applies* to all undertakings. 勤俭节约的原则适用于一切事业。

2. You should *apply* immediately, in person or by letter. 你应该立即申请，亲自去也好，写信也好。

3. A nurse is *applying* some medicine to his wound. 有个护士正在给他的伤口敷药。

【同】 use; ask, request; spread

【派】 applicant *n*. 申请人

application *n*. 申请，请求；应用，运用

appointment [ə'pɔɪntmənt] *n*. 1. 任命，选派；2. 约会，预约

【记】 ap(= ad, to) + point(点) + ment(名词词尾)→到指定的一个点→任命

【例】 1. His promotion to manager was a popular *appointment*. 他升任经理是众望所归的。

2. Otherwise you make an *appointment* to see your doctor at the health centre. 或者你也可以通过预约在保健中心看医生。

【同】 date, engagement

【派】 (逆构)appoint *v*. 任命，委任；指定

apportion [ə'pɔːʃən] *v*. 分派，(根据计划或规定)按比例分配

【记】 ap(= ad, to) + port(= part, 部分) + ion(名词词尾)→分成小部分→按比例分配

【例】 We must *apportion* the money fairly. 我们必须把钱公平地分配。

【同】 allocate, distribute

appraise [ə'preɪz] *v*. 评定，鉴定，评价

【记】 ap(= ad, to) + praise(= price, 价值，价钱)→对…定价值→评价

【例】 It's difficult to *appraise* the damage this might do to his political reputation. 要评定这件事对他的政治声望会造成怎样的损害是困难的。

【同】 estimate, evaluate

【派】 appraisal *n*. 估价，评价

appreciable [ə'priːʃɪəbl] *adj*. (数量或变化等)很大的，值得重视的

【记】 ap(= ad, to) + preci(价值，价钱) + able(形容词词尾)→能体现价值的→值得重视的

【例】 The increase in salary will be *appreciable*. 增加的薪水将会很可观。

【同】 considerable

appreciate [ə'priːʃɪeɪt] *v*. 1. 赏识，欣赏；2. 意识到，觉察；3. 感激；4. 增值，涨价

【记】 ap(= ad, to) + preci(价值，价钱) + ate(动词词尾)→对…有好的评价→赏识

【例】 1. You can't fully *appreciate* foreign literature in translation. 看翻译作品很难欣赏到外国文学的精髓。

2. I *appreciate* that this is not an easy decision for you to make. 我完全理解你作出这项决定是不容易的。

3. We *appreciate* your helping us. 我们感谢你们的帮助。

4. Houses in this area have all *appreciated* in value since the new highway was built. 由于修建了新公路，这一地区的房屋都涨价了。

【同】 admire; realize; acknowledge; revalue

【反】 despise; depreciate

【派】 appreciation *n*. 重视，赏识；评价

appreciative *adj*. 有欣赏力的；感激的

apprehend [ˌæprɪˈhend] *v*. 1. 逮捕；2. 领会，理解

【记】 ap(= ad, to) + prehend(抓取)→去抓取→领会

【例】 1. The thief was *apprehended* by the police in the act of stealing a car. 窃贼在偷汽车时当场被警察抓住。

2. We should not pretend to understand the world only by the intellect; we *apprehend* it just as much by feeling. 我们不应假装仅仅通过智力去理解世界；我们通过感觉理解得一样多。

【同】 arrest; comprehend, understand

apprehensive [ˌæprɪˈhensɪv] *adj*. 1. 有理解力的；2. 忧虑的，担心的

【记】 ap(= ad, to) + prehens(抓取) + ive(形容词词尾)→能抓到的→有理解力的

【例】 1. Judgement is implied in every *apprehensive* act. 每一种理解的行为都说明是运用了判断。

2. She was *apprehensive* about her son's safety. 她很担心儿子的安全。

【同】 discerning; worried

【反】 confident

【派】 apprehension *n*. 忧虑，担心；理解(力)

apprentice [əˈprentɪs] *n*. 学徒，初学者

【记】 ap(= ad, to) + prent(抓取，学习) + ice(名词词尾)→来学习的人→学徒

【例】 The company is taking on four new *apprentices*. 公司收了4个新学徒。

【同】 beginner, novice

【反】 old-hand, veteran

approach [əˈprəʊtʃ] *v*. 靠近，接近 *n*. 1. 靠近，接近；2. 方式，方法

【记】 ap(= ad, to) + proach(接近)→接近

【例】 1. As autumn *approaches*, the beekeepers pack up their hives and go south. 当秋天临近，养蜂人就收拾蜂箱向南方迁移。

2. The lion's *approach* drove away the small animals. 狮子一走近，小动物们都跑开了。

3. A similar *approach* in Hawaii has produced about 8, 000 new speakers of Polynesian languages in the past few years. 在夏威夷采取的类似方法在过去几年带动了大约8000人加入了说波利尼西亚语的行列。

【同】 reach, near; method, means

【派】 approachable *adj*. 可接近的，平易近人的，亲切的

approachability *n*. 可亲近，可接近性

appropriate [əˈprəʊprɪɪt] *adj*. 适当的，恰当的

【记】 ap(= ad, to) + propri(= proper, 适当的) + ate(形容词词尾)→适当的

【例】 You will be informed of the details at the *appropriate* time. 在适当的时候将把详情告诉你。

【同】 suitable, proper

【反】 inappropriate, unsuitable, improper

approve [ə'pruːv] *v*. 1. 赞成, 同意; 2. 批准, 核准

【记】 ap(= ad, to) + prove(证明)→证明(可行)→赞成

【例】 1. She doesn't want to take her new boy-friend home in case her parents don't *approve* of him. 她不愿把新男朋友带回家, 怕父母看不中他。

2. Your application will be processed promptly and you can begin making purchases immediately after your application is *approved*. 你的申请将会被及时处理, 一旦申请获准, 即可购买。

【同】 agree, endorse; ratify

【反】 disapprove, disagree, object

【派】 approval *n*. 赞成; 批准

approximate [əprɒksɪ'mət] *adj*. 近似的, 大约的

【记】 ap(= ad, to) + proxim(接近) + ate(形容词词尾)→接近的→大约的

【例】 This is just an *approximate* figure. 这仅是个大概数字。

【同】 rough, approximative

【反】 exact, precise

【派】 approximately *adv*. 近似地, 大概

apt [æpt] *adj*. 1. 易于…的, 有…倾向的; 2. 恰当的; 3. 聪明的

【例】 1. This kind of shoe is *apt* to slip on wet ground. 这种鞋子在湿地上容易打滑。

2. A comedian will present a situation followed by an unexpected interpretation that is also *apt*. 喜剧演员是表现一种情形, 并随后给出一个意想不到却很恰当的解释。

3. She's one of my *aptest* students. 她是我最聪明的一个学生。

【同】 likely; proper; clever

【反】 improper; foolish, stupid

aptitude ['æptɪtjuːd] *n*. 天资, 才能

【记】 apt(聪明的) + itude(名词词尾)→聪明→天资

【例】 Edison had a remarkable *aptitude* for inventing new things. 爱迪生具有发明创造的非凡才能。

【同】 talent, gift

aquatic [ə'kwætɪk] *adj*. 水生的, 水上的

【记】 aqua(水) + tic(形容词词尾)→水生的

【例】 Many forms of *aquatic* life inhabit ponds. 有很多种水生动植物栖居于池塘。

【派】 aquaculture *n*. 水产养殖

aquarium *n*. 养鱼缸; 水族馆

arable ['ærəbl] *adj*. 可耕的, 适于耕种的

【记】 ar(耕作)+able(形容词词尾)→能够耕种的→可耕的

【例】 In Holland thousands of hectares have been reclaimed from the sea and turned over to *arable* land and pasture. 在荷兰，人们拦海造田，已开垦了成千上万公顷的土地并将它们变成可耕地和牧场。

【同】 cultivable, cultivatable

【派】 arability *n*. 适合耕种，可耕性

arbitrary ['ɑːbɪtrərɪ] *adj*. 武断的，任意的

【记】 arbitr(给出判决)+ary(形容词词尾)→(随意)给出判决的→武断的

【例】 The choice of players for the team seems completely *arbitrary*. 对队员的挑选似乎完全是主观决定的。

【同】 unreasonable, willful

arbitrate ['ɑːbɪtreɪt] *v*. 仲裁，公断

【记】 arbitr(给出判决)+ate(动词词尾)→使给出判决→仲裁

【例】 He was asked to *arbitrate* a serious dispute between management and the unions. 他被邀请在资方与工会之间对一严重争端作出仲裁。

【同】 mediate, intercede

【派】 arbitrator *n*. 仲裁者

arbitration *n*. 仲裁，公断

archaeology [ˌɑːkɪ'ɒlədʒɪ] *n*. 考古学

【记】 archae(=ancient，古代的)+ology(…学)→研究古代的学科→考古学

【例】 *Archaeology* is partly the discovery of the treasures of the past, partly the careful work of the scientific analyst, partly the exercise of the creative imagination. 考古学一部分是发现历史珍宝，一部分是科学分析者细致的工作，一部分是发挥创造性的想象力。

【派】 archaeological *adj*. 考古学的，考古学上的

archaeologist *n*. 考古学家

archaic [ɑː'keɪɪk] *adj*. 古代的，古老的，过时的

【记】 arch(古代的)+(a)ic(形容词词尾)→古代的

【例】 'Thou art' is an *archaic* form of 'you are'. "Thou art"是"you are"的古体。

【同】 antient, antiquated, old-fashioned

【反】 modern, up-to-date

【派】 archaism *n*. 古语，古体

archetype ['ɑːkɪtaɪp] *n*. 原型，典型

【记】 arch(e)(古代的，最先的)+type(类型)→最初的类型→原型

【例】 The House of Commons is the *archetype* of all the representative assemblies. 下议院是所有代议制议会的原型。

【同】 original type

architect ['ɑːkɪtekt] *n*. 建筑师

【记】 archi(主要的)+tect(工匠)→主要的工匠→建筑师

【例】 Now other *architects* know how to design buildings to fit into the land. 现在别的建筑师也知道怎样设计能使建筑物与地形相协调。

【同】 builder

【派】 architecture *n*. 建筑，建筑学

architectural *adj*. 建筑的，建筑学的

archive [ɑːkaɪv] *n*. (通常用复数)档案，大宗记录

【记】 arch(统治)＋ive(本是形容词词尾，但是可以转用做名词)→记录官方的活动的→档案

【例】 The Museum of London has drawn on its *archive* collection to convey a fresh picture with its exhibition. 伦敦博物馆用其收藏的档案举办了一次展览，展示出一幅鲜活的画面。

【同】 file

【派】 archival *adj*. 档案的

archivist *n*. 档案保管员

ardent [ˈɑːdənt] *adj*. 热情的，热心的，热烈的

【记】 ard(燃烧)＋ent(形容词词尾)→像燃烧一样的→热情的

【例】 I am an *ardent* supporter of the local football team. 我是本地足球队的球迷。

【同】 burning，fervent，fiery

【反】 cool

ardor [ˈɑːdə] *n*. 激情，狂热

【记】 ard(燃烧)＋or(名词词尾)→燃烧的东西→热情

【例】 His *ardor* for the cause inspired his followers. 他对事业的热情激励着他的追随者。

【同】 enthusiasm，passion，zeal

arduous [ˈɑːdjʊəs] *adj*. 艰巨的，艰苦的，困难的

【记】 ardu(陡峭的)＋ous(形容词词尾)→难攀登的→艰巨的，困难的

【例】 Negotiating a reduction in nuclear arms is a long and *arduous* undertaking. 有关削减核武器的谈判是一项漫长而艰苦的工作。

【同】 hard，difficult，labourious

arid [ˈærɪd] *adj*. 干旱的，贫瘠的；2. 枯燥的，无趣味的

【例】 1. Nothing grows in these *arid* conditions. 在这些干旱环境中，寸草不生。

2. This is a technically perfect but *arid* musical performance. 这是一场技术上完美但枯燥的音乐演出。

【同】 dry，barren；dull，boring

【反】 wet，fruitful；interesting

【派】 aridity *n*. 干旱，乏味

aristocrat [ˈærɪstəkræt] *n*. 贵族

【记】 aristo(最好的)＋crat(统治)→最好的统治(的人)→贵族

【例】 Her father was an English *aristocrat*. 她的父亲曾是英国贵族。

【同】 patrician，nobleman

【派】 aristocratic *adj*. 贵族的，贵族化的

aristocracy *n*. 贵族，贵族政府，贵族统治

arithmetic [əˈrɪθmətɪk] *n*. 算术，算法

【记】 arithm(数字)+etic(本是形容词词尾，但是可以转用做名词)→与数字有关的→算术

【例】 *Arithmentic* is a basic school subject. 算术是一门基础学科。

【派】 arithmetician *n*. 算术家，精于算术的人

arithmetical *adj*. 算术的，算术上的

armament ['ɑːməmənt] *n*. (常用复数)军备，武器

【记】 arm(武装)+a +ment(名词词尾)→用来武装的东西→军备

【例】 Some observers think that this country's offer to reduce spending on *armaments* is just a hollow promise. 一些观察家认为，这个国家减少军备开支的提议仅仅是一个空口许诺。

【同】 arming, weaponry

【反】 disarmament

armor ['ɑːmə] *n*. 1. 盔甲，装甲；2. 保护物

【记】 arm(武装)+or(名词词尾)→用来武装的东西→盔甲

【例】 1. The film is about a knight in full *armor*. 这部电影是关于一个全身披挂盔甲的骑士。

2. Their sense of justice gave them *armor* against the contempt of others. 他们的正义感保护他们不被别人轻视。

aroma [ə'rəumə] *n*. 1. 香气，芳香；2. 气氛，氛围

【例】 1. The rose gave the room a pleasant *aroma*. 玫瑰给房间带来怡人的芳香。

2. An *aroma* of mystery hung about the place. 这个地方笼罩着一种神秘的气氛。

【同】 fragrance, perfume, scent; atmosphere

【派】 aromatic *adj*. 芬芳的

arouse [ə'rauz] *v*. 唤醒，激起

【记】 a(加强语气)+rouse(唤醒)→唤醒

【例】 He succeeded in *arousing* the nation's sympathy. 他已经激发了全民的同情。

【同】 awaken, stimulate, excite

【反】 calm, quiet

【派】 arousal *n*. 觉醒，激励

array [ə'reɪ] *n*. 1. 展示，陈列，排列；2. 衣服，服装；*v*. 排列，部署；2. 装饰，打扮

【记】 ar(=ad, to)+ray(光线)→把…弄成一束光线→一连串

【例】 1. The myth is that from a disorderly *array* of factual information an orderly, relevant theory will somehow emerge. 这种荒诞的方法是说，从一串杂乱无章的真实信息中总会产生出一个有条理的相关理论。

2. The royal couple appeared in splendid *array*. 王室伉俪身穿盛装出现。

3. His soldiers were *arrayed* along the riverbank. 他的士兵沿着河岸摆开阵势。

4. She was *arrayed* in all her finery. 她打扮得花枝招展的。

【同】 display, arrangement; finery, apparel; align, arrange; adorn, dress

arrogant ['ærəgənt] *adj*. 傲慢的，自大的

【记】 ar(=ad, to)+rog(要求，问)+ant(形容词词尾)→一直提要求的→傲慢的

【例】 One should never be *arrogant* even when he is at his best. 一个人在最得意的时候

也不应傲慢。

【同】 self-important，proud

【反】 modest，humble

【派】 arrogance *n*. 傲慢，自大

arsenal ['ɑːsɪnl] *n*. 兵工厂，军械库

【记】 来自阿拉伯语 ar(= dar，房子) + sen(a)(生产) + al(名词词尾)→生产(武器)的地方→兵工厂

【例】 The police found an *arsenal* in the terrorists' hideout. 警察在恐怖分子藏匿的地方发现了一个军械库。

【同】 armory

article ['ɑːtɪkl] *n*. 1.文章，论文；2.物品，商品；3.项目，条款

【记】 art(艺术，技巧) + icle(名词词尾)→用技巧做出的东西→物品

【例】 1. Have you read the *article* on the Chinese way of life in today's paper? 你读过今天报纸上论述中国生活方式的文章了吗?

2. The burglars took no *articles* of value. 这些盗贼没有拿走值钱的东西。

3. The electoral law has special *articles* dealing with these problems. 选举法关于这些问题有专门的条款。

【同】 essay，writing；object，thing；item，clause

articulate [ɑː'tɪkjʊlɪt] *v*. 1.清晰地发音，清楚地表达；2.用关节连接，接合；*adj*. 1.发音清晰的，表达能力强的；2.有关节的

【记】 articul(关节) + ate(动词兼形容词词尾)→有关节的→接合

【例】 1. He finds it difficult to *articulate* his distress. 他感到很难表达清除自己的痛苦。

2. The bones of our fingers are *articulated*. 我们的手指骨是以关节相连接的。

3. She's unusually *articulate* for a ten-year-old. 对一个10岁的孩子来说，她异乎寻常地能说会道。

4. Many insects are *articulate* animals. 许多昆虫都是节肢动物。

【同】 enunciate；joint；clear，expressive

【反】 inarticulate

【派】 articulation *n*. 发音，表达；关节

artificial [ˌɑːtɪ'fɪʃəl] *adj*. 1.人工的，人造的，假的；2.做作的，虚假的

【记】 art(i)(技巧) + fic(做) + ial(形容词词尾)→用技巧做出来的→人造的

【例】 1. This brand of tinned beans contains no *artificial* colouring. 这种品牌的罐装豆不含人造色素。

2. Her *artificial* gaiety disguised an inner sadness. 她以矫揉造作的快乐掩饰着内心的悲痛。

【同】 man-made，fake，synthetic；pretended

【反】 genuine，real

【派】 artificiality *n*. 人工，人造物

ascend [ə'send] *v*. 上升，升高

【记】 a(= ad，to) + scend(登，爬)→向上爬→上升

【例】 We watched the mists *ascending* from the valley below. 我们看着薄雾从下面的山

谷中升起。
【同】 climb，rise，go up
【反】 descend
【派】 ascent *n*. 上升，提高；上坡路

ascertain [ˌæsəˈteɪn] *v*. 查明，确定
【记】 a(= ad，to) + (s)certain(确定的)→使…确定→查明
【例】 The police are trying to *ascertain* what really happened. 警方正设法查个水落石出。
【同】 confirm，determine
【反】 assume，guess
【派】 ascertainment *n*. 探查，发现

ascetic [əˈsetɪk] *n*. 苦行者，禁欲者；*adj*. 禁欲的，苦行的
【记】 asce(实践者，隐士) + tic(形容词词尾)→隐士的生活的→苦行的
【例】 The hermit followed an *ascetic* life-style. 这个隐士过的是苦行生活。
【同】 abstainer
【反】 self-indulgent
【派】 asceticism *n*. 禁欲主义

ascribe [əsˈkraɪb] *v*. 把…归于
【记】 a(= ad，to) + scribe(写)→把…写上去→归因于
【例】 1. He *ascribed* his failure to bad luck. 他把失败归咎于运气不好。
2. This play is usually *ascribed* to Shakespeare. 这个剧本一般认为是莎士比亚所作。
【同】 attribute
【派】 ascription *n*. 归因，归属

aspect [ˈæspekt] *n*. 1. 样子，容貌；2. (问题、事物等的)方面
【记】 a(加强语气) + spect(看见)→看见的东西→外表
【例】 1. A young woman, of sullen *aspect*, was sitting alone on the bench. 一个面色忧郁的年轻女人独自坐在长凳上。
2. The training program covers every *aspect* of the job. 训练计划的范围包括了这种工作的各个方面。
【同】 appearance，look；view

aspersion [əsˈpɜːʃən] *n*. 诽谤，中伤
【记】 a(= ad，to) + spers(分散，散布) + ion(名词词尾)→散布(谣言)→诽谤
【例】 I strongly resent such unwarranted *aspersions*. 我对这种莫须有的诽谤深恶痛绝。
【同】 defamation，slander
【派】 (逆构)asperse *v*. 诽谤，中伤

aspire [əsˈpaɪə] *v*. 渴望，追求，有志于
【记】 a(= ad，to) + spir(呼吸) + e→对…吐气→渴望
【例】 He *aspired* after a political career. 他追求的是政治生涯。
【同】 desire，seek，strive
【派】 aspiring *adj*. 有抱负的，有理想的

aspiration *n*. 雄心，抱负

assail [ə'seɪl] *v*. (身体上)攻击，(言语上)攻击，批评

【记】 as(= ad, to) + sail(跳)→跳起来→猛扑上去→攻击

【例】 The police were *assailed* with rocks and petrol bombs. 警察遭到石块和汽油弹的猛烈攻击。

【同】 attack, assault

【反】 defend, guard, protect

【派】 assailment *n*. 攻击，痛骂

assassinate [ə'sæsɪneɪt] *v*. 暗杀，行刺

【记】 assassin(刺客) + ate(动词词尾)→使刺客做→暗杀

【例】 The exposure of the plot to *assassinate* the President probably saved his life. 揭发了刺杀总统的阴谋可能救了他一命。

【同】 kill, murder

【派】 (逆构)assassin *n*. 刺客

assassination *n*. 暗杀

assault [ə'sɔːlt] *v*. /*n*. (武力上的)袭击，(口头的)攻击

【记】 as(= ad, to) + sault(= sal, 跳)→猛扑上去→袭击

【例】 1. He got two years' imprisonment for *assaulting* a police officer. 他因袭击警察而遭两年监禁。

2. The roar of city traffic is a steady *assault* on one's nerves. 市区车辆的喧嚣声不停地刺激着神经。

【同】 attack, assail, offense

【派】 assaulter *n*. 攻击者，殴打者

assemble [ə'sembl] *v*. 1. 集合，聚集；2. 装配

【记】 as(= ad, to) + sembl(类似) + e→让类似的在一起→集合

【例】 1. The whole school (was) *assembled* in the main hall. 全校在大礼堂集合。

2. The bookcase can easily be *assembled* with a screwdriver. 这个书柜用一把螺丝刀就可以很容易地安装起来。

【同】 gather, congregate; put together

【反】 dismiss, disassemble

assembly [ə'semblɪ] *n*. 1. 集合，集会；2. 装配，组装

【记】 as(= ad, to) + sembl(类似) + y(名词词尾)→类似的在一起→集合

【例】 1. The national *assembly* has/have met to discuss the crisis. 国民大会已对这一危机进行了讨论。

2. Each component is carefully checked before *assembly*. 每个零件在装配前都经过仔细检查。

【同】 gathering, convention, congregation

【反】 disassembly

assert [ə'sɜːt] *v*. 坚定地断言，主张

【记】 as(= ad, to) + sert(连接，加入)→声明加入→主张

【例】 She *asserted* her innocence/that she was innocent. 她坚称自己很清白/她是无

辜的。

【同】 declare，affirm，insist

【派】 assertion *n*. 主张，断言

assertive *adj*. 断言的；自信的，武断的

assess [ə'ses] *v*. 1.对…进行估价，估计；2.评估，评价

【记】 as(= ad，to) + sess(坐)→使坐下来(说)→定价格→对…进行估价

【例】 1.They *assessed* the value of the house at £60，000. 他们估计这座房子值6万英镑。

2.It's too early to *assess* the effects of the new legislation. 要评价新法令的效果现在还为时过早。

【同】 estimate，evaluate

【派】 assessment *n*. 评价，评估

assessor *n*. 估价员，估税员

asset ['æset] *n*. 1.(通常用复数)资产，财产；2.有价值的或有用的东西

【例】 1.His *assets* included shares in the company and a house in London. 他的财产包括公司的股票和位于伦敦的房子。

2.Good health is a great *asset*. 健康就是莫大的财富。

【同】 property，wealth；benefit

【反】 liability

assiduous [ə'sɪdjʊəs] *adj*. 勤勉的，刻苦的

【记】 as(= ad，to) + sid(坐) + uous(形容词词尾)→(一直)坐在桌子边的→勤勉的

【例】 The book was the result of ten years' *assiduous* research. 那本书是十年苦心钻研的成果。

【同】 diligent，sedulous，hard-working

assign [ə'saɪn] *v*. 1.分配，指派；2.确定，指定

【记】 as(= ad，to) + sign(记号，信号)→在…上面打符号决定→指派

【例】 1.The teacher has *assigned* each of us a holiday task. 老师给我们每个人都分配了假期的工作。

2.Can we *assign* jealousy as the motive for the crime? 我们能否确定这一犯罪动机是出于嫉妒？

【同】 distribute，appoint；ascribe

【派】 assignment *n*. 分派，指定；任务，作业

assimilate [ə'sɪmɪleɪt] *v*. 1.吸收；2.同化

【记】 as(= ad，to) + simli(类似，相同) + ate(动词词尾)→使…相同→同化

【例】 1.Some foods *assimilate*/ are *assimilated* more easily than others. 有些食物比另一些食物容易吸收。

2.The USA has *assimilated* people from many different countries. 美国已经同化了许多来自不同国家的人。

【同】 absorb，integrate

【反】 dissimilate

【派】 assimilation *n*. 吸收；同化，同化作用

assist [ə'sɪst] *v*. 协助，帮助

【记】 as(= ad, to) + sist(站立)→站在一旁→协助

【例】 You will be required to *assist* Mrs Smith in preparing a report. 你将要协助史密斯夫人准备一份报告。

【同】 help, aid

【派】 assistance *n*. 帮助，协助

assistant *adj*. 助理的，辅助的；*n*. 助手

associate [ə'səuʃɪeɪt] *v*. 1. 使联系，联想；2. 交往，交际

【记】 as(= ad, to) + soci(结交) + ate(动词词尾)→使…结合起来→使联系

【例】 1. You wouldn't normally *associate* these two writers—their styles are completely different. 通常不会把这两位作家相提并论——他们两人的风格完全不同。

2. I don't like you *associating* with such people. 我不喜欢你和那些人混在一起。

【同】 connect, combine, unite; socialize

【派】 associated *adj*. 联合的，关联的

association *n*. 联想；协会，社团

assorted [ə'sɔːtɪd] *adj*. 各式各样的，多样混合的

【记】 as(= ad, to) + sort(种类) + ed(形容词词尾)→按种类分的→各式各样的

【例】 This is a bag of *assorted* sweets. 这是一袋什锦糖果。

【同】 classified, various

【派】 assortment *n*. 分类；什锦，各色俱全

assuage [ə'sweɪdʒ] *v*. 缓和，减轻(痛苦等)

【记】 as(= ad, to) + suage(甜的)→使感觉甜的→减轻痛苦

【例】 Nothing can *assuage* the widow's grief. 什么也不能缓和这寡妇的哀伤。

【同】 alleviate, soothe, relieve

【派】 assuagement *n*. 缓和，缓和物

assume [ə'sjuːm] *v*. 1. 假定，以为；2. 承担(责任)，担任

【记】 as(= ad, to) + sum(拿，取) + e→拿取→有了(想法)→以为

【例】 1. We must *assume* him to be innocent until he is proved guilty. 尚未证实他有罪，就得假定他是清白的。

2. You will *assume* your new responsibilities tomorrow. 你明天就任新职。

【同】 suppose, presume

【派】 assumption *n*. 假设，假想

assure [ə'ʃuə] *v*. 确保，向…保证

【记】 as(= ad, to) + sure(确定的)→使…确定→向…保证

【例】 I *assure* you they'll be perfectly safe with us. 我向你保证，他们和我们在一起十分安全。

【同】 guarantee, convince

【派】 assurance *n*. 保证，信心；保险

astonish [æs'tɒnɪʃ] *v*. 使惊讶

【记】 as(= ad, to) + tonish(雷)→使听到雷声→使惊讶

【例】 It *astonishes* me that no one has thought of this before. 以前谁也没想到这一点，

我感到惊讶。

【同】 amaze, astound, surprise

【派】 astonishing *adj*. 惊人的，令人惊讶的

astound [əs'taʊnd] *v*. 使震惊，使惊异

【例】 The news of their divorce *astounded* me. 他们离婚的消息使我大为震惊。

【同】 amaze, astonish, surprise

【派】 astounding *adj*. 使人震惊的

astronaut ['æstrənɔːt] *n*. 宇航员，航天员

【记】 astro(星) + nau(船，航行) + t→星际的航行员→宇航员

【例】 Spaceship manned by trained *astronauts* will launch soon. 载有受过训练的宇航员的太空船马上就要发射了。

【派】 astronautic *adj*. 太空航行的，太空航行员的

astronomy [ə'strɒnəmɪ] *n*. 天文学

【记】 astro(星) + nomy(某一领域的知识，定律)→研究星星的学科→天文学

【例】 *Astronomy* is the scientific study of the sun, moon, stars and other heaven bodies. 天文学是研究太阳、月亮、星星和其他天体的科学。

【派】 astronomical *adj*. 天文的，天文学的；庞大无法估计的

astronomer *n*. 天文学家

astute [ə'stjuːt, ə'stuːt] *adj*. 机敏的，精明的

【例】 It was an *astute* move to sell just before prices went down. 正好在价格下跌前脱手，真是精明之举。

【同】 smart, shrewd, perceptive

【反】 dull, blunt

asymmetry [æ'sɪmətrɪ] *n*. 不对称，不匀称

【记】 a(不) + sym(相同) + metry(测量)→测量不相同的→不对称

【例】 Two American researchers studied the brains of human embryos and discovered that the left-right *asymmetry* exists before birth. 两位美国研究人员研究了人类胚胎的大脑，发现左右不对称现象在出生前就有。

【同】 dissymmetry, imbalance

【反】 symmetry

【派】 asymmetric *adj*. 不对称的，不匀称的

atheism ['eɪθɪɪzəm] *n*. 无神论

【记】 a(无) + the(神) + ism(名词词尾)→无神论

【例】 Anne's *atheism* contrasted with her friend's strong religious beliefs. 安妮的无神论与她朋友强烈的宗教信仰形成鲜明的对比。

【同】 unbelief

【反】 theism

【派】 atheist *n*. 无神论者

athlete ['æθliːt] *n*. 运动员，体育家

【记】 athl(比赛) + ete(名词词尾)→参加比赛的人→运动员

【例】 The Olympic *athletes* came from all over the world. 参加奥运会的运动员来自世

界各地。

【同】 sportsperson

【派】 athletic *adj*. 运动的，体育的；运动员的

athletics *n*. 体育运动(尤指田径运动)

atmosphere [ˈætməsfɪə] *n*. 1.大气，大气层；2.气氛

【记】 atmo(= vapour，气) + sphere(球)→地球周围的气体→大气

【例】 1. We still let harmful gases escape into the *atmosphere*. 我们还在让有害的气体泄漏进大气层。

2. The *atmosphere* over dinner was warm and friendly. 用餐时四周洋溢着热情友好的气氛。

【同】 air；ambience

【派】 atmospheric *adj*. 大气的，空气的

atom [ˈætəm] *n*. 原子

【记】 a(不) + tom(分割)→不能再分割的东西(当时认为原子是无法再分割的东西)→原子

【例】 Two *atoms* of hydrogen combine with one atom of oxygen to form a molecule of water. 两个氢原子和一个氧原子结合而形成一个水分子。

【派】 atomic *adj*. 原子的，关于原子的；核能的

atomization *n*. 原子化；雾化

atrophy [ˈætrəfɪ] *v*./*n*. 萎缩(症)，衰退

【记】 a(无) + troph(滋养) + y(名词词尾)→没有营养了→萎缩

【例】 The disease *atrophied* her leg. 疾病使她的一条腿萎缩了。

【同】 wither，shrink

attach [əˈtætʃ] *v*. 1.系，贴；2.附加，使附属

【记】 at(= ad，to) + tach(栓)→栓上→系，贴

【例】 1. He *attached* labels to all his bags. 他在所有的袋子上都贴上标签。

2. She *attached* a check to the order form. 她在订货单上附了一张支票。

【同】 fasten，tie；affix，append

【反】 detach

【派】 attachment *n*. 附属物

attain [əˈteɪn] *v*. 达到，获得

【记】 at(= ad，to) + tain(接触)→接触到→达到

【例】 The challenge is to *attain* a sustainable balance between population，economic growth and the environment. 我们面临的挑战就是在人口、经济增长和环境之间达到可持续的平衡。

【同】 reach，gain，achieve

【反】 fail

【派】 attainable *adj*. 可以达到的，可以获得的

attainment *n*. 达到，获得；才能，造诣

attempt [əˈtempt] *n*./*v*. 试图，尝试

【记】 at(= ad，to) + tempt(尝试)→尝试

【例】 1. They made no *attempt* to escape/at escaping. 他们并不想逃跑。
2. An astronaut will *attempt* to leave the stationary spaceship and then return to it. 一名宇航员将试着离开停着的宇宙飞船，然后再回到里面去。
【同】 try, endeavor

attend [ə'tend] *v*. 1. 出席，参加；2. 照料，看管，伴随；3. 专心，注意
【记】 at(= ad, to) + tend(伸展)→伸展到→参加
【例】 1. The meeting was well *attended*. 有很多人出席会议。
2. He was constantly *attended* by his bodyguard. 他经常由保镖保护着。
3. Why weren't you *attending* when I explained before? 我以前解释的时候，你怎么不注意听呢?
【同】 participate; serve, assist; observe, concentrate on
【反】 ignore, disregard
【派】 attendance *n*. 出席，参加；照料
attendant *n*. 出席者，参加者；侍从，陪伴者

attire [ə'taɪə] *n*. 穿着，盛装(正规服装总称)；*v*. 穿着，打扮
【记】 at(= ad, to) + tire(服装)→穿上服装→穿着打扮
【例】 1. The singer wears rich *attire*. 歌唱家身着盛装。
2. The graduates *attired* in their academic robes. 毕业生们穿着学位服。
【同】 apparel, clothing; dress

attitude ['ætɪtjuːd] *n*. 态度，看法
【记】 att(= apt, 倾向) + itude(名词词尾)→…的倾向→态度
【例】 People's *attitude* towards the skyscrapers varies widely. 人们对这些摩天大楼的态度很不相同。
【同】 position, standpoint

attorney [ə'tɜːnɪ] *n*. 律师
【记】 at(= ad, to) + torne(转动) + y(名词词尾)→代替者，代理人→律师
【例】 She refused to make a statement until she had spoken to her *attorney*. 她拒绝发表谈话，要先和她的律师谈谈。
【同】 lawyer

attribute ['ætrɪbjuːt; ə'trɪbjuːt] *v*. 1. 把…归因于；2. 认为…属于
【记】 at(= ad, to) + tribut(赠与) + e→赠与→使归属于→把…归因于
【例】 1. She *attributes* her success to hard work and a bit of luck. 她认为她的成功是由于勤奋加上一点儿运气而得来的。
2. This song is usually *attributed* to Bach. 这首歌曲通常被认为是巴赫的作品。
【同】 ascribe, impute, assign
【派】 attributable *adj*. 可归因于的

attrition [ə'trɪʃən] *n*. (逐渐的)损耗，磨损
【记】 at(= ad, to) + trit(擦) + ion(名词词尾)→擦掉→磨损
【例】 The long war of *attrition* exhausted the strength of both countries. 这场长期的消耗战耗尽了两国的力量。
【同】 abrasion, erosion, wearing away

【派】 (逆构)attrite *adj*. 磨损的，削弱的；*v*. 磨损以便使…变小

auction [ˈɔːkʃən] *v*./*n*. 拍卖

【记】 auc(增加) + tion(名词词尾)→渐渐地增加其价值→拍卖

【例】 The house is up for *auction*/will be sold by *auction*. 这所房子将要拍卖。

【同】 vendue

【派】 auctioneer *n*. 拍卖人

audacious [ɔːˈdeɪʃəs] *adj*. 大胆的，敢于冒险的

【记】 aud(大胆) + acious(形容词词尾)→大胆的

【例】 We have made an *audacious* plan. 我们制订了一个大胆的计划。

【同】 brave, fearless, venturous

【反】 careful, prudent

【派】 audacity *n*. 大胆，卤莽

audible [ˈɔːdəbl] *adj*. 听得见的

【记】 aud(听) + ible(形容词词尾)→听得见的

【例】 Her voice was scarcely *audible* above the noise of the wind. 在风中她的声音几乎听不见。

【同】 hearable

audit [ˈɔːdɪt] *v*./*n*. 1.查账，审计；2.旁听

【记】 aud(听) + it(名词词尾)→听的行为→听…汇报账目→审计

【例】 1. The yearly *audit* takes place each December. 年度审计在每年的12月进行。
2. She's not officially registered, so she's just *auditing*. 她并没有正式注册，只是旁听而已。

【同】 scrutinise, inspect

【派】 auditor *n*. 查账员，审计员

audition [ɔːˈdɪʃən] *n*. 试听，面试

【记】 aud(听) + ition(名词词尾)→听觉→试听

【例】 I'm going to the *audition* but I don't expect I'll get a part. 我去试音，可并不指望会给我个角色演出。

【同】 tryout, interview

【派】 auditory *adj*. 听觉的，关于听觉的

auditorium [ˌɔːdɪˈtɔːrɪəm] *n*. (复数 auditoriums 或 auditoria)听众席，观众席；大礼堂

【记】 audi(听) + orium(名词词尾，表场所)→听的地方→大礼堂

【例】 The lecture will be in the biggest *auditorium* in our university. 讲座在我们学校的最大的礼堂里举行。

【同】 assembly hall

augment [ɔːgˈment] *n*./*v*. 扩大，增加，提高

【记】 aug(增加) + ment(名词词尾)→增加

【例】 He *augments* his income by teaching in the evenings. 他晚上去教书以增加收入。

【同】 enlarge, increase

【反】 abate

【派】 augmentation *n*. 扩大，增加，提高

aura [ˈɔːrə] *n*. (复数 auras 或 aurae)气味，气氛，氛围

【例】 She always seems to have an *aura* of happiness about her. 她好像总是喜气洋洋的。

【同】 air, atmosphere

auspice [ˈɔːspɪs] *n*. 1. 前兆；2. (通常用复数)赞助，支持

【记】 au(= avi, 鸟) + spice(= see 看)→以鸟的飞行来预卜吉凶→前兆

【例】 1. The smoothness in your exams is an *auspice* for your future success. 考试进展顺利是你将来成功的先兆。

2. This conference has been arranged under the *auspices* of the United Nations. 本次会议由联合国赞助召开。

【同】 omen, presage; sponsorship

【派】 auspicious *adj*. 预示成功的，有利的，幸运的

authentic [ɔːˈθentɪk] *adj*. 1. 真正的，真实的；2. 可信的，可靠的

【记】 aut(自己) + hent(做的人) + ic(形容词词尾)→自己亲手做的→可信的

【例】 1. Is that an *authentic* Roman statue, or a modern copy? 那是罗马雕塑的原作还是现代的复制品？

2. Can we taste some *authentic* Chinese food there? 在那儿我们能吃上正宗的中国菜吗？

【同】 true, real, genuine; credible

【反】 inauthentic, false

【派】 authenticate *v*. 证明…是确实的；使具有法律上的效力

authority [ɔːˈθɒrɪtɪ] *n*. 1. 权力，权威；2. (常用复数)当局；3. 允许

【记】 auth(使生长) + or(表示"人"的名词词尾) + ity(名词词尾)→使事物产生的根源→权威

【例】 1. She now has *authority* over the people she used to take orders from. 她现在有权力支配那些一贯向她发号施令的人。

2. The health *authorities* are investigating the matter. 卫生当局正调查这件事。

3. I have the boss's *authority* to park here. 我有上司的许可把汽车停在这里。

【同】 right, power; government, administration; approval

【派】 authoritative *adj*. 权威性的，可相信的；官方的，当局的

authorize [ˈɔːθəraɪz] *v*. 授权，批准

【记】 auth(使生长) + or(表示"人"的名词词尾) + ize(动词词尾)→使…具有使事物生长的权力→授权

【例】 I've been *authorized* by the court to repossess this property. 我得到法庭认可重新拥有这笔财产。

【同】 approve, empower, assign

【反】 forbid, prohibit

【派】 authorized *adj*. 权威认可的，经授权的

authorization *n*. 授权，认可

autobiography [ˌɔːtəbaɪˈɒgrəfɪ] *n*. 自传

【记】 auto(自己) + bio(生活) + graph(写) + y→写关于自己的生活的→自传

【例】 Bill Clinton's *autobiography* is a best seller. 比尔·克林顿的自传是一本畅销书。
【同】 life story, memoir
【派】 autobiographer *n*. 自传作者
autobiographical *adj*. 自传的，自传体的，自传作家的

autocratic [ˌɔːtəˈkrætɪk] *adj*. 独裁的，独断专行的
【记】 auto(自己) + crat(统治) + ic(形容词词尾)→自己统治的→独裁的
【例】 His *autocratic* manner made him unpopular. 他的专横态度使他不得人心。
【同】 dictatorial, tyrannical, dominating
【派】 (逆构)autocrat *n*. 独裁者
autocracy *n*. 独裁政治，独裁政府

automate [ˈɔːtəmeɪt] *v*. 自动化，用自动化技术操作
【记】 auto(自己) + mate(行为)→自己做→自动化
【例】 This part of the assembly process is now fully *automated*. 装配过程的这一部分现在是全自动的。
【派】 automatic *adj*. 自动的；不经思索的
automation *n*. 自动化
automaton *n*. 机器人

autonomous [ɔːˈtɒnəməs] *adj*. 自治的，独立自主的
【记】 auto(自己) + nom(法律) + ous(形容词词尾)→使用自己的法律的→自治的
【例】 Health-care came to be seen as one of the fundamental social facilities necessary for people to exercise their other rights as *autonomous* human beings. 保健逐渐被看作是人们作为独立自主的人行使其他权利必要的基本社会设施之一。
【同】 independent, self-governing
【反】 subordinate, dependent
【派】 autonomy *n*. 自由，自主权；自治，自治权

auxiliary [ɔːgˈzɪljərɪ] *adj*. 辅助的，备用的
【记】 auxili(= help, 帮助) + ary(形容词词尾)→辅助的
【例】 We have an *auxiliary* generator in case of power cuts. 我们有一台万一断电时使用的备用发电机。
【同】 subsidiary, supplementary
【反】 chief, main

available [əˈveɪləbl] *adj*. 1. 可利用的，可获得的；2. (某人)有空的
【记】 a(= ad, to) + vail(价值) + able(形容词词尾)→能带来价值的→可利用的
【例】 1. You will be informed when the book becomes *available*. 这本书有货时就通知你。
2. The Prime Minister was not *available* for comment. 首相无暇作出评论。
【同】 usable, accessible; uncommitted
【反】 unavailable
【派】 (逆构)avail *v*. 有益于，有助于；利用
availability *n*. 可用性，有效性

avalanche [ˈævəˌlɑːnʃ] *n*. 雪崩

【记】 来自于法语 lavanch，滑落→雪滑落→雪崩

【例】 Yesterday's *avalanche* killed a party of skiers and destroyed several trees. 昨天的雪崩造成一批滑雪者死亡，并毁坏了一些树木。

【派】 avalanchine *adj*. 雪崩似的，压倒性的

avant-garde [əˌvɒŋ'gɑːd] *adj*. 〔法〕先锋派的；*n*. 先锋派

【例】 It was also at this time that the *avant-garde* film first achieved commercial success. 也正是在这个时期，先锋电影首次获得商业上的成功。

【同】 vanguard, forefront

avenge [ə'vendʒ] *v*. 复仇，报复

【记】 a(= ad, to) + venge(报仇)→复仇

【例】 She *avenged* her father's murder. 她为其父被谋杀而复了仇。

【同】 revenge

【反】 pardon

【派】 avenger *n*. 复仇者

avenue ['ævɪnjuː] *n*. 1. 林荫道，大街；2. 方法，途径

【记】 a(= ad, to) + venu(来) + e→来的时候经过的地方→大街

【例】 1. The *avenues* of the area were crowded with visitors. 这个地区的大街上挤满了参观的人群。

2. Clean coal is another *avenue* for improving fuel conversion efficiency. 净煤的使用是另外一种提高燃料转化效率的方法。

【同】 street, road; approach, way

averse [ə'vɜːs] *adj*. 反对的，不愿意的

【记】 a(= abs, 离开) + vers(转移) + e→把头转开的→反对的

【例】 I'm not *averse* to a drop of whisky after dinner. 我倒不反对饭后喝点儿威士忌。

【同】 hostile, opposed, disinclined

【派】 aversion *n*. 厌恶，憎恨

avert [ə'vɜːt] *v*. 1. 转移(目光、注意力等)；2. 挡开，避免

【记】 a(= abs, 离开) + vert(转移)→转移

【例】 1. She *averted* her eyes from the terrible sight. 她转移目光不看那可怕的情景。

2. He managed to *avert* suspicion. 他设法避嫌。

【同】 shift; prevent, avoid

aviation [ˌeɪvɪ'eɪʃən] *n*. 飞行，航空，航空学

【记】 avi(鸟) + ation(名词词尾)→像鸟一样的→飞行，航空

【例】 He devoted all his life to China's *aviation*. 他把一生都奉献给了中国的航空事业。

【同】 flying, flight

【派】 (逆构)aviate *v*. 飞行

aviator *n*. 飞行员，飞行家

avid ['ævɪd] *adj*. 渴望的，热心的

【例】 She has an *avid* fondness for the limelight. 她热衷于出风头。

【同】 eager, greedy, zealous

【派】 avidity *n*. 热望，贪婪

avocation [ævəˈkeɪʃən] *n*. 副业，业余爱好

【记】 a(无，没有) + vocation(职业)→不是职业→业余爱好

【例】 Breeding birds became his *avocation* after he retired. 退休后养鸟成了他的业余爱好。

【同】 hobby, pastime

【反】 profession, vocation

avow [əˈvaʊ] *v*. 公开承认，公开宣称

【记】 a(= ad, to) + vow(喊叫)→大声说出来→公开承认

【例】 Their *avowed* aim is to overthrow the government. 他们公开声明，他们的目的是推翻政府。

【同】 affirm, assert

【反】 deny, disavow

【派】 avowal *n*. 公开宣称，声明

award [əˈwɔːd] *v*. 1. 把…奖给，授予；2. 判决，裁决 *n*. 1. 奖，奖品；2. 奖学金

【记】 a(= ex, 出去) + ward(观察，调查)→经过调查给出去→把…奖给

【例】 1. For his astonishing achievements he was *awarded* the Nobel Prize. 因为他惊人的成就，他被授予了诺贝尔奖。

2. He was *awarded* his damages in the shipwreck by the court. 法院判给了他沉船事故中的损失赔偿费。

3. She showed us the athletics *awards* she had won. 她给我们看她赢得的体育运动奖。

4. Mary is not eligible for an *award*. 玛丽没有申请助学金的资格。

【同】 give, grant, reward; prize, trophy; scholarship

awkward [ˈɔːkwəd] *adj*. 1. 笨拙的；2. 尴尬的

【记】 awk(向后转的) + ward(方向)→向后走的→笨拙的

【例】 1. I was always an *awkward* dancer. 我跳舞一向是笨手笨脚的。

2. I realized they wanted to be alone together so I felt very *awkward*. 我意识到了他们想要单独在一起，所以觉得很尴尬。

【同】 clumsy; embarrassing

【反】 skillful, graceful

axis [ˈæksɪs] *n*. (复数 axes)轴，中心线

【例】 The earth's *axis* is the line between the North and South Poles. 地轴是南北极之间的线。

B

baby-sit [ˈbeɪbɪsɪt] *v*. (-sat; -tting)担任临时保姆，照顾婴儿

【记】 baby(婴儿) + sit(坐)→坐在婴儿旁边→照顾婴儿

【例】 She *baby-sits* for her friends every Saturday. 她每星期六为她朋友照看婴儿。

【同】 take care of

【派】 baby-sitter *n*. 代人临时照看婴儿者

bachelor [ˈbætʃələ] *n*. 1. 单身男子；2. 学士

【记】 来自古法语 bacheler，年轻的男人→单身男子

【例】 1. He remained a *bachelor* all his life. 他终生未娶。

2. To do the job, you must have at least a *bachelor* degree in chemistry. 要做这项工作至少也要先取得化学学士学位。

【派】 bachelorhood *n*. 独身，独身生活

backbone [ˈbækbəun] *n*. 脊椎，栋梁，支柱

【记】 back(背) + bone(骨)→背部的骨头→脊椎→栋梁

【例】 Such people are the *backbone* of the country. 这样的人是国家的栋梁。

【同】 mainstay, spine

back-up [ˈbækʌp] *n*. 候补，支持

【例】 Well, let's put that down as the first choice and have some *back-ups*. 好吧，我们先把这个记下来作为第一个选择，然后再找一些候补的。

【同】 fill-in

bacterial [bæktɪərɪəl] *adj*. 细菌的

【记】 bacteri(细菌的) + (i)al(形容词词尾)→细菌的

【例】 A mould might prove to be a successful antidote to *bacterial* infection. 一种霉菌可能被证明为一种有效的解毒剂用以对付细菌感染。

【派】 (逆构)bacterium *n*. (复数-ria)细菌

bacterin *n*. 疫苗，菌苗

badge [bædʒ] *n*. 标记，徽章

【例】 Singapore has for a while had a scheme that forces drivers to buy a *badge* if they wish to visit a certain part of the city. 新加坡在一段时间内实施了一个方案，如果汽车司机想到城市某一特定区域，就要被强制购买一个标识。

【同】 emblem, label, sign

baffle [ˈbæfl] *v*. 1. 困惑；2. 阻碍，为难

【记】 baff(公开指责) + le(动词词尾)→公开指责→为难

【例】 1. One of the exam questions *baffled* me completely. 有一道试题把我完全难

住了。

2. She *baffled* all our attempts to find her. 她千方百计不让我们找到她。

【同】 bewilder, confuse, puzzle; frustrate

【派】 baffling *adj*. 使困惑的；令人丧气的，阻碍的

baggage [ˈbæɡɪdʒ] *n*. 行李

【记】 bag(袋子) + g + age(名词词尾)→袋子的总称→行李

【例】 Our *baggage* has cleared customs. 我们的行李已通过海关检查。

【同】 luggage

bait [beɪt] *v*. 以饵引诱(动物)，把饵装上；*n*. 诱饵，引诱物

【例】 1. He is *baiting* a mousetrap with cheese. 他在捕鼠器上放上干酪作诱饵。

2. The shop used free gifts as a *bait* to attract new customers. 商店用赠品作诱饵招徕新顾客。

【同】 tempt, lure; temptation

bald [bɔːld] *adj*. 秃头的，光秃的

【例】 Our dog has a *bald* patch on its leg. 我们的狗的腿上秃了一块。

【同】 bare, hairless

balk [bɔːlk] *v*. 1. 阻碍；2. 犹豫，不愿做

【例】 1. We are *balked* to do what we want to do. 有人阻止我们去做我们想做的事情。

2. His parents *balked* at the cost of the guitar he wanted. 他想要那个吉他，但他父母看到吉他的价格却犹豫不决。

【同】 stop, curb

【反】 continue

【派】 balky *adj*. 停止不前的，倔强的

ballot [ˈbælət] *n*./*v*. 投票，选票

【记】 ball(球) + ot(et，表示"小"的名词词尾)→小球(以前选票都团成小球)→投票

【例】 The club members held a secret *ballot* to choose the chairperson. 俱乐部成员用无记名投票选举主席。

【同】 vote, ticket, poll

【反】 abstention

ban [bæn] *v*./*n*. (-nning; -nned)明令禁止，取缔

【例】 The Government has *banned* the use of chemical weapons. 政府已经禁止使用化学武器。

【同】 bar, forbid, prohibit

【反】 allow, permit

banal [bəˈnɑːl] *adj*. 平凡的，陈腐的

【记】 ban(宣布) + al(形容词词尾)→原义为"宣布属于农奴的"→平凡的，陈腐的

【例】 An exciting film was spoiled by a *banal* ending. 一部动人的电影被平庸的结局糟蹋了。

【同】 timeworn, trite

【反】 original

【派】 banality *n*. 平庸，陈腐，陈词滥调

band [bænd] *n*. 1. 乐队；2. 带子，箍，条；*vi*. 联合，集合

【例】 1. The *band* drowned our conversation. 乐队的演奏声把我们谈话的声音淹没了。

2. She tied her hair back with a rubber *band*. 她用橡皮筋把头发扎到后面。

3. We must *band* ourselves against natural calamities despite the disputes on the working plan. 尽管我们对工作计划存在着分歧，但我们应该联合起来与自然灾害作斗争。

【同】 orchestra; unite

bandit [ˈbændɪt] *n*. 强盗，土匪

【记】 band(捆绑) + it(名词词尾)→被捆绑在一起的一群人→土匪

【例】 Buses driving through the mountains have been attacked by *bandits*. 驶经山区的公共汽车遭到匪徒袭击。

【同】 gangster

bankrupt [ˈbæŋkrʌpt] *adj*. 破产的

【记】 bank(银行) + rupt(打破)→银行被打破了→破产的

【例】 If your liabilities exceed your assets, you may go *bankrupt*. 如果你所负的债超过你的资产，你就会破产。

【同】 insolvent

【派】 bankruptcy *n*. 破产的状况，彻底失败

banner [ˈbænə] *n*. 旗帜，横幅

【例】 The marchers carried *banners* with the words 'No Nuclear Weapons' in large letters. 游行者打着横幅，上有大字"禁止使用核武器"。

【同】 flag

banquet [ˈbæŋkwɪt] *n*. 宴会

【记】 banqu(长凳，桌子) + et(表示"小"的名词词尾)→(摆着菜肴的)小桌子→宴会

【例】 We gave him a farewell *banquet* yesterday. 我们昨天为他举行了告别宴会。

【同】 feast

bar [bɑːr] *n*. 1. 条，横木，(跳高架等的)横杆；2. 障碍，阻碍物；3. 酒吧；*v*. (-rred; -rring)1. 禁止，不许；2. 拦住

【例】 1. They fitted *bars* to their windows to stop burglars getting in. 他们在窗户上加了窗条以防盗贼进入。

2. Poor health may be a *bar* to success in life. 健康状况不佳可能会成为人生取得成功的障碍。

3. There are several *bars* in the hotel. 旅馆中有好几个酒吧。

4. She was *barred* from entering the competition because of her age. 她因年龄的关系而被禁止参加比赛。

5. Soldiers *barred* the road so we had to turn back. 士兵挡住了去路，我们只好折回。

【同】 rod; barrier, obstacle; saloon; ban, prohibit; block, obstruct

barbecue [ˈbɑːbɪkjuː] *n*. 户外烤肉餐，烤烧

【记】 barbe(构架) + cue(棍，棒)→用棍棒支起来的架子→烤肉用的架子→户外烤肉餐

【例】 Membership gives wide access to other activities like basketball and football as well as *barbecues* and other social functions. 会员还可以参加其他的活动，比如篮球、足球、户外烧烤以及其他社交活动。

bare [beə] *adj*. 1.赤裸的，没有保护的；2.仅够的，极少的

【例】 1. Certain plants can cause irritation if you touch them with *bare* skin. 如果你直接使皮肤接触某些植物的话，可能会受到刺激。

2. Just give us the *bare* facts of the case. 你只要向我们提供案件最低限度的事实真相就行。

【同】 naked; mere, scanty

【反】 covered; ample

bargain ['bɑːgɪn] *v*. 交易，讨价还价；*n*. 交易，物美价廉的东西

【例】 1. The salesman refused to *bargain* over the price. 推销员拒绝讨价还价。

2. He made a satisfactory *bargain* with them. 他和他们做了一笔满意的交易。

【同】 barter, deal, sale

barge [bɑːdʒ] *n*. 驳船；*v*. 鲁莽而大力地冲撞，蛮不讲理地闯入

【例】 1. In the 1880s North American beekeepers moved bees on *barges* along the Mississippi. 在19世纪80年代，北美的养蜂人把蜜蜂装上驳船，沿着密西西比河顺水而下。

2. He *barged* his way onto the bus before everyone else. 他左冲右撞，第一个登上公共汽车。

【同】 flatboat; push forward

barometer [bə'rɒmɪtə] *n*. 1.气压计；2.晴雨表

【记】 baro(重量)+meter(测量)→测量空气的重量→气压计

【例】 1. Can you help me read the *barometer*? 你能帮我看一下气压计吗？

2. Tomorrow's by-election will be a *barometer* of the mood in the whole country. 明天的补缺选举将会是国民情绪的晴雨表。

【同】 barograph

【派】 barometric *adj*. 大气压力的

barrage ['bærɑːʒ, bə'rɑːʒ] *n*. 拦阻，拦河坝；2.连珠炮

【记】 bar(r)(横木)+age(名词词尾)→用横木挡住→拦阻

【例】 1. The sun's rays couldn't wedge their way through the *barrage* of foliage. 阳光透不过树叶的屏障。

2. The Premier was under a *barrage* of questions at the press conference. 记者招待会上总理遭到了连珠炮般的发问。

【同】 bombardment

barrel ['bærəl] *n*. 桶

【记】 bar(r)(横木)+el→用木头做成的东西→木桶

【例】 Finally the honey is poured into *barrels* for shipment. 最后蜂蜜被倒入桶中以便装船运输。

【同】 cask

【派】 barrelful *n*. 一桶之量

barren ['bærən] *adj*. 1.贫瘠的，不结果的；2.不能生育的

【例】 Such a *barren* desert can support very few creatures. 在这样荒瘠的沙漠里，很少生物能够存活。

【同】 sterile，infertile；childless

【反】 fertile，rich

barricade [ˌbærɪˈkeɪd] *n*. 路障，障碍物；*v*. 设路障，阻挡

【记】 bar(r)(横木)＋ic(形容词词尾)＋ade(动词词尾)→像横木一样的东西→障碍物

【例】 1. The soldiers stormed the *barricades* erected by the rioting crowd. 士兵们向暴乱分子设置的街垒发起了猛攻。

2. The police *barricaded* off the entrance to the square. 警方在广场的入口处设置了路障。

【同】 barrier，block；impede，obstruct

barrier [ˈbærɪə] *n*. 1. 障碍物，屏障；2. 障碍，妨碍因素

【记】 bar(r)(横木)＋ier(名词词尾)→用栅栏挡住→屏障

【例】 1. The Sahara Desert is a natural *barrier* between North and Central Africa. 撒哈拉沙漠是北非与中非之间的天然屏障。

2. Lack of confidence is the biggest *barrier* to investment in the region. 缺乏信心是这一地区投资的最大障碍。

【同】 block，barricade，obstruction

barter [ˈbɑːtə] *n*. 物品交换，易货贸易；*v*. 物品交换，交换

【例】 1. On these islands a system of *barter* is used. 在这些岛上仍然实行着物物交换的制度。

2. Farmers *bartered* rice for machinery. 农民们用大米换机器。

【同】 exchange，trade，deal

basin [ˈbeɪsn] *n*. 1. 盆，大碗；2. 盆地

【例】 1. He washed his hands in a *basin*. 他在盆里洗了手。

2. The village lay in a peaceful *basin* surrounded by hills. 那村庄坐落在平静的山坳里。

【同】 bowl

bask [bɑːsk] *v*. 1. 晒太阳，取暖；2. 承受他人的恩惠

【例】 1. She lies on the sand，*basking* in the sunshine. 她躺在沙滩上晒太阳。

2. He *basked* in his employer's approval. 他受到雇主的赞许而得意洋洋。

【同】 sunbathe；enjoy

baste [beɪst] *v*. 1. (烤肉时)涂油，把油涂在(肉上)；2. 殴打，公开责骂

【例】 1. Meat is *basted* to keep it from drying out and to improve its flavor. 烤肉时润以脂油使不致烤焦并可增加香味。

2. The paper *basted* the candidate for irresponsible statement. 该报公开指责候选人作不负责任的声明。

batch [bætʃ] *n*. 一批生产量，一批

【例】 The *batch* number is printed on the bottom of each jar. 生产批号均印在罐子底部。

【同】 heap，group

batter [bætə] *v*. 打坏，猛击

【记】 bat(= beat，打) + t + er(表示动作的反复)→连续地打→猛击

【例】 There is someone *battering* at the door. 有人连续用力敲门。

【同】 beat，pound，strike

battery [ˈbætərɪ] *n*. 1.电池；2.一组或一套器具

【记】 batt(打) + t + er(表示动作的反复) + y(名词词尾)→本义是"连续打"→一套，一组→电池

【例】 1.This pocket calculator needs two *batteries*. 这个袖珍计算器需用两节干电池。

2.They've got a *battery* of stainless cooking utensils in their kitchen. 他们在厨房里配备了一套不锈钢的厨房用具。

【同】 set

beam [biːm] *n*. 1.光线，光束；2.笑容，喜色；*v*. 1.愉快地微笑；2.定向发出，播送

【例】 1.The *beams* of the searchlights fingered the sky over the airport. 一道道探照灯光刺破机场的天空。

2.The old lady opened the door with a *beam*. 老太太面带微笑开了门表示欢迎。

3.The winner *beamed* with satisfaction. 获胜者满意地笑了。

4.The news was *beamed* to the whole globe by satellite. 这条新闻由卫星向全世界传送。

【同】 ray，shine；smile；send，broadcast

【派】 beaming *adj*. 照耀的，光亮的；喜气洋洋的

beamy *adj*. 放射光线的，光亮的

bear [bɛə] *v*. (bore，borne)1.运送，携带；2.负担，支撑；3.具有，显示；4.忍受，容忍；5. 生产，生育

【例】 1.The sound of music was *borne* on the wind. 乐声随风飘送。

2.I doubt if that chair will *bear* your weight. 我怀疑那把椅子能否承受得了你的体重。

3.The document *bore* his signature. 这份文件有他的签字。

4.The pain was almost more than he could *bear*. 这样的痛苦几乎使他受不了。

5. Different trees *bear* different fruits. 什么样的树结什么样的果。

【同】 bring，carry；hold，support；show，exhibit；endure，stand；breed，produce

becoming [bɪˈkʌmɪŋ] *adj*. 1.合适的，适当的；2.好看的，有吸引力的

【记】 be(在…上) + com(e)(来) + ing(形容词词尾)→来到…上面的→合适的

【例】 1.His laughter was not very *becoming* on such a solemn occasion. 在如此严肃的场合，他的笑声不太得体。

2.Blue always looks very *becoming* on her. 她穿蓝色的衣服总是很好看。

【同】 decent，proper；comely

【反】 improper

bedrock [ˈbedˈrɒk] *n*. 基础，基石

【记】 bed(床) + rock(岩石)→岩石的床→基岩，基石

【例】 Let's get down to *bedrock*, and find out the truth. 让我们寻根究底，查明真相。

【同】 base

beforehand [bɪˈfɔːhænd] *adv*. 预先，事先

【记】 before(前) + hand(手)→做前手准备→预先

【例】 He warned me *beforehand* what to expect. 他预先提醒过我这件事。

【同】 ahead, in advance

【反】 afterwards, behindhand

befuddle [bɪˈfʌdl] *v*. 1. 使酒醉昏迷；2. 使迷惑，使迷糊

【记】 be(加强语气) + fuddle(灌醉)→使酒醉昏迷

【例】 1. John is very amusing when he is completely *befuddled*. 当约翰喝得完全糊涂了的时候，他非常有趣儿。

2. He also fabricates sensational lies to *befuddle* world opinion. 他也编造危言耸听的谎言欺骗世界舆论。

【同】 fuddle; confuse

beget [bɪˈget] *v*. (begot, begotten/begot; begetting)引起，产生

【记】 be(加强语气) + get(得到)→使…得到→引起

【例】 War *begets* misery and ruin. 战争是苦难与毁灭的祸根。

【同】 generate, bring forth

begrudge [bɪˈgrʌdʒ] *v*. 1. 嫉妒；2. 吝啬，勉强给

【记】 be(加强语气) + grudge(怨恨，妒忌)→ 嫉妒

【例】 1. She *begrudged* her friend the award. 她嫉妒她的朋友获奖。

2. She did not *begrudge* the money spent on her children's education. 她对用在孩子们教育上的费用从不吝啬。

【同】 envy, grudge

beguile [bɪˈgaɪl] *v*. 1. 哄，欺骗；2. 迷住；3. 使(时间等)过得愉快，消遣

【记】 be(使) + guile(狡诈，诡计)→使中计→欺骗

【例】 1. They were *beguiled* into giving him large sums of money. 他们受骗，给了他一大笔钱。

2. The travelers were *beguiled* by the beauty of the landscape. 游客对这美丽的景色赞叹不已。

3. Our journey was *beguiled* with spirited talk. 我们旅行中谈笑风生，过得很愉快。

【同】 cheat, deceive, trick; captivate, fascinate

【派】 beguilement *n*. 欺骗；散心

beguiling *adj*. 欺骗的；消遣的

behalf [bɪˈhɑːf] *n*. 利益，支持

【记】 be(= by) + half(旁边)→站在…的旁边→为了…的利益

【例】 On *behalf* of my colleagues and myself I thank you. 我代表我的同事和我本人向你表示感谢。

【同】 benefit, good

behave [bɪˈheɪv] *v*. 表现，以某种态度对待

【记】 be(动作) + have(有)→(一个人)拥有的动作→表现

【例】 Managers often *behave* very differently outside the office and in it, even to the same person. 经理们在办公室内与办公室外的行为表现往往大相径庭，即便是面

对同一个人也是这样。

【同】 act，do，conduct

【派】 behavior *n*. 行为，举止

behavioral *adj*. 行为的，关于行为的

behold [bɪˈhəʊld] *v*. (beheld，beheld)目睹，看见

【记】 be(在…上)+hold(保持)→把(目光)保持在…上→看见

【例】 They *beheld* the great city of Babylon. 他们看到了雄伟的巴比伦城。

【同】 see，observe

【派】 beholder *n*. 目睹者，旁观者

belie [bɪˈlaɪ] *v*. (-lied；-lying)1. 给人错觉，掩饰；2. 不足以证明，未能实现(希望、诺言等)

【记】 be(使)+lie(撒谎)→撒谎使相信→给人错觉

【例】 1. His cheerful manner *belied* his real feelings. 他那快活的样子掩饰了他的真实感情。

2. The poor sales of the product *belied* our high hopes for it. 产品销路不佳证明当初我们对它期望过高。

【同】 misrepresent

belittle [bɪˈlɪtl] *v*. 轻视，贬低

【记】 be(使)+little(小的，卑微的)→使变得卑微→贬低

【例】 Don't *belittle* yourself. 不要小看你自己。

【同】 depreciate，disparage

belligerent [bɪˈlɪdʒərənt] *adj*. 交战的，好斗的，好战的

【记】 bell(i)(战争)+ger(带来)+ent(形容词词尾)→带来战争的→好战的

【例】 The boys found it hard to get along with Tom，because he always said some very *belligerent* things. 孩子们觉得汤姆很难相处，因为他老是说些十分挑衅性的话。

【同】 aggressive，combative，militant

【派】 belligerence *n*. 交战，好战，斗争性

beneath [bɪˈniːθ] *prep*./*adv*. 在…下方，在下面

【记】 be(在)+neath(下面)→在下面

【例】 1. The boat sank *beneath* the waves. 小船淹没在浪涛中。

2. Her careful make-up hid the signs of age *beneath*. 她的精心化妆掩饰了脂粉下面岁月刻下的痕迹。

【同】 below，under

benefit [ˈbenɪfɪt] *n*. 益处，好处；*v*. 使…受益，得到好处

【记】 bene(好，善)+ fit(做)→做事后的好处→利益

【例】 1. The new regulations will be of great *benefit* to us all. 新规章对我们大家都会大有好处。

2. These facilities have *benefited* the whole town. 这些设施使全城受益。

【同】 good，profit

【反】 damage，harm，loss

【派】 beneficial *adj*. 有益的

beneficiary *n*. 受益人，受惠者

benevolent [bɪˈnevələnt] *adj*. 慈善的，仁义的

【记】 bene(好，善) + vol(愿望) + ent(形容词词尾)→有好的愿望的→慈善的

【例】 Our teachers taught us to be *benevolent*. 我们的老师教导我们应当以仁慈为怀。

【同】 charitable，good-hearted

【反】 malevolent

【派】 benevolence *n*. 仁慈，善行

benign [bɪˈnaɪn] *adj*. 1.(人)亲切和蔼的；2.(病)良性的

【记】 beni(好，善) + gn(产生)→产生好的→亲切的，良性的

【例】 1. My mother's character is very *benign*. 我母亲非常慈祥。
2. A *benign* tumor will not cause you any fatal harm. 良性肿瘤不会对你有致命的伤害。

【同】 kind，genial

【反】 malign；malignant

bequeath [bɪˈkwiːð] *v*. 遗赠，遗留

【记】 be(= by，根据) + queath(说的话)→根据说的话，根据遗言→遗赠

【例】 Her collection of paintings was *bequeathed* to the National Gallery when she died. 她去世的时候，她的全部藏画遗赠给了国家美术馆。

【同】 endow，pass on

【反】 disinherit

【派】 bequest *n*. 遗产，遗赠

bereave [bɪˈriːv] *v*. 剥夺，夺去

【记】 be(加强语气) + reave(剥夺)→剥夺

【例】 He was *bereaved* of his wife last year. 去年他痛失爱妻。

【同】 deprive

【派】 bereavement *n*. (亲人)丧亡，丧亲之痛

besiege [bɪˈsiːdʒ] *v*. 1. 围攻；2. 拥在…周围，围住；3. 困扰

【记】 be(加强语气) + siege(包围，围攻)→围攻

【例】 1. Troy was *besieged* by the Greeks. 特洛伊城被希腊人包围了。
2. Reporters *besieged* the winner for interviews. 记者们团团围住获胜者进行采访。
3. We were *besieged* with requests for help. 我们被一大堆求助的请求所困扰。

【同】 beleaguer，siege；encircle，surround；pester

【反】 release

bestow [bɪˈstəʊ] *v*. 给予，赐赠(祝福、奖励、荣誉等)

【记】 be(在…上) + stow(放)→把东西放在…上→给予

【例】 Several fancy gifts were *bestowed* on the distinguished guests. 向贵宾们赠送了几件精美的礼品。

【同】 award，give，present

【派】 bestowal *n*. 赠予，给予

betray [bɪˈtreɪ] *v*. 1. 出卖，背叛；2. 泄露(秘密)，露出…迹象

【记】 be(使) + tray(交出，移交)→把…交出来→出卖

【例】 1. The resistance group was *betrayed* to the government by one of its own members. 抵抗组织被其内部一名成员出卖给政府了。

2. She said she was sorry, but her eyes *betrayed* her secret delight. 她说她很难过，但从她的眼神里却流露出她内心的喜悦。

【同】 trick; expose, give away

【派】 betrayal *n*. 出卖，暴露

betrayer *n*. 叛徒，背叛者

beverage [ˈbevərɪdʒ] *n*. 饮料

【记】 bever(饮，喝) + age(名词词尾)→喝的东西→饮料

【例】 What *beverage* would you like? 你想喝什么饮料?

【同】 drink

bewilder [bɪˈwɪldə] *v*. 使不知所措，使迷惑

【记】 be(使) + wilder(迷惑)→使迷惑

【例】 The child was *bewildered* by the noise and the crowds. 孩子让噪声和人群给弄得晕头转向。

【同】 confuse, perplex, puzzle

【派】 bewilderment *n*. 困惑，迷乱

bias [ˈbaɪəs] *n*. 偏见，偏好

【例】 Her scientific *bias* showed itself in early childhood. 她在科学方面的偏爱在孩童时代就已显现出来。

【同】 prejudice, prejudgment

【反】 fairness, justice

【派】 biased *adj*. 有偏见的

unbiased *adj*. 无偏见的，公正的

bibliography [ˌbɪblɪˈɒɡrəfɪ] *n*. 书目，文献

【记】 biblio(书) + graph(写) + y(名词词尾)→为书写的东西→书目

【例】 There is a useful *bibliography* at the end of each chapter. 在每一章后面都附有一份有用的参考书目。

【同】 list, reference

bicker [ˈbɪkə] *v*. 口角，斗嘴

【例】 The children are always *bickering* (with each other) over their toys. 孩子们常常为玩具争吵。

【同】 quarrel, squabble

bid [bɪd] (bid/bade, bid/bidden; -dding) *n*./*v*. 出价，投标

【例】 1. Have they put in a *bid* for the contract? 他们有没有投标争取承包合同?

2. He *bid* £10 for an old book at the auction. 在拍卖会上他为一本旧书出价10英镑。

【同】 offer

【派】 bidding *n*. 投标

bidder *n*. 喊价者

bigoted [ˈbɪɡətɪd] *adj*. 固执己见的，顽固的

【记】 bigot(顽固者)+ed(形容词词尾)→顽固的

【例】 He is so *bigoted* that it is impossible to argue with him. 他固执得不可理喻。

【同】 intolerant

【派】 (逆构)bigot *n*. 盲目信仰者，顽固者

bilateral [baɪˈlætərəl] *adj*. 双边的

【记】 bi(二)+later(侧面)+al(形容词词尾)→双边的

【例】 The minister signed a *bilateral* trade agreement. 部长签署了一个双边贸易协议。

【同】 two-sided

【反】 unilateral

bind [baɪnd] *v*.(bound, bound)1.捆绑；2.约束

【例】 1. They *bound* his legs together so he couldn't escape. 他们将他的双腿捆在一起使他无法逃跑。

2. I am *bound* by my promise. 我必须遵守自己的诺言。

【同】 attach, fasten, tie

【反】 loose, undo, untie

【派】 binding *n*. 捆绑，装订；*adj*. 有约束力的，应遵守的

biography [baɪˈɒgrəfɪ] *n*. 传记

【记】 bio(生命，生活)+graph(写)+y(名词词尾)→写关于人的一生→传记

【例】 Boswell wrote a famous *biography* of Dr. Johnson. 鲍斯威尔为约翰逊博士写过一本著名的传记。

【同】 life history

【派】 biographer *n*. 传记作家

biology [baɪˈɒlədʒɪ] *n*. 生物学，生物(总称)

【记】 bio(生命，生活)+logy(…学)→研究生命的学科→生物学

【例】 The *biology* of bacteria can be quite hard to understand. 细菌生物学有时会很难理解。

【派】 biological *adj*. 生物学的

biologist *n*. 生物学家

biosphere [ˈbaɪəsfɪə] *n*. 生物圈，生态体系

【记】 bio(生命)+sphere(范围，圈子)→生物圈

【例】 When there is an imbalance in one part of the *biosphere*, it affects all the other parts as well. 生态体系中的一部分出现不平衡时，会影响所有其他部分。

blackmail [ˈblækmeɪl] *n*./*v*. 勒索，讹诈

【记】 black(黑色的)+mail(信)→给…发黑信→勒索

【例】 The gangsters who knew of Bill's past crimes tried to *blackmail* him. 知道比尔过去所犯的罪的那帮歹徒想要勒索他。

【同】 extortion; extort

bland [blænd] *adj*. 淡味的，无味的

【例】 He eats only *bland* food because of his ulcer. 他患溃疡，只能吃无刺激性的食物。

【同】 flavorless, insipid

【反】 pungent

blast [blɑːst] *n*. 1.一阵(风),一股(气流);2.爆炸,冲击波;*v*. 1.爆炸,毁灭;2.使枯萎,损害

【例】 1. A *blast* of wind blew the window and the door open. 一阵风把门和窗子都吹开了。

2. Several passers-by were killed by (the) *blast*. 数名路人被炸死。

3. They've *blasted* away the rock to build the new road. 他们已炸掉这块岩石以便修一条新的路。

4. The icy wind had *blasted* the new spring growth. 寒冷的风摧毁了春天才生长出来的东西。

【同】 gust; blowout, explosion; burst; destroy

blaze [bleɪz] *n*. 火焰,烈火;*v*. 燃烧,发光

【例】 1. Dry wood makes a good *blaze*. 干木燃起夺目的火焰。

2. When the firemen arrived the whole building was *blazing*. 消防队到达时,整座建筑物正在熊熊燃烧着。

【同】 flame, glare; burn

【派】 blazing *adj*. 炽烧的,闪耀的

bleach [bliːtʃ] *v*. 去色,漂白;*n*. 漂白,漂白剂

【例】 1. Did you *bleach* this tablecloth? 你把这块桌布漂白了吗?

2. My shirt was so dirty that I had to use *bleach* on it. 我的衬衫太脏了,只好用漂白剂来洗。

【同】 whiten, decolor

bleak [bliːk] *adj*. 1.荒凉的;2.无望的,黯淡的

【例】 1. The weather in early December was *bleak* and unpleasant. 十二月初的天气又阴冷又难受。

2. The future of this firm will be very *bleak* indeed if we keep losing money. 要是我们继续亏本的话,我们公司的前途会非常黯淡。

【同】 chilly, dim, dismal

【反】 warm

bleed [bliːd] *v*. (bled, bled)出血,流血

【例】 The cut on my arm *bled* for a long time. 我胳膊上的伤口流了好长时间的血。

【同】 flow

blemish [ˈblemɪʃ] *n*. 缺点,污点;*v*. 玷污

【记】 blem(= bluish,青色的) + ish(动词词尾)→使变成青色的→玷污

【例】 1. The wine glasses were sold at half price because of *blemishes* in the crystal. 这些酒杯半价出售,因为水晶玻璃上有瑕疵。

2. His reputation was *blemished* by a newspaper article alleging he'd evaded his taxes. 报纸上一篇文章说他漏税,他的声誉因而受到玷污。

【同】 flaw, stain

【反】 merit

blend [blend] *n*./*v*. 混合,混杂

【例】 1. Oil does not *blend* with water. 油不溶于水。

2. His manner is a *blend* of charm and politeness. 他的举止既充满魅力，又彬彬有礼。

【同】 intermix, mix

【反】 resolve

bless [bles] *v*. 1. 求神赐福，保佑；2. 赞美神明，颂扬

【例】 1. The priest *blessed* the ship before it left port. 牧师在船离港之前为其祝福。

2. *Bless* the name of the lord! 颂扬天主的圣名!

【同】 bestow; sanctify

【反】 curse

【派】 blessed *adj*. 神圣的；幸运的；带来愉快的

blessing *n*. 祝福，恩赐

blink [blɪŋk] *n*./*v*. 1. 眨眼；2. 视若无睹，无视

【例】 1. She *blinked* her eyes as the bright light shone on her. 亮光照到她时，她直眨眼睛。

2. It's no use *blinking* (at) the fact that unemployment is still rising. 不能无视失业率在不断上升这一事实。

【同】 wink

blister [ˈblɪstə] *n*. 水泡，脓疱；*v*. 起水泡

【例】 1. These tight shoes have given me *blisters* on my ankles. 这双鞋太紧，把我的脚腕磨起了泡。

2. The hot sun *blistered* the paint. 炎热的阳光晒得油漆起了泡。

【同】 bleb

【派】 blistering *adj*. 酷热的；严厉的，刻薄的

blizzard [ˈblɪzəd] *n*. 暴风雪

【记】 bliz(用力的打) + z + ard(名词词尾)→猛烈敲打的东西→暴风雪

【例】 The *blizzard* caused a great damage to the crop. 暴风雪对庄稼造成了严重的损害。

【同】 snowstorm

block [blɒk] *v*. 堵塞，阻塞；*n*. 街区

【例】 1. The accident *blocked* traffic in the town centre. 事故阻塞了市中心的交通。

2. The heating system in this *block* doesn't work well. 这个街区的供暖系统不太好用。

【同】 obstruct, hinder, stop

bloom [bluːm] *n*. 花(尤指观赏的花)；*v*. 开花

【例】 1. These roses have beautiful *blooms*. 这些玫瑰花开得真美。

2. Our friendship is *blooming*. 我们之间情深谊长。

【同】 blossom, flower

【反】 fade, wither, perish

blossom [ˈblɒsəm] *n*. 花(尤指果树或灌木的花)；*v*. 开花

【例】 The cherry trees *blossomed* early this year. 樱桃树今年开花早。

【同】 bloom, flower

B

【反】 fade, wither, perish

blunder [ˈblʌndə] *n.*/*v.* 大错，失策

【例】 1. I've made an awful *blunder*. 我做了一件大错特错的事。

2. The police *blundered* badly by arresting the wrong man. 警方抓错了人，犯了荒唐的大错。

【同】 mistake, flub

blunt [blʌnt] *adj.* 钝的，不尖的；*v.* 把…弄钝，减弱

【例】 1. My pencil is *blunt*; could you lend me a knife to sharpen it? 我的铅笔钝了，你能借我一把刀子削一削吗？

2. The bad weather has rather *blunted* their enthusiasm for going camping. 不作美的天公大大减弱了他们去露营的热情。

【同】 dull

【反】 sharp, keen

blur [blɜː] *v.* (-rred; -rring)使(视线、感觉等)模糊不清

【例】 The steamy windows *blurred* the view. 水蒸气弄湿了窗户，景色都模糊了。

【同】 blear, dim

【派】 blurred *adj.* 模糊的

blush [blʌʃ] *v.* 脸红，羞愧

【例】 She *blushed* at the thought of her stupid mistake. 她因想到自己干的蠢事而脸红。

【同】 flush

board [bɔːd] *n.* 1. 纸板，木板；2. 委员会，董事会；*v.* 登(飞机、车、船等)

【例】 1. You sign your name on the notice *board*. 你把名字签在通知板上。

2. The *board* of the directors unanimously agreed that Mr. White was the best candidate for the job. 董事会一致同意怀特先生是干这项工作的最佳候选人。

3. Please *board* the plane immediately. 请立刻上飞机。

【同】 card, plank; committee; get on

boast [bəust] *n.*/*v.* 吹牛，夸耀

【例】 He's always *boasting* about his children's success at school. 他总是夸耀他的孩子们学习成绩好。

【同】 brag, vaunt

【反】 belittle, depreciate

【派】 boastful *adj.* 喜自夸的，自吹自擂的

boisterous [ˈbɔɪstərəs] *adj.* 喧闹的，欢闹的

【记】 boister(粗鲁的) + ous(形容词词尾)→粗鲁的→喧闹的

【例】 Her sons are nice boys, but rather *boisterous*. 她的几个儿子都是好孩子，就是有点吵闹。

【同】 noisy

【反】 calm

bold [bəuld] *adj.* 1. 大胆的，勇敢的；2. 黑体的，粗体的

【例】 1. The council today announced its *bold* new plans for the city center. 市议会今天宣布了大胆改造市中心的新计划。

2. The headwords in this dictionary are in *bold* type. 本词典的词条用的是粗体字。

【同】 audacious, brave, courageous

【反】 cowardly, shy

bolster [ˈbəulstə] *n*. 垫子，枕垫；*v*. 支持

【例】 1. There is a *bolster* across the head of the bed. 床头上有一个长枕垫。

2. The government borrowed money to *bolster* up the economy. 政府借贷以促进经济发展。

【同】 cushion, pillow; support

bombastic [bɒmˈbæstɪk] *adj*. 夸大的，言过其实的

【记】 bomba(棉花) + st + ic(形容词词尾)→像棉花一样的→夸大的

【例】 He made a *bombastic* speech. 他作了一场夸夸其谈的演说。

【同】 pompous

【派】 (逆构)bombast *n*. 浮夸的言语，高调

bonanza [bəuˈnænzə] *n*. 1. 富矿带；2. 兴旺发达，走鸿运

【记】 bonanz(= bonus, 好) + a(名词词尾)→带来好处→兴旺发达

【例】 1. South Africa's gold and mineral *bonanza* is beginning to tail off. 南非的丰富黄金矿藏量以及其他矿业资源正在日益枯竭。

2. It's been a *bonanza* year for the tourist trade. 对旅游业来说，这是财源滚滚的一年。

【同】 rich mine; prosperity

bond [bɒnd] *v*. 结合，粘合；*n*. 1. 纽带，维系；2. 契约，合同；3. 债券，公债

【例】 1. You need a strong adhesive to *bond* wood to metal. 需要强力胶才能把木料粘在金属上。

2. The trade agreement helped to strengthen the *bonds* between the two countries. 这项贸易协定有助于加强两国之间的联系。

3. We entered into a solemn *bond*. 我们缔结了一项正式协定。

4. The government issued National Savings *bonds*. 政府发行了国家储蓄债券。

【同】 adhere, stick; link, tie; agreement, contract

bondage [ˈbɒndɪdʒ] *n*. 奴役，束缚

【记】 bond(粘合，捆绑) + age(名词词尾)→被捆绑的→束缚

【例】 Lincoln emancipated the slaves from their *bondage*. 林肯把奴隶从枷锁中解放出来。

【同】 slavery

bonus [ˈbəunəs] *n*. 额外给予的东西，奖金，红利

【记】 bon(好) + us(拉丁语名词词尾)→好东西→红利

【例】 The staff got a Christmas *bonus*. 员工在圣诞节拿到了奖金。

【同】 reward, dividend

boom [buːm] *v*. /*n*. 迅速发展，繁荣

【例】 1. The market for tourism in remote areas is *booming* as never before. 偏远地区旅游业的市场从来没有像今天这么火暴过。

2. This *boom* in adult education, in turn, helps to raise the intellectual standard of

the whole country. 而成人教育热反过来又促进了整个国家文化水平的提高。

【同】 flourish, thrive

【反】 depress

【派】 booming *adj*. 迅速发展的，兴旺的

boon [buːn] *n*. 恩惠，好处

【例】 A bicycle is a real *boon* when you live in a small town. 住在小城镇上，有辆自行车确实极为方便。

【同】 benefit, blessing

boost [buːst] *n*./*v*. 推进，提高

【例】 1. Last month saw a tremendous *boost* in sales. 上个月销售额激增。

2. Advertising *boosts* sales. 广告能增加销售额。

【同】 advance, increase, promote

【反】 hinder, depress

【派】 booster *n*. 积极的支持者，推进者；推进器

booth [buːθ] *n*. 摊位，有某种用途的小房间(如电话亭等)

【例】 There is a telephone *booth* near the cinema. 电影院附近有一个电话亭。

【同】 kiosk, stall

border [ˈbɔːdə] *n*. 边界，边境

【记】 bord(边) + er(名词词尾)→边界

【例】 The terrorists escaped across/over the *border*. 恐怖分子越过边境逃走了。

【同】 boundary, edge

【反】 inside, interior

【派】 borderline *n*. 边界线

botany [ˈbɒtənɪ] *n*. 植物学，植物(总称)

【记】 botan(植物) + y(名词词尾)→植物

【例】 The coverage of the subject in his *botany* text is inadequate. 他的植物学教科书中对那题目的叙述不充分。

【派】 botanical *adj*. 植物的，植物学的

bound [baʊnd] *v*. 1. 形成界线，限制；2. 跳跃，蹦着跑；*adj*. 1. 被束缚的，负有义务的；2. 注定的，必然的

【例】 1. The US is *bounded* on the north by Canada and on the south by Mexico. 美国北面与加拿大接壤，南面与墨西哥毗邻。

2. He *bounded* into the room and announced that he was getting married. 他蹦蹦跳跳地跑进房间里，宣布他要结婚了。

3. The priest was *bound* by his position to withhold the information from the police. 身为神父，他有义务不向警方透露这一情况。

4. In a group as big as this, you are *bound* to get occasional disagreement. 在这么大的一个组里，肯定会不时遇到不同的意见。

【同】 border, confine; jump, leap; obligate; doomed

【反】 free, unbound

boundary [ˈbaʊndərɪ] *n*. 边界，界限

【记】 bound(= 拉丁语 bodina，边界) + ary(名词词尾)→边界

【例】 A river forms a *boundary* between the two countries. 河流成了两国的国界。

【同】 border, edge

bouquet [ˈbuːkeɪ, buˈkeɪ] *n*. 花束

【记】 bouqu(= bosc，树木) + et(表示"小"的名词词尾)→小的树木→花束

【例】 At the end of the concert, the singer was presented with a *bouquet* of roses. 音乐会演出结束后，人们向歌唱家献了一束玫瑰花。

【同】 nosegay, posy

bow [baʊ] *n*. 1. 弓，弓形；2. 蝴蝶结；*v*. 鞠躬

【例】 1. Other than *bows*, arrows and crude digging sticks, the only tools the Siriono seemed to possess were 'two machetes worn to the size of pocket-knives'. 除了一些弓、箭和粗糙的挖掘用的棍棒之外，看来西里奥诺人所仅有的工具，就是"两把磨损到只有袖珍折刀那么大的砍刀"。

2. The little girl tied the ribbon in a *bow*. 小女孩把丝带打成个蝴蝶结。

3. Every one *bowed* as the Queen walked into the room. 女王走进房间时，每个人都鞠躬致敬。

【同】 arc; knot; bend, stoop

brace [breɪs] *v*. 1. 支撑，撑牢；2. 振作

【例】 1. He *braced* his foot against the wall. 他把脚顶着墙站稳。

2. *Brace* yourself for a new challenge! 振作起来，迎接新的挑战！

【同】 poise, prop, support; invigorate

【反】 loosen, relax

【派】 bracing *adj*. 令人鼓舞的，提神的

brag [bræg] *v*. (-gged; -gging)夸大，吹牛

【例】 He *bragged* that he had passed the exam easily. 他吹牛说他已轻松地通过了考试。

【同】 boast, exaggerate

【派】 braggart *n*. 吹牛的人

brake [breɪk] *n*./*v*. 刹车

【例】 1. His *brakes* failed on a steep hill. 他的车闸在陡峭的山路上失灵了。

2. The driver *braked* hard as the child ran onto the road in front of him. 那孩子跑到汽车前面的路上，司机猛踩刹车。

【同】 stop

breach [briːtʃ] *v*. 造成缺口，突破；*n*. 1. 破裂，裂口；2. 违背，破坏

【例】 1. Our tanks have *breached* the enemy defenses. 我方坦克突破了敌人的防线。

2. The huge waves made a *breach* in the sea wall. 大浪在堤上冲出一个缺口。

3. This new decision represents a *breach* of our original agreement. 这个新决定意味着破坏我们原来的协议。

【同】 break, rupture

breakthrough [ˈbreɪkˈθruː] *n*. 突破性进展，突破点

【记】 来自动词词组 break through，突围，突破

【例】 For years, AI researchers had implied that a *breakthrough* was just around the corner. 多年以来，人工智能(AI)研究人员一直在暗示，一次突破性的进展就要到来。

B

【同】 progress

breathtaking [ˈbreθˌteɪkɪŋ] *adj*. 1. 惊人的，激动人心的；2. 惊险的，令人毛骨悚然的

【记】 breath(呼吸) + tak(e)(带走) + ing(形容词词尾)→让人无法呼吸的→惊人的，惊险的

【例】 1. The woman is of a beauty almost *breathtaking*. 那个女人美得惊人。

2. It was quite *breathtaking* to ride on the brow of the steep hills. 在陡峭的悬崖边骑马，实在令人胆战心惊。

【同】 exciting, breathless

breed [briːd] *v*. (bred, bred) 1. 养育，繁殖；2. 导致，造成

【例】 1. They've *bred* a new variety of rose with larger flowers. 他们栽培了能开大花朵的新品种玫瑰。

2. Unemployment *breeds* social unrest. 失业会造成社会不安定。

【同】 cultivate, raise; cause, produce

【派】 breeding *n*. 生育，繁殖

breeder *n*. 饲养动物的人，饲养员

brew [bruː] *v*. 1. 酿造，调制；2. 泡(茶)，煮(咖啡等)；3. 即将发生，酝酿

【例】 1. He *brews* his own beer at home. 他在家自己酿造啤酒。

2. We *brewed* (up) a nice pot of tea. 我们沏了一壶好茶。

3. A storm is *brewing*. 暴风雨即将来临。

【同】 make; infuse; prepare

【派】 brewery *n*. 酿酒厂

bribe [braɪb] *n*./*v*. 贿赂

【例】 She was charged with attempting to *bribe* a police officer. 她被控告企图贿赂警官。

【同】 corrupt, buy off

【派】 bribery *n*. 行贿，受贿

brilliant [ˈbrɪljənt] *adj*. 1. 灿烂的；2. 卓越的，才华横溢的

【记】 brilli(宝石) + ant(形容词词尾)→像宝石一样的→灿烂的

【例】 1. Stars are *brilliant* in the clear night sky. 星星在晴朗的夜空闪亮。

2. He has got *brilliant* achievements in the field of physics. 他在物理学方面已经取得了巨大成就。

【同】 bright, glorious, magnificent, splendid

【反】 dismal, gloomy

【派】 brilliance *n*. 光辉，显赫

brim [brɪm] *n*. 边，边缘；*v*. (-mmed; -mming) 满溢

【例】 1. The glass was full to the *brim*. 玻璃杯(里的水)已经满到快溢出来了。

2. Her eyes *brimmed* over with sympathetic tears. 她的眼睛里充满了同情的泪水。

【同】 rim, edge; fill up

【派】 brimful *adj*. 满到边的，充满的

brisk [brɪsk] *adj*. 1. 活泼的，轻快的；2. 兴隆的，繁忙活跃的

【例】 1. A *brisk* walk before breakfast is a good way to start the day. 早饭前轻松地散会步可以很好地开始一天的生活。

2. Business is *brisk* today. 今天生意兴隆。

【同】 active, breezy; busy

【反】 leisurely

brittle ['brɪtl] *adj*. 易碎的，易损坏的

【记】 brit(= break，打破) + tle(形容词词尾)→容易打破的→易碎的

【例】 Geologists consider the earth as having a molten core, surrounded by a semi-molten mantle and a *brittle*, outer skin. 地质学家认为地球有一个熔化的地核，周围包裹着半熔化的地幔和一层易碎的外壳。

【同】 crisp, fragile, frail

【反】 strong, flexible

broadcast ['brɔːdkɑːst] *v*. (-cast, -cast)广播，播送；*n*. 广播，广播节目

【记】 broad(广阔的) + cast(播，投掷)→广泛播种的→广播

【例】 1. The BBC *broadcasts* all over the world. 英国广播公司向全世界播送节目。

2. I'd advise them to pay a lot of attention to the quality of the actual *broadcast* 我得建议他们多注意一下实际广播时候的质量。

【同】 air, send, transmit

【派】 broadcaster *n*. 广播员

broadcasting *n*. 广播

broaden ['brɔːdn] *v*. 放宽，扩大

【记】 broad(广阔的) + en(动词词尾)→使变得广阔→扩大

【例】 His parents hoped the course would *broaden* his horizons. 他的父母希望这门课程能够开阔他的视野。

【同】 widen, extend

brochure [brəʊ'ʃʊər] *n*. 小册子，简介材料

【记】 来自法语 brocher 缝→用线缝在一起的纸→小册子

【例】 The computer's features are detailed in our *brochure*. 该计算机的特点在我们的小册子中有详细介绍。

【同】 booklet, pamphlet

browse [braʊz] *v*. /*n*. 随意翻阅，浏览

【例】 I spent hours *browsing* in the bookstore. 我花了几个小时在书店里浏览图书。

【同】 surf, scan

【派】 browser *n*. 浏览器

bruise [bruːz] *n*./*v*. 瘀伤，擦伤

【例】 He was covered in *bruises* after falling off his bicycle. 他从自行车上跌下来，满身青一块紫一块的。

【同】 hurt, injure

brutal ['bruːtl] *adj*. 野蛮的，残忍的，残酷的

【记】 brut(e)(畜生) + al(形容词词尾)→畜生一般的→野蛮的

【例】 Children were rent from their mothers' arms by the *brutal* soldiers. 凶残的士兵把孩子们从母亲的怀抱中夺走了。

【同】 barbarous, cruel

【反】 civilized

【派】 brutality *n*. 残忍，野蛮的行为

bubble [ˈbʌbl] *n*. 气泡，泡沫；*v*. 汩汩地流；冒泡，起泡

【例】 1. Champagne is full of *bubbles*. 香槟酒有很多气泡。

2. Gases from deep in the earth *bubble* up through the lake. 地下深处的气体从湖底冒了出来。

【同】 foam, froth

bud [bʌd] *n*. 芽，蓓蕾；*v*. 发芽

【例】 1. The magnolia has come into *bud*. 木兰树已长出花蕾。

2. The trees are *budding* early this year. 今年树木发芽早。

【同】 sprout

【派】 budding *adj*. 萌芽的，发育的；初露头角的

budget [ˈbʌdʒɪt] *n*. 预算；*v*. 为…做预算

【记】 budg(e)(袋子)+et(表示"小"的名词词尾)→小袋子，钱包→(保管好)钱包→预算

【例】 1. The sales director is preparing the company's advertisement *budget*. 销售部经理正在制定公司的广告费预算。

2. If we *budget* carefully, we'll be able to afford a new car. 我们精打细算就能买辆新汽车了。

【同】 allowance, ration

buffet [ˈbʌfɪt] *n*. 快餐，自助餐

【例】 Dinner will be a cold *buffet*, not a sit-down meal. 正餐是凉的自助餐，不是坐着让人侍候的那种。

【同】 snack

bulk [bʌlk] *n*. 1. 大批，大部分；2. 大小，体积

【例】 1. We did the *bulk* of the work ourselves. 我们自己做了大部分的工作。

2. It was difficult to move, not because of its weight but because of its *bulk*. 移动它很困难，不是由于它的重量，而是由于它的体积很大。

【同】 majority, mass; volume

【派】 bulky *adj*. 庞大的；笨重的

bulletin [ˈbʊlɪtɪn] *n*. 公告，公报

【记】 bull(公文，法令)+et(表示"小"的名词词尾)+in(名词词尾)→小的公文→公告

【例】 Here is the latest *bulletin* about the President's health. 这是总统健康状况的最新公告。

【同】 report, statement

bump [bʌmp] *v*. 1. 碰，撞；2. 颠簸

【例】 1. I *bumped* my head on a low branch. 我的头撞在了一个低树杈上。

2. The old bus *bumped* along the mountain road. 旧公共汽车沿着山路颠簸行驶。

【同】 hit, collide

【派】 bumper *n*.（机动车辆的）保险杠

bunch [bʌntʃ] *n*. 一串，一束

【例】 The banana *bunches* are picked well before the fruit is ripe. 在香蕉成熟以前就要小心地把一串串香蕉采摘下来。

【同】 cluster

buoy [bɔɪ] *n*. 浮标，航标；*v*. 1. 使…漂浮；2. 给…带来希望，鼓舞

【例】 1. I threw a life *buoy* to him when I saw his struggling. 看到他在挣扎，我给他扔了一个救生圈过去。

2. The raft was *buoyed* up by empty petrol cans. 这木筏依靠空的汽油桶的浮力漂浮。

3. We felt *buoyed* up by the good news. 我们觉得这个好消息很令人鼓舞。

【同】 float

【派】 buoyant *adj*. 能漂浮的；看涨的；轻松愉快的

buoyancy *n*. 浮性，浮力

bureaucracy [bjʊəˈrɒkrəsɪ] *n*. 官僚制度，官僚作风

【记】 bureau（政府机构）+ cracy（统治，管理）→政府机构的管理→官僚制度

【例】 It was hard to understand all the minute gradations of their *bureaucracy*. 很难弄清楚他们那套官僚体制全部细微的层次分别。

【派】 bureaucrat *n*.（常作贬义）官员，官老爷

bureaucratic *adj*. 官僚制度的，官僚的

burgeon [ˈbɜːdʒən] *vi*. 迅速成长，发展

【记】 来自古法语 burjon，嫩芽→萌芽→发展

【例】 To service the *burgeoning* tourist industry, an array of professionals has developed. 为了服务于迅速发展的旅游业，一批专业人员涌现出来。

【同】 grow，flourish

【派】 burgeoning *adj*. 迅速成长的，发展的

burglar [ˈbɜːlə] *n*. 窃贼

【记】 burgl(e)（盗窃）+ ar（名词词尾）→盗窃的人→窃贼

【例】 The *burglar* got into the house through the bedroom window. 窃贼是从卧室的窗户潜入这所房子的。

【同】 thief

【派】 burglary *n*. 行窃行为

burnish [ˈbɜːnɪʃ] *v*. 磨光，使光滑，擦亮

【记】 burn（= brun，闪光的）+ ish（动词词尾）→使闪光→磨光，擦亮

【例】 The craftsman *burnished* the brass plates until they glowed. 那个工匠把铜盘子擦得闪闪发光。

【同】 polish

burrow [ˈbʌrəʊ] *v*. 挖地洞；*n*. 洞穴

【例】 Rabbits had *burrowed* holes in the grassy bank. 兔子在河岸的草地上掘了些洞。

【同】 tunnel

burst [bɜːst] *n*./*v*.（burst，burst）破裂，爆发

【例】 1. There was a *burst* of laughter in the next room. 隔壁房间里突然爆发出一阵笑声。

2. The police *burst* through the door. 警察破门而入。

【同】 explode, break

bust [bʌst] *n*. 半身(雕)像；*v*. (busted 或 bust)打破，弄坏

【例】 1. There is a *bust* of Beethoven in the park. 公园里有一个贝多芬的半身塑像。

2. I dropped my camera on the pavement and *bust* it. 我把照相机掉在人行道上摔坏了。

【同】 statue; break, smash

bypass [ˈbaɪpɑːs, ˈbaɪpæs] *n*. 支路，旁道；*v*. 绕开，忽视

【记】 by(在旁边) + pass(经过)→从旁边经过→绕过

【例】 1. If we take the *bypass* we'll avoid the traffic in the town center. 我们走旁道，就能避开市中心的交通拥堵。

2. I *bypassed* the usual complaints procedure by writing directly to the owner of the company. 我绕过通常的投诉程序，直接写信给公司的老板。

【同】 road; avoid, ignore

by-product [ˈbaɪprɒdʌkt] *n*. 副产品，副作用

【记】 by(在旁边) + product(产品)→顺便生产出来的产品→副产品

【例】 An increase in crime is one of the *by-products* of unemployment. 犯罪增加是失业问题造成的恶果之一。

【同】 spin-off

C

cabin [ˈkæbɪn] *n*. 1. 小屋；2. 船舱

【例】 1. They lived in a little log *cabin* in the mountains. 他们住在山上一座小木屋里。

2. Please book me a *cabin* on the ship. 请替我在船上登记一个房舱。

【同】 cottage, hut; compartment

cabinet [ˈkæbɪnɪt] *n*. 1. 柜，橱柜；2. 内阁

【记】 cabin(小屋) + et(表示"小"的名词词尾)→小的房间→橱柜

【例】 1. I keep my collection of old china in the *cabinet*. 我把古瓷器收藏品存放在橱柜里。

2. Members of the *Cabinet* are chosen by the Prime Minister. 内阁阁员是由首相挑选的。

【同】 cupboard; government

calamity [kəˈlæmɪtɪ] *n*. 灾难，不幸事件

【记】 calam(不幸) + ity(名词词尾)→不幸的事情→灾难

【例】 The earthquake was the worst *calamity* in the country's history. 那次地震是全国有史以来最严重的灾难。

【同】 catastrophe, disaster

calculate [ˈkælkjuleɪt] *v*. 计算，估计

【记】 calc(石灰) + ul(表示小的词尾) + ate(动词词尾)→计算(古时候用小石头来计数)

【例】 The scientists are able to *calculate* accurately when the spaceship will reach the moon. 科学家能准确地计算出太空船什么时候抵达月球。

【同】 compute, reckon, estimate

【派】 calculation *n*. 计算，计算的结果

calendar [ˈkælɪndə] *n*. 1. 日历，历法；2. 日程表

【记】 calend(每月第一天) + ar(名词词尾)→显示每月第一天的东西→日历

【例】 1. According to the *calendar* my birthday falls on a Sunday this year. 按照今年的日历，我的生日恰好是个星期日。

2. The cup final is an important date in the sporting *calendar*. 足总杯决赛在运动日程表中是个重要日子。

【同】 schedule

camouflage [ˈkæmʊflɑːʒ] *v*. (军事上的)伪装，掩饰

【记】 来自意大利语 camuffare，伪装

【例】 The soldiers *camouflaged* themselves with leaves and branches. 士兵们用树枝树叶把自己伪装起来。

【同】 disguise

campaign [kæm'peɪn] *n*. 1.战役；2.运动，活动；*v*. 参加活动、运动

【记】 camp(田野)+aign(名词词尾)→战役，活动

【例】 1. He fought in the North African *campaign* during the last war. 在上次战争中他在北非战役参战。

2. Despite a new advertising *campaign*, they were suffering from falling sales. 尽管有新的广告宣传活动，但是他们的销售额却不断下降。

3. Joan is *campaigning* for women's right to equal pay. 琼正发起为妇女争取同工同酬权利的运动。

【同】 battle, fight; movement

【派】 campaigner *n*. 参加战役或运动的人，活动家

cancel ['kænsəl] *v*. (-cel(l)ed; -cel(l)ing)取消，删去

【例】 The match had to be *canceled* because of bad weather. 比赛因天气不好只得取消。

【同】 erase, call off, delete

【派】 cancellation *n*. 取消

candid ['kændɪd] *adj*. 率直的，坦白而诚实的

【记】 cand(白色的)+id(形容词词尾)→坦白的

【例】 I would like your *candid* opinion of these proposals. 我欢迎你对这些建议提出坦诚的意见。

【同】 direct, frank, straightforward

【反】 devious, insincere

candidate ['kændɪdɪt] *n*. 1.候选人；2.考生，应聘者

【记】 cand(白色的)+id(形容词词尾)+ate(表示人的名词词尾)→穿白衣的人(以前想求取官位的人，总是穿着白衣，到处奔走演说，以求多得选票)→候选人

【例】 1. She had been nominated as *candidate* for the presidency. 她已被提名为总统候选人。

2. They are interviewing *candidates* for the job of sales manager. 他们在面试应聘销售经理的人选。

【同】 campaigner, nominee; applicant

【派】 candidacy *n*. 候选人的资格或身份

canoe [kə'nuː] *n*. 独木舟，轻舟

【例】 We crossed the lake by *canoe*. 我们乘独木舟过湖去。

【同】 boat, pirogue

canteen [kæn'tiːn] *n*. 餐厅，食堂

【例】 The *canteen* was absolutely packed and I had to wait for ages. 餐厅里的人太多了，我等了好长时间。

【同】 dining room, restaurant

canvas ['kænvəs] *n*. 帆布，画布

【例】 The painter stretched the *canvas* on a frame. 画家把油画布紧绷在画框上。

canvass ['kænvəs] *v*. 1.游说，拉票；2.详查，细究

【例】 1. The party claims to have *canvassed* over 70% of the votes. 这个党声称已通过

游说争取到超过70%的选票。

2. The evidence had been repeatedly *canvassed* in American courts. 证据已在美国的法庭中反复被审查过。

【同】 solicit vote; examine, scrutinize

capable ['keɪpəbl] *adj*. 1.有能力的，能干的；2.有可能的，可以…的

【记】 cap(获取)+able(形容词词尾)→能够取得→有能力的

【例】 1. The company was not *capable* of handling such a large order. 公司没有能力应付大批的订货。

2. This tool machine is *capable* of being improved. 这台机床是可以改进的。

【同】 able, competent; susceptible

【反】 incapable, unable

【派】 capability *n*. 能力，技能

capacity [kə'pæsɪtɪ] *n*. 1.(做某事的)能力，资格；2.容量，容积

【记】 cap(获取，抓住)+ city(名词词尾)→可能接受的量→容量

【例】 1. He has a great *capacity* for enjoying himself. 他很会想办法自得其乐。

2. The fuel tank has a *capacity* of 12 gallons. 这个燃料箱的容量是12加仑。

【同】 capability, volume

capacious [kə'peɪʃəs] *adj*. 容积大的，广阔的

【记】 cap(获取)+cious(形容词词尾)→能够获取许多的→容积大的

【例】 He has a *capacious* memory. 他有很好的记忆力。

【同】 spacious, roomy

capsule ['kæpsjuːl] *n*. 1.胶囊，药丸；2.太空舱

【记】 capsu(装)+le(表示"小"的名词词尾)→装…的小东西→胶囊

【例】 1. He explains that it is sold in *capsules*, tablets, lozenges. 他解释说，这种药物以胶囊、药片、糖锭的形式出售。

2. The *capsule* gets very hot on re-entry. 太空舱在重返大气层时产生高热。

caption ['kæpʃən] *n*. (图片、报刊文章等的)说明文字、标题，字幕

【记】 cap(获取)+tion(名词词尾)→能够提出的东西→说明

【例】 The *caption* under the photo said 'The President greets the Chinese delegation'. 照片下面的说明文字写着"总统欢迎中国代表团"。

【同】 subtitle

captivate ['kæptɪveɪt] *v*. 迷惑，迷住

【记】 cap(获取，抓住)+tiv(e)(形容词词尾)+ate(动词词尾)→把(心)抓住→迷住

【例】 He was *captivated* by her beauty. 他被她的美色迷住了。

【同】 bewitch, fascinate

【派】 captivating *adj*. 迷人的，有魅力的

captivation *n*. 迷惑，魅力；着迷

captivity [kæp'tɪvɪtɪ] *n*. 囚禁，拘留

【记】 cap(获取，抓住)+tiv(e)(形容词词尾)+ity(名词词尾)→被抓住的→囚禁

【例】 Wild animals don't breed well in *captivity*. 圈养着的野生动物繁殖不好。

【同】 imprisonment, confinement

C

【反】 release
【派】 (逆构)captive *adj*. 被俘获的；被束缚的，受奴役的

capture [ˈkæptʃə] *n*./*v*. 1.捕获；2.夺取
【记】 capt(抓，取)＋ure(名词词尾)→抓住→捕获
【例】 1. The criminal was *captured* when trying to escape from the city. 罪犯在企图逃离这座城市时被捕获。
2. They *captured* a large share of the market. 他们夺得了很大一部分市场。
【同】 arrest，seize
【反】 release

cardinal [ˈkɑːdɪnəl] *adj*. 首要的，主要的；*n*. 红衣主教
【记】 card(铰链)＋al(形容词词尾)→起铰链作用的→主要的
【例】 1. This is one of the *cardinal* rules of mountain climbing. 这是登山运动的主要规则之一。
2. Wolsey, the great *Cardinal*, was a friend of Henry VIII. 红衣大主教渥西是亨利八世的朋友。
【同】 principal，central，important

cargo [ˈkɑːgəʊ] *n*. (船或飞机装载的)货物
【记】 car(跑的东西，车)＋go→车载的东西→货物
【例】 The captured ship and its *cargo* were condemned. 这艘被俘获的船及其货物均被没收。
【同】 freight，shipment，consignment

carnage [ˈkɑːnɪdʒ] *n*. 大屠杀，残杀
【记】 carn(肉)＋age(名词词尾)→吃肉的时节→大屠杀
【例】 The battlefield was a scene of terrible *carnage*. 战场上是一片可怕的大屠杀景象。
【同】 slaughter，bloodbath

carnal [ˈkɑːnl] *adj*. 肉体的，肉欲的
【记】 carn(肉)＋al(形容词词尾)→肉体的
【例】 *Carnal* pleasures can destroy a man's soul. 肉体的享乐会毁掉人的灵魂。
【同】 physical，corporeal
【反】 mental，spiritual

carnival [ˈkɑːnɪvəl] *n*. 表演会，狂欢节，嘉年华会
【记】 carn(肉)＋v＋al(名词词尾)→吃肉的时节→狂欢节
【例】 They are celebrating their annual *carnival*. 他们正在庆祝一年一度的狂欢节。
【同】 festival，funfair

carnivorous [kɑːˈnɪvərəs] *adj*. 食肉的
【记】 carn(肉)＋vor(e)(＝devour，吞食)＋ous(形容词词尾)→食肉的
【例】 Tigers are *carnivorous* animals; cattle are not. 老虎是食肉动物，牛不是。
【同】 flesh-eating，predacious
【反】 herbivorous
【派】 (逆构)carnivore *n*. 食肉动物

carton [ˈkɑːtən] *n*. 纸(板)盒，纸(板)箱

【记】 cart(= card，纸板) + on(名词词尾)→用纸板做的东西→纸板盒

【例】 He give the foreman a *carton* of cigarette as a sop. 他给工头一条香烟以表心意。

【同】 box

cartoon [kɑːˈtuːn] *n*. 动画片，漫画

【记】 cart(= card，纸板) + oon(名词词尾)→画在纸板上的东西→漫画

【例】 The making of *cartoons* became a separate branch of film-making. 卡通片制作成为电影制作的一个独立的分支。

【派】 cartoonist *n*. 漫画家，动画片画家

carve [kɑːv] *v*. 雕刻，切

【例】 The statue was *carved* out of marble. 这座雕像是用大理石雕刻的。

【同】 cut

【派】 carving *n*. 雕刻物，雕刻品

cascade [kæsˈkeɪd] *n*. 1. 小瀑布；2. 一连串，瀑布状下垂的东西

【记】 casca(落下) + de→落下的东西→瀑布

【例】 1. The water formed a *cascade* down the mountain. 水沿山泻下，形成一条瀑布。

2. Her long hair fell over her shoulders in a *cascade* of curls. 她长长的卷发像瀑布一样披泻在肩上。

【同】 waterfall

cassette [kɑːˈset] *n*. 盒式录音带，录音带盒

【记】 casse(盒子) + (e)tte(表示“小”的名词词尾)→小盒子→盒式录音带

【例】 I'm going to use a *cassette* recorder and record them all. 我想用一台卡式录音机把它们全都录下来。

cast [kɑːst] *v*. (cast，cast) 1. 投，掷，抛；2. 浇铸，铸造；3. 把…投向，投射；*n*. 演员阵容

【例】 1. The angler *cast* his line into the water. 钓鱼的人把鱼线抛入水中。

2. That's where all the metal was smelted and the tools were *cast*. 那就是所有的金属被熔化、工具被制成的地方。

3. The tragedy *cast* a shadow on/over their lives. 这一悲剧在他们的生命中投下了一片阴影。

4. The film has a strong *cast* that includes several famous names. 这部影片有很强的演员阵容，其中包括几位著名的影星。

【同】 throw; mold; project

castigate [ˈkæstɪgeɪt] *v*. 谴责，训斥

【记】 cast(纯洁的) + ig(做) + ate(动词词尾)→使…做好→训斥

【例】 His teacher *castigated* him for his inattentiveness in class. 他的老师因他在课堂上不专心听讲而严厉批评了他。

【同】 chasten, criticize, rebuke

【派】 castigation *n*. 惩罚，苛责

casual [ˈkæʒjuəl] *adj*. 1. 不是安排好的，偶然的；2. 随便的，漫不经心的

【记】 cas(降临，发生) + ual(形容词词尾)→降临的→偶然发生的

【例】 1. The woman is seeking help from *casual* passers-by. 那个女人在向碰巧路过的人求助。

2. The *casual* newspaper reader wouldn't like long articles on serious subjects every day. 随便看看报纸的人不愿每天看那些有关严肃主题的长文章。

【同】 accidental，incidental；indifferent

【反】 deliberate，planned；enthusiastic

casualty [ˈkæʒjuəltɪ] *n*. 死伤者，伤亡人数

【记】 cas(降临，发生)＋ual(形容词词尾)＋ty(名词词尾)→偶然降临的事情→意外→因意外而死伤者

【例】 She read through the *casualty* list anxiously. 她焦急地把伤亡人员名单从头至尾看了一遍。

【同】 victim

cataclysm [ˈkætəklɪzəm] *n*. 大灾难，大变动

【记】 cata(向下)＋clysm(洗)→冲刷而下→洪水→灾难

【例】 The revolution was a *cataclysm* of major importance in that century. 这场革命是那个世纪中一次重大的动荡。

【同】 calamity，catastrophe，disaster

catalog [ˈkætəlɒg] *n*. 目录，总目

【记】 cata(仔细地、详尽地)＋log(说)→被仔细述说的东西→目录

【例】 You can look for the book in the library *catalogue*. 你可以在图书馆的图书目录上查找这本书。

catalyze [ˈkætəlaɪz] *v*. 促使，激励

【记】 cata(向下)＋lyze(＝loose，松开)→向下松开，使释放→促使

【例】 The technology bred of science has *catalyzed* stupendous economic growth. 产生于科学的技术已经促成了巨大的经济发展。

【派】 catalyst *n*. 催化剂；促使事情发展的因素

catastrophe [kəˈtæstrəfɪ] *n*. 大灾难，大灾祸

【记】 cata(向下)＋strophe(转)→转而向下→灾难

【例】 The flood was a major *catastrophe*, causing heavy loss of life. 洪水是一场大灾难，夺去了许多人的生命。

【同】 calamity，cataclysm，disaster

【派】 catastrophic *adj*. 灾难性的

catching [ˈkætʃɪŋ] *adj*. 1. 传染性的；2. 有感染力的，有魅力的

【记】 catch(抓住)＋ing(形容词词尾)→抓住的→传染性的，有感染力的

【例】 1. Bad colds are *catching*. 恶性感冒是有传染性的。

2. Her eyes are the most *catching* I have ever seen. 她的眼睛是我见到过的最迷人的。

【同】 infectious，contagious；charming

categorical [ˌkætɪˈgɒrɪkəl] *adj*. 无条件的，绝对的，明确的

【记】 cate(向下)＋(e)gor(集合)＋ical(形容词词尾)→可以把(相同)的集合在同一个名下的→绝对的，明确的

【例】 The government has issued a *categorical* denial of this rumor. 政府对这一谣言断然否定。

【同】 absolute, unconditional, definite

【反】 tentative, uncertain

categorize [ˈkætɪgəraɪz] *n*. 分类，归类

【记】 cate(向下) + (e)gor(集合) + ize(动词词尾)→把(相同)的集合在同一个名下→分类

【例】 Participants were *categorized* to age and sex. 参加者按年龄和性别分组。

【同】 classify, assort

category [ˈkætɪgərɪ] *n*. 种类，范畴

【记】 cate(向下) + (e)gory(集合)→把(相同)的集合在同一个名下→范畴

【例】 There are different *categories* of books in a library. 图书馆里有各种不同种类的书籍。

【同】 class, sort

cater [ˈkeɪtə] *v*. 1. 提供饮食及服务；2. 满足需要，迎合

【例】 1. Who is *catering* your daughter's wedding? 谁承办你女儿的婚宴？

2. Our newspapers try to *cater* for all opinions. 我们的报纸试图满足各种观点的要求。

【同】 supply, provide; satisfy

【派】 caterer *n*. 酒宴承办人

catering *adj*. 承办酒席的，提供饮食及服务的；*n*. 餐饮，饮食

cathedral [kəˈθiːdrəl] *n*. 总教堂，大教堂

【记】 cat(向下) + hedr(a)(坐) + al(名词词尾)→(主教)坐下的地方→教堂

【例】 They are many *cathedrals* in York. 在约克郡有许多大教堂。

【同】 church

catholic [ˈkæθəlɪk] *adj*. 范围广阔或自由的，广泛的；*n*. [C-] 天主教徒

【记】 cat(向下) + hol(整个) + ic(形容词词尾)→整个(范围)下的→广泛的

【例】 1. Her musical tastes were *catholic* and ranged from classics to jazz. 她的音乐爱好非常广泛，从古典音乐到爵士乐都喜欢。

2. Is she a *Catholic* or a Protestant? 她是天主教徒还是新教徒？

【同】 broad, comprehensive, universal

caustic [ˈkɔːstɪk] *adj*. 1. 腐蚀性的；2. 刻薄的

【记】 caust(燃烧) + ic(形容词词尾)→燃烧的→腐蚀性的

【例】 1. Acid is *caustic*. 酸具有腐蚀性。

2. John's always making *caustic* comments about your work. 约翰总是对你的工作进行尖刻批评。

【同】 corrosive, erosive; acrid, sarcastic

caution [ˈkɔːʃən] *n*. 1. 小心，谨慎；2. 劝告，警告；*v*. 警告

【例】 1. You should exercise extreme *caution* when driving in fog. 在雾中开车要极为小心。

2. I received a *caution* from the doctor about fat in my diet. 医生劝告我注意饮食中的脂肪量。

3. The policeman *cautioned* the prisoners not to play any tricks. 警察正式告诫罪犯不要耍花招。

【同】 care, watchfulness; warning; alert, warn

【反】 incaution

cautious [ˈkɔːʃəs] *adj*. 谨慎的，小心的

【记】 caut(警觉)+ious(形容词词尾)→警觉的→小心的

【例】 The bank is very *cautious* about lending money. 银行在贷款方面十分慎重。

【同】 careful, conservative

【反】 incautious, careless

cease [siːs] *v*. 停止，结束

【例】 It rained all day without *ceasing*. 雨下了一天，一直没停。

【同】 stop, end, discontinue

【反】 start, begin, continue

【派】 ceaseless *adj*. 不停的，不断的

celebrate [ˈselɪbreɪt] *v*. 庆祝，庆典

【记】 celebr(荣誉)+ate(动词词尾)→给…荣誉→庆祝

【例】 These good results have given us something to *celebrate*. 这些好成绩值得我们庆祝一番。

【派】 celebration *n*. 庆祝，庆典

celebrated *adj*. 有名的，大名鼎鼎的

celebrity [sɪˈlebrɪtɪ] *n*. 著名，名人，社会名流

【记】 celebr(荣誉)+ity(名词词尾)→有荣誉的人→社会名流

【例】 She became a *celebrity* overnight. 她一下变成名人了。

【同】 famous person, fame

celestial [sɪˈlestjəl, sɪˈlestʃəl] *adj*. 天体的，天上的

【记】 cele(=caelum, 天空)+st+ial(形容词词尾)→天空中的→天上的

【例】 The sun, the moon and the stars are *celestial* bodies. 太阳、月亮和星星都是天体。

【同】 ethereal, heavenly

【反】 terrestrial, earthly

cellular [ˈseljʊlə] *adj*. 1. 细胞的；2. 蜂窝式无线通讯的

【记】 cell(u)(细胞)+lar(形容词词尾)→细胞的

【例】 1. They're doing *cellular* research, looking at changes in body cells when the body is under stress. 他们在做细胞方面的研究，他们要看看人的身体在处于压力的情况下细胞会发生怎样的变化。

2. The last straw that broke the camel's back was the failure of the Motorola Co. to win a large share of the Japanese *cellular* phone market. 最后令(美国)再也不能容忍的事件就是:摩托罗拉公司未能争取到较大的日本手机市场。

【派】 (逆构)cell *n*. 细胞

cement [sɪˈment] *n*. 水泥，接合剂；*v*. 接合，(用水泥、胶等)粘合

【例】 1. Don't walk on the wet *cement*. 水泥未干时不要在上面行走。

2. He *cemented* the bricks into place. 他用水泥砌砖。

【同】 cementum

censor ['sensə] *n*.（书刊、电影等的）检查员，审查员；*v*. 检查，审查

【记】 cens(判断)+or(名词词尾)→判断之人→审查员

【例】 1. Parts of this film have been banned by the *censor*. 这部电影的某些镜头遭到审查官的删剪。

2. They *censored* the violence. 他们把暴力镜头删去了。

【派】 censorship *n*. 审查员的职能，审查制度

censorious *adj*. 爱挑剔的，吹毛求疵的

censure ['senʃə] *v*./*n*. 指责，谴责

【记】 censure＝拉丁文 censura(意见)→陈述自己的意见→指责

【例】 The policeman was officially *censured* for his handling of the incident. 这名警察由于对事件处理不善，受到正式的谴责。

【同】 criticize, reproach

【反】 praise

【派】 censurable *adj*. 可非难的，该责备的

census ['sensəs] *n*. 人口调查，人口普查

【记】 cens(评估)+us(名词词尾)→调查评估出来的东西→人口调查

【例】 The *census* enumerated eighty-six persons over one hundred years old in this mountain area. 根据人口调查，这一带山区共有 86 位百岁老人。

centennial [sen'tenjəl] *n*. 百年纪念；*adj*. 一百年的

【记】 cent(百)+enn(年)+ial(形容词词尾)→一百年的

【例】 Eminent physicists from all over the world came to the United States to celebrate the *centennial* of Einstein's birth. 全世界著名的物理学家来到美国庆祝爱因斯坦诞生一百周年。

【同】 centenary, 100th anniversary

centigrade ['sentɪgreɪd] *adj*. 百分度的，摄氏温度的

【记】 cent(百)+grade(度)→百分度的

【例】 In the summer, the temperature is sometimes forty degrees *centigrade*. 在夏季，有时候温度可以达到 40 摄氏度。

【同】 Celsius

ceremony ['serɪmənɪ] *n*. 典礼，仪式

【记】 cere(神圣的)+mony(ment 的变体，名词词尾)→神圣的东西→典礼，仪式

【例】 The new graduates receive their degrees at a special *ceremony*. 新一届毕业生在一个特别的典礼上接受颁发的学位。

【同】 ritual

【派】 ceremonious *adj*. 礼节的，合乎礼俗的

ceremonial *adj*. 正式的，仪式上的；*n*. 礼仪，仪式

certificate [sə'tɪfɪkɪt] *n*. 证明，证明书

【记】 certi(确定)+fic(使)+ate(名词词尾)→使…得到确认→证明

【例】 most banks ask you to bring your passport and your *certificate* of enrolment. 大多数银行还会让你带着护照和录取证明书。

【同】 certification, authorization

【派】 certificated *adj*. 授予证明书的，合格的

certify [ˈsɜːtɪfaɪ] *v*. (尤指通过某种检验)证明，保证

C

【记】 certi(确定) + fy(= make 做)→使确定→证明

【例】 The accused has been *certified* to be insane. 被告被证明为精神失常。

【同】 attest, confirm, testify

【反】 decertify

【派】 certification *n*. 证明

chafe [tʃeɪf] *v*. 1.摩擦，擦破；2.(因某事物)恼怒或不耐烦

【例】 1. His shirt collar *chafed* his neck. 他的衬衫领口把脖子磨疼了。

2. The passengers sat *chafing* at the long delay. 乘客们因长时间的耽搁而坐得很不耐烦。

【同】 rub, scratch; annoy, irritate

chain [tʃeɪn] *n*. 链子，锁链；2.一系列的事物；3.连锁店

【例】 1. These poisons can easily enter the food *chain*, affecting the productivity of fishing and farming. 这些毒素很容易就能进入食物链，影响渔业和农业的生产。

2. Eruptions have rifted continents, raised mountain *chains*, constructed islands and shaped the topography of the earth. 火山喷发使大陆断裂，山脉增高，小岛形成，地貌定型。

3. I bought this loaf of bread in the *chain* store opposite the street. 我在街道对面的连锁商店里买了这只面包。

【同】 shackle; string, range; store

chamber [ˈtʃeɪmbə] *n*. 1.室，房间；2.会议厅，议会；3.枪膛

【例】 1. Cases not dealt with in court are sometimes heard in the judge's *chambers*. 不在法庭上处理的案件有时就在法官的专用办公室审理。

2. In Britain the upper *chamber* of parliament is the House of Lords, the lower is the House of Commons. 在英国，议会的上议院叫"贵族院"，下议院叫"众议院"。

3. A rocket motor's 'bullets' are minute, high-speed particles produced by burning propellants in a suitable *chamber*. 火箭助推器的"子弹"是精密而高速的粒子，通过点燃弹膛内的发射火药即可将这些粒子发射出去。

【同】 room, compartment

champagne [ʃæmˈpeɪn] *n*. 香槟酒

【记】 Champagne，香槟省，是法国东北部的一个省

【例】 True *champagne* comes only from one area of France, but sparkling wine from other places is often called champagne, too. 真正的香槟酒只出产于法国的一个地区，但是其他地区生产的冒气泡的酒也常叫做香槟酒。

【同】 bubbly

champion [ˈtʃæmpjən] *n*. 冠军，优胜者

【记】 champ(战场) + on(表示人的名词词尾)→战场上的士兵→冠军

【例】 The final game decides who is the *champion*. 最后一局比赛决定谁是冠军。

【同】 winner

【反】 loser

【派】 championship *n*. 锦标赛

channel [ˈtʃænl] *n*. 1. 渠道，途径；2. 频道

【记】 chann(管) + el(名词词尾)→像管子一样的东西→渠道

【例】 1. Your complaint must be made through the proper *channels*. 你的意见必须通过正当途径投诉。

2. We're doing some market research for a new television *channel* starting in two years' time. 我们正在为一个新开播两年的电视频道做市场调查。

【同】 line, way; TV station

chant [tʃɑːnt] *n*. 圣歌，赞美诗；*v*. (有节奏地、反复地) 唱或喊叫

【例】 1. This is a *chant* to the Hindu god Krishna. 这是一首赞颂印度教上帝克利士那的圣歌。

2. The crowd *chanted* slogans and waved banners. 人群一再有节奏地呼喊口号并挥舞旗帜。

【同】 psalm

chaos [ˈkeɪɒs] *n*. 混乱，紊乱

【例】 The failure of the electricity supplies created complete *chaos* in the city. 停电使这个城市完全陷入混乱状态。

【同】 disorder, confusion, mess

【反】 order, regularity

【派】 chaotic *adj*. 混乱的，杂乱的

chapter [ˈtʃæptə] *n*. 章，节，回

【记】 chapt(主要的) + er(名词词尾)→主要的部分→章

【例】 You have to wait until the last *chapter* to find out who the murderer was. 你要等到看完最后一章才能搞清楚谁是凶手。

【同】 section, subdivision

character [ˈkærɪktə] *n*. 1. (事物的) 性质，特性；2. 性格；3. 人物，角色

【例】 1. The whole *character* of the village has changed since I was last here. 自从我上次到这里以来，这个村庄的特色完全改变了。

2. The twins look alike but have very different *characters*. 这对双胞胎长得很像，但性格很不同。

3. I find all the *characters* in his new play very real. 我觉得他那出新戏中所有的人物都很真实。

【同】 nature, personality, role

【派】 characteristic *adj*. 独特的，典型的；*n*. 特性，特征

characterize [ˈkærɪktəraɪz] *v*. 1. 以…为特征；2. 表现…的特色，刻画…的性格

【记】 character(特色) + ize(动词词尾)→表现…的特色

【例】 1. The education system there is *characterized* by an emphasis on success in exams. 那里的教育制度以强调考试成绩为特征。

2. The novelist *characterizes* his heroine as capricious and passionate. 这位小说家把女主人公刻画成反复无常而又多情的人。

【同】 individuate, mark; describe, depict

charcoal ['tʃɑːkəʊl] *n*. 炭，木炭

【记】 char(改变…的形式)+coal(煤)→把煤的形式改变→炭，木炭

【例】 Some time in the tenth century, black powder was first compounded from its basic ingredients of saltpeter, *charcoal* and sulphur. 在10世纪的某个时期，人们首次用硝石、木炭和硫磺作为基本原料合成黑色炸药。

【同】 wood coal

charge [tʃɑːdʒ] *v*. 1.要(价)，收(费)；2.控告；3.充电；*n*. 1.费用；2.指控；3.电荷；4.主管，责任

【例】 1. How much do you *charge* for a double room? 双人房间你们收费多少？

2. He was *charged* with murder. 他被控犯谋杀罪。

3. The concentration of positively *charged* particles is greater than normal in these winds. 这些风带有超出平常风里的正电荷分子的集结。

4. I'd like to speak to the person in *charge*. 我想和负责人谈谈。

【同】 ask for; accuse; load; bill; accusation; electricity; command

【派】 chargeable *adj*. 可以控诉的；可记在某项账目上的；可充电的

charisma [kə'rɪzmə] *n*. (复数-mas或-mata)(大众爱戴的)领袖气质，魅力

【记】 charis(好感)+ma(名词词尾)→给人好感→有魅力

【例】 He could never be a film star; he's got no *charisma*. 他决没有可能成为电影明星；他一点儿魅力也没有。

【同】 attractiveness

charity ['tʃærɪtɪ] *n*. 1.仁慈，慈善；2.慈善活动，慈善机构

【记】 char(可爱的)+ity(名词词尾)→表达爱的行为→慈善活动

【例】 1. She gave the old woman some shoes out of *charity*. 她出于善心给了老妇人几双鞋。

2. The Red Cross is an international *charity*. 红十字会是个国际性的慈善机构。

【同】 benevolence

【反】 cruelty

【派】 charitable *adj*. 慈善的，慈悲的

chart [tʃɑːt] *n*. 示意图，图表

【记】 chart=card，用纸画的→图表

【例】 Check the *chart* to see which income bracket you are in. 查一下那个图表，看看你属于哪一个收入阶层。

【同】 graph, illustration

charter ['tʃɑːtə] *n*. 1.特许状，执照；2.宪章；3.包租

【记】 chart(纸做的卡片)+er(名词词尾)→一张纸片→执照

【例】 1. A royal *charter* exempted the Massachusetts colony from direct interference by the Crown. 一张皇家的特许状，使马萨诸塞州殖民地免受英王直接干涉。

2. The *Ottawa Charter for Health Promotion* remains as the backbone of health action today. 《渥太华健康促进宪章》在今天仍然是健康行动的支柱。

3. This travel firm specializes in low-cost *charter* flights. 这家旅行社专门从事廉价

包租班机业务。

【同】 treaty，alliance；rent，lease

【派】 chartered *adj*. 特许的，合格的

chase [tʃeɪs] *v*. 追赶，追逐

【例】 He *chased* (after) the burglar but couldn't catch him. 他追赶窃贼却未捉住。

【同】 pursue，follow

chaste [tʃeɪst] *adj*. 1 纯洁的，正派的；2.(思想、言论)朴素的

【例】 1. She was a holy woman，innocent and *chaste*. 她是一个圣洁的女人，天真而忠贞。

2. He wrote in a *chaste* style. 他文笔朴实。

【同】 pure，decent；simple

【反】 unchaste

chat [tʃæt] *v*./*n*. (-tted；-tting)聊天，闲谈

【例】 The two friends sat in a corner and *chatted* away about the price of stocks and shares. 两个朋友坐在角落里聊着股票行情。

【同】 converse，talk

chef [ʃef] *n*. 厨师长，厨师

【例】 *Chefs* wore white because they worked with flour，but the main chef wore a black hat to show his supervision. 厨师们因为和面粉打交道，所以身穿白色，而大厨要头戴黑色帽子以显示他是管理者。

【同】 cook

cherish ['tʃerɪʃ] *v*. 珍爱，爱护

【记】 cher(亲爱) + ish(动词词尾表示"做")→爱护

【例】 The old man *cherished* the girl as if she were his daughter. 老人疼爱那女孩就好像她是自己的女儿一般。

【同】 treasure，value

【反】 abandon，desert

chide [tʃaɪd] *v*. (chided/chid，chided /chid /chidden)斥责，责骂

【例】 She *chided* him for his laziness. 她责备他懒惰。

【同】 rebuke，reproach，scold

chill [tʃɪl] *n*. 寒冷，寒心；*v*. 使…寒心，冷冻

【例】 1. The bad news cast a *chill* over the gathering. 这坏消息使参加聚会的人颇为扫兴。

2. I'd love a really *chilled* mineral water or something. 我想来一瓶冰冻的矿泉水或其他什么的。

【同】 cool，freeze

【反】 warmth

【派】 chilly *adj*. 寒冷的，冷淡的

chilling *adj*. 吓人的

chivalry ['ʃɪvəlrɪ] *n*. 骑士精神，骑士制度

【记】 来自法语 chevalerie，骑士

【例】 The legends of King Arthur represent the apotheosis of *chivalry*. 亚瑟王的传说代表骑士精神的顶峰。

【同】 knighthood

choir ['kwaɪə] *n*. 合唱团，(教堂的)唱诗班

【例】 The church *choir* sing(s) every Sunday morning. 每周星期天上午教堂歌唱队要唱诗。

【派】 choral *adj*. 合唱的，唱诗班的

chorus *n*. 合唱，齐声说的话

choke [tʃəʊk] *v*. 1. 掐住…的脖子，使窒息；2. 堵塞，阻塞

【例】 1. She *choked* to death on a fish bone. 鱼刺把她卡住使她窒息而死。

2. The streets in the centre of the city were *choked* up with traffic. 市中心的街道被车辆堵塞了。

【同】 suffocate, smother; block, obstruct

【反】 breathe

chop [tʃɒp] *v*. (-pped; -pping)砍，劈

【例】 The old man *chopped* the block of wood in two with a single blow.

这老头一斧头把木块劈成两半。

【同】 cleave, cut

【派】 choppy *adj*. (水面)波浪起伏的，(指风)不断改变方向的

chore [tʃɔː] *n*. 1. 日常零星工作，杂务；2. 烦琐之事，令人讨厌的工作

【例】 1. She has to do the daily *chores* of cleaning, cooking and shopping. 她必须要做打扫、做饭、买东西等日常杂活。

2. It's such a *chore* filling in tax forms. 填写纳税表真是令人讨厌的工作。

【同】 duty, task; drudgery

choreograph ['kɔːrɪəgrɑːf] *v*. 设计舞蹈动作

【记】 choreo(舞蹈) + graph(写)→写舞蹈→设计舞蹈动作

【例】 He has *choreographed* a musical comedy. 他为一出歌舞喜剧设计舞蹈动作。

【派】 choreographer *n*. 舞蹈指导

choreographic *adj*. 舞蹈术的，舞蹈的

choreography *n*. 舞蹈编排

chorus ['kɔːrəs] *n*. 合唱，合唱团

【例】 Bill sang the verses and everyone joined in the *chorus*. 比尔先唱独唱部分，然后大家一起合唱。

【同】 ensemble

Christian ['krɪstjən] *n*. 基督教徒；*adj*. 1. 基督教的；2. 以基督为榜样的，宽宏大量的，人道的

【记】 Christ(基督) + ian(形容词词尾)→基督的→基督教的

【例】 1. He is an earnest *Christian*. 他是一个虔诚的基督教徒。

2. Christmas and Easter are *Christian* festivals. 圣诞节和复活节是基督教的节日。

3. It wasn't very *Christian* of you to laugh at the poor child. 你嘲笑穷孩子，那不是基督徒的所为。

chronic ['krɒnɪk] *adj*. 慢性的，久病的

【记】 chron(时间)+ic(形容词词尾)→耗费时间的→慢性的

【例】 They all suffer from *chronic* back pain. 他们都忍受着长期的背部疼痛。

【同】 habitual, constant

【反】 acute

【派】 chronicity *n*. 慢性，长期性

chronology [krə'nɒlədʒɪ] *n*. 年表，年代学

【记】 chron(时间)+ology(…学)→研究时间顺序的学科→年代学

【例】 Do you agree with this *chronology* of events in the 13th century? 你同意这份13世纪的大事年表吗?

【派】 chronological *adj*. 按时间顺序排列的

chuckle ['tʃʌkl] *v*. 咯咯地笑，轻声发笑

【记】 chuck(= choke，窒息)+le(不是动作的反复)→像被掐住脖子一样地笑→轻声发笑

【例】 I could hear him *chuckling* to himself as he read the book. 他看书时，我能听见他轻声发笑。

【同】 laugh, titter

cipher ['saɪfə] *n*. 密码

【例】 The army uses a special *cipher* so that military messages are kept secret. 军队使用一种特殊密码，军事电讯因此得以保密。

【同】 code

circle ['sɜːkl] *n*. 1.圆，圆形物；2.循环；3.圈子，派系；*v*. 环绕，绕行

【记】 circ(环)+le(表示“小”的名词词尾)→小环→圆

【例】 1. They sat in a *circle* round the fire. 他们围着火坐成一圈。

2. But of course that starts up a vicious *circle*. 但是这自然就开始了一种恶性循环。

3. She has a large *circle* of friends. 她交游很广。

4. The moon *circles* the earth every 28 days. 月亮每28天绕地球一圈。

【同】 lap, round; circulation; community

circuit ['sɜːkɪt] *n*. 1.环行，圈；2.电路，线路

【记】 circu(环，四周)+it(走)→走过四周→环行

【例】 1. The old scientist used to run three *circuits* of the track every morning. 老科学家以前每天早晨沿跑道跑三圈。

2. A break in the *circuit* had caused the lights to go out. 电路断路使灯光都熄灭了。

【同】 circle, loop, tour

circuitous *adj*. 迂回的，绕圈子的

circulate ['sɜːkjʊleɪt] *v*. 1.(使)循环；2.散布，传播，流传；3.发行，销售；4.巡回，穿梭

【记】 circul(= circ，圆，圈)+ate(动词词尾)→使形成圈→循环

【例】 1. Blood *circulates* through the body. 血液在体内循环。

2. Gossip tends to *circulate* quickly. 流言传播迅速。

3. These magazines *circulate* mostly in rural areas. 这些杂志大部分在农村地区销售。

4. The host and hostess *circulated* among their guests. 男女主人在客人间走来走去招待客人。

【同】 circle; transmit, spread; go around

【派】 circulation *n*. 循环，流通

circumference [sə'kʌmfərəns] *n*. 圆周，周长

【记】 circum(环绕，周围) + fer(带来) + ence(名词词尾)→从周围带来的东西→周长

【例】 The earth's *circumference* is more than 40000 kilometers. 地球的周长为四万多千米。

【同】 perimeter, circuit

circumscribe ['sɜːkəmskraɪb] *v*. 限制，划分

【记】 circum(环绕，周围) + scribe(写)→写上范围→限制

【例】 His activities has been severely *circumscribed* since his illness. 自从生病以后，他的活动受到了严格的限制。

【同】 limit, confine

【派】 circumscription *n*. 界限

circumspect ['sɜːkəmspekt] *adj*. 慎重的，仔细的

【记】 circum(周围) + spect(看)→看清除四周→慎重的

【例】 I'm surprised he got married in such a hurry—he's usually pretty *circumspect*. 他这样匆匆忙忙就结了婚，我感到很吃惊——他通常是相当慎重的啊！

【同】 discreet, prudent

【派】 circumspection *n*. 细心，慎重

circumstance ['sɜːkəmstəns] *n*. 环境，条件，情况

【记】 circum(周围) + stan(站立) + ce(名词词尾)→所站立周围的(细节)→环境

【例】 Under the *circumstances* he felt unable to accept the job. 在这种情况下，他觉得无法接受这项工作。

【同】 condition, context, situation, state

circumvent [ˌsɜːkəm'vent] *v*. 1. 围绕，包围；2. 用计谋战胜，规避

【记】 circum(周围) + vent(来到)→从周围来→包围

【例】 1. He turned north off the main road, hoping to *circumvent* the city. 他离开大路转而向北，希望绕过这座城市。

2. The company opened an office aboard in order to *circumvent* the tax laws. 公司在国外开设了一个办事处，以避开本国的税法。

【同】 besiege, surround; evade

cite [saɪt] *v*. 引用，援引

【记】 cit(呼叫) + e(词尾)→呼叫过来→引用

【例】 The lawyer *cited* a previous case to support his argument. 律师引用了以前的案例来支持他的论点。

【同】 quote, refer

civil ['sɪvl] *adj*. 1. 平民的；2. 民事的；3. 国内的

【例】 1. He left the army and resumed *civil* life. 他离开军队，恢复平民生活。

2. It was a *civil* case so there was no question of him being sent to prison. 这是一

桩民事案件，因此他没有被送进监狱的可能。

3. This ruined bridge is a relic of the *Civil* War. 这座毁坏的桥是南北战争(内战)时的遗迹。

【同】 civic; public, social; domestic

【反】 uncivil; foreign

【派】 civilian *n./adj.* 平民(的)，文职人员(的)

civilization [sɪvɪlaɪzeɪʃənlɪz] *n.* (US civilisation)文明，文明世界

【记】 civi(城市)+liz(使…化)+ation(名词词尾)→使城市化→文明

【例】 It is generally accepted that the Chinese *civilization* is one of the oldest in the world. 普遍认为华夏文明是世界上最古老的文明之一。

【派】 (逆构)civilize *v.* 使文明，使开化

claim [kleɪm] *v./n.* 1.(根据权利)要求，认领；2.声称，主张

【记】 claim(大叫)→声称

【例】 1. Old people are entitled to *claim* a special heating allowance from the government. 老年人有权向政府索取一笔特别的取暖津贴。

2. They *claim* that they have discovered a cure for the disease, but this had not yet been proved. 他们声称已经发现了治疗此病的一种药物，但此事尚未得到证实。

【同】 demand, require; assert, declare

clamor ['klæmə] *n./v.* 喧闹，叫嚷，大声地要求

【记】 clam(大叫)+or(名词词尾)→叫嚷

【例】 1. The children were *clamoring* to go to the zoo. 孩子们大声吵着要去动物园。

2. The government ignored the *clamor* for a public inquiry into these events. 政府没有理睬要求公开调查这些事件的强烈呼声。

【同】 cry out, exclaim

clarify ['klærɪfaɪ] *v.* 澄清，阐明

【记】 clari(清楚)+fy(动词词尾)→使…清楚→澄清

【例】 I hope that what I say will *clarify* the situation. 我希望我说的话能澄清这一情况。

【同】 elucidate, elaborate, illuminate

【反】 confuse, obscure

【派】 clarification *n.* 澄清，净化

clarity *n.* 清晰，明晰

classify ['klæsɪfaɪ] *v.* 分类，归类

【记】 class(等级)+fy(低潮词尾，做)→分成等级→分类

【例】 Would you *classify* her novels as serious literature or as mere entertainment? 你认为她的小说属于文学类呢，还是属于通俗读物类?

【同】 assort, class, sort

【派】 classification *n.* 分类，归类

cleanse [klenz] *v.* 使清洁，使纯净

【记】 clean(干净的)+se(动词词尾)→使干净，使清洁

【例】 The nurse *cleansed* the wound for the injured before stitching it. 护士先把伤员的

伤口弄干净后再缝合。

【同】 clean, wash

【反】 stain

【派】 cleanser *n*. 清洁剂，去污粉

clergy ['klɜːdʒɪ] *n*. (总称)神职人员；教士，牧师

【例】 All the local *clergy* attended the ceremony. 当地所有的牧师出席了仪式。

【同】 priesthood

【派】 clergyman *n*. 牧师，教士

client ['klaɪənt] *n*. 1.顾客，客户；2.委托人

【例】 1. We guarantee that no single *client* will pay more, even when only double rooms are available for them. 我们保证任何一位顾客都不必多付钱，即使只剩双人间了也不会多要钱的。

2. The lawyer explained the legal technicalities to his *client*. 律师给委托人解释法律上的要点。

【同】 customer, guest

【派】 clientele *n*. (总称)顾客，主顾

climate ['klaɪmɪt] *n*. 1.气候；2.(某一时期社会上的)风气，环境

【记】 clim(= cline, 倾斜) + ate(形容词词尾，此处转用作名词)→古希腊人认为地球是向北极倾斜的，这就影响了各地区的气候→气候

【例】 1. She moved to a warmer *climate*. 她搬到气候较温暖的地方。

2. Since 1979, companies have responded to improvements in the business *climate* by having employees work overtime rather than by hiring extra personnel. 自从1979年以来，各公司对于改善经营风气所作出的反应就是，让现有的员工加班干活也不会多雇佣人员。

【同】 clime, weather; ambience, atmosphere

【派】 climatic *adj*. 气候的

climax ['klaɪmæks] *n*. 顶点，高潮

【记】 cli(弯曲，倾向) + max(最大)→倾向于最大→顶点

【例】 The *climax* of the celebration was a firework display. 庆祝会的高潮是燃放烟火。

【同】 culmination, peak, top

clinch [klɪntʃ] *v*. 1.钉牢，揪住；2.确定，最终决定

【例】 1. He is *clinching* the boards together. 他正在用钉子把木板钉牢在一起。

2. The two companies *clinched* the deal quickly. 两家公司很快地成交了。

【同】 clench, fix; conclude, confirm

cling [klɪŋ] *v*. (clung, clung)粘着，依附

【例】 His wet shirt *clung* to his body. 湿衬衫紧紧贴在他身上。

【同】 adhere, stick

【派】 clinging *adj*. 贴身的；依赖的；坚持的

clinic ['klɪnɪk] *n*. 诊所，门诊部

【记】 clin(床) + ic(形容词词尾，此处转用作名词)→有床的地方→诊所

【例】 He is being treated at a private *clinic*. 他正在私人诊所接受治疗。

【同】 hospital

【派】 clinician *n*. 门诊医师

clip [klɪp] *n*. 夹子，回形针 *v*. (-pped; -pping)修剪

【例】 1. The letters were held together with a paper *clip*. 信是用一枚回形针夹在一起的。

2. The guard on the train *clipped* our tickets. 火车上的列车员给我们剪了票。

【同】 crop, cut

clockwise [ˈklɒkwaɪz] *adj*. /*adv*. 顺时针方向的(地)

【记】 clock(钟表) + wise(方式)→以钟表的方式→顺时针方向的(地)

【例】 Turn the lid *clockwise* if you want to fasten it tightly. 如果要把盖子拧紧，就得顺时针方向拧。

【反】 counterclockwise, anticlockwise

clog [klɒg] *v*. (-gged; -gging)堵塞，阻塞

【例】 1. The pipes were *clogged* with rubbish. 管子里塞满了脏物。

2. The road to the airport is *clogged* with traffic. 去机场的路交通堵塞得厉害。

【同】 block, choke, obstruct

【反】 unclog

clue [kluː] *n*. 线索，提示

【例】 The only *clue* to the identity of the murderer was a half-smoked cigarette. 鉴定谋杀者的唯一线索是一支吸了一半的香烟。

【同】 clew, cue, hint

clumsy [ˈklʌmzɪ] *adj*. 笨拙的，无技巧的

【记】 clums(古英语 clumsen，使麻木) + y(形容词词尾)→使有麻木的性质→笨拙的

【例】 It's not easy walking in these *clumsy* shoes. 穿着这双笨重的鞋走路真难受。

【同】 awkward, unskillful

【反】 clever, skillful

cluster [ˈklʌstə] *n*. 串，丛；*v*. 使成群，聚集

【例】 1. Their villages were little more than *clusters* of thatched huts. 他们的村落只不过是一簇簇的茅草屋。

2. The men *clustered* together for warmth. 那些人挤作一团互相用身体取暖。

【同】 bunch, bundle

clutch [klʌtʃ] *n*./*v*. 紧抓，紧握

【例】 He *clutched* the rope we threw to him. 他急忙抓住我们扔给他的绳子。

【同】 clench, grip

coalesce [ˌkəʊəˈles] *v*. 联合，合并

【记】 co(一起) + alesce(生长)→一起生长→联合

【例】 The views of party leaders *coalesced* to form a coherent policy. 党的领导人的各种观点已统一为一致的政策。

【同】 combine, merge, mix

【派】 coalescence *n*. 合并，联合

coalition [ˌkəʊəˈlɪʃən] *n*. 联合，同盟

【记】 co(一起)+alit(生长)+ion(名词词尾)→一起生长→联合

【例】 Some of the parties in Spain formed a *coalition* government. 西班牙的一些政党组成了一个联合政府。

【同】 alignment, alliance

C

coarse [kɔːs] *adj*. 粗的，粗糙的

【记】 coarse=course 跑过去→粗糙的

【例】 Sandpaper is an extremely *coarse* material. 砂纸是一种非常粗糙的材料。

【同】 crude, rough

【反】 fine, delicate

coax [kəʊks] *v*. 哄诱，巧言诱哄

【例】 The children had to be *coaxed* into going to school. 孩子们得哄着才去上学。

【同】 wheedle, persuade

coddle [ˈkɒdəl] *v*. 娇生惯养，溺爱

【例】 You *coddle* your children too much; they are getting spoiled. 你太娇惯孩子了，他们都要被惯坏了。

【同】 cosset, pamper, spoil

code [kəʊd] *n*. 1.代码，密码；2.规范，准则

【例】 1. We have broken/cracked their *code*! 我们破译出他们的密码了！

2. The new *code* of conduct lays down the ground rules for management-union relations. 新的管理章程为劳资关系确定了基本的原则。

【同】 cipher

coerce [kəʊˈɜːs] *v*. 强制，强迫

【记】 co(一起)+erce(限制)→一起限制→强制

【例】 They were *coerced* into signing the contract. 他们被迫签了合同。

【同】 compel, force

【派】 coercion *n*. 强迫，威压，高压政治

coercive *adj*. 强制的，强迫的

cogent [ˈkəʊdʒənt] *adj*. 强有力的，使人信服的

【记】 co(一起)+g(=ag, 做)+ent(形容词词尾)→(说服)别人一起做的→使人信服的

【例】 He produced *cogent* reasons for the change of policy. 他对改变政策提出了充分的理由。

【同】 potent, forceful, powerful

【派】 cogency *n*. 力量，中肯

cognitive [ˈkɒgnɪtɪv] *adj*. 认识的，认知的

【记】 cognit(知道)+ive(形容词词尾)→认识的

【例】 Not only is more of the brain involved in play than was suspected, but it also seems to activate higher *cognitive* processes. 玩耍不仅涉及的大脑范围比猜测的要多，而且还好像能激活更高的认知过程。

【派】 cognition *n*. 认知，认识，认识力

cohere [kəʊˈhɪə] *v*. 1.粘着，附着；2.连贯，紧凑

【记】 co(一起)+here(粘)→粘在一起→粘着

【例】 1. When you squeeze a handful of snow, the flakes *cohere* to make a snowball. 你把一团雪捏紧，雪就黏合成雪球。

2. The movie as a whole failed to *cohere*. 这部电影从整体上不连贯。

【同】 adhere, cling

【派】 coherence *n*. 一致

coherent *adj*. 粘在一起的；连贯的，有条理的

cohesion [kəʊ'hiːʒən] *n*. 团结，内聚力

【记】 co(一起) + hes(粘着) + ion(名词词尾)→粘在一起→团结

【例】 We need greater *cohesion* in the party if we're going to win the next election. 我们如果想赢得下次选举，就需要党内有更加紧密的团结。

【同】 coherence, coherency

【派】 cohesive *adj*. 有结合力的，产生内聚力的

coil [kɔɪl] *v*. 盘绕，卷曲

【例】 The snake *coiled* round the tree. 蛇盘绕在树上。

【同】 curl, roll, spiral

【反】 uncoil

coin [kɔɪn] *n*. 硬币，钱币；*v*. 1. 铸币，铸造；2. 创造(新词等)

【例】 1. These teller machines accept any denomination of *coins* or notes up to 50 dollars. 这些柜员机可识别 50 美元以内的纸币和硬币。

2. It's a serious offence to *coin* money. 私自铸造钱币是严重的罪行。

3. Do not *coin* terms that are intelligible to nobody. 不要生造谁也不懂的词语。

【同】 specie, nickel; mint; originate

【派】 coinage *n*. (总称)硬币；新创造的词语

coincide [ˌkəʊɪn'saɪd] *v*. 1 同时发生；2. 相符，一致

【记】 co(一起) + in(在…上) + cid(降临，发生) + e→一起发生→同时发生

【例】 1. Her arrival *coincided* with our departure. 她来到时我们正好离开。

2. Her taste in music *coincides* with her husband's. 她在音乐方面的爱好与她丈夫一致。

【同】 concur; accord, agree

【反】 differ

【派】 coincidence *n*. 一致，巧合

coincident *adj*. 一致的，巧合的

collaborate [kə'læbəreɪt] *v*. 1. 协作，合作；2. 通敌

【记】 col(= com，一起) + labor(工作) + ate(动词词尾)→一起工作→合作

【例】 1. Our company is *collaborating* with a Japanese firm in designing a new computer. 我们公司和一家日本公司正合作设计一种新型计算机。

2. Anyone who had *collaborated* with the enemy was shot. 所有通敌分子都被枪决了。

【同】 cooperate; collude

【派】 collaboration *n*. 合作，协作；通敌

collapse [kəˈlæps] *n*. 1.倒塌，塌陷；2.垮掉，崩溃；*v*. 1.倒塌，瓦解；2.倒下，昏倒

【记】 col(= com，一起) + laps(滑) + e→一起滑落→倒塌

【例】 1. The unexpected rainstorm caused the *collapse* of the roof. 突然来临的暴风雨使屋顶塌了。

2. He suffered from a nervous *collapse*. 他的精神崩溃了。

3. The roof of the old house *collapsed*. 这座旧房子的房顶塌了。

4. He *collapsed* in the street and died on the way to hospital. 他在大街上晕倒，在送往医院途中死去。

【同】 break down，crumble，fall

collate [kɒˈleɪt] *v*. 核对，校勘

【记】 col(= com，一起) + late(带来)→集合在一起→核对

【例】 The editor is *collating* a new edition with an earlier one. 编辑正把新版本与旧版本进行核对。

【同】 compare，check

【派】 collation *n*. 1.核对，校勘；2.冷食小吃，便餐

collateral [kəˈlætərəl] *adj*. 1.并行的，附属的，伴随的；2.旁系的；*n*. 抵押品，担保物

【记】 col(= com，一起) + later(侧面) + al(名词词尾)→侧面在一起→并行的

【例】 1. A *collateral* aim of the government's industrial strategy is to increase employment. 政府工业战略的一个附带目的是增加就业。

2. Cousins are *collateral* relatives but brothers are directly related. 堂表兄弟是旁系亲戚，而兄弟则是直系亲属。

3. The bank will insist on *collateral* for a loan of that size. 银行坚决要求这样的大笔贷款一定要有抵押物。

【同】 parallel；indirect；guarantee

【反】 lineal

colleague [ˈkɒliːg] *n*. 同事，同僚

【记】 col(= com，一起，共同) + league(选择)→共同选出的人→同事

【例】 Well you can discuss that with my *colleague* in a moment. 过一会儿你可以和我的同事讨论那个问题。

【同】 co-worker，workfellow

collective [kəˈlektɪv] *adj*. 集体的，共同的；*n*. 集体，集体组织

【记】 col(= com，一起) + lect(集合) + ive(形容词词尾)→描绘集合在一起的→集体的

【例】 1. We all bear *collective* responsibility for this decision. 我们大家共同承担这项决定的责任。

2. Another successful project，The Shoe Shine *Collective*，was a partnership program with the Dominican Republic. 另一个成功的项目叫做“擦鞋合作社”，这是一个和多米尼加共和国的合作项目。

【同】 corporate，common；group，collectivity

【反】 individual，distributive

【派】 collectivism *n*. 集体主义

collectivity *n*. 集体，总体

collide [kəˈlaɪd] *v*. 1. 互撞，碰撞；2. 冲突，抵触

【记】 col(= com，一起) + lide(打)→打在一起→互撞

【例】 1. As the bus turned the corner, it *collided* with a van. 公共汽车转过拐角时与一辆货车相撞。

2. The President *collided* with Congress over his budget plan. 总统在预算计划上和国会发生了冲突。

【同】 clash, conflict

【派】 collision *n*. 碰撞；冲突，抵触

colloquial [kəˈləʊkwɪəl] *adj*. 口语的，通俗语的

【记】 col(= com，一起) + loqu(说) + ial→一起说的→口语的

【例】 The teacher deleted the *colloquial* expressions in Bob's formal writing. 老师把鲍勃的正式写作里面的口语表达删除了。

【同】 informal

【反】 formal

【派】 colloquialism *n*. 俗话，白话，口语

colossal [kəˈlɒsl] *adj*. 巨大的，庞大的

【记】 colloss(巨像，巨人) + al(形容词词尾)→巨大的

【例】 It requires government spending on a *colossal* scale. 这要求政府付出巨额开支。

【同】 enormous, gigantic, huge, immense

【反】 tiny, small

column [ˈkɒləm] *n*. 1. 圆柱，柱状物；2. 专栏

【例】 1. Nelson's *Column* is a famous monument in London. 纳尔逊纪念碑是伦敦著名的纪念碑。

2. I always read her *column* in the local paper. 我经常在当地报纸上看她的专栏文章。

【同】 cylinder, pillar

【派】 columnar *adj*. 柱形的；分栏印刷或书写的

columnist *n*. 专栏作家

combine [kəmˈbaɪn] *v*. 结合，联合

【记】 com(一起) + bine(两个)→把两个结合起来→联合

【例】 Circumstances have *combined* to ruin our plans for a holiday. 各种情况凑在一起破坏了我们的假日计划。

【同】 merge, unite

【反】 divide, part

【派】 combination *n*. 结合，联合

combustion [kəmˈbʌstʃən] *n*. 燃烧

【记】 comb(= com，完全) + ust(燃烧) + tion(名词词尾)→完全燃烧→燃烧

【例】 Superclean coal has the potential to enhance the *combustion* efficiency of conventional pulverized fuel power plants. 超级纯净碳有可能提高传统的粉碎燃料电厂的燃烧率。

【同】 burning

【派】 (逆构)combust *v*. 燃烧，消耗
combustible *adj*. 易燃的，可燃的

comedy [ˈkɒmɪdɪ] *n*. 喜剧，喜剧性事件，喜剧作品

【例】 I prefer *comedy* to tragedy. 我喜欢喜剧，不喜欢悲剧。
【反】 tragedy
【派】 comic *adj*. 喜剧的，滑稽的
comedian *n*. 喜剧演员，滑稽人物

comet [ˈkɒmɪt] *n*. 彗星
【例】 *Comets* move around the sun like planets, but in long oval course. 彗星像行星一样绕太阳运转，然而其轨道呈狭长的椭圆形。

command [kəˈmɑːnd] *n*./*v*. 1.命令，指挥；2.掌握，掌管
【记】 com(一起)+mand(命令)→一起命令→指挥
【例】 1.The general *commanded* his men to attack the city. 将军下令部下攻城。
2.A government minister *commands* the services of many officials. 政府部长掌管许多官员的工作。
【同】 order, instruct; control, dominate
【反】 comply, obey
【派】 commanding *adj*. 指挥的，发号施令的
commandment *n*. 1.命令，指挥；2.(十诫之一的)诫律

commemorate [kəˈmeməreɪt] *v*. 纪念，庆祝
【记】 com(一起)+memor(记忆)+ate(动词词尾)→一起记忆→纪念
【例】 This memorial *commemorates* those who died in the war. 这座纪念碑是纪念战争中牺牲者的。
【同】 remember, celebrate
【派】 commemoration *n*. 纪念，纪念仪式

commence [kəˈmens] *v*. 开始，着手
【记】 com(一起)+mence(着手)→一起着手→开始
【例】 Now before we *commence* our tour I'd just like to tell you a little bit about the history of the museum. 在我们正式参观之前，我先向各位简要介绍一下这个博物馆的历史。
【同】 begin, start
【反】 conclude, end, finish
【派】 commencement *n*. 开始，发端

commend [kəˈmend] *v*. 1.称赞，颂扬；2.委托，托付
【记】 com(共同)+mend(委托)→共同委托→委托，托付
【例】 1.She was highly *commended* for her organizational skills. 她的组织才能受到高度赞赏。
2.The dying woman *commended* her five children to their aunt. 那个临终的妇女把她五个孩子托付给孩子们的阿姨。
【同】 compliment, praise; trust
【反】 criticize

【派】 commendable *adj*. 值得表扬的
commendation *n*. 赞扬，荣誉；奖状

comment [ˈkɒment] *n*./*v*. 评论，(发表)意见

【记】 com(彻底)+ment(心智，想)→彻底想到，论及→评论

【例】 1. He made several unfavorable *comments* about their candidate. 他对他们的候选人发表了一些不利的言论。
2. The minister refused to *comment* on the rumors of his resignation. 部长拒绝就他辞职一事的传闻发表评论。

【同】 observe, remark

【派】 commentary *n*. 评论；实况报道
commenter *n*. 批评家，评论家
commentator *n*. 评论员，讲解员

commerce [ˈkɒməːs] *n*. 商业，贸易

【记】 com(一起)+merce(交易)→一起交易→贸易

【例】 We must promote *commerce* with neighboring countries. 我们必须促进与邻国的贸易。

【同】 business, trade

【派】 commercial *adj*. 商业的，营利的
commercialize *v*. 使商业化，使商品化

commission [kəˈmɪʃən] *n*. 1.(委托)任务，工作；2.委员会；3.佣金

【记】 com(一起)+miss(送)→被一起送→任务

【例】 1. The *commission* to build the new theater was given to a well-known architect. 建造新剧院的任务委托给了一位著名的建筑师。
2. The government has set up a *commission* to suggest improvements in the educational system. 政府成立了一个委员会来提出改进教育制度的计划。
3. He gets a 10% *commission* on everything he sells. 他每卖一件东西得10%的佣金。

【同】 mission; committee; reward

【派】 commissioner *n*. 委员，长官

commit [kəˈmɪt] *v*. (-tted, -tting) 1.犯(错误，罪行等)；2.承诺

【记】 com(一起)+mit(送)→一起送→做

【例】 1. They may not even realize they're *committing* a crime. 他们可能根本就没有意识到他们在犯罪。
2. The government has *committed* itself to improving health education. 政府承诺改善健康教育。

【同】 dedicate, do; promise

【派】 commitment *n*. 信奉，支持；许诺，承诺
committed *adj*. 忠心耿耿的，效忠的；坚定的
committee *n*. 委员会

commodity [kəˈmɒdɪtɪ] *n*. 商品，(尤指)日用品

【记】 com(共同)+mod(方法，方式)+ity(名词词尾)→共同具有各种样式的东西→

商品

【例】 Air conditioners are one of the many *commodities* that Japan sells abroad. 空调是日本许多出口商品中的一种。

【同】 goods, article

C

commonplace ['kɒmənpleɪs] *adj*. 平凡的，普通的；*n*. 平常的事，平常的话，套话

【记】 common(普通的，公共的) + place(地方)→普通地方都有的→平凡的

【例】 1. We exchanged a few *commonplaces* about our work and the weather. 我们相互寒暄了几句有关工作和天气的套话。

2. Heart transplant operations are becoming fairly *commonplace*. 心脏移植正在成为相当常见的手术。

【同】 ordinary, banal; banality

【反】 distinguished, extraordinary

communal ['kɒmjʊnl] *adj*. 集体公用(或参加)的，共同的

【记】 commun(= common，共同的) + al(形容词词尾)→共同的

【例】 The apartment has four separate bedrooms and a *communal* kitchen. 这个单元有四间卧室和一间共用的厨房。

【同】 common

【反】 individual

【派】 (逆构)commune *n*. 公社

communicate [kə'mjuːnɪkeɪt] *v*. 1. 传达，传递；2. 交流，沟通

【记】 com(一起，共同) + muni(服务) + ate(名词词尾)→一起享有→交流

【例】 1. This poem *communicates* the author's despair. 这首诗流露出作者的绝望心情。

2. He is a shy boy who can't *communicate* well. 他是一个腼腆的孩子，不太善于同别人交流。

【同】 convey, transmit; converse, talk

【派】 communication *n*. 交流；通讯

communicative *adj*. 通信的；交际的

community [kə'mjuːnɪtɪ] *n*. 社区，团体

【记】 commun(= common，共同的) + ity(形容词词尾)→共同的地方→社区

【例】 The whole *community* was astir when the news came that the enemy bombing would be restored. 敌人将恢复轰炸的消息传来，整个社区都骚动起来。

【同】 group

commute [kə'mjuːt] *v*. (尤指市郊之间)乘公交车辆上下班，通勤

【记】 com(一起，共同) + mute(改变)→一起变换→通勤

【例】 She *commutes* from Oxford to London every day. 她每天往返于牛津和伦敦之间。

【派】 commuter *n*. (尤指市郊之间)乘公交车辆上下班者，通勤者

compact ['kɒmpækt] *adj*. 紧密的，密集的；2. 简洁的，紧凑的

【记】 com(一起) + pact(系紧)→紧密地结合在一起→紧密的

【例】 1. Stamp the soil down so that it's *compact*. 把泥土踩结实。

2. This is a *compact* encyclopedia. 这是一本简本百科全书。

【同】 dense, thickset; concise

【反】 loose

companion [kəm'pænjən] *n*. (相伴的)人或动物，伙伴

【记】 com(一起)+pani(面包)+on(指人的名词词尾)→一起吃面包的人→同伴

【例】 My fellow prisoners made good *companions*. 我的狱中难友成了我的好伙伴。

【同】 comrade, friend

【反】 antagonist, enemy

【派】 companionate *adj*. 伙伴的，友爱的

companionship *n*. 伙伴关系，友谊

compare [kəm'pɛə] *v*. 1. 比较，对照；2. 比喻

【记】 com(一起)+par(相等)→把…放在一起看是否相等→比较

【例】 1. I *compared* the copy with the original, but there was not much difference. 我比较了复印件和原件，但是差别不是很大。

2. Life is poetically *compared* to the morning dew. 在诗歌中，人生被比喻为朝露。

【同】 match, contrast; liken

【派】 comparable *adj*. 可比较的，类似的

comparative *adj*. 比较的，相比较而言的

comparison *n*. 比较，对照

compassion [kəm'pæʃən] *n*. 同情，怜悯

【记】 com(共同的)+pass(感情)+ion(名词词尾)→ 有共同的感情→同情

【例】 She felt great *compassion* for the sick children. 她深深同情那些生病的孩子。

【同】 mercy, sympathy

【反】 coldness, cruelty

【派】 compassionate *adj*. 有同情心的；照顾性的

compatible [kəm'pætəbl] *adj*. 1. 协调的，可以并存的；2. 相容的，可协同使用的

【记】 com(一起)+pat(忍受)+ible→能一起忍受的→可以并存的

【例】 1. Their marriage came to an end because they were simply not *compatible* with each other. 他们简直无法和睦相处，所以就离婚了。

2. This printer is *compatible* with most computers. 这台打印机是与大多数电子计算机兼容的。

【同】 harmonious, congenial

【反】 incompatible

compatriot [kəm'pætrɪət] *n*. 同国人，同胞

【记】 com(共同的)+patr(父辈，祖先)+iot(名词词尾)→有共同祖先的人→同胞

【例】 He tried to avoid spending too much time with his *compatriots* when he lived abroad. 他住在国外的时候，尽量避免与同胞经常呆在一起。

【同】 countryman

compel [kəm'pel] *v*. (-lled; -lling)强迫，迫使

【记】 com(一起)+pel(驱使)→一起驱使→迫使

【例】 His conscience *compelled* him to admit his part in the affair. 他的良心驱使他承认自己曾参与该事件。

【同】 force, oblige, press

C

【反】 free

【派】 compelling *adj*. 扣人心弦的，强制性的

compensate [ˈkɒmpənseɪt] *v*. 补偿，弥补

【记】 com(一起)+pens(支付)+ate(动词词尾)→一起支付的东西→补偿

【例】 Nothing can *compensate* for the loss of one's health. 失去健康是无法补偿的。

【同】 counterbalance, recompense

【派】 compensation *n*. 补偿，赔偿

compensatory *adj*. 补偿性的

compete [kəmˈpiːt] *v*. 比赛，竞争

【记】 com(一起)+pet(寻求)→一起寻求一样东西→争夺，竞争

【例】 Several companies are *competing* for the contract. 几家公司正为争取一项合同而互相竞争。

【同】 contend, contest, vie

【派】 competition *n*. 竞争，竞赛

competitive *adj*. 竞争的，竞赛的

competent [ˈkɒmpɪtənt] *adj*. 有能力的，胜任的

【记】 com(完全)+pet(寻求)+ent(形容词词尾)→完全能寻求→有能力的

【例】 We know you are *competent* in doing this job. 我们知道你可以胜任这项工作。

【同】 able, capable, fit, qualified

【反】 incapable, incompetent

【派】 competence *n*. 能力

compile [kəmˈpaɪl] *v*. 编写，编撰

【记】 com(一起)+pile(堆)→汇集在一起→编写

【例】 It takes years of hard work to *compile* a good dictionary. 编一部好词典需要多年的艰苦工作。

【同】 compose, edit

【派】 compiler *n*. 编辑者，编译器

complacent [kəmˈpleɪsnt] *adj*. 自满的，自鸣得意的

【记】 com(完全)+plac(取悦)+ent→被完全取悦的→自满的

【例】 We must not be *complacent* about our achievements; there is still a lot to be done. 我们绝不能满足于自己的成绩，还有很多事情要做。

【同】 self-satisfied, contented

【派】 complacence *n*. 自满，自以为是

complain [kəmˈpleɪn] *v*. 抱怨，诉苦

【记】 com(一起)+plain(捶胸)→一起捶胸→抱怨

【例】 Almost immediately he began to *complain* about the weather. 他几乎马上就开始抱怨起天气来了。

【同】 grumble, whine

【派】 complaint *n*. 抱怨，诉苦

complement [ˈkɒmplɪmənt] *n*. 补充，补足物；*v*. 补足，补充

【记】 com(完全)+ple(充满)+ment(名词词尾)→完全充满的东西→补充

【例】 1. A fine wine is a *complement* to a good meal. 美食加美酒才算完备。

2. His business skill *complements* her flair for design. 他的经营技巧和她的设计才能相辅相成。

【同】 supplement

【派】 complementary *adj*. 补充的，互补的

complex [ˈkɒmpleks] *adj*. 复杂的，错综的；*n*. 1. 复合体；2. 夸大的情绪反应，情结

【记】 com(一起) + ple(倍，重叠)→重叠在一起的→复杂的

【例】 1. At first glance, playing animals do appear to be practicing the *complex* maneuvers they will need in adulthood. 乍一看，玩耍的动物真的像是在练习长大后需要的各种复杂的技能。

2. He has a *complex* about his weight/has a weight *complex*. 他对自己的体重提心吊胆/他有体重情结。

【同】 complicated, intricate

【反】 simple

【派】 complexity *n*. 复杂性

complicated [ˈkɒmplɪkeɪtɪd] *adj*. 复杂的，难解的

【记】 com(一起) + plic(重叠) + ate(动词词尾) + ed(由分词来的形容词)→重叠在一起的→复杂的

【例】 It's rather *complicated* to explain, but I'll try. 这事解释起来相当复杂，不过我试试看吧。

【同】 intricate, complex

【反】 simple, simplified

【派】 (逆构)complicate *v*. 使复杂化

complication *n*. 复杂错综的状态、情况；(复数)并发症

compliment [ˈkɒmplɪmənt] *n*./*v*. 1. 称赞，赞美；2. 致意，问候

【记】 com(用，使) + pli(充满) + ment(名词词尾)→使对方满足的东西→赞美

【例】 1. One likes to hear *compliments* on one's appearance. 人人都爱听夸奖自己容貌的话。

2. The flowers are with the *compliments* of the management. 这鲜花是主管部门送的礼物。

3. I must *compliment* you on the way you handled the meeting. 我应当夸奖你主持会议的方法。

【同】 commend, flatter, praise, congratulate

【反】 insult

【派】 complimentary *adj*. 表示赞美的；赠送的

comply [kəmˈplaɪ] *v*. 答应，遵守

【记】 com(完全) + ply(充满)→满足要求→遵守

【例】 The rules must be *complied* with. 这些规章制度必须遵守。

【同】 abide, conform, follow

【反】 refuse, reject, defy

component [kəmˈpəʊnənt] *n*. 组成部分，成分

【记】 com(一起)+pon(放置)+ent(名词词尾)→放在一起之物→组成部分

【例】 Revenues from oil are the biggest single *component* in the country's income. 来源于石油的收益是这个国家收入中最高的一项。

【同】 constituent, element, part

compose [kəm'pəuz] *v*. 1. 组成，构成；2. 创作，为…谱曲

【记】 com(一起)+pose(放置)→放在一起→组成

【例】 1. Water is *composed* of hydrogen and oxygen. 水是由氢和氧组成的。

2. She began to *compose* (songs) at an early age. 她年轻时就已开始创作(歌曲)。

【同】 constitute; write

【反】 decompose

【派】 composite *adj*. 合成的，复合的；*n*. 合成物

composer *n*. 创作者，作曲家

composition [kɒmpə'zɪʃən] *n*. 1. 组成，构成；2. 作品，乐曲

【记】 com(一起)+posit(放置)+ion(名词词尾)→放在一起的东西、行为→组成

【例】 1. Over the past century, the *composition* of the human gene pool has not changed appreciably. 在过去一个世纪里，人类基因库的构成没有发生显著的变化。

2. 'Swan Lake' is one of Tchaikovsky's best-known *compositions*. "天鹅湖"是柴可夫斯基最著名的作品之一。

【同】 combination, mixture; writing, script

composure [kəm'pəuʒə] *n*. 镇静，沉着

【记】 com(一起)+pos(放置)+ure→(把情绪)放置在一起的→镇静

【例】 He showed great *composure* in a difficult situation. 他在困难环境中表现得极沉着。

【同】 calmness, peace, quiet

【反】 discomposure

compound ['kɒmpaund] *n*. 化合物；*adj*. 复合的，混合的；*v*. 1. 使混合，使合成；2. 使严重，使更复杂

【记】 com(一起)+pound(放置)→放在一起→合成

【例】 1. Cigarette smoke contains more than 4, 700 chemical *compounds*, including 43 cancer-causing substances. 卷烟烟雾含有4700多种化合物，包括43种致癌物。

2. The increasing concentration of greenhouse gases is largely related to the *compound* effects of increased population, improved living standards and changes in lifestyle. 温室气体的混合物越来越多，在很大程度上与人口增加、生活水平提高以及生活方式的改变等复杂因素有关。

3. This medicine was *compounded* from several drugs. 这药是由几种药物合成的。

4. Our difficulties were *compounded* by shortage of petrol supply. 石油供应短缺增加了我们的困难。

【同】 mixture; complex; combine; aggravate

comprehend [ˌkɒmprɪ'hend] *v*. 1. 理解，领会；2. 包含，包括

【记】 com(一起)+prehend(捉住，握取)→一起捉住→理解

【例】 1. I cannot *comprehend* how you could have been so stupid. 我真不明白你怎么那

么蠢。

2. The park *comprehends* all the land on the other side of the river. 这个公园的范围包括了河那边所有的土地。

【同】 apprehend, grasp; cover, encompass

【派】 comprehension *n*. 理解(力)

comprehensive *adj*. 广泛的，全面的，综合的

compress [kəm'pres] *v*. 1.压缩，浓缩；2.使简练，精简

【记】 com(一起)+press(压)→压在一起→压缩

【例】 1. He is *compressing* straw into blocks for burning. 他正将干草压成块供燃烧。

2. He *compressed* his report into three pages. 他把报告压缩成三页。

【同】 compact, condense; abbreviate

【派】 compression *n*. 压缩，浓缩

comprise [kəm'praɪz] *v*. 包含，包括

【记】 com(一起)+prise(捉住，握取)→捉在一起→包含

【例】 This album *comprises* the best hits of the year. 这张唱片集收录了本年度最佳的流行歌曲。

【同】 consist of, include, contain

compromise ['kɒmprəmaɪz] *v*. 1.妥协，让步；2.危及…的安全

【记】 com(一起)+pro(前面)+mise(投，掷)→彼此提前约定→妥协

【例】 1. I wanted to go to Greece, and my wife wanted to go to Spain, so we *compromised* on Italy. 我想去希腊，可我妻子想去西班牙，于是我们折衷了一下，去意大利。

2. Lack of sleep can *compromise* the immune system, muddle thinking, cause depression, promote anxiety and encourage irritability. 缺乏睡眠会危及免疫系统，干扰思考能力，产生沮丧情绪，助长忧虑，使人烦躁易怒。

【同】 concede, yield; endanger

compulsive [kəm'pʌlsɪv] *adj*. 强迫的，强制的

【记】 com(一起)+puls(驱使)+ive→一起驱使的→强迫的

【例】 *Compulsive* drinking is bad for one's health. 不加节制的饮酒有害健康。

【同】 compelling, irresistible

【派】 compulsion *n*. 强迫，强制

compulsory [kəm'pʌlsərɪ] *adj*. 强制的，必修的

【记】 com(一起)+puls(驱使)+ory(形容词词尾)→一起驱使的，必须要做的→强制的

【例】 Is English a *compulsory* subject? 英语是必修科目吗?

【同】 mandatory, required, obligatory

【反】 voluntary, elective

compute [kəm'pjuːt] *v*. 计算，推断

【记】 com(一起)+pute(思考)→把数字一起考虑→计算

【例】 Scientists have *computed* the probable course of the rocket. 科学家用计算机计算了火箭可能运行的轨道。

【同】 calculate, reckon

【派】 computer *n*. 计算机
computational *adj*. 计算的

conceal [kən'siːl] *v*. 隐藏，隐瞒
【记】 com(完全)+ceal(隐藏)→完全隐藏→隐藏
【例】 He tried to *conceal* his heavy drinking from his family. 他极力对家人隐瞒自己酗酒的事。
【同】 hide, cover, veil
【反】 reveal, disclose

concede [kən'siːd] *v*. 勉强承认，让步
【记】 con(一起)+cede(让步)→一起让步→勉强承认
【例】 I was forced to *concede* that she might be right. 我不得不承认她可能是对的。
【同】 confess, admit, yield
【反】 deny, reject

conceit [kən'siːt] *n*. 自负，自高自大
【记】 con(全部)+ceit(拿)→一起拿走→全包了→自负
【例】 This young man is full of *conceit*. 这个年轻人非常自负。
【同】 pride, vanity

conceive [kən'siːv] *v*. 1. 构思，设想；2. 怀胎
【记】 con(一起)+ceive(拿)→拿来放在一起→构思
【例】 1. It was then that I *conceived* the notion of running away. 就在那时我产生了逃跑的念头。
2. The baby was *conceived* in March and born in December. 孩子是3月怀的，12月出生。
【同】 ideate, imagine, think; become pregnant
【派】 conceivable *adj*. 可想到的，可理解的

concentrate ['kɒnsentreɪt] *v*. 集中注意力，专心
【记】 con(一起)+centr(中心)+ate(动词词尾)→一起到中心→集中注意力
【例】 I can't *concentrate* on my studies with all that noise going on. 吵闹声不绝于耳，我的精神无法集中于学习。
【同】 focus
【反】 distract
【派】 concentration *n*. 集中，专心；浓缩，浓度

concept ['kɒnsept] *n*. 概念，观念
【记】 con(一起)+cept(获取)→以一定程度的理解获得的想法→概念
【例】 It is difficult to grasp the *concept* of infinite space. 掌握无限空间的概念是很难的。
【同】 conception, notion
【派】 conceptual *adj*. 概念的
conception *n*. 思想，观念

concerted [kən'sɜːtɪd] *adj*. 协定的，共同的
【记】 con(一起)+cert(结合)+ed(形容词词尾)→团结在一起的→共同的

【例】 He woke his audience to the need for *concerted* action. 他使听众意识到有必要采取一致的行动。

【同】 collaborative, combined, united

concession [kən'seʃən] *n*. 让步，妥协

【记】 con(一起) + cess(服从) + ion(名词词尾)→一起服从→让步

【例】 Employers made *concessions* to the workers in negotiations. 资方在与工人谈判中作出了让步。

【同】 conceding, yielding

conciliate [kən'sɪlɪeɪt] *v*. 安抚，调和

【记】 con(一起) + cil(i)(召集) + ate(动词词尾)→召集在一起→调和

【例】 She *conciliated* her crying little boy with a toy car. 她拿玩具汽车哄她哭叫的孩子。

【同】 pacify, reconcile

【反】 alienate, estrange

【派】 conciliatory *adj*. 调和的，抚慰的

concise [kən'saɪs] *adj*. 简明的，简练的

【记】 con(一起) + cise(切)→一起切→简明的

【例】 Teaching content should be *concise*. 教学内容要少而精。

【同】 brief, short, terse

【反】 redundant

conclude [kən'klu:d] *v*. 1. 推断出，推论出；2.(最后)决定

【记】 con(一起) + clude(关闭)→一起关闭→得出结论

【例】 1. From his appearance we may safely *conclude* that he is a chain smoker. 从他的外表，我们可以有把握地断定他烟抽得很凶。

2. Once the price had been agreed, a deal was quickly *concluded*. 价格一经商定，交易很快就达成了。

【同】 infer; close, finish

【反】 begin, commence, start

【派】 conclusion *n*. 结论，推论

conclusive *adj*. 决定性的；最后的

concoct [kən'kɒkt] *v*. 1. 调制；2. 编造，虚构

【记】 con(一起) + coct(烹调)→一起烹调→调制，编造

【例】 1. Jean *concocted* a splendid meal from the leftovers. 琼用残羹剩菜做了一顿可口的饭。

2. John *concocted* an excuse for being late and the manager believed him. 约翰编造了一个迟到的借口，经理却相信了。

【同】 cook, make; contrive, create, invent

【派】 concoction *n*. 调合，混合；调合物

concoctive *adj*. 调合的；捏造的，策划的

concord ['kɒŋkɔ:d] *n*. 和谐一致，和睦

【记】 con(一起) + cord(心)→心在一起→和谐一致

【例】 These neighboring states had lived in *concord* for centuries. 这些相互毗邻的国家几个世纪以来一直和睦相处。

【同】 harmony, peace

【反】 discord

concrete [ˈkɒnkriːt] *adj*. 具体的，有形的

【记】 con(一起) + crete(生长)→共同生存的→凝结的，具体的

【例】 Physics deals with the forces acting on *concrete* objects. 物理学研究作用于具体物体上的力。

【同】 solid, substantial

【反】 abstract

concur [kənˈkɜː] *v*. (-rred; -rring) 1. 意见一致，同意；2. 同时发生

【记】 con(一起) + cur(流动)→一起流动→一致

【例】 1. The two judges *concurred* with one another on the ruling. 两位法官对这个判决意见一致。

2. Everything *concurred* to produce a successful result. 所有的事都同时发生而产生了圆满的结果。

【同】 coincide

【派】 concurring *adj*. 同时发生的，并发的

concurrence *n*. 同时发生，同时存在

condemn [kənˈdem] *v*. 1. 谴责，责备；2. 判刑

【记】 con(一起) + demn(伤害)→谴责

【例】 1. We all *condemn* cruelty to children. 我们一致谴责虐待儿童的行为。

2. The judge *condemned* her to spend six years in prison. 法官判处她 6 年徒刑。

【同】 blame, censure, reproach; convict

【派】 condemnation *n*. 谴责；定罪

condense [kənˈdens] *v*. 浓缩，精简

【记】 con(一起) + dense(使稠密)→使粘在一起→浓缩

【例】 Steam *condenses*/is *condensed* into water when it touches a cold surface. 蒸汽接触冷的表面而凝结成水珠。

【同】 compress, concentrate

condiment [ˈkɒndɪmənt] *n*. 调味品

【记】 con(一起) + di(放) + ment(名词词尾)→一起放进去的东西→调味品

【例】 Pepper and salt are *condiments*. 辣椒和盐都是调味品。

【同】 flavor, spice

condolence [kənˈdəʊləns] *n*. 哀悼，吊唁

【记】 con(一起) + dol(e)(痛苦) + ence(名词词尾)→一起分担痛苦→哀悼

【例】 Please accept my *condolence* on your mother's death. 请接受我对令堂故去的吊慰。

【同】 commiseration, sympathy

condone [kənˈdəʊn] *v*. 宽恕，宽容，容忍

【记】 con(完全) + don(给予) + e→完全给予→宽恕

【例】 People cannot *condone* the use of violence. 人们不能宽恕使用暴力的行为。

【同】 forgive, pardon

conducive [kən'dʌktɪv] *adj*. (常与 to 连用)有助于…的，有益于…的

【记】 con(一起)+duc(领导)+ive(形容词词尾)→一起引导→有助于…的

【例】 These noisy conditions aren't really *conducive* to concentrated work. 这嘈杂的环境实在不利于专心工作。

【同】 contributive, contributing

【派】 (逆构)conduce *v*. 有助于，导致

conduct ['kɒndʌkt] *v*. 1.进行，实施；2.指挥，引导；3.表现，为人

【记】 con(一起)+duct(领导)→共同引导→指挥

【例】 1. The company *conducted* a survey to find out local reaction to the leisure center. 公司进行了一项调查以了解当地对游乐活动中心的反应。

2. A guide *conducted* the visitors round the museum. 导游带领游客参观博物馆。

3. I think he *conducted* himself admirably, considering the difficult circumstances. 考虑到那种困难的情况，我认为他的表现令人钦佩。

【同】 do; direct, guide, lead; act, behave

【派】 conduction *n*. 引导，输送

conductivity *n*. 导电率；传导率

conductor *n*. 导(电、热等)体

confederate [kən'fedərɪt] *v*. (使)联盟，(使)联合；*n*. 同盟者，盟友；*adj*. 同盟的，联合的

【记】 con(一起)+feder(联盟)+ate(动词词尾)→联盟

【例】 1. The country agreed to *confederate* with the neighboring country for mutual safety. 这个国家同意为了共同的安全而与邻国结盟。

2. The thief was arrested, but his *confederate* escaped. 小偷被逮住了，但他的同伙却逃之夭夭。

【同】 ally, unite

【派】 confederacy *n*. 联盟

confer [kən'fɜː] *v*. (-rred; -rring)1.讨论，商谈；2.授予，赠与

【记】 con(一起)+fer(带，运)→一起带来→讨论

【例】 1. She withdrew to *confer* with her advisers before announcing a decision. 她先去请教顾问然后再来宣布决定。

2. An honorary degree was *conferred* on him by the university. 这所大学授予他荣誉学位。

【同】 consult, discuss; bestow

【派】 conference *n*. 协商，谈判；会议

confess [kən'fes] *v*. 承认，坦白

【记】 con(完全)+fess(说)→完全说出来→承认

【例】 He *confessed* himself to be totally ignorant of their plans. 他承认自己对于他们的计划一无所知。

【同】 acknowledge, admit

【反】 conceal

C

【派】 confession *n*. 承认，招供

confide [kən'faɪd] *v*. 1. 委托，信赖；2. 吐露(心事)，倾诉

【记】 con(完全)+fid(信任)+e→完全信任→信赖

【例】 1. Can I *confide* my children to your care? 托你照顾一下我的孩子好吗？

2. She *confided* her troubles to a friend. 她向朋友倾吐了内心的烦恼。

【同】 entrust, consign; reveal

【反】 conceal

confidence ['kɒnfɪdəns] *n*. 信心，把握

【记】 con(完全)+fid(信任)+ence(名词词尾)→完全信任→信心

【例】 We have full *confidence* that we shall succeed. 我们完全有把握取得成功。

【同】 sureness, trust

【反】 diffidence, distrust

【派】 confident *adj*. 有信心的，自信的

confidential [ˌkɒnfɪ'denʃəl] *adj*. 秘密的，机密的

【记】 confident(有信心的)+ial(形容词词尾)→能够获得信任的→秘密的

【例】 Please keep what I am about to tell you *confidential*. 请对我将要告诉你的话严守秘密。

【同】 secret

configuration [kənˌfɪgjʊ'reɪʃən] *n*. 某物的构造，配置

【记】 con(完全，整个)+figur(形状)+ation(名词词尾)→整个形状→结构

【例】 The *Configuration Handbook* comprises two volumes. 配置手册共有上下两册。

【同】 shape

confine ['kɒnfaɪn] *v*. 限制，使局限

【记】 con(共同)+fine(结束，界限)→共有的界限→限制

【例】 I wish the speaker would *confine* himself to the subject. 我希望演说者不要离题。

【同】 limit, restrict

【反】 free

【派】 confinement *n*. 限制，幽禁

confining *adj*. 狭窄的

confirm [kən'fɜːm] *v*. 确认，证实

【记】 con(完全)+firm(坚固的)→做得十分坚固→证实

【例】 Please *confirm* your telephone message by writing to me. 请给我来封信，好进一步证实你在电话中传达的消息。

【同】 affirm, prove, substantiate

【反】 deny

【派】 confirmation *n*. 确认，证实

confiscate ['kɒnfɪskeɪt] *v*. 没收，充公

【记】 con(完全)+fisc(宝藏，金库)+ate(动词词尾)→完全收入国库→没收

【例】 If you are caught smuggling goods into the country, they will probably be *confiscated*. 假若查出你向该国走私货物，你的货物准得没收。

【同】 impound, seize

【派】 confiscation *n*. 没收，充公，征用

conform [kən'fɔːm] *v*. 使一致，符合

【记】 con(共同)+form(形状)→做成共同的形状→使一致

【例】 The building does not *conform* to safety regulations. 这座建筑物不符合安全条例。

【同】 adapt, adjust, comply

【反】 deviate

【派】 conformity *n*. 遵照，符合

confront [kən'frʌnt] *v*. 1.勇敢地面对，正视；2.面临，遭遇

【记】 con(一起)+front(正面)→使正面在一起→面对

【例】 1. They have *confronted* the problem of terrorism with great determination. 他们以极大的决心对付恐怖活动问题。

2. A soldier often has to *confront* danger. 士兵常常要身临险境。

【同】 encounter, face

【反】 avoid

【派】 confrontation *n*. 面对，对抗

confuse [kən'fjuːz] *v*. 1.使困惑，把…搞糊涂；2.搞乱，混淆

【记】 con(共同)+fuse(倾倒)→共同注入→使混乱

【例】 1. They *confused* me by asking so many questions. 他们提了一大堆问题，把我都弄糊涂了。

2. Don't *confuse* Austria and/with Australia. 不要把奥地利跟澳大利亚弄混淆了。

【同】 muddle, bewilder, confound

【反】 clarify

【派】 confused *adj*. 困惑的，混乱的

confusion *n*. 混乱，混淆

congenial [kən'dʒiːnjəl] *adj*. 1.彼此合得来的，志趣相投的；2.适意的

【记】 con(共同)+geni(天生的)+al(形容词词尾)→有共同的天生的气质的→志趣相投的

【例】 1. In this small village he found few persons *congenial* to him. 在这个小村子里他发现很少有人与他志趣相投。

2. I find this aspect of my job particularly *congenial*. 我觉得我的工作的这一方面特别适合于我。

【同】 compatible, harmonious; agreeable, pleasant

【反】 uncongenial

congenital [kɒn'dʒenɪtl] *adj*. 先天的，天生的

【记】 con(完全)+genit(天生的)+al(形容词词尾)→完全天生的→先天的

【例】 The child's brain disorder is *congenital*. 这个小孩的脑病是先天性的。

【同】 inborn, innate

【反】 acquired

congestion [kən'dʒestʃən] *n*. 挤满，拥塞

【记】 con(一起)+gest(运，载)+ion(名词词尾)→承载在一起→拥塞

【例】 Increasing the number of people in a car would be an effective way of reducing emissions as well as easing *congestion*. 增加每辆车里的人数是减少排放和缓解拥堵的有效手段。

【同】 over-crowding, jam

【派】 (逆构)congest *v*. (使)充满，(使)拥塞

congratulate [kən'grætjʊleɪt] *v*. 祝贺，庆祝

【记】 con(一起)+gratul(满意，感谢)+ate(动词词尾)→使一起高兴→祝贺

【例】 You can *congratulate* yourself on having done a good job. 你的工作做得很出色，你应该感到自豪。

【同】 compliment, commend, praise

【派】 congratulation *n*. 祝贺，贺辞

congregate ['kɒŋgrɪgeɪt] *v*. 聚集，集合

【记】 con(一起)+gregat(聚集)+e→聚集在一起→集合

【例】 A crowd quickly *congregated* round the speaker. 大群的人迅速地在演说者周围聚集起来。

【同】 assemble, gather

【派】 congregation *n*. 集合，集会

congress ['kɒŋgres] *n*. 1. 大会，会议；2. [C～](美国等国的)国会，议会

【记】 con(一起)+gress(行走)→一起去→集合，开会

【例】 1. This matter will be discussed in *congress* tomorrow. 这个问题将在明天的大会上讨论。

2. The American *Congress* corresponds to the British Parliament. 美国的国会相当于英国的议会。

【同】 conference, convention, session

【派】 congressman *n*. 国会议员，众议院议员

congressional *adj*. 会议的，大会的；国会的

conjunction [kən'dʒʌŋkʃən] *n*. 联合，关联

【记】 con(一起)+junct(连接)+ion(名词词尾)→连接在一起→结合

【例】 The *conjunction* of workmanship and artistry in making jewelry decides the value of the jewelry. 在珠宝饰物的制造中，手工与艺术的结合决定了珠宝的价值。

【同】 alignment, junction

【派】 (逆构)conjunct *adj*. 结合的，共同的

conjunctive *adj*. 连接的

conjure ['kʌndʒə] *v*. 1. 变魔术，变戏法；2. 想象，推想；3. 恳求，祈求

【记】 con(共同)+jur(发誓)+e→共同发誓，念咒语→变魔术

【例】 1. The magician *conjured* a duck out of an empty box. 魔术师从空盒子里变出一只鸭子。

2. This place *conjures* up vivid memories. 这个地方使人回忆起许多生动的往事。

3. I *conjure* you most earnestly to reconsider your position. 我最诚恳地请求你重新考虑一下你的立场。

【同】 bewitch, enchant; plead, entreat

【派】 conjurer *n*. 魔术师

connect [kəˈnekt] *v*. 连接，联系

【记】con(一起)+nect(绑，连结)→连接在一起→连接

【例】Corporate crime is the crime which, as the name suggests, is *connected* with companies, with business organizations. 顾名思义，企业犯罪就是一种和公司、商业机构相联系的犯罪活动。

【同】associate, combine, unite

【反】disconnect

【派】connection *n*. 连接，关系；线路

connive [kəˈnaɪv] *v*. 1.默许，纵容；2.共谋，暗中合作

【记】来自拉丁语 connivere，闭上眼睛→默许

【例】1. Not to protest is to *connive* at the destruction of the environment. 对于破坏环境的行为不加反对就等于纵容。

2. The student tried to *connive* with her friend to cheat in the examination. 那个学生企图和她的朋友串谋考试作弊。

【同】assent; intrigue, collude

【派】connivance *n*. 默许，共谋

connoisseur [ˌkɒnɪˈsɜː] *n*. 鉴赏家，行家

【记】con(完全)+noiss(知道)+eur(表示"人"的法文名词词尾)→什么都知道的人→鉴赏家，行家

【例】He is a *connoisseur* of antiques. 他是个古董鉴定家。

【同】expert

conscience [ˈkɒnʃəns] *n*. 良心，良知

【记】con(完全)+sci(知道)+ence(名词词尾)→完全知道(是非)→良心

【例】His *conscience* troubled him after he took the money. 他拿走了钱以后，他的良心使他不安。

【同】qualm, compunction

【派】conscientious *adj*. 尽责的，一丝不苟的；凭良心的

conscious [ˈkɒnʃəs] *adj*. 1.神志清醒的，有意识的；2.故意的

【记】con(完全)+sci(知道)+ous(形容词词尾)→完全知道的→有意识的

【例】1. He is badly hurt but still *conscious*. 他伤得很重，不过神志还清醒。

2. I had to make a *conscious* effort not to be rude to him. 我得刻意约束自己不要对他粗鲁。

【同】sensitive; intended

【反】unconscious

【派】consciousness *n*. 意识，观念；觉悟

consecrate [ˈkɒnsɪkreɪt] *v*. 1.使神圣，给…祝圣；2.奉献，贡献

【记】con(完全)+secr(神圣)+ate(动词词尾)→使神圣

【例】1. This battlefield is *consecrated* to the memory of the soldiers who died here. 这个战场被视为圣地以纪念战死在这里的战士。

2. He *consecrated* his life to helping the poor. 他献身于帮助穷人。

【同】enthrone; devote, sanctify

【反】 desecrate

【派】 consecration *n*. 供献，奉献，献祭仪式

consecratory *adj*. 使神圣化的，奉献的

consecutive [kən'sekjʊtɪv] *adj*. 连续的

【记】 con(一起) + secut(跟随) + ive(形容词词尾)→一起跟随的→连续的

【例】 We shall have meetings on two *consecutive* days, Monday and Tuesday. 周一周二连续两天我们都将开会。

【同】 continuous, successive, sequent

【反】 interrupted, inconsecutive

【派】 consecution *n*. 连续，一连串

consensus [kən'sensəs] *n*. 一致同意，共识

【记】 con(共同) + sens(感觉) + us(拉丁语名词词尾)→共同的感觉→共识

【例】 There is broad *consensus* of opinion in the country on this issue. 对这一问题举国上下舆论普遍一致。

【同】 agreement, unanimity

【反】 disagreement, difference

consent [kən'sent] *n*./*v*. 同意，赞成

【记】 con(共同) + sent(感觉)→共同感觉→同意

【例】 Her father reluctantly *consented* to the marriage. 她父亲勉强答应了这桩婚姻。

【同】 agree, assent, approve

【反】 dissent, refuse

consequence ['kɒnsɪkwəns] *n*. 结果，后果

【记】 con(一起) + sequ(跟随) + ence(名词词尾)→跟随一起的→后果

【例】 Her investment had disastrous *consequences*: she lost everything she owned. 她的投资结果很惨，血本无归。

【同】 result, outcome

【反】 cause

【派】 consequent *adj*. 结果的

consequently ad*v*. 从而，因此

conserve [kən'sɜːv] *v*. 保存，保护

【记】 con(一起) + serve(保存)→一起保存→保存，保护

【例】 We must *conserve* our forests and woodlands for future generations. 我们必须为子孙后代保护森林资源。

【同】 preserve, save

【反】 waste

【派】 conservation *n*. 保存，保护

conservative [kən'sɜːvətɪv] *adj*. 1.保守的，传统的；2.谨慎的，避免过激的

【记】 con(完全) + serv(保存) + ative(形容词词尾)→完全保存的→保守的

【例】 1. Old people are usually more *conservative* than young people. 老年人通常比年轻人保守。

2. There must have been a thousand people there, at a *conservative* estimate. 按照

保守的估计，那里一定有一千人。

【同】 conventional，traditional；cautious

【反】 progressive；extreme

【派】 conservatism *n*. 保守主义，守旧性

conservatory [kən'sɜːvətrɪ] *n*. 1. 温室；2. 音乐学院

【记】 con(完全) + serv(保存) + atory(形容词或名词词尾)→把(植物)完全保护的地方→温室

【例】 1. It's got a sort of *conservatory* tacked on at the back. 这房子背后附近建了一个类似温室的棚子。

2. One does not learn to straddle a cello that way at a *conservatory*. 音乐学院是不会教人这样骑着大提琴演奏的。

【同】 greenhouse；schoolhouse

considerable [kən'sɪdərəbl] *adj*. 相当大(或多)的，相当可观的

【记】 consider(考虑) + able(形容词词尾，表示"值得…的")→值得考虑的→相当可观的

【例】 This essay represents a *considerable* improvement on your recent work. 这篇论文说明你最近的工作取得了相当大的改进。

【同】 important，much，significant

【反】 inconsiderable

considerate [kən'sɪdərɪt] *adj*. 考虑周到的，体贴的

【记】 consider(考虑) + ate(形容词词尾，表示"有…性质的")→具有考虑的性质的→考虑周到的

【例】 It was *considerate* of you not to play the piano while I was asleep. 在我睡觉时你不弹钢琴，真是体贴入微。

【同】 thoughtful，kind

【反】 inconsiderate

【派】 consideration *n*. 体谅，考虑

consign [kən'saɪn] *v*. 1. 寄售，托运；2. 委托，交付

【记】 con(一起) + sign(标记)→一起做标记→一起签署→交付

【例】 1. The goods were *consigned* to you by railway. 货物已由铁路托运到你处。

2. The captured criminals were *consigned* to the dungeons. 抓到的罪犯被送进了地牢。

【同】 convey，deliver；entrust

【派】 consignee *n*. 收件人；受托者

consigner *n*. 发货人；委托人

consignment *n*. 交货，发货；交托；寄存物

consistent [kən'sɪstənt] *adj*. 一致的，协调的

【记】 con(一起) + sist(站立) + ent(形容词词尾)→站在一起的→一致的

【例】 The last five years have seen a *consistent* improvement in the country's economy. 在最近的 5 年里，这个国家的经济状况一直在好转。

【同】 accordant，coherent

【反】 inconsistent

【派】 consistency *n*. 一致，连贯

console [kən'səʊl] *v*. 安慰，慰藉；*n*. 控制台，操纵台

【记】 con(共同) + sole(单独)→共同孤单，共同寂寞→安慰

【例】 1. Nothing could *console* him when his pet dog died. 他的爱犬死后，什么事情也不能使他宽慰。

2. There are many lights and electrical instruments on the computer *console*. 电脑控制板上有许多小灯和电子设备。

【同】 comfort, solace, soothe

【派】 consolation *n*. 安慰，慰藉

consolidate [kən'sɒlɪdeɪt] *v*. 巩固，强化

【记】 con(完全) + solid(单独的) + ate(动词词尾)→完全结合成一体→巩固

【例】 The time has come for the firm to *consolidate* after several years of rapid expansion. 公司经过几年的迅速发展之后，该整顿一下了。

【同】 solidify, strengthen

【反】 weaken

【派】 consolidation *n*. 巩固，加强；联合，统一

consort ['kɒnsɔːt] *v*. 陪伴，结交

【记】 con(共同的) + sort(种类)→共同种类→结交

【例】 He'd been *consorting* with known criminals. 他一直与那些臭名昭著的罪犯有交往。

【同】 associate, companion

【派】 consortium *n*. 协会，联盟；(国际)财团

conspicuous [kən'spɪkjʊəs] *adj*. 显著的，显而易见的

【记】 con(完全) + spicu(看见) + ous(形容词词尾)→能够完全看清楚的→显著的

【例】 If you're walking along a badly-lit road at night you should wear *conspicuous* clothes. 晚上在照明很差的路上行走，应该穿显眼的衣物。

【同】 obvious, prominent, noticeable

【反】 inconspicuous

【派】 conspicuousness *n*. 显著，卓越

conspire [kən'spaɪə] *v*. 1. 共谋，阴谋；2. 巧合，凑在一起

【记】 con(一起) + spire(呼吸)→一起呼吸→共谋

【例】 1. A group of men were charged *conspiring* against the duly elected government. 一伙人被指控阴谋推翻选举产生的合法政府。

2. Bad weather and car trouble *conspired* to ruin our vacation. 恶劣的气候连同汽车故障断送了我们的假日。

【同】 collude, plot; combine

【派】 conspiracy *n*. 阴谋

constant ['kɒnstənt] *adj*. 不变的，持续的，经常的

【记】 con(一起) + st(a)(站立) + ant(形容词词尾)→始终不变地站在一起→不变的

【例】 The machinery requires *constant* maintenance. 这些机器需要经常保养维修。

【同】 ceaseless, continual, continuous

【反】 inconstant, changeable

【派】 constancy *n*. 坚定不移，始终如一

constellation [kɒnstəˈleɪʃən] *n*. 1. 星座；2. 灿烂的一群

【记】 con(一起) + stell(星星) + ation(名词词尾)→星星聚集在一起→星座

【例】 1. My *constellation* is the Great Bear. 我的星座是大熊星座。

2. They are *constellation* of Hollywood talent. 他们是好莱坞的一群才俊。

【同】 star

constituent [kənˈstɪtjuənt] *n*. 1. 成分，要素；2. 选民

【记】 con(一起) + stitu(站立) + ent(名词词尾)→站在一起的人→选民

【例】 1. Do you know the *constituents* of the mixture? 你知道这种混合物的成分吗？

2. The congressman voted for the bill most favorable to his *constituents*. 那个议员投票支持对他的选民最有利的议案。

【同】 component, element; elector, voter

constitute [ˈkɒnstɪtjuːt] *v*. 组成，构成

【记】 con(一起) + stitute(站立)→站在一起→组成

【例】 Twelve months *constitute* one year. 12个月构成一年。

【同】 compose, comprise, form

【派】 constitution *n*. 构成，构造；宪法

constrain [kənˈstreɪn] *v*. 强迫，抑制

【记】 con(一起) + strain(拉紧)→拉在一起→强迫，强制

【例】 I felt *constrained* to do what I was unwilling to do myself. 我觉得是被迫去做我自己不愿去做的事情。

【同】 compel, force, press

【反】 free

【派】 constrained *adj*. 被约束的，被迫的

constraint *n*. 强制，约束

constrict [kənˈstrɪkt] *v*. 1. 收缩，压紧；2. 约束，限制

【记】 con(一起) + strict(拉紧)→拉紧在一起→收缩

【例】 1. The tight collar *constricted* his neck. 紧领子勒着他的脖子。

2. The regulations *constrict* the chairman in his duties. 这些规定限制了主席的职责。

【同】 compress, tighten, constringe

【派】 constriction *n*. 压缩，收缩；限制，约束

construct [kənˈstrʌkt] *v*. 建造，构成

【记】 con(一起) + struct(建筑)→建在一起→建造

【例】 This factory was *constructed* by our company. 这家工厂是由我们公司建设的。

【同】 build, manufacture

【反】 demolish, destroy

【派】 construction *n*. 建筑，建设

constructive *adj*. 建设性的，有积极意义的

construe [kənˈstruː] *v*. 解释，把…理解为

【记】 con(一起)+stru(建筑，堆积)+e→把(理由)堆积在一起→解释
【例】 I think my remarks have been wrongly *construed*. 我想我的话被曲解了。
【同】 interpret

consult [kən'sʌlt] *v*. 请教，咨询，商议

【记】 con(一起)+sult(坐)→坐在一起→商议，咨询
【例】 If you wish good advice, *consult* an old man. 若要主意好，老人须请教。
【派】 consultation *n*. 征求意见，咨询；会诊
consultant *n*. 顾问，咨询者

consume [kən'sjuːm] *v*. 消费，消耗
【记】 con(完全)+sume(取)→完全取用→消费
【例】 Each year Americans *consume* a high percentage of the world's energy. 每年美国人都消耗掉世界能源的很大比例。
【同】 exhaust, spend, waste
【派】 consumer *n*. 消费者，顾客
consumerism *n*. 用户至上主义
consumption *n*. 消费，消耗

contagious [kən'teɪdʒəs] *adj*. 传染性的，会感染的
【记】 con(一起)+tag(接触)+ious(形容词词尾)→接触在一起的→传染性的
【例】 Scarlet fever is highly *contagious*. 猩红热传染性很强。
【同】 catching, epidemic, infectious
【派】 contagion *n*. 传染，传染病

contain [kən'teɪn] *v*. 包含，容纳
【记】 con(一起)+tain(保持)→保持在一起→容纳
【例】 This book *contains* all the information you need. 这本书包含你所需的一切资料。
【同】 comprise, include, involve
【派】 container *n*. 容器，集装箱

contaminate [kən'tæmɪneɪt] *v*. 弄脏，污染
【记】 con(一起)+tamin(接触)+ate(动词词尾)→接触在一起→弄脏
【例】 The oil spill *contaminated* the sea. 溢出的油污染了海面。
【同】 foul, pollute
【反】 decontaminate
【派】 contamination *n*. 玷污，污染
contaminant *n*. 致污物，污染物

contemplate ['kɒntempleɪt] *v*. 凝视，沉思
【记】 con(完全)+templ(庙)+ate(动词词尾)→像庙中人一样深思→沉思
【例】 She stood *contemplating* the painting. 她站着审视那幅图画。
【同】 consider, meditate, ponder
【派】 contemplation *n*. 凝视，沉思
contemplator *n*. 沉思者，静观者

contemporary [kən'tempərərɪ] *adj*. 当代的，同时代的；*n*. 同代人，同龄人
【记】 con(共同)+tempor(时间)+ary(形容词词尾)→时代相同的→当代的

【例】 1. My parents think that the *contemporary* young people have no respect for authority. 我父母认为现在的年轻人不尊重权威。

2. He is a *contemporary* of mine, but our experiences are completely different. 他和我是同龄人，但我们的经历截然不同。

【同】 contemporaneous, current, modern

【反】 ancient

contempt [kən'tempt] *n*. 轻视，轻蔑

【记】 contem(n)(蔑视) + pt(名词词尾)→蔑视，轻视

【例】 I shall treat that suggestion with the *contempt* it deserves. 我对那项建议理所当然嗤之以鼻。

【同】 disdain, disrespect

【反】 honor, respect

【派】 contemptible *adj*. 可鄙的，令人轻视的

contemptuous *adj*. 藐视的，傲慢的

contend [kən'tend] *v*. 1. 斗争，竞争；2. 争辩，声称

【记】 con(一起) + tend(伸展)→一起朝某个方向伸展→竞争

【例】 1. They are *contending* for the championship. 他们为争夺冠军而拼搏。

2. The man *contended* that it was not his fault. 那人争辩说这不是他的过错。

【同】 fight, compete; argue, allege

【派】 contention *n*. 争论，争辩；竞争

content [kən'tent] *n*. 内容，目录；*v*. 使满足；*adj*. 满足的，满意的

【记】 con(一起) + tent(保持)→保持在一起的东西→内容

【例】 1. At the front of the book is a table of *contents*, giving details of what is in the book. 书的前部有目录，详列了书中的内容。

2. We should never *content* ourselves with a little book knowledge only. 我们切不可满足于仅有的一点点书本知识。

3. He is *content* to stay in his present job. 他对现在的工作心满意足。

【同】 satisfy, please; contented, happy, pleased

【反】 discontent, displease

【派】 contented *adj*. 满足的，心安的

contentment *n*. 满足，满意

contest ['kɒntest] *n*./*v*. 竞赛，竞争

【记】 con(一起) + test(证据)→一起拿出证据加以争论→竞赛

【例】 1. How many people are *contesting* the seat on the council? 有多少人在争夺市议会中那个席位？

2. Although he had only entered the *contest* for fun, he won first prize. 尽管他参加这次竞赛只不过是闹着玩儿而已，却赢得了头奖。

【同】 competition, contention; contend, compete

【派】 contestant *n*. 竞争者，争论者

context ['kɒntekst] *n*. 1. 背景，环境；2. 上下文

【记】 con(一起) + text(编织)→编织在一起的→和本文联系在一起的→上下文

【例】 1. The report should be considered within its social *context*. 这个报告应该结合其社会背景加以考虑。

2. It is usually easier to pick out the meaning of a phrase in a given *context*. 在特定的上下文中理解一个短语的含意往往要更容易些。

【同】 circumstance

【派】 contextual *adj*. 上下文的

continent ['kɒntɪnənt] *n*. 大陆

【记】 con(一起)+tin(保持)+ent(名词词尾)→连在一起的东西→陆地

【例】 The Antarctica is a *continent* centered roughly on the South Pole. 南极洲是一片大致以南极为中心的大陆。

【反】 island, isle

【派】 continental *adj*. 大陆的，大陆性的

contingent [kən'tɪndʒənt] *adj*. 偶然发生的，依条件而定的；*n*. 小分队，先遣队

【记】 con(一起)+ting(接触)+ent(形容词词尾)→(偶然)接触在一起→偶然发生的

【例】 1. Whether or not we arrive on time is *contingent* on the weather. 我们是否按时到达要视天气情况而定。

2. His *contingent* was sent to Saudi Arabia. 他的分遣队被派往沙特阿拉伯。

【同】 conditional, uncertain; force, group

【反】 certain

【派】 contingency *n*. 偶然，可能性；意外事故

continual [kən'tɪnjʊəl] *adj*. (动作的重复或反复出现)连续的，频繁的

【记】 con(一起，一直)+tin(保持)+ual(形容词词尾)→一直保持着→连续的

【例】 Her proposal met with *continual* rejections. 她的建议一再遭到拒绝。

【同】 constant, continuing

【反】 sporadic

【派】 continuation *n*. 继续，延长

continuum *n*. 连续统一体；一系列

continuous [kən'tɪnjʊəs] *adj*. (在时间或顺序上)连续不断的，接连的

【记】 con(一起，一直)+tin(保持)+uous(形容词词尾)→一直保持着→连续不断的

【例】 The brain needs a *continuous* supply of blood. 大脑需要不间断的供血。

【同】 uninterrupted

【反】 discontinuous

【派】 continuity *n*. (时间、空间上的)连续性，连贯性

contour ['kɒntʊə] *n*. 1. 轮廓；2. 周线，等高线

【记】 con(一起)+tour(迂回)→迂回到一起→轮廓

【例】 1. The *contour* of that mountain looks like a dragon. 那座大山的轮廓看上去像一条龙。

2. A *contour* line is a line drawn on a map connecting points of equal height. 等高线就是地图上把高度相同的点连成的线。

【同】 form, profile, outline

contract ['kɒntrækt] *n*. 合同，契约；*v*. 1. 订约；2. 缩小，缩约

【记】 con(一起)+tract(拉)→拉在一起→订合同

【例】 1. You shouldn't enter into a *contract* until you have studied its provisions carefully. 你应该先仔细研究合同的条款，然后再签订。

2. Metals *contract* as they get cooler. 金属遇冷则收缩。

【同】 agreement, treaty; compress

【派】 contractor *n*. 订约人，承包人

contradiction [ˌkɒntrəˈdɪkʃən] *n*. 矛盾(性)，对立(性)

【记】 contra(相对，相反)+dict(说)→说相反的话→对立

【例】 I find no *contradiction* between his publicly expressed opinions and his private actions. 我觉得他的公开言论与私下行为并无二致。

【同】 conflict, oppose, dispute

【反】 acknowledge, admit, recognize

【派】 (逆构)contradict *v*. 与…矛盾，违背

contradictory *adj*. 反对的，矛盾的

contrary [ˈkɒntrərɪ] *adj*. 相反的，对抗的

【记】 contra(相对，相反)+ary(形容词词尾)→相反的

【例】 My sister's taste in dresses is *contrary* to my own. 在服装方面，我妹妹的爱好和我完全不同。

【同】 adverse, conflicting, opposite

【反】 coincident, consistent

contrast [ˈkɒntræst] *n*./*v*. 对比，成对照

【记】 contra(相对，相反)+st(站立)→立于对面→对照

【例】 1. Careful *contrast* of the two plans shows up some key differences. 把这两个计划仔细地加以对比就可以看出一些关键性的差异。

【同】 compare, match

contravene [ˌkɒntrəˈviːn] *v*. 违反，抵触

【记】 contra(相反)+ven(来)+e→反着来→违反

【例】 You are *contravening* the regulations. 你违反了规定。

【同】 conflict, contradict

【派】 contravention *n*. 违反，违背，矛盾

contribute [kənˈtrɪbjuːt] *v*. 1. 捐助；2. 促成，有助于；3. 是…的部分原因

【记】 con(一起)+tribute(赠予)→一起赠予→捐助

【例】 1. To achieve the benefits of recycling, the community must also *contribute*. 为了实现循环利用带来的好处，社区也必须进行捐助。

2. Honesty and hard work *contribute* to success and happiness. 诚实加苦干有助于成功和幸福。

3. Only a few of the pupils mentioned that rainforest destruction may *contribute* to global warming. 只有少部分学生提到热带雨林的破坏可能是全球变暖的原因之一。

【同】 donate, provide; attribute

【派】 contributor *n*. 贡献者，捐助者，投稿者

contribution *n*. 贡献

contrive [kən'traɪv] *v*. 1.设计，发明；2.图谋，谋划

【记】 con(一起)+trive(风格，方式)→一样的风格→设计

【例】 1.They managed to *contrive* a means of escape. 他们想出了一个逃跑的办法。

2.He *contrived* to gain their votes. 他图谋获得他们的选票。

【同】 devise，invent，scheme；plot，conspire

【派】 contrived *adj*. 人为的，策划好的

C

controversy ['kɒntrəvɜːsɪ] *n*. 论争，辩论

【记】 contro(相反)+vers(转向)+y(名词词尾)→转而反对的行为→争论

【例】 The appointment of the new director aroused a lot of *controversy*. 新负责人的任命引起了激烈的争论。

【同】 argument，dispute

【派】 controversial *adj*. 引起争论的，有争议的

convene [kən'viːn] *v*. 召集，集合

【记】 con(一起)+ven(来)+e→来到一起→集合

【例】 People were *convened* here for an emergency meeting. 人们被召集到这里举行紧急会议。

【同】 assemble，gather，convoke

convenient [kən'viːnjənt] *adj*. 省力的，方便的

【记】 con(一起)+ven(来)+ient(形容词词尾)→易于来到一块的→方便的

【例】 A bicycle's often far more *convenient* than a car in busy cities. 在热闹的都市里骑自行车往往比坐汽车方便得多。

【同】 handy，labor-saving

【反】 inconvenient

【派】 convenience *n*. 方便，合宜

convention [kən'venʃən]*n*. 1.会议，集会；2.传统，习俗

【记】 con(一起)+vent(来)+ion(名词词尾)→来到一起→会议

【例】 1.She redeemed her reputation with a powerful speech to the party *convention*. 她由于向党代表大会作了有力的演说而挽回了自己的声誉。

2.By *convention* the deputy leader is always a woman. 按照惯例这一领导人的副职总是由女子担任。

【同】 assembly，meeting；custom，tradition

【派】 conventional *adj*. 传统的，习俗的，依照惯例的

conversation [ˌkɒnvə'seɪʃən] *n*. 谈话，交谈

【记】 con(一起)+vers(转)+ation(名词词尾)→转身和某人面对面→交谈

【例】 It is impossible to carry on a *conversation* with all this noise in the background. 在这样喧闹的环境中谈话是不可能的。

【同】 chat，discussion，talk

converse [kən'vɜːs] *n*. 相反的事物，反面说法；*v*. 谈话，交谈

【记】 con(一起)+verse(转)→转向面对面→相反的事物

【例】 1.This statement is *converse* to that one. 这个声明和那个相反。

2. Would you give me half an hour to *converse* with you? 我想跟你谈谈，半小时就行。

convert [kən'vɜːt] *v*. 1. 转变，转化；2. 改变信仰

【记】 con(一起)+vert(转，改变)→一起改变→转变

【例】 1. We *converted* the attic to a games-room. 我们把顶楼改为游戏室。

2. My mother has *converted* to Catholicism. 我母亲已转而信仰天主教。

【同】 change, transform

【派】 conversion *n*. 变换，转化；改变信仰

converter *n*. 炼钢用的转炉；转换器

convey [kən'veɪ] *v*. 1. 传递，传达；2. 运送，传送

【记】 con(完全)+vey(路)→使完全在路上→运送

【例】 1. The ambassador personally *conveyed* the president's message to the premier. 大使亲自向总理转达了总统的问候。

2. Pipes *convey* hot water from the boiler to the radiators. 通过管道把热水从锅炉输送到散热器里。

【同】 carry, deliver, transport

convict ['kɒnvɪkt] *v*. 证明…有罪，宣判…有罪

【记】 con(完全)+vict(征服)→完全征服→使(罪犯)深知有罪→证明…有罪

【例】 He was *convicted* of murder. 他被判犯有谋杀罪。

【同】 condemn, sentence

【反】 absolve, acquit

【派】 conviction *n*. 确信，深信；定罪，宣告有罪

convince [kən'vɪns] *v*. 使确信，使明白

【记】 con(完全)+vince(征服)→完全征服对方→使确信

【例】 Your argument is too weak to *convince* me. 你的论点太薄弱了，说服不了我。

【同】 assure, guarantee, reassure

【派】 convinced *adj*. 确信的，深信的

convincible *adj*. 可说服的，可使信服的

convincing *adj*. 令人信服的，有力的

convoy ['kɒnvɔɪ] *v*. 护航，护送

【记】 con(共同的)+voy(路)→走同一条路→护送

【例】 The troop ships were *convoyed* across the Atlantic. 运兵船被护送渡过大西洋。

【同】 accompany, escort

cooperate [kəʊ'ɒpəreɪt] *v*. 合作，协作

【记】 co(一起)+oper(工作)+ate(动词词尾)→一起工作→合作

【例】 I advise you not to *cooperate* with that deceitful businessman. 我建议你不要和那个不诚实的商人合作。

【同】 collaborate

【派】 cooperation *n*. 合作，协作

cooperative *adj*. 合作的；*n*. 合作机构，合作社

coordinate [kəʊ'ɔːdɪnɪt] *v*. 协调，调整

【记】 co(一起) + ordin(顺序) + ate(动词词尾)→使处于同一次序→协调

【例】 We must *coordinate* our efforts to help the flood victims. 我们应该同心协力以援助遭水灾的灾民。

【同】 harmonize

【派】 coordinator *n*. 协调员

coordination *n*. 协调，协同

copyright ['kɒpɪraɪt] *n*. 版权，著作权

【记】 copy(复制) + right(权利)→复制的权利→版权

【例】 *Copyright* expires 50 years after the death of the author. 版权在作者死后 50 年即行终止。

【同】 proprietary

core [kɔː] *n*. 中心，核心

【例】 The earth has a *core* and a mantle around it. 地球的中心是地核，地核的周围是地幔。

【同】 center, kernel, nucleus

【反】 fringe

corporation [ˌkɔːpə'reɪʃən] *n*. 公司，企业

【记】 corpor(身体) + ation(名词词尾)→构成一个整体→团体→公司

【例】 John works for a large American chemical *corporation*. 约翰为一家美国大化学公司工作。

【同】 business, company, enterprise

【派】 (逆构)corporate *adj*. 团体的，公司的

corpse [kɔːps] *n*. 尸体

【记】 corp(身体) + se→尸体

【例】 The girl screamed when she suddenly saw the *corpse*. 突然看到尸体，女孩尖叫起来。

【同】 cadaver, body

corpulent ['kɔːpjulənt] *adj*. 肥胖的，肥大的，臃肿的

【记】 corp(身体，肉体) + ulent(形容词词尾)→肉体的→肥胖的

【例】 He is a *corpulent* man who loves to eat. 他是一个贪吃的大胖子。

【同】 fat, obese, plump

【反】 thin, lean

【派】 corpulence *n*. 肥胖

corpus ['kɔːpəs] *n*. (复数 corpora)资料，汇编，语料库

【例】 A representative sample of language, compiled for the purpose of linguistic analysis, is known as a *corpus*. 一个为语言分析编写的具有代表性的语言样本就是所谓的语料库。

correlate ['kɒrɪleɪt] *v*. 使…相互关联，使相互影响

【记】 cor(= com, 一起) + re(回来) + late(带)→一起带回来→使…相互关联

【例】 The results of this experiment do not *correlate* with the results of earlier ones. 这次试验的结果与以往试验的结果毫不相干。

【同】 associate, relate

【派】 correlated *adj*. 有相互关系的

correlation *n*. 相互关系，相关(性)

correlative *adj*. 相关的，关联的

correspond [kɒrɪs'pɒnd] *v*. 1. 与…一致，符合；2. 通信

【记】 cor(= com，一起) + re(回) + spond(约定)→一起应允约定→与…一致

【例】 1. Your account of events *corresponds* with hers. 你说的情况跟她说的相符。

2. We've *corresponded* (with each other) for years but I've never actually met him. 我们已(互相)通信多年了，可是我从未见过他本人。

【同】 agree, match, fit

【派】 correspondence *n*. 通信，信件；相当，类似

correspondent *n*. 通信者，通讯记者

corresponding *adj*. 符合的；相应的，对应的；通信的

corrode [kə'rəʊd] *v*. 使腐蚀，侵蚀

【记】 cor(= com，完全，彻底) + rod(咬) + e→彻底地咬→腐蚀

【例】 Rust *corroded* the steel rails. 锈侵蚀了钢轨。

【同】 deteriorate, rot, rust

【派】 corrosion *n*. 腐蚀，侵蚀

corrosive *adj*. 腐蚀的，腐蚀性的

corrupt [kə'rʌpt] *adj*. 被破坏的，腐败的，贪污的

【记】 cor(= com，完全) + rupt(打破)→完全受损→腐败的

【例】 She wrote a book declaiming against our *corrupt* society. 她写了一本书抨击我们这腐败的社会。

【同】 rotten, wicked, evil

【反】 incorrupt

【派】 corruption *n*. 贪污，腐败

cosmic ['kɒzmɪk] *adj*. 宇宙的

【记】 cosm(宇宙) + ic(形容词词尾)→宇宙的

【例】 Physics is governed by *cosmic* laws. 物理学受宇宙法则的制约。

【同】 universal

【反】 chaotic

【派】 (逆构)cosmos *n*. 宇宙

cosmopolitan [ˌkɒzmə'pɒlɪtən] *adj*. 世界性的，遍布全世界的

【记】 cosm(o)(宇宙，世界) + polit(= polis，城市) + an(形容词词尾)→世界性城市的→世界性的

【例】 London is a *cosmopolitan* city. 伦敦是一个国际性的大都市。

【同】 universal, worldwide

【派】 (逆构)cosmopolis *n*. 国际大都市

costume ['kɒstjuːm] *n*. 服装，戏装

【例】 The kimono is part of the national *costume* of Japan. 和服是日本民族服装的一部分。

C

【同】 dress，suit

council ['kaʊnsɪl] *n*. 委员会，理事会，议会

【记】 coun(= com，共同) + cil(召集)→共同召集→议会

【例】 We should submit our plans to the *council* for approval. 我们应该向理事会提交计划以求批准。

【同】 committee

counsel ['kaʊnsəl] *v*. (-l(l)ed；-l(l)ing)劝告，忠告；*n*. 1.意见，忠告；2.辩护律师，法律顾问

【记】 coun(= com，共同) + sel(提，拿)→共同提出→商议

【例】 1. He *counseled* the committee to proceed slowly. 他建议委员会从缓进行。

2. I sought his *counsel* before applying for promotion. 申请晋升之前我征求过他的意见。

3. Each side of a case in court has its own *counsel*. 法庭上原告和被告双方都有各自的律师。

【同】 advise，suggest；advice，suggestion；attorney，lawyer

【派】 counselor *n*. 顾问

counterfeit ['kaʊntəfɪt] *n*. 赝品，伪造品；*adj*. 伪造的，假冒的

【记】 counter(= contra，相反) + feit(做)→(源于法文拼法)仿照着真品做的东西→假冒的

【例】 This ten-dollar bill is a *counterfeit*. 这张十元钞票是一张假钞。

【同】 fake，forgery，artificial，false

【反】 genuine

counterpart ['kaʊntəpɑːt] *n*. 对应的人(或物)

【记】 counter(相对的) + part(部分)→对应的人(或物)

【例】 The new Russian president came to Washington to meet his *counterpart*. 俄罗斯新总统来华盛顿会见美国总统。

【同】 equivalent

couple ['kʌpl] *n*. 两个，一对(夫妇)；2.几个，一些；*v*. 1.结合，伴随；2.联合，连接

【例】 1. A young *couple* views a deserted old house that they are interested in buying. 一对年轻的夫妇去看一座他们有兴趣购买的废弃老屋。

2. I'll be back in a *couple* of days. 我过几天就回来。

3. The bad light，*coupled* with the wet ground，made play very difficult. 光线不足兼之地面潮湿，比赛难以进行。

4. They *coupled* the carriages of the train together. 他们把火车的车厢连接好。

【同】 pair，mate；several；accompany；attach

courier ['kʊrɪə] *n*. (递送急件、外交信件的)信使

【记】 couri(跑) + er(指人的名词词尾)→跑步行进的人→送消息的人→信使

【例】 A *courier* delivered the parcels to our office. 送急件的人将包裹送到我们办公室了。

【同】 messenger

court [kɔːt] *n*. 1.法庭，法院；2.球场；*v*. 向…献殷勤，追求

【例】 1. The prisoner was brought to *court* for trial. 囚犯被提到法庭受审。

2. We also have an arrangement with the local tennis club, entitling our students to use their *courts* on weekday mornings in the Summer. 我们还和当地的网球俱乐部有约定，我们的学生在夏季工作日的上午有权使用他们的网球场。

3. He had been *courting* Jane for six months. 他追求简已有6个月之久。

【同】 courtroom; chase, pursue

【派】 courtship *n*. 求婚，求爱

coverage [ˈkʌvərɪdʒ] *n*. 1. 覆盖，覆盖范围；2. 新闻报道

【记】 cover(掩盖) + age(名词词尾)→覆盖范围

【例】 1. The *coverage* of the subject in his botany text is inadequate. 他的植物学教科书中对那题目的叙述不充分。

2. This is surprising considering the high level of media *coverage* on this issue. 从媒体对这个问题连篇累牍的报道来看，这是很令人吃惊的。

【同】 reportage

【派】 (逆构)cover *v*. 覆盖，掩护

covetous [ˈkʌvɪtəs] *adj*. 贪婪的，贪心的

【记】 covet(贪求) + ous(形容词词尾)→贪求的→贪婪的

【例】 He is looking with *covetous* eyes at his neighbor's beautiful wife. 他贪婪地盯着邻人漂亮的妻子。

【同】 greedy, desirous

【派】 (逆构)covet *v*. 垂涎，觊觎

cower [ˈkaʊə] *v*. 畏缩，退缩

【例】 He *cowered* away as she raised her hand to hit him. 她扬手打他，他立即退开。

【同】 cringe, crouch, squat

cozy [ˈkəʊzɪ] *adj*. 舒适的，安逸的

【例】 The room has a nice *cozy* feel. 这房间给人非常温暖舒适的感觉。

【同】 comfortable, homey, snug

【派】 coziness *n*. 安逸，舒适

crack [kræk] *n*. 裂缝，缝隙；*v*. 1. 砸开，裂开；2. 摧毁，重击

【例】 1. There is a *crack* in this window. 这扇窗户上有个裂纹。

2. You can *crack* this toughened glass, but you can't break it. 这种韧化玻璃只裂不碎。

3. Police are *cracking* down on drug dealers. 警方现对贩毒分子严惩不贷。

【同】 break, slit, split

craft [krɑːft] *n*. 工艺，手艺

【例】 The workers are trying to apply modern techniques to this traditional *craft*. 工人们试图将现代技术用于这项传统工业。

【同】 handicraft

【派】 craftsman *n*. 工匠，手艺精巧的人

craftsmanship *n*. 技能，技术

crafty *adj*. 灵巧的，巧妙的，机灵的

cram [kræm] *v*. (-mmed; -mming) 1. 填塞; 2. 匆忙准备(考试)

【例】 1. He *crammed* as much candy into his pockets as they would hold. 他把口袋都塞满了糖果。

2. She *crammed* for her history exam. 她死记硬背以应付历史考试。

【同】 fill, pack, stuff

crash [kræʃ] *v./n*. 碰撞, 坠落; *adj*. 应急的, 快速的, 速成的

【例】 1. The car *crashed* into a tree and burst into flames. 汽车突然撞在一棵树上并燃烧起来。

2. He attended High School *Crash* Course 11 – 25 Jan. 他参加了1月11日至25日高中生速成班。

【同】 break, smash; speeded-up

crave [kreɪv] *v*. 渴望, 渴求

【例】 I was *craving* for a cigarette. 我很想抽一支烟。

【同】 covet, desire, lust, want

crawl [krɔːl] *n./v*. 1. 爬行; 2. 缓慢地行进

【例】 1. A baby *crawls* before it can walk. 婴儿先能爬, 然后才会走。

2. The heavy traffic *crawled* through the narrow tunnel. 拥挤的车辆慢吞吞地穿过狭窄的隧道。

【同】 creep

crayon [ˈkreɪən] *n*. 彩色笔, 蜡笔或其绘画

【记】 cray(= chalk, 粉笔) + on(名词词尾)→像粉笔一样的东西→蜡笔

【例】 The child colored in all the shapes on the page with a *crayon*. 那孩子用蜡笔把这页上所有的图形都涂上了颜色。

credential [krɪˈdenʃəl] *n*. (常用复数)凭证, 文凭

【记】 cred(相信) + ent(形容词词尾) + ial(形容词兼名词词尾)→使人相信的东西→凭证

【例】 She has the perfect *credentials* for the job. 她做这工作完全够格。

【同】 certificate, certification

credible [ˈkredəbl] *adj*. 可信的, 可靠的

【记】 cred(相信) + ible(形容词词尾)→可信的

【例】 Is there a *credible* alternative to the nuclear deterrent? 是否有可以取代核威慑力量的可靠方法?

【同】 believable, convincing

【反】 incredible

【派】 credibility *n*. 可信性, 可靠性

credit [ˈkredɪt] *n*. 1. 信用, 信贷; 2. 学分; 3. 荣誉; *v*. 1. 信任; 2. 把…归功于

【记】 cred(相信) + it(名词词尾)→信用

【例】 1. The bank refused further *credits* to the company. 银行拒绝再贷款给这家公司。

2. She hasn't enough *credits* to get her degree. 她没有足够的学分获得学位。

3. Her success brought *credit* to the school. 她的成功给学校带来荣誉。

4. You won't *credit* her far-fetched story. 你不会相信她胡扯的话的。

5. Most historians of technology *credit* the Chinese with its discovery. 大多数技术

史专家把它的发现归功于中国人。
【同】 loan; glory, honor; trust, believe; attribute, ascribe
【反】 discredit, distrust
【派】 creditable *adj*. 值得赞扬的，可归功于…的
creditor *n*. 债权人

credulous [ˈkredjʊləs] *adj*. 轻信的，易信的
【记】 cred(相信)+ulous(形容词词尾)→容易相信的→轻信的
【例】 They are *credulous* people who believe in the advertisement. 他们是一些轻信广告的人。
【同】 gullible
【反】 incredulous
【派】 credulity *n*. 易信，轻信

creed [kriːd] *n*. 信仰，信条
【例】 What is your political *creed*? 你的政治信仰如何？
【同】 belief, doctrine

creep [kriːp] *v*. 慢慢、偷偷行进，爬行
【例】 We *crept* upstairs so as not to wake the baby. 为了不吵醒婴儿，我们蹑手蹑脚地上了楼梯。
【同】 crawl, sneak
【派】 creepy *adj*. 爬行的，匍匐的；令人毛骨悚然的

cripple [ˈkrɪpl] *v*. 1. 使残废；2. 削弱，损坏
【例】 1. She was *crippled* in the car accident. 她在汽车出事时把腿伤成了残废。
2. The ship was *crippled* in the storm. 那船在暴风雨中受到严重损坏。
【同】 disable, injure; damage, weaken
【派】 crippling *adj*. 有害健康的；破坏性的

crisp [krɪsp] *adj*. 脆的，易碎的
【例】 It tastes sweet and *crisp*. 吃起来又甜又脆。
【同】 brittle, fragile
【反】 soft

criterion [kraɪˈtɪərɪən] *n*. (复数-ria 或-rions)(评判的)标准，尺度
【记】 criter(判断)+ion(名词词尾)→判断的标准→尺度
【例】 We knew the *criteria*, so we had to think about clarity, organization, and so on. 我们知道评分标准，所以我们必须要考虑表达清楚，组织严密等等。
【同】 standard, touchstone

critical [ˈkrɪtɪkəl] *adj*. 1. 批评的；2. 关键性的，重大的
【记】 crit(判断)+ical(名词词尾)→经过判断以后的→批评的
【例】 1. The inquiry was *critical* of her work. 该项调查对她的工作提出了批评。
2. The *critical* question now is whether this can become the norm, rather than the exception. 当前最为关键的问题是这样的做法能否成为制度，而不只是临时之举。
【同】 fault-finding; decisive, crucial, vital
【反】 complimentary, uncritical

【派】 (逆构)critic *n*. 批评家，评论家

criticize *v*. 批评，责备

crooked ['krʊkɪd] *adj*. 1. 弯曲的，歪的；2. 不老实的，欺诈的

【记】 crook(弯曲)+ed(形容词词尾)→弯曲的

【例】 1. A glance in the mirror reassured him that his tie wasn't *crooked*. 他照了一下镜子，领带确实没有戴歪。

2. That is a *crooked* deal. 那是一笔非法交易。

【同】 bent，curved，twisty；dishonest

【反】 straight；honest

crucial ['kruːʃəl] *adj*. 关键的，至关重要的

【记】 cruc(十字，交叉)+ial(形容词词尾)→交叉的地方→极重要的

【例】 Getting this contract is *crucial* to the future of our company. 签订此项合同对本公司的前途至关重要。

【同】 all-important，determinant，essential

【反】 noncrucial

crude [kruːd] *adj*. 天然的，未加工的，粗糙的

【例】 China is a country rich in *crude* oil. 中国是一个原油丰富的国家。

【同】 raw，coarse

【反】 refined

crumble ['krʌmbl] *v*. 1. 粉碎，弄碎；2. 崩溃，瓦解

【记】 crumb(碎屑)+le(表示动作反复的动词词尾)→把…弄成碎屑→粉碎

【例】 1. He *crumbled* the bread in his fingers. 他用手指把面包捏碎了。

2. Our hopes *crumbled* when the business went bankrupt. 商行破产了，我们的希望也破灭了。

【同】 disintegrate；collapse

crumple ['krʌmpl] *v*. 弄皱，扭弯

【记】 crump(卷)+le(动词词尾)→使卷起来→弄皱

【例】 Silk dresses are easy to *crumple* up if not carefully handled. 真丝衣服若不能正确处理，很容易起皱。

【同】 crinkle，crease，wrinkle

crush [krʌʃ] *v*. 压(或挤)坏，倒塌

【例】 The people *crushed* through the gate. 人们挤进了大门。

【同】 press，squeeze

crutch [krʌtʃ] *n*. 1. (跛子用的)拐杖；2. 支撑，帮助

【例】 1. When he broke his leg he had to walk on *crutches*. 他摔断腿后，只好拄着拐杖走路。

2. He uses his wife as a kind of *crutch* because of his lack of confidence. 他缺乏自信心，总把妻子当做主心骨。

【同】 prop，support

cryptic ['krɪptɪk] *adj*. 1. 秘密的，神秘的；2. 有隐义的，含义模糊的

【记】 crypt(隐藏的)+ic(形容词词尾)→隐藏的→神秘的

【例】 1. The linguist converted the *cryptic* massage into intelligible language. 那个语言学家把密码转变成了明白易懂的语言。

2. I do not understand your *cryptic* remarks. 我不能理解你那有言外之意的话。

【同】 cabalistic, mysterious, inscrutable

【反】 intelligible, plain

crystal [ˈkrɪstl] *n*. 水晶，晶体；*adj*. 清澈的；结晶状的

【记】 来自希腊语 krustallos，冰→像冰一样的→水晶

【例】 1. This set of *crystal* wine cups is very expensive. 这套水晶玻璃酒杯非常昂贵。

2. She made her meaning *crystal* clear. 她把她的意思解释得清清楚楚。

【派】 crystalline *adj*. 水晶制的，透明的

crystallize *v*. 明确；形成结晶体，使结晶

crystallization *n*. 结晶化

cube [kjuːb] *n*. 立方体

【例】 when it breaks, this glass shatters into tiny *cubes* rather than large, razor-sharp shards. 这种玻璃破裂时，会碎成细小的立方体，而不是那种大块的如剃刀一样锋利的碎片。

【派】 cubic *adj*. 立方的

cue [kjuː] *n*. 暗示，提示

【例】 When I nod my head, that's your *cue* to interrupt the meeting. 我一点头，就是暗示你把会议中断。

【同】 clue, hint

cuisine [kwiːˈziːn] *n*. 烹饪，烹饪术

【例】 This is a training restaurant which offers good quality *cuisine* in pleasant surroundings. 这是一家培训餐厅，这里饭菜可口，环境幽雅。

【同】 cooking

culminate [ˈkʌlmɪneɪt] *v*. (使)达到高潮，达到极点

【记】 culmin(顶点) + ate(动词词尾)→达到顶点→达到高潮

【例】 The gala *culminated* in a firework display. 晚会以大放烟火告终。

【同】 climax, terminate, top

【派】 culmination *n*. 顶点

culpable [ˈkʌlpəbl] *adj*. 有罪的，该受谴责的

【记】 culp(过失，责备) + able(形容词词尾)→应该责备的→该受谴责的

【例】 I cannot be held *culpable* for their mistakes. 不能把他们的错误归咎于我。

【同】 blamable, guilty

【派】 culpability *n*. 有罪性，有过失

culprit [ˈkʌlprɪt] *n*. 1. 犯过者，犯罪者；2. 不良后果的根源，祸根

【记】 culp(过失) + rit→犯过失的人→犯过者

【例】 1. Police are searching for the *culprits*. 警方正在搜捕罪犯。

2. Tourism is not always the *culprit* behind such changes. 这些变化不应该都归咎于旅游业。

【同】 offender, criminal, perpetrator

cult [kʌlt] *n*. 1. 膜拜，狂热崇拜；2. 一群信徒

【例】 1. His music has become something of a *cult*. 他的音乐已经成为一种时尚。

2. The *cult* promised revenge for putting its leader in jail. 追随者发誓要对监禁他们的领袖进行报复。

【同】 craze，enthusiasm，furor；cultist

cultivate [ˈkʌltɪveɪt] *v*. 1. 耕作，培养；2. 结交，寻求建立友谊

【记】 culti(v)(耕种)+ate(动词词尾)→耕种

【例】 1. According to my research，the Cavendish banana，which is a type of banana and the first type to be *cultivated* here，actually originated in China. 根据我的研究，这种 Cavendish 香蕉——它是香蕉的一种，并且是最先在这儿培育的，实际上原产于中国。

2. John always tries to *cultivate* people who are useful to him. 约翰经常设法和对他有用的人结交。

【同】 develop，farm，civilize；develop，foster

【派】 cultivation *n*. 耕种；培养

cumbersome [ˈkʌmbəsəm] *adj*. 1. 笨重的；2. 讨厌的，麻烦的

【记】 cumber(阻碍，妨碍)+some(形容词词尾)→妨碍的→笨重的

【例】 1. The desk was too *cumbersome* to pick up and move. 写字台太重了，抬不动。

2. I can't endure the university's *cumbersome* administrative procedures. 我无法忍受这所大学拖拖拉拉的行政工作。

【同】 awkward，clumsy；troublesome

cure [kjʊə] *n*./*v*. 治愈，治疗

【例】 1. The doctor cannot guarantee a *cure*. 医生不能保证治愈。

2. The doctors *cured* of her cancer. 医生治好了她的癌症。

【同】 heal，remedy，treat

【派】 curable *adj*. 可医治的，医得好的

curious [ˈkjʊərɪəs] *adj*. 好奇的

【记】 cur(注意，留心)+ious(形容词词尾)→非常留心的→好奇的

【例】 People are clearly more *curious* about bad news than good. 公众对坏消息显然要比对好消息更加好奇。

【同】 inquisitive，inquiring

【反】 incurious，indifferent

【派】 curiosity *n*. 好奇心

currency [ˈkʌrənsɪ] *n*. 1. 通货，货币；2. 流通，流行

【记】 curr(流，跑)+ency(名词词尾)→流动→流通，货币

【例】 1. The president proclaimed that a new *currency* would be issued. 总统宣布将发行新货币。

2. Reports about the president's illness are gaining *currency* among foreign journalists. 总统生病的消息在外国记者中传播开来。

【同】 money；prevalence

current [ˈkʌrənt] *adj*. 目前的，现在的；*n*. 1. (水、气的)流，流动；2. 潮流

【记】 curr(流，跑)+ent(名词或形容词词尾)→流动

【例】 1. This word is no longer in *current* use. 这个词现在已经不再使用。

2. The *current* is strongest in the middle of the river. 河中央的水流最急。

3. We must try to counteract the present *current* of anti-government feeling. 我们应该努力消除目前的这股反政府情绪。

【同】 present，prevalent；flow

【派】 currently adv. 现时，当今

curriculum [kəˈrɪkjʊləm] *n*.(复数-lums或-la)(全部)课程

【记】 cur(流，跑)+iculum(拉丁语里表名词的词尾)→按照…流→按照…进行→课程

【例】 Is German on your school's *curriculum*? 你们学校有德语课吗?

【同】 course，program

【派】 curricular *adj*. 课程的

extracurricular *adj*. 正课以外的，课外的

curse [kɜːs] *v./n*. 诅咒，咒骂

【例】 1. He *cursed* (at) his bad luck. 他咒骂自己运气不好。

2. The witch put a *curse* on him. 女巫念咒诅咒他。

【同】 damn，swear

【反】 bless

cursory [ˈkɜːsərɪ] *adj*. 仓促的，粗略的，草率的

【记】 curs(跑，流)+ory(形容词词尾)→跑一样的→粗略的

【例】 Even a *cursory* glance at the report showed that it was full of mistakes. 这报告只要粗略一看就会发现到处是错误。

【同】 brief，casual，quick

【反】 thorough

curtail [kɜːˈteɪl] *v*. 缩短，削减

【记】 cur(流动，进行)+tail(切割)→把…切开→缩短

【例】 We must try to *curtail* our spending. 我们必须尽力缩减开支。

【同】 abbreviate，abridge，cut，reduce

【反】 extend

【派】 curtailment *n*. 缩减，缩短

curve [kɜːv] *n*. 曲线，弧线

【例】 The falling star described a long *curve* in the sky. 流星在空中画出了一道长长的弧线。

【同】 bend，curl，twist

cushion [ˈkʊʃən] *n*. 垫子，软垫

【记】 cush(臀部)+ion(名词词尾)→臀部用的东西→垫子

【例】 She made a *cushion* out of odd bits of material. 她用碎布头做了个靠垫。

【同】 pillow

custom [ˈkʌstəm] *n*. 习惯，风俗

【例】 It is difficult to get used to another country's *customs*. 要适应另一国家的风俗习惯是很困难的。

【同】 tradition, practice

【派】 customary *adj*. 合乎习俗的，习惯的

customer [ˈkʌstəmə] *n*. 顾客，消费者

C

【记】 custom(习惯) + er(名词词尾)→去(某个地方)成习惯的人→顾客

【例】 The new shop across the road has taken away most of my *customers*. 马路对面那家新开的店把我的大部分顾客都抢走了。

【同】 client, buyer

【派】 customize *v*. 定制，用户化

customization *n*. 用户化，定制

cylinder [ˈsɪlɪndə] *n*. 圆筒，圆柱体，汽缸

【记】 cylind(滚动) + er(名词词尾)→可以滚动的东西→圆筒，圆柱体

【例】 The *cylinder* is a crucial part of the washing machine. 滚筒是洗衣机必不可少的部分。

cynical [ˈsɪnɪkəl] *adj*. 愤世嫉俗的，挑剔挖苦的

【记】 cynic(愤世嫉俗的人) + al(形容词词尾)→愤世嫉俗的

【例】 His *cynical* attitude gave us a surprise. 他那愤世嫉俗的态度让我们惊奇。

【同】 misanthropic

【派】 (逆构)cynic *n*. 玩世不恭的人，愤世嫉俗者

cynicism *n*. 犬儒主义，玩世不恭

D

dagger [ˈdæɡə] *n*. 短剑，匕首

【例】 He fell a victim to the *dagger* of the assassin. 他死于刺客的匕首之下。

【同】 dirk

dairy [ˈdeərɪ] *n*. 牛奶场，奶品场

【例】 Dung beetles have become an integral part of the successful management of *dairy* farms in Australia over the past few decades. 在过去几十年中，金龟子已经成为对澳大利亚牛奶场进行有效管理工作中的一个不可或缺的部分。

damp [dæmp] *adj*. 潮湿的

【例】 These *damp* matches won't strike. 这些潮湿的火柴划不着。

【同】 dampish，moist

【反】 dry

【派】 dampish *adj*. 含湿气的，稍湿的

dampen *v*. 使潮湿

dangle [ˈdæŋɡl] *v*. 悬摆

【例】 Huge earrings *dangled* from her ears. 她的耳朵上吊着巨大的耳环。

【同】 hang，swing

dash [dæʃ] *v*. 1. 猛冲，冲撞；2. 匆忙完成

【例】 1. He *dashed* across the street and ran towards me. 他冲过马路，向我跑过来。

2. Well, I spent about two or three weeks reading and doing general research and then I *dashed* the writing off very quickly. 我花了两到三周的时间阅读并且做一般的研究工作，然后匆匆忙忙地就把论文写完了。

【同】 rush，hasten

data [ˈdeɪtə] *n*. (datum 的复数)资料，数据

【例】 The *data* stored in a computer can be protected. 存储在计算机里的数据能被保护起来。

【同】 information

【派】 database *n*. 数据库，资料库

daunting [dɒntɪŋ] *adj*. 使人畏缩的

【记】 daunt(畏惧) + ing(形容词词尾)→使人畏缩的

【例】 The prospect of meeting the President is quite *daunting*. 一想到要会见总统就足以令人心悸。

【同】 discouraging

【反】 encouraging

【派】 dauntless *adj*. 勇敢的，无畏的

daze [deɪz] *v*. 使发昏，使眩晕

【例】 The blow on the head *dazed* him for a moment. 头上受了一击后，他昏过去了一会儿。

【同】 bewilder, muddle

D

dazzle ['dæzl] *v*. 1.(使)眩目，(使)眼花；2.使(某人)赞许，称奇

【记】 daz(e)(眩晕)+z+le(动词词尾)→(使)眩目

【例】 1. The bright light of the car *dazzled* me. 这汽车的灯光使我目眩。

2. The star *dazzled* his audience. 这位明星的风采使观众为之倾倒。

【同】 flash, glare, glow

【派】 dazzling *adj*. 眼花缭乱的；耀眼的

deal [diːl] *n*. 交易，协定；*v*. (dealt, dealt)处理，应付

【例】 How would you *deal* with an armed burglar? 你怎样对付闯进来的持有武器的强盗？

【同】 bargain, trade; address, cope, handle

debate [dɪ'beɪt] *n*./*v*. 辩论，争论

【记】 de(向下)+bat(打)+e→将对方打倒→辩论

【例】 1. After a long *debate* the bill was passed. 经长时间的辩论，议案获得通过。

2. We're just *debating* what to do next. 我们正讨论下一步该做什么事。

【同】 argue

【派】 debatable *adj*. 可争议的

debt [det] *n*. 债务，欠款

【记】 deb(欠债)+t(名词词尾)→债务

【例】 If I pay all my *debts* I'll have no money left. 我若还清所有欠债就分文不剩了。

【同】 liability

【派】 debtor *n*. 债务人

decadent ['dekədənt] *adj*. 颓废的，衰落的

【记】 de(向下)+cad(落下)+ent(形容词词尾)→向下落的→颓废的

【例】 Many conservatives in the early 1900s thought impressionistic art was *decadent*. 20世纪初，许多保守主义者认为印象派的艺术是颓废的。

【同】 declining

【派】 decadence *n*. 堕落，颓废

decay [dɪ'keɪ] *v*. 1.变坏，腐烂；2.衰退

【记】 de(向下)+cay(降落)→落下→衰退

【例】 1. The dampness of the climate *decayed* the books. 气候潮湿，把书都霉坏了。

2. What caused the Roman Empire to *decay*? 是什么促使罗马帝国衰落的？

【同】 decompose, rot

deceit [dɪ'siːt] *n*. 欺骗，欺诈

【记】 de(离去)+ceit(=ceive，取，拿)→(偷偷地)拿走→欺骗

【例】 He got the money by *deceit*. 他靠欺骗弄到了钱。

【同】 deception, fraudulence

【派】 deceitful *adj*. 惯于欺骗的

deceive [dɪˈsiːv] *v*. 欺骗，蒙蔽

【记】 de(离去)+ceive(取，拿)→(偷偷地)拿走→欺骗

【例】 We were *deceived* into believing that he could help us. 我们受骗了，还以为他能帮助我们。

【同】 betray, cheat, trick

【反】 undeceive

【派】 deception *n*. 欺骗，诡计

deceptive *adj*. 骗人的

deceivable *adj*. 易受骗的，可欺诈的

decelerate [diːˈseləreɪt] *v*. 减速

【记】 de(向下，不)+celer(快速的)+ate(动词词尾)→使不快速→减速

【例】 The car *decelerated* when apptoaching the corner. 驶近拐角的时候，车子减速了。

【同】 slow down, retard

【反】 accelerate

【派】 deceleration *n*. 减速

decent [ˈdiːsnt] *adj*. 1. 适当的，可接受的；2. 得体的，体面的

【记】 decen(适合)+t→适合的→得体的

【例】 1. We must provide *decent* housing for the poor. 我们必须为穷苦人提供适当的住房。

2. He dreamed of living in *decent* conditions. 他梦想着过体面的生活。

【同】 adequate, proper

【反】 indecent

【派】 decency *n*. 庄重

decimal [ˈdesɪməl] *adj*. 十进制的

【记】 decim(十分之一)+al(形容词词尾)→十分之一的→十进制的

【例】 Most countries have a *decimal* currency. 大多数国家使用十进制货币。

【同】 denary

declaim [dɪˈkleɪm] *v*. 1. 高谈阔论，慷慨陈词；2. 谴责，以言词攻击

【记】 de(充分)+claim(喊叫)→大声喊出来→慷慨陈词

【例】 1. A preacher stood *declaiming* in the town centre. 传教士站在市镇中心慷慨陈词。

2. She wrote a book *declaiming* against our corrupt society. 她写了一本书抨击我们这腐败的社会。

【同】 speak, perorate

【派】 declamation *n*. 雄辩

declamatory *adj*. 雄辩家式的，朗读式的

declare [dɪˈkleə] *v*. 宣言，声明

【记】 de(充分)+clare(清楚)→十分清楚→宣言

【例】 I now *declare* this meeting open. 我现在宣布会议开幕。

【同】 announce, assert, proclaim

【派】 declaration *n*. 宣言，公告，声明

decline [dɪˈklaɪn] *n./v*. 1.下降，减少；2.拒绝，谢绝

【记】 de(向下)+clin(弯曲)+e→向下弯曲→下降

【例】 1.She is on the *decline*, and may die soon. 她的健康每况愈下，可能不久于人世。
2.I invited her to join us, but she *declined*. 我邀请她和我们在一起，可是她婉言谢绝了。

【同】 descent, fall; refuse, reject

【反】 rise, flourish; accept, agree

【派】 declining *adj*. 倾斜的，衰退中的

decode [ˌdiːˈkəʊd] *v*. 解码，译解

【记】 de(=dis，分开)+code(密码)→拆开密码→解码

【例】 We *decoded* the enemy's telegram. 我们破译了敌人的电报密码。

【同】 decipher

【反】 encode

decompose [ˌdiːkəmˈpəʊz] *v*. 分解，(使)腐烂

【记】 de(=dis，分开)+com(一起)+pose(放)→使放在一起的分开→分解

【例】 The eggs began to *decompose* after a day in the sun. 鸡蛋在太阳下放了一天后开始变坏。

【同】 decay, disintegrate

【反】 compose

【派】 decomposable *adj*. 可分解的，会腐败的
decomposer *n*. 分解剂，分解者
decomposition *n*. 分解，腐烂

decorate [ˈdekəreɪt] *v*. 装饰，修饰

【记】 decor(装饰)+ate(动词词尾)→装饰

【例】 We *decorated* the house for Christmas. 我们装饰房屋过圣诞节。

【同】 adorn, ornament

【派】 decoration *n*. 装饰，装饰品
decorative *adj*. 装饰的，可做装饰的

decorum [dɪˈkɔːrəm] *n*. 正派得体，稳重大方

【记】 decor(装饰)+um(名词词尾)→装饰了的→得体

【例】 In the presence of elderly visitors our son was a model of *decorum*. 我们的儿子在来访的长辈面前彬彬有礼。

【同】 decency, etiquette

【反】 indecorum

【派】 decorous *adj*. 端庄得体的

decrease [diːˈkriːs] *v./n*. 减少，减小

【记】 de(向下)+crease(增长)→向下增加→减少

【例】 His interest in this subject gradually *decreases*. 他对这门学科的兴趣逐渐减退。

【同】 diminish, lessen, reduce

【反】 increase

decree [dɪˈkriː] *n*. 1.法令，政令；2.判决；*v*. 颁布

【记】 de(向下)+cree(详审)→结果仔细审议→法令，判决

【例】 1. The government issued a *decree* that political activities should be resitricted. 政府颁布了一项限制政治活动的法令。

2. This *decree* has the force of law behind it. 这一裁决有法律的力量作后盾。

3. The dictator *decreed* that his birthday would be a public holiday. 该独裁者发布命令，将其生日定为公众假期。

【同】 edict，act；rule；command，dictate

decry [dɪˈkraɪ] *v*. 非难，谴责

【记】 de(充分)+cry(喊叫)→大声喊出来→谴责

【例】 The mayor *decried* gambling in all its form. 市长谴责各式各样的赌博。

【同】 condemn，denounce

【派】 decrial *n*. 责难，诽谤

dedicate [ˈdedɪkeɪt] *v*. 奉献，致力于

【记】 de(向下)+dic(宣称)+ate(动词词尾)→宣称处于对方之下→奉献

【例】 She *dedicated* her life to science. 她毕生致力于科学。

【同】 devote

【派】 dedication *n*. 贡献，奉献

dedicated *adj*. 献身的；专注的

deduce [dɪˈdjuːs] *v*. 演绎，推断

【记】 de(向下)+duc(领导，引导)+e→向下引导→推断

【例】 From the presence of so many people at the party, we can *deduce* that it is a welcomed one. 从参加聚会的人数之多我们可以看出，这次聚会是受人欢迎的。

【同】 infer，conclude

【反】 induce

deem [diːm] *v*. 认为，相信

【例】 He *deems* it his duty to help his needy friends. 他认为帮助穷朋友是他的义务。

【同】 believe，suppose，think

defect [dɪˈfekt] *n*. 过失，不足；*v*. 变节，背叛

【记】 de(离开)+fect(做)→对于好的行为与做法的偏离→过失

【例】 1. The new car had to be withdrawn from the market because of a mechanical *defect*. 那种新汽车因有机械缺陷只好撤出市场。

2. One of our spies has *defected* to the enemy. 我们的一名特工已叛变投敌。

【同】 fault，flaw，shortcoming

【反】 merit

【派】 defective *adj*. 有缺点的，有缺陷的

defection *n*. 缺陷；脱党，变节

defend [dɪˈfend] *v*. 1.防守，保卫；2.辩护，辩解

【记】 de(向下)+fend(打击)→打倒敌人→防守

【例】 1. When the dog attacked me, I *defended* myself with a stick. 那狗扑向我时，我用棍子自卫。

2. You'll need stronger evidence to *defend* your claim to the inheritance. 你需要更强有力的证据才能为你的财产继承权辩护。

【同】 protect, safeguard; support

【反】 attack; charge

【派】 defendant *n*. 保护；被告

defense *n*. 防御，保护；辩护

defensive *adj*. 防御用的，防御性的

defer [dɪˈfɜː] *v*. (-rred; -rring) 1. 拖延，推迟；2. 遵从，服从

【记】 de(离开) + fer(运，带)→运到远方→拖延

【例】 1. I shall *defer* replying till I hear from home. 我将等接到家信以后再给你答复。

2. On technical matters, I *defer* to the experts. 在技术问题上，我遵从专家的意见。

【同】 postpone, delay

【反】 advance, hurry

【派】 deference *n*. 遵从，顺从；敬意

deferential *adj*. 顺从的；敬意的

deficiency [dɪˈfɪʃənsɪ] *n*. 缺乏，不足

【记】 de(离开) + fici(做) + ency(名词词尾)→未达完美时所处的状态→不足

【例】 *Deficiency* in vitamins/Vitamin *deficiency* can lead to illness. 身体缺乏维生素就会生病。

【同】 insufficiency, lack

【反】 abundance, plenty, excess

【派】 deficient *adj*. 缺乏的，不足的

deficit [ˈdefɪsɪt] *n*. 缺乏，赤字，逆差

【记】 de(向下，不够) + fic(做) + it(名词词尾)→做得不够→缺乏

【例】 Tax was low and state spending was high, resulting in a budget *deficit*. 税率低而政府支出大，结果出现预算赤字。

【同】 shortage, shortfall

【反】 surplus

define [dɪˈfaɪn] *v*. 给…下定义，限定；2. 阐释，详细说明

【记】 de(向下) + fine(结束，限制)→定下界限→下定义

【例】 1. His work was to *define* new words that were not yet in the dictionaries. 他的工作是给尚未收入词典的新词下定义。

2. This book attemps to *define* the position of the national government in local affairs. 这本书试图阐明国民政府在地方事物中的地位。

【同】 clarify, describe, explain

【派】 definite *adj*. 肯定的，明确的，限定的

definition *n*. 定义，释义

definitive *adj*. 权威性的，确定的

deforestation [dɪˌfɒrɪsˈteɪʃən] *n*. 砍伐森林

【记】 de(向下) + forest(森林) + ation(名词词尾)→让森林倒下→砍伐森林

【例】 They demonstrated agsainst *deforestation* of the Amazon. 他们举行示威游行反对砍伐亚马孙河流域的森林。

【同】 disforestation

【反】 forestation

【派】 (逆构)deforest *v*. 采伐森林，清除树木

deform [diːˈfɔːm] *v*. 使变形

【记】 de(离开) + form(形状)→离开本来的形状→使变形

【例】 Shoes that are too tight *deform* the feet. 太紧的鞋子会使脚变形。

【同】 distort disfigure

【反】 form

【派】 deformable *adj*. 可变形的

deformation *n*. 变形

defy [dɪˈfaɪ] *v*. 蔑视，反抗

【记】 de(=dis，不) + fy(=fid，相信)→不相信→蔑视

【例】 They *defied* their parents and got married. 他们违抗父母的意愿而结婚了。

【同】 disobey，challenge，resist

【反】 obey

【派】 defiance *n*. 挑战，蔑视

defiant *adj*. 挑战的，挑衅的

degenerate [dɪˈdʒenəreɪt] *v*. 衰退，退化

【记】 de(向下) + gener(种族) + ate(动词词尾)→种族变得很低→衰退

【例】 His health is *degenerating* rapidly. 他的健康状况迅速恶化。

【同】 degrade，deteriorate

【反】 develop，evolve

【派】 degeneration *n*. 退化，恶化

degrade [dɪˈgreɪd] *v*. 降级，降低，退化

【记】 de(向下) + grade(行走)→使由现有状态向下行走→降级

【例】 It was very *degrading* to be punished in front of the whole class. 在全班同学面前受罚是非常丢脸的。

【同】 demote，reduce，degenerate

【反】 uplift

【派】 degradation *n*. 降级，退化

deify [ˈdiːɪfaɪ] *v*. 奉为神，崇拜

【记】 dei(神) + fy(动词词尾)→使成为神→奉为神

【例】 Primitive peoples *deified* the sun. 原始民族将太阳奉作神。

【同】 worship，idolize

【反】 curse swear

【派】 deity *n*. 神；被奉若神明的人(物)

deject [dɪˈdʒekt] *v*. 使沮丧，使灰心

【记】 de(向下) + ject(投，掷)→向下投→使沮丧

【例】 He was *dejected* when she turned down his proposal. 当她拒绝了他的求婚时，他

很沮丧。

【同】 depress, dismay, discourage

【反】 encourage

【派】 dejected *adj*. 沮丧的，灰心的

delay [dɪˈleɪ] *v*. 耽搁，延迟

D

【记】 de(离开)+lay(搬运)→运往远处→耽搁

【例】 The breeding season of some plants can be *delayed* to extraordinary lengths. 一些植物的繁殖季节可以被拖得很长。

【同】 detain, postpone

【反】 hasten, hurry

delegate [ˈdelɪgət] *n*. 代表；*v*. 委派…做代表，授权

【记】 de(出去)+leg(任命)+ate(动词词尾)→任命派遣出去→委派…做代表

【例】 1. He was elected as a *delegate* to the annual conference. 他被选为年会代表。

2. The new manager was *delegated* to reorganize the department. 派这位新经理重新组织该部门。

【同】 representative, agent; assign, depute

【派】 delegation *n*. 代表团；授权，委托

delete [dɪˈliːt] *v*. 删除

【记】 delet(擦掉)+e→擦掉→删除

【例】 *Delete* his name from the list. 把他的名字从名单上删去。

【同】 erase, cancel

【派】 deletion *n*. 删除，删除部分

deliberate [dɪˈlɪbəreɪt] *adj*. 1. 周密计划的，蓄意的；2. 从容而谨慎的；*v*. 考虑，研究，讨论

【记】 de(完全，彻底)+liber(测量重量)+ate(动词词尾)→彻底地测量重量→考虑

【例】 1. It had more the appearance of a *deliberate* crime than an accident. 那很像是蓄意的罪行，而不像是意外的事故。

2. He entered the room with *deliberate* steps. 他从容不迫地走进室内。

3. The committee *deliberated* whether to approve our proposal. 委员会讨论是否批准我们的建议。

【同】 intentional, willful; careful; consider, think

【反】 impulsive

【派】 deliberately *adv*. 故意地

deliberation *n*. 熟思，商议，考虑

delicate [ˈdelɪkɪt] *adj*. 1. 柔软的，娇嫩的；2. 细致的，精密的

【记】 de(表强调)+lic(引诱)+ate(形容词词尾)→一再引诱人的→美好的→娇嫩的

【例】 1. Her *delicate* health needs great care. 她娇弱的身体需要小心照料。

2. The scientist needs some *delicate* instruments. 这位科学家需要一些精密的仪器。

【同】 fine, soft, tender, fragile

【反】 coarse, crude, rough

delicious [dɪˈlɪʃəs] *adj*. 美味的，好吃的

【记】 de(表强调)+lic(引诱)+ious(形容词词尾)→(食品)一再引诱人的→美味的

【例】 She can produce *delicious* meal from very simple ingredients. 她能用简单配料烹调出美味的饭菜。

【同】 tasty, toothsome

【反】 distasteful, tasteless

delineate [dɪˈlɪnɪeɪt] *v*. 1. 勾画，划出；2. 描述，刻画

【记】 de(表强调)+line(线)+ate(动词词尾)→一再划线→勾画

【例】 1. He *delineated* the State of Texas on the map with a red pencil. 他用红铅笔在地图上勾画出得克萨斯州的边界。

2. He *delineated* a few of his proposals for the budget. 他描述了他对预算的一些建议。

【同】 outline; describe, depict

【派】 delineation *n*. 勾画；描绘

delinquency [dɪˈlɪŋkwənsɪ] *n*. 行为不良，错失

【记】 de(离开)+linqu(=leave，离开)+ency(名词词尾)→离开(正务)→行为不良

【例】 Now she returned to the subject of juvenile *delinquency* in that country. 现在她又回过来讲那个国家少年犯罪的问题。

【派】 delinquent *n*. 失职者，违法者(特指少年犯罪)

delight [dɪˈlaɪt] *n*. 高兴，快乐；*v*. 使高兴，使快乐

【记】 de(表强调)+light(明亮)→使更明亮→使高兴

【例】 1. To our great *delight*, the day turned out fine. 我们感到高兴的是，天气转晴了。

2. Plato expressed the idea that humour is simply a *delighted* feeling of superiority over others. 柏拉图认为，幽默仅仅是一种因自己比他人优越而感到高兴的感觉。

【同】 pleasure, joy

【反】 grief, sadness, sorrow

【派】 delighted *adj*. 喜欢的，高兴的

delightful *adj*. 令人愉快的，可喜的

deliver [dɪˈlɪvə] *v*. 1. 传送，投递；2. 发表，宣布

【记】 de(出去)+liver(=liberate，自由)→把…放出去，使自由→传送

【例】 1. We *deliver* your order to your door! 我们送货上门！

2. She *delivered* a talk on philosophy to the society. 她给学会作了一次有关哲学的讲话。

【同】 transfer, send; express, say

【派】 delivery *n*. 投递，传送；讲话方式，风度

delude [dɪˈluːd] *v*. 欺骗，迷惑

【记】 de(表强调)+lude(游戏，玩)→玩耍，玩弄→欺骗

【例】 Candidates running for president often *delude* the voters with election promises. 参加总统竞选的候选人往往以竞选许诺来哄骗选民。

【同】 deceive, beguile, cozen

【派】 delusion *n*. 错觉，幻想

D

democratic [ˌdeməˈkrætɪk] *adj*. 民主的，民主主义的

【记】 dem(民众) + crat(统治) + ic(形容词词尾)→民众统治的→民主的

【例】 Many people were elected to take part in *democratic* involvement. 很多人被选举参与民主管理。

【反】 undemocratic

【派】 democracy *n*. 民主政治，民主主义

demographic [deməˈgræfɪk] *adj*. 人口的，人口统计的

【记】 demo(民众) + graph(写，记录) + ic(形容词词尾)→记录下民众的数目→人口统计的

【例】 Measures were designed to change the *demographic* composition. 改变人口组成的措施已经制定。

【派】 demography *n*. 人口学，人口统计学

demolish [dɪˈmɒlɪʃ] *v*. 破坏，摧毁

【记】 de(表否定) + mo(建设) + ish(动词词尾)→把建设好的变成相反的→破坏

【例】 They have *demolished* the slum district. 贫民区已被拆除。

【同】 destroy, dismantle, wreck

【派】 demolition *n*. 破坏，拆除

demonstrate [ˈdemənstreɪt] *v*. 1.示范，演示；2.证明，论证；3.示威

【记】 de(完全，充分) + monstr(表示) + ate(动词词尾)→充分表示→证明

【例】 1. An assistant *demonstrated* the washing machine to customers. 店员向顾客示范如何使用洗衣机。

2. How do you *demonstrate* that the pressure remains constant? 你怎样证明压力一直不变?

3. Thousands *demonstrated* against the price increases. 数以千计的人举行示威，抗议物价上涨。

【同】 display, illustrate, manifest

【派】 demonstration *n*. 示范，演示

denote [dɪˈnəʊt] *v*. 表示，是…的标志

【记】 de(下) + note(标示)→标示于下方→是…的标志

【例】 A smile often *denotes* pleasure and friendship. 微笑常常表示高兴和友善。

【同】 indicate, mean

【派】 denotable *adj*. 可指示的，可表示的

denotative *adj*. 指示的，外延的

denotation *n*. 指示

denounce [dɪˈnaʊns] *v*. 公开指责，谴责

【记】 de(下，贬低) + nounce(讲话，报告)→讲贬低人的话→公开指责

【例】 Union officials *denounced* the action as a breach of the agreement. 工会负责人谴责这一行动破坏了协议。

【同】 blame, condemn, reproach

【反】 praise

【派】 denouncement *n*. 指责，谴责

dense [dens] *adj*. 密集的，浓厚的

【例】 I can't see anything in this *dense* mist. 这样的浓雾里，我什么也看不见。

【同】 compact, thick

【反】 sparse, thin, weak

【派】 density *n*. 稠密，密度

deny [dɪ'naɪ] *v*. 否认，拒绝

【例】 The accused man *denies* that he has ever met her. 被告否认他曾经遇到过她。

【同】 refuse, reject

【反】 admit, affirm, confirm

【派】 denial *n*. 否认，拒绝

depart [dɪ'pɑːt] *v*. 走开，离开

【记】 de(= dis, 分开) + part(部分)→部分分开→离开

【例】 The 10:15 train to Leeds *departs* from platform 4. 10点15分开往利兹的火车从第四站台开出。

【同】 leave, go, exit

【反】 arrive, stay

【派】 departure *n*. 离开，离去

depict [dɪ'pɪkt] *v*. 描绘，描述，描写

【记】 de(完全，充分) + (描画)→充分描画→描写

【例】 The drawing *depicts* her sitting on a sofa. 这幅画画的是她坐在沙发上的姿势。

【同】 describe, illustrate, portray

【派】 depiction *n*. 描写，叙述

deplete [dɪ'pliːt] *v*. 大量削减，使衰竭

【记】 de(离开) + plete(充满)→从充满的状态下取走→耗尽

【例】 Our stock of food is greatly *depleted*. 我们的食物储备已消耗殆尽。

【同】 consume, exhaust

【反】 renew

【派】 depletion *n*. 削减，消耗

deploy [dɪ'plɔɪ] *v*. 部署，调度

【记】 de(= dis, 分开) + ploy(折叠)→将折叠的东西分开→部署

【例】 The infantry began to *deploy* at dawn. 步兵黎明时开始进入战斗位置。

【同】 distribute, arrange, position

【派】 deployment *n*. 部署

deposit [dɪ'pɒzɪt] *v*. 1.(淤泥等)沉积，堆积；2.存放，储蓄；*n*. 存款，保证金，押金

【记】 de(向下) + posit(放置)→放置于下方→沉积

【例】 1. The Nile floods the fields and *deposits* mud on them. 尼罗河泛滥，在田野上淤积了一层泥。

2. He *deposits* a sum of money in the bank each month. 他每月在银行存一笔钱。

3. I had to pay a 500 *deposit* to the landlord before I could move into the house. 我得付给房东500英镑押金才能搬进房里去。

【同】 lay, place, store; bank

【派】 deposition *n*. 沉积作用，沉积物
depository *n*. 存放处

deprave [dɪˈpreɪv] *v*. 使堕落，使道德败坏
【记】 de(向下)+prave(欺骗的，狡猾的)→欺骗使堕落→使堕落
【例】 Do you believe that these films are likely to *deprave* young people? 你认为这些影片会使年轻人堕落吗?
【同】 corrupt, debase, demoralize
【反】 improve
【派】 depravation *n*. 堕落
depraved *adj*. 堕落的，颓废的，邪恶的

deprecate [ˈdeprɪkeɪt] *v*. 不赞成，反对
【记】 de(去掉)+prec(=pray，祈祷)+ate(动词词尾)→祈祷去掉…→反对
【例】 He *deprecates* changing the party's policy. 他不赞成改变党的方针。
【同】 disapprove, reject
【派】 deprecation *n*. 强烈不赞成，反对

depreciate [dɪˈpriːʃɪeɪt] *v*. 1. 贬值；2. 贬低，轻视
【记】 de(向下)+preci(价值)+ate(动词词尾)→降低…的价值→贬值
【例】 1. Our currency will not be *depreciated*. 我们的货币不会贬值。
2. Don't *depreciate* my efforts to help. 不要轻视我为帮忙所付出的努力。
【同】 devaluate; deprecate
【反】 appreciate
【派】 depreciation *n*. 贬值，轻视

depress [dɪˈpres] *v*. 1. 使沮丧，使消沉；2. 使萧条，削弱
【记】 de(向下)+press(压)→向下压→使消沉
【例】 1. They become so *depressed* and lacking in energy that their work and social life are affected. 他们变得非常郁闷，无精打采，以至于他们的工作和社交生活都受到了影响。
2. The threat of war has *depressed* business activity. 战争的威胁使经济萧条。
【同】 discourage, dispirit, dismay
【反】 encourage, inspire, cheer
【派】 depression *n*. 沮丧，消沉；萧条；低气压，低压

deprive [dɪˈpraɪv] *v*. 夺去，使丧失
【记】 de(=dis，离开)+prive(单个，私有)→从个人身边拿走→剥夺
【例】 If you do not drive carefully, I shall be obliged to *deprive* your licence. 如果您不谨慎驾驶，我将不得不没收您的执照。
【同】 dispossess, divest
【派】 deprivation *n*. 缺乏；剥夺

deputy [ˈdepjʊtɪ] *n*. 代理人，代表
adj. 代理的，副的
【记】 de(向下)+put(思考)+y(名词词尾)→把自己的想法置于其下→代表
【例】 1. I'm acting as *deputy* till the headmaster returns. 我在校长回来前代行他的

职务。

2. By convention the *deputy* leader is always a woman. 按照惯例这一领导人的副职总是由女子担任。

【同】 agent, delegate, representative; assistant

deride [dɪˈraɪd] *v*. 讥讽，嘲笑

【记】 de(表强调)+rid(笑)+e→笑…→嘲笑

【例】 He *derides* her naive attitude. 他嘲弄她天真的态度。

【同】 mock

【派】 derision *n*. 嘲笑

derive [dɪˈraɪv] *v*. 得自，起源于

【记】 de(离开)+rive(溪流)→从河里引水→起源

【例】 Thousands of English words *derive* from Latin. 英语中有成千上万的词源自拉丁文。

【同】 acquire, obtain, originate

【派】 derivative *n*. 派生的事物，派生词

descend [dɪˈsend] *v*. 1. 下来，下降；2. 传下，遗传

【记】 de(向下)+scend(爬，登)→向下爬→下降

【例】 1. The balloon *descended* gradually as the air came out. 气球空气外溢而缓缓下降。

2. The title *descends* to me from my father. 这个头衔是由我父亲传给我的。

【同】 decline, drop, fall

【反】 ascend, rise

【派】 descent *n*. 降下，降落；世系，血统

descendant *n*. 子孙，后裔

desert [dɪˈzɜːt] *v*. 离弃，抛弃

【记】 de(离开)+sert(结合)→脱离结合→离弃

【例】 He *deserted* his wife and children and went abroad. 他抛弃了妻子儿女，出国去了。

【同】 abandon, forsake

【派】 deserted *adj*. 荒芜的，荒废的

deserve [dɪˈzɜːv] *v*. 值得，应得

【记】 de(完全，充分)+serve(服务)→给以充分服务→值得(重视)

【例】 The article *deserves* careful study. 这篇文章值得仔细研究。

【同】 earn, merit

【派】 deserving *adj*. 应得的，该受奖赏的

designate [ˈdezɪneɪt] *v*. 指定，指派

【记】 de(向下)+sign(做记号)+ate(动词词尾)→在下面做上记号→指定

【例】 The chairman has *designated* Christina as his successor. 主席已指定克里斯蒂娜做他的继任人。

【同】 assign, appoint, nominate

【派】 designation *n*. 指定，选派；名称

desire [dɪˈzaɪə] *n*./*v*. 愿望，欲望，要求

【例】 1. I am filled with *desire* to go back home. 我心中充满了回家的渴望。

2. We all *desire* happiness. 我们都渴望幸福。

【同】 lust, want, wish

【反】 disappoint, despair

【派】 desirable *adj*. 令人渴望的，可取的

desirous *adj*. 渴望的

desist [dɪ'zɪst] *v*. 停止，中止

【记】 de(向下)+sist(停留)→停留下来→停止

【例】 I wish he'd *desist* from entertaining his friends at all hours of the day and night. 但愿他别再昼夜不分地招待他的朋友。

【同】 cease, end, halt, stop

【反】 continue

【派】 desistance *n*. 停止，断念

desolate ['desəlɪt] *adj*. 1.(地方)荒凉的；2.孤独凄凉的，不幸的；*v*. 使凄惨，使忧伤

【记】 de(加强语气)+sol(孤独)+ate(动词兼形容词词尾)→孤独的→凄凉的

【例】 1. The forest looked *desolate* after the fire. 火灾后，整个森林看起来很荒凉。

2. We all felt absolutely *desolate* when she left. 她走后，我们都觉得万分孤寂。

3. She was *desolated* by his death. 他的去世使她极为忧伤。

【同】 barren, bleak

【派】 desolation *n*. 荒芜，荒废；忧伤，悲哀

desperate ['despərɪt] *adj*. 不顾一切的，拼死的，绝望的

【记】 de(去掉)+sper(希望)+ate(形容词词尾)→去掉希望→绝望的

【例】 He was rifling through her desk in a *desperate* search for the letter. 他拼命在她的书桌里搜寻那封信。

【同】 despairing, mad, wild

【反】 hopeful

【派】 desperation *n*. 绝望

despise [dɪs'paɪz] *v*. 轻视，鄙视

【记】 de(向下)+spise(=spic，看)→向下看→轻视，鄙视

【例】 I *despise* his refusing to accept responsibility. 他拒不承担责任，我鄙视他。

【同】 contemn, disdain, scorn

【反】 appreciate, respect, value

【派】 despicable *adj*. 可鄙的，卑劣的

despoil [dɪs'pɔɪl] *v*. 夺取，掠夺

【记】 de(离开)+spoil(剥夺)→拿走→掠夺

【例】 Museums have *despoiled* India of many priceless treasures. 博物馆里有许多从印度掠夺来的无价之宝。

【同】 loot, plunder, rob

【派】 despoiler *n*. 掠夺者

dessert [dɪ'zɜːt] *n*. 甜点，饭后点心

【记】 des(=dis，不)+sert(=serve，服务)→不服务了(甜点是最后上的)→甜点

【例】 Then for *dessert* there's traditional plum pudding or apple pie, plus coffee. 然后就是饭后甜点，有传统的李子布丁、苹果馅饼，还有咖啡。

【同】 afters

destination [ˌdestɪˈneɪʃən] *n*. 目的地，终点

【记】 de(离开)+stin(站)+ation(名词词尾)→站到远处的地方→目的地

【例】 Once a location is established as a main tourist *destination*, the effects on the local community are profound. 一旦某个地区被确定为主要的旅游目的地，就会给当地生活带来深远的影响。

【同】 end, goal, terminus

destiny [ˈdestɪnɪ] *n*. 命运，定数

【记】 de(离开)+stin(站)+y(名词词尾)→站到远处的地方→最终的→命运

【例】 *Destiny* drew us together. 命运把我们连在一起了。

【同】 fate, fortune

【派】 (逆构)destine *v*. 注定，命定

destruction [dɪsˈtrʌkʃən] *n*. 破坏，毁灭

【记】 de(向下)+struct(建筑)+ion(名词词尾)→使建筑物倒下→破坏

【例】 The *destruction* of these big forests could have serious ecological consequences. 这些大森林的毁坏会带来生态上的严重后果。

【同】 devastation, ruin

【反】 construction, establishment

【派】 destructive *adj*. 破坏性的，毁灭性的

detach [dɪˈtætʃ] *v*. 1.(将连接的部分)分离，分开；2.分遣，派遣(军队)

【记】 de(分开)+tach(拴)→把拴的分开→分离

【例】 1. You can *detach* the handle by undoing this screw. 你拧开螺丝钉就可拆下把手。
2. A number of men were *detached* to guard the right flank. 派遣了一些士兵守卫右翼。

【同】 disconnect, separate

【反】 attach

【派】 detached *adj*. 分开的，分离的；超然的，冷淡的

detain [dɪˈteɪn] *v*. 1.使延迟；2.拘留，扣押

【记】 de(加强语气)+tain(拿，抓)→抓住→拘留

【例】 1. She was *detained* in the office by unexpected callers. 有些临时访客把她耽搁在办公室里了。
2. The police *detained* him for questioning. 警方对他进行拘留审问。

【同】 delay; confine

【反】 free, liberate

detect [dɪˈtekt] *v*. 发现，查明

【记】 de(离开)+tect(遮蔽)→拿走遮蔽物→发现

【例】 They *detected* no defect in the product. 他们没发现产品有任何问题。

【同】 discover, find

【反】 conceal, hide

【派】 detective *n*. 侦探；*adj*. 侦探的，侦查的

detectable *adj*. 可发觉的；可查明的

deter [dɪˈtɜː] *v*. (-rred; -rring)使不敢，阻止

【记】 de(加强语气)+ter(使害怕)→使害怕而退缩→阻止

【例】 Failure did not *deter* him from making another attempt. 他并未因失败而畏缩不前。

【同】 discourage, hinder, prevent

【反】 encourage

【派】 deterrent *n*. 制止物，威慑力量

detergent [dɪˈtɜːdʒənt] *n*. 清洁剂

【记】 de(去掉)+terg(擦)+ent(名词词尾)→把脏污擦掉用的东西→清洁剂

【例】 Be careful to rinse the *detergent* from these dishes. 注意务必冲洗掉这些盘子上的清洁剂。

【同】 cleanser, detersive

deteriorate [dɪˈtɪərɪəreɪt] *v*. 恶化，变坏，质量(或价值)下降

【记】 deterior(=worse，更坏)+ate(动词词尾)→使更坏→恶化

【例】 Relations between the two countries have *deteriorate* sharply in recent weeks. 最近几周那两个国家间的关系严重恶化了。

【同】 degenerate, worsen

【反】 improve

【派】 deterioration *n*. 变坏，退化，堕落

determine [dɪˈtɜːmɪn] *v*. 决定，决心

【记】 de(完全，充分)+termine(结束，边界)→定出清楚的界限→决定

【例】 Before entry to the school, students must take an entry test to *determine* the level of class they enter. 入学之前，学生要先参加入学考试，然后决定他们在哪一个等级的班级就读。

【同】 decide, resolve

【派】 determination *n*. 决心，果断

determinant *n*. 决定因素

detest [dɪˈtest] *v*. 深恶，憎恶

【记】 de(离开)+test(作证)→字面意义是远离作证，实际上是指召唤神祇作证来诅咒→憎恶

【例】 She *detests* having to talk to people at parties. 她讨厌在宴会上为应酬而和人交谈。

【同】 despise, dislike, hate

【反】 adore, love

detract [dɪˈtrækt] *v*. 诽谤，贬低

【记】 de(向下)+tract(拉)→向下拉→贬低

【例】 All the decoration *detracts* from the beauty of the building's shape. 这一切装饰有损于大厦的外形美。

【派】 detraction *n*. 诽谤

detriment ['detrɪmənt] *n*. 伤害，危害

【记】 de(离开) + tri(摩擦) + ment(名词词尾)→擦掉→危害

【例】 This tax can not be introduced without *detriment* to the economy.
这一税收制度一旦施行，必定会危害国民经济。

【同】 hurt，harm

【派】 detrimental *adj*. 有害的

devastate ['devəsteɪt] *v*. 毁坏，摧毁

【记】 de(完全) + vast(= waste，荒废的) + ate(动词词尾)→使完全荒废的→毁坏

【例】 War *devastated* the country. 战争摧毁了这个国家。

【同】 crush

【派】 devastating *adj*. 破坏性的，毁灭性的
devastation *n*. 毁坏

develop [dɪ'veləp] *v*. 1.发展，开发；2.展开，详细阐述；3.逐渐产生，培养起来

【记】 de(去掉) + velop(包，裹)→把包的东西去掉→开发，展开

【例】 1. From small beginnings it has *developed* into a big multinational company. 它开始规模很小，现已发展成一家大型跨国公司。
2. I'd like to *develop* this idea a little more fully before I go on to my next point. 在谈下一点之前，我想把这一想法进一步阐述一下。
3. She has *developed* an interest in international affairs. 她对国际事物逐渐产生了兴趣。

【同】 advance，progress；elaborate，explicate；acquire，train

【反】 decay

【派】 development *n*. 发展，开发；形成，出现

deviate ['diːvɪeɪt] *v*. 离开，偏离

【记】 de(离开) + vi(路) + ate(动词词尾)→离开原来的路→偏离

【例】 She never *deviates* from her regular habits. 她从不偏离自己的日常习惯。

【同】 diverge，divert

【反】 conform

【派】 deviation *n*. 背离

device [dɪ'vaɪs] *n*. 1.设备，装置；2.策略，方法

【记】 de(完全，充分) + vice(= vise，看)→用来充分看的东西→装置

【例】 1. The missile has a heat-seeking *device* which enables it to find its target. 导弹里有一种热跟踪装置使它能找到目标。
2. They use television advertising as a *device* for stimulating demand. 他们利用电视广告作为刺激需求的方法。

【同】 apparatus，equipment；manoeuvre，tactic

devise [dɪ'vaɪz] *v*. 设计，发明，策划

【记】 de(完全，充分) + vise(看)→充分看→策划

【例】 The government *devised* a scheme for redeveloping the city center. 政府制定了市中心重建计划。

【同】 contrive，create，invent

devoid [dɪˈvɔɪd] *adj*. 全无的，缺乏的

【记】 de(加强语气) + void(空)→完全空的→全无的

【例】 The article is *devoid* of substantial matter. 这篇文章缺乏实质性的内容。

【同】 lacking, empty, vacant

devote [dɪˈvəʊt] *v*. 1. 把…专用于；2. 投身于，献身于

【记】 de(加强语气) + vote(发誓)→拼命发誓→献身

【例】 1. Beforehand, several months were *devoted* to planning, and there was also a training period of approximately six months. 之前有几个月专门用于制定计划，还有大约半年的培训期。

2. He *devoted* himself entirely to music. 他将一生奉献给了音乐。

【同】 apply; dedicate

【派】 devotee *n*. 皈依者，狂热者

devotion *n*. 热爱，忠诚

devour [dɪˈvaʊə] *v*. 贪婪地吃，吞食

【记】 de(加强语气) + vour(吃)→大口地吃→吞食

【例】 The flames *devoured* the entire building. 火焰吞没了整栋大楼。

【同】 swallow, gulp

devout [dɪˈvaʊt] *adj*. 虔诚的，诚恳的

【记】 de(加强语气) + vout(= vot, 发誓)→发誓的→虔诚的

【例】 She was a *devout* catholic. 她曾是个虔诚的天主教徒。

【同】 earnest, pious

dexterous [ˈdekstərəs] *adj*. 灵巧的，熟练的

【记】 dexter(右手的) + ous(形容词词尾)→用右手的→灵巧的

【例】 She untied the knots with *dexterous* fingers. 她用灵巧的手指解开绳结。

【同】 adroit, deft, handy

【反】 awkward, clumsy, unskillful

【派】 dexterity *n*. 灵巧，机敏

diagnose [ˈdaɪəgnəʊz] *v*. 诊断，判断

【记】 dia(通过) + gnose(知道)→通过…而得知→诊断

【例】 The doctor *diagnosed* measles. 医生诊断出麻疹。

【同】 deduce, analyse

【派】 diagnosis *n*. (复数-ses)诊断

diagram [ˈdaɪəgræm] *n*. 图表，图解

【记】 dia(通过，穿过) + gram(书写)→从这边画到那边→交叉着画→图表

【例】 He pointed at the *diagram* to illustrate his point. 他指着图表来说明他的论点。

【同】 illustration, drawing

dialect [ˈdaɪəlekt] *n*. 方言，语调

【记】 dia(在…之间) + lect(说，讲)→在一部分人之间说的话→方言

【例】 The *dialect* is spoken principally in the rural areas. 这种方言主要在农村地区使用。

【同】 accent

dialogue ['daɪəlɒg] *n*. (US dialog)对话，(小说、戏剧中的)对白

【记】 dia(在…之间)+logue(说话)→在两人之间的谈话→对话

【例】 Most plays are written in *dialogue*. 大多数戏剧都是用对话体写的。

【同】 conversation

diameter [daɪ'æmɪtə] *n*. 直径

【记】 dia(通过，穿过)+meter(测量)→从这边量到那边→直径

【例】 The *diameter* of the tree-trunk is about 2 meters. 这树干的直径大约是2米。

【反】 radius(半径)

dictate [dɪk'teɪt] *v*. 1.独裁，强令；2.听写，口授

【记】 dict(说)+ate(动词词尾)→说话→口授，命令

【例】 1. The victorious nations were able to *dictate* peace terms. 战胜国能够在制定和平条款上说了算。

2. The teacher *dictated* a passage to the class. 老师给全班同学听写了一段文章。

【同】 demand, instruct, order

【反】 obey, submit

【派】 dictation *n*. 听写，口述

dictator *n*. 独裁者，口授令他人笔录者

dictatorial *adj*. 独裁的，专断的

dictatorship *n*. 独裁政治，专政

diet ['daɪət] *n*. 饮食，食谱，通常吃的食物；*v*. 节食，吃限定食物

【例】 1. Proper *diet* and exercise are both important for health. 适当的饮食和运动对身体健康都很重要。

2. You ought to *diet* and take more exercise. 你应该节食并多做运动。

【派】 dietary *adj*. 饮食的，有关饮食的

dietician *n*. 饮食学家，膳食学家

dietectics *n*. 营养学

differ ['dɪfə] *v*. 有区别，持不同看法

【记】 dif(=dis, 分开)+fer(运，拿)→一个一个分别搬运→区别

【例】 If archaeology deals with the past, in what way does it *differ* from history? 如果考古学研究的是过去，那么它和历史的区别是什么呢？

【同】 disagree, vary

differentiate [ˌdɪfə'renʃɪeɪt] *v*. 区别，区分

【记】 dif(=dis, 分开)+fer(运，拿)+ent(形容词词尾)+iate(动词词尾)→分别搬往不同的地方→区别

【例】 It is wrong to *differentiate* between people according to their family background. 根据出身不同而区别待人是不对的。

【同】 distinguish, separate

【派】 differentiation *n*. 区别

diffidence ['dɪfɪdəns] *n*. 缺乏自信

【记】 dif(=dis, 离开)+fid(信心)+ence(名词词尾)→离开自信→缺乏自信

【例】 It is with *diffidence* and hesitation that I approach this work. 我是带着懦怯和犹

D

像接近这部作品的。
【同】 self-distrust，self-doubt
【反】 assurance，confidence
【派】 diffident *adj*. 羞怯的，缺乏自信的

diffuse [dɪ'fjuːz] *v*. 传播，扩散
【记】 dif(= dis，分开) + fuse(倾倒)→注入不同的地方→传播，扩散
【例】 A drop of milk *diffused* in the water, and it became cloudy. 一滴奶在水中扩散开来，使水变得混浊不清了。
【同】 distribute，spread
【派】 diffusible *adj*. 可传播的，扩散性的
diffusion *n*. 扩散，传播

digest [daɪ'dʒest] *v*. 消化(食物)；*n*. 文摘，摘要
【记】 di(= dis，分开) + gest(运，载)→分开搬运→分解成块→消化
【例】 1. This rich food doesn't *digest* easily. 这种油腻的食物不易消化。
2. This is a thirty-page *digest* of the news. 这是一份 30 页的新闻简报。
【同】 absorb；summary
【反】 indigest
【派】 digestive *adj*. 消化的，有消化力的
digestion *n*. 消化力，领悟

digital ['dɪdʒɪtl] *adj*. 数字的
【记】 digit(数字) + al(形容词词尾)→数字的
【例】 Most of the computers we are using are *digital* computers. 我们正在使用的计算机大多数是数字计算机。
【同】 numeral
【派】 (逆构)digit *n*. 阿拉伯数字
digitize *v*. 使数字化

dignify ['dɪgnɪfaɪ] *v*. 使尊荣，使显贵
【记】 dign(价值) + ify(动词词尾)→使有价值→使尊荣
【例】 The broad steps in front of the mansion made it look very *dignified*. 宽阔的台阶使大厦的正面显得有气派。
【同】 ennoble，honor
【反】 humiliate，disgrace，dishonor
【派】 dignified *adj*. 有尊严的，庄严的，高贵的
dignity *n*. 尊严，高贵

digress [daɪ'gres] *v*. 离开本题
【记】 di(= dis，离开) + gress(走)→走开→离开本题
【例】 I'll tell you a funny story, if I may *digress* for a moment. 如果我可以暂时离开一下话题，我将讲一个有趣的故事给你听。
【同】 stray，divagate
【派】 digression *n*. 离题，扯到枝节上
digressive *adj*. 离题的，枝节的

dilate [daɪˈleɪt] *v*. 使膨胀，使扩大

【记】 di(离开) + lat(线，边) + e→把边缘扩到远处→使扩大

【例】 The pupils of your eyes *dilate* when you enter a dark room. 进入黑暗的房间时，瞳孔就会扩大。

【同】 enlarge, expand, magnify, widen

【派】 dilation *n*. 膨胀，扩张，扩大

dilemma [dɪˈlemə] *n*. 进退两难的困境

【记】 di(二) + lemma(假设)→在两项假设之间→进退两难的困境

【例】 Faced with that *dilemma*, he was perplexed. 他面对进退两难的局面，不知如何是好。

【同】 quandary

diligent [ˈdɪlɪdʒənt] *adj*. 勤勉的，勤奋的

【记】 di(= dis, 分开) + lig(选择) + ent(形容词词尾)→很快地选出来→勤勉的

【例】 She is more *diligent* than any other students in her class. 她是班上最用功的学生。

【同】 industrious

【反】 idle, lazy

【派】 diligence *n*. 勤奋

dilute [daɪˈljuːt] *v*. 稀释，淡化

【记】 di(= dis, 分开) + lut(洗) + e→洗掉→稀释

【例】 The nurse *diluted* the drug with saline water. 护士用生理盐水把药加以稀释。

【同】 adulterate

【反】 concentrate

【派】 diluter *n*. 稀释剂

dilution *n*. 稀释，稀释法

dim [dɪm] *adj*. 暗淡的，模糊的

【例】 The light was too *dim* for me to read easily. 光线太暗，我看书有困难。

【同】 darkish, faint, indistinct, vague

【反】 bright, light

dimension [dɪˈmenʃən] *n*. 1.尺寸，大小；2.方面

【记】 di(= dis, 分开) + mens(测量) + ion(名词词尾)→分开测量→尺寸，大小

【例】 1. What are the *dimensions* of the room? 这房间的面积是多少？

2. There is a *dimension* to the problem that we have not discussed. 这问题还有一方面我们没讨论过。

【同】 measurement, size

diminish [dɪˈmɪnɪʃ] *v*. 减少，缩减，降低

【记】 di(= dis, 分开) + min(小的) + ish(动词词尾)→分别变小→减少

【例】 His strength has *diminished* over the years. 经过这许多年月，他的体力不如从前了。

【同】 decrease, lessen, reduce

【反】 increase, raise

dingy [ˈdɪndʒɪ] *adj*. 1.肮脏的；2.颜色发暗的，无光泽的

【记】 ding(= dung，粪便) + y(形容词词尾)→肮脏的
【例】 1. The clothes were *dingy* and needed bleaching. 这些衣服很脏，需要漂白一下。
2. Rooms in cheap hotels are often *dingy*. 在低级旅馆中全是又黑又脏的房间。
【同】 dirty，grimy；dark，dull
【反】 clean

diploma [dɪˈpləʊmə] *n*. 毕业文凭，学位证书
【记】 di(二) + ploma(折叠的)→折叠的纸→证书，文凭
【例】 The college was nothing more than a *diploma* mill. 这个学院只不过是个文凭制造厂。
【同】 certificate

diplomat [ˈdɪpləmæt] *n*. 外交官，外交家
【记】 di(二) + ploma(折叠的) + t(名词词尾)→拿着折叠的纸的人→外交官
【例】 The *diplomat* solved the international problem by negotiating. 外交官通过谈判解决了那个国际问题。
【同】 envoy
【派】 diplomacy 外交，外交手段
diplomatic *adj*. 外交的，老练的

disable [dɪsˈeɪbl] *v*. 使丧失能力，使残废
【记】 dis(分开，除去) + able(能力)→除去能力→使丧失能力
【例】 He was *disabled* from walking by the accident. 由于车祸，他不能走路了。
【同】 disenable，cripple
【反】 enable
【派】 disabled *adj*. 伤残的，残疾的
disability *n*. 残疾，伤残

disadvantage [ˌdɪsədˈvɑːntɪdʒ] *n*. 劣势，短处
【记】 dis(表否定，不) + advantage(优点，优势)→劣势
【例】 The other candidate's main *disadvantage* is her age. 另一候选人的主要不利条件是她的年龄问题。
【同】 handicap，inconvenience
【反】 advantage

disappoint [ˌdɪsəˈpɔɪnt] *v*. 使失望，使扫兴
【记】 dis(离开) + appoint(指派)→不被指派→失望
【例】 I can't *disappoint* my public by retiring. 我可不能退休，否则大家会失望的。
【同】 displease，dissatisfy，dismay
【反】 encourage
【派】 disappointment *n*. 失望

disapprove [ˌdɪsəˈpruːv] *v*. 不赞成，不同意
【记】 dis(不) + approve(同意)→不同意
【例】 She wants to be an actress, but her parents *disapprove* of her intentions. 她想当演员，但她父母不赞成她的想法。
【同】 disagree，object，oppose

【反】 approve，agree

【派】 disapproval *n*. 不赞成

disarm [dɪsˈɑːm] *v*. 1. 缴械，解除武装；2. 缓和，消除(敌意、疑虑等)

【记】 dis(去掉) + arm(武器)→去掉武器→解除武装

【例】 1. Five hundred rebels were captured and *disarmed*. 500 名造反者被俘获并缴了械。

2. We didn't trust him at first，but his charming manner completely *disarmed* us. 我们开始时并不信任他，但他令人愉快的举止完全消除了我们的疑虑。

【同】 demilitarize

【反】 arm

【派】 disarming *adj*. 使解除警戒心的，消除敌意的

disarrange [ˌdɪsəˈreɪndʒ] *v*. 打乱，搅乱

【记】 dis(离开) + arrange(排列)→离开排列→打乱

【例】 Her sudden departure has *disarranged* my plans. 她突然离去，打乱了我的计划。

【同】 disarray，disorder

【反】 arrange

disarray [ˌdɪsəˈreɪ] *n*. 混乱，漫无秩序

【记】 dis(离开) + array(排列)→离开排列→混乱

【例】 Changing offices has left my papers in complete *disarray*. 办公室搬迁，使我的文件全部乱了套了。

【同】 confusion，disorder

【反】 order

disaster [dɪˈzɑːstə] *n*. 灾难，灾祸

【记】 dis(离开) + aster(星)→原意是注定命运的星宿已离开，人就要遭不幸→灾难

【例】 Losing your job needn't be such a *disaster*. 你不必把丢了工作看成是大难临头。

【同】 calamity，catastrophe，tragedy

【反】 fortune

【派】 disastrous *adj*. 灾难性的，悲惨的

disburse [dɪsˈbɜːs] *v*. 支付，支出

【记】 dis(离开) + burse(袋子，钱包)→从钱包拿出(钱)→支付

【例】 Salaries are *disbursed* by the paymaster's office. 薪水由出纳室发放。

【同】 pay out，expend

discard [dɪsˈkɑːd] *v*. 丢弃，抛弃

【记】 dis(离开，丢开) + card(纸牌)→丢出无用的纸牌→抛弃

【例】 We *discarded* some old clothes. 我们扔了一些旧衣服。

【同】 abandon，desert，throw away

discern [dɪˈsɜːn] *v*. 看出，觉察，识别

【记】 dis(分开) + scern(分离)→一个一个分开→识别

【例】 In the gloom I could only just *discern* the outline of a building. 在黑暗中我只能依稀分辨出一座建筑物的轮廓来。

【同】 distinguish，detect，recognize

D

【派】 discerning *adj*. 眼力好的，有洞察力的
discernment *n*. 辨别(力)，眼力
discernible *adj*. 可识别的

discharge [dɪsˈtʃɑːdʒ] *v*. 1. 卸下，放出；2. 准许离开

【记】 dis(离开)+charge(车)→离开车→卸掉

【例】 1. How long will the *discharge* of the cargo take? 卸货需要多久？
2. The accused man was found not guilty and *discharged*. 被告男子被判无罪而获释。

【同】 dump，unload；dismiss，release

【反】 load，charge

discipline [ˈdɪsɪplɪn] *n*. 1. 纪律；2. 学科，科目

【例】 1. The teacher can't keep *discipline* in her class. 那位老师无法维持教室纪律。
2. How does archaeology relate to *disciplines* such as anthropology and history, that are also concerned with the human story? 考古学与人类学、历史学之类同样和人类历史有关的学科有什么联系呢？

【同】 subject(学科)

【反】 indiscipline

【派】 disciplinary *adj*. 训练的，纪律的

disclaim [dɪsˈkleɪm] *v*. 放弃权利，否认

【记】 dis(表否定)+claim(喊叫)→喊叫不要→否认

【例】 The manufacturers *disclaim* all responsibility for the damage caused by misuse. 因使用不当造成的损坏，生产厂家不负任何责任。

【同】 deny，refuse，reject

【反】 claim

discord [ˈdɪskɔːd] *n*. 不一致，不协调

【记】 dis(离开)+cord(心脏)→心意不同→不一致

【例】 Various *discords* have arisen over this question. 人们在这个问题上发生了不少争执。

【同】 disagreement，dissonance

【反】 accord，agreement，harmony

【派】 discordant *adj*. 不一致的，不调和的

discount [ˈdɪskaʊnt] *n*. 折扣，打折；*v*. 不重视，不相信，不理会

【记】 dis(去掉)+conunt(数，计算)→计算时去掉→折扣

【例】 1. We give (a) 10% *discount* for cash. 现金付款，我们予以九折优惠。
2. You can *discount* what Jack said; he's a dreadful liar. 杰克说的话你不必当真，他可是个说谎大王。

【同】 reduction，decrease；ignore

【反】 premium

discourse [dɪsˈkɔːs，ˈdɪskɔːs] *n*. 1. 交谈，谈话；2. 讲道，演讲

【记】 dis(离开)+course(流)→流向不同的方向→交谈

【例】 1. The judges had solemn *discourse* together. 法官们在一起严肃地交谈。

2. They listened to his *discourse* on human relations. 他们听他作关于人际关系的演讲。

【同】 conversation, talk; lecture, speech, preach

discreet [dɪ'skriːt] *adj*. 言谈举止谨慎的，慎重的

【记】 dis(分开) + creet(区分)→区分开来的→慎重的

【例】 Be more *discreet* or you'll get yourself talked about. 要更谨慎些——否则你就会成为人们的话柄。

【同】 cautious, prudent, thoughtful

【反】 indiscreet

【派】 discretion *n*. 辨别(力)，判断(力)；自行处理，自行决定

discrete [dɪ'skriːt] *adj*. 分离的，离散的

【记】 dis(分开) + cret(区分) + e→一个一个分开的→分离的

【例】 The picture consisted of a lot of *discrete* spots of color. 这幅画由许多互不相连的色点组成。

【同】 distinct, separate

discriminate [dɪs'krɪmɪneɪt] *v*. 分别，区分，歧视

【记】 dis(分开) + crimin(空间) + ate(动词词尾)→在…之间造空间→区别待遇

【例】 Society still *discriminates* against women. 社会上仍然歧视女性。

【同】 separate, distinguish

【派】 discrimination *n*. 辨别(力)，区别，歧视

disdain [dɪs'deɪn] *v*. 轻视，忽视

【记】 dis(离开) + dain(= dign，价值)→不承认其价值→轻视

【例】 He *disdained* that man for snobbishness and was unwilling to talk to him. 他鄙视那个势利小人，不愿和他说话。

【同】 despise, scorn

【反】 admire, respect

【派】 disdainful *adj*. 轻蔑的，倨傲的

disgruntled [dɪs'grʌntəld] *adj*. 不高兴的，不满意的

【记】 dis(表否定) + grunt(咕哝) + le(表示动作的反复) + (e)d(形容词词尾)→一直咕哝的→不满意的

【例】 She's still *disgruntled* about missing the party. 她因错过了这一聚会而仍耿耿于怀。

【同】 dissatisfied, discontented

【反】 satisfied, contented

disguise [dɪs'gaɪz] *n*./*v*. 假装，掩饰

【记】 dis(分开) + guise(举止)→改变行为→假装

【例】 The raiders *disguised* themselves as security guards. 袭击者都装扮成了保安人员。

【同】 camouflage, conceal

【派】 disguiser *n*. 伪装者，假装者

disgust [dɪsgʌstɪŋ] *v*. 令人厌恶，令人作呕

【记】 dis(离开) + gust(品尝) + →不能品尝→令人恶心，令人厌恶

【例】 The use of torture must *disgust* any civilized person. 施用酷刑必为文明社会的人所不齿。
【同】 distasteful, loathsome
【反】 pleasing, delightful
【派】 disgusting *adj*. 令人厌恶的，令人反感的

disillusion [ˌdɪsɪˈluːʒən] *v*. 使醒悟，使不再抱幻想
【记】 dis(离开)+illusion(幻想)→离开幻想→幻想破灭
【例】 She still believes in Santa Claus and it would be cruel to *disillusion* her. 她仍然相信有圣诞老人，要是使她这一幻想破灭就于心不忍了。
【同】 disenchant
【派】 disillusionment *n*. 幻灭，觉醒

dismal [ˈdɪzməl] *adj*. 1. 暗的，凄凉的；2. 忧郁的，沮丧的
【记】 dis(=di，日，日子)+mal(坏)→日子坏的、不吉利的→昏暗的
【例】 1. We were all depressed by the *dismal* weather. 阴沉的天气让我们都感到压抑。
2. The future looks pretty *dismal*. 前景看来相当暗淡。
【同】 bleak, dark, gloomy; depressing, miserable
【反】 cheerful, merry

dismantle [dɪsˈmæntl] *v*. 拆开，拆除
【记】 dis(去掉)+mantle(披风，引申为覆盖)→去掉覆盖→拆开
【例】 This toy machine gun *dismantles* easily. 这种玩具机关枪很容易拆卸。
【同】 disassemble, demolish
【反】 assemble
【派】 dismantlement *n*. 拆卸，拆除的行动

dismay [dɪsˈmeɪ] *v*. 使惊慌，使沮丧；*n*. 沮丧，惊慌
【记】 dis(加强语气)+may(害怕)→使非常害怕→使惊慌，使沮丧
【例】 1. We watched in blank *dismay* as she packed her bags. 我们瞧着她打行李，感到无可奈何。
2. We were all *dismayed* at his refusal to co-operate. 他不肯合作使我们感到非常失望。
【同】 depress, discourage, disturb; discouragement, disheartenment

dismiss [dɪsˈmɪs] *v*. 1. 解散；2. 解雇，开除；3. (法官)驳回，不受理
【记】 dis(离开)+miss(送)→送走→解散
【例】 1. The teacher *dismissed* the class early. 老师提早下课了。
2. If you are late again, you will be *dismissed*. 如果你再迟到，你将被解雇。
3. The judge *dismissed* all the charges agaist Smith. 法官驳回了对史密斯的一切指控。
【同】 release, free; disband, fire; discharge

disparage [dɪsˈpærɪdʒ] *v*. 轻视，贬低
【记】 dis(表否定)+par(相等)+age(名词词尾)→使不平等→贬低
【例】 Don't *disparage* his attempts to become a doctor. 别嘲笑他为成为一名医生而做的努力。

【同】 belittle, criticize, depreciate
【反】 flatter
【派】 disparagement *n*. 轻视，轻蔑

disparate [ˈdɪspərɪt] *adj*. 迥然不同的
【记】 dis(离开)+par(相等，相同)+ate(形容词词尾)→离开相同的→迥然不同的
【例】 The five experiments gave quite *disparate* results. 这五次试验所获得的结果迥然不同。
【同】 different, heterogeneous
【反】 comparable, analogous
【派】 disparatity *n*. 不同，差异

dispatch [dɪsˈpætʃ] *v*./*n*. (紧急)派遣，分配
【记】 dis(表否定)+patch(阻止)→不再阻止→派遣
【例】 American warships have been *dispatched* to the area. 美国军舰已派往该地区。
【同】 discharge, send
【派】 dispatcher *n*. 发报机

dispel [dɪsˈpel] *v*. (-lled; -lling)驱散，驱逐
【记】 dis(离开)+pel(驱赶)→赶走→驱逐
【例】 How can we *dispel* their doubt? 我们怎么才能驱散他们的疑虑呢?
【同】 disperse, drive away

dispense [dɪsˈpens] *v*. 施予，分配
【记】 dis(分开)+pense(衡量)→分称于秤的两端→分配
【例】 On Saturday morning my father solemnly *dispensed* pocket money to each of the children. 星期六上午我父亲郑重其事地给每个孩子发零花钱。
【同】 allot, distribute
【派】 dispenser *n*. 自动售货机
dispensable *adj*. 能分配的，可有可无的，不重要的

disperse [dɪsˈpɜːs] *v*. 分散，散开
【记】 di(=dis, 离开)+sperse(=scatter, 散开)→分散
【例】 The police *dispersed* the crowd. 警方驱散群众。
【同】 dispel, distribute, scatter
【派】 dispersal *n*. 疏散，散开

displace [dɪsˈpleɪs] *v*. 取代，转移
【记】 dis(分开，除去)+place(位置)→使失去位置→取代
【例】 Moderates have *displaced* the extremists on the committee. 在委员会中，稳健派人士取代了激进派人士。
【同】 replace, transfer
【反】 place
【派】 displacement *n*. 转移，置换

display [dɪˈspleɪ] *v*./*n*. 陈列，展示
【记】 dis(分开)+play(折叠)→把折叠的东西打开使能看到→展示
【例】 It's the first time the painting has been *displayed* to the public. 这是该画首次公

开展出。

【同】 demonstrate, exhibit, illustrate

【反】 conceal, hide

dispose [dɪsˈpəʊz] *v*. 处理，处置

【记】 dis(分开) + pose(放置)→分开放置→处理

【例】 Let's *dispose* of this matter once and for all. 让我们一劳永逸解决这件事情吧。

【同】 settle, treat

【派】 disposable *adj*. 可任意使用的，一次性的

disposal *n*. 垃圾倾倒；处置

disposed *adj*. 有…倾向的

disposition [dɪspəˈzɪʃən] *n*. 1.部署，安排；2.性情

【记】 dis(分开) + pos(放置) + ition(名词词尾)→分开放置→部署

【例】 1. A defector revealed the *disposition* of the enemy fleet. 有一名叛变者透露了敌方舰队的部署。

2. She has a calm and introverted *disposition*. 她性格文静内向。

【同】 temperament, tendency

disproportionate [ˌdɪsprəˈpɔːʃənɪt] *adj*. 不成比例的

【记】 dis(表否定) + pro(前) + port(部分) + ion(名词词尾) + ate(形容词词尾)→和前面的部分不一样的→不成比例的

【例】 You spend a *disproportionate* amount of your time on sport. 你在运动方面花费的时间过多。

【同】 incommensurate, unbalanced

【反】 proportionate

【派】 (逆构)disproportion *n*. 不均衡，不成比例

disprove [dɪsˈpruːv] *v*. 反驳，证明…有误

【记】 dis(表否定) + prove(证明)→证明…有误→反驳

【例】 Theallegations have been completely *disproved*. 这些指控证明完全是无中生有。

【同】 confute, controvert

【反】 prove

dispute [dɪsˈpjuːt] *n*. 争论，争端；*v*. 对…表示异议

【记】 dis(分开) + pute(思考)→想法不一致→争论

【例】 1. It is a matter of *dispute* whether they did the right thing. 他们做得对还是不对，这是有争议之处。

2. They *disputed* at great length what they should do. 他们对应该做什么这一问题进行了长时间的争论。

【同】 argument, conflict, quarrel; argue, debate

【反】 agreement

disquisition [ˌdɪskwɪˈzɪʃən] *n*. 长篇演讲，专题论文

【记】 dis(分开) + quis(寻求) + ition(名词词尾)→分开探究→专题论文

【例】 The professor wrote a learned *disquisition* on anthropology. 那位教授写了一篇关于人类学的学术专论。

【同】 speech，essay

disregard [ˌdɪsrɪ'gɑːd] *v*. 不理会，漠视

【记】 dis(表否定) + re(再) + gard(看)→不再看一眼→不理会

【例】 He completely *disregarded* my point of view. 他完全不理会我的观点。

【同】 ignore，neglect

【反】 regard

disreputable [dɪs'repjʊtəbl] *adj*. 声名狼藉的，品行不端的

【记】 dis(表否定) + reput(e)(名声) + able(形容词词尾)→名声不好的→声名狼藉的

【例】 I've had nothing to do with him since he got in with that rather *disreputable* clique. 自从他和那个声名狼藉的集团鬼混在一起之后，我就同他断绝了往来。

【同】 dishonorable，ill-famed

【反】 reputable

【派】 (逆构)disrepute *n*. 坏名声，不光彩

disrupt [dɪs'rʌpt] *v*. 使中断，扰乱

【记】 dis(分开) + rupt(打破)→使破裂分开→使中断

【例】 An accident has *disrupted* railway services into and out of the city. 一次交通事故使进出这座城市的铁路交通陷于混乱。

【同】 break，interrupt，disturb

【派】 disruption *n*. 中断，破坏

dissect [dɪ'sekt] *v*. 1. 解剖(动、植物等)；2. 详细研究，剖析

【记】 dis(分开) + sect(切)→切开→解剖，剖析

【例】 1. We *dissected* a rabbit yesterday. 我们昨天解剖了一只兔子。

2. Commentators are still *dissecting* the election results. 评论家仍然在剖析此次选举的结果。

【同】 cut；analyze

【派】 dissection *n*. 解剖，切开；仔细分析，详细研究

dissemble [dɪ'sembl] *v*. 掩盖，掩饰

【记】 dis(表否定) + semble(相似)→使不相→掩盖

【例】 You can always tell if he's *dissembling*; his voice trembles when he lies. 你总能判断他是否在掩饰什么，他说谎时声音会颤抖。

【同】 pretend，mask，feign

【派】 dissembler *n*. 伪君子，伪善者

disseminate [dɪ'semɪneɪt] *v*. 传播，散布

【记】 dis(分开) + semin(= sow，播种) + ate(动词词尾)→分散播种→散布

【例】 They use the press to *disseminate* right-wing views. 他们利用报刊来传播右翼观点。

【同】 broadcast，diffuse，propagate

【派】 dissemination *n*. 传播；分发

dissent [dɪ'sent] *v*. /*n*. 不同意，异议

【记】 dis(表否定) + sent(感觉)→没有感觉→不同意

【例】 1. I *dissent* from what you said. 我不同意你所说的。

2. They expressed their *dissent* from official policy. 他们对官方的政策表示出异议。

【同】 differ, disagree

【反】 assent, consent

【派】 dissenter *n*. 不同意者，反对者

dissenting *adj*. 不同意的

dissertation [ˌdɪsɜːˈteɪʃən] *n*. (学位)论文

【记】 dis(离开)+sert(结合)+ation(名词词尾)→离开群体→个别分开详细论述→论文

【例】 I'm working my notes up into a *dissertation*. 我正在把我的笔记修改成论文。

【同】 thesis

dissimulate [dɪˈsɪmjʊleɪt] *v*. 隐藏，假装

【记】 dis(表否定)+simul(=simil，相似的)+ate(动词词尾)→使不相似→假装

【例】 They were just *dissimulating*, pretending to be friendly. 他们是在装模作样地表示友好。

【同】 disguise, pretend

【派】 dissimulation *n*. 掩饰，虚伪，装糊涂

dissimulator *n*. 伪君子，假好人

dissipate [ˈdɪsɪpeɪt] *v*. 1. 消失，消散；2. 挥霍，浪费

【记】 dis(离开)+sip(扔)+ate(动词词尾)→随便扔掉→挥霍

【例】 1. The mist quickly *dissipated* as the sun rose. 太阳升起时雾很快就消散了。

2. He soon *dissipated* his fortune. 他很快就把财产挥霍光了。

【同】 dispel, disperse

【反】 accumulate

【派】 dissipation *n*. 消散，分散；挥霍，浪费

dissolve [dɪˈzɒlv] *v*. 溶解，解散

【记】 dis(分开)+solve(松散)→松开分散→溶解

【例】 Salt *dissolves* in water. 盐在水中溶解。

【同】 melt, disintegrate

dissuade [dɪˈsweɪd] *v*. 劝阻，阻止

【记】 dis(离开)+suade(劝告)→劝告不要做→劝阻

【例】 The police managed to *dissuade* him from jumping off the building. 警方已设法劝他不要从大楼上跳下来。

【同】 discourage

【反】 persuade

【派】 dissuasion *n*. 劝阻

distant [ˈdɪstənt] *adj*. 1. 远离的，遥远的；2. 疏远的，冷淡的

【记】 di(分开)+stan(站立)+t(形容词词尾)→分开站立→远离的

【例】 1. We could hear the *distant* drone of the traffic. 我们可以听到远处传来的车辆往来的嗡嗡声。

2. She passed by with only a *distant* nod. 她只冷淡地点了一下头就走了过去。

【同】 remote

【反】 close, near

distill [dɪˈstɪl] *v*. 蒸馏，提取

【记】 di(=dis, 去掉)+still(滴下)→一滴滴往下滴→蒸馏

【例】 Water can be made pure by *distilling* it. 水可以通过蒸馏而提纯。

【同】 extract, purify

【派】 distillation *n*. 蒸馏

distinct [dɪsˈtɪŋkt] *adj*. 清楚的，明显的，截然不同的

【记】 di(s)(分开)+stinct(刺)→把刺分开→清楚地分开→明显的

【例】 There was a *distinct* sense of embarrassment in the air. 周围的气氛中有一种明显的局促不安的感觉。

【同】 clear, obvious, definite, different

【反】 indistinct, ambiguous

【派】 distinction *n*. 差别，区别

distinctive *adj*. 特殊的，与众不同的

distinguish [dɪsˈtɪŋgwɪʃ] *v*. 区分，辨别

【记】 di(s)(分开)+stingu(=sting, 刺)+ish(动词词尾)→把刺明白分开→区分

【例】 People who cannot *distinguish* between colours are said to be colour-blind. 不能辨别颜色的人被称为色盲。

【同】 differentiate, discriminate

【反】 confuse

【派】 distinguished *adj*. 卓著的，高贵的

distort [dɪsˈtɔːt] *v*. 歪曲，扭曲

【记】 dis(离开)+tort(拧，扭曲)→由…扭曲开去→歪曲

【例】 How dare he *distort* the facts so brazenly! 他怎么敢如此肆无忌惮地歪曲事实！

【同】 deform, twist

【派】 distortion *n*. 歪曲，扭曲

distract [dɪsˈtrækt] *v*. 转移(注意力)，使分心

【记】 dis(离开)+tract(拉)→拉往别的方向→使分心

【例】 Don't *distract* my attention, I'm trying to study! 别分散我的注意力——我正要学习呢！

【同】 disturb, divert

【反】 attract

【派】 distraction *n*. 分心，分散注意力的东西

distribute [dɪsˈtrɪbjuːt] *v*. 分布，分发

【记】 dis(分开)+tribute(赠予，给予)→分开给→分配

【例】 Some types of plants are widely *distributed*. 有些植物分布得很广。

【同】 allot, dispense, spread

【反】 assemble, collect, gather

【派】 distribution *n*. 分发，分配

disturb [dɪsˈtɜːb] *v*. 打扰，扰乱

【记】 dis(分开)+turb(搅动)→搅开了→搅乱了→扰乱

【例】 As mining ceases in one section of the open-cut, the *disturbed* area is reshaped. 一个地方的露天开采结束后，该地被扰乱的地方就恢复原状。
【同】 annoy, bother, trouble
【派】 disturbance *n*. 干扰，困扰
disturbing *adj*. 令人不安的，引起烦恼的

dive [daɪv] *v*./*n*. 1.潜水，跳水；2.下潜，俯冲
【例】 1.Throw your arms out in front of you as you *dive*. 跳水时手臂要迅速前伸。
2.The eagle *dived* down on the rabbit. 那只鹰向兔子猛扑下来。
【同】 plunge
【派】 diver *n*. 潜水者

divergent [daɪ'vɜːdʒənt] *adj*. 有分歧的，有差异的
【记】 di(= dis，分开) + verg(倾斜) + ent(形容词词尾)→倾斜开去→有分歧的
【例】 I tried to combine their *diverment* views. 我试图把他们不同的观点结合起来。
【同】 different
【派】 (逆构)diverge *v*. (道路等)分叉，(意见等)分歧

diverse [daɪ'vɜːs] *adj*. 多种多样的，多变化的
【记】 di(离开) + verse(转移，转向)→从…移开→多变化的
【例】 They are the people from *diverse* cultures. 他们是些有着不同文化背景的人。
【同】 different, various
【反】 same, similar

diversify [daɪ'vɜːsɪfaɪ] *v*. 使多样化，从事多种经营
【记】 di(离开) + verse(转移，转向) + fy(动词词尾，表示"使")→使从…移开→使多样化
【例】 A factory must try to *diversify* for further development. 一个工厂要获得进一步发展就要努力使产品多样化。
【同】 vary
【反】 specialize
【派】 diversification *n*. 经营多样化
diversity *n*. 多样性

divert [dɪ'vɜːt] *v*. 使转向，转移
【记】 di(离开) + verse(转移，转向)→使转向
【例】 They *diverted* the river to supply water to the town. 他们使河流改道以便向城市供水。
【同】 detract, distract
【反】 attract
【派】 diversion *n*. 转向，转移；消遣，娱乐

divorce [dɪ'vɔːs] *n*./*v*. 离婚
【记】 di(离开) + vorce(= vert，转向)→从(丈夫或妻子身边)转开→离婚
【例】 1.She got a *divorce* after years of unhappiness. 经过多年的不幸之后，她终于离了婚。
2.He *divorced* his wife. 他和他妻子离了婚。
【同】 disjoin, separate

divulge [daɪˈvʌldʒ] *v*. 泄露(秘密)，透露

【记】 di(离开)＋vulge(＝vulgus，普通百姓)→使在普通百姓中流传→泄露秘密

【例】 I cannot *divulge* how much it cost. 我不能把价钱泄露出来。

【同】 reveal，disclose

【派】 divulgence *n*. 透露，泄露

dizzy [ˈdɪzɪ] *adj*. 头晕目眩的，困惑的

【例】 After another glass of whisky I began to feel *dizzy*. 我又喝了一杯威士忌酒之后，就觉得头晕目眩。

【同】 light-headed，giddy；confused

【派】 dizziness *n*. 头晕，眩晕

docile [ˈdəusaɪl] *adj*. 驯服的，温顺的

【记】 doc(教导)＋ile(形容词词尾)→容易教导的→驯服的

【例】 That pony is very *docile*. 那匹小马很温顺。

【同】 obedient，tame

【反】 obstinate，stubborn

doctrine [ˈdɒktrɪn] *n*. 教义，教旨

【记】 doc(教导)＋tr(＝tor，表示人)＋ine(名词词尾)→教导的人所教的东西→教义

【例】 Christian and Muslim *doctrines* are very different. 基督教教义和穆斯林教义极为不同。

【同】 belief，creed

document [ˈdɒkjumənt] *n*. 文件，文档；*v*. 用文件证明，为…提供文件(或证据等)

【记】 docu(＝doc 教)＋ment(名词词尾)→用来教的东西→文件

【例】 1. Let me see all the official *documents* concerning the sale of this land. 让我看看买卖这块土地的所有官方文件。

2. Can you *document* these claims? 你能为这些要求提供证件吗?

【同】 paper，file

【派】 documentary *n*. 纪录片

documentation *n*. 文件或证据的提供或备办

dodge [dɒdʒ] *v*. 闪开，躲避，逃避

【例】 He *dodged* the falling rock and escaped unhurt. 他闪身躲过了滚落的岩石，安然脱险了。

【同】 avoid，recoil

dogma [ˈdɒgmə] *n*. 教条，教义

【例】 Beliefs have ossified into rigid *dogma*. 信仰已僵化为不可更动的教条。

【同】 belief，tenet

【派】 dogmatic *adj*. 武断的，教条的，固执己见的

doleful [ˈdəulful] *adj*. 悲哀的，忧愁的

【记】 dole(痛苦，悲伤)＋ful(形容词词尾)→充满痛苦的→悲哀的

【例】 He always shows a *doleful* expression. 他总是露出忧郁的表情。

【同】 dismal，dreary，mournful，sad

domain [dəuˈmeɪn] *n*. 领域，范围

【记】 dom(统治)+ain(动词词尾转用做名词)→有特定主人的区域→领域
【例】 The kitchen is my wife's *domain*, she doesn't like me going into it. 厨房是我妻子的领地，她不愿让我进去。
【同】 field, realm, region

domestic [də'mestɪk] *adj*. 1. 家的，家庭的；2. 国内的，本国的

【记】 dome(房屋)+stic(形容词词尾)→家里的
【例】 1. My husband loves adventurous life while I enjoy a more peaceful *domestic* life. 我丈夫喜欢充满冒险的生活，而我则喜欢宁静的家居生活。
2. The newspaper provides more foreign news than *domestic* news. 这家报纸刊登的国外消息多于国内消息。
【同】 family, home, household; national, internal
【反】 foreign, international

domesticate [də'mestɪkeɪt] *v*. 1. 驯养，驯化；2. 使喜爱家居，使专注于家务
【记】 domestic(家的)+ate(动词词尾)→使变成家里的→驯养
【例】 1. Cows were *domesticated* to provide us with milk. 人们饲养奶牛来为我们提供牛奶。
2. He's become a lot more *domesticated* since his marriage. 他婚后已非常恋家了。
【同】 cultivate, tame

dominate ['dɒmɪneɪt] *v*. 支配，占优势
【记】 domin(统治)+ate(动词词尾)→统治→支配
【例】 She *dominated* the meeting by sheer force of character. 她单凭个人气势就镇住了会场。
【同】 control, rule
【派】 dominant *adj*. 支配的，首要的，占优势的
dominance *n*. 支配地位，优势

domineer [ˌdɒmɪ'nɪə] *v*. 压制
【记】 domin(统治)+eer(=er，表是动作的反复)→一再统治→压制
【例】 He *domineered*, and the rest of us hated it. 他行事专横，我们大家都讨厌他这种作风。
【同】 tyrannize
【派】 domineering *adj*. 盛气凌人的，专权的

donate [dəʊ'neɪt] *v*. 捐献，捐赠
【记】 don(给予)+ate(动词词尾)→给予→捐赠
【例】 The government calls on the youth to *donate* their blood voluntarily. 政府号召青年义务献血。
【同】 contribute, give, present
【派】 donation *n*. 捐赠，捐款
donor *n*. 捐助者

doomed [du:md] *adj*. 命定的，注定失败的
【记】 doom(命运，厄运)+ed(形容词词尾)→有厄运的→注定失败的
【例】 The project is *doomed* to fail. 这计划注定要失败。
【同】 fated

dormant [ˈdɔːmənt] *adj*. 静止的，休眠的

【记】 dorm(睡) + ant(形容词词尾)→睡眠的→静止的，休眠的

【例】 Many *dormant* branches of our organization are now springing to active life. 我们组织中有许多沉寂的部门现在突然活跃起来。

【同】 inactive, sleeping

【反】 active

【派】 dormancy *n*. 睡眠，休眠

downcast [ˈdaʊnkɑːst] *adj*. 意志消沉的，沮丧的

【记】 down(向下的) + cast(投)→投向下的→意志消沉的

【例】 He seemed very *downcast* at the news. 那消息似乎使他非常难过。

【同】 depressed, discouraged, gloomy, low-spirited

draft [drɑːft] *n*. 草稿，草案；*v*. 起草，设计

【例】 1. He drew a *draft* of the car. 他画了一张汽车的草图。

2. Who will *draft* the indictment? 谁将起草起诉状？

【同】 drawing, outline, sketch

drag [dræg] *v*. /*n*. (-gged; -gging)拖曳，缓慢而费力地行动

【例】 The protesters were *dragged* away by the police. 抗议者被警察拖走了。

【同】 draw, pull

【派】 dragging *adj*. 拖曳用的，拖延的

drainage [ˈdreɪnɪdʒ] *n*. 排水，排水装置

【记】 drain(排干) + age(名词词尾)→排水

【例】 He came to look at the *drainage*. 他是来检查排水设备的。

【同】 exhaustion

【派】 (逆构)drain *v*. 慢慢排去，渐渐耗尽

dramatic [drəˈmætɪk] *adj*. 引人注目的，令人吃惊的，突然的

【记】 drama(戏剧) + tic(形容词词尾)→戏剧般的→令人吃惊的

【例】 The government is alarmed by the *dramatic* increase in violent crime. 政府对暴力犯罪案件的急剧增加感到恐慌。

【同】 notable, remarkable

【派】 (逆构)drama *n*. 戏剧

drastic [ˈdræstɪk] *adj*. 激烈的，严厉的

【记】 dra(表演) + stic(形容词词尾)→表演出来的→激烈的

【例】 *Drastic* measures will have to be taken to restore order. 为恢复秩序必须采取严厉措施。

【同】 fierce, intense, extreme

【反】 mild

【派】 drastically *adv*. 非常地，激烈地

drawback [ˈdrɔːˌbæk] *n*. 缺点，不利条件，障碍

【记】 draw(拉) + back(回)→把…向后拉→缺点

【例】 The great *drawback* to living near a main road is noise. 住在大街旁最大的缺点是噪音(很大)。

【同】 disadvantage, obstacle, shortcoming
【反】 advantage
dread [dred] *n*. 畏惧，恐怖
【例】 The Jews lived in *dread* of being caught. 这些犹太人生活在会遭到拘捕的恐惧之中。
【同】 fear
【派】 dreadful *adj*. 可怕的；[口]糟透了的
drift [drɪft] *v*. /*n*. 漂流，漂泊
【例】 1. A tiny fishing boat was *drifting* slowly along. 一只小小的渔船在缓缓地漂去。
2. We must stop this *drift* towards war. 我们必须制止这种战争趋势。
【同】 float, wander
drill [drɪl] *v*. 1. 钻(孔)，打眼；2. 训练，操练；*n*. 1. 练习；2. 钻头，钻机
【例】 1. The dentist's *drill* made a lot of noise. 牙钻发出很大的噪音。
2. The workman is *drilling* in the wall. 工人正在墙上打孔。
3. You should finish your English grammar *drills* in the class. 你应该在课堂上完成语法练习。
【同】 penetrate; discipline, exercise
drizzle ['drɪzl] *v*. 下毛毛雨；*n*. 细雨
【记】 driz(露珠落下) + z + le(动词词尾)→像露珠一样落下的→毛毛雨
【例】 1. It had been *drizzling* all day. 下了一整天的毛毛雨。
2. Would you like to go for a walk in the *drizzle*? 想去毛毛雨里散会儿步吗？
【同】 rain
drought [draʊt] *n*. 干旱，旱灾
【例】 The crops failed because of the *drought*. 干旱造成农作物歉收。
【同】 dryness
【反】 flood
drowsy ['draʊzɪ] *adj*. 昏昏欲睡的
【例】 The medicine made me *drowsy*. 这药使我昏昏欲睡。
【同】 dozy, sleepy
【反】 awake
drudgery ['drʌdʒərɪ] *n*. 苦工，苦差事
【记】 drudger(辛苦工作) + ry(名词词尾)→苦差事
【例】 Labor-saving devices have emancipated women from kitchen *drudgery*. 许多节省劳力的设备让妇女摆脱掉乏味的厨房杂役。
【同】 labor, work
dual ['djuːəl] *adj*. 二重的，两层的
【记】 du(二) + al(形容词词尾)→两个的→二重的
【例】 His *dual* role as a composer and a conductor made him very busy. 他作曲家和指挥家的双重身份使他非常繁忙。
【同】 double, duplicate, twofold
dub [dʌb] *v*. (-bbed; -bbing) 1. 授予…称号，给…起绰号；2. (电影)配音

【例】 1. The region is *dubbed* the paradise on earth. 这个地方被称为人间天堂。

2. Is the film *dubbed* or does it have subtitles? 这部影片是经过配音的还是配上字幕的？

【同】 name，nickname

dubious [ˈdjuːbjəs] *adj*. 怀疑的

【记】 du(二) + b + ious(形容词词尾)→向两个方向的→不确定的→怀疑的

【例】 I remain *dubious* about her motives. 我对她的动机仍存疑念。

【同】 doubtful，questionable，uncertain

【反】 certain，undoubtful

dump [dʌmp] *v*. 1. 倾倒，丢弃；2. 倾销，抛售

【例】 1. Some people just *dump* their rubbish in the river. 有些人径直往河里倒垃圾。

2. The company *dumped* large quantities of substandard machines on the market at cut-rate price. 那家公司将大量次品机器削价向市场抛售。

【同】 discard，empty，unload

【反】 load

duplicate [ˈdjuːplɪkeɪt] *v*. 重复，复制；*n*. 复制品，副本

【记】 du(二) + plic(折叠，倍) + ate(动词词尾)→重复第二份→复制

【例】 1. This research merely *duplicates* work already done elsewhere. 这项研究仅仅是重复别人已经做过的工作。

2. Is this a *duplicate* or the original? 这是复制件还是原件？

【同】 copy，repeat，reproduce

【反】 original

【派】 duplication *n*. 副本，复制

durable [ˈdjʊərəbl] *adj*. 耐用的，持久的

【记】 dur(持续，持久) + able(形容词词尾)→持久的

【例】 This pair of shoes is *durable*. 这双鞋很耐磨。

【同】 long-lasting，enduring，serviceable

【反】 disposable

【派】 duration *n*. 持续，持续期间

dusk [dʌsk] *n*. 薄暮，黄昏

【例】 The street lights come on at *dusk* and go off at dawn. 路灯在黄昏时开，拂晓时关。

【同】 evening，nightfall，sunset，twilight

【反】 dawn

【派】 dusky *adj*. 微暗的，肤色黑的

duty [ˈdjuːtɪ] *n*. 1. 责任，义务；2. 税，关税

【记】 du(= debt，负债) + ty(名词词尾)→应该背负的东西→责任

【例】 1. It's not something I enjoy. I do it purely out of a sense of *duty*. 那并不是我喜欢做的事，我纯粹是出于责任感才做的。

2. Coffee and bananas are *duty*-free imports there. 咖啡和香蕉在那里都是免税进口产品。

【同】 obligation，responsibility；tariff

【派】 duty-bound *adj*. 义不容辞的

duty-free *adj*. 免税的，免关税的

dwarf [dwɔːf] *n*. 侏儒；*v*. 把…显得矮小

【例】 1. The kind *dwarf* asked the little princess to have dinner with him. 善良的小矮人邀请小公主和他一起吃晚饭。

2. Our little dinghy was *dwarfed* by the big yacht. 我们的小船跟大游艇一比显得很小。

【同】 midget, runt, pygmy

【反】 giant

dwell [dwel] *v*. 1.居住；2.细想，详述

【例】 1. He decided to *dwell* on our island. 他决定到我们的岛上居住。

2. Let's not *dwell* on your past mistakes. 我们不要再细说你过去的错误了。

【同】 inhabit, live, reside

【派】 dweller *n*. 居民，居住者

dwelling *n*. 住处，住宅

dwindle ['dwɪndl] *v*. 减少

【记】 dwind(消瘦) + le(表动作的反复)→逐渐消瘦下去→减少

【例】 The number of people going to the cinema seems to *dwindle* steadily. 看电影的人数似乎在逐渐下降。

【同】 decline, decrease, diminish, lessen

【反】 increase

dye [daɪ]*n*. 颜料，染料；*v*. 染色

【例】 1. A good *dye* will not fade. 染得好的颜色不会褪色。

2. The wounded soldier's blood *dyed* the ground red. 受伤士兵的血染红了地面。

【同】 stain, tint

【反】 bleach

dynamic [daɪ'næmɪk] *adj*. 充满活力的，精力充沛的

【记】 dynam(力量) + ic(形容词词尾)→有力量的→充满活力的

【例】 We are looking for *dynamic* persons to be salesmen. 我们正在寻找充满活力的销售人员。

【同】 active, energetic, vigorous

【反】 undynamic, static

【派】 dynamics *n*. 动力学

dynasty ['dɪnəstɪ] *n*. 王朝，朝代

【记】 dyna(力量) + sty(名词词尾)→拥有力量的事物→王朝

【例】 How many *dynasties* are there in China's history? 中国历史上有多少个朝代？

E

eager ['iːə]*adj*. 渴望的，热心的

【例】 The company is *eager* to expand into new markets. 那家公司急欲开辟新的市场。

【同】 anxious, desirous, keen

earnest ['ɜːnɪst] *adj*. 认真的，真诚的

【例】 I'm sure he was *earnest* when he said he would come. 我相信他说他会来是认真的。

【同】 serious, sincere, resolute

【反】 insincere

ebb [eb] *n*. 退潮；*v*. 退潮，衰退

【例】 A crab was left stranded on the beach when the tide *ebbed*. 退潮时，一只蟹被困留在沙滩上。

【同】 recede, retreat

【反】 flow

earthquake ['ɜːθkweɪk] *n*. 地震

【记】 earth(土地) + quake(震动)→地震

【例】 The wall declined slightly on account of the *earthquake*. 墙壁因地震而倾斜。

【同】 seism

ease [iːz] *n*. 不费力，舒适，安逸；*v*. 解除，减轻(痛苦、忧虑等)

【例】 1. I don't feel at *ease* in the strange place. 在这个陌生的地方，我觉得很不自在。

2. It would *ease* my mind to know where he was. 要知道他在哪儿我就放心了。

【同】 comfort, relaxation; soothe, relieve

【反】 difficulty, anxiety

eccentric [ɪk'sentrɪk] *adj*. 古怪的，怪僻的；*n*. 古怪的人，怪僻的人

【记】 e(= ex 出去) + centr(中心) + ic(形容词词尾)→脱离中心的→不和别人一起的→古怪的

【例】 1. The club seemed full of *eccentrics*. 这个俱乐部里好像都是怪人。

2. She is an *eccentric* old lady. 她是个古怪的老太太。

【同】 odd, peculiar, queer

【反】 common, general, normal, ordinary

【派】 eccentricity *n*. 古怪，怪僻

eclipse [ɪ'klɪps] *n*. 日食，月食

【记】 ec(= ex 出去) + lipse(离开)→减掉光亮→日食，月食

【例】 It was reported that there would be an annular *eclipse* tomorrow. 据报道说，明天

有日环食。

【同】 overcast, shadow

ecology [iːˈkɒlədʒɪ] *n*. 生态，生态学

【记】 eco(家) + logy(…学)→研究家庭环境的学问→生态学

【例】 He started to study *ecology* and decided to devote his whole life to the science. 他开始研究生态学，并决心将他的一生献身于这门科学。

【同】 bionomics

【派】 ecological *adj*. 生态学的

ecologist *n*. 生态学家

economy [iːˈkɒnəmɪ] *n*. 1. 经济；2. 节省，节约

【记】 eco(家) + nomy(定律，理论)→关于家务的理论→经济，节约

【例】 1. The state of the *economy* is very worrying. 目前的经济状况令人十分担忧。

2. We are trying to make a few *economies*. 我们正想办法节省一些。

【同】 frugality, thrift

【反】 luxury

【派】 economic *adj*. 经济的，经济学的

economical *adj*. 经济的，节约的

economics *n*. 经济学

economist *n*. 经济学家

economize *v*. 节约，节省

ecosystem [iːkəˈsɪstəm] *n*. 生态系统，生态体系

【记】 eco(生态) + system(系统)→生态系统

【例】 Ecologists have assumed that tropical *ecosystems* were shaped entirely by natural forces. 生态学家们已作出假设，热带生态体系完全是由自然力量形成的。

ecstasy [ˈekstəsɪ] *n*. 狂喜，入迷

【记】 ec(= ex 出去) + stasy(站立)→立于(理性)之外→狂喜，入迷

【例】 We were in *ecstasy* at the thought of going home. 一想到回家，我们就兴奋不已。

【同】 exaltation, delight

【派】 ecstatic *n*. 狂喜的人；*adj*. 狂喜的，心醉神迷的，入迷的

edge [edʒ] *n*. 边缘，棱

【例】 Please sharpen the *edge* of this axe. 请把这把斧头的刃磨快。

【同】 border, fringe, verge

【反】 center, core

【派】 edging *n*. 边饰

edible [ˈedɪbl] *adj*. 可食用的

【记】 ed(吃) + ible(形容词词尾)→可以吃的→可食用的

【例】 Throw that tainted meat away; it's not *edible*. 把那块腐烂的肉扔掉，不能再吃了。

【同】 eatable

【反】 inedible, uneatable

【派】 edibility *n*. 适食性，可食性

edict [ˈiːdɪkt] *n*. 法令，布告

【记】 e(= ex 出去) + dict(说)→说出去的话→法令，布告

【例】 The king issued an *edict* forbidding the wearing of swords within the city. 国王颁布了一项在市内不得佩带剑的法令。

【同】 decree, order

edify [ˈedɪfaɪ] *v*. 启发，陶冶

【记】 ed(吃) + ify(动词词尾)→使能吃的，能消化的→启发

【例】 Travel is an *edifying* experience, especially for young people. 旅游可以使人增长见闻，尤其对年轻人。

【同】 enlighten

【派】 edification *n*. 教诲，启迪，熏陶

efface [ɪˈfeɪs] *v*. 擦掉，抹去

【记】 ef(= ex 去掉) + face(脸)→从脸上去掉→擦掉，抹去

【例】 Time alone will *efface* those unpleasant memories. 只有时间才能使人淡忘那些不快的记忆。

【同】 erase, obliterate, wipe

【派】 effacement *n*. 抹消，抹杀

effect [ɪˈfekt] *n*. 结果，效力，作用

【记】 ef(= ex 出去) + fect(做)→做出来→结果

【例】 A new system of taxation will be brought into *effect* next year. 新的税收制度将于明年实行。

【同】 consequence, influence

【反】 cause

【派】 effective *adj*. 有效的，产生预期结果的
effectuate *v*. 实行，完成

efficient [ɪˈfɪʃənt] *adj*. 有效的，效率高的

【记】 ef(= ex 出去) + fic(做) + ient(形容词词尾)→能做出事来→有效率的

【例】 The heating system has recently been modified to make it more *efficient*. 最近供暖设备已稍加改动以提高效率。

【同】 effective

【反】 inefficient

【派】 efficiency *n*. 效率，功效

effluent [ˈefluənt] *adj*. 流出的，发出的；*n*. 流出物，废水

【记】 ef(= ex 出去) + flu(流) + ent(形容词词尾)→流出的

【例】 Dangerous *effluent* is being poured into our rivers. 有害的废水正流入我们的江河里。

【同】 outflowing; wastewater, sewage

effrontery [eˈfrʌntərɪ] *n*. 厚颜无耻，放肆(的行为)

【记】 ef(= ex 去掉) + front(面，脸) + ery(名词词尾)→使没有脸面的行为→厚颜无耻

【例】 The politician had the *effrontery* to ask the people he had insulted to vote for him. 这个政客竟厚颜地要求受过他侮辱的人投他一票。

E

【同】 audacity

effuse [ɪ'fjuːz] *v*. 流出，散布

【记】 ef(= ex 出去) + fuse(倾泻)→泻出→流出

【例】 The town *effuse* warmth and hospitality. 这市镇洋溢着人情味和好客精神。

【同】 flow out

【派】 effusive *adj*. 感情横溢的，流出的

ego ['iːgəʊ] *n*. 自我，自己

【例】 He's my alter *ego*, we go everywhere together. 他是我的知己——彼此形影不离。

【同】 self

【派】 egoism *n*. 利己主义

egoist *n*. 自我主义者

eject [ɪ'dʒekt] *v*. 射出，逐出

【记】 e(= ex 出去) + ject(投掷)→把…投出去→射出，逐出

【例】 As the plane fell rapidly towards the ground, the pilot had to *eject*. 在飞机迅速落向地面时，驾驶员只得弹射出来。

【同】 discharge, expel

elaborate [ɪ'læbərət] *adj*. 精心制作的，复杂的，精细的；*v*. 精心制作，详细阐述

【记】 e(= ex 出去) + labor(做，制作) + ate(动词词尾)→努力做出来的→精心制作的

【例】 1. The curtains had an *elaborate* pattern of flowers. 窗帘上绘有精美的花卉图案。

2. What you've told me of your plan sounds most interesting; would you care to *elaborate*? 你给我讲的这个计划很有意思，你能详细地谈一谈吗？

【同】 detailed, intricate; develop, detail

【反】 plain, simple

【派】 elaboration *n*. 精心制作，详细阐述

elapse [ɪ'læps] *v*. 过去，消逝

【记】 e(= ex 出去) + lapse(滑)→滑出去→时光流出→过去

【例】 Three years have *elapsed* since we last met. 我们上次相见至今已过了三年。

【同】 pass, slip by

elastic [ɪ'læstɪk] *adj*. 有弹性的，有弹力的

【记】 elast(推进) + ic(形容词词尾)→可以推进的→有弹性的

【例】 1. Rubber is *elastic*. 橡皮是有弹性的。

2. Our plans are fairly *elastic*. 我们的计划相当有弹性。

【同】 flexible, pliable

【反】 rigid, stiff

【派】 elasticity *n*. 弹力，弹性

elate [ɪ'leɪt] *v*. 使得意洋洋，使兴高采烈

【记】 e(= ex 外面) + late(带着)→使把(心情)表现在外面→使得意洋洋

【例】 The crowds in the square were *elated* by the news. 这消息使广场上的人群欢欣鼓舞。

【同】 exhilarate, stimulate

【反】 depress

【派】 elation *n*. 得意洋洋，兴高采烈

elbow ['elbəʊ] *n*. 肘，肘部

【记】 el(arm，前臂) + bow(弯曲)→前臂弯曲的地方→肘部

【例】 He had a patch on the *elbow* of his jacket. 他的夹克衫肘部有一块补丁。

electricity [ɪlek'trɪsɪtɪ] *n*. 电，电力

【记】 electr(琥珀) + ic(形容词词尾) + ity(名词词尾)→最初是摩擦琥珀产生电→电力

【例】 After the failure of the *electricity* supplies the city was in chaos. 电力供应中断，城市陷于混乱之中。

【同】 power

【派】 electrical *adj*. 电的

electronic [ɪlek'trɒnɪk] *adj*. 电子的，电子器件的

【记】 electr(电的) + onic(形容词词尾)→用电的→电子器件的

【例】 This dictionary is available in *electronic* version. 这部词典有电子版。

【派】 (逆构)electron *n*. 电子

electronics *n*. 电子学，电子设备

elegant ['elɪgənt] *adj*. 优美的，优雅的

【记】 e(= ex 出去) + leg(= lig 选择) + ant(形容词词尾)→选出的→好的，高雅的

【例】 I like my clothes to be simple but *elegant*. 我喜欢朴素但漂亮雅致的衣服。

【同】 graceful，exquisite

【反】 inelegant

【派】 elegance *n*. 优美，雅致

element ['elɪmənt] *n*. 基本部分，要素

【例】 Honesty，industry and kindness are *elements* of a good life. 诚实、勤劳和善良是幸福生活的要素。

【同】 component，constituent，ingredient

【派】 elementary *adj*. 基础的，初级的

elevate ['elɪveɪt] *v*. 提高，举起

【记】 e(= ex 出去) + lev(举) + ate(动词词尾)→举出去→升高

【例】 Either iron or gold will *elevate* the position of the country in the family of nations. 强权或经济实力都可以提高一个国家在国际中的地位。

【同】 lift，promote，raise

【反】 lower，degrade

【派】 elevation *n*. 提高，晋级

elevator *n*. 电梯，升降机

elicit [ɪ'lɪsɪt] *v*. 引起，抽出

【记】 e(= ex 出来) + lic(诱使) + it(动词词尾)→引诱出来→抽出

【例】 At last we have *elicited* the truth from him. 我们终于从他那里探得真相。

【同】 arouse，educe，extract，evoke

【派】 elicitation *n*. 引出，启发

eligible ['elɪdʒəbl] *adj*. 有资格当选的，合格的

【记】 e(= ex 出来) + lig(选择) + ible(形容词词尾)→挑选出来的→合格的

【例】 Is she *eligible* for sickness pay? 她有资格获得病假工资吗？
【同】 fit，qualified，suitable
【反】 ineligible
【派】 eligibility *n*. 有条件被选中，有资格当选

eliminate [ɪˈlɪmɪneɪt] *v*. 消除，排除，淘汰
【记】 e(=ex 出去)+limin(门槛)+ate(动词词尾)→ate→赶出门槛→消除
【例】 Their team was *eliminated* in the first round. 他们队在第一轮就被淘汰了。
【同】 exclude，remove
【反】 add
【派】 elimination *n*. 排除，除去

elite [eɪˈliːt] *n*. (总称)出类拔萃的人，精英
【记】 elit(=elect 选择)+e→选出的人物→精英
【例】 Only the *elite* were there. 只有上层人士在场。
【同】 cream(精华)
【派】 elitist *adj*. 上等的，高级的

eloquent [ˈeləkwənt] *adj*. 雄辩的，有口才的
【记】 e(=ex 出去)+loqu(说话)+ent(形容词词尾)→很清楚地说出来的→雄辩的
【例】 He is *eloquent* and humorous as well. What he says never fails to please us. 他口才好又幽默，他所说的一定能使我们高兴。
【同】 expressive，fluent，well-spoken
【派】 eloquence *n*. 雄辩，口才

elucidate [ɪˈljuːsɪdeɪt] *v*. 阐明，讲明
【记】 e(=ex 出去)+lucid(光，明亮的)+ate(动词词尾)→闪耀在外面的→阐明
【例】 You have not understood; allow me to *elucidate*. 你没理解，让我解释一下。
【同】 clarify，explicate，illuminate
【派】 elucidation *n*. 阐明，讲明

elusive [ɪˈljuːsɪv] *adj*. 难懂的，难捉摸的
【记】 e(=ex 出去)+lus(扮演)+ive(形容词词尾)→扮演出来的样子→让人难懂的
【例】 Immediate solutions for solving problems surrounding poverty remain *elusive*. 立即解决贫困问题的办法仍然是难以捉摸的。

emaciate [ɪˈmeɪʃɪeɪt] *v*. 使憔悴，使消瘦
【记】 e(=ex 出去)+maci(瘦的)+ate(动词词尾)→使瘦下去→使消瘦
【例】 A long illness had *emaciated* my father. 长期卧病使我父亲很瘦弱了。
【派】 emaciated *adj*. 瘦弱的，憔悴的

emancipate [ɪˈmænsɪpeɪt] *v*. 解放，释放
【记】 e(=ex 出去)+man(手)+cipate(拿)→把手中的东西拿出来→释放，解放
【例】 we must *emancipate* our minds and think independently. 我们必须解放思想，独立思考。
【同】 free，liberate，release
【派】 emancipation *n*. 释放，解放

embalm [ɪmˈbɑːm] *v*. 1. 以香膏涂抹，保存；2. 使不朽

【记】 em(= en 使) + balm(香膏)→使有香膏→保存

【例】 1. The Egyptians used to *embalm* the bodies of their dead kings. 埃及人以前用药物保存国王的尸体。

2. We will *embalm* him forever. 我们永远怀念他。

embark [ɪm'bɑːk] v. 1. 上船(飞机、汽车等); 2. 着手, 从事

【记】 em(= en 进入) + bark(船)→上船

【例】 1. Passengers with cars must *embark* first. 带汽车的乘客必须先上船。

2. He is about to *embark* on a new business venture. 他就要开始新的商业冒险活动了。

【同】 board; start

【反】 disembark

embarrass [ɪm'bærəs] v. 使窘迫, 使尴尬

【记】 em(= en 进入) + barr(棒) + ass(名词词尾)→被拦住→使难堪

【例】 I was *embarrassed* by his comments about my clothes. 他评论我的衣服使我很尴尬。

【同】 abash, bewilder

【派】 embarrassment n. 尴尬

embellish [ɪm'belɪʃ] v. 1. 装饰, 修饰; 2. 给(叙述)添加细节, 对…加以渲染

【记】 em(= en 使) + bell(= bellus 美丽的) + ish(动词词尾)→使更美丽→装饰, 修饰

【例】 1. My daughter wears a dress *embellished* with lace and ribbons today. 今天我女儿穿了一件有花边和饰带的连衣裙。

2. Just tell the truth and don't *embellish* the story by any means. 你只要讲清事实, 千万不要添枝加叶。

【同】 adorn, beautify, decorate

【派】 embellishment n. 装饰, 修饰; 润色

embezzlement [ɪm'bezlmənt] n. 盗用, 挪用(公款), 侵吞(财物)

【记】 em(= en, in 里面) + bezzle(破坏) + ment(名词词尾)→在里面搞破坏→盗用, 挪用

【例】 The judge sent him to prison for *embezzlement*. 法官因他贪污将其送入监牢。

【同】 defalcation, peculation

【派】 (逆构)embezzle v. 盗用, 挪用(公款), 侵吞(财物)

emblem ['embləm] n. 象征, 标志, 徽章

【记】 em(= en, in 里面) + blem(投, 抛)→把(含义)投在里面→象征

【例】 The ring was important to her as an *emblem* of their love. 这枚戒指是他们爱情的象征, 对她是重要的。

【同】 symbol, token, badge

embody [ɪm'bɒdɪ] v. 具体表现, 体现

【记】 em(= en 使成为) + body(身体)→使变成一个身体→体现

【例】 To me he *embodies* all the best qualities of a teacher. 在我看来, 他本身体现了教师应有的一切优秀品质。

【同】 personify

【派】 embodiment *n*. 体现，具体化

embrace [ɪm'breɪs] *v*. 拥抱，接受

【记】 em(= en 进入) + brace(胳膊)→在双臂之中→拥抱

【例】 She eagerly *embraced* the offer of a trip to Europe. 她热情地接受了到欧洲旅行的建议。

【同】 hug, hold, accept, adopt

embroider [ɪm'brɔɪdə] *v*. 绣花，刺绣

E

【记】 em(= en, in 里面) + broider(刺绣)→绣进去→刺绣

【例】 She *embroidered* her initials on the handkerchief. 她把她姓名的起首字母绣在手帕上。

【派】 embroidery *n*. 刺绣

embryo ['embrɪəʊ] *n*. 胚胎，胚芽；*adj*. 胚胎的，初期的

【记】 em(= en 使成为) + bry(发芽) + o→使成为胚芽→胚芽

【例】 1. Two American researchers studied the brains of human *embryos* and discovered that the left-right asymmetry exists before birth. 两个美国研究员研究了人类胚胎的大脑，发现人的大脑的不对称性在出生前就有了。

2. The plans are still in *embryo*. 计划仍在酝酿中。

【派】 embryological *adj*. 胚胎学的

embryonic *adj*. 胚胎的，萌芽期的

emend [iː'mend] *v*. 修订，校订

【记】 e(= to) + mend(修补)→修订

【例】 Many men are needed to *emend* this book. 修订这本书需要许多人手。

【同】 alter, improve

emerge [ɪ'mɜːdʒ] *v*. 出现，露出

【记】 e(= ex 出去) + merge(没入水里)→露出水面→出现

【例】 The sun *emerged* from behind the clouds. 太阳从云层后面露出来了。

【同】 appear, come out

【反】 submerge

【派】 emergent *adj*. 在出现过程中的，新兴的

emergence *n*. 出现，暴露

emergency [ɪ'mɜːdʒnsɪ] *n*. 紧急情况，突发事件，急诊

【记】 emerg(出现) + ency(名词词尾)→突然出现的事情→紧急情况

【例】 In case of *emergency*, break the glass and press the button. 遇到紧急情况时，击碎玻璃并按下按钮。

【同】 crisis, pinch

emigrate ['emɪreɪt] *v*. 移居外国

【记】 e(= ex 出去) + migr(移动) + ate(动词词尾)→向外移动→移居外国

【例】 He *emigrated* from Britain to Australia in order to find a better job. 他从英国移居到澳大利亚，想找一份更好的工作。

【同】 leave, migrate

【反】 immigrate

【派】 emigrant *n*. 移居外国的人，移民

eminent ['emɪnənt] *adj*. 突出的，著名的，卓越的

【记】 e(= ex 出去) + min(突出) + ent(形容词词尾)→向外面突出→著名的

【例】 He is *eminent* both as a sculptor and as a portrait painter. 他既是著名的雕塑家又是著名的肖像画家。

【同】 famous, outstanding, prominent

【反】 nameless, unknown

【派】 eminence *n*. 出众，著名；要人

emit [ɪ'mɪt] *v*. (-tted; -tting)发出，散发(光、热、气味等)

【记】 e(= ex 出去) + mit(送)→送出去→放出

【例】 The cheese was *emitting* a strong smell. 干酪散发出强烈的气味。

【同】 give off

【反】 absorb

【派】 emission *n*. 散发，发射，(烟、气等)排放

emotion [ɪ'məʊʃən] *n*. 感情，情感

【记】 e(= ex 出去) + mot(移动) + ion(名词词尾)→移动出来的东西→感情

【例】 Chopin aroused very complicated *emotions* in her. 肖邦的乐曲唤起了她极其复杂的感情。

【同】 feeling, sentiment

【派】 emotional *adj*. 感情上的，情绪上的

emphasize ['emfəsaɪz] *v*. 强调，重视

【记】 em(= en, in 里面) + phas(出现) + ize(动词词尾)→把里面的也表现出来→强调

【例】 He *emphasized* the importance of careful driving. 他强调小心驾驶的重要性。

【同】 stress, underline

【反】 deemphasize

【派】 emphasis *n*. (复数-ses)强调，重点
emphatic *adj*. 强调的，语调强的

empire ['empaɪə] *n*. 帝国

【记】 empir(= emper, 命令，统治) + e→帝国

【例】 I am reading a book about the rise and fall of the Roman *Empire*. 我正在看一本关于罗马帝国兴衰的书。

empirical [em'pɪrɪkəl] *adj*. 以经验或实验为根据的，经验主义的

【记】 em(= en, in 里面) + piri(通过) + cal(形容词词尾)→在通过的过程中→在实验中→经验主义的

【例】 Some of these scholars found the Royal Society in 1660 in order to promote *empirical* scientific research. 他们当中的一些学者在 1660 年为促进经验主义的科学研究创立了皇家社团。

【同】 experiential, experimental

【反】 theoretical

【派】 empiricism *n*. 经验主义
empiricist *n*. 经验主义者

empower [ɪm'paʊə] *v*. 给…权利，赋权

【记】 em(= en，使进入…状态) + power(权利)→进入有权利的状态→给…权利

【例】 The new laws *empower* the police to stop anybody in the street. 新法令授予警察可以在街上截停任何人的权利。

【同】 authorize，enable，warrant

enact [ɪ'nækt] *v*. 制定法律，颁布

【记】 en(使) + act(法令)→使成为法令→制定法律

【例】 Several bills were *enacted* at the end of this session of Parliament. 这届国会结束时，好几个议案制定成为法律。

【同】 legislate，ordain

encase [ɪn'keɪs] *v*. 装入，包住

【记】 en(进入) + case(箱子)→装入箱子里→装入

【例】 His broken leg was *encased* in plaster. 他骨折的腿打上了石膏。

enchant [ɪn'tʃɑːnt] *v*. 施魔法，使迷惑

【记】 en(进入) + chant(圣歌)→唱圣歌给…听→施魔法

【例】 Her performance *enchanted* the audience. 她的表演迷住了观众。

【同】 captivate，charm，fascinate

【反】 disenchant

【派】 enchantment *n*. 迷惑，着迷；魔法

enclose [ɪn'kləʊz] *v*. 1. 装入，放入封套；2. 围绕

【记】 en(使) + close(关闭)→使封起来→装入，围绕

【例】 1. I *enclose* herewith two copies of the contract. 随函寄上合同副本两份。

2. He *enclosed* the land with a hedge. 他用篱笆把地圈起来。

【同】 envelop；encircle，surround

【反】 disclose

【派】 enclosure *n*. 围绕；围墙

encompass [ɪn'kʌmpəs] *v*. 1. 包围，环绕；2. 包含，包括

【记】 en(进入) + com(完全) + pass(通过)→完全进入通过→包围

【例】 1. The prison is *encompassed* by high walls. 监狱被高墙围绕着。

2. The general arts course at the university *encompasses* a wide range of subjects. 大学文科包括的科目非常广泛。

【同】 encircle，enclose，surround

encounter [ɪn'kaʊntə] n/*v*. 遭遇，遇到

【记】 en(进入…状态) + counter(冲突)→进入冲突状态→遭遇

【例】 1. An example was America's *encounter* with El Nino in 1997 and 1998. 一个例子是美国在 1997 和 1998 年遭遇了厄尔尼诺现象。

2. I *encountered* an old friend at Rome. 我在罗马邂逅了一个老朋友。

【同】 confront，meet

encourage [ɪn'kʌrɪdʒ] *v*. 鼓励

【记】 en(使进入…状态) + courage(勇气)→使进入有勇气的状态→鼓励

【例】 Her success *encouraged* me to try the same thing. 她的成功鼓励我试着做同样

的事。

【同】 inspire, promote, promote

【反】 discourage

【派】 encouragement *n*. 鼓励

encumber [ɪn'kʌmbə] *v*. 阻碍，妨碍

【记】 em(= en, in 里面) + cumb(横躺) + er(此处用作动词词尾)→横躺在里面→阻碍

【例】 Travelling is difficult when you're *encumbered* with two small children and a heavy suitcase. 旅行时带着两个孩子和一个沉重的手提箱，真是寸步难行。

【同】 hamper, hinder, impede

【派】 encumbrance *n*. 阻碍，累赘，妨害物

endanger [ɪn'deɪndʒə] *v*. 使遭危险，危害

【记】 en(使进入…状态) + danger(危险)→使进入危险的状态→使遭危险

【例】 The widespread use of pesticides and fertilisers may also have *endangered* the glow-worm. 杀虫剂和肥料的广泛使用可能也会危及萤火虫。

【同】 imperil, hazard, risk

【反】 safeguard, protect

endeavour [ɪn'devə] *v*./*n*. 尝试，竭力做到

【记】 en(里面) + deavour(责任)→在本分中→竭力

【例】 On account of your health, you must *endeavour* to shift off the care of your children. 由于你身体不好，你必须尽量避免为孩子们操心。

【同】 attempt, effort, strive, struggle

【反】 neglect

endorse [ɪn'dɔːs] *v*. 在…签字，赞同，支持

【记】 en(= on, …上) + dorse(背)→写于背面→在…签字

【例】 I am afraid I can't *endorse* your opinion. 很抱歉，我不赞成你的意见。

【同】 approve, support, sign

【反】 disapprove

【派】 endorsement *n*. 签注(文件)，认可

endow [ɪn'daʊ] *v*. 1. 捐赠；2. 赋予

【记】 en(使) + dow(= don 给)→给，拥有→捐赠

【例】 1. He *endowed* the hospital with a large fortune. 他捐赠一笔巨款给这家医院。
2. He is *endowed* with literary talent. 他有文学天分。

【同】 contribute; empower

【派】 endowment *n*. 禀赋；捐款

endure [ɪn'djʊə] *v*. 忍耐，耐久

【记】 en(= in, 处于…状态) + dure(持续)→处于持续的状态→耐久

【例】 I cannot *endure* listening to that any longer. 我再也不耐烦听那一套了。

【同】 bear, last, tolerate

【派】 endurable *adj*. 可忍受的，能忍耐的
endurance *n*. 忍耐，忍耐力

energy ['enədʒɪ] *n*. 1. 活力，精力；2. 能量，能源

E

【记】 en(进入)+erg(工作)+ y(名词词尾)→能让人进入工作的东西→能量

【例】 1. Young people usually have more *energy* than the old. 青年人通常比老年人精力充沛些。

2. The solar cell can convert the *energy* of sunlight into electric energy. 太阳能电池能把阳光的能量转化为电能。

【同】 force, power, vigor

【派】 energetic *adj*. 充满活力的，精力充沛的

enervate ['enɜːveɪt] *v*. 使虚弱，使无力

【记】 e(= ex 出去)+nerv(神经)+ate(动词词尾)→使神经失效→使虚弱

【例】 He was *enervated* by his long illness. 他因为长期生病而身体衰弱。

【同】 weaken, unnerve

enforce [ɪn'fɔːs] *v*. 1. 实施，使生效；2. 加强，支持

【记】 en(= in, 进入)+force(力量)→把力量加进去→强行

【例】 1. Policemen and judges *enforce* the law. 警察与法官执行法律。

2. Have you any statistics that would *enforce* your argument? 你有任何统计资料可以加强你的论点吗?

【同】 compel, execute, force

【反】 exempt

【派】 enforcement *n*. 实施；强制执行

enfranchise [ɪn'fræntʃaɪz] *v*. 给…公民权(或选择权)

【记】 en(使进入…状态)+franchise(公民权)→使处于有公民权状态→给…公民权

【例】 In Britain women were *enfranchised* in 1918. 1918 年英国妇女获得议会选举权。

【同】 franchise

【反】 disfranchise

【派】 enfranchisement *n*. 给…公民权(选择权)

engender [ɪn'dʒendə] *v*. 产生，引起

【记】 en(使)+gen(d)(产生)+er(此处是动词词尾)→使产生→产生，引起

【例】 Crime is sometimes *engendered* by poverty. 犯罪有时是由贫困引起的。

【同】 breed, generate, produce

engrave [ɪn'greɪv] *v*. 1. 雕上，雕刻；2. 铭记

【记】 en(= in 里面)+grave(切，刻)→刻在里面→雕刻，铭记

【例】 1. It is difficult to *engrave* in marble. 在大理石上雕刻是困难的。

2. The terrible scene was *engraved* on his memory. 那可怕的情景铭记在他的记忆里。

【同】 carve, inscribe

【派】 engraving *n*. 雕刻术，雕版，雕版图

engross [ɪn'grəʊs] *v*. 使全神贯注于，吸引

【记】 en(使)+gross(大)→使大部分进入→使全神贯注于

【例】 I was so *engrossed* in my work that I completely forgot the time. 我专心致志地工作，以至于全然忘记了时间。

【同】 absorb, engage, fascinate

enhance [ɪnˈhɑːns] *v*. 提高，增强

【记】 en(使成为)+hance(高)→使高→提高

【例】 He made many efforts to *enhance* his reputation. 他做了许多努力来提高他的声誉。

【同】 better, improve, uplift

【反】 diminish, decrease

【派】 enhancement *n*. 增进，增加

enigma [ɪˈnɪgmə] *n*. 谜，谜一样的东西

【例】 He is an *enigma* to all of us. 对我们而言，他是个神秘莫测的人物。

【同】 mystery, puzzle, riddle

【派】 enigmatic *adj*. 谜一般的，高深莫测的

enlarge [ɪnˈlɑːdʒ] *v*. 扩大，扩展

【记】 en(使成为)+large(大)→使变大→扩大

【例】 The police had the photograph of the missing girl *enlarged*. 警方把失踪姑娘的照片放大了。

【同】 broaden, expand, magnify

【反】 diminish, reduce, shrink

enlighten [ɪnˈlaɪtn] *v*. 启发，教导

【记】 en(使)+light(光)+en(动词词尾)→把光给…→启发

【例】 How can I *enlighten* your wooden head? 我怎么才能让你这木头疙瘩开窍呢?

【同】 acquaint, educate, instruct, illuminate

【派】 enlightenment *n*. 启发，启迪；[E～]启蒙运动

enlist [ɪnˈlɪst] *v*. 1. 入伍，征募；2. 得到(支持、帮助等)

【记】 en(使)+list(单子)→使在单子上→征募

【例】 1. He *enlisted* when he was 18. 他 18 岁时入伍。

2. This book is planned to *enlist* your active cooperation. 这本书的出版是建立在你会积极合作的基础上的。

【同】 enroll, recruit; obtain

enmity [ˈenmɪtɪ] *n*. 敌意，仇恨，不和

【记】 en(=in 不)+m(=am 爱)+ity(名词词尾)→不爱的→敌意，仇恨

【例】 They are at *enmity* with each other. 他们彼此不和。

【同】 dislike, hostility

【反】 amity

enormous [ɪˈnɔːməs] *adj*. 巨大的，庞大的

【记】 e(=ex 出去)+norm(规则)+ous(形容词词尾)→超出规则之外的→巨大的

【例】 Long ago *enormous* animals lived on the earth. 很久以前，地球上生活着巨大的动物。

【同】 colossal, huge, tremendous, vast

【反】 little, small, tiny

enrage [ɪnˈreɪdʒ] *v*. 激怒

【记】 en(使)+rage(愤怒)→使愤怒→激怒

【例】 Mary is *enraged* to find that he has left home. 玛丽万分气恼地发现他离家出走了。
【同】 anger, infuriate

enrapture [ɪn'ræptʃə] v. 使狂喜，使兴高采烈
【记】 en(使)+rapture(狂喜)→使出于狂喜的状态→使狂喜
【例】 We were *enraptured* by the view of the mountains. 我们看到山峦景色，心花怒放。
【同】 enchant, delight

E

enrich [ɪn'rɪtʃ] v. 使丰富，使土地肥沃
【记】 en(使)+rich(富)→使丰富
【例】 The expanding economy *enriched* the peasants. 不断发展的经济使农民们富裕起来。
【同】 better, improve

enroll [ɪn'rəʊl] v. 登记，注册
【记】 en(=in，进入)+roll(名册)→进入名册中→注册
【例】 I am preparing to come to *enroll* in early September. 我正在为9月初来报到做准备。
【同】 enlist, recruit, register
【派】 enrollment n. 登记，注册，入学

ensue [ɪn'sjuː] v. 跟着发生，继起
【记】 en(使进入…状态)+sue(跟随)→跟着发生
【例】 Many troubles *ensued* from this misunderstanding. 由此误会产生了许多麻烦。
【同】 follow, result, succeed

ensure [ɪn'ʃʊə] v. 保证，确保
【记】 en(使)+sure(确定的)→使确定→确保
【例】 This medicine will *ensure* you a good night's sleep. 这药保证能让你好好睡一觉。
【同】 assure, guarantee

entail [ɪn'teɪl] v. 使成为必要，牵涉
【记】 en(使)+tail(剪，切割)→使切开→牵涉
【例】 That will *entail* an early start tomorrow morning. 那就需要明晨很早动身。
【同】 implicate, involve

enterprise ['entəpraɪz] n. 企业，公司
【记】 enter(在…之间)+prise(抓，握取)→把(事业)掌握在手中→公司
【例】 The *enterprise* is an applicant of this credit. 这家企业是信用证的申请者。
【同】 business, undertaking
【派】 enterprising adj. 有事业心的，有进取心的
enterpriser n. 企业家

entertainment [entə'teɪnmənt] n. 娱乐，消遣
【记】 enter(在…之间)+tain(保持)+ment(名词词尾)→保持在其中→消遣
【例】 Television provides universal *entertainment*. 电视提供大众化的娱乐。
【同】 amusement, recreation

【派】 (逆构)entertain *v*. 给…娱乐，消遣

enthrall [ɪn'θrɔːl] *v*. 迷惑，迷住

【记】 en(使)+thrall(奴隶)→使成为奴隶→使着迷

【例】 The boy was *enthralled* by the stories of adventure. 这孩子被冒险故事迷住了。

【同】 captivate，enchant，fascinate

enthusiasm [ɪn'θjuːzɪæzəm] *n*. 热情，热心

【记】 en(进入…状态)+thus(=theo，神)+iasm(名词词尾)→进入像神一样的状态→热情

【例】 His *enthusiasm* breathed new life into the company. 他的热情给公司注入了新的生命力。

【同】 passion，warmth，zeal

【反】 apathy

【派】 enthusiastic *adj*. 满腔热情的，极感兴趣的

entitle [ɪn'taɪtl] *v*. 1. 给…以权利，给…以资格；2. 给(书、文章等)加标题

【记】 en(使)++title(题目)→使…有题目→给…加标题→给…以权利

【例】 1. All students at the college are *entitled* to become members of the Sports Centre, for an annual fee of £9.50. 所有本学院学生都有权利成为运动中心的会员，每年的会费是9.5英镑。

2. She read a poem *entitled* "The Apple Tree". 她读了一首题为"苹果树"的诗。

【同】 authorize，empower，enable；name，title

【反】 deprive

【派】 entitlement *n*. 权利

entity ['entɪtɪ] *n*. 实体，实在物

【记】 ent(存在)+ity(名词词尾)→存在的东西→实体

【例】 Since the war the country has been divided; it is no longer one political *entity*. 这个国家自战争爆发以来不再是一个统一的政治实体了。

【同】 being

entrepreneur [ˌɒntrəprə'nɜː] *n*. 企业家，创业者

【记】 entre(在…之间)+pren(抓，握取)+eur(法语名词词尾)→把(事业)掌握在手中的人→企业家

【例】 He will not have succeeded in such a risky business if he has not been such a clever *entrepreneur*. 假若他不是那么精明强干的企业家，就不会在这样冒险的事业中取得成功。

【同】 enterpriser

【派】 entrepreneurship *n*. 企业家的身份、地位、能力等

entrust [ɪn'trʌst] *v*. 信托，委托，托付

【记】 en(=to)+trust(信任)→信任→委托

【例】 He's *entrusted* his children to my care for a day. 他托我照看一天孩子。

【同】 confide，trust

entry ['entrɪ] *n*. 1. 进入，进入许可；2. 条目

【例】 Before *entry* to the school, students must take an entry test to determine the level of class they enter. 入学之前，学生要先参加入学考试，然后决定他们在哪一个等级的班级就读。

【同】 entrance，admission，admittance

【反】 exit

enumerate [ɪ'njuːməreɪt] *v*. 列举，枚举

【记】 e(= ex 出来) + numer(= number 数) + ate(动词词尾)→给出数来→列举

【例】 The teacher *enumerated* many examples to us for understanding. 为了让我们理解，老师列举了很多事例。

【同】 count，list，number

enunciate [ɪ'nʌnsɪeɪt] *v*. 1.清晰地发音；2.清楚地表达，宣布

【记】 e(= ex 出来) + nunci(报告) + ate(动词词尾)→报告出来→发音

【例】 1. She *enunciated* each word slowly for her students. 她把每个字都给学生慢慢念清楚。

2. He is always willing to *enunciate* his opinions on the subject of politics. 他总是愿意对政治问题发表意见。

【同】 pronounce；express，speak

【派】 enunciation *n*. 阐明

envelop [ɪn'veləp] *v*. 笼罩，包围

【记】 en(= in，里面) + velop(包，裹)→包在里面→包围

【例】 The building was soon *enveloped* in flames. 那幢建筑物很快就陷入了火海之中。

【同】 cover，embrace，encompass，wrap

environment [ɪn'vaɪərənmənt] *n*. 环境，自然环境

【记】 en(= in，里面) + viron(周围) + ment(名词词尾)→环绕在周围→环境

【例】 The house itself is not particularly to my mind，but I like its *environment*. 这房子本身并不特别合我的心意，但我喜欢它周围的环境。

【同】 circumstance，setting，situation，surroundings

【派】 environmental *adj*. 环境的，有关环境(保护)的

environmentalist *n*. 环保主义者，环境保护论者

envisage [ɪn'vɪzɪdʒ] *v*. 设想，预见

【记】 en(使) + vis(看见) + age(名词词尾转用作动词)→使看见→设想

【例】 Nobody can *envisage* the consequences of total nuclear war. 没有人能想象出全面核战争的后果。

【同】 picture，envision，visualize

envision [ɪn'vɪʒən] *v*. 想象，预想

【记】 en(使) + vis(看见) + ion(名词词尾转用作动词)→使看见→想象

【例】 You will achieve precisely the success you can *envision* for yourself. 你将会达成你为自己设定的目标。

【同】 picture，envisage，visualize

envoy ['envɔɪ] *n*. 外交使节，使者

【记】 en(使) + voy(路)→使在路上→派遣→使节

【例】 The special *envoy*'s visit established a link between the two countries. 特使的出访

在两国间建立了联系。

【同】 diplomat, messenger

envy [ˈenvɪ] *n*. / *v*. 羡慕，嫉妒

【记】 en(= to) + vy(= vid 看见)→看见了→羡慕

【例】 1. He was filled with *envy* at my success. 他对我的成功满怀羡慕。

2. They *envy* him his good fortune. 他们羡慕他的好运气。

【同】 jealousy; begrudge

【派】 envious *adj*. 嫉妒的，羡慕的

ephemeral [ɪˈfemərəl] *adj*. 短暂的，转瞬即逝的

【记】 ep(= epi 在…之中) + hemer(天) + al(形容词词尾)→在一天之中→短暂的，转瞬即逝的

【例】 Such novels came forward to enjoy *ephemeral* popularity only. 这样的小说只是昙花一现的东西而已。

【同】 transient, temporary

【反】 eternal, lasting

epic [ˈepɪk] *n*. 史诗，惊人之举；*adj*. 史诗般的，宏伟的

【例】 1. Have you read another *epic* about the Roman Empire? 你读过另一部关于罗马帝国的史诗吗?

2. This story is about the *epic* fight of one small ship against six enemy ships. 这是关于一艘小船对抗六艘敌舰的英勇战斗的故事。

【同】 poem, verse; heroic, splendid

【反】 lyric

epidemic [ˌepɪˈdemɪk] *adj*. 流行的，传染的；*n*. 流行病，时疫

【记】 epi(在…之间) + dem(人民) + ic(形容词词尾)→流行于人民之中的→流行病

【例】 1. Violence is reaching *epidemic* levels in some of the films and TV plays. 在一些电影和电视剧中暴力已经快到泛滥程度了。

2. A flu *epidemic* raged through the school for weeks. 流感在这所学校里蔓延了几个星期。

【同】 contagious, infectious, prevalent

episode [ˈepɪsəʊd] *n*. 片断，插曲

【记】 epi(在…之间) + sode(进入)→在…之间插入的东西→插曲

【例】 That is one of the funniest *episodes* in my life. 那是我生活中最有趣的插曲之一。

【同】 section, incident, occurrence

epitomize [ɪˈpɪtəmaɪz] *v*. 摘要，为…的典型表现

【记】 epi(在…上) + tom(剪) + ize(动词词尾)→在原来的基础上修剪→摘要

【例】 This strike *epitomizes* what's wrong with industrial relations in this country. 这次罢工是这个国家在劳资关系方面问题的表现。

【同】 abstract

【派】 (逆构)epitome *n*. 摘要，概括

epoch [ˈiːpɒk, ˈepɒk] *n*. 时代，纪元

【记】 epi(在…上) + och(保持)→在原来的时间上加上新的→纪元

【例】 Einstein's theory marked a new *epoch* in physics. 爱因斯坦的理论开创了物理学的新纪元。

【同】 age, era, period

equality [iː'kwɒlɪtɪ] *n*. 相等，平等

【记】 equ(相等的) + al(形容词词尾) + ity(名词词尾)→相等，平等

【例】 I do not believe in *equality* of capacity, but I do believe in equality of opportunity. 我不相信能力均等，但我确实相信机会均等。

【同】 equivalent, parallel; match

【派】 (逆构)equal *adj*. 相同的，相等的；*v*. 与…相同或相等

equation [ɪ'kweɪʃən] *n*. 1. 等式，公式，方程式；2. 相等，平衡

【记】 equ(相等的) + ation(名词词尾)→相等的东西→等式

【例】 1. I can't make this *equation* come out. 我不会解这个方程式。

2. The *equation* of wealth with happiness can be dangerous. 把财富与幸福等同起来是很危险的。

【同】 equilisation

equator [ɪ'kweɪtə] *n*. 赤道

【记】 equa(相等的) + tor(名词词尾)→把地球等分的东西→赤道

【例】 Singapore is near the *equator*. 新加坡位于赤道附近。

equilibrium [ˌiːkwɪ'lɪbrɪəm] *n*. 均衡，平衡

【记】 equi(相等的) + libr(平衡) + ium(名词词尾)→均衡

【例】 The *equilibrium* of force must be established in Europe. 必须确立欧洲的均势。

【同】 balance

equip [ɪ'kwɪp] *v*. (-pped; -pping)装备，配备

【例】 English was not well *equipped* to deal with scientific argument. 英语不太适合于进行科学论证。

【同】 furnish, outfit

【派】 equipment *n*. 设备，器材

equity ['ekwɪtɪ] *n*. 公平，公正的裁判；2. (一般用复数 equities)证券

【记】 equ(相等的) + ity(名词词尾)→相等的状况→公平

【例】 1. They shared the work of the house with perfect *equity*. 他们很公平地分担屋内的工作。

2. Once again *equities* were hard hit. 股票再次受到严重打击。

【同】 fairness, justice

【派】 equitable *adj*. 公平合理的，公正的

equivalent [ɪ'kwɪvələnt] *adj*. 相等的，相同的；*n*. 相等物，等价物

【记】 equi(相等的) + val(价值) + ent(形容词词尾)→价值相等的→等价物

【例】 1. He changed his pounds for the *equivalent* amount in dollars. 他把英镑兑换成等值的美元。

2. Some American words have no British *equivalents*. 一些美国英语在英国英语中没有对应的词。

【同】 equal, same; substitute, match

【派】 equivalence *n*. 同等，等值

era ['ɪərə] *n*. 时期，年代，纪元

【例】 We are living in the computer *era*. 我们正生活在计算机时代。

【同】 age, epoch, period

eradicate [ɪ'rædɪkeɪt] *v*. 根除，杜绝

【记】 e(= ex 出来) + radi(c)(根) + ate(动词词尾)→把根拔出来→根除

【例】 Smallpox has almost been *eradicated*. 天花几乎已经被消灭了。

【同】 eliminate, exterminate

【派】 eradication *n*. 根除，杜绝

erase [ɪ'reɪz] *v*. 擦掉，消除

【记】 e(= ex 离开) + rase(刮，擦)→擦掉

【例】 She couldn't *erase* the incident from her memory. 她难以忘记那次事件。

【同】 cancel, delete

【反】 record

【派】 eraser *n*. 橡皮

erect [ɪ'rekt] *adj*. 直立的，竖立的；*v*. 建立，创立

【记】 e(= ex 出去) + rect(直立的)→使笔直向上→使竖立

【例】 1. She held her head *erect* and her back straight. 她昂着头，把背挺得笔直。

2. They *erected* their tent at the foot of the mountain. 他们在山脚下支起了帐篷。

【同】 straight, upright, vertical; build, construct

【派】 erection *n*. 直立，竖起；建筑物

erode [ɪ'rəʊd] *v*. 腐蚀，侵蚀

【记】 e(= ex 离开) + rode(咬)→咬掉→侵蚀

【例】 Metals are *eroded* by acids. 金属易被酸所腐蚀。

【同】 corrode, disintegrate

【派】 erosion *n*. 腐蚀，侵蚀

err [ɜː] *v*. 做错，出差错

【例】 To *err* is human. 人都会犯错误。

【同】 misbehave

【派】 error *n*. 错误

erroneous *adj*. 错误的，不正确的

erratic [ɪ'rætɪk] *adj*. 1. 古怪的；2. 不稳定的，不规则的

【记】 err(漫游，走) + atic(形容词词尾)→到处游走的→不稳定的

【例】 1. Jack is a good man, but then he is so *erratic*. 杰克是个好人，但他为人相当怪僻。

2. She is a very *erratic* tennis player. 她是一个技术非常不稳定的网球手。

【同】 queer; changeable, irregular

eruption [ɪ'rʌpʃən] *n*. (火山)喷发，(战争等)爆发

【记】 e(= ex 离开) + rupt(打破) + ion(名词词尾)→打破而出→喷发

【例】 The *eruption* of volcano makes many people lose their lives. 火山的爆发使许多人丧失了生命。

【同】 blast, explosion

【派】 (逆构)erupt *v*. (火山)喷发, (战争等)爆发

escort [ɪs'kɔːt] *v*. 护送, 伴随

【记】 es(= ex 出去) + cort(直的)→使直着出去→护送

【例】 The troop ship was *escorted* by two warships. 运兵船由两艘军舰护航。

【同】 accompany, usher

essence ['esns] *n*. 精华, 实质

【记】 ess(存在) + ence(名词词尾)→存在的东西→实质

【例】 The two things are the same in outward form but different in *essence*. 那两样东西在外表上相同, 但在本质上不同。

【同】 significance, substance

【派】 essential *adj*. 本质的, 基本的, 非常重要的

establish [ɪs'tæblɪʃ] *v*. 1. 建立, 设立; 2. 证实, 确定

【记】 e(表示强调) + stabli(站立) + sh(名词词尾)→站在…之上→建立

【例】 1. Our company was *established* in 1994. 我们的公司成立于 1994 年。

2. His second novel *established* his fame as a writer. 他的第二部小说确立了他的作家之名。

【同】 build, found, constitute; prove

【反】 demolish, destroy, ruin

【派】 establishment *n*. 建立, 确立, 建立的机构

established *adj*. 已建立的, 已确定的

estate [ɪ'steɪt] *n*. 房地产, 财产; 2. 住宅区

【记】 e(表示强调) + state(站立)→站在那里的东西→不动产, 财产

【例】 1. Her *estate* was divided between her four children. 她的遗产分给了她的四个子女。

2. In some California housing *estates*, a key alone is insufficient to get someone in the door. 在加利弗尼亚的一些居民区, 一个人只有钥匙是进不了房门的。

【同】 land, property

esteem [ɪs'tiːm] *v*. / *n*. 尊敬, 敬重

【例】 1. We *esteem* him to be worthy of trust. 我们认为他值得信任。

2. We all have great *esteem* for you. 我们都非常敬重您。

【同】 appreciate, respect, treasure, value

【反】 despise

estimate ['estɪmeɪt] *v*. / *n*. 估计, 评估

【记】 estim(价值) + ate(动词词尾)→评出价值→评估

【例】 1. My *estimate* of the length of the room was 10 feet. 我估计房间的长度为 10 英尺。

2. He is highly *estimated* among his colleagues. 他在同事中受到的评价很高。

【同】 evaluate, value, assess

【派】 estimation *n*. 估计, 评价, 判断

estimable *adj*. 可估计的; 值得尊敬的

eternal [iː'təːnl] *adj*. 永久的，永恒的

【记】 etern(时代) + al(形容词词尾)→经过时代的→永恒的

【例】 She felt *eternal* gratitude to him for saving her life. 她终生感激他的救命之恩。

【同】 endless, everlasting, perpetual, permanent

【反】 momentary, temporary, transient

【派】 eternity *n*. 永远，不朽

ethical ['eθɪkəl] *adj*. 道德的，伦理的

【记】 ethic(伦理) + al(形容词词尾)→伦理的

【例】 You can't divorce science from *ethical* questions. 不能把科学与伦理问题截然分开。

【同】 moral

【反】 unethical

【派】 (逆构)ethic *n*. 道德规范，伦理

ethnic ['eθnɪk] *adj*. 种族的，民族的

【记】 ethn(人种，民族) + ic(形容词词尾)→种族的

【例】 This music would sound more *ethnic* if you played it on steel drums. 如果你用钢鼓演奏，这首乐曲将更具有民族特色。

【同】 ethnical

ethnography [eθ'nɒrəfɪ] *n*. 人种学，民族志学

【记】 ethno(人种，民族) + graph(写) + y(名词词尾)→写关于人种或民族的→人种学，民族志学

【例】 The Department of *Ethnography* was created as a separate department within the British Museum in 1946. 人种史馆是作为大英博物馆的一个单独的机构于1946年设立的。

【派】 ethnographic *adj*. 人种论的，民族志的

ethnographer *n*. 人种论学者，民族志研究者

etiquette [etɪ'ket, 'etɪket] *n*. 礼仪，礼节

【记】 etiqu(标签) + ettee(加在名词后面，表示"小")→小的标签→礼节

【例】 According to *etiquette*, you shall stand up to meet a guest. 按照礼节你应该站起来接待客人。

【同】 manners

eulogy ['juːlədʒɪ] *n*. 颂词，歌功颂德的话

【记】 eu(好) + log(说) + y(名词词尾)→说好话→颂词

【例】 He pronounced a *eulogy* upon the hero. 他向英雄致颂词。

【同】 praise

【派】 eulogize *v*. 称赞，颂扬

euphemism ['juːfɪmɪzəm] *n*. 委婉说法，婉辞

【记】 eu(好) + phem(= phon 声音) + ism(名词词尾)→听起来舒服的说法→委婉说法

【例】 "Pass away" is a *euphemism* for "die". "去世"是"死"的委婉语。

【同】 locution

【派】 euphemistic *adj*. 委婉的

euphonious [juːˈfəʊnɪəs] *adj*. 悦耳的

【记】 eu(好)+phon(声音)+ious(形容词词尾)→好听的→悦耳的

【例】 I like her *euphonious* Southern speech. 我喜欢她那柔和的南方语音。

【同】 silvery, soft

【反】 cacophonous

evade [ɪˈveɪd] *v*. 逃脱，躲开

【记】 e(=ex 出去)+vade(走)→走出去→躲开

【例】 The policeman *evaded* all the difficult questions. 那警察回避了所有难以答复的问题。

【同】 avoid, escape, miss

【反】 face, confront

【派】 evasion *n*. 逃避，借口

evasive *adj*. 逃避的，推托的

evaluate [ɪˈvæljʊeɪt] *v*. 评价，估价

【记】 e(加强语气)+valu(e)(价值)+ate(动词词尾)→评出价值→评价

【例】 The school has only been open for six months, so it's hard to *evaluate* its success. 那所学校仅开办了六个月，现在还很难估计它的成就。

【同】 appraise, estimate, value

【派】 evaluation *n*. 估价，评价

evaporate [ɪˈvæpəreɪt] *v*. 蒸发，消失

【记】 e(=ex 出去)+vapor(蒸汽)+are(动词词尾)→放出蒸汽→蒸发

【例】 The water soon *evaporated* in the sunshine. 水在阳光下不久就蒸发了。

【同】 disappear, vanish

【派】 evaporation *n*. 蒸发，消散

eventuality [ɪˌventjʊˈælɪtɪ] *n*. 可能发生的事，可能出现的结果

【记】 e(=ex 出去)+vent(来到)+ual(形容词词尾)+ity(名词词尾)→来到的事情→结果

【例】 We must be prepared for any *eventuality*. 我们必须做好应付各种情况的准备。

【派】 (逆构)eventual *adj*. 最终的，最后的

eventually *adv*. 终于，最后

evident [ˈevɪdənt] *adj*. 明显的，清楚的

【记】 e(=ex 外面)+vid(看见)+ent(形容词词尾)→从外面可以看见的→明显的

【例】 It was *evident* that the policy was a failure. 显然这项政策是失败的。

【同】 distinct, obvious, apparent, clear

【反】 doubtful, uncertain

evoke [ɪˈvəʊk] *v*. 唤起，引起

【记】 e(=ex 外面)+voke(喊叫)→唤起

【例】 The book *evoked* memories of his boyhood. 此书唤起了他对童年的回忆。

【同】 arouse, provoke, stimulate

evolution [ˌiːvəˈluːʃən] *n*. 进化，演变

【记】 e(=ex 外面)+volu(滚)+tion(名词词尾)→向外滚→进化

【例】 Do you know about the *evolution* of a seed into a plant? 你知道从种子发展成为植物的过程吗?

【同】 development, progress

【反】 devolution(退化, 衰落)

【派】 (逆构)evolve *v*. 发展, 进化

evolutionary *adj*. 演变的, 演化的

exacerbate [eks'æsɜːbeɪt] *v*. 使加剧, 使恶化

【记】 ex(出去)+acerb(酸的)+ate(动词词尾)→使酸了→使恶化

【例】 Her mother's interference *exacerbated* the difficulties in their marriage. 她母亲从中干预使他们的婚姻雪上加霜。

【同】 aggravate, worsen

【派】 exacerbation *n*. 恶化, 增剧

exaggerate [ɪ'zædʒəreɪt] *v*. 夸张, 夸大

【记】 ex(出去)+ag(to)+ger(运, 载)+ate(动词词尾)→向外扩张→夸张

【例】 The seriousness of the situation has been much *exaggerated* by the press. 形势的严重性被报纸夸大了。

【同】 enlarge, magnify, overstate

【反】 understate

【派】 exaggeration *n*. 夸张, 夸大

exalt [ɪ'zɔːlt] *v*. 1. 晋升, 提升; 2. 赞扬, 歌颂

【记】 ex(出去)+alt(高)→使高出去→提升

【例】 1. He was *exalted* to the position of general manager. 他被提升到总经理的职位。

2. Songs of *exalting* the motherland are ringing far and near. 颂扬祖国的歌声响彻四方。

【同】 elevate, raise; extol, praise

【派】 exalted *adj*. 崇高的, 高贵的

exasperate [ɪ'zɑːspəreɪt] *v*. 激怒

【记】 ex(出去)+asper(粗糙)+ate(动词词尾)→把粗糙的(脾气)展示出去→激怒

【例】 Constant interruption of his work *exasperated* him. 对他工作不断的干扰使他恼怒。

【同】 aggravate, infuriate, irritate

exceed [ɪk'siːd] *v*. 超过, 胜过

【记】 ex(出去)+ceed(走)→走出去→超过

【例】 Demand began to *exceed* supply. 开始供不应求。

【同】 excel, overtake, surpass

【派】 exceeding *adj*. 超过的, 非常的

exceedingly *adv*. 非常, 极其

excel [ɪk'sel] *v*. (-lled; -lling)胜过, 擅长

【记】 ex(出去)+cel(上升)→比…高出→胜过

【例】 They each *excel* in their respective fields. 他们在各自领域里都是出类拔萃的。

【同】 exceed, surpass

【派】 excellent *adj*. 优秀的，卓越的
excellence *n*. 优秀，卓越

exception [ɪk'sepʃən] *n*. 除外，例外

【记】 except(除…外)+ion(名词词尾)→除外

【例】 All students without *exception* must take the English examination. 所有的学生毫无例外，都必须参加英语考试。

【同】 exclusion

【反】 inclusion

【派】 exceptional *adj*. 例外的，独特的；杰出的

excerpt ['eksɜːpt] *n*. 摘录，节选，引用

【记】 ex(出来)+cerpt(挑选)→挑选出来→摘录

【例】 One of the Sunday newspapers is publishing *excerpts* from her new book. 其中一家星期日报纸正在刊登她新书的节选。

【同】 extract, selection

excess [ɪk'ses, 'ekses] *n*. 过度，超过

【记】 ex(外面)+cess(走)→向外走多了→过度

【例】 She was charged an *excess* of 4 pounds over the amount stated on the bill. 向她索取的比账单上显示的数额多出4英镑。

【同】 additional, extra, surplus

【派】 excessive *adj*. 过分的，过度的

exclaim [ɪks'kleɪm] *v*. 呼喊，惊叫

【记】 ex(外面)+claim(大叫)→向外面大叫→呼喊

【例】 She *exclaimed* in delight when she saw the present. 她见到礼物高兴得叫了起来。

【同】 clamour, shout

【派】 exclamation *n*. 惊呼，感叹
exclamatory *adj*. 叫喊的，感叹的

exclude [ɪks'kluːd] *v*. 把…排斥在外，不包括

【记】 ex(外面)+clude(关闭)→关在外面→不包括

【例】 We cannot *exclude* the possibility that he killed his wife. 我们不能排除他杀了他妻子的可能性。

【同】 bar, forbid, prohibit

【反】 include

【派】 exclusive *adj*. 排他的，专有的
exclusion *n*. 排除，除外

excursion [ɪks'kɜːʃən] *n*. 远足，短途旅行

【记】 ex(外面)+cur(跑)+sion(名词词尾)→到外面走走→短途旅行

【例】 The *excursion* was the high spot of our holiday. 我们那个假日的最大乐趣是远足。

【同】 outing, journey, tour

【派】 (逆构)excurse *v*. 远足，短程旅行

executive [ɪg'zekjʊtɪv] *adj*. 执行的，行政的；*n*. 执行者，经理，行政官

【记】 ex(出去)+(s)ecut(跟随)+ive(形容词词尾)→跟随出去的→执行的

【例】 1. He is a man of great *executive* ability. 他是个具有极高管理才能的人。
2. The President of the United States is the chief *executive*. 美国总统是行政首脑。
【同】 administrative, managing; administrator
【派】 (逆构)execute *v*. 实行，执行
execution *n*. 实行，执行

exemplary [ɪɡ'zemplərɪ] *adj*. 模范的，典范的，可仿效的
【记】 exempl(来自拉丁语 exemplum 样板) + ary(形容词词尾)→样板的→模范的
【例】 He led an *exemplary* life. 他的一生堪作楷模。
【同】 admirable, typical

exemplify [ɪɡ'zemplɪfaɪ] *v*. 例证，例示
【记】 exempl(来自拉丁语 exemplum 样板) + ify(动词词尾)→使成为样板→例证
【例】 The recent oil price rises *exemplify* the difficulties which the motor industry is now facing. 最近的石油涨价是汽车工业正面临的困难的一个例子。
【同】 demonstrate, illustrate, show
【派】 exemplification *n*. 例证，范例

exempt [ɪɡ'zempt] *v*. 豁免，免除；*adj*. 被豁免的，被免除的
【记】 ex(出去) + empt(拿)→拿出去，拿掉→免除
【例】 1. Poor eyesight will *exempt* you from military service. 视力不佳将使你免服兵役。
2. These houses are *exempt* from paying rates. 这些房子是免付捐税的。
【同】 excuse, free, release
【反】 enforce
【派】 exemption *n*. 免除，免税

exert [ɪɡ'zɜːt] *v*. 用力，行使，发挥
【记】 ex(外面) + (s)ert(放在一起)→把(力量)全拿出来→用力
【例】 He *exerted* all his influence to make them accept his plan. 他用尽一切影响力使他们接受他的计划。
【同】 exercise, use
【派】 exertion *n*. 努力，尽力

exhaust [ɪɡ'zɔːst] *v*. 用完，耗尽
【记】 ex(外面) + haust(拉，抽)→抽出去→耗尽
【例】 The long cycle ride *exhausted* her. 她因长途骑车而疲惫不堪。
【同】 consume, spend, use up
【反】 supply, provide
【派】 exhaustible *adj*. 可耗尽的，会枯竭的

exhibit [ɪɡ'zɪbɪt] *v*. 展现，展览
【记】 ex(外面) + hibit(拥有)→将自己拥有的东西拿出来→展览
【例】 Many unearthed cultural relics were *exhibited* at the museum. 博物馆展出了许多出土文物。
【同】 display
【派】 exhibition *n*. 展览，展览会

exhilarate [ɪɡ'zɪləreɪt] *v*. 使高兴，使兴奋

【记】 ex(出来)+hilar(高兴)+ate(动词词尾)→使高兴

【例】 I was *exhilarated* by my ride in the sports car. 乘坐赛车使我感到很刺激。

【同】 cheer, excite

【派】 exhilarating *adj*. 爽快的，使人愉快的，令人兴奋的

exhilaration *n*. 令人高兴，愉快

exist [ɪg'zɪst] *v*. 存在，生存

【记】 ex(外面)+(s)ist(站)→站出来→存在

【例】 Men cannot *exist* without air. 没有空气人就不能生存。

【同】 be, live

【派】 existence *n*. 存在，实在，生活

existent *adj*. 存在的，生存的

exit ['eksɪt] *n*. 出口，通道

【记】 ex(外面)+it(行走)→向外走的地方→出口

【例】 There are four emergency *exits* in the department store. 这家百货公司有四个紧急出口。

【同】 outlet

【反】 entrance

exonerate [ɪg'zɒnəreɪt] *v*. 免除罪过，确定无罪

【记】 ex(出去)+oner(负担)+ate(动词词尾)→使去掉负担→免除罪过

【例】 The report on the accident *exonerates* the bus driver from any responsibility. 事故的报告认为公共汽车司机是没有任何责任的。

【同】 acquit, exculpate

【反】 inculpate

exorbitant [ɪg'zɔːbɪtənt] *adj*. 过高的，过分的

【记】 ex(出去)+orbit(圆周，轨道)+ant(形容词词尾)→超出范围的→过高的，过分的

【例】 That seaside hotel charges *exorbitant* prices during the summer holidays. 那家海滨旅馆在夏天休假期间漫天要价。

【同】 excessive, unreasonable

【反】 moderate

exotic [ɪg'zɒtɪk] *adj*. 外来的，异国情调的

【记】 exo(外面)+tic(形容词词尾)→从外面来的→外来的

【例】 The film retains much of the book's *exotic* flavour. 这部电影保存了原著的许多异国情调。

【同】 foreign

【反】 indigenous, native

【派】 exoticism *n*. 异国情调，对外国事物的兴趣

expand [ɪks'pænd] *v*. 扩大，扩展

【记】 ex(向外)+pand(伸展)→向外伸展→扩展

【例】 Once over the age of three, children continue to *expand* on existing knowledge of the world. 一旦过了3岁，孩子们将继续扩展他们现有的关于这个世界的知识。

【同】 enlarge, extend, broaden

【反】 condense, shrink

【派】 expansion *n*. 扩充，扩张

expansive *adj*. 可扩展的；广泛的，全面的

expedient [ɪks'piːdɪənt] *adj*. (指行动)权宜之计的，有利的，有用的

【记】 ex(出去) + ped(足) + ient(形容词词尾)→能让脚出去的→有助于行进的→有利的

【例】 He thought it *expedient* not to tell his wife where he had been. 他认为不告诉妻子他去过哪里是适宜的。

【同】 appropriate, helpful, sensible

【反】 inexpedient

expedite ['ekspɪdaɪt] *v*. 使加速，促进

【记】 ex(出去) + ped(足) + ite(动词词尾)→脚跨出去→加速

【例】 They promised to *expedite* payment. 他们承诺尽快付款。

【同】 hasten, hurry

【派】 expeditious *adj*. 迅速的，敏捷的

expedition [ˌekspɪ'dɪʃən] *n*. 探险，考察

【记】 ex(出去) + ped(足) + ition(名词词尾)→脚走出去→探险，考察

【例】 They planned to organize a scientific *expedition*. 他们计划组织一次科学考察。

【同】 exploration, journey

expel [ɪks'pel] *v*. (-lled; -lling)赶走，驱逐

【记】 ex(出去) + pel(驱赶，驱使)→驱赶出去→驱逐

【例】 Two attaches at the embassy were *expelled* from the country. 大使馆的两名随员已被驱逐出境。

【同】 discharge, dismiss

expertise [ˌekspə'tiːz] *n*. 专门知识(或技能)，专长

【记】 ex(完全) + perti(= peri 通过) + se→完全经历过的，积累的知识→专门知识

【例】 We were amazed at his *expertise* on the ski slopes. 他斜坡滑雪的技能使我们赞叹不已。

【同】 knowledge, professionalism

expire [ɪks'paɪə] *v*. 1.呼气，断气；2.(因到期而)失效，终止

【记】 ex(外面) + spire(呼吸)→向外呼气→呼气

【例】 1. He *expired* at midnight. 他半夜死去。

2. Our present lease on the flat *expires* next month. 我们这套公寓的租约下月到期。

【同】 exhale, perish; terminate

【反】 inspire

【派】 expiry *n*. (期限)到期，终止

expiration *n*. 呼气，满期

explicit [ɪks'plɪsɪt] *adj*. 详述的，清楚明白的

【记】 ex(外面) + plicit(折叠)→向外折叠→表现在外→清楚明白的

【例】 He gave me *explicit* directions on how to get there. 他清清楚楚地告诉我怎样到达那里。

【同】 clear，definite，specific

【反】 ambiguous，implicit，vague

explode [ɪks'pləʊd] *v*. 爆炸，爆发

【记】 ex(出来)+plode(鼓掌)→雷鸣般的掌声就像爆炸→爆炸

【例】 When the boiler *exploded* many people were injured. 因锅炉爆炸，许多人受了伤。

【同】 blast，burst，erupt

【派】 explosion *n*. 爆炸，激增

explosive *adj*. 爆炸的，爆发的

exploit [ɪks'plɔɪt] *v*. 1.开拓，开发；2.利用，剥削

【记】 ex(外面)+ploit(=plic 折叠)→向外折叠→开→开发

【例】 1. People should read the related regulations before they *exploit* natural resources. 在开发自然资源前，人们应该先了解相关的规定。

2. Television advertisers can *exploit* a captive audience. 电视广告商能利用被动观众。

【同】 explore；utilize

【派】 exploitation *n*. 1.开发，开采；2.利用，剥削

exploitative *adj*. 剥削的，榨取的

explore [ɪks'plɔː] *v*. 1.探险；2.探索，探究

【记】 ex(出来)+plore(流出)→流出来→探索

【例】 1. The experts are *exploring* every part of the island. 专家们正在勘查这个岛的各个部分。

2. We must *explore* all the possibilities. 我们必须要探讨所有的可能性。

【同】 exploit，probe，search；examine，research

【派】 exploration *n*. 探索，探究

explorer *n*. 探险者

expose [ɪks'pəʊz] *v*. 暴露，使遭受

【记】 ex(外面)+pose(放)→放在外面→暴露

【例】 Some Russian scientists claim that children learn better after being *exposed* to ultraviolet light. 一些俄罗斯科学家声称孩子在接触紫外线之后会学习得更好。

【同】 disclose，reveal

【反】 conceal，cover，hide

【派】 exposed *adj*. 易受攻击的，无保护的

exposure *n*. 暴露，面临

exposition [ˌekspə'zɪʃən] *n*. 博览会，展览会

【记】 ex(外面)+pos(放置)+ition(名词词尾)→把东西放在外面→博览会

【例】 The industrial *exposition* will be held in September. 工业博览会将于9月召开。

【同】 exhibition

expound [ɪks'paʊnd] *v*. 解释，详细说明

【记】 ex(外面)+pound(放)→把…放在外面→详细说明

【例】 He *expounded* the reasons why he did it. 他阐述了他做这件事的理由。

【同】 elaborate，explain，clarify

express [ɪks'pres] *v*. 表达，表示；*adj*. 快的，直达的；*n*. 快递，快运

【记】 ex(出去)+press(压)→把(思想)压出来→表达

【例】 1. I can't *express* how grateful I am. 我说不出我有多么感激。

2. The parcel was sent by *express* (delivery). 这包裹是用快邮寄的。

【同】 convey，indicate，show

【派】 expression *n*. 表情

expressive *adj*. 表现的，表达的

exquisite ['ekskwɪzɪt] *adj*. 优美的，精致的

【记】 ex(出来)+quis(寻求)+ite(形容词词尾)→被寻求出来的→被选出的→精致的

【例】 The girl came up with a set of *exquisite* stamps. 那姑娘拿出一套精美的邮票。

【同】 delicate，elegant，fine

extant [eks'tænt] *adj*. 现存的，尚存的

【记】 ex(出来)+t(=st 站)+ant(形容词词尾)→仍能站出来的→尚存的

【例】 The earliest *extant* manuscript of this poem has been kept in the museum. 此诗现存最早的原稿收藏在这座博物馆里。

【同】 surviving，remaining

【反】 extinct

extemporize [eks'tempəraɪz] *v*. 即席演说，即兴演奏，当场作成

【记】 ex(=at 在)+tempor(时间)+ize(动词词尾)→使在当时做→即席演说

【例】 He had to *extemporize* because he had forgotten to bring his notes. 他因为忘了带讲稿，只好即席发言。

【派】 (逆构)extempore *adj*./*adv*. 即席(的)，当场(的)；*n*. 即席之作

extemporaneous *adj*. 即席的，无准备的

extend [ɪks'tend] *v*. 扩大范围，延伸

【记】 ex(外面)+tend(伸张)→向外伸张→扩大

【例】 At the same time, however, scholars also began to test and *extend* this knowledge. 然而同时，学者还开始检验并扩展这些知识。

【同】 broaden，expand，enlarge，stretch

【反】 contract，shrink

【派】 extendable *adj*. 可延伸的

extensive *adj*. 广大的，广阔的，广泛的

extension *n*. 延长，延期

extent [ɪks'tent] *n*. 广度，范围，程度

【记】 ex(外面)+tent(伸张)→向外伸张→广度

【例】 I was amazed at the *extent* of his knowledge. 我对他知识的渊博感到惊奇。

【同】 degree，expanse，level

extenuate [ɪks'tenjʊeɪt] *v*. 减轻，使(罪过)等显得轻微

【记】 ex(出去)+tenu(细的，稀薄的)+ate(动词词尾)→使细下去→减轻

【例】 He stole the money, but there were *extenuating* circumstances. 他的确偷了钱，但有可以减轻罪责的情况。

【同】 mitigate，palliate

【派】 extenuating *adj*. 使减轻的，情有可原的

extenuation *n*. 减轻罪孽的借口，酌情减轻

exterior [eks'tɪərɪə] *adj*. 外面的，外部的

【记】 exter(外面，出去)+ior(表示比较级的形容词词尾)→比较靠外面的→外部的

【例】 Not only will all the roofs need insulating, the *exterior* walls will be required to be double brick. 不仅所有的屋顶都需要绝缘材料，所有的外墙也都必须用双层砖。

【同】 external，outer，outside

【反】 interior

exterminate [ɪks'tɜːmɪneɪt] *v*. 根除，灭绝

【记】 ex(出去)+termin(界限)+ate(动词词尾)→使…超出界限以外→全部消灭→根除

【例】 We've made great efforts to *exterminate* mosquitoes and flies. 我们做了很大努力来消灭蚊蝇。

【同】 eradicate，eliminate，uproot

【派】 extermination *n*. 消灭，灭绝

external [eks'tɜːnl] *adj*. 外部的，外面的

【记】 extern(外面，出去)+ al(形容词词尾)→外面的

【例】 This news program only covers *external* events. 这一新闻节目只报道国外消息。

【同】 exterior，outer，outside

【反】 internal

extinct [ɪks'tɪŋkt] *adj*. 灭绝的，绝种的

【记】 ex(出去)+ stinct(刺)→把刺拿出去→灭绝的

【例】 Dinosaurs have been *extinct* for millions of years. 恐龙已绝种几百万年了。

【同】 dead，gone

【反】 extant，living

【派】 extinction *n*. 消亡，灭绝

extinguish [ɪks'tɪŋgwɪʃ] *v*. 熄灭，消灭

【记】 ex(出去)+ stingu(刺)+ ish(动词词尾)→把刺拿出去→刺引申为火焰→灭火

【例】 They tried to *extinguish* the flames. 他们竭力要把火焰扑灭。

【同】 quench，crush，smother

【反】 ignite

【派】 extinguisher *n*. 灭火器

extol [ɪks'tɒl] *v*. (-lled；-lling)赞美，颂扬

【记】 ex(出去)+tol(举)→高举→赞美

【例】 He keeps *extolling* the merits of his new car. 他对他的新车赞不绝口。

【同】 exalt，glorify，laud，praise

extort [ɪks'tɔːt] *v*. 勒索，强夺

【记】 ex(出来)+tort(扭，拧)→拧出来→勒索

【例】 They accused him of trying to *extort* money with menaces. 他们控告他企图通过恐吓勒索钱财。

【同】 bully，extract

extra [ˈekstrə] *adj*. 额外的，外加的

【例】 A small *extra* charge is made for electricity. 如果用电的话，需要额外再付费。

【同】 additional, excess

extract [ɪksˈtrækt] *v*. 提出，提取；*n*. 摘录，选段

【记】 ex(出去) + tract(拉)→拉出来→提取

【例】 1. The oil is *extracted* from the seeds of certain plants. 油是从某些植物的种子里榨出来的。

2. I would like to quote two *extracts* from the book. 我很想引用这本书的两段文字。

【同】 elicit, excerpt, extort

【派】 extraction *n*. 抽出，取出；萃取法

extracurricular [ekstrəkəˈrɪkjʊlə] *adj*. 正课以外的，课外的

【记】 extra(超出) + curricula(课程的)→超出课程的→课外的

【例】 Nathan has *extracurricular* activities. He's on the basketball team. 纳森参加了很多课外活动，他是个篮球队员。

extraordinary [ɪkˈstrɔːdnrɪ] *adj*. 非常的，特别的，非凡的

【记】 extra(超出) + ordinary(普通的)→超出普通的→非凡的

【例】 An act was passed giving the army *extraordinary* powers. 这项法案的通过赋予军队特别的权力。

【同】 exceptional, marvelous, remarkable, unusual

【反】 ordinary, common, general

extraterrestrial [ˌekstrətəˈrestrɪəl] *adj*. 地球外的，外星球的

【记】 extra(超出) + terrestrial(陆地的)→超越地球的→外星球的

【例】 Does *extraterrestrial* life exsist? 外星球有生命存在吗？

extravagant [ɪksˈtrævəgənt] *adj*. 奢侈的，挥霍的

【记】 extra(超出) + vag(流浪) + ant(形容词词尾)→走过头→奢侈的

【例】 She was pilloried in the press for her *extravagant* parties. 她的聚会十分铺张，新闻界对她大加嘲弄。

【同】 excessive, luxurious, wasteful

【反】 economical, frugal, thrifty

【派】 extravagance *n*. 奢侈品

extreme [ɪksˈtriːm] *adj*. 极度的，极端的；*n*. 极端

【记】 extr(超出) + eme(形容词词尾)→超出的→极端的

【例】 1. His political views are rather *extreme*. 他的政治观点相当极端。

2. She's been generous in the *extreme*. 她一直非常慷慨。

【同】 terminal, utmost, supreme

【反】 moderate, proper, temperate

【派】 extremity *n*. 末端；极度；[pl](人的)手足

extricate [ˈekstrɪkeɪt] *v*. 救出，使解脱

【记】 ex(出去) + tric(障碍) + ate(动词词尾)→冲出障碍→使解脱

【例】 How can we *extricate* the firm from this trouble? 我们该如何拯救公司脱离困

境呢?

【同】 free, release

【派】 extrication *n*. 救出，解脱

exuberant [ɪg'zjuːbərənt] *adj*. 丰富的，精力旺盛的

【记】 ex(出来)+uber(很多的)+ant(形容词词尾)→多到满出来→丰富的

【例】 Play may look like a carefree and *exuberant* way to pass the time before the adulthood comes along. 玩可能看起来是长大成熟之前一种无忧无虑、兴高采烈地打发时间的方式。

【同】 profuse, energetic, luxuriant

【反】 sterile

exude [ɪg'zjuːd] *v*. 使慢慢流出，渗出

【记】 ex(出去)+ude(=sude 汗)→汗出来→渗出

【例】 The hot sun made him *exude* sweat. 烈日晒得他汗流浃背。

【同】 ooze, seep

exultant [ɪg'zʌltənt] *adj*. 欢腾的，狂欢的

【记】 ex(出去)+ult(=sult 跳)+ant(形容词词尾)→跳出(高兴)的范围→狂欢的

【例】 They gave an *exultant* shout of victory. 他们发出胜利的欢呼声。

【同】 joyful, cheerful

【反】 sad, sorrowful

【派】 (逆构)exult *v*. 非常高兴，欢跃

eyesight ['aɪsaɪt] *n*. 视力，视野

【记】 eye(眼睛)+sight(看见)→眼睛能看见→视力

【例】 You must stop taking the medicine if your *eyesight* is affected. 如果你的视力受到影响，一定要停止用药。

【同】 sight, vision

F

fable [ˈfeɪbl] *n*. 寓言，神话，传说

【记】 fabl(说) + e→人们传说的故事→寓言

【例】 *Fables* often have animals as the main characters. 寓言常以动物为主角。

【同】 allegory, fiction, legend, myth

【反】 fact

fabric [ˈfæbrɪk] *n*. 1.织物，织品；2.结构，构造

【记】 fabr(工匠) + ic(形容词词尾此处转用作名词)→工匠做的东西→织物，织品

【例】 1. Chiffon is a kind of thin, almost transparent *fabric*. 雪纺绸是一种几乎透明的丝质薄织物。

2. The cost of repairing the *fabric* of the church was very high. 修理教堂结构的花费非常大。

【同】 cloth, textile; framework, structure

fabricate [ˈfæbrɪkeɪt] *v*. 1.制作，构成；2.捏造，虚构

【记】 fabric(结构) + ate(动词词尾)→制作

【例】 1. The finest craftsmen *fabricated* this clock. 这只钟是手艺最好的工匠制作的。

2. It turned out that he had *fabricated* the whole story. 结果证明，整件事都是他编造出来的。

【同】 construct, manufacture; invent, make up

【派】 fabrication *n*. 制作，构成；伪造物，装配工

fabulous [ˈfæbjʊləs] *adj*. 惊人的，极好的，难以置信的

【记】 fabul(说) + ous(形容词词尾)→说故事的→难以置信的

【例】 The little boy's performance is *fabulous*. 那个小孩的表演真是精彩。

【同】 amazing, marvelous, remarkable

【反】 awful

facade [fəˈsɑːd] *n*. 正面，表面

【记】 fac(脸) + ade(名词词尾)→脸的那一面→正面

【例】 Squalor and poverty lay behind the city's glittering *facade*. 这城市表面繁华，背后却肮脏和贫困。

【同】 face, front

facelift [feɪslɪft] *n*./*v*. 1.翻新，表面修改；2.整容

【记】 face(脸) + lift(抬起)→使脸能够抬起→翻新

【例】 The town center certainly needs a *facelift*. 市中心可真该装修一下了。

2. If you want an idea of what a *facelift* could do for you, look in the mirror and use your hands to pull back the skin on your face. 如果你想知道什么是面部整容术，就对着镜子用自己的手把脸部的皮肤往后拉一下就知道了。

【同】 improvement, renovation; rhytidectomy

facet [ˈfæsɪt] *n*. (多面体的)面，方面

【记】 fac(脸，面) + et(表示"小"的名词词尾)→小的一面→方面

【例】 There are many *facets* to this question. 这个问题有很多方面。

【同】 aspect, side

F

facetious [fəˈsiːʃəs] *adj*. 幽默的，好开玩笑的

【记】 facet(面) + ious(形容词词尾)→有许多面的→幽默的

【例】 She kept interrupting our discussion with *facetious* remarks. 她不断用开玩笑的话干扰我们的讨论。

【同】 humorous, amusing

facile [ˈfæsaɪl] *adj*. 1. 轻率浅薄的，非发自衷心的；2. 容易做的

【记】 fac(做) + ile(形容词词尾)→容易做的

【例】 1. What he said is a *facile* remark. 他说的话全是信口开河。

2. I'm bored at work because my boss only gives me *facile* assignments. 我现在厌烦了自己的工作，因为老板总是给我安排简单的任务。

【同】 smooth-spoken, superficial; easy

facilitate [fəˈsɪlɪteɪt] *v*. 1. 使变得容易，使便利；2. 有助于，促进

【记】 fac(做) + ili(t)(使…容易) + ate(动词词尾)→使做起来容易→使便利

【例】 1. The new underground railway will *facilitate* the journey to the airport. 新建的地下铁道将会使去机场变得更方便。

2. Tractors and other agricultural machines greatly *facilitate* farming. 拖拉机及其他农业机械大大促进了农业耕作。

【同】 assist, ease; help

【派】 facilitation *n*. 简易化，助长

facility [fəˈsɪlɪtɪ] *n*. (常用复数-ties)设备，设施

【记】 fac(做) + ili(t)(使…容易) + ty(名词词尾)→使做起来容易的东西→设备

【例】 The house is well situated in reach of good shopping and transport *facilities*. 这所房子的位置很好，离商店和交通设施都不远。

【同】 amenity

facsimile [fækˈsɪmɪlɪ] *n*. 摹本，复制品

【记】 fac(做) + simile(相似)→做成相似的→复制品

【例】 Many of the drawings are reproduced in *facsimile* in the catalogue. 许多图画的复制品都载在这本目录里。

【同】 autotype, reproduction

faction [ˈfækʃən] *n*. 派别，小集团

【记】 fact(做) + ion(名词词尾)→为做…而聚在一起→派别

【例】 The *faction* from the extreme left is trying to elbow its way into power by short-cutting the democratic process. 这个极左小集团试图通过走民主程序的捷径，设

法挤进有影响的机构。

【同】 group，party

【派】 factious *adj*. 好搞派系的

factor [ˈfæktə] *n*. 因素，要素

【记】 fact(做) + or(名词词尾)→做成…的东西→构成物→要素

【例】 The committee's support is an important *factor* in the success of the project. 委员会的支持是该项目取得成功的一个重要因素。

【同】 element，ingredient

factual [ˈfæktjʊəl] *adj*. 事实的，实际的

【记】 fact(事实) + ual(形容词词尾)→事实的

【例】 From a disorderly array of *factual* information an orderly, relevant theory will somehow emerge. 从一串杂乱无章的真实信息中总会产生出一个有条理的相关理论。

【同】 actual

【反】 fictional

【派】 (逆构)fact *n*. 事实
factuality *n*. 实在性

faculty [ˈfækəltɪ] *n*. 1. 全体教员，(大学的)系、学院；2. 官能，能力

【记】 fac(做) + ul(形容词词尾) + ty(名词词尾)→做事的人或能力→全体教员

【例】 1. I'm an undergraduate, and I'm in the Business *faculty*. 我是一个本科生，是商学院的。
2. This boy has a *faculty* of making friends easily. 这个男孩有交友的能力。

【同】 staff，department；aptitude，capacity

fade [feɪd] *v*. 1. 逐渐消失；2. 褪色，枯萎

【例】 1. As evening came, the coastline *faded* into darkness. 夜晚来临，海岸线融入茫茫夜色中。
2. The strong sunlight had *faded* the curtains. 强烈的阳光把窗帘晒得褪了色。

【同】 bleach，decline

【反】 bloom

faint [feɪnt] *adj*. 微弱的，模糊的

【例】 The sounds of music grew *fainter* in the distance. 音乐的声音在远处逐渐模糊了。

【同】 vague，weak，dim

【反】 strong

faith [feɪθ] *n*. 信心，信任

【例】 Belief in a life after death is the keystone of her religious *faith*. 她的宗教信仰的基础是相信死后有来生。

【同】 belief，confidence，trust

【反】 doubt

【派】 faithful *adj*. 守信的，忠实的，可靠的

fake [feɪk] *adj*. 伪造的，假的；*n*. 假货，赝品

【例】 This is a *fake* video camera which you fix to your wall to scare off burglars. 这是

一个假的摄像机，安装在墙上是为了吓唬盗贼。

【同】 artificial, false, counterfeit

【反】 genuine, real

fallible ['fæləbl] *adj*. 易错的，可能犯错的

【记】 fall(欺骗)+ible(形容词词尾)→易骗人的→可能犯错的

【例】 We are *fallible* beings. 我们都难免犯错误。

【同】 frail, erring

【反】 infallible

【派】 fallibility *n*. 易错，不可靠，易误

falter ['fɔːltə] *v*. 1. 蹒跚；2. 犹豫，退缩

【记】 falt(犹豫)+er(动词词尾，表示动作的重复)→犹豫

【例】 1. The sick man *faltered* a few steps and then fell. 这个病人摇摇晃晃地走了几步，然后就跌倒了。

2. The manager never *falters* in his determination. 我们经理的决心从不动摇。

【同】 stagger, stumble; hesitate

familiarize [fə'mɪljəraɪz] *v*. 使熟悉

【记】 familiar(熟悉的)+ize(动词词尾)→使熟悉

【例】 The first repetition drill serves to *familiarize* the students with the sounds in the dialogue. 第一部分的背诵练习是为了使学生熟悉一下对话的语调。

【同】 acquaint

famine ['fæmɪn] *n*. 饥荒，饥饿

【记】 fam(=faim，饥饿)+ine(名词词尾)→饥荒

【例】 The long drought was followed by months of *famine*. 久旱之后出现长达数月的饥荒。

【同】 hunger, starvation, dearth

【反】 plenty

【派】 famish *v*. 使挨饿

fanatical [fə'nætɪkəl] *adj*. 狂热的，入迷的

【记】 fana(=fanum，庙)+t+ical(形容词词尾)→在庙里的，被神召唤的→狂热的

【例】 She's *fanatical* about keeping fit. 她对健身如醉如痴。

【同】 zealous, passionate

【反】 moderate

【派】 fanaticism *n*. 狂热，盲信

fancy ['fænsɪ] *adj*. 1. 想象出来的，奇异的；2. 精美的，昂贵的；*v*. 1. 想象，认为；2. 喜欢，爱好

【例】 1. People in western countries sometimes went to the party in *fancy* dress. 在西方国家人们有时化了装去参加舞会。

2. That's a very *fancy* pair of shoes! 那是一双非常别致的鞋！

3. I *fancy* (that) it's going to rain today. 我看今天要下雨。

4. I don't *fancy* going all that way in such bad weather. 我不喜欢在这样的坏天气里一直这么走着。

【同】 fanciful; elaborate; imagine; like, love

【反】 plain

fantasy ['fæntəsɪ, 'fæntəzɪ] *n./v.* 想象，幻想

【记】 fanta(出现) + sy(名词词尾)→浮现在眼前的东西→幻想

【例】 The young always live in a world of *fantasy*. 年轻人总是生活在幻想中。

【同】 fancy, fiction, illusion, imagination

【派】 fantastic *adj.* 了不起的，很好的

fare [fɛə] *n.* 费用，车费

【例】 When you did your expenses, did you reckon in your taxi *fares*? 你计算费用时，把计程车费算进去了吗?

【同】 charge, fee

fascinate ['fæsɪneɪt] *v.* 强烈地吸引，使着迷

【记】 fascin(符咒，魔力) + ate(动词词尾)→对…使用魔力→使着迷

【例】 The children were *fascinated* by the toys in the shop window. 孩子们让商店橱窗里的玩具给吸引住了。

【同】 attract, charm, enchant

【派】 fascinating *adj.* 迷人的，极有吸引力的

fascination *n.* 魅力，迷恋

fashion ['fæʃən] *n.* 1.样子，方式；2.流行，时尚

【记】 fash(= fac, 做) + ion(名词词尾)→做出来的东西→样子

【例】 1. The children lined up in an orderly *fashion*. 孩子们整整齐齐排好队。

2. Long skirts have come into *fashion* again. Faded jeans are still in *fashion* too. 长裙子又流行起来。漂褪色的牛仔裤也还很时髦。

【同】 form, mode, mold; style

【派】 fashionable *adj.* 流行的，时髦的

fasten ['fɑːsn] *v.* 系牢，拴紧

【记】 fast(牢固的) + en(动词词尾)→使…牢固→系牢

【例】 We shall be landing shortly please *fasten* your seat-belts. 我们马上就要着陆——请大家系好座位上的安全带。

【同】 attach, bind, tie

【反】 loosen, unfasten

fastidious [fæs'tɪdɪəs] *adj.* 挑剔的，难于讨好的

【记】 fast(骄傲，蔑视) + tid(厌烦的) + ious(形容词词尾)→因为骄傲而惹人烦的→挑剔的

【例】 She is so *fastidious* about her food that I never invite her for dinner. 她对食物过于挑剔，因此我从不请她吃饭。

【同】 choosy, critical

fatal ['feɪtl] *adj.* 致命的，毁灭性的

【记】 fat(说) + al(形容词词尾)→本意是指神说的话，神决定人的命运→致命的

【例】 Death is instantaneous in a *fatal* accident. 在致命的事故中，死亡是即刻发生的。

【同】 deadly, disastrous

【派】 fatality *n*. 命运决定的事物，不幸，灾祸
fatalism *n*. 宿命论

fatigue [fəˈtiːg] *n*. 疲劳，劳累
【记】 来自拉丁语 fatigare，疲倦→疲劳
【例】 They make better use of the time they have, and they are less likely to succumb to *fatigue* in stressful jobs. 他们更好地利用自己的时间，这样在工作压力很大的时候就不太感觉疲劳了。
【同】 exhaust, tire

F

fatuous [ˈfætjuəs] *adj*. 愚昧的
【记】 来自拉丁语 fatuus，愚蠢的
【例】 What a *fatuous* remark! 多么愚蠢的话呀！
【同】 foolish
【反】 sensible

faucet [ˈfɔːsɪt] *n*. 水龙头
【记】 fauc(= false，假的) + et(表示"小"的名词词尾)→管子上的假的东西→插口，水龙头
【例】 Water was falling from the *faucet*. 水正从水龙头流出。
【同】 tap, spigot

fault [fɔːlt] *n*. 1. 地质学的断层；2. 过错，缺点
【例】 1. There are huge *faults* in southern California. 加利福尼亚州南部有巨型断层。
2. He has many *faults*, but vanity is not one of them. 他有很多缺点，但并没有虚荣心。
【同】 defect, error, flaw
【反】 merit, virtue
【派】 faulty *adj*. 有缺点的，有错误的
faultfinding *n*./*adj*. 挑剔，吹毛求疵

favorable [ˈfeɪvərəbl] *adj*. (US favorable)令人高兴的，有利的
【记】 favor(= 拉丁语 favere，待之若友) + able(形容词词尾)→像对待朋友一样的→令人高兴的
【例】 The conditions are *favorable* for opening a new business. 各种条件有利于开办新企业。
【同】 positive, pleasing
【反】 unfavorable
【派】 (逆构)favor *v*./*n*. 喜爱，偏爱

favorite [ˈfeɪvərɪt] *adj*. 最喜欢的，偏爱的；*n*. 最喜爱的事物(或人)
【记】 favor(喜爱) + ite(形容词词尾)→最喜欢的
【例】 1. My *favorite* pastime is reading. 我最喜爱的消遣是读书。
2. I like all the books on the shelf but this one is my *favorite*. 我喜欢书架上所有的书，但这本是我最喜欢的。
【同】 beloved, precious

feasible [ˈfiːzəbl] *adj*. 可行的，行得通的

【记】 feas(做)+ible(形容词词尾)→能够做的→可行的

【例】 It's quite clear that the electric car is technically *feasible*. 很清楚，电动汽车在工艺技术上是可行的。

【同】 practicable, workable

【反】 infeasible

【派】 feasibility *n*. 可行性，可能性

feast [fiːst] *n*. 盛宴，宴会

【例】 Christmas is an important *feast* for Christians. 圣诞节是基督教徒的一个重要节日。

【同】 banquet

F

feat [fiːt] *n*. 技艺，功绩，壮举

【记】 feat=fact，已经做或者完成的事→功绩

【例】 Apparently impossible *feats* are now accomplished by science. 许多看起来不可能的伟大业绩现在已经由科学实现了。

【同】 accomplishment, achievement, deed

feature [ˈfiːtʃə] *n*. 1.特色，特征；2.面部的一部分，(经常用复数)面貌，相貌；*v*. 1.以…为特色，特写；2.起重要作用，作为主要角色

【记】 feat(做)+ ure(名词词尾)→做事的状态→做事特征

【例】 1. The *feature*, which makes fireflies and glow-worms so appealing, is their ability to produce an often dazzling display of light. 萤火虫之所以很吸引人的主要特征是因为它们能够发出耀眼的光芒。

2. His eyes are his most striking *feature*. 他面部最突出的部分是那双眼睛。

3. Fireflies often *featured* in Japanese and Arabian folk medicine. 萤火虫是日本和阿拉伯民间药物中很有特色的一味药。

4. Does a new job *feature* in your future plans? 新的工作在你的未来计划中十分重要吗？

【同】 characteristic; part

federation [ˌfedəˈreɪʃən] *n*. 联盟，(社团、工会等)联合会

【记】 feder(联盟)+ation(名词词尾)→联盟

【例】 The small countries joined together into a *federation*. 小国联合起来组成一个联盟。

【同】 confederation, union

feeble [ˈfiːbl] *adj*. 微弱的，衰弱的

【例】 Grandmother has been getting *feebler* lately. 近来祖母愈益衰弱了。

【同】 frail, powerless, weak

【反】 intense, strong, tough

feed [fiːd] *v*. 喂养，饲养；*n*. 饲养，饲料

【例】 1. She has a large family to *feed*. 她要养活一大家人。

2. There isn't enough *feed* left for the hens. 母鸡的饲料不够了。

【同】 eat, nourish, nurture

feedback [ˈfiːdbæk] *n*. 反馈，反应

【记】 来自动词词组 feed back，反馈

【例】 We need more *feedback* from the consumer in order to improve our goods. 我们需要从消费者那里多得到些反馈信息以提高产品质量。

feign [feɪn] *v*. 假装，伪装

【例】 Her efforts to *feign* cheerfulness weren't convincing. 她的强颜欢笑并不使人信服。

【同】 fake，pretend

feminine [ˈfemɪnɪn] *adj*. 妇女(似)的，阴性的，女性的

【记】 femin(妇女) + ine(形容词词尾)→具有女性性质的→女性的

【例】 Jewelry and lace are mostly *feminine* belongings. 珠宝和蕾丝大多是女性用品。

【同】 womanly，female

【反】 masculine，virile

【派】 feminist *n*. 女权主义者

ferment [ˈfɜːmənt] *v*. (使)发酵；2. (使)激动，(使)动乱

【记】 fer(= ferv，沸腾) + ment(名词词尾转用做动词)→使…沸腾起来→(使)发酵

【例】 1. When wine is *fermented* it gives off bubbles of gas. 酒发酵时会放出气泡。

2. The news *fermented* trouble among the factory workers. 那则消息在工人中引起骚动。

【同】 convert；agitate，provoke，stir

【派】 fermentation *n*. 发酵

ferret [ˈferɪt] *v*. 搜索，查获

【记】 fer(= fur，贼) + r + et(本是名词词尾此处转用做动词)→小贼做的事情→搜索

【例】 I spent the day *ferreting* about in the attic for old photographs. 我一整天都在阁楼上翻找旧照片。

【同】 hunt，search

ferry [ˈferɪ] *n*. 渡口，渡船

【记】 fer(搬运) + ry(名词词尾)→搬运的东西或地方→渡口，渡船

【例】 1. The *ferry* leaves for France at one o'clock. 渡船于一点钟开往法国。

2. He went down to the *ferry* but found the boat on the other side. 他到了渡口，却发现渡船在对岸。

【同】 boat

fertile [ˈfɜːtaɪl, ˈfɜːtɪl] *adj*. 1. (指土地)肥沃的，富饶的；2. (指动植物)能结果实的，能生育的

【记】 fert(= fer，运，带来) + ile(形容词词尾)→能带来东西的→肥沃的，能结果实的

【例】 1. We have irrigated the desert area to make it *fertile*. 我们已经灌溉了荒芜地区使它肥沃。

2. Some fish are very *fertile*; they lay thousands of eggs. 有些鱼是非常多产的，它们产下数以千计的卵。

【同】 fruitful，productive

【反】 infertile，barren，sterile

【派】 fertility *n*. 肥沃，多产，丰富

fertilize [ˈfɜːtɪlaɪz] *v*. 1. 施肥，使肥沃；2. 使受精，使受粉

【记】 fertil(e)(肥沃的)+ize(动词词尾)→使肥沃

【例】 1. The peasants *fertilize* the field by using manure. 农民们施肥来使土地肥沃。

2. Flowers are often *fertilized* by bees as they gather nectar. 蜜蜂采蜜时常使花受粉。

【派】 fertilizer *n*. 肥料，化肥

fertilized *adj*. 受精的

fertilization *n*. 授精，受胎

fervent [ˈfɜːvənt] *adj*. 热情的，强烈的

【记】 ferv(沸腾)+ent(形容词词尾)→像沸腾的一样→热情的

【例】 She had a *fervent* farewell speech. 她发表了热情的告别演说。

【同】 ardent, passionate, zealous

【反】 apathetic

【派】 fervor *n*. 热情，热烈

fetch [fetʃ] *v*. 去拿来，去请来

【例】 The chair is in the garden, please *fetch* it in. 椅子在花园里，请把它搬进来。

【同】 bring

fetter [ˈfetə] *n*./*v*. (带)脚镣，束缚

【记】 fet(=ped，脚)+t+er(名词词尾)→绑住脚的东西→脚镣

【例】 He was *fettered* by his family and could not travel any longer. 他被家庭束缚，不能再到处去旅游了。

【同】 bind, chain, shackle

feverish [ˈfiːvərɪʃ] *adj*. 1. 发烧的；2. 兴奋的

【记】 fever(发烧)+ish(形容词词尾)→发烧一样的→兴奋的

【例】 1. The child's body felt *feverish*. 这孩子身上发烧。

2. They worked with *feverish* haste to finish the job. 为了做完这件事情，他们赶做了一阵子。

【同】 febrile, fevered; excited, agitated

fiber [ˈfaɪbə] *n*. 纤维，纤维制品

【例】 And the pulses would travel over glass *fibers*, not copper wire. 脉冲将通过玻璃纤维而不是铜线传播。

fickle [ˈfɪkl] *adj*. 易变的，反复无常的

【记】 来自古英语 ficol 欺骗的→易变的

【例】 It's the third time that he changed his mind; he's so *fickle*! 他改变主意已经是第三回了，他这人太反复无常了！

【同】 changing, unfaithful

【反】 faithful, constant

【派】 fickle-minded *adj*. 易变的，不专一的

fiction [ˈfɪkʃən] *n*. 1. 小说；2. 虚构，编造

【记】 fict(假装)+ion(名词词尾)→不真实的假话→编造

【例】 1. Truth is often stranger than *fiction*. 事实往往比小说更离奇。

2. It's important to distinguish fact from *fiction*. 把现实与虚构区分开来是很重要的。

【同】 fantasy, invention, myth

【反】 fact, nonfiction

【派】 fictional *adj*. 虚构的

fictitious *adj*. 假想的，编造的；虚伪的

fidelity [fɪˈdelɪtɪ] *n*. 忠实，忠诚

【记】 fid(信任) + el + ity(每次词尾)→值得信任的→忠实

【例】 His *fidelity* and industry brought him speedy promotion. 他的忠于职守和勤于工作使他得到迅速晋升。

【同】 faithfulness, loyalty

【反】 infidelity, disloyalty

figure [ˈfɪgə] *n*. 1.外形，轮廓，人物；2.数字，图表；*v*. 算出，估计

【例】 1. Mahatma Gandhi was both a political and a religious *figure* in Indian history. 甘地在印度历史上是政治和宗教要人。

2. He has an income of six *figures* /a six-*figure* income. 他有六位数字的收入。

3. They figured it was better to stay where they were. 他们断定还是呆在原地好。

【同】 shape, outline; diagram, drawing; reckon

file [faɪl] *n*. 1.档案，文件夹；*v*. 1.归档；2.列队行进；3.提出申请

【例】 1. Where's the *file* of our recent correspondence? 我们近期的信件卷宗在哪里？

2. Please *file* those letters. 请把这些信件存档。

3. The pupils *filed* out of the room during the fire drill. 在消防演习中，学生们排成纵队走出房间。

4. They *filed* an application to have their case heard early. 他们正式提交了一份申请书以期案件早日得到审理。

【同】 document; store; march; initiate

filter [ˈfɪltə] *n*./*v*. (使)漏过，过滤

【例】 It won't take long to *filter* the coffee. 用不了多少时间就可以把咖啡过滤好。

【同】 screen

【派】 filtration *n*. 过滤，筛选

filthy [ˈfɪlθɪ] *adj*. 1.肮脏的，污秽的；2.邪恶的，猥亵的

【记】 filth(污秽) + y(形容词词尾)→肮脏的，污秽的

【例】 1. This place is *filthy*; I don't believe anyone can live here. 这个地方脏极了，我不相信有人能住在这。

2. He is always telling *filthy* jokes. 他老是说些下流的笑话。

【同】 dirty, nasty

finance [faɪˈnæns] *n*. 财政，金融；*v*. 为…供给资金

【例】 1. He is an well-known expert in *finance*. 他是知名的金融专家。

2. The scheme is partly *financed* by a government grant. 此计划有一部分是政府资助的。

【同】 banking; fund

【派】 financial *adj*. 财政的，金融的

fiscal ［ˈfɪskəl］ *adj*. 财政的，国库的

【例】 We are trying to get a thorough understanding of the government's *fiscal* policy. 我们正努力对政府的财政政策进行全面的了解。

【同】 financial

fishery ［ˈfɪʃərɪ］ *n*. 渔业，渔场

【记】 fish(鱼)+ery(名词词尾)→与鱼有关的→渔业，渔场

【例】 The ship is engaged in pelagic *fishery*. 这艘船从事远洋渔业。

fitful ［ˈfɪtfʊl］ *adj*. 一阵阵的，间歇的，不定的

【记】 fit(病的一阵发作)+ful(形容词词尾)→一阵阵的，间歇的

【例】 I worried half the night and have a *fitful* sleep. 我半个晚上都在担心，故而时睡时醒。

【同】 disconnected，broken

fitness ［ˈfɪtnɪs］ *n*. 1.合适；2.健康

【记】 fit(适合)+ness(名词词尾)→合适

【例】 1. Her *fitness* for the job should not be questioned. 她能胜任这项工作是毋庸质疑的。

2. Good muscles are one of the prerequisites of physical *fitness*. 肌肉发达是身体健康的一个必备条件。

【同】 suitability；good condition

【反】 unfitness

【派】 fitting *adj*. 适合的，适宜的

fix ［fɪks］ *v*. 1.固定，安装；2.修理；3.确定，决定

【例】 1. He *fixed* a picture to the wall. 他往墙上贴了张画。

2. I must get the radio *fixed*. 我必须找人把收音机修理好。

3. Have you *fixed* on a date for the wedding? 你们选定结婚日期了吗？

【同】 pose，stabilize；mend，repair；settle

【反】 alter，modify

【派】 fixed *adj*. 固定的，不变的

fixture *n*. 固定物；设备

flag ［flæg］ *n*. 旗，标记；*v*. 衰退，低落

【例】 1. *Flags* are fluttering in the breeze. 旗子在风中飘扬。

2. My strength，interest，enthusiasm，etc is *flagging*. 我的力气、兴趣、热情等正在减退。

【同】 banner；fade，weaken

flagrant ［ˈfleɪgrənt］ *adj*. 罪恶昭彰的，明目张胆的

【记】 flagr(燃烧)+ant(形容词词尾)→像燃烧一样的→明目张胆的

【例】 We cannot bear his *flagrant* disregard for the law. 我们不能忍受他那么明目张胆地漠视法律。

【同】 glaring，obvious

flamboyant ［flæmˈbɔɪənt］ *adj*. 火焰似的，艳丽的，炫耀的

【记】 flam(火焰)+boy(buoy，浮)+ant(形容词词尾)→像火焰一样浮着的→艳丽的

【例】 With a *flamboyant* gesture he threw off the covering to reveal the new statue. 他炫耀而自负地揭掉覆盖物，让新的塑像露出来。

【同】 florid, showy

flame [fleɪm] *n*. 火焰，火苗；*v*. 燃烧，发出火焰

【例】 1. How and where man learnt how to produce *flame* at will is unknown. 人们根据自己的意愿生火是怎样学会的，在哪儿学会的，这一点还不可知。

2. The evening sky *flamed* with red and orange. 傍晚天空的颜色是一片火红和橘黄相间。

【同】 blaze, fire, flare

flare [flɛə] *n*./*v*. 闪光，闪耀

【例】 The fire *flared* up as I put more logs onto it. 我加了几块木材，火顿时亮了起来。

【同】 blaze, flame, glow

flash [flæʃ] *v*./*n*. 闪光，反射

【例】 Lightning *flashed* during the storm. 暴风雨中闪电大作。

【同】 blink, flare, twinkle

【派】 flashlight *n*. 手电筒；闪光灯

flatter [ˈflætə] *v*. 恭维，奉承

【例】 If you *flatter* your mother a bit she might invite us all to dinner. 你要是奉承你母亲几句，说不定她会把我们全请去吃饭。

【同】 compliment, praise

【派】 flattery *n*. 谄媚，阿谀奉承

flavor [ˈfleɪvə] *n*. 味道，风味

【例】 I don't like the *flavor* of onion. 我不喜欢洋葱的味道。

【同】 spice

flaw [flɔː] *n*. 缺陷，瑕疵

【例】 This vase would be perfect but for a few small *flaws* in its base. 这花瓶底部没有那几个小斑点就十全十美了。

【同】 defect, fault, weakness

【派】 flawless *adj*. 无瑕疵的，无缺点的

flee [fliː] *v*. (fled, fled)逃跑，逃离

【例】 The customers *fled* from the bank when the alarm sounded. 警铃响起，顾客纷纷从银行逃走。

【同】 fly, run away

flexible [ˈfleksəbl] *adj*. 有弹性的，可变通的，灵活的

【记】 flex(弯曲)+ible(形容词词尾)→可以弯曲的→有弹性的

【例】 We need a foreign policy that is more *flexible*. 我们需要一个更为灵活的外交政策。

【同】 elastic, pliable

【反】 inflexible

【派】 flexibility *n*. 灵活性，弹性

flicker [ˈflɪkə] *v*. 闪烁

【记】 flick(忽然摇动)+er(表示动作的重复)→不停地摇动→闪烁

【例】 A slender hope still *flickered* within him. 他心中仍闪出一线希望。

【同】 blink, glimmer

【派】 flickering *adj*. 闪烁的，摇曳的

flimsy [ˈflɪmzɪ] *adj*. 轻而薄的，不结实的

【记】 flim(=film, 薄膜，薄层)+s+y(形容词词尾)→像薄膜一样的→轻而薄的

【例】 It is a *flimsy* cardboard box. 那是一个不结实的纸箱。

【同】 delicate, fragile, frail

flip [flɪp] *v*. (-pped; -pping)(以手指)弹，投

【例】 They *flipped* a coin to decide who would go first. 他们用抛硬币的方法决定谁先去。

【同】 cast, flick, throw

float [fləʊt] *v*. 漂浮，使漂浮

【例】 The raft was *floating* gently down to the river. 筏子顺河水缓缓漂流。

【同】 drift, sail

【反】 sink

flock [flɒk] *n*. (禽、畜等的)群，大量；*v*. 蜂拥，群集

【例】 1. There is a black sheep in every *flock*. [谚]人多必有败类。

2. People are *flocking* to the cinema to see the new film. 人们正蜂拥到电影院去看这部新电影。

【同】 crowd, group

flop [flɒp] *n*./*v*. (-pped; -pping)扑，拍，跳动

【例】 The fish we'd caught *flopped* around in the bottom of the boat. 我们捕到的鱼在船底乱蹦。

【同】 droop, slump

【派】 floppy *adj*. 松软的，下垂的

flora [ˈflɔːrə] *n*. 某一地区或时期的植物总称，植物群

【例】 My professor studies *flora* of the Palaeozoic Era. 我的教授研究古生代的植物群。

【同】 plant, vegetation

【反】 fauna

flourish [ˈflʌrɪʃ] *v*. 茂盛，繁荣

【记】 flour(花)+ish(动词词尾)→如繁花盛开一般→茂盛

【例】 1. This species of flower *flourishes* in a warm climate. 这种花在温暖的气候中长得茂盛。

2. No new business can *flourish* in the present economic climate. 在目前的经济气候中，任何新生意都兴旺不起来。

【同】 bloom, boom, thrive

【反】 decay, decline

【派】 flourishing *adj*. 繁茂的，欣欣向荣的

flout [flaʊt] *v*. 愚弄，藐视

【例】 No one can *flout* the rules and get away with it. 谁也不能违反这些规则而不被处分。

【同】 disdain, scoff

flow [fləʊ] *n.*/*v.* 流，流动

【例】 1. This river *flowed* southwest to the Atlantic Ocean. 这条河流向西南，汇入大西洋。

2. The *flow* of traffic is always slow at rush hours. 在交通高峰时间，路上的车流总是很慢的。

【同】 run, stream

fluctuate [ˈflʌktjʊeɪt] *v.* 变动，波动

【记】 fluctu(= 拉丁语 fluctus，波) + ate(动词词尾)→像波浪一样波动→变动

【例】 In the temperate zone in spring, temperatures *fluctuate* greatly from day to day. 春天的温带地区，气温每天变化不定。

【同】 swing, waver

【派】 fluctuation *n.* 波动，起伏

fluent [ˈflu:ənt] *adj.* 说话流利的，熟练自如的

【记】 flu(流动) + ent(形容词词尾)→流动的样子→说话流利的

【例】 She speaks *fluent* and idiomatic French. 她说得一口又流利又地道的法语。

【同】 eloquent, smooth

【反】 faltering

【派】 fluency *n.* 流利，流畅

fluffy [flʌfɪ] *adj.* 绒毛的，松软的

【记】 fluff(绒毛) + y(形容词词尾)→绒毛一样的→绒毛的，松软的

【例】 Most animals are soft and *fluffy* when first born. 大多数动物刚出生时都很软，身上有绒毛。

【同】 downy, feathery

【派】 (逆构)fluff *n.* 软毛，绒毛

fluid [ˈflu:ɪd] *adj.* 流动的，流体的

【记】 flu(流) + id(拉丁文的形容词词尾)→流动的

【例】 Air is a *fluid* but not a liquid, while water is both a fluid and a liquid. 空气是流体不是液体，水是流体也是液体。

【同】 flowing, running

【反】 solidity

flush [flʌʃ] *n.* 脸红；*v.* 1. 变红，发红；2. 冲洗

【记】 flu(流) + sh(动词词尾)→使流动→冲洗

【例】 1. She shows a *flush* of joy at his coming. 对他的到来她表现出一阵兴奋。

2. Mary *flushed* crimson with embarrassment. 玛丽羞得脸红了。

3. Please *flush* the toilet after you've used it. 便后请冲水。

【同】 blush; redden; wash out

fluster [ˈflʌstə] *v.*/*n.* 使困惑，慌乱

【记】 flust(匆忙) + er(动词词尾，表示动作的重复)→一直匆忙的→慌乱

【例】 1. The honking of horns *flustered* the boy. 汽车喇叭的叫声使男孩感到慌乱。
2. I got in an awful *fluster* at some traffic lights, so I failed my driving test. 我被一些交通信号弄得忙乱紧张，因此未能通过驾驶考试。

【同】 confuse, disconcert

foam [fəʊm] *n*. 泡沫，泡沫状物

【例】 The breaking waves left the beach covered with *foam*. 浪花弄得海滩都是泡沫。

【同】 bubble, froth

focus [ˈfəʊkəs] *n*. (复数-cuses或-ci)焦点，中心；*v*. 聚焦，将(注意力等)集中于

【例】 1. Air pollution is increasingly becoming the *focus* of government and citizen concern around the globe. 空气污染正日益成为全世界政府和平民关注的焦点。
2. If you *focus* the sun's rays through a magnifying glass on a dry leaf, it will start to burn. 用放大镜把阳光聚到干叶子上，叶子就能燃烧。

【同】 concentrate

【反】 distract

【派】 focal *adj*. 焦点的，在焦点上的

fold [fəʊld] *v*. 折叠，包

【例】 The paper should be *folded* in half. 这张纸应该对折。

【同】 enclosure

【反】 unfold

【派】 folder *n*. 文件夹，折叠器，折叠式印刷品

foliage [ˈfəʊlɪɪdʒ] *n*. 树叶，植物

【记】 foli(叶子)+age(名词词尾)→树叶

【例】 My flower arrangement needs more *foliage*. 我的插花作品还得多要些枝叶。

【同】 leafage

folk [fəʊk] *adj*. 民间的；*n*. 人们

【例】 1. He is a very popular *folk* singer. 他是一位很受欢迎的民歌手。
2. They are just simple country *folk*. 他们只不过是普通的村民。

【同】 public; people

【派】 folklore *n*. 民间传说

foment [fəʊˈment] *v*. 煽动，助长

【例】 His words finally *foment* her hostility. 他的言词终于引发了她的敌意。

【同】 agitate, stir up

footnote [ˈfʊtnəʊt] *n*. 脚注，说明

【记】 foot(脚，底部)+note(记录)→在书页的底部记录的东西→脚注

【例】 That biography is an illuminate *footnote* to the history of our times. 那篇传记对我们这个时代是一个很有启发性的说明。

【同】 annotation

forbid [fəˈbɪd] *v*. (forbad(e), forbidden; -dding)不许，禁止

【例】 I can't *forbid* you/your seeing that man again. 我无法禁止你再和那个男人来往。

【同】 ban, prevent, prohibit

【反】 allow, permit

【派】 forbidding *adj*. 可怕的，令人难亲近的，令人生畏的

forebear [ˈfɔːbeə] *n*. (一般用复数)祖先

【记】 fore(在…之前) + bear(具有)→在前面有的→祖先

【例】 My *forebears* lived in the west of Scotland. 我的祖先居住在苏格兰西部。

【同】 ancestor, antecedent, predecessor

forecast [ˈfɔːkɑːst] *v*. /*n*. (-cast, -cast)预报，预测

【记】 fore(提前) + cast(投掷)→预先投下→预报

【例】 1. The *forecast* said there would be sunny intervals and showers. 预报说将会晴间阵雨。

2. They tried to *forecast* the result of the football match. 他们试图预测这场足球比赛的结果。

【同】 predict, foretell, foresee

F

foremost [ˈfɔːməust] *adj*. 最初的，最重要的

【记】 fore(在…之前) + most(最)→在最前面的→最初的，最重要的

【例】 First and *foremost*, I think you should work harder on your biology. 首先，我认为你应该多在生物学上下工夫。

【同】 first, primary, principal

foresee [fɔːˈsiː] *v*. (-saw, -seen)预见，预料

【记】 fore(提前) + see(看)→提前看→预见

【例】 They could not have *foreseen* how things would turn out. 他们不可能预知事情的结果。

【同】 forecast, foretell, predict

【派】 foreseeable *adj*. 可预见的

foresight [ˈfɔːsaɪt] *n*. 远见，深谋远虑

【记】 fore(在…之前) + sight(看)→在…之前看→远见

【例】 The couple had the *foresight* to plan their retirement wisely. 他们夫妇很有远见，精心安排了退休后的生活。

【同】 anticipation, forethought

【反】 hindsight

【派】 foresighted *adj*. 有先见之明的，深谋远虑的

forestall [fɔːˈstɔːl] *v*. 抢先一步，预先阻止

【记】 fore(在…之前) + stall(放)→放在前面→预先阻止

【例】 He *forestalled* all his competitors. 他比所有的竞争者都抢先了一步。

【同】 foreclose, prevent

foretell [fɔːˈtel] *v*. (-told, -told)预言，预示

【记】 fore(在…之前) + tell(讲，说)→提前说出来→预言

【例】 No one could have *foretold* such strange events. 谁也料不到有这些奇怪的事情。

【同】 forecast, predict

forge [fɔːdʒ] *v*. 锻造，制作；*n*. 锻造，锻造车间

【例】 1. They *forged* their manager's signature on the check. 他们在支票上伪造了经理的签名。

2. At that time, local craftsmen first built an iron *forge* just behind the village here. 那时候，当地的工匠首先在村庄的后面建立了一个铁匠铺。

【同】 mold; workplace

【派】 forgeable *adj*. 可锻造的

format [ˈfɔːmæt] *n*. 格式，式样

【记】 form(形状) + at(名词词尾)→有…形状→格式

【例】 Official reports are usually written to a set *format*. 官方报告通常按固定格式写成。

【同】 mode, fashion

formidable [ˈfɔːmɪdəbl] *adj*. 令人敬畏的，可怕的

【记】 formid(恐惧) + able(形容词词尾)→令人恐惧的→令人敬畏的

【例】 They climbed up the last part of the mountain in *formidable* weather conditions. 他们在恶劣的天气条件下登上了山的顶峰。

【同】 difficult, hard, tough

formula [ˈfɔːmjʊlə] *n*. (复数-las 或-lae) 1. 分子式，公式；2. 配方，药方；3. 方法，计划

【记】 form(u)(形成) + la(拉丁语名词词尾)→形成…的东西→分子式

【例】 1. The *formula* for water is H_2O. 水的分子式为 H_2O。

2. They are working on the perfection of their new paint *formula*. 他们正在努力研制尽善尽美的新颜料配方。

3. Managers and workers are still working out a peace *formula*. 劳资双方仍在商谈制订和解方案。

formulate [ˈfɔːmjʊleɪt] *v*. 1. 用公式表示；2. 明确地表达

【记】 formula(公式，方法) + (a)te(动词词尾)→用公式表示

【例】 1. The contract was *formulated* in difficult legal language. 该合同是用深奥的法律术语订立的。

2. He *formulated* his thought clearly. 他清楚确切地表达了自己的思想。

【同】 define, explicate

【派】 formulation *n*. 格式化；确切地表达

forsake [fəˈseɪk] *v*. (-sook, -saken) 遗弃，抛弃

【记】 for(分离) + sake(努力)→努力脱离→遗弃

【例】 He has *forsaken* the bad habit of smoking. 他已改掉了吸烟的坏习惯。

【同】 abandon, quit, give up

【反】 conserve, maintain, preserve

forthcoming [fɔːθˈkʌmɪŋ] *adj*. 即将到来的，即将出现的

【记】 forth(朝，向) + com(来) + ing→朝这个方向来的→即将到来的

【例】 The *forthcoming* talks hold out the hope of real arms reductions. 即将举行的会谈给实现真正的裁军带来了希望。

【同】 approaching, upcoming, imminent

forthright [ˈfɔːθˈraɪt] *adj*. 坦白的，直率的

【记】 forth(朝，向) + right(径直)→径直向前的→直率的

【例】 He has a reputation for being a *forthright* critic. 他是以直率著称的评论家。

【同】 candid, frank, outspoken, straightforward
【反】 cautious

fortify ['fɔːtɪfaɪ] *v*. 1. 设防于；2. 增强(体力等)
【记】 forti(强壮的) + fy(动词词尾)→使…强壮→设防于，增强
【例】 1. The medieval town is *fortified* with a high wall and a deep moat. 这座中世纪的城市用高墙深沟来加强防御。
2. Good eating habits help to *fortify* the body against disease. 好的饮食习惯有助于强身防病。
【同】 defend, reinforce; invigorate, strengthen
【反】 demilitarize; weaken
【派】 fortification *n*. 防御工事，要塞

F

fortitude ['fɔːtɪtjuːd] *n*. 坚忍，刚毅，勇气
【记】 forti(强壮的) + tude(名词词尾)→强壮的状态→坚忍，刚毅
【例】 He bore the pain with great *fortitude*. 他以极大的毅力忍受了痛苦。
【同】 courage, bravery, strength

fortress ['fɔːtrɪs] *n*. 要塞，城堡
【记】 fort(强壮的) + ress(名词词尾)→强壮的东西→要塞，城堡
【例】 The easiest way to capture a *fortress* is from within. 堡垒最容易从内部攻破。
【同】 fort

fortuitous [fɔː'tjuːɪtəs] *adj*. 偶然的，意外的
【记】 fortu (ne)(运气) + itous(形容词词尾)→与运气有关的→偶然的
【例】 A series of *fortuitous* circumstances advanced her career. 一系列的幸运事使她的事业一帆风顺。
【同】 accidental, unintended
【反】 intentional

fortunate ['fɔːtʃənɪt] *adj*. 幸运的，幸福的
【记】 fortun(e)(运气) + ate(形容词词尾)→有运气的→幸福的
【例】 She is *fortunate* enough to enjoy good health. 她身体好，真有福气。
【同】 blessed, lucky
【反】 unfortunate

fortune ['fɔːtʃən] *n*. 1. 命运，运气；2. 财富，运气
【记】 fort(机会) + une(名词词尾)→有机会的→运气
【例】 1. These two brothers decided to go to America to try their *fortunes*. 这兄弟俩决定去美国碰碰运气。
2. He dreamed of making a *fortune*. 他梦想发大财。
【同】 destiny; reasure
【反】 misfortune

fossil ['fɒsl] *n*. 化石
【记】 来自拉丁语 fossus，被掘出的东西→化石
【例】 This *fossil* may be over 2 million years old. 这化石可能超过二百万年了。
【同】 relic, remains

【派】 fossilize *v*. 使成化石，使…过时或固定不变

foster [ˈfɒstə] *v*. 1. 培养，培育；2. 鼓励，促进

【记】 fost(= food，食物) + er(表示动作重复的动词词尾)→不断地给食物→培养

【例】 1. The mother tried to *foster* her son's interest in music. 母亲设法培养儿子对音乐的兴趣。

2. Frequent cultural exchange will certainly help *foster* friendly relations between our two universities. 经常的文化交流肯定有助于发展我们两校之间的友好关系。

【同】 cultivate，nurture；encourage，promote

【派】 fosterage *n*. 养育，助长

fowl [faʊl] *n*. 鸡，家禽

【例】 There are many kinds of *fowl*. 家禽的种类很多。

【同】 poultry

fraction [ˈfrækʃən] *n*. 小部分，碎片

【记】 fract(打破) + ion(名词词尾)→打破的部分→碎片

【例】 You can now buy this software at only a *fraction* of the original cost. 你现在买这个软件只需要花原价的一小部分钱。

【同】 part，fragment，segment

fracture [ˈfræktʃə] *n*. 1. 裂缝，裂痕；2. 骨折

【记】 fract(打破) + ure(名词词尾)→打破的地方→裂缝

【例】 1. These *fracture* zones，where the collisions occur，are where earthquakes happen. 这些发生碰撞的断裂带是发生地震的地方，而且经常会有火山爆发。

2. He had several injuries，including three *fractures*. 他多处受伤，其中三处骨折。

【同】 break，crack，rupture

fragile [ˈfrædʒaɪl] *adj*. 易碎的，脆弱的

【记】 frag(打破) + ile(形容词词尾)→易于打破的→易碎的

【例】 This glass plate is very *fragile*. 这个玻璃盘子很容易碎。

【同】 delicate，frail

【反】 solid，strong，tough

【派】 fragility *n*. 脆弱，虚弱

fragment [ˈfrægmənt] *n*. 碎片，断片

【记】 frag(打破) + ment(名词词尾)→打破的东西→碎片

【例】 She dropped the vase on the floor and it broke into *fragments*. 她把花瓶掉在地上，摔成了碎片。

【同】 part，fraction，segment

【派】 fragmentary *adj*. 由碎片组成的，断断续续的

fragrant [ˈfreɪgrənt] *adj*. 香的，芬芳的

【记】 来自拉丁语 fragrans，发出香味的→香的，芬芳的

【例】 The flowers gave off a *fragrant* odor. 花发出一阵幽香。

【同】 aromatic，odorous，sweet-scented

【反】 malodorous

【派】 fragrance *n*. 芬芳，香味

frail [freɪl] *adj*. 脆弱的，意志薄弱的

【记】 frail = fract，打碎，是法语拼写→易打碎的→脆弱的

【例】 The *frail* wooden bridge cracked. 这座不牢固的木桥断裂了。

【同】 delicate, fragile, weak

【反】 solid, strong, sturdy

frame [freɪm] *n*. 1. 框架；2. 骨架；*v*. 1. 帧，加外框；2. 提出，制定

【例】 1. This old bed has a copper *frame*. 这张旧床的床架是铜的。

2. This athlete has a powerful *frame*. 这位运动员有着魁梧的体格。

3. I'm having this picture *framed*, so that I can hang it on the wall. 我要给这幅画装个框，才可以把它挂在墙上。

4. The government is *framing* a new bill to control gambling. 政府在制定新的法案以控制赌博。

【同】 skeleton; enclose; compose

【派】 framework *n*. 框架，体系

F

fraternal [frəˈtɜːnl] *adj*. 兄弟的，友善的

【记】 frater(兄弟) + n + al(形容词词尾)→兄弟般的

【例】 The party sent its *fraternal* greetings to the trade union meeting. 党向工会大会致以亲切的问候。

【同】 brotherly

【派】 fraternity *n*. 兄弟关系，友爱，兄弟会

fraud [frɔːd] *n*. 欺骗，诈骗

【例】 She went through the company's accounts, looking for evidence of *fraud*. 她仔细审核公司的账目，查找欺骗作弊的证据。

【同】 swindle, trickery

【反】 honesty

【派】 fraudulent *adj*. 欺诈的，欺骗性的

fraught [frɔːt] *adj*. 1. (作表语)充满某事物；2. 使人忧虑的，烦恼的

【例】 1. The expedition through the jungle was *fraught* with difficulties and danger. 穿越森林的探险充满了艰辛和危险。

2. But translating corporate philosophies into the right mix of color, style, degree of branding and uniformity can be a *fraught* process. 但是要把企业宗旨正确地体现在颜色、式样、创新和证实程度的混合之中，这个过程会令人忧虑。

【同】 full, loaded; annoying, anxious

fray [freɪ] *v*. 1. 磨损，磨破；2. 烦躁，紧张；*n*. 吵架，冲突

【例】 1. Constant rubbing will *fray* even the thickest rope. 再粗的绳子也经不住磨。

2. Relations between us have become *frayed* through a series of misunderstandings. 我们之间产生了一连串的误解，因而关系紧张了。

3. He rushed into the *fray*. 他冲上前去，投入战斗。

【同】 rub, fret; affray

freeze [friːz] *v*. (froze, frozen)结冰，冻结

【例】 Water *freezes* at the temperature of 0 degrees Celsius. 水在摄氏零度结冰。

【同】 chill

【反】 melt

【派】 freezing *adj*. 冰冻的，严寒的

freight [freɪt] *n*. 货物，运货

【例】 Heavy *freight* could only be carried by water or rail. 大宗的货物只能通过水路或铁路运输。

【同】 cargo，goods

【派】 freighter *n*. 货船；运输飞机

frenzy [ˈfrenzɪ] *n*. 狂暴，狂怒，极为激动的状态

【记】 fren(心智) + z + y(名词词尾)→(没有)心智→狂怒

【例】 The fans at the rock concert worked themselves up into a *frenzy*. 摇滚音乐会上的音乐迷们激动到了疯狂的地步。

【同】 fury，rage

【派】 frenetic *adj*. 狂乱的，发狂的

frequent [ˈfriːkwənt] *adj*. 时常发生的，频繁的

【例】 Production in the factories stopped because of *frequent* power failures. 频繁的停电使工厂停产。

【同】 regular，prevailing

【反】 infrequent，rare

【派】 frequency *n*. 频率，次数

fret [fret] *v*. (-tted；-tting) 1. (使)磨损；2. (使)烦恼，焦虑

【例】 1. The stream from the mountain slope *fretted* a channel through the soft earth along the mountain foot. 山坡上下来的小溪流侵袭着松软的土地，沿着山脚形成了一条沟渠。

2. What are you *fretting* about? 你在烦躁什么？

【同】 rub，erode；fuss，worry

friction [ˈfrɪkʃən] *n*. 摩擦，摩擦力

【记】 fric(摩擦) + tion(名词词尾)→摩擦

【例】 Studies of primitive societies suggest that the earliest method of making fire was through *friction*. 对原始社会的研究表明人们最早的生火的方法是通过摩擦。

【同】 rubbing，conflict

frighten [ˈfraɪtn] *v*. (使)惊吓，惊恐

【记】 fright(惊吓) + en(动词词尾)→使人受到惊吓

【例】 News of the robberies *frightened* many people into fitting new locks to their doors. 发生抢劫的消息把许多人吓得装上新门锁。

【同】 scare，terrify

【反】 calm，soothe

【派】 (逆构)fright *n*. 惊骇，吃惊

frightful *adj*. 可怕的，非常的

frigid [ˈfrɪdʒɪd] *adj*. 1. 严寒的；2. 冷淡的

【记】 frig(冷) + id(形容词词尾)→冷的→严寒的，冷淡的

【例】 1. The parts of the world near the North and South Poles are called the *frigid* zones. 靠近南北极的地带被称为严寒带。

2. She returned his smile with a *frigid* glance. 她对他的微笑报之以冷冰冰的一瞥。

【同】 cold, frosty, icy; aloof, wintry

fringe [frɪndʒ] *n*. 边缘，外围

【例】 It was easier to move about on the *fringe* of the crowd. 在人群外围移动比较容易。

【同】 edge, border

【反】 center

frisky [ˈfrɪskɪ] *adj*. 活泼的，精力充沛的

【记】 firsk(欢跃，跳跃) + y(形容词词尾)→跳跃的→活泼的

【例】 The morning fresh air makes me feel quite *frisky*. 早晨清新的空气使我感到十分愉快。

【同】 lively, spirited

frost [frɒst, frɔːst] *n*. 霜，霜冻，严寒天气

【例】 Thousands starved as the harvests failed, after snow in June and *frosts* in August. 由于六月下雪、八月霜冻，庄稼歉收，成千上万的人忍饥挨饿。

【同】 freezing

【派】 frostbite *n*. 霜寒，冻伤

frown [fraʊn] *v*. 皱眉，表示不悦

【例】 The teacher *frowned* angrily at the noisy class. 老师对那班吵吵嚷嚷的学生皱起了眉头。

【同】 scowl

【反】 smile

frowzy [ˈfraʊzɪ] *adj*. 不整洁的，污秽的

【例】 At London I am pent up in *frowzy* lodgings, where there is not enough room to swing a cat. 在伦敦，我守在肮脏的住所里面，那地方狭窄得无法转身。

【同】 untidy

frugal [ˈfruːəl] *adj*. 节约的，节俭的

【记】 frug(果实，美德) + al(形容词词尾)→有果实的，有美德的→节约的

【例】 They lived a very *frugal* existence, avoiding all luxuries. 他们生活非常俭朴，力避奢华。

【同】 economical, saving, thrifty

【派】 frugality *n*. 节俭，俭省

frustrate [frʌsˈtreɪt] *v*. 1. 挫败，破坏；2. 使沮丧

【记】 frustr(犯错误) + ate(动词词尾)→使犯错误→挫败

【例】 1. He had hoped to set a new world record, but was *frustrated* by bad weather. 他本希望能创造新的世界纪录，但因天气恶劣而未果。

2. He was *frustrated* by his poverty. 他因贫穷而灰心丧气。

【同】 defeat, depress

【反】 encourage

【派】 frustrating *adj*. 令人沮丧的

frustration *n*. 沮丧，挫折

fulminate ［ˈfʌlmɪneɪt］ *v*. 猛烈抨击，严厉谴责

【记】 fulmin(闪电，雷声)＋ate(动词词尾)→像雷声一样的→猛烈抨击

【例】 The preacher *fulminated* against the use of alcohol. 那位传道的人强烈反对饮用含酒精的饮料。

【同】 denounce

fume ［fjuːm］ *n*. (常用复数～s)(有害、浓烈、或难闻的)烟，气，汽

【例】 Even Moscow has joined the list of capitals afflicted by congestion and traffic *fumes*. 甚至莫斯科也成了受交通堵塞和汽车尾气之苦的首都之一。

【同】 smoke

function ［ˈfʌŋkʃən］ *n*. 1. 功能，作用；2. 典礼，重大聚会；*v*. 具有功能，起作用

【记】 func(做，完成)＋tion(名词词尾)→做…的能力→功能

【例】 1. One *function* of the dictionary was to enable its student to convey an impression of fine learning. 这部词典的功能之一就是让使用它的学生能够给人留下受过良好教育的印象。

2. Membership gives wide access to other activities like basketball and football as well as barbecues and other social *functions*. 会员还可参与其他活动，比如篮球、足球、户外烧烤以及其他社交活动。

3. The machine won't *function* properly if you don't oil it well. 如果你不给机器好好加油的话，它就不会正常运转。

【同】 role；ritual，gathering；operate，work

【反】 malfunction

【派】 functional *adj*. 官能的，有功能的

fund ［fʌnd］ *n*. 资金，基金；*v*. 为…提供资金，资助

【例】 1. The factory has built up reserve *fund*. 这个工厂已积累了后备基金。

2. The Government has been *funding* a loans scheme for students in Higher Education since September 1990. 政府自1990年9月起为接受高等教育的学生贷款计划提供资金。

【同】 investment，funding；supply，invest

【派】 funding *n*. 专款，基金

fund-raising *n*. 资金筹集，募捐

fundamental ［ˌfʌndəˈmentl］ *adj*. 基本的，根本的

【记】 fund(a)(基础)＋ment(名词词尾)＋al(形容词词尾)→基础的→基本的

【例】 There are *fundamental* differences between your religious beliefs and mine. 你我的宗教信仰根本不同。

【同】 basic，elementary，essential

【派】 fundamentality *n*. 基本性，重要性

furnace ［ˈfɜːnɪs］ *n*. 火炉，熔炉

【记】 furn(热)＋ace(名词词尾)→产生热的地方→火炉

【例】 Just a tenth of a gram of nickel in the *furnace* can create up to 50, 000 crystals. 在熔炉中，十分之一克的镍可以产生五万个晶体。

【同】 oven, stove

furnish ['fɜːnɪʃ] *v*. 为…配备家具，提供

【记】 furn(备有) + ish(动词词尾)→为…备有→为…配备家具

【例】 The room was *furnished* with the simplest essentials, a bed, a chair, and a table. 房间里只布置了最简单的必需品，一张床、一把椅子和一张桌子。

【同】 equip, provide, supply

【派】 furniture *n*. 家具

F

further ['fɜːðə] *adj*. 更远的，更多的，深一层的；*v*. 促进，增进

【记】 far 的比较级变体

【例】 1. The lungs and brains of children who grow up in polluted air offer *further* evidence of its destructive power. 在污染空气中长大的儿童的肺部和大脑更加证明了空气污染的毁灭能力。

2. The society was dedicated to *furthering* the cause of world peace. 该协会致力于推动世界和平事业。

【同】 beyond, farther; promote

【反】 hinder

furthermore [fɜːðə'mɔːr] *adv*. 此外，而且

【记】 further(更远的) + more(更多的)→此外

【例】 *Furthermore* the high divorce rates in North America are creating a poverty cycle for women. 此外，北美的高离婚率也造成了妇女贫困的恶性循环。

【同】 again, in addition

fury ['fjʊərɪ] *n*. 愤怒，激烈

【例】 She flew into a *fury* when I wouldn't lend her any money. 我不借给她钱，她顿时勃然大怒。

【同】 craze, rage, intensity

【派】 furious *adj*. 暴怒的，激烈的

fuse [fjuːz] *v*. 熔合，使融合

【例】 Lead *fuses* at a low temperature. 铅在低温下就熔化。

【同】 blend, merge

【反】 defuse

【派】 fusion *n*. 1.【原子】核聚变；2.熔化；3.联合

futile ['fjuːtaɪl] *adj*. 无益的，徒劳的

【记】 fut(流) + ile(形容词词尾)→流出去的→无益的

【例】 On the whole, our efforts did not prove to be *futile*. 总体说来，我们的努力没有白费。

【同】 ineffective

【反】 profitable, useful

【派】 futility *n*. 无益，无用

fuzzy ['fʌzɪ] *adj*. 1.绒毛般的，有绒毛的；2.不清楚的，模糊的

【记】 fuzz(细毛，绒毛)+y(形容词词尾)→绒毛般的

【例】 1. I tied it with *fuzzy* white yarn, and admired my work. 我用毛茸茸的白纱线把它系好，然后欣赏着自己的杰作。

2. The television picture is *fuzzy* tonight. 今晚电视图像不清晰。

【同】 downy, feathery; blurred, unclear

【反】 clear

G

gabble ['gæbl] *v*. 急促而不清楚地说

【记】 gab(喋喋不休地说) + b + le(表是动作的重复)→急促而不清楚地说

【例】 Mary *gabbled* out her prayers and jumped into bed. 玛丽急匆匆说过祈祷词就跳上了床。

【同】 chatter，jabber，mutter

gadget ['gædʒɪt] *n*. 小器械，小装置

【记】 gadg(锁里面的一个部件) + et(表示"小"的名词词尾)→小部件→小装置

【例】 I've been investigating four new household *gadgets* and sorting out the advantages and disadvantages. 我对四个新的家用小装置进行了调查，并且整理出了它们的优点和缺点。

【同】 apparatus，appliance，device

gainsay [geɪn'seɪ] *v*. 否认，反驳

【记】 gain(= against，反对) + say(说)→反对着说→反驳

【例】 There is no *gainsaying* her ability. 她的能力是无可否认的。

【同】 deny，contradict

【反】 admit

galaxy ['gæləksɪ] *n*. 星系，银河

【记】 galax(= milk，牛奶) + y(名词词尾)→银河的英语名称就是 Milky Way→银河

【例】 There may be millions of worlds in the Milky Way *Galaxy*. 银河系中也许有几百万个世界。

gale [geɪl] *n*. 大风，(突发的)一阵

【例】 The ship lost its masts in the *gale*. 这船的桅杆都在风暴中刮掉了。

【同】 wind

gallant ['gælənt] *adj*. 1.(对女子)殷勤的；2.勇敢的，英勇的

【记】 gall(胆) + ant(形容词词尾)→有胆的→勇敢的

【例】 1. He was very *gallant* at the ball. 他在舞会上对妇女大献殷勤。

2. These *gallant* soldiers will protect our country. 这些勇敢的士兵会保卫我们的国家的。

【同】 chivalrous；bold，brave，courageous

【反】 rude；cowardly，timid

【派】 gallantry *n*. 勇敢

gallery ['gælərɪ] *n*. 长廊，画廊

【记】 来自拉丁语 galeria，长的柱廊→长廊→画廊

【例】 Her collection of paintings was bequeathed to the National *Gallery* when she died. 她去世时，她的全部藏画都遗赠给了国家美术馆。

【同】 balcony，corridor

gamble [ˈgæmbl] *v*./*n*. 赌博，投机

【例】 He *gambled* all his winnings on the last race. 他把赢得的钱全都压在最后一场赛马上了。

【同】 bet，risk，speculate

【派】 gambler *n*. 赌博的人，赌徒

gap [gæp] *n*. 缺口，差距

【例】 Reducing the *gap* between rich and poor is one of the main challenges facing the government. 缩小贫富之间的差距是政府面临的主要难题之一。

【同】 break，cleft，crack

garbage [ˈgɑːbɪdʒ] *n*. 废物，垃圾(箱)

【例】 Throw any left-over food in the *garbage*. 把剩下的食物倒进垃圾箱里。

【同】 junk，rubbish，waste

garment [ˈgɑːmənt] *n*. 衣服，外衣

【记】 gar(= garnir，装备，装饰) + ment(名词词尾)→用来装饰的东西→衣服

【例】 Is this *garment* made of pure wool, or of wool mixed with nylon? 这件衣服是纯羊毛的，还是羊毛与尼龙混纺的？

【同】 apparel，robe，clothes，garb

garnish [ˈgɑːnɪʃ] *v*. 配菜，装饰；*n*. 食物上的装饰物

【记】 garn(= garnir，装备，装饰) + ish(动词词尾)→装饰

【例】 The chicken was *garnished* with coriander and red chili. 这道鸡配上了芫荽和红辣椒。

【同】 adorn，decorate，embellish

gash [gæʃ] *n*. 深的切口，创口

【例】 He *gashed* his foot on a piece of broken glass. 他的脚在一块碎玻璃上划了一个大口子。

【同】 cut，wound

gasp [gɑːsp] *v*./*n*. 喘息，气喘

【例】 I *gasped* with surprise at the unexpected news. 听到意外的消息，我惊讶地吸了一口气。

【同】 pant，puff

gauge [gedʒ] *n*./*v*. 量度，测量

【例】 We must *gauge* the diameter of wire first. 我们必须先测量电线的直径。

【同】 measure

gaunt [gɔːnt] *adj*. 1. 憔悴的；2. 荒凉的

【例】 1. He had *gaunt* cheeks and hollow eyes after his long illness. 他长时间生病后，脸

颊憔悴，双目凹陷。

2. The old house stood *gaunt* and empty, a complete ruin. 那栋旧房子荒凉空洞地伫立着，像一堆废墟。

【同】 bony; bleak, desolate

gaze [geɪz] *v.* / *n.* 盯，凝视

【例】 She *gazed* at me in disbelief when I told her the news. 我告诉她这消息时，她以怀疑的目光注视着我。

【同】 stare, look

gear [gɪə] *n.* 齿轮，传动装置，排档；*v.* 调整，(使)适合，换档

【例】 1. Careless use of the clutch may damage the *gears*. 离合器使用不慎可能损坏传动装置。

2. Education should be *geared* to the children's needs and abilities. 教育应适应儿童的需要和能力。

【同】 equipment; adjust, adapt

G

gem [dʒem] *n.* 宝石，珠宝

【例】 The price of this *gem* is expensive—as much so as astronomical figures. 这个宝石的价格十分昂贵——简直是个天文数字。

【同】 jewel, treasure

gender [ˈdʒendə] *n.* 性别，〈语法〉性

【记】 gen(d)(种，种族) + er(名词词尾)→不同种的→性别

【例】 There are three *genders* in German: masculine, feminine and neuter. 德语中有三性：阳性、阴性和中性。

【同】 sex

gene [dʒiːn] *n.* 基因

【例】 Over the past century, the composition of the human *gene* pool has not changed appreciably. 在过去一个世纪的时间里，人类基因库的构成没有发生显著的变化。

【派】 genetic *adj.* 遗传的，起源的

genetics *n.* 遗传性，遗传学

genome *n.* 基因组，染色体组

generalize [ˈdʒenərəlaɪz] *v.* 归纳，概括

【记】 general(一般的) + ize(动词词尾)→把…一般化→概括

【例】 You cannot *generalize* about the effects of the drug from one or two cases. 你不能根据一两个病例就得出该药是否有效的结论。

【反】 specialize

【派】 generalization *n.* 概括

generate [ˈdʒenəˌreɪt] *v.* 产生，发生

【记】 gener(生产，产生) + ate(动词词尾)→产生

【例】 This hatred was *generated* by racial prejudice. 这种仇恨是由种族偏见引起的。

【同】 create, originate, produce

【派】 generation *n*. 产生，发生；代，一代人
generative *adj*. 生成的

generous [ˈdʒenərəs] *adj*. 慷慨的，大方的

【记】 gener(生产，产生) + ous(形容词词尾)→产生许多的→慷慨的

【例】 It was *generous* of her to contribute such a large sum. 她很大方，捐助了这么大笔钱。

【同】 munificent

【反】 ungenerous, stingy

【派】 generosity *n*. 慷慨，宽大

genesis [ˈdʒenɪsɪs] *n*. 创始，起源

【记】 gene(= gener，生产，产生) + sis(名词词尾)→产生的地方→起源

【例】 We cannot yet satisfactorily explain the *genesis* of the universe. 我们还不能满意地解释宇宙的起源。

【同】 origin, beginning

genetic [dʒɪˈnetɪk] *adj*. 遗传的，起源的

【记】 gene(基因) + tic(形容词词尾)→从基因上的→遗传的

【例】 *Genetic* engineering will have revolutionary consequences for mankind. 遗传工程将对人类产生深远的影响。

【同】 hereditary, inherited

【派】 genetics *n*. 遗传学

genial [ˈdʒɪnjəl] *adj*. 和蔼可亲的

【记】 gen(生产，产生) + ial(形容词词尾)→生来就有的→和蔼可亲的

【例】 Her *genial* smile made every guest feel at home. 她亲切的笑容使每个人都感觉宾至如归。

【同】 amiable, cordial, kindly, friendly

【反】 austere, unfriendly

genius [ˈdʒiːnjəs] *n*. 天才，天赋

【记】 geni(出生) + us(名词词尾)→出生(就有)→天才

【例】 Johnson was a poet and critic who raised common sense to the heights of *genius* 约翰逊当时是诗人兼批评家，他能够把常识提升到天才的高度。

【同】 gift, talent

【反】 idiot

genre [ˈʒɒŋrə] *n*. [法]种类，类型，流派

【例】 Many of his finest works belong to the *genre* of nature poetry. 他的许多优秀作品属于自然诗歌类。

【同】 style

genteel [dʒenˈtiːl] *adj*. 有教养的，属于上流社会的

【记】 gentle 的变体

【例】 Although she was poor, she was living in *genteel* poverty. 尽管她贫穷，但她总想

G

装出上流社会阶层的样子。

【同】 cultivated, polite, well-bred

【派】 gentility *n*. 有教养，文雅

gentry ['dʒentrɪ] *n*. 绅士，上等人

【记】 gent(出生)+ry(名词词尾)→出身(高贵)的→贵族

【例】 The English *gentry* is next below the nobility. 英国绅士的地位仅次于贵族。

【同】 upper class

genuine ['dʒenjʊɪn] *adj*. 真的，非人造的

【记】 genu(出生)+ine(形容词词尾)→出生就有的→真的

【例】 It appears to be *genuine*, but I have my suspicions (about it). 这看来好像是真的，不过我(对此)有怀疑。

【同】 authentic, real, true

【反】 artificial, false, fake

geography [dʒɪ'ɒgrəfɪ] *n*. 地理，地理学

【记】 geo(土地)+graph(写)+y(名词词尾)→记录有关土地的→地理学

【例】 I have only a sketchy knowledge of *geography*. 我对地理只是一知半解。

【派】 geographic(al) *adj*. 地理(学)的

geographer *n*. 地理学者

geology [dʒɪ'ɒlədʒɪ] *n*. 地质学，地质概况

【记】 geo(土地)+logy(…学)→研究土地的学科→地质学

【例】 Although the UK is a fairly small country, the *geology* and climate vary a good deal from region to region. 尽管英国是一个相当小的国家，它的地质和气候却因为地区的不同而差别很大。

【派】 geologic(al) *adj*. 地质学的，地质的

geologist *n*. 地质学者

geometry [dʒɪ'ɒmɪtrɪ] *n*. 几何学，几何图形

【记】 geo(土地)+metry(测量)→丈量土地→几何学

【例】 The higher division of the seven liberal arts in the Middle Ages, is composed of *geometry*, astronomy, arithmetic, and music. 中世纪7个文科中较高级的学科，由几何、天文、算术以及音乐组成。

【派】 geometric(al) *adj*. 几何学的，几何的

geometrician *n*. 几何学者

germ [dʒɜːm] *n*. 微生物，细菌

【例】 *Germs* are invisible to the naked eye. 细菌用肉眼看不见。

【同】 microorganism

giant ['dʒaɪənt] *n*. 巨人，伟人；*adj*. 巨大的，庞大的

【例】 1. Shakespeare is a *giant* among writers. 莎士比亚是作家中的大文豪。

2. The *giant* packet gives you more for less money. 特大的包装，使你用便宜的价钱买到超值的分量!

【同】 colossal，gigantic，huge

【反】 dwarf；small，tiny

gibe [dʒaɪb] *v*. 嘲弄，讥笑

【例】 It's easy enough for you to *gibe* at them，but could you do any better?
笑话人家很容易，可是你能做得更好吗?

【同】 jeer，mock，scoff，sneer

gigantic [dʒaɪ'gæntɪk] *adj*. 巨大的

【记】 gigant(= giant，巨人)+ic(形容词词尾)→巨人一般的→巨大的

【例】 The company has made *gigantic* losses this year，and will probably be out of business. 这个公司今年亏损巨大，有可能倒闭。

【同】 colossal，enormous，huge，immense

【反】 little，small

gild [gɪld] *v*. (-ed 或 gilt，gilt)镀金

【例】 He bought her a *gilt* brooch. 他给她买了一枚镀金胸针。

【同】 coat，cover，paint

gist [dʒɪst] *n*. 要旨，主旨

【例】 I haven't time to read the report；can you give me the *gist* of it? 我没时间看这份报告，你能把要点告诉我吗?

【同】 core，essence，theme

glacier ['glæsjə，'gleɪʃə] *n*. 冰河，冰川

【例】 Mr Forster and his guide entered upon this portion of the *glacier*. 福斯特先生和他的向导进入了冰河地区。

【派】 glacial *adj*. 冰的，冰河的
glaciated *adj*. 冻结成冰的

glamour ['glæmə] *n*. 魅力，魔力，迷人的力量

【记】 glam(= magic，魔法)+our(名词词尾)→魔力→魅力

【例】 She added a touch of *glamour* by wearing a beautiful dress. 她换上一件漂亮衣服，增添了一分魅力。

【同】 enchant，charm

【派】 glamorous *adj*. 迷人的，富有魅力的

glare [gleə] *n*. 眩目的光；*v*. 发出刺目的光

【例】 1. The sun *glared* on the sea. 太阳在海上发出令人目眩的光芒。
2. The windows were tinted to reduce the *glare*. 窗户上涂上了浅色以减少强光。

【同】 brilliance；blaze，shine

【派】 glaring *adj*. 耀眼的，刺目的

glaze [gleɪz] *v*. 上釉，使表面光滑

【例】 He is *glazing* the table. 他正在给桌子上釉。

【同】 cover，coat

gleam [gliːm] *n*. 亮光，闪光；*vi*. 闪烁，隐约地闪现

【例】 1. The lighthouse of the island *gleamed* in the distance. 远处岛上的灯塔在闪耀着。

2. I could see the faint *gleam* of light in the distance. 我能看见远处微弱的灯光。

【同】 beam; glimmer, sparkle, twinkle

glean [gliːn] *v*. 点滴搜集，拾

【例】 Much of the information you have *gleaned* is of no practical use. 你收集到的大部分情报没有实用价值。

【同】 gather, collect, harvest

glide [glaɪd] *v*. 滑动，滑行

【例】 The figure skater *glided* gracefully over the ice. 花样滑冰者在冰上优雅地滑行。

【同】 slide

G

glimmer ['glɪmə] *v*. /*n*. 闪烁，闪光

【记】 glimm(光) + er(表示"动作的反复"的动词词尾)→光一直动的→闪烁

【例】 From the cottage window a few lamps were *glimmering* in the distance. 远处的农舍窗户闪烁着几盏微弱的灯。

【同】 blink, flicker, glitter

glimpse [glɪmps] *v*. /*n*. 瞥见，看一眼

【记】 glimp(光) + se(动词词尾)→目光的移动→瞥见

【例】 I *glimpsed* at her among the crowd before she disappeared from sight. 就在她即将消失在人群里之前，我瞥见了她。

【同】 glance, skim

【反】 gaze, stare

glitter ['glɪtə] *v*/*n*. 闪闪发光，闪烁

【记】 glitt(光) + er(动词词尾，表示动作的反复)→光一直动的→闪烁

【例】 All that *glitters* is not gold. [谚]闪闪发光的东西不一定都是金子。

【同】 blink, flicker, glimmer

global ['gləʊbəl] *adj*. 全球的，全世界的

【记】 glob(球) + al(形容词词尾)→全球的

【例】 *Global* climatic changes may have been responsible for the extinction of the dinosaurs. 全球性的气候变化也许是造成恐龙灭绝的原因。

【同】 worldwide, international

【派】 globalize *v*. 使全球化

globalization *n*. 全球化，全球性

gloomy ['gluːmɪ] *adj*. 阴沉的，阴郁的，令人沮丧的

【例】 *Gloomy* weather can cause depression, but sunshine appears to raise the spirits. 天气阴郁可能导致人们的情绪低沉，而晴空万里似乎会使人情绪高涨。

【同】 bleak, melancholy; depressing, sad

【反】 bright, clear; delightful, pleasant

glory ['glɔːrɪ] *n*. 光荣，荣誉，辉煌

【例】 His brave deeds in the battle earned him everlasting *glory*. 他在那场战斗中的英勇事迹为他赢得了永恒的荣誉。

【同】 honor

【反】 dishonor, disgrace, shame

【派】 glorify *v*. 使光荣，赞美

glorious *adj*. 光荣的，壮丽的

glossary [ˈglɒsərɪ] *n*. 词汇表

【记】 gloss(= glot，舌头) + ary(形容词词尾)→舌头说出来的→词汇

【例】 He put a tick beside each word in the *glossary* that he had learnt by heart. 他在词表中每一个已熟记的生词旁做个记号。

【同】 vocabulary, wordlist

glossy [ˈglɒsɪ] *adj*. 平滑的，有光泽的

【记】 gloss(光泽) + y(形容词词尾)→有光泽的

【例】 The old man has *glossy* hair. 那位老人头发很有光泽。

【同】 silky, lustrous

【反】 dull

glow [gləʊ] *v*. 发出光和热，燃烧

【例】 The cat's eyes *glowed* in the darkness. 猫的眼睛在黑暗中发亮。

【同】 blaze, glare

【派】 glowing *adj*. 白热的，通红的，热烈的

gnaw [nɔː] *v*. 1. 咬，啃；2. 折磨，侵蚀

【例】 1. The rat *gnawed* a hole through the wall. 耗子在墙上啃了一个洞。

2. Anxiety *gnawed* at his heart. 他忧心如焚。

【同】 bite, chew, grind; erode

goal [gəʊl] *n*. 1. 球门；2. 努力的对象，目标

【例】 1. Who is keeping *goal*/is in *goal* for Arsenal? 谁给阿森纳队守球门？

2. He has achieved his *goal*. 他已经实现了他的目标。

【同】 aim, objective

【派】 goalkeeper *n*. 守门员

gorge [gɔːdʒ] *n*. 峡谷；*v*. 贪婪地吃

【例】 1. A deep *gorge* separates the two halves of the city. 有一道深谷把这座城市分成两部分。

2. The fat man *gorged* himself constantly with enormous desserts. 那个胖子经常大吃甜食。

【同】 gully, valley; gulp, devour

gorgeous [ˈgɔːdʒəs] *adj*. 华丽的，灿烂的

【记】 gorge(法语，喉咙) + ous(形容词词尾)→令人从喉咙发出感叹的→华丽的

【例】 In the evening the rosy clouds were *gorgeous*. 傍晚的云霞绚丽多彩。

【同】 beautiful, glorious, splendid

G

gossip ['gɒsɪp] *n*. 闲话，小道传闻

【记】 go(= god，上帝) + s + sip(= sib，亲属)→本义是指教父、教母→引申为和教父、教母说话→闲话

【例】 There has been much *gossip* in political circles. 政界里有许多流言蜚语。

【同】 chat，prattle，tattle

gourmet ['guəmeɪ] *n*. 美食家

【记】 古法语 groumet 的变体，本义是指餐桌上倒酒的男仆→美食家

【例】 Mr Bowen，you're lucky to have such a *gourmet* cook as your wife. 伯恩先生，你真有福气，有这么一位美食家做你的妻子。

【同】 epicure

govern ['gʌvən] *v*. 1.统治，控制；2.治理，管理

【例】 1. You must not be *governed* by the opinions of others. 你决不要受别人意见的支配。

2. They demand the right to *govern* themselves. 他们要求自治权。

【同】 control，rule；manage，minister

【反】 misgovern，misrule

【派】 governance *n*. 统治，控制，治理

government *n*. 政府

governor *n*. 总督，州长

grab [græb] *v*. (-bbed；-bbing)攫取，抓住

【例】 The thief *grabbed* the shoulder bag from the woman and ran off. 贼抓了那个妇女的挂包就跑。

【同】 seize，catch

grace [greɪs] *n*. 优美，优雅

【例】 She had the *grace* to admit that I was right. 她很有气度地承认我是对的。

【同】 beauty，refinement

【反】 disgrace

【派】 graceful *adj*. 优美的，优雅的

grand [grænd] *adj*. 壮观的，显赫的

【例】 How *grand* the mountains look in the early evening! 暮色中群山是多么壮丽！

【同】 impressive，magnificent，prominent

【反】 modest

【派】 grandeur *n*. 庄严，伟大

granite ['grænɪt] *n*. 花岗岩，花岗石

【记】 gran(颗粒) + ite(名词词尾)→颗粒组成的东西→花岗岩

【例】 The valley ended in a perpendicular rim of *granite*. 那山谷的尽头是花岗石的断崖。

【同】 rock，stone

grant [grɑːnt] *v*. 同意给予，授予；*n*. 授予物，(尤指政府的)拨款，助学金

【例】 1. They *granted* him permission to go. 他们准许他去。

2. The government has rescued the firm from bankruptcy by giving them a *grant*. 政府拨款给这家公司使其免于破产。

【同】 give, award

graph [grɑːf] *n*. 图表，曲线图

【记】 graph，本义是写，画→画出的东西→图表

【例】 The *graph* flattens out gradually after a steep fall. 图表上的曲线突降之后逐渐趋于平稳。

【同】 chart, diagram, drawing

【派】 graphic *adj*. 图表的，书写的

grasp [grɑːsp] *v*. 抓住，全面理解

【例】 I don't think you've quite *grasped* the seriousness of the situation. 我认为你对情况的严重性理解得还不透彻。

【同】 take, apprehend, comprehend

grateful ['greɪtfʊl] *adj*. 感激的，感谢的

【记】 grat(高兴，喜欢) + e + ful(形容词词尾)→充满欢喜的→感激的

【例】 We are *grateful* to you for your bounteous gifts. 对您给予的丰厚礼物，我们不胜感激。

【同】 appreciative, thankful

【反】 ungrateful

【派】 gratitude *n*. 感激，感谢

gratify ['grætɪfaɪ] *v*. 使高兴，使满足

【记】 grat(高兴，喜欢) + ify(动词词尾)→使高兴

【例】 Now that she has a job in France she can *gratify* her desire to see Europe. 既然现在她在法国工作，那就可以满足她游览欧洲的愿望了。

【同】 satisfy, please

【派】 gratification *n*. 满意

gratuitous [grə'tjuːɪtəs] *adj*. 1. 免费的；2. 无缘无故的，不必要的

【记】 grat(高兴，喜欢) + u + itous(形容词词尾)→高兴地去做的→自愿的→免费的

【例】 1. At the current stage, most of people's sports entertaining consumption is non-*gratuitous*. 现阶段来看，人们的体育娱乐消费，绝大部分还是有偿服务。

2. This is an unpleasant film with a lot of *gratuitous* violence in it. 这是一部充斥着不必要的暴力镜头的令人不快的电影。

【同】 free, voluntary; needless, unnecessary

【反】 charged; justifiable

gravity ['grævɪtɪ] *n*. 1. 重力，地心引力；2. 重要性，严重性

【记】 grav(重) + ity(名词词尾)→重的东西→重量，重力

【例】 1. Anything that is dropped falls towards the ground because of the force of *gravity*. 落下的东西因为地心引力的缘故，都会掉到地上。

2. I don't think you realize the *gravity* of the situation. 我认为你没有意识到局势的严重。

【同】 gravitation; graveness

【反】 levity

【派】 (逆构)grave *adj*. 严重的，黯淡的

graze [greɪz] *v*. (牲畜)吃草，放牧

【例】 We are *grazing* the sheep in the next field. 我们在旁边的地里放羊。

【同】 browse, pasture

grease [griːs] *n*. 油脂，脂肪

【例】 You put *grease* on a wheel to make it turn more easily. 把润滑油涂在轮子上使它转起来更灵活一些。

【同】 oil

【派】 greasy *adj*. 多脂的，油脂的

greedy ['griːdɪ] *adj*. 贪吃的，贪婪的，渴望的

【记】 greed(贪婪) + y(形容词词尾)→贪婪的

【例】 He looked at the shop window with *greedy* eyes. 他用贪婪的眼光看着商店的橱窗。

【同】 grabby, desirous

greenhouse ['griːnhaus] *n*. 温室，花房

【记】 green(绿色) + house(房子)→培养绿色植物的房子→温室，花房

【例】 Most vegetables we buy in winter are nurtured in the *greenhouse*. 我们冬天买的大多数蔬菜都是在温室里培育的。

【同】 glasshouse, hothouse

grieve [griːv] *v*. 悲伤，伤心

【记】 griev(= grav, 重) + e→心情沉重→悲伤

【例】 Their daughter died over a year ago, but they are still *grieving*. 他们的女儿死去已一年多了，但他们现在仍很悲痛。

【同】 lament, mourn, sorrow

【反】 delight, please

【派】 grief *n*. 悲伤，伤心

grievance *n*. 委屈，怨恨

grind [graɪnd] *v*. (ground, ground)磨碎，碾碎

【例】 We *grind* up the wheat to make flour. 我们把小麦磨成面粉。

【同】 crumble, crush, grate

grip [grɪp] *v*. (-pped; -pping)紧握，紧抓

【例】 The frightened child *gripped* his mother's arm. 这个受惊的孩子紧紧地抓着妈妈的胳膊。

【同】 clutch, grasp, hold, seize

【反】 loosen, free, release

grocery ['grəusərɪ] *n*. 食品杂货店，食品，杂货

【记】 groc(大批的) + er(表示“人”的名词词尾) + y(表示“地点”的名词词尾)→大批买卖东西的地方→杂货店

【例】 A new supermarket opened across the street, and Peter's *grocery* business was soon in a bad way. 在街对面开了一家新的超级市场，这使彼得的杂货店的生意马上萧条下来。

grope [grəʊp] *v*. 摸索，探索

【例】 We *groped* our way through the dark streets. 我们摸索着走过黑暗的街道。

【同】 fumble, search blindly

grouch [graʊtʃ] *v*. /*n*. 发牢骚，抱怨

【例】 1. Stop *grouching* about everything! 别再事事都抱怨了！

2. He's always having a *grouch* about something. 他总是发脾气抱怨这个抱怨那个。

【同】 grumble, complain

【派】 grouchy *adj*. 不悦的，愠怒的

G

grudge [grʌdʒ] *v*. /*n*. 吝啬，不满，恶意

【例】 1. I always feel he has a *grudge* against me, although I don't know why. 我总觉得他讨厌我，但我不知道为什么。

2. He *grudged* my success. 他嫉妒我成功。

【同】 dislike, resent

【派】 grudging *adj*. 吝啬的；不愿的，勉强的

grumble ['grʌmbl] *v*. /*n*. 发牢骚，抱怨

【例】 1. They will *grumble* about having to do the work. 他们将为不得不干那项工作而抱怨。

2. He has everything he needs, but he is still full of *grumbles*. 他需要的一切都得到了，却还牢骚满腹。

【同】 complain, grouch

guarantee [ˌgærən'tiː] *n*./*v*. 保证，确保

【记】 guarant(= warrant，保证，担保) + ee(= y，名词词尾)→保证，确保

【例】 1. This radio has a two-year *guarantee*. 这台收音机保修两年。

2. We cannot *guarantee* the punctual arrival of trains in fogy weather. 雾天我们不能保证火车准时到达。

【同】 assure, ensure, warrant

guile [gaɪl] *n*. 欺骗，狡诈

【例】 He persuaded her to sign the document by *guile*. 他用欺骗手段说服她在文件上签字。

【同】 cunning, deceit, trickery

【派】 guileless *adj*. 不狡猾的，诚实的

guilty ['gɪltɪ] *adj*. 有罪的，证明(或判决)有罪的

【记】 guilt(罪责，过失) + y(形容词词尾)→有罪的

【例】 A man is accounted innocent until he is proven *guilty*. 一个人未被证明有罪前，被视为是清白的。

【同】 criminal, culpable

【反】 innocent

【派】 (逆构)guilt *n*. 罪行，内疚

guise [gaɪz] *n*. 1. 外观，装束；2. 伪装

【例】 1. It's an ancient tale which appears in various *guises* in several languages. 那是一个以几种语言叙述的古老的故事。

2. He cheated us under the *guise* of friendship. 他以友谊为掩护欺骗了我们。

G

【同】 apparel, appearance; pretence

gullible [ˈgʌlɪbəl] *adj*. 轻信的，易受骗的

【记】 gull(欺骗，哄骗) + ible(形容词词尾)→易受骗的

【例】 He must have been pretty *gullible* to fall for that old trick. 他准是有点儿傻，才落入那惯用的圈套。

【同】 credulous, deceivable, naive

gush [gʌʃ] *v*. 1. 喷涌，涌流；2. 滔滔不绝地讲

【例】 1. Oil *gashed* out from the broken pipe. 油从断裂的管道中喷出来。

2. Young mothers are *gushing* over their babies. 年轻的母亲滔滔不绝地谈论她们的婴儿。

【同】 pour, flow, surge; chatter

gym [dʒɪm] *n*. (= gymnasium)体操馆，健身房

【例】 After several sessions at the *gym*, I feel a lot fitter. 我在健身房锻炼了几次以后，觉得身体好多了。

【派】 gymnastic *adj*. 体操的，体育的

gymnastics *n*. 体操，体育

H

habitat [ˈhæbɪtæt] *n*.（动植物的）生活环境，栖息地

【记】habit(有) + at(表示地方)→拥有的地方→生活环境

【例】The polar bear's *habitat* is the icy waters of the Arctic. 北极熊的栖息地是冰冷的北极海域。

【同】environment, surroundings

【派】habitation *n*. 居住

habitual [həˈbɪtjuəl] *adj*. 习惯性的，惯常的

【记】habit(习惯) + ual(形容词词尾)→习惯性的

【例】His *habitual* place at the table was occupied by a stranger. 他习惯常坐的桌旁的位置被一个陌生人占据了。

【同】customary, regular, usual

【反】occasional

【派】(逆构)habit *n*. 习惯，习性

haggle [ˈhægl] *v*. 争论，讨价还价

【例】It's not worth *haggling* over a few pence. 为几便士争论不休实在不值得。

【同】chaffer, bargain

hail [heɪl] *n*. 冰雹 *v*. 呼喊，向…欢呼

【例】1. It *hailed* last night. 昨夜下雹子了。

2. An old friend *hailed* me from the other side of the street. 一个老朋友在街的对面喊我。

【同】greet, call

hallmark [ˈhɔːlmɑːk] *n*. 标志，特征

【记】hall(庄园里的主要建筑) + mark(标记)→主要的标记→标志，特征

【例】The plan has all the *hallmarks* of being a total failure. 这个方案具有彻底失败的一切标志。

【同】characteristic, marking

halt [hɔːlt] *v*. /*n*. 中止，停止

【例】1. The car came to a *halt* just in time to prevent an accident. 汽车及时停下，避免了一场车祸。

2. The officer *halted* his troops for a rest. 军官下令部队停下来休息。

【同】cease, stop

【反】march

hamper [ˈhæmpə] *v*. 妨碍，使困难

【例】 Our progress was *hampered* by the bad weather. 我们前进时受到了恶劣天气的阻碍。

【同】 hinder, impede, obstruct

handicap [ˈhændɪkæp] *n*. 生理上或智力上的缺陷，残疾；*v*. (-pped; -pping)加障碍于，妨碍

【记】 = hand in cap 原来指赌马时把钱放入帽子里；为了比赛公平，为强者(马或者人)设置障碍→加障碍于

【例】 1. Deafness can be a serious *handicap*. 耳聋算是严重的缺陷。

2. He was *handicapped* by lack of education. 他因文化水平低而吃了亏。

【同】 disability, hindrance

【派】 handicapped *adj*. 残疾的，身体有缺陷的

handicraft [ˈhændɪkrɑːft] *n*. 手工艺，手工艺品

【记】 hand(i)(手) + craft(工艺，手艺)→手工艺

【例】 The place is known for its *handicraft* products. 这地方因出手工艺品而出名。

【同】 handiwork

【派】 handicraftsman *n*. 手艺人，工匠

handle [ˈhændl] *n*. 手柄，把手；*v*. 操纵，管理，处理

【记】 hand(手) + le(名词词尾)→手抓的东西→手柄

【例】 1. It works by squeezing the *handle* to generate the power. 它靠挤压手柄产生能量来工作。

2. I was impressed by her *handling* of the affair. 我觉得她对此事的处理很了不起。

【同】 grip, hold; address, deal

haphazard [ˈhæpˈhæzəd] *adj*. 偶然的，随便的

【记】 hap(运气) + hazard(一种掷色子的游戏)→靠掷色子决定运气→偶然的，随便的

【例】 The town grew in a *haphazard* way. 这个城镇无计划地随意发展。

【同】 accidental, disorderly

harass [ˈhærəs] *v*. 侵扰，骚扰

【例】 Political dissidents complained of being *harassed* by the police. 持不同政见者申诉他们受到警方的不断骚扰。

【同】 bother, disturb, molest

【派】 harassment *n*. 骚扰，侵袭

harbor [ˈhɑːbə] *n*. 港口，港湾 *v*. 心怀，怀藏

【例】 1. Several boats lay at anchor in the *harbor*. 港湾里停泊着几只船。

2. Many studies have shown that children *harbor* misconceptions about 'pure' curriculum science. 许多研究表明，孩子们对"纯"课程科学怀有一些错误想法。

【同】 port, shelter, wharf; hold

hardware [ˈhɑːdweə] *n*. 1. 五金制品；2. (计算机) 硬件

【记】 hard(硬) + ware(器皿)→硬的器皿→五金制品

【例】 1. There is a *hardware* store at the corner of the street. 街道拐角处有家五金商店。

2. I know nothing about computer *hardware*. 我对计算机硬件一窍不通。

【同】 ironware

hardy [ˈhɑːdɪ] *adj*. 1. 能吃苦耐劳的，强壮的；2. 耐寒的

【例】 1. A few *hardy* people swam in the icy water. 一些强壮的人在冰冷的水中游泳。

2. Strawberry is *hardy* and easy to grow in all soil. 草莓耐寒，各种土壤里都容易生长。

【同】 doughty，stout，robust，tough

【反】 tender

harmony [ˈhɑːmənɪ] *n*. 一致，和谐

【记】 来自拉丁语 harmonia，原义指声音的和谐→和谐，一致

【例】 There was not much *harmony* in international affairs during those years. 那些年国际事态不太协调。

【同】 concordance

【反】 disharmony，dissonance

【派】 harmonious *adj*. 和谐的，融洽的

harness [ˈhɑːnɪs] *n*. (全套)马具；*v*. 1. 套上马具，套车；2. 利用(河流、瀑布等)产生动力

【例】 1. The parachutist was buckled into his *harness*. 跳伞者扣上了背带。

2. The farmer *harnessed* the horse. 农夫给马套上挽具。

3. We can *harness* the power of the wind to make electricity. 我们可以利用风力发电。

【同】 saddlery；rein，control

harsh [hɑːʃ] *adj*. 1. 粗糙的，严酷的，恶劣的；2. 严厉的，残酷的

【例】 1. An important characteristic is their marked seasonality, with *harsh* conditions prevailing for many months each year. 它们的一个重要特征就是显著的季节性，一年好几个月都持续着恶劣的环境。

2. The punishment was too *harsh* for him. 这种惩罚对他来说太严厉了。

【同】 rough，coarse；cruel

【反】 gentle，mild

harvest [ˈhɑːvɪst] *n*./*v*. 收获，成果

【例】 1. We have a plenteous *harvest* this year. 我们今年取得了大丰收。

2. The farmers are out *harvesting* the corn. 农民们在地里收割作物。

【同】 crop，reap，yield

hasten [ˈheɪsn] *v*. 加速，加紧

【记】 haste(匆忙) + (e)n(动词词尾)→使匆忙→加紧

【例】 She *hastened* home after hearing the news. 听到这个消息后，她匆匆忙忙地回家。

【同】 hurry，rush

H

【反】 delay

【派】 (逆构)haste *n*. 匆忙，急忙；草率

hasty *adj*. 急急忙忙的，草率的

hatch [hætʃ] *v*. 孵化

【例】 Hen's eggs take 21 days to *hatch* out. 鸡蛋需要21天才孵化。

【同】 brood，incubate

【派】 hatchery *n*. 孵卵所

hatred [ˈheɪtrɪd] *n*. 憎恶，憎恨

【记】 hat(恨)＋red(＝古英语 reden，状况)→恨的状况→憎恶，憎恨

【例】 He looked at me with *hatred*. 他带有敌意地望着我。

【同】 hate

【反】 love，affection

haughty [ˈhɔːtɪ] *adj*. (指人或态度)高傲自大的

【记】 haught(＝high，高)＋y(形容词词尾)→高傲自大的

【例】 The nobles treated the common people with *haughty* contempt. 贵族对待平民趾高气扬不可一世。

【同】 disdainful，arrogant

【反】 modest

haul [hɔːl] *v*. 用力拖或拉

【例】 They *hauled* the boat up the beach. 他们把船拖上岸。

【同】 drag，draw，pull

【反】 push

【派】 haulage *n*. 拖运

haunting [ˈhɔːntɪŋ] *adj*. 萦绕于心头的，使人不安的

【记】 haunt(鬼魂常出没于)＋ing(把动词变成形容词)→(鬼魂)常出没的→萦绕于心头的

【例】 Separatism and racial conflict has been *haunting* the post- cold war community. 分离主义和种族冲突一直困扰着后冷战时代的国际社会。

【同】 unforgettable，preoccupying

【反】 forgettable

【派】 (逆构)haunt *v*. (鬼魂)常出没于

haven [ˈheɪvn] *n*. 避难所，安全地

【例】 They have made their home a *haven* for the homeless orphans. 他们把自己的家变成了无家可归的孤儿们的避难所。

【同】 refuge，safety，shelter

hazard [ˈhæzəd] *n*. 危险，危害

【记】 来自古法语 hasard 色子→冒险→危险

【例】 In Mexico City，vehicle pollution is a major health *hazard*. 在墨西哥城，车辆造成的污染是最主要的健康危害。

【同】 danger, risk, venture

【派】 hazardous *adj*. 有危险的，有危害的

headline [ˈhedlaɪn] *n*. (书刊、报纸的)头条

【记】 head(头) + line(字行)→头一行字→标题

【例】 A newspaper *headline* caught his attention. 报纸的大标题引起了他的注意。

【同】 heading

headquarters [ˈhedˌkwɔːtəz] *n*. 1. 指挥部；2. (企业、团体、机关等的)总部

【记】 head(头，首脑) + quarters(住处，营房)→首脑住的地方→总部

【例】 1. The town hall was requisitioned as army *headquarters*. 市政厅被征用做了军队的指挥部。

2. The company wants to situate its *headquarters* in the north. 公司想把总部设在北方。

【同】 base

H

heal [hiːl] *v*. 愈合，治愈

【例】 The medicine and rest will soon *heal* your wound. 药物治疗和休息会使你的伤口很快愈合。

【同】 cure, mend

【反】 hurt, injure

【派】 healing *adj*. (可)愈合的，有疗效的

heap [hiːp] *n*. 堆，大量；*v*. 堆积，给予

【例】 1. The books lay in a *heap* on the floor. 书堆放在地板上。

2. He *heaped* the plate with food. 他在盘子里堆满了食物。

【同】 load, pile, stack

heave [hiːv] *v*. (用力)举起，提升

【例】 I *heaved* the heavy box up the steps. 我用力把这个重箱子搬上楼梯。

【同】 lift, raise, elevate

hectic [ˈhektɪk] *adj*. 激动的，兴奋的，紧张的

【记】 hect(= habit, 习惯) + ic(形容词词尾)→习惯的，忙碌的→紧张的

【例】 The journalist lead a *hectic* life. 新闻记者过着紧张兴奋的生活。

【同】 feverish, exciting, frantic

heed [hiːd] *n*. 关心，注意

【例】 A good leader should always pay *heed* to the voice of the masses. 一位好领导应该经常注意倾听群众的呼声。

【同】 attentiveness, attention

【派】 heedless *adj*. 不注意的

hegemony [hiˈgemənɪ] *n*. 霸权，领导权

【记】 hegemon(领导) + y(名词词尾)→领导权→霸权

【例】 China opposes hegemonism, and China will never seek *hegemony*. 中国反对霸权主义，中国永远不称霸。

【同】 dominance
【派】 hegemonism *n*. 霸权主义

heighten ['haɪtn] *v*. 增高，增加，增强
【记】 height(高度) + en(动词词尾)→使变高→增高
【例】 When she heard the news she was *heightening* tension. 当她听到那则消息后，她变得越来越紧张。
【同】 raise，enhance
【反】 lower
【派】 (逆构)height *n*. 高度

heir [ɛə] *n*. 继承人，后嗣
【例】 He is the only legal *heir* of the rich man. 他是这位富翁的唯一法定继承人。
【同】 heritor，inheritor
【派】 heirship *n*. 继承权

H

hemisphere ['hemɪsfɪə] *n*. (地球的)半球，大脑半球
【记】 hemi(半) + sphere(球，球状物)→半球
【例】 In the northern *hemisphere*，spring is in March and April. 在北半球，春季是3月和4月。

hence [hens] *adv*. 因此，由此(其后动词常略去不用)
【例】 It's handmade and *hence* expensive. 这是手工制作的，因此价格昂贵。
【同】 therefore，thus

herb [hɜːb] *n*. 草药
【例】 I had to take the *herb* tea although it's bitter. 虽然汤药很苦，我还是不得不喝了。
【派】 herbal *adj*. 草本植物的，药草的
herbalism *n*. 药草学，草本植物学
herbalist *n*. 草药医生

heredity [hɪ'redɪtɪ] *n*. 遗传
【记】 her(继承) + ed + ity(名词词尾)→继承下来的东西→遗传
【例】 Do *heredity* and environment determine one's character? 遗传与环境可以决定一个人的性格吗?
【同】 inheritance
【派】 hereditary *adj*. 世袭的，遗传的

heresy ['herəsɪ] *n*. 异端，邪说
【记】 heres(= hairesis，选择) + y(名词词尾)→选择(其他的)东西→异教邪说
【例】 He gave a speech on the *heresies* of the early Protestants. 他就早期新教徒的异端邪说作了演讲。
【同】 unorthodoxy
【反】 orthodoxy

heritage ['herɪtɪdʒ] *n*. 继承物，遗留物，传统
【记】 herit(继承) + age(名词词尾)→继承的东西→继承物

【例】 These beautiful old palaces are part of our national *heritage*. 这些美丽的古老宫殿是我们民族遗产的一部分。

【同】 birthright，heredity

【派】 (逆构)heir *n*. 继承人

hermit [ˈhɜːmɪt] *n*. 隐士，隐居者

【记】 h + ermit(生活在沙漠)→生活在沙漠里→与世隔绝→隐士

【例】 A *hermit* used to live in the cave. 一位隐士曾经住在那个山洞里。

【同】 recluse，anchorite

hesitate [ˈhezɪteɪt] *v*. 犹豫，踌躇

【记】 hest(粘着) + ate(动词词尾)→粘着不易分开→犹豫

【例】 She *hesitated* for a moment，and then gave her agreement. 她迟疑了一会儿，随即表示同意。

【派】 hesitation *n*. 犹豫，踌躇

hesitant *adj*. 迟疑的，犹豫不定的

heterogeneous [ˌhetərəʊˈdʒiːnɪəs] *adj*. 异类的，不同的

【记】 hetero(异的，不同的) + gen(种) + ious(形容词词尾)→不同种类的→异类的，不同的

【例】 There is a *heterogeneous* mass of papers in the teacher's office. 老师的办公室里堆满了大批不同的论文。

【同】 assorted，miscellaneous

【反】 homogeneous

heyday [ˈheɪdeɪ] *n*. 全盛期，年富力强时期

【记】 hey(高兴、惊奇的时候发出的声音) + day(日，天)→一个人最兴奋的时候→全盛期

【例】 The 1930s were the *heyday* of the big Hollywood musical. 20世纪30年代是好莱坞歌舞片的全盛时期。

【同】 bloom，peak，prime

hibernate [ˈhaɪbəneɪt] *v*. 冬眠

【记】 hibern(冬季的) + ate(动词)→使处于冬季→冬眠

【例】 Bears wake for spring，summer，and fall，and *hibernate* for the winter. 熊在春天、夏天和秋天保持清醒，在冬季冬眠。

【同】 sleep，slumber

【反】 aestivate(夏眠)

【派】 hibernation *n*. 过冬，冬眠

hierarchy [ˈhaɪərɑːkɪ] *n*. 等级制度，等级森严的组织

【记】 hier(= hiero，神圣的) + arch(为首的) + y(名词词尾)→本意指在神里面负责的祭司长，大主教→有权力的阶级→等级制度

【例】 She's high up in the management *hierarchy*. 她在管理阶层中地位很高。

【派】 hierarchically *adv*. 等级森严地，等级制度地

highlight [ˈhaɪlaɪt] *n*. 最突出的部分；*v*. 使显著，强调

【记】 high(高的)+light(光)→把高处照亮→使显著，使突出

【例】 1. The *highlights* of the match will be shown on TV tonight. 比赛的最精彩场面将在今晚的电视节目中播放。

2. The paper *highlights* the difficulties of the working poor. 报纸突出了劳苦大众的艰难困苦。

【同】 spotlight; emphasize

hike [haɪk] *v*. /*n*. 远足，旅行

【例】 The storm upset their plans for a *hike*. 暴风雨破坏了他们的远足计划。

【同】 excurse, outing, walk

【派】 hiker *n*. 徒步旅行者

hiking *n*. 徒步旅行

hilarious [hɪˈleərɪəs] *adj*. 十分有趣的，欢闹的

【记】 hilar(高兴)+ious(形容词词尾)→高兴的→有趣的，欢闹的

【例】 The party got quite *hilarious* after they brought more wine. 当他们拿来更多葡萄酒后聚会变得十分热闹起来。

【同】 gleeful, joyful

【派】 hilarity *n*. 欢乐，热闹

hinder [ˈhɪndə] *v*. 阻碍，妨碍

【例】 Heavy snow *hindered* the construction work. 大雪妨碍了这项建筑工程的进行。

【同】 block, curb, impede, obstruct

hint [hɪnt] *n*. 暗示，提示，线索

【例】 The calm sea gave no *hint* of the storm that was coming. 平静的海上没有一点迹象显示暴风雨即将来临。

【同】 clue, cue, signal

hoarse [hɔːs] *adj*. 嘶哑的，沙哑的

【例】 We shouted ourselves *hoarse* at the football match. 足球比赛时我们把嗓子都喊哑了。

【同】 gruff, husky

hoe [həʊ] *v*. 用锄耕地，锄

【例】 I would rather *hoe* in the garden than run about on the playground. 我宁愿在花园锄草，也不愿在运动场上跑来跑去。

【同】 till

holistic [həʊˈlɪstɪk] *adj*. 整体的，全面的

【记】 holis(=holo，完全，全部)+tic(形容词词尾)→全面的

【例】 *Holistic* medicine attempts to treat both the mind and the body. 整体医学试图身心并治。

hollow [ˈhɒləʊ] *adj*. 1. 空的；2. 无价值的，虚伪的

【记】 hollo(=hole，洞)+w→像洞的→空的

【例】 1. This tree looks high and strong but actually its trunk is *hollow*. 这棵树看起来又

高又壮，实际上树干是空的。

2. His protests on human rights sound *hollow*. 他就人权问题提出的抗议听来很空洞。

【同】 empty, vacant

【反】 solid

holocaust ['hɒləkɔːst] *n*. 大毁灭，大屠杀，浩劫

【记】 holo(全) + caust(烧)→全烧了→大毁灭，浩劫

【例】 It is unthinkable that we shall allow a nuclear *holocaust* to occur. 我们如果让核武器大屠杀的惨剧发生，那简直是不可想象。

【同】 destruction, devastation, conflagration

homage ['hɒmɪdʒ] *n*. 敬意

【记】 hom(= homo，人) + age(名词词尾)→对人表现的东西→敬意

【例】 We pay *homage* to the genius of Shakespeare. 我们对莎士比亚的天才表示敬仰。

【同】 esteem, honor, respect, reverence

homicide ['hɒmɪsaɪd] *n*. 杀人

【记】 homi(人) + cide(杀)→杀人

【例】 There were two *homicides* in this area last year. 去年这个地区有两起杀人案件。

【同】 murder, slaying

homogeneous [ˌhɒməʊ'dʒiːnjəs] *adj*. 同种类的，同性质的

【记】 homo(相同) + gene(种类，来源) + ous(形容词词尾)→有相同来源的→同种类的

【例】 Japan has a largely *homogeneous* population. 日本的人口主要由同一种族构成。

【同】 uniform

【反】 heterogeneous

【派】 homogeneity *n*. 同种，同质

horizon [hə'raɪzn] *n*. 1. 地平(线)，水平(线)；2. (知识、经验、兴趣等的)范围，眼界

【记】 horiz(限制) + on(名词词尾)→有限的地方→地平线

【例】 1. The sun sank below the *horizon*. 太阳已沉入地平线。

2. Travel broadens one's *horizons*. 旅行可开阔人的眼界。

【同】 skyline; perspective

【派】 horizontal *adj*. 与地平线平行的，水平的

horticulture ['hɔːtɪkʌltʃə] *n*. 园艺，园艺学

【记】 horti(= 拉丁语 hortus，花园) + culture(栽培，培养)→在花园里栽培→园艺学

【例】 This classification is commonly used in forestry and *horticulture*. 这种分类办法在林业和园艺业也是广泛应用的。

【同】 gardening

hospitable ['hɒspɪtəbl] *adj*. 好客的，殷勤的

【记】 hospit(= 拉丁语 hospes，客人) + able(形容词词尾)→招待客人的→好客的

【例】 She is always *hospitable* to visitors from abroad. 她总是殷勤招待外宾。

【同】 cordial, friendly, neighborly

【反】 inhospitable

【派】 hospitality *n*. 好客，盛情

hostile ['hɒstaɪl] *adj*. 敌对的，敌方的

【记】 host(=拉丁语 hostis，敌人) + ile(形容词词尾)→敌对的

【例】 I don't know why she is *hostile* to me. 我不知道她为什么对我抱有敌意。

【同】 unfriendly，aggressive

【反】 amicable，friendly

【派】 hostility *adj*. 敌对，敌方

household ['haushəuld] *adj*. 家庭的，家常的

【记】 house(家) + hold(主持，操持)→操持家的→家庭的

【例】 I disputed with my wife on *household* expenses. 我跟太太争论有关家庭费用的问题。

【同】 family，domestic

hover ['hɒvə] *v*. 翱翔，徘徊

【例】 The hawk is *hovering* overhead. 鹰在头顶上盘旋。

【同】 linger，hang over

hovercraft ['hɒvəkrɑːft] *n*. 气垫飞行器，气垫船

【记】 hover(盘旋，翱翔) + craft(船)→气垫飞行器

【例】 The *hovercraft* is able to skim over the water. 气垫船能掠过水面飞速行驶。

【同】 watercraft

howl [haʊl] *v*. 吠，咆哮

【例】 The wolf was *howling* at the moon. 狼对着月亮嚎叫。

【同】 bark，roar

hub [hʌb] *n*. 中心，核心

【例】 The city was the manufacturing *hub*. 该城市是制造业中心。

【同】 center，core，nucleus

huddle ['hʌdl] *v*. 缩成一团，挤成一团

【例】 The boys *huddled* together in the cave to keep warm. 男孩子们在山洞里挤成一团取暖。

【同】 converge，gather，squeeze

【反】 scatter

humane [hjuː'meɪn] *adj*. 仁慈的，人道的

【记】 是 human 的变体→人道的

【例】 People have found many *humane* methods of killing animals. 人们已经发明了很多宰杀动物的人道方法。

【同】 humanistic

【反】 inhumane

humanity [hjuː'mænɪtɪ] *n*. 人类，人性，人道

【记】 human(人) + ity(名词词尾)→人类

【例】 He treated the prisoners with *humanity*. 他人道地对待俘虏。

【同】 humankind, humanness

【派】 humanist *adj*. 人文主义的

humanistic *adj*. 人文学科的，人文主义(者)的

humble [ˈhʌmbl] *adj*. 低下的，谦逊的；*v*. 降低…的地位，使卑贱

【记】 hum(地面)+ble(形容词词尾)→接近地面的→低下的

【例】 1. Defeat and failure make people *humble*. 挫折与失败使人谦卑。

2. The politician was *humbled* by defeat in the last election. 那位政治家因在上次选举中被击败而有失尊严。

【同】 modest; humiliate, disgrace

【反】 proud, noble; magnify

humid [ˈhjuːmɪd] *adj*. 潮湿的，湿润的

【例】 Foods are easily to be moldy in *humid* days. 潮湿的日子里，食物很容易发霉。

【同】 damp, moist, wet

【反】 dry

【派】 humidify *v*. 使潮湿，使湿润

humiliate [hjuːˈmɪlɪeɪt] *v*. 羞辱，使丢脸

【记】 humili(=humble，低下的)+ate(动词词尾)→使低下→羞辱

【例】 He felt *humiliated* by her scornful remarks. 他听到她那些嘲讽的话而感到屈辱。

【同】 disgrace, dishonor, shame

【反】 honor

【派】 humiliation *n*. 羞辱，耻辱

hurl [hɜːl]] *v*. 用力投掷

【例】 The best way to forget your sadness is to *hurl* yourself into your work. 忘掉悲伤的最好方法是将自己投入到工作中去。

【同】 cast, throw, thrust

hurricane [ˈhʌrɪkən] *n*. 飓风，暴风雨

【记】 hurri(印第安语，=wind，风)+cane(印第安语，=thunder，雷)→ 风雷交加→暴风雨

【例】 The *hurricane* destroyed the whole village. 飓风把整个村子都毁掉了。

【同】 cyclone, storm

husbandry [ˈhʌzbəndrɪ] *n*. 1.农牧业，饲养业；2.管理

【记】 hus(房子)+band(屋主)+ry(名词词尾)→屋主做的事情→农牧业

【例】 1. The animal *husbandry* in this area has developed greatly in recent years. 最近几年这个地区的畜牧业得到了巨大的发展。

2. To let the roof leak would be bad *husbandry*. 屋漏不修，不是个好管家的办法。

【同】 agriculture, farming; management

hustle [ˈhʌsl] *n*./*v*. 拥挤喧嚷，粗野地推

【例】 1. The mother *hustled* the children off to school and started working. 母亲打发孩

子们赶快去上学，然后就开始干起活来。

2. It seems that he enjoys the *hustle* and bustle of life in the big city. 看起来他似乎很喜欢大城市的热闹繁忙的生活。

【同】 bustle, push

hybrid [ˈhaɪbrɪd] *n*. 1.杂种，混血儿；2.混合物

【记】 来自拉丁语 hybrida，杂种

【例】 1. A mule is a *hybrid* of a donkey and a horse. 骡子是公驴和母马交配而生的杂种。

2. The work is a *hybrid* of classical and rock music styles. 此作品是古典音乐和摇滚乐的混合产物。

【同】 crossbreed, mongrel; mixture

H

hydrogen [ˈhaɪdrəudʒən] *n*. 氢

【记】 hydro(水) + gen(产生)→能变成水的→氢

【例】 Water is composed of *hydrogen* and oxygen. 水由氢和氧组成。

hygiene [ˈhaɪdʒiːn] *n*. 卫生

【例】 People should wash regularly to ensure personal *hygiene*. 人们应经常洗澡以保证个人卫生。

【同】 sanitation, cleanliness

hypothesis [haɪˈpɒθɪsɪs] *n*. (复数-ses)假设，假说

【记】 hypo(下面) + thes(放) + (s)is(希腊语中表示状态的名词词尾)→放在下面，还不能作为正式理论→假说

【例】 Science continued to throw up discoveries which further backed up his *hypothesis*. 科学不断地提供新的发现，从而进一步证实了他的假设。

【同】 theory, supposition

【派】 hypothetical *adj*. 假设的，假定的

I

iceberg ['aɪsbəg] *n*. 冰山

【记】 ice(冰)+berg(山丘)→冰山

【例】 Most of the *iceberg* is under the water. 冰山的大部分在水面以下。

ideal [aɪ'dɪəl] *adj*. 理想的，完美的

【例】 He is looking for a wife but he hasn't found his *ideal* mate. 他正在寻找未来的妻子，但还没有找到理想人选。

【同】 model, perfect

【反】 real

【派】 idealism *n*. 理想主义，唯心论

identical [aɪ'dentɪkəl] *adj*. 完全相同的，一模一样的

【记】 ident(相同)+ical(形容词词尾)→相同的→一模一样的

【例】 Even among *identical* twins who have exactly the same genes, one in six pairs will differ in their handedness. 即使是在基因完全一样的一模一样的双胞胎里面，6 对里面就有 1 对在使用左右手的习惯上是不同的。

【同】 alike, duplicate, same

【反】 different

identify [aɪ'dentɪfaɪ] *v*. 确定，识别

【记】 ident(相同)+ify(动词词尾)→使…相同→使…有关系从而识别

【例】 She *identified* that the man was her attacker. 她认出那个男人就是袭击过她的人。

【同】 distinguish, recognize

【派】 identification *n*. 识别，身份证明

identity [aɪ'dentɪtɪ] *n*. 身份，个性

【记】 ident(相同)+ity(名词词尾)→和本人完全相同的事物→(自己的)身份

【例】 The *identity* of the murdered man has not yet been established. 那名被害人的身份尚未确定。

【同】 individuality, personality

ideology [ˌaɪdɪ'ɒlədʒɪ] *n*. 意识形态，思想体系

【记】 ideo(思想，意识)+log(说)+y(名词词尾)→说出自己的思想的→意识形态

【例】 His attitude to ownership is rooted in communist *ideology*. 他的所有制观点源自共产主义思想。

【派】 ideological *adj*. 意识形态的

idiom ['ɪdɪəm] *n*. 习语，惯用语

【记】 idio(个人的，特别的)+(o)m(名词词尾)→某一民族的特别的用法→惯用语

【例】 To my knowledge, there is no such *idiom* in English. 据我所知，英文里并没有这样的成语。

【同】 phrase

【派】 idiomatic *adj*. 惯用的，合乎语言习惯的

idiosyncrasy [ˌɪdɪəˈsɪŋkrəsɪ] *n*. 特质，特性

【记】 idio(个人的)+syn(一起)+cras(混合)+y(名词词尾)→把个人的特质混合在一起→特质

【例】 One of her little *idiosyncrasies* is always washing in cold water. 她有个怪习惯，就是洗什么都爱用冷水。

【同】 individual

【派】 idiosyncratic *adj*. 特有的，独特的

idiot [ˈɪdɪət] *n*. 愚蠢的人，白痴

I

【记】 idio(个人的)+t→(特殊的)个人→白痴

【例】 She always makes a mess of things; she's a prize *idiot*. 她总是把事情弄糟；她是个不折不扣的大白痴。

【同】 fool, moron

【派】 idiotic *adj*. 愚蠢的

idle [ˈaɪdl] *adj*. 闲散的，无工作的；*v*. 虚度，游手好闲

【例】 1. Many people were *idle* during the depression. 在那萧条时期，很多人都无事可做。

2. Don't *idle* away your time. 不要虚度光阴。

【同】 lazy, jobless

【反】 diligent, industrious

【派】 idler *n*. 游手好闲者

idol [ˈaɪdl] *n*. 偶像，崇拜物

【例】 The fans of the actress craned their necks to catch a glimpse of their *idol*. 那位女演员的崇拜者们伸长了脖子想看一看他们崇拜的偶像。

idolize *v*. 把…当偶像崇拜，极度羡慕

ignite [ɪgˈnaɪt] *v*. 使某物燃烧，着火

【记】 ign(火)+ ite(动词词尾)→着火

【例】 The liquid *ignited* when somebody dropped a match in it accidentally. 有人无意中往这种液体里扔了一根火柴，它就燃烧起来了。

【同】 burn, kindle

【反】 extinguish

【派】 ignition *n*. 着火，燃烧

ignoble [ɪgˈnəʊbl] *adj*. 卑鄙的，下流的

【记】 ig(= in 不)+noble(高尚的)→不高尚的→卑鄙的，下流的

【例】 To betray a friend is *ignoble*. 背弃朋友是卑鄙的。

【同】 disgraceful, mean

【反】 noble

ignominious [ɪɡnə'mɪnɪəs] *adj*. 可耻的，不名誉的

【记】 ig(= in 不) + nomin(名字) + ious(形容词词尾)→毁坏名字的→可耻的

【例】 The conspiracy frittered away to an *ignominious* conclusion. 那个阴谋以可耻的失败而告终。

【同】 disgraceful, inglorious, shameful

【反】 graceful, glorious

【派】 ignominy *n*. 耻辱

ignore [ɪɡ'nɔː] *v*. 忽视，不理

【记】 i(= in, 不) + gnore(知道)→不知道→不理睬

【例】 He's his own man, but he doesn't *ignore* other advice. 他虽然自有主张，但并不轻视别人的意见。

【同】 disregard, overlook

【反】 notice

【派】 ignorant *adj*. 无知的，愚昧的

ignorance *n*. 无知，愚昧

illegal [ɪ'liːɡəl] *adj*. 违法的，不合规定的

【记】 il(= in, 不) + leg(法律) + al(形容词词尾)→不合乎法律的→违法的

【例】 He admitted that he was an *illegal* immigrant. 他承认他是非法移民。

【同】 illegitimate, unlawful

【反】 legal

illegible [ɪ'ledʒəbl] *adj*. 难以辨认的，(字迹)模糊的

【记】 il(= in, 不) + leg(读) + ible(形容词词尾)→不可以读的→难以辨认的

【例】 Her signature was an *illegible* scrawl. 她的签字潦草难辨。

【同】 indistinct, unclear, unreadable

【反】 legible

illiterate [ɪ'lɪtərɪt] *adj*. 不识字的，缺乏教育的；*n*. 文盲(指人)

【记】 il(= in, 不) + liter(字母) + ate(形容词词尾)→不认识字母的→不识字的

【例】 1. The boy is an *illiterate* child. 那个孩子不识字。

2. About half the population is still *illiterate*. 大约一半人口仍是文盲。

【同】 ignorant, uncultured, uneducated

【反】 literate

【派】 illiteracy *n*. 文盲(抽象名词)

illuminate [ɪ'ljuːmɪneɪt] *v*. 照亮，照明

【记】 il(= on, …上) + lumin(光) + ate(动词词尾)→光线照在…上→照明

【例】 The streets were *illuminated* for the celebration. 街道灯火通明以示庆祝。

【同】 brighten, light

【派】 illumination *n*. 照亮，照明

illusion [ɪ'luːʒən] *n*. 幻想，错误的观念

【记】 il(= on, …上) + lus(玩) + ion(名词词尾)→在…上面玩耍→幻想

【例】 We're left with few *illusions* about our ally. 我们的处境已不容我们对盟友再存多少幻想了。

I

【同】 fantasy, misconception
【反】 disillusion
【派】 illusive *adj*. 迷惑人的，错觉的

illustrate [ˈɪləstreɪt] *v*. 阐明，举例说明
【记】 il(= on, …上) + lustr(光) + ate(动词词尾)→光线照在…上→阐明
【例】 He pointed at the diagram to *illustrate* his point. 他指着图表来说明他的论点。
【同】 clarify, exemplify
【派】 illustration *n*. 说明，例证，插图
illustrative *adj*. 说明性的，例证性的

illustrious [ɪˈlʌstrɪəs] *adj*. 辉煌的，著名的
【记】 il(= on, …上) + lustr(光) + ious(形容词词尾)→有光亮的→辉煌的，著名的
【例】 His *illustrious* accomplishments made him one of the greatest men in this century. 他的杰出成就使他成为本世纪最伟大的人物之一。
【同】 famous, glorious, great, outstanding

I

image [ˈɪmɪdʒ] *n*. 图像，肖像，形象
【例】 How can we improve our *image*? 我们该怎样来改善自己的形象呢?
【同】 picture, appearance
【派】 imagery *n*. (艺术、文学中)肖像，形象；形象化的比喻

imagine [ɪˈmædʒɪn] *v*. 想象，设想
【记】 imag(e)(图像) + ine(动词词尾)→勾画出图像→想象
【例】 You can *imagine* how surprised I was. 你可以想象我是多么惊讶。
【同】 conceive, envision, fancy
【派】 imaginable *adj*. 可想象的，可能的
imaginary *adj*. 想象中的，虚构的
imaginative *adj*. 想象的，虚构的
imagination *n*. 想象，想象力

imbibe [ɪmˈbaɪb] *v*. 1. 饮；2. 吸入，吸收
【记】 im(= in 进入) + bib(饮) + e→饮，吸入
【例】 1. What are you *imbibing*? 你正在喝什么?
2. I always *imbibe* fresh air in the woods. 我经常在树林里呼吸新鲜空气。
【同】 drink, suck; absorb, assimilate

imbue [ɪmˈbjuː] *v*. (一般用被动态)浸透，使…充满
【记】 来自拉丁语 imbuere，湿润→浸透
【例】 A President should be *imbued* with a sense of responsibility for the nation. 一位总统应该充满对国家的责任感。
【同】 permeate, saturate

imitate [ˈɪmɪteɪt] *v*. 模仿，仿效
【记】 imit(形象，相象) + ate(动词词尾)→做得相像→模仿
【例】 Decide what you want to do; don't just *imitate* others. 想做什么自己决定，不要一味学别人的样。
【同】 mimic, simulate

【派】 imitation *n*. 模仿，效法，仿造物

immediate [ɪˈmiːdjət] *adj*. 直接的，立刻的

【记】 im(不，没) + medi(中间) + ate(形容词词尾)→没有间隔→立刻的

【例】 Her arrest produced an *immediate* reaction from the press. 她被捕的事立刻在新闻界引起反应。

【同】 prompt，direct，quick

【反】 mediate

【派】 immediately *adv*. 立即，马上

immense [ɪˈmens] *adj*. 巨大的，无限的

【记】 im(不，没) + mense(测量)→无法测量的→无限的

【例】 It's almost impossible to find him in the *immense* ocean. 在无边无际的海洋中要找到他几乎是不可能的。

【同】 huge，enormous，vast

【反】 finite，limited

【派】 immensity *n*. 广大，无限，浩瀚

immerse [ɪˈməːs] *v*. 1. 浸，浸没；2. 沉浸于

【记】 im(= in 进入) + merse(沉)→沉进去→浸没

【例】 1. He lay *immersed* in a hot bath. 他躺在浴缸中，把身子浸泡在热水里。
2. He *immersed* himself in work so as to stop thinking about her. 他埋头于工作以不再思念她。

【同】 drown，plunge，sink；engage

【派】 immersion *n*. 沉浸

immigrate [ˈɪmɪgreɪt] *v*. (从外国)移入，移居入境

【记】 im(= in，进入) + migr(移动) + ate(动词词尾)→移动进来→移居入境

【例】 People from many countries *immigrated* to the United States and Canada. 许多国家的人移居到美国和加拿大。

【同】 migrate，enter

【反】 emigrate

【派】 immigration *n*. 移民
immigrant *n*. (外来)移民，侨民

imminent [ˈɪmɪnənt] *adj*. 即将来临的，逼近的

【记】 im(= on，…上) + min(突出) + ent(形容词词尾)→突出于…上面→逼近的

【例】 An announcement of further cuts in government expenditure is *imminent*. 最近将发布进一步削减政府开支的公告。

【同】 forthcoming，impending

【派】 imminence *n*. 迫切，迫近的危险(或祸患)

immortal [ɪˈmɔːtl] *adj*. 不朽的，流芳百世的

【记】 im(不) + mort(死) + al(形容词词尾)→不死的→不朽的

【例】 He left behind an *immortal* example to all posterity. 他给后世留下了不朽的典范。

【同】 deathless，eternal，everlasting

【反】 mortal

【派】 mortality *n*. 致命性；死亡率

immune [ɪ'mjuːn] *adj*. 有免疫力的，豁免的

【记】 im(不，没) + mune(服务)→不必服务→免除的

【例】 I'm *immune* to smallpox as a result of vaccination. 我种过牛痘了，所以对天花有免疫力。

【同】 exempt，free

【派】 immunity *n*. 免疫性

impact ['ɪmpækt] *n*. 影响，作用

【记】 im(= in，进入) + pact(紧的)→压进去的力量→影响

【例】 All these activities may have damaging environmental *impacts*. 所有这些活动都可能会产生破坏环境的影响。

【同】 affect，shock，influence

impair [ɪm'peə] *v*. 削弱，损害

【记】 im(= in，使处于…状态) + pair(更糟)→使处于更糟的状态→损害

【例】 Today's attack has seriously *impaired* attempts to achieve peace in the area. 今日发动的攻击严重损害了在该地区谋求和平的努力。

【同】 damage，harm，weaken

【派】 impairment *n*. 损害，损伤

impale [ɪm'peɪl] *v*. 刺穿，钉住

【记】 im(= in，进入) + pale(= pole，竹竿)→用竹竿穿过→刺穿

【例】 In former times, prisoners' heads were *impaled* on pointed stakes. 从前的人把犯人的头钉在尖桩上。

【同】 transfix，pierce

impart [ɪm'pɑːt] *v*. 传授，传达

【记】 im(= in，进入) + part(部分)→把自己的一部分给→传授

【例】 A good teacher *imparts* wisdom to his pupils. 一个好的教师把智慧赋予学生。

【同】 convey，give，pass on

impartial [ɪm'pɑːʃəl] *adj*. 公平的，公正的

【记】 im(不) + part(部分) + ial(形容词词尾)→不偏向某一部分的→公平的

【例】 People in the city held the *impartial* judge in high regard. 这个城市的人们都很尊敬这位公正的法官。

【同】 fair，unbiased

【反】 partial

【派】 impartiality *n*. 不偏不倚，公正，公平

impatient [ɪm'peɪʃənt] *adj*. 不耐烦的，不耐心的

【记】 im(= in，不) + patient(忍耐的)→不能忍耐的→不耐烦的

【例】 They say he's very good with elderly people, but he does tend to get a bit *impatient* with children. 他们说他对老人特别好，但是对孩子有点不够耐心。

【同】 eager，intolerant

【反】 patient

【派】 impatience *n*. 不耐烦，急躁

impeach [ɪm'piːtʃ] *v*. 指责，控告，弹劾

【记】 im(= in，进入) + peach(脚镣)→使…戴上脚镣→控告

【例】 The Parliament decided to *impeach* the President. 国会决定弹劾总统。

【同】 accuse，arraign，charge

impeccable [ɪm'pekəbl] *adj*. 无瑕疵的

【记】 im(= in，不) + pecc(犯罪) + able(形容词词尾)→不犯罪的→无瑕疵的

【例】 As your company's representative，your phone manners should be *impeccable*. 作为公司的代表，你打电话的举止应该是无可挑剔的。

【同】 faultless，perfect

impede [ɪm'piːd] *v*. 阻碍，妨碍

【记】 im(= in，进入) + pede(脚)→把脚放进去→妨碍

【例】 What *impedes* you to make progress? 什么事妨碍你取得进步?

【同】 block，inhibit，obstruct

【派】 impediment *n*. 妨碍，阻碍

impel [ɪm'pel] *v*. (-lled；-lling)推进，驱使

【记】 im(= in) + pel(推，驱使)→在里面推→驱使

【例】 I felt *impelled* to investigate the matter further. 我觉得自己有责任对事情作进一步调查。

【同】 compel，drive，force，propel

impending [ɪm'pendɪŋ] *v*. 行将发生的，逼近的

【记】 im(= on，在…上) + pend(悬挂) + ing(形容词词尾)→悬在上面的→行将发生的

【例】 The news of the *impending* storm sobered them down. 关于暴风雨即将来临的消息使他们冷静下来。

【同】 imminent，forthcoming

【派】 (逆构)impend *v*. 悬挂，逼近

imperative [ɪm'perətɪv] *adj*. 必要的，强制的；*n*. 需要，必要的事

【记】 imper(指挥，命令) + ative(形容词词尾)→命令的→强制的

【例】 1. It's *imperative* that you apologize to him immediately. 你必须立即向他道歉。
2. Job creation has become an *imperative* for the government. 创造就业机会是政府必须做的事。

【同】 compelling，compulsory，mandatory，necessary

impersonate [ɪm'pɜːsəneɪt] *v*. 模仿，扮演

【记】 im(= in，以) + person(人) + ate(动词词尾)→以…什么人的方式→模仿

【例】 He can *impersonate* many well-known politicians. 他能饰演许多著名政治家的角色。

【同】 imitate，personate

【派】 impersonation *n*. 扮演，模仿

impertinent [ɪm'pɜːtɪnənt] *adj*. 不礼貌的，莽撞的

【记】 im(= in，不) + per(完全彻底的) + tin(保持) + ent(形容词词尾)→不完全保持(良好)行为的→不礼貌的

【例】 I've had enough of your *impertinent* words. 你说话太不礼貌了，我已受够了。

【同】 impolite, rude

【反】 pertinent, polite

【派】 impertinence *n*. 不适宜，鲁莽，无礼

impetus ['ɪmpɪtəs] *n*. 刺激，促进，推动力

【记】 im(= in, 内) + pet(追求) + us(名词词尾)→内在的追求→推动力

【例】 The *impetus* behind the development of these early plastics was generated by a number of factors. 发展这些早期塑料的推动力来自几个因素。

【同】 momentum, impulsion

implement ['ɪmplɪmənt] *n*. 工具，器具；*v*. (使)生效，实施，执行

【记】 im(= in, 内) + ple(充满) + ment(名词词尾)→用来把里面充满的东西→工具

【例】 1. Man's earlist *implements* were carved from stone and bone. 人类最早的工具是用石头和骨头制成的。

2. The government is *implementing* a new policy to help the unemployed. 政府正在实施一项新的帮助失业者的政策。

I

【同】 tool, utensil; execute, enforce

【派】 implementation *n*. 执行

implicate ['ɪmplɪkeɪt] *v*. 使牵连其中，涉及

【记】 im(= in, 内) + plic(折叠) + ate(动词词尾)→把…折叠在里面→使牵连其中

【例】 The police found a letter which *implicated* him in the robbery. 警察发现了一封信，这封信把他牵连到抢劫案中。

【同】 entail, imply

【派】 implication *n*. 牵连，含意，暗示

implicit [ɪm'plɪsɪt] *adj*. 不明确的，含蓄的

【记】 im(= in, 内) + plic(折叠) + it(名词词尾)→折叠在里面的→ →不明确的

【例】 Her attitude was *implicit* in the answer she gave us. 她在给我们的答复中的态度是含蓄的。

【同】 implied, tacit, unexpressed

【反】 explicit

imply [ɪm'plaɪ] *v*. 暗示，意味

【记】 im(= in, 内) + ply(折叠)→折叠在里面→暗示

【例】 I don't wish to *imply* that you are wrong. 我无意暗示你错了。

【同】 hint, mean, suggest

import [ɪm'pɔːt] *n*. / *v*. 进口，输入

【记】 im(= in, 进入) + port(搬，运)→运进来→进口

【例】 The government has an interest in *importing* scientific equipment. 政府对引进科学设备非常感兴趣。

【反】 export

impose [ɪm'pəuz] *v*. 把…强加于，强迫

【记】 im(= on, …上) + pose(放置)→放置在…上面→把…强加于

【例】 Don't try to *impose* your wishes on us. 不要试图把你的愿望强加给我们。

【同】 force, place, put

【反】 liberate

【派】 imposing *adj*. 使人难忘的，壮丽的

impotent [ˈɪmpətənt] *adj*. 无力的，无能的

【记】 im(= in，不) + potent(强有力的)→ 没有力量的→无力的

【例】 Without the chairman's support, the committee is *impotent*. 没有主席的支持，委员会是无能为力的。

【同】 powerless

【反】 potent

【派】 impotence *n*. 无力，虚弱；[医]阳萎

impoverished [ɪmpɒvərɪʃt] *adj*. 贫困的，赤贫的

【记】 im(= in，使处于…状态) + pover(贫穷) + ish(动词词尾) + ed→被处于贫穷的状态的→贫困的

【例】 We lived in an *impoverished* African country. 我们生活在一个贫穷的非洲国家。

【同】 needy，poor，poverty-stricken

【反】 enriched

【派】 (逆构)impoverish *v*. 使贫穷，使枯竭

impress [ɪmˈpres] *v*. 给…深刻的印象

【记】 im(= in，进入) + press(压)→把…压入心里→给…深刻的印象

【例】 His words are strongly *impressed* on my memory. 他的话使我深深铭记心头。

【同】 affect，imprint，engrave

【派】 impression *n*. 印象，影响

impressive *adj*. 给人深刻印象的

impressionism *n*. 印象派，印象主义

imprison [ɪmˈprɪzn] *n*. 监禁，坐牢

【记】 im(= in，进入) + prison(监狱)→投入监狱→监禁

【例】 He was *imprisoned* for two years. 他被关押了两年。

【同】 confine，jail，lock up

【反】 free，liberate

【派】 imprisonment *n*. 监禁

impromptu [ɪmˈprɒmptjuː] *adj*./*adv*. 即席的(地)，临时的(地)

【记】 im(= in，不) + promptu(被准备好的)→没有准备的→即席的

【例】 It usually take me more than three weeks to prepare a good *impromptu* speech. 为了准备一则即席的好演讲，我通常需要三个星期以上的时间。

【同】 unprepared

improvident [ɪmˈprɒvɪdənt] *adj*. 无远见的，浪费的

【记】 im(= in，不) + pro(提前) + vid(看) + ent(形容词词尾)→提前没有看到的→无远见的

【例】 Her *improvident* speech at the meeting has set a stone rolling. 她在会上的发言缺乏远见，已产生严重后果。

【同】 shortsighted

【反】 provident

I

【派】 improvidence *n*. 目光短浅

improvise [ˈɪmprəvaɪz] *v*. 即席创作，即兴表演

【记】 im(= in，不) + pro(提前) + vis(看) + e→提前没有看到的→即席创作

【例】 I forgot to bring the words of my speech，so I had to *improvise*. 我忘了带发言稿，所以只得即兴发挥。

【同】 extemporize，ad-lib

impulse [ˈɪmpʌls] *n*. 推动，冲动

【记】 im(= in，内) + pulse(驾驶，驱使)→内心的驱动→冲动

【例】 He bought the house on an *impulse*. 他凭一时冲动买下了这所房子。

【同】 impetus，momentum，push

【派】 impulsive *adj*. 冲动的

impulsion *n*. 冲动

impunity [ɪmˈpjuːnɪtɪ] *n*. 免受处罚

【记】 im(= in，不) + pun(= pen 惩罚) + ity(名词词尾)→不受惩罚→免受处罚

【例】 Wit sometimes enables us to act rudely with *impunity*. 机智有时可以使我们做出失礼的行为而不受惩罚。

【同】 exemption

impute [ɪmˈpjuːt] *v*. 归于，(尤指不公正地)归咎于

【记】 im(= in = to) + put(认为) + e→认为是→归咎于

【例】 They *imputed* the accident to the driver's carelessness. 他们把事故归咎于驾驶员的疏忽。

【同】 ascribe，attribute

inanimate [ɪnˈænɪmɪt] *adj*. 无生命的

【记】 in(不) + anim(呼吸) + ate(形容词词尾)→不呼吸的→无生命的

【例】 Rocks and stones are *inanimate*. 岩石是无生命的。

【同】 nonliving

【反】 animate

【派】 inanimation *n*. 没有生命，不活动

inaugurate [ɪˈnɔːɡjʊreɪt] *v*. 创立，举行就职典礼

【记】 in(以，用) + augur(占卜) + ate(动词词尾)→用卜卦算出吉辰→举行就职典礼

【例】 He was *inaugurated* as the President of the USA. 他就任美国总统。

【同】 initiate，introduce，launch

【派】 inauguration *n*. 就职典礼，开幕式

incentive [ɪnˈsentɪv] *n*. 刺激，鼓励，动机

【记】 in(进入) + cent(唱) + ive(形容词兼名词词尾)→把(力量)唱进去→激励

【例】 They don't try very hard if there is no *incentive*. 没有奖励，他们工作就不太努力。

【同】 encouragement，motive，stimulus

【反】 disincentive

incessant [ɪnˈsesnt] *adj*. 不停的，连续的

【记】 in(不) + cess(屈服，放弃) + ant(形容词词尾)→不放弃的→不停的

【例】 We are tired of his *incessant* complaining. 我们对他没完没了的埋怨感到厌烦。

【同】 ceaseless, constant, endless, never-ending

【派】 incessancy *n*. 持续不断，连续性

incident ['ɪnsɪdənt] *n*. 事情，事件

【记】 in(= on，…上) + cid(降落) + ent(名词词尾)→降临在…上的事物→事件

【例】 The police are connecting this *incident* with last week's terrorist bombing. 警方认为这次事件和上周的恐怖分子爆炸事件有关。

【同】 event, occurrence

【派】 incidental *adj*. 附带的，偶然的

incidentally *adv*. 偶然地，顺便提一句

incipient [ɪn'sɪpɪənt] *adj*. 初始的，初期的

【记】 in(进入) + cip(拿) + ient(形容词词尾)→刚拿进来的→初期的

【例】 Ache is a sign of *incipient* tooth decay. 牙疼是初期蛀牙的一个标志。

【同】 beginning, initial

【派】 incipience *n*. 起初，发端

incline [ɪn'klaɪn] *v*. 倾斜，倾向

【记】 in(向，朝) + cline(斜，靠)→向…倾斜→倾斜，倾向

【例】 She *inclines* towards depression. 她动不动就情绪低落。

【同】 bend, tend

【派】 inclination *n*. 倾斜，倾向

include [ɪn'kluːd] *v*. 包括，包含

【记】 in(内) + clude(关闭)→关在里面 →包括，包含

【例】 Is service *included* in the bill? 账单中包含服务费吗？

【同】 comprise, involve

【反】 exclude

【派】 inclusion *n*. 包含，内含物

inclusive *adj*. 包括的，包含的

incoherent [ˌɪnkəʊ'hɪərənt] *adj*. 不连贯的，不清楚的

【记】 in(不) + coherent(连贯的)→不连贯的

【例】 He was so drunk that he was quite *incoherent*. 他喝得这样醉，说起话来语无伦次。

【同】 disconnected, disjointed, illogical

【反】 coherent

incorporate [ɪn'kɔːpəreɪt] *v*. 包含，使并入

【记】 in(进入) + corpor(身体，团体) + ate(动词词尾)→使成为一个团体→使并入

【例】 Many of your suggestions have been *incorporated* in the new plan. 你的很多建议已经被纳入新计划中。

【同】 combine, join, integrate

【派】 incorporation *n*. 合并，公司

incredible [ɪn'kredəbl] *adj*. 难以置信的，不可思议的

【记】 in(表否定，不) + cred(信用，信任) + ible(形容词词尾)→不能相信的→难以置信的

【例】 That's the most *incredible* coincidence I've ever heard of! 那是我听说过的最难以

I

置信的巧合!

【同】 unbelievable

【反】 credible

【派】 incredulity *n*. 怀疑，不相信

increment [ˈɪnkrɪmənt] *n*. 增加，增量

【记】 in(内)+cre(生长)+ment(名词词尾)→里面在生长→增加

【例】 Your salary will be £12,000 a year, with annual *increments* of £500. 你的年薪为12000英镑，每年增加500英镑。

【同】 growth, increase

【反】 decrement

incriminate [ɪnˈkrɪmɪˌneɪt] *v*. 控告，连累

【记】 in(在…里)+crimin(=crim 罪)+ate(动词词尾)→使有罪→控告

【例】 He *incriminated* the thief to the judge. 他向法官控告了那个偷窃的人。

【同】 accuse, inculpate, charge

【派】 incrimination *n*. 连累，控告

I

incubator [ˈɪnkjʊbeɪtə] *n*. 恒温箱，孵化器

【记】 in(内)+cub(躺)+at(e)(动词词尾)+or(名词词尾)→躺在里面的东西→孵化器

【例】 The farmer needs special equipment such as *incubators* for the eggs. 农民需要特殊的设备，比如说用来孵蛋的孵化器。

【同】 brooder

【派】 (逆构)incubate *v*. 孵卵

incubation *n*. 孵化，培育

incur [ɪnˈkɜː] *v*. (-rred; -rring)招致，引起

【记】 in(进入)+cur(跑，流)→跑进来→招致

【例】 The company *incurred* heavy losses in its first year. 这家公司第一年经营就蒙受惨重损失。

【同】 catch, contract

indefinite [ɪnˈdefɪnɪt] *adj*. 模糊的，不明确的

【记】 in(无)+de(向下)+fin(结束，界限)+ite(名词词尾)→没有一定的界限的→不确定的

【例】 He has rather *indefinite* views on the question. 他对该问题的看法很不明确。

【同】 indistinct, obscure, unclear, vague

【反】 definite

indemnify [ɪnˈdemnɪfaɪ] *v*. 赔偿，补偿

【记】 in(不)+demn(=harm 损害)+i+fy(动词词尾)→使没有损害→补偿

【例】 I will *indemnify* you for any expenses you may incur on my behalf. 我会偿付你为了我而负担的任何花费。

【同】 compensate

【派】 indemnity *n*. 赔偿

indent [ɪnˈdent] *v*. 1. 切割成锯齿状；2. 缩进

【记】 in(进入)+dent(牙齿)→用牙齿咬进去→切割成锯齿状，缩进

【例】 1. There are long *indented* coastlines in the South Sea. 在南海有犬牙交错的海岸线。

2. Please *indent* the first line of each paragraph. 请于每段第一行缩格书写。

【同】 cut, dent

【派】 indenture *n*. 契约，合同

index [ˈɪndeks] *n*. (复数-dexes或-dices)索引，指数

【记】 in(向，朝)+dex(=dic，宣称)→向…宣称→通知，指示→索引

【例】 1. The *index* is arranged in alphabetical order. 这索引是按字母顺序排列的。

2. Do you know the price *index* in the city? 你知道这个城市的物价指数吗？

【同】 indicator, exponent

indicate [ˈɪndɪkeɪt] *v*. 1. 指示，指出；2. 表明，显示

【记】 in(向，朝)+dic(宣称)=ate(动词词尾)→向…宣称→表明

【例】 1. A signpost *indicated* the right road for us to follow. 一个路标给我们指出应走的路。

2. The committee *indicated* that it might take action. 委员会表示可能采取行动。

【同】 demonstrate, show, suggest

【派】 indication *n*. 暗示，象征

indicator *n*. 标志物

indicative *adj*. 指示的，预示的

indict [ɪnˈdaɪt] *v*. 起诉

【记】 in(=against，反对)+dict(说)→说话反对…→起诉

【例】 He was *indicted* on three counts of murder. 他被控三项谋杀罪。

【同】 accuse, charge

【派】 indictment *n*. 控告

indifferent [ɪnˈdɪfərənt] *adj*. 不感兴趣的，冷淡的

【记】 in(表否定，不)+ different(不同)→没有不同的→平常的→冷漠的

【例】 How can you be *indifferent* to the sufferings of starving people? 你怎能对饥疾苦无动于衷呢？

【同】 detached, apathetic

【反】 concerned, interested

【派】 indifference *n*. 不关心，冷漠

indigenous [ɪnˈdɪdʒɪnəs] *adj*. 本地的，土生土长的

【记】 indi(内部)+gen(出生)+ous(形容词词尾)→内部出生的→土生土长的

【例】 Indians were the *indigenous* inhabitants of America. 印第安人是美洲的土著居民。

【同】 native, original

【反】 exotic

【派】 (逆构)indigen(e) *n*. 土生的动植物，土著

indignant [ɪnˈdɪgnənt] *adj*. 愤怒的，愤慨的

【记】 in(表否定，不)+dign(值得)+ant(形容词词尾)→对没有价值的东西生气→愤怒的

【例】 She was most *indignant* with me when I suggested she might try a little harder. 我

建议她不妨再努力一些，她竟大为恼火。

【同】 angry，irate

【派】 indignation *n*. 愤怒，愤慨

indignity [ɪn'dɪgnɪtɪ] *n*. 侮辱，侮辱性的做法

【记】 in(表否定，不)+dign(值得)+ity(名词词尾)→不承认价值→侮辱

【例】 They inflicted all kinds of *indignities* on their captives. 他们对俘虏百般侮辱。

【同】 affront，insult

indispensable [ˌɪndɪs'pensəbl] *adj*. 必不可少的，必需的

【记】 in(表否定，不)+dispensable(可有可无的)→必不可少的

【例】 Air is *indispensable* to life. 空气是生命所必需的东西。

【同】 essential，necessary

【反】 dispensable

individual [ˌɪndɪ'vɪdjʊəl] *n*. 个人，个体；*adj*. 个人的，个体的

【记】 in(不)+divid(分割)+ual(形容词词尾)→不能再分的→一个整体→个体

【例】 1. The welfare of the *individual* is bound up with the welfare of the community. 个人的福利与社会的福利有着密切的关系。

2. These styles can be adapted to suit *individual* tastes. 这些式样均可改动以适应个人不同的爱好。

【同】 human，person；private，single

【反】 entire，common，whole

【派】 individually *adv*. 各自地，分别地

individualism *n*. 个人主义

indolent ['ɪndələnt] *adj*. 懒惰的

【记】 in(不)+dol(感到疼痛)+ent(形容词词尾)→不感到疼痛的→反应慢的→懒惰的

【例】 I don't want to make friends with *indolent* persons. 我不喜欢和懒惰的人交朋友。

【同】 lazy，slothful

【反】 industrious，diligent

【派】 indolence *n*. 懒惰，好逸恶劳

indomitable [ɪn'dɒmɪtəbl] *adj*. 不屈不挠的

【记】 in(不)+domit(驯服的)+able(形容词词尾)→不能驯服的→不屈不挠的

【例】 my greatest reason for confidence is the *indomitable* spirit of the people of Hong Kong themselves. 我感到信心十足，主要是因为香港人那种不屈不挠的精神。

【同】 unconquerable

induce [ɪn'djuːs] *v*. 劝诱，促使

【记】 in(进入)+duce(领导，引导)→引导进入→劝诱

【例】 What *induced* you to do such a foolish thing? 是什么引诱你做这样的傻事？

【同】 persuade，prompt，stimulate

【派】 inductive *adj*. 诱导的，归纳的

inducement *n*. 诱导，诱因，刺激物

indulge [ɪn'dʌldʒ] *v*. 沉溺，放纵

【记】 in(向，朝)+dulge(友好，顺从)→对…很顺从→放纵

I

【例】 He no longer *indulged* himself in smoking. 他不再过度吸烟了。

【同】 wallow, spoil

【派】 indulgence *n*. 放任

indulgent *adj*. 放纵的，溺爱的

industrialize [ɪn'dʌstrɪəlaɪz] *n*. 使工业化，使产业化

【记】 industrial(工业的) + ize(动词词尾，使…化)→使工业化

【例】 In many other *industrialized* countries, orthodox and alternative medicine have worked "hand in glove" for years. 在许多其他工业化国家，传统医学和另类医学已经"亲密地"工作了好多年。

【派】 industrialisation *n*. 工业化

industrialized *adj*. (实现了)工业化的

industrious [ɪn'dʌstrɪəs] *adj*. 勤勉的，努力的

【记】 indu(= in，进入) + str(站) + ious(形容词词尾)→使劲站进去→努力的

【例】 The Chinese are *industrious* people. 中国人民是勤劳的人民。

【同】 diligent, hardworking, untiring, tireless

【反】 idle, indolent, lazy

ineligible [ɪn'elɪdʒəbl] *adj*. 无资格的，不合适的

【记】 in(不) + e(= ex，出去) + lig(选) + ible(形容词词尾)→不能被选出的→无资格的

【例】 He was *ineligible* to vote, because he didn't belong to the club. 他无资格投票，因为他不是那个俱乐部的成员。

【同】 unqualified, unentitled, unsuitable

【反】 eligible

inert [ɪ'nɜːt] *adj*. 惰性的，不活泼的

【记】 in(无) + ert(= art，技巧)→没有技巧的→笨拙的→懒惰的

【例】 There is an *inert* management team in our company. 我们公司的管理阶层死气沉沉。

【同】 inactive, lifeless, slow, stagnant

【反】 active

【派】 inertia *n*. 惰性

inevitable [ɪn'evɪtəbl] *adj*. 不可避免的，必然的

【记】 in(不) + evitable(可避免的)→不可避免的

【例】 An argument was *inevitable* because they disliked each other so much. 争论是不可避免的，因为他们彼此非常厌恶。

【同】 certain, doomed, sure

【反】 evitable

infallible [ɪn'fæləbl] *adj*. 没有错误的，确实可靠的

【记】 in(不) + fallible(可能犯错的)→不可能犯错的→可靠的

【例】 His judgment in this matter was by no means *infallible*. 在这件事上他的判断决不是无可指摘的。

reliable, sure, unerring

infant ['ɪnfənt] *n*. 婴儿

【记】 in(不)+fant(说)→不会说话的人→婴儿
【例】 She gazed at the newborn *infant* and smiled. 她望着这个初生的婴儿笑了。
【同】 baby
【派】 infancy *n*. 婴儿期，幼年时代

infection [ɪnˈfekʃən] *n*. 传染，感染
【记】 in(内)+fect(做)+ion(名词词尾)→在内部做，常指病菌侵入体内→传染
【例】 People catch all kinds of *infections* in the winter. 冬天人们易患多种传染病。
【同】 contagion, transmission
【派】 (逆构)infect *v*. 传染，感染
infectious *adj*. 传染性的，易传染的

infer [ɪnˈfɜː] *v*. (-rred; -rring)(根据已知事实等)推断，得出结论
【记】 in(进入)+fer(运，带)→带进(意义)→推断
【例】 It is possible to *infer* two completely opposite conclusions from this set of facts. 从这些事实中可能推断出两种截然相反的结论。
【同】 deduce, conclude, indicate
【派】 inferential *adj*. 推论性的

inferior [ɪnˈfɪərɪə] *adj*. 低的，差的，次要的
【记】 infer(下面)+ior(拉丁语中用来表示比较级的词尾)→处于比较靠下面的→低的
【例】 These people occupy an *inferior* position in local society. 这些人在当地社会居于下等地位。
【同】 lower, secondary, subordinate
【反】 superior
【派】 inferiority *n*. 自卑，次等

inflation [ɪnˈfleɪʃən] *n*. 通货膨胀，(物价)暴涨
【记】 in(进入)+flat(吹)+ion(名词词尾)→吹入空气，使膨胀→通货膨胀
【例】 There appears to be a growing discontent about *inflation*. 对通货膨胀似乎有一种日渐增长的不满情绪。
【反】 deflation
【派】 (逆构)inflate *v*. 充气，膨胀
inflatable *adj*. 可充气的，膨胀的

inflict [ɪnˈflɪkt] *v*. 强加给，使遭受(痛苦、损伤等)
【记】 in(=on 在…上)+flict(敲打)→打在…上→强加于
【例】 Don't *inflict* your belief on me. 不要把你的想法强加于我。
【同】 impose, bring about
【派】 infliction *n*. 施加，使负担

influence [ˈɪnfluəns] *n*./*v*. 影响，对…起作用
【记】 in(进入)+flu(流)+ence(名词词尾)→流入其中→影响
【例】 1. He is a man of some *influence* in the government circles. 他是个在政府内有一定势力的人。
2. Don't let me *influence* your decision. 不要让我影响你的决定。
【同】 affect, impact

【派】 influential *adj*. 有影响力的，有势力的

influenza [ˈɪnflʊˈenzə] *n*.（略作 flu）流行性感冒

【记】 in(进入) + flu(流) + za(名词词尾)→病毒流入→生病

【例】 She was taken down with *influenza*. 她患了流行性感冒。

inform [ɪnˈfɔːm] *v*. 通知，告知

【记】 in(在…内) + form(形状)→在心里塑成形状→提前成形的→通知

【例】 I wasn't *informed* of the decision until too late. 等到我得知这项决定时，已经太迟了。

【同】 notify，report，tell

【派】 information *n*. 通知，信息，消息

informative *adj*. 提供大量资料或信息的，增进知识的

informed *adj*. 见多识广的

informal [ɪnˈfɔːməl] *adj*. 非正式的，随便的

【记】 in(表否定，不) + formal(正式的)→非正式的

【例】 We have made preliminary, *informal* approaches to the committee. 我们已同委员会进行了初步的、非正式的接触。

【同】 casual，colloquial，free-and-easy

【反】 formal

【派】 informality *n*. 非正式

infringe [ɪnˈfrɪndʒ] *v*. 破坏，侵犯，违反

【记】 in(进入) + fringe(打破)→打破进入→破坏

【例】 The publisher *infringed* his copyright. 出版社侵犯了他的版权。

【同】 break，violate

【派】 infringement *n*. 违反，侵害

infuse [ɪnˈfjuːz] *v*. 注入，灌输

【记】 in(进入) + fuse(流)→流入→注入

【例】 The news *infused* the workers with new life. 那条消息使工人获得了新的活力。

【同】 impregnate，instill

【派】 infusion *n*. 注入

ingenious [ɪnˈdʒiːnjəs] *adj*. 有发明天才的，有独创性的

【记】 in(加强语气) + gen(出生) + ious(形容词词尾)→天生有才的→有独创性的

【例】 This book shows that he is an *ingenious* author. 这本书表明他是一个有创造力的作家。

【同】 clever，creative，imaginative，inventive

【派】 ingenuity *n*. 机灵，灵巧

ingredient [ɪnˈgriːdɪənt] *n*.（混合物的）组成部分，成分

【记】 in(进入) + gredi(行走) + ent(名词词尾)→进入的东西→组成部分

【例】 There is a list of *ingredients* on the side of the packet. 包装袋的边上印有所含配料表。

【同】 component，constituent，part

inhabit [ɪnˈhæbɪt] *v*. 居住于，栖息于

【记】 in(内) + habit(居住)→居住在里面→居住于

【例】 Only a few people *inhabited* the island. 只有少数人在这个岛上居住。

【同】 dwell, live, reside

【派】 inhabitant *n*. 居民，栖息的动物

inhale [ɪnˈheɪl] *v*. 吸入，吸气

【记】 in(进入) + hal(呼吸)→吸入

【例】 Do you *inhale* when you smoke? 你抽烟时是否把烟吸入肺里？

【同】 breathe in

【反】 exhale

【派】 inhalation *n*. 吸入，吸入物

inherent [ɪnˈhɪərənt] *adj*. 固有的，与生俱来的

【记】 in(内) + her(e)(粘着) + ent(形容词词尾)→粘着在体内的→与生俱来的

【例】 Weight is an *inherent* property of matter. 重量是物质固有的特性。

【同】 instinctive, internal, natural

【反】 acquired

【派】 inherence *n*. 内在，固有，天赋

inherit [ɪnˈherɪt] *v*. 继承，遗传而得

【记】 in(内) + herit(后嗣，继承人)→在继承人之间进行的→继承

【例】 Research has shown that there is a genetic or *inherited* element to handedness. 研究表明，人们使用左手还是右手的习惯，有一个原因是基因或者遗传的因素引起的。

【同】 receive

【派】 inheritance *n*. 遗传，遗产
inheritor *n*. 继承人，后继者
inheritrix *n*. 女继承人

inhibit [ɪnˈhɪbɪt] *v*. 抑制，阻止

【记】 in(里面) + hold(抓住，控制)→从里面控制→抑制

【例】 The mild weather has *inhabited* the sales of winter clothing. 暖和的天气妨碍了冬季服装的销路。

【同】 curb, restrain

【派】 inhibited *adj*. 拘谨的，内向的
inhibition *n*. 禁止，阻止

initial [ɪˈnɪʃəl] *adj*. 最初的，开始的；*n*. 词首大写字母

【记】 in(进入) + it(走) + ial(形容词词尾)→走进的地方→开始的

【例】 1. After she'd overcome her *initial* shyness, she became very friendly. 她克服了开始时的羞涩之后，就变得非常友善。
2. Please write down your *initials* on each page of the paper. 请在每页考卷上写下名字的首字母。

【同】 beginning, primary

【派】 initially *adv*. 最初，首先

initiate [ɪˈnɪʃieɪt] *v*. 开始，发起

【记】 in(进入) + it(走) + ate(动词词尾)→走进→开始

【例】 The book was written to *initiate* outsiders into the mysteries of the trade. 写这本书的目的是为了让外行初步了解这一行业的奥秘。

【同】 begin, launch, originate

【派】 initiative *n*. 为解决困难而采取的行动，倡议

initiation *n*. 开始

injection [ɪnˈdʒekʃən] *n*. 注射，投入

【记】 in(进入) + ject(投掷) + ion(名词词尾)→投掷进来→注射

【例】 The doctor gave her an *injection* to alleviate the pain. 医生给她注射以减轻疼痛。

【同】 shot

【派】 (逆构)inject *v*. 注射

injury [ˈɪndʒərɪ] *n*. 受伤，伤害

【记】 in(表否定，不) + jury(法律，正义)→做不正当的行为→伤害

【例】 He suffered serious *injuries* to the arms and legs. 他的双臂和双腿严重受伤。

【同】 harm, hurt

【派】 (逆构)injure *v*. 损害，伤害

innate [ˈɪneɪt] *adj*. 先天的，天生的

【记】 in(内) + nate(出生)→出生就有的→天生的

【例】 Ability is not *innate*, but comes through practice. 本事不是天生的，是锻炼出来的。

【同】 inborn, congenital

innocent [ˈɪnəsnt] *adj*. 无辜的，清白的

【记】 in(表否定，不、没) + noc(伤害) + ent(形容词词尾)→没有伤害的→无辜的

【例】 He was charged with murder but found *innocent* later. 他被控杀人，但后来发现他是无罪的。

【同】 blameless, guiltless

【反】 guilty

【派】 innocence *n*. 清白，无辜

innovate [ˈɪnəuveɪt] *v*. 创新，革新

【记】 in(进入) + nov(新的) + ate(动词词尾)→放入新的东西→创新

【例】 The scientist *innovated* new ways of research. 那个科学家创立了新的研究方法。

【同】 initiate, introduce

【派】 innovation *n*. 创新，革新

innovative *adj*. 革新的，富有创新精神的

innumerable [ɪˈnjuːmərəbl] *adj*. 无数的，数不清的

【记】 in(不) + number(数) + able(形容词词尾)→不能数的→无数的

【例】 The stars in the night sky are *innumerable*. 夜空中的星星数不清。

【同】 countless, infinite, numberless

input [ˈɪnput] *n*. 输入，(资金、材料等的)投入

【记】 in(进入) + put(放)→放进去→投入

【例】 As the *input* of energy is increased, the volume gets louder. 随着能量的输入增

I

加，音量变得更大。
【同】 import
【反】 output

inquiry [ɪn'kwaɪərɪ] *n*. 1. 询问，质问；2. 调查
【记】 in(进入)+quir(探求)+y(名词词尾)→深入探求→询问，调查
【例】 1. The police are making *inquiries* about the crime. 警方正在询问罪案的情况。
2. They've promised a thorough *inquiry* into the plane crash. 他们答应对这次飞机失事进行彻底的调查。
【同】 enquiry, investigation
【派】 (逆构)inquire *v*. 询问，调查

inquisitive [ɪn'kwɪzɪtɪv] *adj*. 好奇的，多管闲事的
【记】 in(进入)+quis(探求)+itive(形容词词尾)→爱探求的→好奇的
【例】 She is *inquisitive* to other people's affairs. 她过分好奇别人的事情。
【同】 speculative, questioning, wondering

I

insane [ɪn'seɪn] *adj*. 发狂的，精神错乱的
【记】 in(不)+san(健康)+e→精神不健康的→发狂的
【例】 He must be *insane* to drive his car so fast. 他把车开得这么快，一定是疯了。
【同】 crazy, mad
【反】 sane
【派】 insanity *n*. 精神错乱，疯狂

insert [ɪn'sɜːt] *v*. 插入，嵌入
【记】 in(进入)+sert(放置)→置于其中→插入
【例】 He *inserted* the key into the lock but could not open the door. 他把钥匙插入锁中但没能打开门。
【同】 enter, inject
【派】 insertion *n*. 插入

insight ['ɪnsaɪt] *n*. 见识，洞察力
【记】 in(内)+sight(看)→向深处看→洞察力
【例】 The book is filled with remarkable *insights*. 这本书很有真知卓见。
【同】 perception, penetration

insinuate [ɪn'sɪnjʊeɪt] *v*. 暗示，迂回进入
【记】 in(进入)+sinu(弯曲)+ate(动词词尾)→拐弯抹角地进入→暗示
【例】 1. He *insinuated* his doubt of the reply. 他暗示他对这答复有怀疑。
2. What are you *insinuating*? 你旁敲侧击，究竟指的是什么？
【同】 hint, imply, indicate

insist [ɪn'sɪst] *v*. 坚持，坚决主张
【记】 in(=on, …上)+sist(站)→站在…上不动→坚持
【例】 He *insisted* that he had done right. 他坚决认为自己做对了。
【同】 stress, assert
【派】 insistent *adj*. 坚持不懈的
insistence *n*. 坚持，坚决主张

insolent [ˈɪnsələnt] *adj*. 傲慢的，无礼的

【记】 in(不) + sol(习惯) + ent(形容词词尾)→不合乎习惯的→傲慢的，无礼的

【例】 His staff is *insolent* to our manager. 他的员工对我们的经理很无礼。

【同】 arrogant, bodacious, haughty, rude

【反】 polite

【派】 insolence *n*. 傲慢

inspect [ɪnˈspekt] *v*. 检查，审视

【记】 in(内) + spect(看)→向里面看→检查

【例】 Police were called out to keep at the airport, and *inspect* the arriving planes. 警察们被紧急召集起来去守卫机场，并对到达的飞机进行检查。

【同】 examine, scrutinize

【派】 inspection *n*. 检查，审视

inspire [ɪnˈspaɪə] *v*. 激励，鼓舞，赋予灵感

【记】 in(进入) + spire(吹气)→把气吹进去→鼓舞

【例】 The Lake District scenery *inspired* Wordsworth to write his greatest poetry. 英格兰湖区的美景给了华兹华斯灵感而使他创作出最伟大的诗篇。

【同】 encourage, prompt

【派】 inspiration *n*. 灵感

inspirational *adj*. 灵感的，给予灵感的

install [ɪnˈstɔːl] *v*. 安装，安置

【记】 in(内) + stall(放置)→放入其中→安装

【例】 The workers are *installing* a heating system. 工人们正在安装供暖系统。

【同】 establish, fix

【派】 installation *n*. 安装，装置

installment [ɪnˈstɔːlmənt] *n*. 分期付款

【记】 instal(来自拉丁语 estall，安排付款) + ment(名词词尾)→分期付款

【例】 If you can't pay for the house in cash, you can buy it on *installment*. 如果你不能用现金购房，也可以分期付款。

【同】 payment

instance [ˈɪnstəns] *n*. 例子，事例

【记】 in(= on，在…上) + stan(站) + ce(名词词尾)→在现场站着的东西→例子

【例】 This is only one *instance* out of many. 这不过是许多例子中的一个。

【同】 case, example, illustration

instant [ˈɪnstənt] *adj*. 1. 紧急的，立即的；2. 速溶的，方便的

【记】 in(= on，在…上) + stan(站) + t(形容词词尾)→在现场站着→即时的→立即的

【例】 1. The medicine gives *instant* relief from pain. 这药服了立刻见效。

2. I don't like to drink *instant* coffee. 我不喜欢喝速溶咖啡。

【同】 immediate, urgent; fast

【派】 instantly *adv*. 立即

instantaneous [ˌɪnstənˈteɪnjəs] *adj*. 瞬间的，即刻的

【记】 instant(立即的) + an + eous(形容词词尾)→立即的→瞬间的

【例】 Death is *instantaneous* in a fatal accident. 在致命的事故中，死亡是即刻发生的。

【同】 instant

instigate ['ɪnstɪgeɪt] *v*. 鼓动，煽动，怂恿

【记】 in(进入)+stig(=sting，刺)+ate(动词词尾)→刺进去→煽动

【例】 The police have *instigated* a search for the missing boy. 警方已经开始了寻找那个失踪男孩的行动。

【同】 incite，inspire，stir up

【派】 instigation *n*. 教唆，鼓动，煽动

instigator *n*. 煽动者

instill [ɪn'stɪl] *v*. 灌输，滴注

【记】 in(进入)+still(滴)→慢慢滴入→灌输

【例】 Fear of the father is *instilled* into some children from their infancy. 有的小孩从小就慢慢养成害怕父亲的心理。

I

【同】 inculcate，infuse

【派】 instillation *n*. 灌输，滴下

instinct ['ɪnstɪŋkt] *n*. 本能，直觉

【记】 in(内)+stinct(刺)→内部的刺→内部兴起的东西→本能

【例】 1. Birds learn to fly by *instinct*. 鸟会飞是出自本能。

2. When I saw the flames I acted on *instinct* and threw a blanket over them. 我看见火焰时便本能地把一张毯子扑在火焰上。

【同】 intuition

【派】 instinctual *adj*. 本能的

institute ['ɪnstɪtjuːt] *n*. 组织，机构，学会

【记】 in(=on，在…上)+stitut(建立，放)+e→建立在…上→设立

【例】 He graduated from a famous foreign language *institute*. 他毕业于一所知名的外语学院。

【同】 association，organization

【派】 institution *n*. 公共机构，协会，制度

institutional *adj*. 制度上的

instruct [ɪn'strʌkt] *v*. 指示，指导

【记】 in(进入)+struct(建立，建筑)→把(知识)建立进去→指导

【例】 I've been *instructed* to wait here until the lecturer arrives. 我得到指示在这儿等到讲课老师到来。

【同】 dictate，direct，guide

【派】 instruction *n*. 指令，指导，用法说明

instrument ['ɪnstrʊmənt] *n*. 工具，仪器

【记】 in(以…)+stru(=struct，建筑)+ment→建筑用的东西→工具

【例】 A new generation of optical *instruments* is emerging that can provide detailed imaging of the inner workings of cells. 新一代的光学仪器出现了，它可以为细胞的内部活动提供详细的成像。

【同】 apparatus，implement，utensil

【派】 instrumental *adj*. 仪器的，器械的

insufficient [ˌɪnsəˈfɪʃənt] *adj*. 不充足的，缺乏的

【记】 in(表否定，不) + sufficient(充足的)→不充足的

【例】 Our wood supply proved *insufficient*. 我们的木材供应证明是不够的。

【同】 deficient，inadequate

【反】 sufficient

insulation [ˌɪnsjʊˈleɪʃən] *n*. 绝缘，隔绝

【记】 insul(岛屿) + ation(名词词尾)→使变成岛的状态→隔绝

【例】 Foam rubber provides good *insulation*. 泡沫橡胶隔绝性能良好。

【同】 detachment

【派】 (逆构)insulate *v*. 绝缘，隔离

insult [ˈɪnsʌlt] n/*v*. 侮辱，凌辱

【记】 in(= on，在…上) + sult(跳)→在…上跳→侮辱

【例】 You will *insult* her if you don't go to her party. 你要是不去参加她举办的聚会，就对她太无礼了。

【同】 humiliate

【反】 honor，respect

insurance [ɪnˈʃʊərəns] *n*. 保险，保险业

【记】 in(进入) + sur(确定的，安全的) + ance(名词词尾)→使进入安全的状态→保险

【例】 This unbeatable program fee includes 3 months' *insurance* cover. 这个无与伦比的活动的费用包括3个月的保险费。

insurmountable [ˌɪnsəˈmaʊntəbl] *adj*. 不能克服的，不能超越的

【记】 in(不) + sur(在…上) + mount(山) + able(形容词词尾)→无法攀登过去的→不能超越的

【例】 But the difficulties of sending goods out are not entirely *insurmountable*. 但是这种出口困难，不是完全不可克服的。

【同】 insuperable，surmountable

【反】 surmountable

intact [ɪnˈtækt] *adj*. 无损伤的，完整的

【记】 in(不) + tinct(接触)→未被触碰的→无损伤的，完整的

【例】 Despite his misfortunes, his faith and optimism remained *intact*. 虽然他遭到一连串的不幸，他的信心和乐观丝毫未减。

【同】 integral，unchanged，untouched

intangible [ɪnˈtændʒəbl] *adj*. 触摸不到的，无形的

【记】 in(不) + tang(= touch，触摸) + ible(形容词词尾)→触摸不到的

【例】 We felt an *intangible* presence in the conference room. 我们感到会议室里有一种难以捉摸的东西。

【同】 unsubstantial，untouchable

【反】 tangible

integral [ˈɪntɪgrəl] *adj*. 构成整体所必需的，完整的

【记】 in(不) + tegr(触动) + al(形容词词尾)→未动过的→完整的

【例】 Steel is an *integral* part of a modern skyscraper. 钢铁是现代摩天大厦的主干。

【同】 entire, intact

integrate ['ɪntɪgreɪt] *v*. 使成为整体，使一体化

【记】 in(不)+tegr(触动)+ate(动词词尾)→不触动→使成为整体

【例】 Many suggestions are needed to *integrate* the plan. 需要许多建议使计划更加完整。

【同】 coordinate, incorporate

【反】 disintegrate

【派】 integration *n*. 综合，整体

integrity *n*. 完整；正直，诚实

intellectual [ˌɪntɪ'lektjʊəl] *adj*. 知识的，智力的；*n*. 知识分子

【记】 intel(=inter, 在…之间)+lect(选择，收集)+ual(形容词词尾)→能够在…之间做出选择的→有知识的

【例】 1. The argument was too *intellectual* for me; I couldn't follow a word of it. 这场争论对我来说太深奥了，我一点都搞不明白。

2. These views were common among *intellectuals*. 这些观点在知识分子中很普遍。

【同】 mental

【派】 (逆构)intellect *n*. 智力，理解力

intelligence [ɪn'telɪdʒəns] *n*. 1. 智力，智能；2. 情报，消息

【记】 intel(=inter, 在…之间)+lig(选择)+ence(名词词尾)→善于选择的品质→智力

【例】 1. She has more *intelligence* than we suspected her to possess. 她的智慧比我们想象的要高。

2. Our *intelligence* reports indicate that rebel groups are planning an attack. 我们的情报表明叛乱分子正在部署一场进攻。

【同】 intellect, wit; information

【派】 intelligent *adj*. 有才智的，理解力强的

intelligible *adj*. 可以理解的

intense [ɪn'tens] *adj*. 剧烈的，极度的

【记】 in(不)+tens(延伸)+e→拉到了不能再拉的程度→极度的

【例】 My work is so *intense* that I even have no time to take a rest. 我的工作非常紧张，以致于我没有时间休息。

【同】 acute, drastic, extreme

【反】 mild

intensify [ɪn'tensɪfaɪ] *v*. 加强，加剧

【记】 in(向)+tens(延伸)+ify(表示"做"的动词词尾)→使向…努力延伸→加强

【例】 My first failure only *intensify* my desire to succeed. 我的初次失败只是更加强了我成功的信念。

【同】 escalate, deepen

【反】 weaken

【派】 intensity *n*. 强烈，强度

intensive [ɪn'tensɪv] *adj*. 集中的，密集的

【记】 in(向)+tens(延伸)+ive(形容词词尾)→向一个方向延伸的→集中的
【例】 Ahead of us lay ten days of *intensive* training. 我们当前有10天的强化训练。
【反】 extensive

intention [ɪn'tenʃən] *n*. 目的，意图
【记】 in(内)+tent(延伸)+ion(名词词尾)→在内心延伸的东西→意图
【例】 They have no *intention* of getting married at present. 他们目前没有结婚的打算。
【同】 aim, intent, purpose
【派】 intentional *adj*. 有意的，故意的

interact [ˌɪntə'rækt] *v*. 互相作用，互相影响
【记】 inter(在…之间)+act(行动)→在两者之间活动→互相作用
【例】 Mother and baby *interact* in a very complex way. 母亲与婴儿以非常复杂的方式相互影响。
【派】 interaction *n*. 一起活动，配合

intercede [ˌɪntɜː'siːd] *v*. 调停，求情
【记】 inter(在…之间)+cede(走)→走到…之间→干涉→调停
【例】 The lawyer has promised to *intercede* for the prisoner, hoping to free him from prison. 律师答应为那囚犯说情，放他出狱。
【同】 mediate, intervene
【派】 intercession *n*. 求情，调解

intercept [ˌɪntə'sept] *v*. 中途拦截，阻止
【记】 inter(在…之间)+cept(拿)→在…之间拿走→中途拦截
【例】 Reporters *intercepted* him as he tried to leave by the rear entrance. 他想从后门溜走，记者把他截住了。
【同】 stop, block
【派】 interception *n*. 中途夺取，拦截

interdependent [ˌɪntɜːdɪ'pendənt] *adj*. 相互依赖的，互助的
【记】 inter(在…之间)+dependent(依靠的)→相互之间依靠的
【例】 All nations are *interdependent* in the modern world. 当今世界上所有国家都是互相依存的。
【同】 dependent
【派】 interdependence *n*. 相互依赖

interface ['ɪntɜːˌfeɪs] *n*. 界面，结合部位，边缘区域
【记】 inter(在…之间)+face(面)→面和面之间的东西→界面
【例】 Can you give me an explanation of the man-machine *interface*? 你能给我解释一下人机接口吗?

interfere [ˌɪntə'fɪə] *v*. 干涉，介入，干预
【记】 inter(在…之间)+fere(打击)→打入…之间 →干涉
【例】 He tries not to let his business *interfere* with his home life. 他尽量不让日常工作妨碍他的家庭生活。
【同】 interrupt, intervene, intrude
【派】 interference *n*. 干涉，冲突

I

interior [ɪn'tɪərɪə] *adj*. /*n*. 内部(的)，内地(的)

【记】 inter(内的)+ior(表示比较级的词尾)→内部的

【例】 1. The secret of the versatility of glass lies in its *interior* structure. 玻璃的多功能的秘密在于它的内部结构。

2. This causes the outer layer of the pane to contract and solidify before the *interior*. 这会导致玻璃板外层先于内层收缩并固化。

【同】 inner, inside

【反】 exterior, foreign

interject [ˌɪntɜː'dʒekt] *v*. 插嘴，突然插入

【记】 inter(在…之间)+ject(投掷)→投在…之间→插嘴

【例】 When I brought up the question of funding, he quickly *interjected* that it had been settled. 我刚提出筹集基金的问题，他急忙插嘴说问题已经解决了。

【同】 inject, interpose, insert

I

interlude ['ɪntɜːluːd] *n*. 间隔，暂休，插曲

【记】 inter(在…之间)+lude(=play，表演)→在演出之间→间隔

【例】 There will now be a 15-minute *interlude*. 现在有15分钟的中场休息。

【同】 break, interval

intermediary [ˌɪntə'miːdɪərɪ] *n*. 媒介物，居间者

【记】 inter(在…之间)+medi(中间)+ary(名词词尾)→从中间介入的→媒介物，居间者

【例】 They disliked each other too much to meet, so they conducted all their business through an *intermediary*. 他们彼此交恶不愿相见，有事均通过中间人处理。

【同】 go-between, mediator

intermediate [ˌɪntə'miːdjət] *adj*. 中等水平的，中级的

【记】 inter(在…之间)+medi(中间)+ate(形容词词尾)→在两者之间的中间→中等水平的

【例】 I've passed the *intermediate* level exam of Japanese. 我已经通过了日语的中级水平考试。

【同】 medium, middle

intermittent [ˌɪntɜː'mɪtənt] *adj*. 间歇的，断断续续的

【记】 inter(在…之间)+mitt(=send，发出()+ent(形容词词尾)→在…之间发出的→间歇的，断断续续的

【例】 They saw the *intermittent* flashes from a lighthouse. 他们看见了灯塔发出一闪一闪的光。

【同】 broken, irregular

【反】 continuous

【派】 intermission *n*. 间歇

internal [ɪn'tɜːnl] *adj*. 内在的，内部的，国内的

【记】 inter(n)(内的)+al(形容词词尾)→内部的

【例】 The doctor x-rayed her to see if there were any *internal* injuries. 医生给她做了X光检查，看看有没有内伤。

【同】 inner, inside, interior

【反】 external

interpret [ɪn'tɜːprɪt] *v*. 1.理解，解释；2.翻译，口译

【记】 inter(在…之间)+pret(=price，价格)→在买卖双方间调停→解释，翻译

【例】 1. We *interpreted* his silence as a refusal. 我们认为他的沉默是拒绝的表示。

2. Would you please *interpret* for me? 请你为我翻译一下好吗？

【同】 explain；translate

【派】 interpretation *n*. 解释，理解，口译

interpreter *n*. 译员，口译者

interrogate [ɪn'terəgeɪt] *v*. 审问，询问

【记】 inter(在…之间)+rog(问)+ate(动词词尾)→在…之间问→询问

【例】 The police *interrogated* the suspect for several hours. 警察盘问了那个嫌疑犯好几个钟头。

【同】 question

【派】 interrogation *n*. 讯问，审问

interrupt [ˌɪntə'rʌpt] *v*. 打断，打扰

【记】 inter(在…之间)+rupt(打破)→在(讲话)中间打断→打断

【例】 Trade between the two countries was *interrupted* by the war. 两国间贸易因战争而中断。

【同】 break，interfere

【派】 interruption *n*. 中断，打断

intersection [ˌɪntɜː'sekʃən] *n*. 十字路口，交叉点

【记】 inter(在…之间)+sect(切割)+ion(名词词尾)→相互切割→交叉点

【例】 Turn right at the first *intersection*. 第一个十字路口向右转。

【同】 crossroad，crossing

interval ['ɪntəvəl] *n*. (时间、空间上的)间隔，间距

【记】 inter(在…之间)+val(=wall，墙壁)→两个墙壁之间的→间隔

【例】 He comes back to see us at regular *intervals*. 他每隔一段时间就回来看看我们。

2. The proper *intervals* should be maintained between vehicles. 车辆之间应保持适当的间距。

【同】 break，pause

intervene [ˌɪntə'viːn] *v*. 介入，在其间

【记】 inter(在…之间)+ven(来到)+e→来到…中间→介入

【例】 When rioting broke out, the police were obliged to *intervene*. 暴乱发生时，警察有责任干预。

【同】 interfere

【派】 intervention *n*. 干涉，干预

interview ['ɪntəvjuː] *v*./*n*. 面试，采访

【记】 inter(在…之间)+view(观看)→相互观看→面谈，面试

【例】 1. All the applicants were *interviewed* one by one. 所有的申请者一个接着一个参加面试。

2. As he had nothing to tell, he refused to give any *interviews* to the journalists.

他由于无可奉告，拒绝了记者采访。

【同】 audience

【派】 interviewer *n*. 面试者，采访者

interviewee *n*. 被面试者，被采访者

intimate [ˈɪntɪmɪt] *adj*. 亲密的，私密的

【记】 intim(= inter，内的) + ate(形容词词尾)→内部的→亲密的

【例】 Do you believe these two *intimate* friends used to be mutual sworn enemies? 这两位亲密朋友彼此间过去曾经是不共戴天的死敌，你相信吗？

【同】 close，bosom，familiar

intoxicate [ɪnˈtɒksɪkeɪt] *v*. 喝醉，使陶醉

【记】 in(进入) + tox(毒) + ic(形容词词尾) + ate→进入(酒精)中毒状态→喝醉

【例】 1. He was fined for driving while *intoxicated*. 他因醉酒开车被罚款。

2. The businessman was *intoxicated* by his success. 这个商人因为成功而狂喜。

I

【同】 befuddle

【派】 intoxication *n*. 陶醉

intrepid [ɪnˈtrepɪd] *adj*. 勇敢的

【记】 in(不) + trep(警觉) + id(形容词词尾)→不是警觉的→不是小心的→勇敢的

【例】 He is not really satisfied with his *intrepid* action. 他没有真正满意他的无畏行动。

【同】 bold，brave，courageous，fearless

intricate [ˈɪntrɪkɪt] *adj*. 复杂的，错综的

【记】 in(里面) + tric(障碍) + ate(形容词词尾)→里面有障碍的→复杂的

【例】 This is a novel with an *intricate* plot. 这是一本情节错综复杂的小说。

【同】 complex，complicated，elaborate

【反】 simple

intrigue [ɪnˈtriː] *v*. 用诡计迷住，激起…的好奇心(或兴趣)

【记】 in(内部) + trigue(= tric，妨碍)→原义为在内部妨碍，使阴谋→用诡计迷住

【例】 You *intrigue* me; tell me more. 你引起了我的兴趣，给我多讲一些吧。

【同】 fascinate，plot

【派】 intriguing *adj*. 吸引人的，引起兴趣(或好奇心的)

intrinsic [ɪnˈtrɪnsɪk] *adj*. 固有的，本质的

【记】 intrin(= intra，内部的) + sic(旁边)→在内部的旁边的→固有的

【例】 He admitted the *intrinsic* merits of of my idea. 他承认了我提的意见的内在价值。

【同】 essential，inherent

【反】 extrinsic

introspection [ˌɪntrəʊˈspekʃən] *n*. 内省，自省，反省

【记】 intro(向内，入内) + spect(看) + ion(名词词尾)→向内看→内省

【例】 In my opinion，30th birthday is the day of *introspection* and reflection for many people. 依我看，30岁生日对许多人来说都是反省和深思的时候。

【同】 meditation，reflection

【派】 (逆构)introspect *v*. 自省，反省

intrude [ɪnˈtruːdə] *v*. 闯入，入侵

【记】 in(进入)+trude(插入)→插进去→入侵

【例】 He had no wish to *intrude* on their privacy. 他原本就不想触犯他们私人活动的自由。

【同】 invade

【派】 intruder *v*. 闯入者，侵入者

intrusion *n*. 闯入，侵扰

intuition [ˌɪntjuːˈɪʃən] *n*. 直觉，直觉力

【记】 in(内)+tuit(观察)+ion(名词词尾)→从心里观察→直觉

【例】 My *intuitions* proved correct. 我的直觉确实是正确的。

【同】 instinct

inure [ɪˈnjuə] *v*. 使习惯

【记】 in(进入)+ure(使用，练习)→经常练习→使习惯

【例】 After living here for years I've become *inured* to the cold climate. 我在此地居住多年，已习惯寒冷的气候。

【同】 accustom, habituate

invade [ɪnˈveɪd] *v*. 侵略，侵犯

【记】 in(进入)+vade(走)→走进去→入侵

【例】 Alexander the Great *invaded* India with a large army. 亚历山大大帝曾率领大军入侵印度。

【同】 attack, infringe, intrude

【派】 invader *n*. 侵略者，侵入物

invalid [ɪnˈvælɪd] *adj*. 无效的，作废的；*n*. 病人

【记】 in(不)+valid(有效的)→无效的

【例】 1. This ticket has passed its expiration date, and so it is now *invalid*. 这张票已过了有效期，现在作废了。

2. He helps to look after his grandfather who is an *invalid*. 他帮助照看他病弱的祖父。

【同】 expired, void; patient, sufferer,

【派】 invalidate *v*. 使作废

inventory [ˈɪnvəntrɪ] *n*. 存货清单，财产目录

【记】 in(进入)+ vent(来到)+ory(名词词尾)→来到里面的东西→存货清单

【例】 I regret not completing the *inventory* on time. 我很遗憾没有按时填好库存单。

【同】 list, stock

inverse [ˈɪnˈvɜːs] *adj*. 逆的，反的

【记】 in(=on, …上)+vers(转移)+e→使(下部朝上)的→反过来的→逆的，反的

【例】 This is the *inverse* of his earlier proposition. 这和他早些时候提的建议截然相反。

【同】 opposite, reverse

invert [ɪnˈvɜːt] *v*. 使颠倒，使转换

【记】 in(=on, …上)+vert(转移)→使(下部)朝上→颠倒

【例】 The little boy caught the insect by *inverting* the cup over it. 小男孩把杯子倒过来就逮住了那只昆虫。

【同】 reverse

invest [ɪn'vest] *v*. 投资，投入(时间、金钱、精力等)

【记】 in(使处于…状态) + vest(衣服)→给…穿衣服→给…付钱→投资

【例】 I won't *invest* my money in his company. 我不会把我的钱投资到他的公司。

【同】 input

【派】 investment *n*. 投资

investigate [ɪn'vestɪgeɪt] *v*. 调查，研究

【记】 in(进入) + vestig(踪迹) + ate(动词词尾)→根据踪迹进入→调查

【例】 The police are *investigating* the murder. 警察正在调查这件谋杀案。

【同】 examine, inspect, study

【派】 investigation *n*. 调查，研究

investigative *adj*. 调查的，调查研究的

invoice ['ɪnvɔɪs] *n*. 发票，发货清单

【记】 in(= on, …上) + voi(路) + ce(名词词尾)→已经送上路的东西→发的货物(清单)

【例】 The work entailed the processing of accounts and generating of *invoices*. 工作必须涉及财务流程和由此产生的发票的处理。

【同】 bill

invoke [ɪn'vəʊk] *v*. 恳求，祈求

【记】 in(= on, …上) + voke(喊叫)→大声喊叫→恳求

【例】 They *invoked* help in the desperate situation. 他们在走投无路的情况下恳求援助。

【同】 appeal, beg, plead

involve [ɪn'vɒlv] *v*. 1.包含，包括；2.使陷入，涉及

【记】 in(进入) + volve(滚，卷)→卷入其中→包含

【例】 1. The job *involves* travellving abroad for three months each year. 这份工作需要每年去国外三个月。

2. Don't *involve* other people in your mad schemes. 不要把别人卷入你的疯狂计划中去。

【同】 encompass, include; entail, implicate

【派】 involvement *n*. 卷入，牵连

irony ['aɪərənɪ] *n*. 反语，冷嘲

【例】 It was a real *irony* that my former boss was asking me for a job. 具有讽刺意味的是，我以前的老板向我求职。

【同】 satire

【派】 ironic(al) *adj*. 冷嘲的，具有讽刺意味的

irrigation [ˌɪrɪ'geɪʃən] *n*. 灌溉

【记】 ir(= in, 使处于…状态) + rigat(湿润) + ion(名词词尾)→使处于湿润的状态→灌溉

【例】 We used the money to set up an *irrigation* project. 我们把钱用在兴建灌溉工程上了。

【派】 (逆构)irrigate *v*. 灌溉，修水利

irritate ['ɪrɪteɪt] *v*. 激怒，使恼怒

【记】 ir(= in, 使处于…状态) + rit(擦) + ate(动词词尾)→进入磨擦→激怒

【例】 Don't *irritate* her, she's on a short fuse today. 别惹她，她今天动不动就发火。
【同】 annoy, bother, provoke
【反】 soothe, calm
【派】 irritable *adj*. 易怒的，急躁的
irritation *n*. 激怒，恼怒，生气
irritability *n*. 易怒

isolate ['aɪsəleɪt] *v*. 使隔离，使孤立
【记】 isol(= island, 岛) + ate(动词词尾)→使在岛上→使隔离
【例】 Several villages have been *isolated* by the floods. 洪水使好几座村庄与外界隔绝了。
【同】 insulate, seclude, separate
【派】 isolated *adj*. 隔离的，孤立的
isolation *n*. 隔绝，孤立

issue ['ɪsjuː] *n*. 1. 问题，难题；2.(报刊的)期；*v*. 发布，发行
【例】 1. This is surprising considering the high level of media coverage on this *issue*. 从媒体对这个问题连篇累牍的报道来看，这是很令人吃惊的。
2. The Christmas *issue* of the magazine had a picture of carol singers on its cover. 圣诞节那期杂志的封面上刊有唱圣诞颂歌者的照片。
3. Banknotes of this design were first *issued* 10 years ago. 这种图案的钞票是10年前首次发行的。
【同】 point, problem; publish, release
【反】 recall(召回)

item ['aɪtem, 'aɪtəm] *n*. 条，项目；2. 物品
【例】 1. Let us go on to the next *item* on the agenda. 让我们继续讨论议程上的下一个项目。
2. The Museum of London's exhibition is largely visual, with a huge number of *items* on show. 伦敦博物馆的展览比较直观，其中展示了大量物品。
【同】 article, piece

ivory ['aɪvərɪ] *n*. 象牙
【记】 ivor(= ebor, 大象) + y(名词词尾)→大象身上的东西→象牙
【例】 Living in your *ivory* tower at Oxford, you can't imagine what it's like to go hungry. 你生活在牛津的象牙塔中，想象不到挨饿是什么滋味。

J

jam [dʒæm] *n*./*v*. (-mmed; -mming)拥挤，堵塞

【例】 1. Their car was stuck in a traffic *jam* for hours. 他们的车子因交通堵塞而被耽搁了好几个小时。

2. The crowds *jammed* the streets, and no cars can pass. 大街上挤满了人，汽车都无法通过。

【同】 block, cram, crowd

jar [dʒɑː] *n*. 罐子，坛子

【例】 No payment will be made far empty *jars*, which do not need to be returned. 空罐恕不退费，亦无须退回。

【同】 vessel

jealous [ˈdʒeləs] *adj*. 羡慕的，嫉妒的

【例】 When she kisses the baby, it makes the older child *jealous*. 她亲吻那个婴儿的时候，引起了那个大一点的孩子的嫉妒。

【同】 green-eyed, envious

【派】 jealousy *n*. 嫉妒，羡慕

jeer [dʒɪə] *v*. 揶揄，嘲笑

【例】 They all *jeered* at the foolish speaker. 他们都嘲笑那个愚蠢的演说者。

【同】 mock, scoff

jeopardy [ˈdʒepədɪ] *n*. 危险

【记】 jeo(= joke, game 游戏) + pard(= part, 部分) + y(名词词尾)→游戏的一部分→危险

【例】 His foolish remark and behavior may put his whole future in *jeopardy*. 他愚蠢的言词和行为可能毁了他的前程。

【同】 danger, hazard, risk

【反】 safety

【派】 jeopardize *v*. 危害，危及

jerk [dʒɜːk] *v*. 猝然一动

【例】 The bus *jerked* to a stop. 公共汽车猛然刹车停住了。

【同】 jolt, flip

jewelry [dʒuːəlrɪ] *n*. 珠宝，珠宝饰物

【记】 jewel(宝石) + ry(名词词尾)→珠宝

【例】 My aunt bequeathed me all her *jewelry*. 我姑妈把她所有的珠宝都遗赠给我了。

【派】 jeweler *n*. 珠宝商，钟表商

jolt [dʒəʊlt]n. 震动，颠簸；*v*. 使颠簸，猛击

【例】 1. The sudden *jolt* plunged her forward. 突然颠了一下，她向前打了个趔趄。
2. The cart *jolted* along over the rough road. 马车在崎岖的路上颠簸而行。
【同】 jerk, shake

journal [ˈdʒɜːnl] *n*. 定期刊物，杂志
【记】 journ(日) + al(名词词尾)→每天的东西→日志→杂志
【例】 The *journal* makes its appearance once two months. 这本刊物两个月出版一次。
【同】 magazine
【派】 journalist *n*. 记者，新闻工作者
journalism *n*. 新闻业，报章杂志

judge [dʒʌdʒ] *v*. 1. 判断，认为；2. 审理，判决；*n*. 法官，审判员，评委
【记】 jud(判断) + ge(名词词尾)→进行判断→审理
【例】 1. You can't *judge* a book by its cover. 你不能根据封面判断一本书。
2. Who will judge the next case? 下一个案子由谁来审理？
3. The judge sentenced her to 12 months' imprisonment. 法官判她一年监禁。
【同】 estimate, consider; try
【派】 judg(e)ment *n*. 审判，判决；看法，评价

judicial [dʒuːˈdɪʃəl] *adj*. 司法的，法院的
【记】 jud(判断) + ic(形容词词尾) + ia(形容词词尾)→与判断有关的→司法的，法院的
【例】 The workers decided to take *judicial* proceedings against the company. 工人们决定对公司正式提起诉讼。
【同】 legal
【派】 judiciary *adj*. 司法的，法院的；*n*. 司法部，司法官，审判员

judicious [dʒuːˈdɪʃəs] *adj*. 头脑精明的，贤明的
【记】 jud(判断) + ic(形容词词尾) + ious(形容词词尾)→能判断的→头脑精明的
【例】 Our leaders made a *judicious* decision for our company's future. 我们公司的领导为我们公司做出了明智的抉择。
【同】 sensible, thoughtful, wise

juice [dʒuːs] *n*. (水果)汁，液
【例】 And there's your bottle of orange *juice*. 这是你要的橘子汁。
【派】 juicy *adj*. 多汁的，有趣的

jumble [ˈdʒʌmbl] *v*. 使混乱，混杂；*n*. 混乱，杂乱的一堆
【例】 1. Details of the accident were all *jumbled* up in his mind. 该事故的详情在他头脑中已混在一起。
2. There is a *jumble* of books and papers on the table. 桌子上凌乱地堆着一堆书和报纸。
【同】 mingle, mix, muddle
【反】 order

junction [ˈdʒʌŋkʃən] *n*. 连接处，交叉口
【记】 junct(连接) + ion(名词词尾)→连接的地方→连接处
【例】 The accident happened at one of the country's busiest railway *junctions*. 事故发生在该国一个极繁忙的铁路交叉点处。
【同】 connection, juncture, intersection

jungle [ˈdʒʌŋgl] *n*. 丛林

【例】 The new road was hacked out of the *jungle*. 这条新路是在丛林地带开辟出来的。

【同】 forest

junior [ˈdʒuːnjə] *n*. 1. 年少者，下级；2. 大学三年级学生；*adj*. 1. 年少的；2. 下级的，后进的

【记】 jun(年轻)＋ior(表示比较级)→比较年轻的→年少的

【例】 1. She is my *junior* by three years. 她比我小三岁。

2. Mike is already a *junior*. 迈克已经大学三年级了。

3. He is three years *junior* to me. 他比我小三岁。

4. He has *junior* position in the company. 他在这家公司担任一个低级职务。

【同】 lower，younger

【反】 senior

jurisdiction [ˌdʒuərɪsˈdɪkʃən] *n*. 权限，管辖范围；2. 司法权，审判权

【记】 juris(法律)＋dict(说)＋ion(名词词尾)→陈述关于法律→司法权

【例】 1. This affair is within his *jurisdiction*. 这件事情在他的管辖权限之内。

2. The court has no *jurisdiction* over foreign diplomats living in this country. 法院对居住在本国的外交官无裁判权。

【同】 power，territory，authority

jury [ˈdʒuərɪ] *n*. 陪审团，评判委员会

【记】 jur(发誓)＋y(名词词尾)→发誓的人→陪审团

【例】 The *jury* found the prisoner not guilty. 陪审团认定该囚犯无罪。

justice [ˈdʒʌstɪs] *n*. 1. 正义，公平；2. 司法，审判

【记】 just(法律)＋ice(名词词尾)→法律所维护的→正义，公平

【例】 1. Everyone should be treated with *justice*. 每个人都应受到公正的对待。

2. The police must do all they can to bring criminals to *justice*. 警方必须竭尽全力追捕罪犯，将他们绳之以法。

【同】 fairness，justness；trial

【反】 injustice

justify [ˈdʒʌstɪfaɪ] *v*. 提出正当理由，证明…有道理

【记】 just(法律)＋ify(动词词尾)→证明是符合法律的→证明…是正当的

【例】 Nothing can *justify* your cheating on an exam. 任何事情都不能成为你考试作弊的理由。

【同】 warrant

【派】 justification *n*. (做某事的)正当理由

juvenile [ˈdʒuːvɪnaɪl] *adj*. 少年的，未成年的

【记】 juven(年轻)＋ ile(形容词词尾)→年轻的→青少年的

【例】 Now she returned to the subject of *juvenile* delinquency in that country. 现在她又回过来讲那个国家少年犯罪的问题。

【同】 adolescent，immature

【反】 adult

K

keen [kiːn] *adj*. 1. 敏锐的，敏捷的；2. 热衷于，渴望的

【例】 1. The blind have a *keen* sense of touch. 盲人有敏锐的触觉。

2. I'm not very *keen* on westerns, although my father likes them. 我不是特别喜欢西部片，尽管我父亲很喜欢。

【同】 acute, sharp; eager

【反】 blunt, dull

ken [ken] *n*. 视野，知识领域

【例】 His ideas are quite beyond my *ken*. 我很不理解他的想法。

【同】 knowledge

kernel [ˈkɜːnl] *n*. 1. 仁，果仁；2. 核心，要点中心

【例】 1. Are *kernels* of apricots edible? 杏仁能吃吗？

2. I think there is a *kernel* of truth in these otherwise frivolous comments. 我认为在这些本来是无关紧要的评论中含有一定的真实性。

【同】 core; heart

kidnap [ˈkɪdnæp] *v*. (-p(p)ed; -p(p)ing)诱拐，绑架

【记】 kid(孩子)+nap(偷)→偷走孩子→诱拐，绑架

【例】 Two businessmen have been *kidnapped* by terrorists. 有两个商人让恐怖分子绑架了。

【同】 abduct

kidney [ˈkɪdnɪ] *n*. 肾，肾脏

【例】 Each man has a pair of *kidneys*. 每个人有一对肾脏。

kingdom [ˈkɪŋdəm] *n*. 王国，领域

【记】 king(国王)+dom(表示"状态，领域"的名词词尾)→国王的领域→王国

【例】 The king is the most important person in a *kingdom*. 国王是一个王国中最重要的人物。

【同】 realm

kit [kɪt] *n*. 成套工具，用品箱

【例】 The nurse has taken a first-aid *kit*. 护士已经带上了一套急救用品。

【同】 equipment, outfit

kneel [niːl] *v*. (knelt, knelt 或 -ed, -led)屈膝，跪下

【例】 Everyone in church *knelt* in prayer. 教堂里每个人都跪着祈祷。

knowledge [ˈnɒlɪdʒ] *n*. 知识，学问

【记】 know(知道)+ledge(= leche, 东西)→知道的东西→知识

【例】 Once over the age of three, children continue to expand on existing *knowledge* of the world. 一旦过了 3 岁，孩子们将继续扩展他们现有的关于这个世界的知识。

【派】 knowledgeable *adj*. 有学问的，消息灵通的

L

label [ˈleɪbl] *v*. /*n*. (-lled; -lling)标记，标签

【例】 1. Have you attached *labels* to the luggage? 你给行李系上标签了吗？

2. The bottle is *labeled* poison. 瓶上标明有毒。

【同】 mark, tag

laborious [ləˈbɔːrɪəs] *adj*. 费力的，艰难的

【记】 labor(劳动) + ious(形容词词尾)→劳动的→费力的

【例】 Breaking up the stones was a *laborious* task. 打碎这些石头是一项吃力的活。

【同】 arduous, hard, tough

【反】 easy

【派】 (逆构)labor *n*. 劳动，努力工作

labyrinth [ˈlæbərɪnθ] *n*. 迷宫，错综复杂的事件

【记】 layr(= labor, 劳动) + in(进入) + th(名词词尾)→需要很费力才能进去的→迷宫

【例】 The old building was a *labyrinth* with dark corridors. 那座古老建筑是一座长廊纵横光线昏暗的迷宫。

【同】 complex, maze, tangle

lag [læg] *n*./*v*. (-gged; -gging)落后，迟延

【例】 1. The children always *lag* behind when we go for a walk. 我们出去散步时，孩子们总是落在后面。

2. I felt completely disorientated with the jet *lag*. 我乘长途飞机后因生理节奏失调而感到昏昏沉沉的。

【同】 delay

【反】 hasten, hurry

lament [ləˈment] *v*. 为…悲痛，痛惜

【例】 He deeply *lamented* the death of his wife. 他对妻子的去世深感悲痛。

【同】 bemoan, grieve, mourn

【反】 rejoice

landmark [ˈlændmɑːk] *n*. 地标，里程碑

【记】 land(土地) + mark(记号)→土地的记号→地标

【例】 The discovery of penicillin was a *landmark* in the history of medicine. 青霉素的发现是医学史上的里程碑。

【同】 milestone

landscape [ˈlændskeɪp] *n*. (陆上)风景，景色

【记】 land(土地) + scape(= ship, …的样子)→土地的样子→风景

【例】 Tourists are drawn to these regions by their natural *landscape* beauty and the unique cultures of their indigenous people. 吸引旅游者来到这些地区的是它们美丽的天然景色和当地土著居民独特的文化。

【同】 scenery

languish ['læŋgwɪʃ] *v*. 1.衰弱，枯萎；2.受苦，受煎熬

【记】 langu(虚弱)+ish(动词词尾)→使变得虚弱→衰弱，枯萎

【例】 1.The plants are *languishing* because of lack of water. 植物因缺水而渐渐枯萎。

2.She *languished* in prison for fifteen years. 她在狱中受苦15年。

【同】 fade，wither；suffer

【反】 flourish

【派】 languid *adj*. 疲倦的，没精打采的

laser ['leɪzə] *n*. 激光

【记】 是 Light Amplification by Stimulated Emission of Radiation 的首字母缩写

【例】 *Lasers* can be used to perform operations nowadays. 现在激光可以用来做手术。

latent ['leɪtənt] *adj*. 潜伏的，隐藏的

【记】 来自拉丁语 latere(潜伏)的现在分词

【例】 The manager did not find her *latent* abilities. 经理没有发现她潜在的才能。

【同】 potential，hidden，undiscovered

【派】 latency *n*. 潜伏，潜在，潜伏物

L

lateral ['lætərəl] *adj*. 侧面的，旁边的；2.水平的，对等的

【记】 later(侧面)+al(形容词词尾)→侧面的

【例】 1.In pushing back the *lateral* rocks，he lost his point of support. 在把侧面的石头向后推的时候，他失去了支撑点。

2.The company offered her a *lateral* move but not a promotion. 公司对她的职位进行了同级调整，但是没有提升她。

【同】 side，sidelong；equivalent

latitude ['lætɪtjuːd] *n*. 纬度，范围

【记】 lat(侧，横)+itude(名词词尾)→横着的线→维度

【例】 Our position is *latitude* 40 degrees north. 我们的位置是北纬40度。

【同】 parallel

【反】 longitude

launch [lɔːntʃ，lɑːntʃ] *v*. 1.发射(导弹、火箭等)；2.使开始，发动

【记】 来自拉丁语 lancea，长矛→掷出长矛→发射

【例】 1.They have *launched* a man-made satellite successfully. 他们成功地发射了一颗人造卫星。

2.They *launched* an aggressive election campaign. 他们发起了一次大张旗鼓的竞选活动。

【同】 fire；start

【派】 launcher *n*. 发射装置，发射器

laundry ['lɔːndrɪ] *n*. 洗衣店，所(送)洗的衣物

【记】 lau(nd)(洗)+ry(表地点的名词词尾)→洗衣服的地方→洗衣店

【例】 When does the wash come back from the *laundry*? 送到洗衣店的衣服什么时候取回来?

【同】 washhouse

laurel ['lɒrəl] *n*. 月桂树，桂冠

【例】 Our team won the regional *laurels*. 我们的球队赢得了地区冠军。

lavish ['lævɪʃ] *adj*. 过分丰富的，浪费的

【记】 lav(洗) + ish(形容词词尾)→如水一般的→浪费的

【例】 That is a vast and *lavish* party. 那是个规模盛大、极其铺张的宴会。

【同】 abundant，extravagant，wasteful

【反】 economical

lawn [lɔːn] *n*. 草地，草坪，草场

【例】 My mother asked me to mow the *lawn*. 妈妈让我去剪草坪。

【同】 grass

lawsuit ['lɔːsuːt，'lɔːsjuːt] *n*. 诉讼(尤指非刑事案件)

【记】 law(法律) + suit(诉讼)→诉讼

【例】 The victims have started a *lawsuit* to get compensation for their injuries. 受害者已经开始诉讼，要求得到损害赔偿。

【同】 case，suit

layout ['leɪˌaʊt] *n*. 格局，规划，版面设计

【记】 来自动词词组 lay out，摆开，展示→布局，规划

【例】 Please fax me the *layout* for the new catalogue. 请用传真机把新目录的版面编排图样传送给我。

【同】 design，plan

league [liːg] *n*. 同盟，联盟，联合会

【记】 leag(= lig 绑) + ue→绑在一起→同盟

【例】 Our club is a member of the Football *League*. 我们的俱乐部是足球联合会的一员。

【同】 association，federation，union

leak [liːk] *v*. /*n*. 1.漏，渗；2.泄露

【例】 1. Can you smell a gas *leak*? 你能闻到煤气漏气吗?

2. Who *leaked* the news to the press? 谁将新闻泄露给新闻界的?

【同】 drip，seep，trickle；disclose，reveal

【派】 leaky *adj*. 漏的

leap [liːp] *v*. (leapt，leapt 或-ed，-ed)跳，跳跃

【例】 1. The thief *leaped* the wall and ran away. 小偷越墙逃跑了。

2. His name *leapt* out at me from the newspaper. 报纸上他的名字一下子跳入我的眼帘。

【同】 bound，jump，spring

【派】 leapyear *n*. 闰年

lease [liːs] *n*. 租约；*v*. 出租，租借

【例】 1. The *lease* on our flat runs out in a few months. 我们公寓的租约还有几个月就到期了。

2. We will *lease* you the house for one year. 我们将把这房子租给你一年。

【同】 rent

leather ['leðə] *n*. 皮革，皮制品

【例】 Plastic is sometimes used instead of *leather*. 塑胶有时可以替代皮革。

【同】 hide, skin

legal ['liːgəl] *adj*. 法律的，属于法律范围的

【记】 leg(法律)+al(形容词词尾)→法律的

【例】 The sale of firearms is subject to many *legal* restrictions. 出售枪支受到许多法律限制。

【同】 judicial, legitimate

【派】 legally *adv*. 从法律上解释地，符合法律条文地

legacy ['legəsɪ] *n*. 遗产，遗物

【记】 leg(a)(指定)+cy(名词词尾)→被指定的东西→遗产

【例】 These are the cultural *legacies* of the Renaissance. 这些是文艺复兴时期的文化遗产。

【同】 bequest

legend ['ledʒənd] *n*. 传说，传奇

【记】 leg(读)+end(名词词尾)→被诵读的东西→传奇

【例】 The musician made the *legend* into a beautiful ballad. 这位音乐家把传说编成了一首美丽的民谣。

【同】 fable, fiction, folklore

【派】 legendary *adj*. 传奇的

legislation [ˌledʒɪs'leɪʃən] *n*. 立法，法律的制定(或通过)

【记】 legis(=leg, 法律)+lat(带来)+ion(名词词尾)→带来法律→立法

【例】 *Legislation* will be difficult and take time. 立法将是困难而又费时的。

【同】 lawmaking, enactment

【派】 (逆构)legislate *v*. 制定法律，立法

legislature *n*. 立法机关

lengthen ['leŋθən] *v*. 延长，(使)变长

【记】 length(长，长度)+en(动词词尾)→使变长

【例】 The days *lengthened* as summer approached. 随着夏天的到来，白昼变长了。

【同】 grow

【反】 shorten

【派】 (逆构)length *n*. 长度，长

legitimate [lɪ'dʒɪtɪmɪt] *adj*. 合法的，合理的

【记】 leg(法律)+itim(表示最高级)+ate(形容词词尾)→最符合法律的→合法的

【例】 I'm not sure that his business is strictly *legitimate*. 我说不好他的生意是否全部合法。

【同】 lawful, authentic

【反】 illegitimate

【派】 legitimacy *n*. 合法性，合理性，正统性

leisure ['leʒə, 'liːʒə] *adj*. 空闲的，悠闲的；*n*. 空闲，闲暇

【记】 leis(=lic, 允许)+ure(名词词尾)→(时间上)允许→空闲

【例】 1. How do you usually spend your *leisure* time? 你通常是怎样度过你的空闲时间？

2. Do it at your *leisure*; it is not urgent. 这事不急，你方便时再做。

【同】 free, easy, relaxing; vacation, spare time

【反】 busy

lethal ['li:θəl] *adj*. 致死的，会致死的

【记】 leth(Lethe 是希腊神话中冥府的河流，忘川，人饮其水，就忘却过去) + al(形容词词尾)→让人去喝忘川水的→去冥府的→致死的

【例】 A hammer can be a *lethal* weapon. 铁锤是可以致命的武器。

【同】 deadly, fatal

lexical ['leksɪkəl] *adj*. 词汇的

【记】 lexic(词，词汇) + al(形容词词尾)→词汇的

【例】 Lexicology is a branch of linguistics that deals with the *lexical* component of language. 词汇学是语言学的一个分支，主要研究构成一种语言的词汇。

【派】 (逆构)lexis *n*. (复数-xes)词，词汇

lexicon *n*. 词典，词汇手册

liability [ˌlaɪə'bɪlɪtɪ] *n*. 1.责任，义务；2.债务；3.妨碍，不利

【记】 lia(= lig，绑) + b + ility(名词词尾)→绑住的东西→责任，义务

【例】 1. The new law exempts them from all *liability* in these matters. 新的法律免除了他们在这些事上的所有责任和义务。

2. If your *liabilities* exceed your assets, you may go bankrupt. 如果你所负的债超过你的资产，你就会破产。

3. Bad pronunciation is a *liability* in being a narrator. 不良的发音是做解说员的不利条件。

【同】 obligation; indebtedness; limit

liable ['laɪəbl] *adj*. 1.有责任的，有义务的；2.有… 倾向的，很有可能的

【记】 lia(= lig，绑) + ble(形容词词尾)→被绑住的→有责任的

【例】 1. Be careful — if you have an accident I'll be *liable*. 小心——你要是出事故，我要负责的。

2. We are all *liable* to make mistakes. 我们都易犯错误。

【同】 accountable, responsible; apt, likely

【派】 liability *n*. 责任，义务；倾向

liaise [li:'eɪz] *v*. [法](英国口语中使用)做联络人，联络

【例】 What you can do is phone them up — we will, of course, *liaise* between you — and discuss your concerns with them. 您可以给他们打电话——当然，我们也会在你们之间做联络人——和他们讨论您关心的问题。

【派】 (逆构)liaison *n*. 联络

liberal ['lɪbərəl] *adj*. 自由主义的，宽松的

【记】 liber(自由) + al(形容词词尾)→自由的，宽松的

【例】 He returned from abroad with very *liberal* ideas. 他带着非常开明的思想从国外回来了。

【同】 free, tolerant

【反】 conservative, compulsory

L

【派】 liberty *n*. 自由，独立自主

liberation *n*. 解放，释放

license [ˈlaɪsəns] *v*. 批准、许可(从事某行业或活动)；*n*. 许可证，执照

(注意在美语中名词和动词均为 license，而在英语中 license 是动词，而名词则为 licence。)

【记】 licen(允许)＋se(动词词尾)→批准

【例】 1. They are only *licensed* for beer and expensive wine. 他们仅获准出售啤酒和昂贵的葡萄酒。

2. His *license* was suspended for six months. 他的执照被吊销 6 个月。

【同】 approve, authorize, permit

【反】 disapprove

【反】 licensed *adj*. 特许的，领有许可证的

liken [ˈlaɪkən] *v*. 把…比作

【记】 lik(e)(像…一样)＋en(动词词尾)→使像…一样→把…比作

【例】 Life can be *likened* to a journey with an unknown destination. 生命可以被比作一次不知目的地的旅行。

【同】 compare

limb [lɪm] *n*. 肢，臂，腿

【例】 Men and women have four *limbs*: two arms and two legs. 人都有四肢，两只胳膊两条腿。

limp [lɪmp] *v*./*n*. 蹒跚，瘸着走

【例】 1. His *limp* is the result of an accident. 他腿瘸是事故所致。

2. He *limped* off the football field. 他一瘸一拐地走出足球场。

【同】 hobble

linger [ˈlɪŋgə] *v*. 逗留，徘徊，缓慢消失

【例】 The beautiful melody is *lingering* in my mind. 美妙的音乐在我心中回荡。

【同】 dawdle, tarry, hover

【反】 rush

linguist [ˈlɪŋgwɪst] *n*. 语言学家

【记】 lingu(舌头，语言)＋ist(表示"人"的名词词尾)→会说多种语言的人→语言学家

【例】 The *linguist* went to study tribal language in the field. 语言学家去实地研究部落语言了。

【派】 linguistic *adj*. 语言的，语言学的

linguistics *n*. 语言学

link [lɪŋk] *v*./*n*. 联系，连接

【例】 1. Is there a *link* between smoking and lung disease? 吸烟与肺部疾病之间有关系吗?

2. Television stations around the world are *linked* by satellite. 全世界的电视台通过卫星联系一起。

【同】 associate, connect, join

【派】 linkage *n*. 联接

liquid [ˈlɪkwɪd] *adj*. 液体的，液态的；*n*. 液体，液态

【记】 liqu(液体)+id(形容词词尾)→液体的

【例】 1. The doctor recommended that the patient be fed *liquid* food. 医生建议病人应吃流质食物。

2. The *liquid* was 5 liters in volume. 该液体的体积为5升。

【同】 fluid

【反】 gaseous, solid

【派】 liquidity *n*. 流动性，流畅

literal [ˈlɪtərəl] *adj*. 字面上的，没有夸张的

【记】 liter(文字)+al(形容词词尾)→用文字表达的→字面上的

【例】 A *literal* translation is not always the closest to the original meaning. 逐字翻译不一定最接近原义。

【同】 actual, exact

【派】 literally *adv*. 字面意义地，真正地，不加夸张地

literate [ˈlɪtərɪt] *adj*. 有文化的，有阅读和写作能力的

【记】 liter(文字)+ate(形容词词尾)→能用文字表达的→有文化的

【记】 Every *literate* person should read this book. 凡有文化的人都该读一读此书。

【同】 educated, learned

【反】 illiterate

【派】 literacy *n*. 读写能力

literature [ˈlɪtərɪtʃə] *n*. 1. 文学，文学作品；2. 文献，资料

【记】 litera(文字)+ture(名词词尾)→写成文字的东西→文学

【例】 1. This book is titled *An Introduction to American Literature*. 这本书名为《美国文学指南》。

2. There is now extensive *literature* dealing with the First World War. 现有大量关于第一次世界大战的文献。

【派】 literary *adj*. 文学(上)的，文艺的

lithe [laɪð] *adj*. (指人、身体等)柔软的，易弯曲的

【例】 She has the *lithe* grace of a gymnast. 她有体操运动员轻盈而优美的体态。

【同】 flexible, lissome

【反】 rigid

litter [ˈlɪtə] *v*. 使凌乱，乱扔东西于

【例】 He was fined for *littering* on the sidewalks. 他因在人行横道上乱扔杂物而被罚款。

【同】 clutter, scrap

livestock [ˈlaɪvstɒk] *n*. 家养动物，家畜

【记】 live(活的)+stock(家畜)→家养动物

【例】 In the severe winter of 1947, farmers had to dig their *livestock* out of huge snowdrifts. 在1947年严峻的冬天，农民们不得不挖开大雪堆把他们的家畜救出来。

【同】 stock, cattle

load [ləʊd] *v*. 装载，使担负；*n*. 负荷，装载量

【例】 1. *Load* the furniture into the van. 把这些家具装上货车。

2. Her grief is a heavy *load* to bear. 她心情沉重得难以忍受。

【同】 burden，lade；cargo，shipment

【反】 unload

loan [ləʊn] *n*./*v*. 贷款，借

【例】 1. How much interest do they charge on *loans*? 他们贷款收多少利息？

2. The bank *loaned* me some money. 银行贷给了我一些钱。

【同】 lend

【派】 loanword *n*. 外来词，借用词

loath [ləʊθ] *adj*.（用作表语）不愿意的，厌恶的

【例】 He is *loath* to get out of bed on cold morning. 在寒冷的早晨他不愿意起床。

【同】 reluctant，unwilling

【反】 willing

【派】 loathe *v*. 厌恶，憎恶

loathsome *adj*. 令人讨厌的，令人厌恶的

lobby [ˈlɒbɪ] *n*./*v*. 游说；*n*. 大厅，休息室

【例】 1. The group tried to *lobby* the bill through. 这个集团企图通过游说议员通过该项法案。

2. The *lobby* was filled with partygoers. 门厅内挤满了参加聚会的人。

local [ˈləʊkəl] *adj*. 当地的，地方性的

L

【记】 loc(场所) + al(形容词词尾)→场所的→当地的

【例】 I suggest that he put an advertisement in the *local* paper. 我建议他在当地的报纸上登条广告。

【同】 regional，restricted

【派】 locality *n*. 地区

localize *v*. 使地方化，使本土化

locate [ləʊˈkeɪt] *v*. 1. 找到…位置，找到；2. 将(某物)设置在某处，使坐落于

【记】 loc(场所) + ate(形容词词尾)→使位于某个场所→使坐落于

【例】 1. We *located* the shops and the post office as soon as we moved into the town. 我们一搬进城里，就找到了商店和邮局的所在地。

2. The company wished to *locate* its new factory beside the river. 这家公司希望把新工厂设在河边。

【同】 find，identify；place，settle

【派】 location *n*. 位置，场所，地点

locomotive [ˌləʊkəˈməʊtɪv] *adj*. 移动的，运动的；*n*. 机车，火车头

【记】 loc(o)(位置) + mot(移动) + ive(形容词词尾)→位置发生移动的→移动的

【例】 1. It may be that the founding fathers overestimated the *locomotive* force of the collective and mutual self-interest. 开国功勋们可能过高地估计了集体的和相互的个人利益所能起的推动作用。

2. The US could no longer serve as the *locomotive* for the world economy. 美国再也无力承担世界经济推动力的重任了。

【同】 movable，moving；engine

【派】 locomotion *n*. 运动，移动

lodge [lɒdʒ] *v*. 临时住宿，寄宿

【例】 I'm *lodging* at Mrs Brown's house / with Mrs Brown. 我在布朗太太家寄宿。

【同】 accommodate, stay

【派】 lodging *n*. 寄宿处，寄宿；(通常用复数)出租的房间、住房

logic ['lɒdʒɪk] *n*. 逻辑，逻辑学

【例】 There's no *logic* in spending money on things you don't need. 把钱花在不需要的东西上是没有道理的。

【派】 logical *adj*. 合乎逻辑的，合理的
illogical *adj*. 不合逻辑的，不合理的

logistics [lə'dʒɪstɪks] *n*. 物流，后勤(学)

【记】 log(= lodge, 提供住宿) + ist(名词词尾) + ics(表示…学)→研究提供食宿的学科→后勤学

【例】 The *logistics* of supplying food to all the famine areas were very complex. 为向所有遭受饥荒的地区提供食物而做的后勤工作是非常复杂的。

【同】 provision, supply

【派】 logistical *adj*. 后勤的，物流的

logo ['lɒgəʊ] *n*. (logotype 的缩写)(公司或机构的)标志，徽标

【例】 The Longman *logo*, a small sailing ship, is on the cover of this book. 本书的封面上印有朗文公司的小帆船标志。

【同】 emblem, mark

longevity [lɒn'dʒevɪtɪ] *n*. 长寿

【记】 long(长的) + ev(年龄) + ity(名词词尾)→年龄长的→长寿

【例】 Proper rest and enough sleep contribute to *longevity*. 适当的休息和足够的睡眠有益于长寿。

longitude ['lɒndʒɪtju:d] *n*. 经度，经线

【记】 long(长的) + itude(名词词尾)→长的线，纵的线→经度

【例】 The town is at *longitude* 24 degrees east. 这个镇位于东经 24 度。

【反】 latitude

loom [lu:m] *v*. 隐隐呈现，(危险、忧虑等)逼近

【例】 The prospect of war *loomed* large in everyone's mind. 战事将起的庞大阴影威慑人心。

【同】 emerge, hover

loosen ['lu:sn] *v*. 松开，放松

【记】 loos(e)(松的) + en(动词词尾)→使变得松→松开

【例】 The government's control over the newspapers has *loosened* in recent years. 近年来政府已放松了对报纸的控制。

【同】 slacken, relax

【反】 tighten

【派】 (逆构)loose *adj*. 宽松的，松散的

loot [lu:t] *v*. 掠夺，抢劫

【例】 Rioters *looted* the shops. 暴动的人洗劫店铺。

L

【同】 plunder, rob

【派】 looter *n*. 掠夺者，抢劫者

lottery ['lɒtərɪ]n. 彩票，抽彩给奖法

【记】 lot(签，阄) + ter + y(名词词尾)→靠抽签的→彩票

【例】 She had the prize-winning *lottery* ticket. 她抽到了中奖的彩票。

【同】 drawing, raffle

lounge [laʊndʒ] *n*. 休息室

【记】 15 世纪苏格兰方言，懒洋洋地倚(靠，躺)→懒洋洋地倚(靠，躺)的地方→休息室

【例】 She is waiting for me in the departure *lounge*. 她在候机室等我。

【同】 waiting room

loyalty ['lɔɪəltɪ] *n*. 忠诚，忠心耿耿

【记】 loyal(忠诚的) + ty(名词词尾)→忠诚

【例】 All the men took a vow of *loyalty* to their leader. 所有士兵都发誓效忠他们的指挥官。

【同】 faithfulness, allegiance

【反】 disloyalty

【派】 (逆构)loyal *adj*. 忠诚的，忠心的

lucid ['luːsɪd] *adj*. 表达清楚的，易懂的

L

【记】 luc(明亮的) + id(形容词词尾)→明亮的→清楚易懂的

【例】 He is erudite and *lucid* about political affairs. 他对政治事物知识渊博，观点清晰。

【同】 clear, explicit

【反】 ambiguous, implicit

【派】 lucidity *n*. 明朗，清晰，透明

lucrative ['luːkrətɪv] *adj*. 获利的，赚钱的，合算的

【记】 lucr(钱) + ative(形容词词尾)→有钱的→获利的

【例】 Her husband is reaching after a more *lucrative* situation. 她丈夫正在谋求一个待遇较好的职位。

【同】 profitable

lumber ['lʌmbə] *n*. 木材，木料；*v*. 缓慢地移动

【例】 1. He has a *lumber*-mill. 他有一个锯木厂。
2. The old car *lumbered* up the hill. 那辆旧车摇摇晃晃地开上了小山。

【同】 timber, wood; pound

luminous ['ljuːmɪnəs] *adj*. 发光的，明亮的

【记】 lumin(光) + ous(形容词词尾)→发光的

【例】 There are many *luminous* road signs along the roads. 沿着路有许多夜光路标。

【同】 bright, glowing, shining

【反】 dark, dim

【派】 luminosity *n*. 【物】亮度，发光度；光辉

luggage ['lʌgɪdʒ] *n*. 行李

【记】 lug(g)(用力拖、拉) + age(名词词尾)→用力拖拉的东西→行李

【例】 Have you attached labels to the *luggage*? 你给行李系上标签了吗？

【同】 baggage, suitcase

lunar ['ljuːnə] *adj*. 月的，阴历的

【记】 lun(a)(月) + ar(形容词词尾)→月的→阴历的

【例】 It was reported that there would be a *lunar* eclipse tomorrow evening. 据报道说，明天晚上有月食。

lure [ljʊə] *n*./*v*. 引诱，诱惑

【例】 1. He left home because of the *lures* of the life in the city. 由于受到城市生活的诱惑，他离开了家。

2. The travel brochure *lured* me into taking a Caribbean vacation. 这本旅游小册子诱使我去加勒比地区度假。

【同】 attract, tempt

luster ['lʌstə] *n*. 1. 光彩，光泽；2. 声望

【记】 lust(光) + er(名词词尾)→闪光的东西→光彩

【例】 1. Her eyes lost their *luster*. 她的眼睛失去了光泽。

2. The company hopes that this prestigious publication will add a new *luster* to their image. 这家公司希望这一有声誉的出版物将给他们的形象增加新的光彩。

【同】 brightness, brilliance, splendor

【派】 lustrous *adj*. 有光泽的；光辉的

luxuriant [lʌg'zjʊərɪənt] *adj*. 丰富的，肥沃的，华丽的

【记】 luxuri(奢侈的) + ant(形容词词尾)→近乎奢侈的→华丽的

【例】 There is *luxuriant* tropical vegetation in our country. 我们国家有很多繁茂的热带植物。

【同】 abundant, exuberant

【反】 scanty, sterile

【派】 luxuriance *n*. 茂盛，丰富

luxurious [lʌg'zjʊərɪəs] *adj*. 豪华的，奢侈的

【记】 luxury(i)(奢侈的) + ious(形容词词尾)→奢侈的

【例】 This car is our most *luxurious* model. 这种汽车是我们最豪华的型号了。

【同】 sumptuous

【反】 economical, modest

【派】 (逆构)luxury *n*. 豪华，奢侈

lyric ['lɪrɪk] *n*. 抒情诗

【记】 lyr(古希腊弦乐器) + ic(学术用语的名词词尾)→用乐器唱的→歌→抒情诗

【例】 This is a good example of Shelley's *lyric* poetry. 这首诗是雪莱抒情诗的范例。

【同】 poem

【派】 lyricist *n*. 抒情诗人

M

magical ['mædʒɪkəl] *adj*. 神奇的，不可思议的

【记】 magic(魔法，魔术)＋al(形容词词尾)→魔术的→神奇的

【例】 She has a *magical* touch with the baby; he never cries when she is holding him. 她的手像有魔法似的，这个婴儿由她抱着就一声不哭。

【同】 charming, enchanting

【派】 (逆构)magic *n*. 魔术，魔力

magician *n*. 魔术师，术士

magnetic [mæg'netɪk] *adj*. 1.磁的，有磁性的；2.有吸引力的

【记】 magnet(磁铁)＋ic(形容词词尾)→有磁性的

【例】 1. The loop becomes *magnetic* when the current is switched on. 通电时线圈就会有磁性。

2. He has *magnetic* personality. 他有吸引人的个性。

【同】 alluring, attractive, drawing

【派】 magnetism *n*. 磁，磁力

magnetize *v*. 使磁化；吸引

magnificent [mæg'nɪfɪsnt] *adj*. 华丽的，高尚的，宏伟的

【记】 magni(大的)＋fic(做)＋ent(形容词词尾)→被做得很大的→宏伟的

【例】 These *magnificent* palaces impressed the foreigners deeply. 这些宏伟的宫殿给外宾们留下了深刻的印象。

【同】 grand, glorious, splendid

【派】 magnificence *n*. 华丽，富丽堂皇

magnify ['mægnɪfaɪ] *v*. 放大，夸大，夸张

【记】 magni(大的)＋fy(动词词尾，做)→放大

【例】 A microscope will *magnify* these germs, so that you can actually see them. 显微镜会放大这些细菌，使你能实际上看见它们。

【同】 amplify, enlarge, exaggerate

【反】 diminish, minify

【派】 magnification *n*. 扩大，放大

magnitude ['mægnɪtjuːd] *n*. 1.大小，数量；2.重要，重要性

【记】 magn(大的)＋itude(名词词尾)→大小

【例】 1. The *magnitude* of the epidemic was frightening. 这种流行病传播范围之广令人惶惶不安。

2. You don't appreciate the *magnitude* of her achievement. 你没有认识到她这一

成就的重大意义。

【同】 dimension，amount；importance

mainstream ［ˈmeɪnstriːm］ *adj*. 主流的；*n*. 主流，主要倾向

【记】 main(主要的)＋stream(河流)→主要的河流→主流

【例】 Their views lie outside the *mainsteam* of current medical opinion. 他们的观点不属于当前医学界观点的主流。

maintain ［menˈteɪn］ *v*. 保持，维持，保养

【记】 main(＝man，手)＋tain(拿，抓住)→用手拿住→保持

【例】 Part of my job is to *maintain* good relationship with our suppliers. 我的部分工作是同我们的供应商保持良好的关系。

【同】 keep，preserve，sustain

【派】 maintenance *n*. 维修，保养

majestic ［məˈdʒestɪk］ *adj*. 壮观的，庄严的

【记】 maj(大的)＋estic(形容词词尾)→宏大的→壮观的

【例】 Openings and closings were all accomplished with *majestic* rituality. 开幕和闭幕都是用隆重的仪式来完成的。

【同】 grand，imposing，imperial，magnificent

【派】 majesty *n*. 威严，最高权威

major ［ˈmeɪdʒə］ *adj*. 1.主要的，重大的；*n*. /*v*. (主修)专业

【例】 1. We have encountered *major* problems. 我们已遇到重大的问题。
2. Her *major* is French. 她的主修科目是法语。

【同】 greater，larger；subject

【反】 minor

【派】 majority *n*. 大多数

makeup ［meɪkʌp］ *n*. 1.补考；2.化妆，化妆品

【记】 来自词组 make up 弥补，化妆

【例】 1. The *makeup* was held in a huge auditorium. 补考在大礼堂进行。
2. I cannot tell who's who when the women take off their *makeup*. 女士们卸了妆，我就分辨不出谁是谁。

【同】 exam；cosmetics

malady ［ˈmælədɪ］ *n*. 疾病，弊病

【记】 mal(坏的，不好)＋ady(处于)→处于不好的状态→生病，疾病

【例】 Violent crime is only one of the *maladies* afflicting modern society. 暴力犯罪仅仅是危害社会的弊病之一。

【同】 illness，ailment

malfunction ［mælˈfʌŋkʃən］ *n*. 故障，失灵

【记】 mal(坏的)＋function(功能)→功能坏了→故障

【例】 Results have been delayed owing to a *malfunction* in the computer. 由于电脑发生故障，计算结果被推迟了。

【同】 failure，fault

M

malice [ˈmælɪs] *n*. 恶意，怨恨

【记】 mali(坏的) + ce(名词词尾)→坏的行为或状态→恶意

【例】 He got no advantage out of it; he did it from pure *malice*. 他并没有从中得到什么好处，他做此事纯粹出于恶意。

【同】 ill-will, spite

【反】 goodness

【派】 malicious *adj*. 怀恶意的，恶毒的

malign [məˈlaɪn] *v*. 诽谤，中伤；*adj*. 有害的，恶毒的

【记】 mali(坏的) + gn(= gen, 产生)→产生恶意→诽谤

【例】 1. She likes to *malign* innocent people. 她爱诋毁那些清白的人。

2. A *malign* tumour was found in his stomach. 在他的胃部发现了一个恶性肿瘤。

【同】 defame, slander; harmful

【反】 benign

【派】 malignant *adj*. 有害的，恶毒的，邪恶的

malnutrition [ˈmælnjuːˈtrɪʃən] *n*. 营养不良

【记】 mal(坏的) + nutri(营养) + tion(名词词尾)→坏的营养状况→营养不良

【例】 Most people in the area suffer from *malnutrition* at the best of times. 该地区里的多数人即使是在生活景况最好的时仍患有营养不良症。

mammal [ˈmæməl] *n*. 哺乳动物

【记】 mamma(乳房) + (a)l(名词词尾)→有乳房的→哺乳动物

【例】 Monkeys and dogs are *mammals*. 猴子和狗都是哺乳动物。

M

mandate [ˈmændeɪt] *n*. 命令，指令；*v*. 托管，授权

【记】 mand(命令) + ate(动词词尾)→给…下命令→托管

【例】 1. The government gave the police a *mandate* to reduce crime. 政府命令警方进一步打击犯罪活动。

2. Britain was *mandated* to govern the former colony of German East Africa. 英国受权代管德国在东非的前殖民地。

【同】 command, order; depute

【派】 mandatory *adj*. 命令的，强制的，托管的

maneuver [məˈnjuːvə] *n*. 策略，花招；*v*. 调遣，移动

【记】 man(手) + euv(操纵) + er(名词词尾)→用手操纵的东西→花招

【例】 1. There were secret *maneuvers* to get him removed out of from the job. 有秘密的手段把他撤职。

2. It was difficult to *maneuver* the bed into the room. 要把这张床搬进房里是很困难的。

【同】 tactic, trick

mangle [ˈmæŋgl] *v*. 撕裂，毁坏

【记】 man(手) + g + le(动词词尾)→用手弄坏→撕裂

【例】 There are many badly *mangled* bodies of those killed by the explosion. 那有许多在爆炸中被炸得残缺不全的尸体。

【同】 lacerate, mutilate, tear

manifest ['mænɪfest] *adj*. 显然的，明白的；*v*. 显示，表示

【记】 mani(手)+fest(打)→用手敲打，使…更明显→显然的

【例】 1. Fear was *manifest* on his face. 他脸上分明露出了恐惧的神色。

2. The symptoms *manifested* themselves ten days later. 十天后出现了症状。

【同】 apparent，evident；demonstrate，show

【反】 obscure；hide

【派】 manifestation *n*. 显示，表现

manipulate [mə'nɪpjuleɪt] *v*. (熟练地)操作，操纵

【记】 mani(手)+pul(填满)+ate(动词词尾)→用手填满→用手控制→操作

【例】 He accused the government of *manipulating* public opinion. 他谴责政府操纵公众舆论。

【同】 handle，manage，operate

【派】 manipulation *n*. 操作，操纵

mansion ['mænʃən] *n*. 大厦，公寓

【记】 mans(居住)+ion(名词词尾)→居住的地方→房屋，大厦

【例】 The broad steps in front of the *mansion* made it look very dignified. 宽阔的台阶使大厦的正面显得有气派。

【同】 house，palace

mantle ['mæntl] *n*. 1. 地幔；2. 覆盖物，披风

【例】 1. The earth has a core and a *mantle* around it. 地球的中心是地核，地核的周围是地幔。

2. The mountain was covered with a *mantle* of snow. 山上覆盖着一层雪。

【同】 cloak，cover，robe

manual ['mænjʊəl] *n*. 手册，指南；*adj*. 手的，手动的，体力的

【记】 manu(手)+al(形容词词尾)→与手有关的→手动的，体力的

【例】 1. A workshop *manual* gives diagrams and instructions for repairing your car. 维修手册向您提供修理汽车所需的图表和说明。

2. I've never driven a car with *manual* gears. 我从来没有开过手动档的车。

【同】 guidebook，handbook；hand-operated

【反】 automatic

manufacture [ˌmænjʊ'fæktʃə] *n*. / *v*. 生产，制造

【记】 manu(手)+fact(做)+ure(名词词尾)→用手做→制造

【例】 1. This firm *manufactures* cars. 这家公司大量生产汽车。

2. The *manufacture* of these small components is expensive. 制造这些小部件是非常昂贵的。

【同】 create，make，produce

【派】 manufacturer *n*. 生产者，制造商

manufacturing *adj*. 制造业的，制造的

manuscript ['mænjʊskrɪpt] *n*. 手稿，原稿

【记】 manu(手)+script(书写)→用手写的→手稿

【例】 The earliest extant *manuscript* of this poem has been kept in the museum. 此诗现

M

存最早的原稿收藏在这座博物馆里。

【同】 writing

march [mɑːtʃ] *n*. /*v*. 行进，行军

【例】 1. The soldiers had a long *march* in front of them to reach the camp before nightfall. 士兵们要经过长途行军，才能在黄昏前抵达营地。

2. The soldiers *marched* along the street. 士兵们行进在街道上。

【同】 walk，parade

margin [ˈmɑːdʒɪn] *n*. 1. 页边的空白，边缘；2. 盈余，利润

【记】 marg(= mark，记号) + in(名词词尾)→用来做记号的地方→页边的空白

【例】 1. I've made some suggestions in the *margins*. 我在空白处写了一些建议。

2. So it's possible，once the initial outlay has been made，for the farmer to be looking at very good profit *margins* indeed. 所以，对于农民来说，一旦做了初步的投资，他们可能关注的是有非常好的盈利空间。

【同】 border，edge

【派】 marginal *adj*. 边缘的，边际的

marginalize *v*. 使边缘化

marine [məˈriːn] *adj*. 海的，海中的，海船的

【记】 marin(海) + e→与海有关的→海的，海中的

【例】 *Marine* creatures are those which live in the sea. 海洋生物是生存在海里的生物。

【同】 maritime

【派】 mariner *n*. 船员，水手

M

maritime [ˈmærɪtaɪm] *adj*. 海上的，海事的，海运的

【记】 mari(海) + tim(来源不明) + e→与海有关的→海事的

【例】 Good morning everyone，and welcome to the *Maritime* Museum. 各位早上好！欢迎大家来到海事博物馆。

【同】 marine

marsh [mɑːʃ] *n*. 湿地，沼泽

【例】 It's dangerous to be alone in the *marsh*. 一个人在沼泽地里是很危险的。

【同】 wetland

【派】 marshy *adj*. 沼泽的

marshal [ˈmɑːʃəl] *v*. (-l(l)ed; -l(l)ing)排列，集结；*n*. 司仪，指挥

【例】 1. The route will be signposted and the participants will be *marshalled*. 路线将用路标标示出，参加者将被编成纵队。

2. If you need help along the route，please inform one of the *marshals*. 如果您在行走中需要帮助，请告诉其中的一位司仪。

【同】 arrange，gather；usher，guide

marvel [ˈmɑːvəl] *n*. 奇迹，奇异的事

【记】 marv(= mir，惊奇) + el(名词词尾)→令人惊奇的事情→奇迹

【例】 It was a real *marvel* that the baby was unhurt when he fell from the fifth floor. 那婴儿从五楼摔下来竟没受伤真是一个奇迹。

【同】 wonder

【派】 marvelous *adj*. 不可思议的，非凡的

mass [mæs] *adj*. 大量的，大规模的；*n*. 团，大量，大批

【例】 1. It's a *mass* extinction, and whether we will ever rebound from the loss is difficult to know. 这是一种大规模的消失，我们能否挽回这种局面现在很难说。

2. The quantity of these gases, again multiplied over 3, 500 million years, is enough to explain the *mass* of the world's atmosphere. 这些气体的量同样在 35 亿年的时间里成倍增加，足以说明世界的大气之多。

【同】 large-scale; chunk, heap

【反】 bit

【派】 massive *adj*. 大而重的，大块的，厚实的

massacre ['mæsəkə] *n*. 残杀，大屠杀

【记】 来自古法语 macecle 屠杀

【例】 The press has reported the *massacre* of thousands of people for their religious beliefs. 新闻界报道了那场因宗教信仰原因而对数以千计的人的大屠杀。

【同】 butchery, carnage, killing, slaughter

massage ['mæsɑːʒ] *n*./*v*. 按摩

【记】 massa(抚摸) + (a)ge(名词词尾)→抚摸→按摩

【例】 I want somebody to *massage* my shoulders. 我想要有人给我按摩肩膀。

【同】 knead

masterpiece ['mɑːstəpiːs] *n*. 杰作，名著

【记】 master(主人，大师) + piece(一件作品)→大师的一件作品→杰作

【例】 Technically the building is a *masterpiece*, but few people like it. 就技术而言那座建筑物是杰作，但却没人喜欢。

match [mætʃ] *n*. 1. 火柴；2. 比赛；*v*. 搭配，使…相配

【例】 1. She lit a cigar with a *match*. 她用一根火柴点燃了雪茄。

2. Our team has won the football *match*. 我们队赢得了足球赛。

3. The curtains don't *match* the paint. 窗帘和油漆不相配。

【同】 contest, game; correspond, pair

【派】 matchable *adj*. 可匹敌的，对等的

matchless *adj*. 无敌的，无比的

mate [meɪt] *n*. 朋友，伙伴；*v*. 成配偶，(鸟、兽)交配

【例】 1. The light is used by the adult fireflies as a signal to attract a *mate*. 成年萤火虫用这种光作为求偶的信号。

2. Birds mate in the spring. 鸟儿在春天交配。

【同】 partner; copulate, match

maternal [mə'tɜːnl] *adj*. 母亲的，母性的，母系的

【记】 mater(母亲) + nal(形容词词尾)→描述母亲般的特性→母性的

【例】 Your *maternal* instincts go deeper than you think. 你的母性本能远比你想象的强。

【同】 motherly

【反】 paternal

mature [mə'tjuə] *adj*. 成熟的，充分考虑的

M

【例】 You are a *mature* man now; you are no longer a boy. 你现在是成人了，不再是孩子了。

【同】 full-grown, ripe

【反】 immature

【派】 maturity *n*. 成熟，完备

maxim [ˈmæksɪm] *n*. 格言，普遍真理

【记】 max(伟大的) + im(主张)→伟大的主张→真理，格言

【例】 "Waste not, want not" is her favorite *maxim*. "不浪费则不匮乏"是她特别喜爱的格言。

【同】 adage, proverb

maximum [ˈmæksɪməm] *n*. (复数-ma 或 - mums)最大量，最大值；*adj*. 最大的

【记】 max(大的) + mum(拉丁文的最高级词尾)→最大的

【例】 1. Students on a visitor visa or work permit may study for a *maximum* of 3 months. 持有访问签证或工作许可的学生最多可以学习三个月。

2. The *maximum* temperature in July may be 36 degrees Celsius. 七月份最高温度可能达到 36 摄氏度。

【同】 greatest, utmost, maximal

【反】 minimum

【派】 maximal *adj*. 最大的，最高的

maximize *v*. 使(某事物)增至最大值

M

maze [meɪz] *n*. 迷宫，迷惑

【例】 She was lost in the *maze* for several hours. 她在迷宫中迷了路，浪费了好几个小时。

【同】 labyrinth

meadow [ˈmedəʊ] *n*. 草地，牧场

【记】 mead(古英语用来指草地) + ow(名词词尾)→草地

【例】 There are lambs frisking in the *meadow*. 那儿有些在草地上跳来跳去的小羊。

【同】 grassland, pasture

meager [ˈmiːɡə] *adj*. 贫乏的，不足的

【记】 merg(瘦的) + er(形容词词尾)→瘦的→贫乏的

【例】 He had to support his family with his *meager* income. 他只能靠微薄的收入来养家。

【同】 poor, scanty

【反】 ample, plentiful

meander [mɪˈændə] *v*. 1. 蜿蜒曲折，漫步；2. 漫谈，闲聊

【记】 来自希腊语，本是一条河的名字，以蜿蜒曲折而著称

【例】 1. We usually *meander* down to the pub after dinner. 晚饭之后我们经常漫步去酒吧。

2. The discussion *meandered* (on) for hours. 讨论会漫无边际地进行了几小时。

【同】 twist, wander; stray

mechanical [mɪˈkænɪkl] *adj*. 机械的，与机械有关的

【记】 mechan(机器) + ic(表示人的名词词尾) + al(形容词词尾)→与机器有关的→机械的

【例】 The new car had to be withdrawn from the market because of a *mechanical* defect. 那种新汽车因有机械缺陷只好撤出市场。

【同】 automatic

【反】 manual

【派】 (逆构)mechanic *n*. 机械师，技工

mechanism *n*. 【生】机制，机理

meddle ['medl] *v*. 干涉，管闲事

【记】 medd(混合) + le(动词词尾)→混合进去→干涉

【例】 Don't *meddle* in my affairs. 别干预我的事情。

【同】 interfere，trespass

media ['miːdjə] *n*. (medium 的复数)新闻媒介，媒体

【例】 A third source of confusion is the attitude of the *media*. 媒体的态度是造成混乱的第三个根源。

mediate ['miːdɪeɪt] *v*. 斡旋，调停

【记】 medi(中间) + ate(动词词尾)→进入中间→调停

【例】 He cooled the situation down by offering to *mediate* between the disputing parties. 他提出愿为争执的双方调停，情况因此缓和下来。

【同】 arbitrate，intercede，intervene

【派】 mediator *n*. 调停者

M

medieval [ˌmedɪ'iːvəl] *adj*. 中世纪的

【记】 medi(中间) + ev(时代) + al(形容词词尾)→中时代的→中世纪的

【例】 Knighthood was an ideal in *medieval* Europe. 在中世纪的欧洲，骑士是一种风范。

meditate ['medɪteɪt] *v*. 想，(尤指宗教上的)沉思

【记】 med(治疗) + it + ate(动词词尾)→治疗内心→沉思

【例】 He sat there *meditating* on his misfortunes. 他坐在那儿思索着自己不幸的事。

【同】 deliberate，ponder，reflect，think

【派】 meditative *adj*. 深思的

meditation *n*. 沉思，冥想

megacity ['megəsɪtɪ] *n*. 特大城市，巨型城市

【记】 mega(兆，大的) + city(城市)→大城市

【例】 The United Nations has estimated that in the year 2000 there will be twenty-four *megacities*. 联合国预测在2000年将有24个特大城市。

melancholy ['melənkəlɪ] *n*. 忧郁，悲哀；*adj*. 忧郁的，悲伤的，令人消沉的

【记】 melan(黑色) + chol(胆汁) + y(形容词词尾)→分泌黑色胆汁多的→忧郁的(苏格拉底认为忧郁是因为黑色胆汁太多的缘故，所以给了 melancholia(忧郁症)这个名字。)

【例】 There is a vein of *melancholy* in his character. 他的性格中有少许忧郁的气质。

【同】 blue，depressing，gloomy

【反】 cheerful，delightful，happy

melody [ˈmelədɪ] *n*. 美妙的音乐，旋律

【记】 mel(= 希腊文 melos，歌曲) + ody(歌，歌唱)→歌唱歌曲→旋律

【例】 The beautiful *melody* is lingering in my mind. 美妙的音乐在我心中回荡。

【同】 song，tune

【派】 melodic *adj*. 有旋律的，调子美妙的

melt [melt] *v*. (melted，molten；melting)融化，熔化，溶解

【例】 These chocolates really *melt* in your mouth. 这些巧克力真正是入口即化。

【同】 dissolve，liquefy

【反】 freeze，solidify

【派】 meltability *n*. 可融性，可熔性

meltage *n*. 熔化，融化，溶解

memorandum [ˌmeməˈrændəm] *n*. (= memo)(复数-dums 或-da)备忘录，便笺

【记】 memor(记忆) + and(= be，是) + um(名词词尾)→成为记忆的→备忘录

【例】 His suggestion was contained in a *memorandum* published here today. 他的建议是今天在这里发表的一项备忘录中提出的。

【同】 memo，memoire

memory [ˈmemərɪ] n 记忆力，记忆

【记】 memor(记忆) + y(名词词尾)→记忆

【例】 We first met in New York，if my *memory* serves me. 如果我没记错的话，我们第一次相遇是在纽约。

M

【同】 remembrance，recollection

【派】 memorize *v*. 记住，记忆

memorization *n*. 记住，背诵

memorable *adj*. 值得纪念的，难忘的

memorial *adj*. 纪念的，记忆的；*n*. 纪念物，纪念馆

menace [ˈmenəs] *n*. 威胁，恐吓

【记】 mena(= mina，突出，伸出) + (a)ce(表示抽象名词的词尾)→伸出以恐吓→威胁

【例】 That film creates an atmosphere of *menace*. 那部影片营造出吓人的气氛。

【同】 threat

mend [mend] *v*. 修补，改进

【例】 Can you *mend* the hole in my shirt? 你能补一下我衬衫上的洞吗？

【同】 patch，repair

mental [ˈmentl] *adj*. 精神的，智力的

【记】 ment(想) + al(形容词词尾)→思想上的→心理的，精神的

【例】 His problem is *mental*，not physical. 他的问题是心理的而不是身体的。

【同】 intellectual，moral

【反】 material，physical

【派】 mentality *n*. 智力，精神，心理

mention [ˈmenʃən] *v*. /*n*. 提及，提到

【记】 ment(想) + ion(名词词尾)→从心里发出来→想到→提到

【例】 You never *mentioned* that you are married. 你从没有提起过你已经结了婚了。

【同】 note, name, observe

menu ['menjuː] *n*. 菜单，饭菜

【例】 They say with such large numbers we have to choose the *menu* in advance. 他们说因为人比较多，我们必须提前选好菜单。

【同】 list

merchandise ['mɜːtʃəndaɪz] *n*. 商品，货物；*v*. 推销，销售

【记】 merch(= merc，贸易) + and(= ant，表示人的名词词尾) + ise(表示物品的名词词尾)→人用来做贸易的东西→商品

【例】 1. The store has the best *merchandise* in town. 这家商店有镇上最好的商品。
2. If this product is properly *merchandised*, it should sell very well. 这种产品如果推销得好，就会很好卖。

【同】 goods; trade

【派】 merchandising *n*. 新产品计划和开发，销售规划

merchant ['mɜːtʃənt] *n*. 商人，贸易商

【记】 merch(= merc，贸易) + ant(表示人的名词词尾)→做贸易的人→商人

【例】 The *merchant* decided to use camels to carry his goods across the desert. 商人决定用骆驼载运货物穿过沙漠。

【同】 businessman, seller, trader

mercy ['mɜːsɪ] *n*. 仁慈，怜悯，宽恕

【记】 merc(贸易，报酬) + y(名词词尾)→给予他人的东西→怜悯

【例】 The king showed no *mercy* and killed all the prisoners. 这个国王没有宽容之心，杀死了所有的犯人。

【同】 compassion, pity, sympathy

【反】 cruelty

【派】 merciful *adj*. 仁慈的，慈悲的

merge [mɜːdʒ] *v*. 兼并，合并

【记】 merge→沉没，没入→合并

【例】 The bank *merged* with its major rival. 该银行与其主要对手合并了。

【同】 combine, mingle, mix

【派】 merger *n*. 合并，归并

merit ['merɪt] *n*. 美德，优点，价值

【记】 来自拉丁语 merere，值得→值得赞扬的→美德

【例】 There is little *merit* in passing the examination if you cheated. 如果你考试作弊了，那么考试及格也就没有一点价值。

【同】 excellence, value, worth

【反】 demerit, fault

message ['mesɪdʒ] *n*. 信息，消息

【记】 mess(送) + age(名词词尾)→送给人的东西→信息

【例】 Wittingly or unwittingly, how we look sends all sorts of powerful subliminal *messages* to other people. 我们的外表有意无意地在向其他人传递各种强烈的潜意识信息。

M

【同】 letter，note，word

【派】 messenger *n*. 报信者，使者

messy ['mesɪ] *adj*. 肮脏的，凌乱的

【记】 mess(混乱)+y(形容词词尾)→混乱的→凌乱的

【例】 The kitchen's always so *messy* after we've had guests. 家里来了客人之后，厨房总是那么乱。

【同】 mussy，untidy

【反】 clean，tidy

【派】 (逆构)mess *v*. /*n*. 混乱，弄乱

metabolism [me'tæbəlɪzəm] *n*. 新陈代谢

【记】 meta(变化)+bol(投掷)+ism(名词词尾)→变化之后再投入→用新的代替旧的→. 新陈代谢

【例】 The dosage was geared down to a level which would work on the infected cells but not upset their *metabolism*. 药剂量要减少到既能对受感染细胞起作用，又不损害它们的代谢作用。

【派】 metabolic *adj*. 新陈代谢的

metal ['metl] *n*. 金属，金属制品

【例】 Copper and gold are both *metals*. 铜和金都是金属。

【派】 metallic *adj*. (似)金属的

metaphor ['metəfə] *n*. 比喻，象征

【记】 meta(变化)+phor(带来)→(语言)改变着说→比喻

【例】 We have found that the blind understand other kinds of visual *metaphors* as well. 我们发现，盲人还能理解其他类型的视觉比喻。

【同】 figure，symbol

【派】 metaphorical *adj*. 比喻的，比喻意义的

meteor ['miːtjə] *n*. 流星

【记】 met(在…中)+eor(悬浮的东西)→在空中飞的东西→流星

【例】 It is said that if you make a wish when you see a *meteor* in the sky your wish will be realized. 据说如果你在看见流星时许个愿，愿望就会实现。

【派】 meteorite *n*. 陨星，陨石

meteorologist [ˌmiːtjə'rɒlədʒɪst] *n*. 气象学家

【记】 meteor(流星，引申为天气)+olog(…学)+ist(名词词尾)→研究天气的学科的人→气象学家

【例】 TV weather forcaters prefer to be called *meteorologists*. 电视天气预报员更愿意人们称自己气象学家。

【派】 (逆构)meteorology *n*. 气象学

meteorological *adj*. 气象学的

methodology [meθə'dɒlədʒɪ] *n*. 方法学，方法论

【记】 method(方法)+ology(…学)→研究方法的学科→方法学

【例】 One *methodology* is chosen and others discarded. 一种方法被选用了，而其他方法被舍弃了。

M

【派】 methodological *adj*. 方法的

methodologist *n*. 方法论学者，方法学家

metropolitan [metrə'pɒlɪtən] *adj*. 大城市的，大都会的，属大城市的

【记】 metro(母亲) + polit(= polis，城市) + an(形容词词尾)→城市之母的→大城市的

【例】 She left the small island and became famous in *metropolitan* France. 她离开小岛而在法国的大都市中成名。

【同】 municipal，urban

【派】 (逆构)metropolis *n*. 主要都市，大城市，首都

microcosm ['maɪkrəkɒzəm] *n*. 微观世界，缩影

【记】 micro(小的) + cosm(宇宙)→小的宇宙→微观世界

【例】 This town is a *microcosm* of our world. 这个市镇是我们这个世界的缩影。

【反】 macrocosm

microscope ['maɪkrəskəup] *n*. 显微镜

【记】 micro(小的) + scope(看)→观察小东西之物→显微镜

【例】 The *microscope* magnified the object 100 times. 这台显微镜将物体放大了100倍。

【派】 microscopic *adj*. 用显微镜可见的；极小的

mighty ['maɪtɪ] *adj*. 强大的，巨大的

【记】 might(力量) + y(形容词词尾)→有力量的→强大的

【例】 The United Kingdom was a *mighty* empire before World War I. 英联邦在第一次世界大战前曾是一个强大的帝国。

【同】 powerful，strong

【反】 weak

migrate [maɪ'greɪt 'maɪgreɪt] *v*. 迁移，移动

【记】 migr(移动) + ate(动词词尾)→移动

【例】 In some developing countries more and more people *migrate* to urban areas. 在某些发展中的国家，越来越多的人向市区迁移。

【同】 move

【反】 remain

【派】 migration *n*. 迁徙

migrant *n*. 候鸟；移民

migratory *adj*. 迁移的；流浪的

milestone ['maɪlstəun] *n*. 里程碑，重大事件

【记】 mile(英里) + stone(石头)→里程碑

【例】 Each birthday is a *milestone* we touch along life's way. 每个生日都是我们人生之旅的一个里程碑。

【同】 milepost，landmark

military ['mɪlɪtərɪ] *adj*. 军事的，军用的；*n*. (集合名词)军队，军人

【记】 milit(士兵) + ary(形容词词尾)→与士兵有关的→军事的，军用的

【例】 In some countries all the young men do a year's *military* service. 有些国家，所有年轻男子都要服一年兵役。

【同】 army，martial

M

【反】 civil, civilian

millennium [mɪ'lenɪəm] *n*.（复数-ia）一千年，千禧年

【记】 mill(e)(千)+enn(年)+ium(名词词尾)→一千年

【例】 How did you celebrate the *Mellennium*? 你们是怎样庆祝千禧年的?

mimic ['mɪmɪk] *v*.（-micked；-micking）模仿，摹拟

【记】 mim(e)(模仿)+ic(形容词词尾此处转用作动词)→模仿

【例】 The goal they shared was an attempt to capture or *mimic* human abilities using machines. 它们的一个共同目标就是试图运用机器捕捉或者是模仿人类的能力。

【同】 imitate, copy

【派】 mimical *adj*. 模仿的，假装的

mimicry *n*.【生物】拟态，模仿

mineral ['mɪnərəl] *n*. 无机物，矿物；*adj*. 矿物的，含矿物的，无机的

【记】 miner(a)(=mine，矿)+al(形容词词尾)→矿物的

【例】 1. Few coaches, for instance, understand how deficiencies in trace *minerals* can lead to injuries. 比方说，很少有教练明白缺少微量元素怎么能导致受伤。

2. I'd love a really chilled *mineral* water or something. 我想来点冰冻的矿泉水或者别的什么。

mingle ['mɪŋgl] *v*.（使）混合，（使）结合

【记】 ming(混合)+le(动词词尾)→使混合

【例】 She accepted the money with *mingled* feelings. 她悲喜交集地收下了这笔钱。

【同】 blend, mix

M

minimum ['mɪnɪməm] *n*. 最少量，最小值

【记】 mini(小的)+mun(拉丁文的最高级词尾)→最小值

【例】 Repairing your car will cost a *minimum* of 100 dollars. 修理你的汽车最低限度要100美元。

【同】 least, lowest

【反】 maximum

【派】 minimize *v*. 将…减到最少，最小化

minimal *adj*. 最小的，最少的

minor ['maɪnə] *adj*. 较小的，无关紧要的

【记】 min(小的)+or(比较级词尾)→较小的

【例】 She acted as a *minor* role in the play. 她在剧中扮演了一个次要的角色。

【同】 lesser, lower

【反】 major

【派】 minority *n*. 少数，少数民族

minute ['mɪnɪt] *n*. 分钟，片刻；[maɪ'njuːt] *adj*. 微小的，仔细而准确的

【记】 min(小的)+ute(名词词尾)→把一小时分成小片段→分钟

【例】 1. The park is only five *minutes* from downtown. 这个花园离市中心只有五分钟的路程。

2. I had remembered in *minute* detail everything that had happened. 我对发生的每件事的细枝末节都记得清清楚楚。

【同】 moment, instant; small, tiny

【反】 broad, immense

miracle [ˈmɪrəkl] *n*. 奇迹，奇事

【记】 mir(a)(惊讶)＋cle(名词词尾)→让人惊奇的东西→奇迹

【例】 It's a *miracle* you weren't killed in that car crash! 你在那次汽车撞车事故中大难不死，真不可思议！

【派】 miraculous *adj*. 奇迹的，不可思议的

mirage [ˈmɪrɑːʒ] *n*. 海市蜃楼，幻景

【记】 mir(惊讶)＋age(名词词尾)→令人吃惊的东西→海市蜃楼

【例】 A *mirage* is an optical illusion. 海市蜃楼是一种视错觉。

【同】 illusion

miserable [ˈmɪzərəbl] *adj*. 痛苦的，可怜的

【记】 miser(可怜)＋ able(形容词词尾)→可怜的

【例】 There are still many people whose living conditions are *miserable*. 仍有许多人的生活条件是很艰苦的。

【同】 dismal, sorry, unhappy

【反】 happy

【派】 misery *n*. 痛苦，悲惨

misgiving [mɪsˈgɪvɪŋ] *n*. 疑惧，疑虑

【记】 mis(错的)＋giv(给)＋ing(加在动词后面变名词)→错误的感觉→疑虑

【例】 I have many *misgivings* about taking the job. 我对是否接受那项工作顾虑重重。

【同】 mistrust, suspicion

【派】 (逆构)misgive *v*. (-gave, -given)疑虑，怀疑

mishap [ˈmɪshæp, mɪsˈhæp] *n*. 不幸，灾祸

【记】 mis(坏的)＋hap(运气)→坏的运气→不幸

【例】 My whole morning's work has been put out of gear by that *mishap*. 我一个上午的工作全让这倒霉的事给弄得乱了套。

【同】 accident, misfortune

【反】 fortune, luck

mislead [mɪsˈliːd] *v*. (-led, -led)引入歧途，误导

【记】 mis(错误)＋lead(引导)→错误地引导→误导

【例】 He *misled* me into thinking he was rich. 他使我误以为他很有钱。

【同】 misdirect

【反】 lead

【派】 misleading *adj*. 使人产生误解的，误导的

missile [ˈmɪsaɪl, -səl] *n*. 导弹，发射物

【记】 miss(投掷)＋ ile(名词词尾)→被投掷上去的东西→发射物

【例】 A defect in the fuel lines prevented the *missile* from blasting off. 燃料管路上的一个缺陷妨碍了导弹的发射。

【同】 projectile

mission [ˈmɪʃən] *n*. 1. 使命，任务；2. 使团，代表团

M

【记】 miss(送，投)+ion(名词词尾)→奉命送达→使命

【例】 1. He has been on confidential *missions* to Berlin. 他前往柏林执行秘密任务。

2. An official *mission* was sent to settle the dispute. 一个官方使团被派去解决争端。

【同】 assignment; delegation

mitigate [ˈmɪtɪgeɪt] *v*. 使减轻，使缓和

【记】 mit(温和)+ig(做)+ate(动词词尾)→使变得温和→使减轻

【例】 The government is trying to *mitigate* the effects of inflation. 政府正试图缓和通货膨胀的影响。

【同】 alleviate, lessen

【反】 aggravate, deteriorate

【派】 mitigation *n*. 缓解，减轻，平静

mixture [ˈmɪkstʃə] *n*. 混合，混合物

【记】 mix(混合)+ture(名词词尾)→混合，混合物

【例】 Air is a *mixture*, not a compound of gases. 空气是气体的混合物，不是化合物。

【同】 combination, blend

【派】 (逆构)mix *v*. (使)混和，混淆

mobile [ˈməʊbaɪl] *adj*. 可移动的，易变的

【记】 mob(移动)+ile(形容词词尾)→可移动的

【例】 It was a great relief to the patient with the broken leg when he finally became *mobile* again after two months. 这位腿骨骨折患者经过两个多月的治疗又能行动了，这对他真是莫大的安慰。

M

【同】 movable, changeable

【反】 immobile, stabile

【派】 mobility *n*. 活动性，灵活性

mode [məʊd] *n*. 方式，模式，风格

【例】 Yet cars easily surpass trains or buses as a flexible and convenient *mode* of personal transport. 然而，作为一种灵活而又方便的个人交通方式，小汽车很轻易地就超过了火车和公共汽车。

【同】 fashion, form, manner, style

moderate [ˈmɒdərɪt] *adj*. 适度的，中等的

【记】 mod(模式)+er+ate(形容词词尾)→能放在一个模式里的→适度的

【例】 Tomorrow winds will be light to *moderate*. 明天的风力为轻度到中度。

【同】 medium, modest, temperate

【反】 immoderate

【派】 moderation *n*. 适度，合理

modest [ˈmɒdɪst] *adj*. 1.适度的，适中的；2.谦虚的

【记】 mod(模式)+est→放在一个模式里的→适度的

【例】 1. I bought the house at a *modest* price. 我以适中的价格买下了这所房子。

2. The young actress is very *modest* about her success; she says it's as much the result of good luck as of her own talent. 这位年轻的女演员对她的成功表现得很谦

虚，她说，她的成功一半靠自己的天赋，一半也靠运气好。

【同】 humble, lowly, moderate

【反】 immodest

【派】 modesty *n*. 谦逊，虚心

modify [ˈmɒdɪfaɪ] *v*. 修改，更改

【记】 mod(模式)＋ify(动词词尾，做)→为适合模式而加以改变→更改

【例】 The policy was agreed by the committee, but only in a *modified* form. 那项政策经修改后才获得委员会同意。

【同】 change, alter, vary

【派】 modification *n*. 修改，改变

modified *adj*. 改良的，改进的

modulate [ˈmɒdjʊleɪt] *v*. 调整，调节

【记】 mod(模式)＋ul＋ate(动词词尾)→使 符合…模式→调整

【例】 He has a very monotonous voice; he should *modulate* it more. 他的声音很单调，应该加以调整。

【同】 adjust, change

【派】 modulation *n*. 调制，调整

moisture [ˈmɔɪstʃə] *n*. 湿度，水分

【记】 moist(潮湿的)＋ure(名词词尾)→潮湿

【例】 The plants drink in *moisture* from the atmosphere. 植物从大气中吸取水分。

【同】 wet

【反】 dry

【派】 (逆构)moist *adj*. 潮湿的

mold [məʊld] *n*. 模子，铸型；*v*. 浇铸，塑造

【例】 1. He is cast in his father's *mold*. 他长得和他父亲一模一样。

2. Children *mold* figures out of clay. 孩子们用粘土做泥人。

【同】 container, model; form, shape

molecule [ˈmɒlɪkjuːl, ˈməʊ-] *n*. 分子

【记】 mole(堆，一团)＋cule(表示"小"的名词词尾)→小团团→分子

【例】 A *molecule* is made up of atoms. 分子由原子组成。

【派】 molecular *adj*. 分子的

mollify [ˈmɒlɪfaɪ] *v*. 抚慰，平息

【记】 moll(软的)＋ify(动词词尾)→使软下来→平息

【例】 He bought his angry wife a gift, but she refused to be *mollified*. 他买了一件礼物给生气的妻子，但她不肯就此息怒。

【同】 appease, pacify

【反】 exasperate

【派】 mollification *n*. 缓和

momentum [məʊˈmentəm] *n*. (复数-ta 或－ tums)动力，要素

【记】 mom(移动)＋ent(名词词尾)＋um(名词词尾)→使移动的力量→动力

【例】 The movement was gaining *momentum*. 这运动势头越来越大。

【同】 force，impetus

【派】 momentous *adj*. 极重要的，严重的

monarch ['mɒnək] *n*. 君主，帝王

【记】 mon(一) + arch(统治)→一个人统治→君主

【例】 They attempted to overthrow the *monarch*. 他们企图推翻国王。

【同】 emperor，king，ruler

【派】 monarchy *n*. 君主政体，君主政治

monetary ['mʌnɪtərɪ] *adj*. 货币的，金钱的

【记】 moneta(= money，钱) + ry(形容词词尾)→货币的

【例】 The *monetary* system of some countries used to be based on gold. 过去有些国家的货币制度是金本位制的。

【同】 pecuniary

monitor ['mɒnɪtə] *n*. 1. 班长；2. 监视器，监控器；*v*. 监测，监控

【记】 monit(忠告，提醒) + or(名词词尾)→提出劝告的人或物→监视器

【例】 1. Jimmy has been made dinner money *monitor*. 吉米被选为班上收餐费的班长。

2. The *monitors* showed the patient's heartbeats to be above normal. 监视器显示病人的心跳次数超过了正常值。

3. We *monitor* the enemy's radio broadcasts for political information. 我们为了收集政治情报而监听敌方的电台广播。

【同】 reminder；supervise

M

monolog ['mɒnəlɒg] *n*. 独白(= monologue)

【记】 mono(一个) + log(说)→一个人说→独白

【例】 There will be a conversation between two speakers and then a *monologue*. 先是两个人的谈话，然后是一段独白。

【同】 soliloquy

【反】 dialogue

monopoly [mə'nɒpəlɪ] *n*. 垄断，专利事业

【记】 mono(一个) + poly(卖)→一个人卖→垄断

【例】 In some countries tobacco is a government *monopoly*. 在有些国家烟草是政府的专卖品。

【同】 control，possession

【派】 monopolize *v*. 独占，垄断

monotonous [mə'nɒtənəs] *adj*. 单调的，单一得令人厌倦的

【记】 mono(一个) + ton(语调) + ous(形容词词尾)→语调单一的→单调的

【例】 I only heard a *monotonous* voice of the singer. 我只听到那个歌唱家单调的声音。

【同】 boring，dull，monotonic

【反】 various

【派】 monotony *n*. 单调，乏味

monster ['mɒnstə] *n*. 怪物，怪兽

【记】 monst(表示) + er(名词词尾)→表示出来的东西→醒目的东西→怪物

【例】 She dreamt that terrible *monsters* with flaming eyes and sharp teeth were chasing her. 她梦见一些眼中冒火、尖牙利齿的的怪物在追逐她。

【派】 monstrous *adj*. 巨大的，怪异的

monument ['mɒnjʊmənt] *n*. 纪念碑，纪念性建筑物

【记】 monu(忠告，提醒)+ment(名词词尾)→提醒的东西→纪念碑

【例】 A *monument* was built to commemorate the victory. 为了纪念胜利，建造了一座纪念碑。

【同】 memorial

【派】 monumental *adj*. 杰出的，不朽的

mood [muːd] *n*. 思想倾向，情绪

【例】 She's in a good *mood* today. 她今天心情很好。

【同】 disposition, temper

【派】 moody *adj*. 喜怒无常的，忧郁的

moral ['mɒrəl] *adj*. 道德的，精神的

【记】 mor(风俗，习惯)+al(形容词词尾)→风俗习惯上的→道德的

【例】 We differ about *moral* standards. 我们对道德标准看法不一致。

【同】 ethical, mental

【反】 immoral

【派】 morality *n*. 道德，道义

morbid ['mɔːbɪd] *adj*. 病态的，不正常的

【记】 morb(=mort，死)+id(形容词词尾)→使死的→病态的

【例】 She always has a *morbid* imagination. 她总在做病态的想像。

【同】 unhealthy, unwholesome

【反】 healthy

【派】 morbidity *n*. 病态，不健全；发病率

morphology [mɔː'fɒlədʒɪ] *n*. 形态学，形态论

【记】 morph(形态，形状)+ology(…的学科)→研究形态的学科→形态学

【例】 *Morphology* is the field within linguistics that studies the internal structure of words. 词汇形态学是语言学的一个领域，研究词的内部结构。

【派】 morphological *adj*. 形态学(上)，语形学的

morphologist *n*. 形态学者

mortal ['mɔːtl] *adj*. 终有一死的，凡人的

【记】 mort(死)+al(形容词词尾)→终有一死的

【例】 All human beings are *mortal*. 人总有一死。

【同】 earthly, fatal

【反】 immortal

【派】 mortality *n*. 必死性，死亡率

mortgage ['mɔːgɪdʒ] *n*. 按揭，抵押

【记】 mort(死)+gage(=pledge，担保)→涉及财产和死亡之事→抵押

【例】 We've got a *mortgage* of £40000. 我们得到40000英镑的抵押借款。

mortify ['mɔːtɪfaɪ] *v*. 1.使难堪或受辱；2.禁欲，苦行

【记】 mort(死)+ify(动词词尾)→使想死→使难堪

【例】 1. The teacher was *mortified* by his inability to answer the question. 老师因为自己答不出这个问题而感到羞怒。

2. Hermits of the Middle Ages rejected all the comforts of life, intent on *mortifying* the flesh. 中世纪的隐士们热衷于苦行禁欲，摒弃了一切生活享受。

【同】 disgrace, humiliate; abstain

【反】 honor; indulge

【派】 mortification *n*. 羞辱；禁欲

motion [ˈməʊʃən] *n*. 1. 动，运动；2. 动议，提议；*v*. 示意，打手势

【记】 mot(移动) + ion(名词词尾)→动，移动

【例】 1. Parts of the film were shown again in slow *motion*. 影片的一些部分以慢动作重放。

2. His *motion* was rejected. 他的提议遭到了拒绝。

3. He opened the door and *motioned* me to come in. 他打开了门，招手让我进去。

【同】 action, movement

【反】 inaction, rest

【派】 motionless *adj*. 不动的，静止的

motivate [ˈməʊtɪveɪt] *v*. 激发…的积极性，做…的动机

【记】 motiv(动机) + ate(动词词尾)→使…有做事的动机→激发…的积极性

【例】 Pictures are also used to help *motivate* children to read because they are beautiful and eye-catching. 图片还被用来激发孩子阅读的积极性，因为它们很漂亮，很吸引人。

M

【同】 excite, stimulate

【派】 (逆构)motive *adj*. (引起)运动的；发动的，推动的

motivation *n*. 动机，动力

motivational *adj*. 激发积极性的；动机的，有关动机的

mount [maʊnt] *v*. 1. 爬上，登上；2. 增加，增长

【例】 1. He *mounted* his bicycle and rode away. 他骑上脚踏车走了。

2. Their debts continued to *mount* up. 他们的债务不断增长。

【同】 climb, grow, increase

【反】 dismount

mountain [ˈmaʊntɪn] *n*. 山，山脉

【记】 mount(山) + ain(名词词尾)→山脉

【例】 He looks down from the top of the *mountain* to the valley far below. 他从山顶向下眺望下面幽深的山谷。

【同】 hill

【派】 mountaineer *n*. 山地人，登山运动员

mountainous *adj*. 多山的，山一般的；巨大的

mourn [mɔːn] *v*. 哀悼，忧伤

【例】 The old woman still *mourns* for her son. 这位老太太还在为儿子的死伤心。

【同】 bemoan, grieve, lament

【反】 rejoice

【派】 mournful *adj*. 悲痛的，悲哀的
mourning *n*. 悲恸，服丧

movement [ˈmuːvmənt] *n*. 1.移动，动作；2.活动，运动

【记】 move(移动)+ment(名词词尾)→移动

【例】 1. Her every *movement* is very graceful. 她的一举一动都很优美。
2. The Trade Union *Movement* works to obtain higher wages and better conditions. 工会运动旨在争取更高的工资和更好的工作条件。

【同】 motion, action; campaign

【派】 (逆构)move *v*. 移动，运行

muddle [ˈmʌdl] *v*. 使某人糊涂，弄乱

【例】 Stop talking, or you'll *muddle* me (up) completely. 别说了，要不你把我全搞糊涂了。

【同】 confuse, disorder, mess

multiple [ˈmʌltɪpl] *adj*. 多重的，多种多样的

【记】 multi(多)+ple(倍，重)→多重的→多种多样的

【例】 A *multiple* crash can often be seen on that motorway. 那条公路上的连环撞车事故很多。

【同】 manifold

multiply [ˈmʌltɪplaɪ] *v*. 1.乘；2.增加；3.繁殖

【记】 multi(多)+ply(折叠)→折叠多次→繁殖

【例】 1. Four *multiplied* by seven is twenty-eight. 7乘4等于28。
2. Spending on military equipment has *multiplied* in the last five years. 在过去五年中军事装备的开支大大增加。
3. When animals have more food, they generally *multiply* faster. 动物在有较多的食物时，一般繁殖得较快。

【同】 increase; breed, reproduce

【反】 divide

multitude [ˈmʌltɪtjuːd] *n*. 大量，多数

【记】 multi(多)+tude(名词词尾)→许多的→大量

【例】 A *multitude* of people gathered at the gate of the exhibition hall. 大群人聚集在展览大厅的门口。

【同】 crowd, mass, throng

mundane [ˈmʌndeɪn] *adj*. (常做贬义)世俗的，平凡的，单调的

【记】 来自拉丁语 mandus→世界的→世俗的

【例】 It was hard to return to *mundane* matters after such excitement. 经过这样紧张的情形，很难回来做例行的公事。

【同】 earthly, worldly

【反】 heavenly

municipal [mjuːˈnɪsɪpəl] *adj*. (常作定语)市的，市政的

【记】 muni(公共的)+cip(带来)+al(形容词词尾)→为公众带来服务的→市政的

【例】 She works in a *municipal* library. 她在一所市立的图书馆工作。

M

【同】 civic, metropolitan, urban

【派】 municipality *n*. 市政当局，自治市

munificent [mjuː'nɪfɪsnt] *adj*. 慷慨的，大方的

【记】 muni(= munus，礼物) + fic(做) + ent(形容词词尾)→给做礼物的→慷慨的

【例】 I am so happy to get *munificent* birthday presents from my friends. 我很高兴从我朋友那里收到慷慨的生日礼物。

【同】 generous

【反】 stingy

muscle ['mʌsl] *n*. 肌肉

【记】 mus(= mouse，老鼠) + cle(表示"小"的名词词尾)→小老鼠(原来认为肌肉及其活动与老鼠相似)→肌肉

【例】 Some of my friends develop their arm *muscles* by playing tennis. 我的一些朋友通过打网球锻炼他们胳膊的肌肉。

【同】 sinew

【派】 muscular *adj*. 肌肉发达的，强壮的

mushroom ['mʌʃrʊm] *n*. 蘑菇；*v*. 迅速生长，迅速增加

【例】 1. I gathered many *mushrooms* after rain. 雨后我采了很多蘑菇。

2. New houses have *mushroomed* on the edge of the town. 城市边缘的新建房屋犹如雨后春笋。

【同】 grow

M

mutate [mjuː'teɪt] *v*. 变异，突变

【记】 mut(改变) + ate(动词词尾)→变化→变异

【例】 The plant must have *mutated*. 这株植物一定是发生了突变。

【同】 change

【派】 mutation *n*. 变化，(生物物种的)突变

mute [mjuːt] *adj*. 哑的，无声的，沉默的

【例】 They were *mute* when I asked them who was the thief. 当我问他们谁是贼时，他们一言不发。

【同】 dumb, silent, speechless

mutual ['mjuːtʃʊəl] *adj*. 互相的，彼此的

【记】 mut(改变) + ual(形容词词尾)→彼此改变以适合→互相的

【例】 I believe this is an agreement that will be for our *mutual* benefit. 我相信这是一份对我们双方都会有利的协议。

【同】 reciprocal

myriad ['mɪrɪəd] *adj*. 无数的，种种的

【记】 myri(万，多) + ad→无数的

【例】 As their eyes adjusted to the darkness they saw *myriad* lights reflecting off the water. 当眼睛逐渐适应那里的黑暗之后，他们看见数不清的光芒反射在水面上。

【同】 many, numerous

【反】 calculable

mysterious [mɪs'tɪərɪəs] *adj*. 神秘的，奇怪的

【记】 myst(神秘)+er(y)(名词词尾)+ious(形容词词尾)→神秘的

【例】 We must pay special attention to the *mysterious* stranger. 我们必须对那个神秘的陌生人严加注意。

【同】 mystical, incomprehensible

【派】 (逆构)mystery *n*. 神秘，神秘的事物

mystic [ˈmɪstɪk] *adj*. 神秘的，奥秘的(=mystical)

【记】 myst(神秘)+ic(形容词词尾)→神秘的

【例】 They held a *mystic* religious ceremony. 他们举行了一个神秘的宗教仪式。

【同】 mysterious

【派】 mysticism *n*. 神秘，神秘主义

myth [mɪθ] *n*. 神话，神话故事，荒诞的说法

【例】 His account of the event is pure *myth*. 他对事件的叙述纯属凭空捏造。

【同】 fable, fiction

【派】 mythical *adj*. 神话的，虚构的

mythology [mɪˈθɒlədʒɪ] *n*. 神话，神话学

【记】 myth(神话)+ology(…学科)→关于神话的学说→神话学

【例】 A satyr is half man and half goat in Greek and Roman *mythology*. 在希腊和罗马神话中，森林之神是半人半羊的样子。

【派】 mythological *adj*. 神话学的，神话的

mythologist *n*. 神话学者，神话作者

N

naive [nɑːˈiːv] *adj*. 天真的，幼稚的

【例】 Where is your *naive*, pure and objective researcher now? 你那天真的、纯理论的、客观的研究者现在在哪里呢?

【同】 childlike, innocent, unworldly

【反】 sophisticated

naked [ˈneɪkɪd] *adj*. 裸体的，无遮盖的

【例】 These little boys swim *naked* in the river. 这些小孩光着身子在河里游泳。

【同】 bare, nude

【反】 covered, clothed

narrative [ˈnærətɪv] *adj*. 叙述性的，叙事体的；*n*. 叙述，描述，记叙文

【记】 narrat(告诉) + ive(形容词词尾)→告诉的→叙述性的

【例】 1. This work is largely *narrative* in style, based on a transcript of oral demonstrations and lectures. 这项工作主要是叙述性的，主要内容来自口头演示和讲座的手稿。

2. *Narrative* makes up most of the book. 这本书的大部分篇幅都是叙述性的。

【同】 story

【派】 (逆构)narrate *v*. 叙述，讲述

narration *n*. 讲述，叙述

nasty [ˈnæstɪ] *adj*. 污秽的，肮脏的，不堪的

【例】 He is a person with a *nasty* mind. 他是个思想肮脏的人。

【同】 dirty, disgusting, repulsive

【反】 clean

nationality [ˌnæʃəˈnælɪtɪ] *n*. 1. 国籍，国家；2. 部落，民族

【记】 nation(国家) + al(形容词词尾) + ity(名词词尾)→与国家有关→国籍

【例】 1. She has dual *nationality*. 她有双重国籍。

2. There are two main *nationalities* in our village. 我们村子有两大民族。

【同】 nation; people

nationwide [ˈneɪʃənwaɪd] *adj*./*adv*. 全国范围的(地)，全国性的(地)

【记】 nation(国家) + wide(宽的)→在全国那么宽的范围内→全国性的

【例】 The chairman's speech will be broadcast *nationwide*. 主席的讲话将向全国广播。

【同】 countrywide

naughty [ˈnɔːtɪ] *adj*. 顽皮的，淘气的

【记】 naught(无) + y(形容词词尾)→没有(礼貌)的→淘气的

【例】 His dog scared that *naughty* boy off the garden. 他的狗把那个顽皮的孩子从花园里吓走了。

【同】 mischievous

【反】 well-mannered

naval [ˈneɪvəl] *adj*. 海军的，军舰的

【记】 nav(船) + al(形容词词尾)→与船有关的→海军的，军舰的

【例】 He was expelled from the country for spying on their *naval* bases. 他因刺探该国海军基地的情报而被驱逐出境。

【派】 (逆构)navy *n*. 海军

navigate [ˈnævɪgeɪt] *v*. 航行，航海

【记】 nav(船) + ig(驱使) + ate(动词词尾)→驱使船向前→航行

【例】 Which officer in the ship *navigates*? 舰上哪个军官引航?

【同】 pilot, sail, steer

【派】 navigation *n*. 航行，航海(术)

necessitate [nɪˈsesɪteɪt] *v*. 使需要，成为必要

【记】 ne(不) + cess(走开) + it + ate(动词词尾)→不能离开的→成为必要

【例】 The increase in population *necessitates* a greater food supply. 人口的增加需要更多食物供应。

【同】 demand, involve, need

【反】 obviate

【派】 necessity *n*. 必要性，必需品

needy [ˈniːdɪ] *adj*. 贫穷的，生活艰苦的

【记】 need(需要) + y(形容词词尾)→需要的→贫穷的

【例】 There are many *needy* families in our village. 我们村子有很多贫困家庭。

【同】 poor, indigent

negative [ˈnegətɪv] *adj*. 1. 否定的，消极的；2. 负的

【记】 neg(否定) + ative(形容词词尾)→否定的

【例】 1. I have a *negative* opinion on the value of this idea. 我对这个主意持反对意见。
2. These small machines raise the number of *negative* ions in the air in a room. 这些小型仪器可以提高一个房间里空气中负离子的数量。

【反】 affirmative, positive

【派】 negativity *n*. 否定性，消极性

neglect [nɪˈglekt] *v*. / *n*. 忽视，忽略

【记】 neg(否定) + lect(收集，聚集)→拒绝集合→忽视

【例】 Don't *neglect* to lock the door when you leave. 你走时别忘了锁门。

【同】 disregard, ignore

【反】 attend

【派】 negligent *adj*. 疏忽的，粗心大意的
negligible *adj*. 可忽略的，无关紧要的；很小的，几乎没有的
neglectful *adj*. 忽略的，疏忽的

negotiate [nɪˈgəʊʃɪeɪt] *v*. 谈判，洽谈

N

【记】 neg(否定)+oti(闲暇的，多余的)+ate(动词词尾)→没有多余的→谈判

【例】 The company has *negotiated* a new contract with its staff. 公司已经和全体员工商定了一项新合同。

【同】 discuss, confer, bargain

【派】 negotiation *n*. 谈判，洽谈

nerve [nɜːv] *n*. 1. 神经；2. 胆量，勇气

【例】 1. Light stimulates the optic *nerve*. 光刺激视神经。

2. You'll need plenty of *nerve* to sit beside him when he is driving. 他开车的时候，你得有足够的胆量才敢坐在他旁边。

【派】 nervous *adj*. 神经紧张的

neural *adj*. 神经的，神经系统的，神经中枢的

neutral ['njuːtrəl] *adj*. 中立的，不偏不倚的

【记】 neutr(= neither, 两者都不)+al(形容词词尾)→两者都不的→中立的

【例】 That country remained *neutral* in the war. 那个国家在那场战争中保持中立。

【同】 impartial, unprejudiced

【反】 partial, biased

【派】 neutralize *v*. 使中立

nevertheless [ˌnevəðə'les] *adv*. 仍然，不过

【记】 never(决不)+the+less(little 的比较级，少的)→一点也不少的→仍然

【例】 The news may be unexpected; *nevertheless*, it's true. 这消息也许是出乎预料，但它是真的。

【同】 although, anyway, notwithstanding

N

newsletter ['njuːzletər] *n*. 简讯，时事通讯

【记】 news(新闻)+letter(用字母标出来的)→用字母标出来的新闻→时事通讯

【例】 If you have any information that may be useful, please let David know so that it can be included in these *newsletters*. 如果你们还有什么有用的信息，请告诉大卫，以便于能写进我们这些简讯里。

【同】 newssheet

newsreel ['njuːzriːl] *n*. 新闻短片

【记】 news(新闻)+reel(胶片、磁带等一盘)→一盘胶片的新闻→新闻短片

【例】 The film contained some old *newsreel* footage. 这部影片中有些旧新闻片的镜头。

nickel ['nɪkl] *n*. 镍，(五分)镍币

【例】 Can you give me a dime for two *nickels*? 你能不能用两个五分镍币给我换一个一毛的镍币？

nickname ['nɪkneɪm] *n*. 绰号，昵称；*v*. 给…取绰号

【记】 nick(附加的)+name(名字)→附加的名字，另外的名字→绰号

【例】 1. Jess is just my *nickname* - my real name is Jessica. 杰西只是我的昵称，我的真名是杰西卡。

2. They *nicknamed* him "Lofty" because he was so tall. 他们给他起了个绰号叫"高个儿"，因为他身材很高。

【同】 moniker, sobriquet

nightmare ['naɪtmeər] *n*. 梦魇，噩梦，可怕的事物

【记】 night(夜)+mare(鬼)→夜里看到鬼→噩梦

【例】 I have *nightmares* about falling off a cliff. 我常做恶梦梦见从悬崖上摔下来。

【同】 dream

nominal ['nɒmɪnl] *adj*. 名义上的，象征性的

【记】 nomin(名字)+al(形容词词尾)→名义上的

【例】 1. The chairman is only the *nominal* ruler of the country. 主席只是那个国家名义上的统治者。

2. She charged only a *nominal* fee for her work. 她为所做的工作只收取象征性的费用。

【反】 real，veritable

nominate ['nɒmɪneɪt] *v*. 提名，推荐，任命

【记】 nomin(名字)+ate(动词词尾)→提出某人的名字→提名

【例】 She had been *nominated* as candidate for the presidency. 她已被提名为总统候选人。

【同】 appoint，name

【派】 nomination *n*. 提名，任命

nominator *n*. 提名者，任命者

nominee *n*. 被提名的人，被任命者

nostalgia [nɒs'tældʒɪə] *n*. 思乡病，怀旧

【记】 nost(回家)+alg(痛)+ia(名词词尾)→为想回家而痛苦→思乡病

【例】 The sight inspired him with *nostalgia*. 这景象激起了他的怀旧之情。

【同】 homesickness

【派】 nostalgic *adj*. 乡愁的，怀旧的

notify ['nəʊtɪfaɪ] *v*. 通报，通知

【记】 not(标示)+ify(表示"做"的动词词尾)→做出标示→通知

【例】 Have the authorities been *notified* of this? 当局是否已得知此事？

【同】 inform，report，tell

【派】 notification *n*. 通知，布告，告示

notion ['nəʊʃən] *n*. 观念，概念

【记】 not(标示)+ion(名词词尾)→标示出来应该记住的想法→概念

【例】 He didn't have a slightest *notion* of what I meant. 他对我指的是什么没有一点儿概念。

【同】 belief，conception，opinion

【派】 notional *adj*. 概念的，想象的

notorious [nəʊ'tɔːrɪəs] *adj*. 声名狼藉的，坏名声的

【记】 not(标示，注意)+orious(形容词词尾，多…的)→多得惹人注意的→声名狼藉的

【例】 Hitler is a *notorious* dictator. 希特勒是一个臭名昭著的独裁者。

【同】 ill-famed，disreputable

【反】 famous，reputable

【派】 notoriety *n*. 声名狼藉，坏名声

nourish [ˈnʌrɪʃ] *v*. 滋养，使健壮

【记】 nour(营养)+ish(动词词尾)→滋养

【例】 Milk is all we need to *nourish* a small baby. 我们供给婴儿营养只需喂奶就够了。

【同】 feed，nurture

【派】 nourishment *n*. 食物，营养品

novelty [ˈnɒvəltɪ] *n*. 新奇，新颖

【记】 nov(新的)+el(形容词词尾)+ty(名词词尾)→新的东西→新奇

【例】 At first I enjoyed all the parties, but the *novelty* soon wore off. 起初我喜欢参加一切社交聚会，但这种新奇感很快就消失了。

【同】 freshness，originality

【派】 (逆构)novel *adj*. 新颖的，珍奇的

novice [ˈnɒvɪs] *n*. 生手，新手

【记】 nov(新的)+ice(名词词尾，表示"行为者")→新手

【例】 She's a complete *novice* as a reporter. 她初任记者，完全是个生手。

【同】 beginner，rookie

noxious [ˈnɒkʃəs] *adj*. 有毒的，有害的

【记】 nox(伤害)+ious(形容词词尾)→造成伤害的→有害的

【例】 Fumes from the exhaust of an automobile are *noxious*. 汽车排出的废气是有害的。

【同】 harmful，poisonous，toxic

【反】 wholesome

nuclear [ˈnjuːklɪə] *adj*. 核的，原子能的

【例】 They decided to establish a *nuclear* power station. 他们决定建立一所核电站。

【派】 (逆构)nucleus *n*. (复数 nuclei)核，核心

null [nʌl] *adj*. 无效的，无价值的；*n*. 零

【例】 The marriage was declared *null* and void. 婚事已宣告无效了。

【同】 void，invalid

【反】 valid

【派】 nullify *v*. 使无效

nullity *n*. (尤指法律上的)无效，无效的行为

numb [nʌm] *adj*. 麻木的

【例】 My fingers were *numb* with cold. 我的手指因寒冷而冻僵了。

【同】 dull，insensitive

numerous [ˈnjuːmərəs] *adj*. 许多的，大量的

【记】 numer(数字，数目)+ous(形容词词尾)→数目众多的→许多的

【例】 The Earth is only one of the *numerous* planets in the universe. 地球只是宇宙中众多星球中的一个。

【同】 abundant，many，plentiful

【反】 few

nursery [ˈnɜːsərɪ] *n*. 托儿所，婴儿室

【记】 nurse(保育员)+ry(名词词尾)→保育员工作的地方→+托儿所

【例】 She sent her little son to a *nursery* when she was working. 她工作的时候就把小儿

子送到托儿所。

nurture [ˈnɜːtʃə] *n.*/*v.* 养育，培养

【记】 nur(营养) + ture(名词词尾)→给予营养→养育

【例】 Most vegetables we buy in winter are *nurtured* in the greenhouse. 我们冬天买的大多数蔬菜都是在温室里培育的。

【同】 feed, foster, nourish, raise

nutrition [njuːˈtrɪʃən] *n.* 营养，滋养

【记】 nutri(营养) + tion(名词词尾)→营养

【例】 *Nutrition* is another area that sports trainers have failed to address adequately. 营养是运动教练员没有充分发挥作用的另一个领域。

【同】 nourishment

【派】 nutrient *n.* 营养品，食物

nutritional *adj.* 营养的，滋养的

nutritious *adj.* 有营养的

N

O

oasis [əʊˈeɪsɪs] *n*. (复数 oases)(沙漠中的)绿洲

【例】 The caravan stopped for the night at an *oasis*. 旅行队在沙漠中的绿洲停下来过夜。

obedient [əˈbiːdjənt, -dɪənt] *adj*. 服从的，孝顺的

【记】 ob(无特殊意义) + edi(听) + ent(形容词词尾)→听…的→听从的，顺从的

【例】 My brother is an *obedient* boy. 我弟弟是一个听话的男孩。

【同】 compliant, submissive

【反】 disobedient, resistant

【派】 (逆构)obey *v*. 服从，顺从

obedience *n*. 服从，顺从

object [ˈɒbdʒɪkt] *n*. 1. 物体；2. 目标，对象；*v*. 反对

【记】 ob(对，向) + ject(扔，投)→对…投掷东西→反对

【例】 1. There were several *objects* on the floor of the room. 房间的地板上有几样东西。

2. She has become an *object* of contempt. 她已变成一个受人鄙视的对象。

3. However, others strongly *object* to developing private cars. 然而，另有一些人强烈反对发展私人小汽车。

【同】 aim; oppose

【反】 subject; agree

【派】 objection *n*. 反对意见

objective *adj*. 客观的，中肯的

obligation [ˌɒblɪˈgeɪʃən] *n*. 义务，责任

【记】 ob(向，对) + lig(绑) + ation(名词词尾)→把…绑起来→束缚

【例】 The company has to fulfill the terms of its *obligation*. 这个公司必须履行合同条款。

【同】 duty, responsibility

【派】 (逆构)oblige *v*. 强制，强迫

obligatory *adj*. 强制性的，义务的

obscure [əbˈskjʊə] *adj*. 朦胧的，晦涩的；*v*. 使不分明

【记】 ob(在…之上) + scure(覆盖住的)→全部覆盖住的→朦胧的

【例】 1. Her poetry is full of *obscure* literary allusions. 她的诗里用了很多晦涩的文学典故。

2. The moon was *obscured* by clouds. 月亮被云遮住了。

【同】 vague, ambiguous

【反】 clarify，clear
【派】 obscurity *n*. 阴暗，偏僻

observe [əbˈzɜːv] *v*. 1.看到，注意到；2.遵守
【记】 ob(为了)+serve(保留)→保留在眼前→看守
【例】 1. She *observed* that he'd left but made no comment. 她看见他离去，但未置一词。
2. We should *observe* the laws of the land. 我们应该遵守该国法律。
【同】 notice；obey
【反】 violate，break
【派】 observation *n*. 观察，观测(数据)
observance *n*. 惯例，仪式
observatory *n*. 观测所，气象台，天文台

obsession [əbˈseʃən] *n*. 着迷，困扰
【记】 ob(向着)+sess(坐下)+ion(名词)→面向…而坐→着迷
【例】 His *obsession* with computers began six months ago. 他半年前就迷上了计算机了。
【同】 attraction
【派】 (逆构)obsess *v*. 迷住，使困扰
obsessive *adj*. 强迫性的，分神的

obsolete [ˈɒbsəliːt] *adj*. 废弃的，过时的
【记】 ob(相反)+sol(习惯)+ete(形容词词尾)→与习惯相违的→过时的
【例】 Our service is *obsolete*，requiring root and branch reform. 我们的服务已经过时，需要从根本上进行改革。
【同】 outdated，out-of-date

obstacle [ˈɒbstəkl] *n*. 障碍，妨碍物
【记】 ob(相反)+st(a)(站立)+cle(名词词尾)→反着站立的东西→障碍物
【例】 She felt that her family were an *obstacle* to her work. 她觉得家庭对她的工作是个障碍。
【同】 impediment，obstruction
【反】 help，assistance

obstinate [ˈɒbstɪnɪt] *adj*. 倔强的，顽固的
【记】 ob(相反)+stin(使…站)+ate(动词词尾)→对抗着站在那里→倔强的
【例】 This child is *obstinate* and rebellious. 这个孩子倔强，难以管束。
【同】 stubborn，headstrong，inflexible
【反】 docile，amenable

obstruct [əbˈstrʌkt] *v*. 阻塞，妨碍
【记】 ob(相反)+struct(建造，构造)→反着建在那里→阻碍
【例】 The road was *obstructed* by a fallen tree. 路被一棵倒下的树堵住了。
【同】 block，hamper，hinder，impede
【反】 free
【派】 obstruction *n*. 阻塞，妨碍；障碍物

obtain [əbˈteɪn] *v*. 获得
【记】 ob(接近)+tain(掌握)→在身边的→获得

O

【例】 I haven't been able to *obtain* that book anywhere. 我到处都没买到那本书。
【同】 acquire, gain
【反】 lose
【派】 obtainable *adj*. 能得到的，可到手的
obtainer *n*. 获得

obvious [ˈɒbvɪəs,-vjəs] *adj*. 显然的，醒目的
【记】 ob(在…附近) + vi(路) + ous(形容词)→横放在路上的→明显的
【例】 The embassy is an *obvious* target for terrorist attacks. 大使馆是恐怖分子攻击的明显目标。
【同】 apparent, distinct
【反】 obscure, unobvious

occasion [əˈkeɪʒən] *n*. 1. 场合；2. 时机，机会
【记】 oc(在…之前) + cas(发生，降临) + ion(名词)→发生在眼前的事→场合
【例】 1. I only wear a tie on special *occasions*. 我只在特殊场合才打领带。
2. You should go there if *occasion* arises. 如果有机会，你应当到那里去。
【同】 incident; opportunity
【派】 occasional *adj*. 偶然的，非经常的

occidental [ɒksɪˈdəntəl]n. 欧美人，西方人；*adj*. 西洋的，西方的
【记】 oc(下) + cid(落) + ent(名词词尾) + al(形容词词尾)→太阳落下的地方的→西方的
【例】 1. Whether they are oriental or *occidental*, they all love peace. 不管是东方人还是西方人，他们都爱和平。
2. The doctoral student has study all religion, oriental and *occidental*. 这位博士生研究过东西方的所有宗教。
【同】 western
【反】 oriental
【派】 (逆构)occident *n*. 西方，欧美；西欧诸国

O

occupation [ˌɒkjʊˈpeɪʃən] *n*. 1. 职业；2. 占领，占有
【记】 occup(y)(占有) + ation(名词词尾)→占有
【例】 1. I haven't entered your name and *occupation* yet. 我尚未记下你的名字和职业。
2. He returned from Paris and found his office was under someone else's *occupation*. 他从巴黎回来，发现他的办公室被别人占了。
【同】 business, employment; ownership, possession
【派】 occupational *adj*. 职业的，工作的

occupy [ˈɒkjʊpaɪ] *v*. 1. 居住；2. 占用，占据(时间、地点)
【记】 oc(在) + cupy(捕捉)→进行捕捉→俘获→占有
【例】 1. The family has occupied the farm for many years. 这一家在农场已居住多年。
2. Reading occupies most of my free time. 阅读占去了我大部分的闲暇时间。
【同】 inhabit; engage, take
【派】 occupant *n*. 占有者，居住者

occur [əˈkɜː] *v*. (-rred; -rring)发生，存在
【记】 oc(向着) + cur(奔跑)→流向→发生

【例】 1. Death *occurred* about midnight, the doctor says. 医生说大约是在半夜死的。

2. Misprints *occur* on every page. 每页都有印刷错误。

【同】 happen, emerge

【派】 occurrence *n*. 发生的事情,出现

odor [ˈəʊdə] *n*. 气味

【例】 The unspeakable *odor* clung to the room. 一股难以形容的气味充斥着房间散不出去。

【同】 aroma, scent, smell

【派】 odorless *adj*. 无臭的,没有气味的

offend [əˈfend] *v*. 犯罪,冒犯

【记】 of(=ob, 相反) + fend(打击)→对着打→冒犯

【例】 She may be *offended* if you don't reply to her invitation. 她请你,你要是不回个信儿就可能把她得罪了。

【同】 affront, infract

【派】 offensive *adj*. 讨厌的,冒犯的;进攻(性)的

offender *n*. 犯法者,犯规者

offer [ˈɒfə] *v*. 提供,(主动)给予

【记】 of(在附近) + fer(搬运)→拿到面前→提供

【例】 The company has *offered* a high salary. 公司已提出高薪相聘。

【同】 proffer, tender

【反】 accept, receive

【派】 offering *n*. 提供,奉献物

offertory *n*. 捐款

offhand [ˈɔːfˈhænd, ˈɒf-] *adj*. 临时的,无准备的

【记】 off(离开) + hand(手)→不在手边→临时的

【例】 He's a good salesman, but his *offhand* manner does tend to put people off. 他是个很好的推销员,可是他那随便的态度容易使人产生反感。

【同】 extemporaneous, unprepared

【反】 prepared

official [əˈfɪʃəl] *adj*. 1. 职务上的;2. 官方的,正式的;*n*. 官员,公务员

【记】 of(要) + fic(做) + ial(形容词)→关于要做的事情的→职务的

【例】 1. Although the retired architects of the party do not occupy any *official* positions, they have a lot of authority. 虽然党的缔造者们现在不担任正式职务,但他们很有一些影响。

2. The news is almost certainly true although it is not *official*. 尽管消息是非官方的,但是几乎确凿无疑。

3. An *official* of the local government called to see him. 当地政府一位官员来看他。

【同】 functionary

【反】 unofficial

【派】 (逆构)office *n*. 办公室,职责

offset ['ɔːfset] *n./v.* (-set, -set)弥补，抵销

【记】 off(分离)+set(设置)→设置使…分离→抵消

【例】 Higher mortgage rates are partly *offset* by increased tax allowances. 抵押款提高了，其中一部分可由免税额增加而抵消。

【同】 countervail, counteract

offshore ['ɔːfʃɔː] *adj./adv.* 近岸(的)，离岸一定距离(的)

【记】 off(离开)+shore(岸)→离开海岸的→离岸一定距离的

【例】 The ship anchored five miles *offshore*. 那船在离岸五英里处抛锚。

【反】 onshore, inshore

offspring ['ɒfsprɪŋ, 'ɔːf-] *n.* (单复数同形)子孙后代

【记】 off(离开)+spring(长出)→长出来的(新)东西→后代

【例】 How do parents pass genes on to their *offspring*? 父母是怎样把基因遗传给自己的子女的?

【同】 descendant, child

【反】 ancestor, forebear

omen ['əʊmen] *n./v.* 预兆，征兆

【例】 When it rained on their wedding day, she took it as a bad *omen*. 他们举行婚礼的那天下雨了，她认为这是个不祥的预兆。

【同】 indication, portent

omit [əʊ'mɪt] *v.* (-tted; -tting)遗漏，省略

【记】 o(出)+mit(送出)→把…送出去→省略

【例】 This chapter may be *omitted*. 这一章可以省略。

【同】 neglect, overleap

【反】 insert

【派】 omissible *adj.* 可省略的，可删节的

omission *n.* 省略

omnipotent [ɒm'nɪpətənt] *adj.* 全能的，万能的

【记】 omni(所有)+potent(力量)→具有所有的力量→全能的

【例】 The *omnipotent* God will help us. 万能的上帝会帮助我们的。

【同】 almighty, powerful

【反】 impotent

oncoming ['ɒnkʌmɪŋ] *adj.* 即将来临的，接近的

【记】 on(在…上)+com(e)(来)+ing(加在动词后面使其变为形容词)→在来的路上→即将来临的

【例】 Remember to ease up as you approach the bridge; *oncoming* traffic has the right of way. 记住，靠近大桥时开慢一些，迎面来的车流有先行权。

【同】 approaching, advance

onset ['ɒnset] *n.* (病)发作，开始

【记】 来自词组 set on(攻击)

【例】 He went to see a doctor at the *onset* of a fever. 他开始发烧时便去看医生了。

【同】 attack, start

opaque [əu'peɪk] *adj*. 不透明的，迟钝的

【记】 op(不同)+aque(水)→不像水那样→不透明的

【例】 I felt his report was deliberately *opaque*. 我觉得他的报告故意含糊其辞。

【同】 dull, vague

【反】 clear

opera ['ɒpərə] *n*. 歌剧

【记】 oper(工作)+a(名词词尾)→通过创作而来的→歌剧

【例】 They planned to go to the *opera* this Sunday. 他们计划这个星期天去看歌剧演出。

【派】 opera-house *n*. 歌剧院，(尤指乡间的)剧场

operate ['ɒpəreɪt] *v*. 1.操作，运行；2.做手术

【记】 oper(工作)+ate(动词词尾)→工作→操作

【例】 1. The lift doesn't *operate* properly. 这台电梯运转不正常。

2. The doctors decided to *operate* on her immediately. 医生决定马上给她动手术。

【同】 conduct, handle

【派】 operational *adj*. 实施时的，操作上的

operation *n*. 运转，操作；手术

opinion [ə'pɪnjən] *n*. 意见，看法

【记】 op(相反的)+inion(名词词尾)→相反的东西→意见

【例】 In my opinion and in the opinion of most people, it is a very sound investment. 照我的和大多数人的看法，这是很可靠的投资。

【同】 thought, view

【派】 opinioned *adj*. 有意见的

opponent [ə'pəunənt] *n*. 对手，反对者

【记】 op(相反的)+pon(地方)+ent(名词词尾)→站在相反的地方的人→对手

【例】 She is one of the strongest *opponents* of tax reform. 她是税收改革最强烈的反对者之一。

【同】 adversary, enemy

【反】 ally

opportunity [ˌɒpə'tjuːnɪtɪ] *n*. 机会，时机

【记】 op(靠近)+port(门)+(u)nity(名词词尾)→靠近门的地方→机会，时机

【例】 Don't hesitate; seize the first *opportunity* that comes along! 别再犹豫了，一有机会就抓住它！

【同】 chance, occasion

【派】 (逆构)opportune *adj*. 凑巧的，及时的

oppose [ə'pəuz] *v*. 反对，使对立

【记】 op(相反的)+pose(放置)→处于相反的→反对，反抗

【例】 It was courageous of him to *oppose* his chief. 他敢反对他的上司，真是勇敢。

【同】 object, resist

【反】 agree, correspond

【派】 opposite *adj*. 对面的，截然相反的；*prep*. 在…对面 opposition *n*. 反对，反对意见

O

opt [ɒpt] *v*. 决定做某事，选择

【例】 They *opt* for more holiday instead of more pay. 他们选择了延长假期而不是增加工资。

【同】 choose，select

【反】 decline，reject

【派】 option *n*. 选项，选择

optical [ˈɒptɪkəl] *adj*. 光学的，视觉的

【记】 opt(眼睛) + ical(形容词词尾)→眼睛的→视觉的

【例】 I thought I saw a ghost but it was just an *optical* illusion. 我以为我看见鬼了，其实只是一种幻觉.

【同】 visual，ocular

【派】 optician *n*. 眼镜商；光学仪器制造商

optimism [ˈɒptɪmɪzəm] *n*. 乐观主义，乐观

【记】 opt(希望) + im(拉丁文最高级字尾) + (i)sm(主义)→认为处于最有希望的状态→乐观主义

【例】 Her mood varied from *optimism* to extreme depression. 她的情绪由乐观一变而为极度消沉。

【反】 pessimism

【派】 optimistic *adj*. 乐观的

optimist *n*. 乐天派，乐观者

optimum [ˈɒptɪməm] *n*. (复数-ma 或-mums)最佳条件

adj. 最优的，最佳的

【记】 opt(希望) + im(拉丁文最高级词尾) + um(名词)→最有希望的状态 →最佳条件

O

【例】 The market offered *optimum* conditions for sale. 市场为销售提供了最佳条件。

【同】 optimal

【派】 optimal *adj*. 最佳的，最理想的

optimize *v*. 使最优化

optimization *n*. 最佳化，最优化

opulence [ˈɒpjʊləns] *n*. 富裕，豪华

【记】 opul(财富)ence(名词词尾)→拥有财富→富裕

【例】 He owes his *opulence* to hard work. 他的财富乃辛勤工作得来。

【同】 luxury，sumptuousness

【反】 poverty

【派】 opulent *adj*. 富裕的，繁茂的

oracle [ˈɒrəkl] *n*. 神谕，先知

【记】 ora(说) + cle(名词词尾)→(神)说的话→神谕

【例】 In times of difficulty, she prays for an *oracle* to guide her. 在困难的时候，她祈祷神谕来指引她。

【同】 prophet

oral [ˈɔːrəl] *adj*. 口头的

【记】 ora(说) + (a)l(形容词词尾)→说的→口头的

【例】 The old man told us a story passed on by *oral* tradition. 老人给我们讲述了一个口头流传的故事。

【同】 spoken, verbal

【反】 written

oration [ə'reɪʃən] *n*. 正式演说，演讲

【记】 ora(说)+tion(名词词尾)→说的话→演讲

【例】 He was asked to deliver an *oration* at the meeting. 他被邀请在会议上发表演说。

【同】 speech

orbit ['ɔːbɪt] *n*. 轨道；*v*. 绕…轨道而行

【例】 1. How many satellites have been put into *orbit* round the earth? 有多少颗人造卫星已送入绕地球轨道？

2. How many spacecraft have *orbited* the moon? 有多少航天器绕月球轨道运行？

【同】 circle, track

【派】 orbital *adj*. 轨道的

orbiter *n*. 盘旋物，人造卫星

orchestra ['ɔːkɪstrə,-kes-] *n*. 管弦乐队

【记】 来自拉丁语 *orchestra*，本义是指剧院里舞台前为合唱队留出的空间→乐队演奏的地方→管弦乐队

【例】 The orchestra were all in position, waiting for the conductor. 管弦乐队队员都已各就各位，等待着指挥。

【同】 band, ensemble

ordeal [ɔː'diːl,-'diːəl] *n*. 严峻考验，痛苦的经历

【例】 His courage was severely tried by his *ordeal*. 他的勇气在艰难困苦中经受了严峻的考验。

【同】 experience, tribulation, trial

ordinance ['ɔːdɪnəns] *n*. 法令，条例

【记】 ordin(=order，命令)+ance(名词词尾)→下的命令→法令

【例】 Everyone should obey the government *ordinance*. 每个人都必须遵守这条政府法令。

【同】 decree, regulation, rule

ore [ɔːr] *n*. 矿石，矿砂

【例】 After chemical assay, we have known the composition of the *ore*. 经过化学分析，我们知道了矿石的构成。

【同】 mineral

organ ['ɔːgən] *n*. 1. 器官；2.(党派、集团等的)工具，喉舌

【例】 1. The heart is a vital *organ*. 心脏是维持生命必须的器官。

2. This paper is the official *organ* of the Labor Party. 这份报纸是工党的官方喉舌。

【同】 apparatus, mouthpiece

【派】 organic *adj*. 有机的

organism *n*. 生物体，有机体

O

organize [ˈɔːgənaɪz] *v*. 组织，创办

【记】 organ(器官) + ize(动词词尾)→组织成为一个有机体→组织，创办

【例】 They planned to *organize* a scientific expedition. 他们计划组织一次科学考察。

【同】 arrange, group

【反】 jumble

【派】 organization *n*. 组织，团体

organizer *n*. 组织者，建立者

orientation [ˌɔːrienˈteɪʃən] *n*. 1. 熟悉情况，指南；2. 方向，倾向

【记】 ori(升起，开始) + ent(形容词词尾) + ation(名词词尾)→太阳升起的地方→向东方

【例】 1. The librarian made a twenty-minute *orientation* to the library facilities. 那个图书馆管理员作了20分钟的图书馆设施情况介绍。

2. His political *orientation* is clearly radical. 他的政治倾向显然是激进的。

【派】 (逆构)orientate *v*. 向东，朝向

oriental [ˌɔːrɪˈentl]n. 东方人(尤指中国人和日本人)；*adj*. 东方诸国的，亚洲的

【记】 ori(升起) + ent(名词词尾) + al(形容词词尾)→太阳升起的地方的→东方的

【例】 China is an *oriental* country with a long history. 中国是一个有着悠久历史的东方国家。

【同】 eastern

【反】 occidental

original [əˈrɪdʒənəl] *adj*. 1. 起初的，原始的；2. 独创的，原版的

【记】 ori(开始) + gin(名词词尾) + al(形容词词尾)→开始的→原始的

【例】 1. The *original* owner of the house moved out. 房子原先的主人搬出去了。

2. The *original* picture is in the British Museum. 这幅画的原作在大英博物馆内。

【反】 copy, imitative

【派】 (逆构)origin *n*. 起源，由来；出身，血统

originality *n*. 创意，新奇

originate [əˈrɪdʒɪneɪt] *v*. 来自，发源

【记】 origin(起源) + ate(动词词尾)→起源于→发源

【例】 The hot dog did not *originate* in the United States, but in Germany. 热狗不是起源于美国，而是德国。

【同】 arise, initiate

【派】 origination *n*. 发源

originator *n*. 发起人，创办人

ornament [ˈɔːnəmənt] *n*./*v*. 装饰，修饰

【记】 orna(装饰) + ment(…的东西)→装饰用的东西→装饰品

【例】 The clock is simply for *ornament*; it doesn't actually work. 那时钟纯粹是为了装饰，其实不能走。

【同】 adorn, decoration

【反】 unorthodox, heathen

【派】 ornamental *adj*. 装饰性的

ornamentation *n*. 装饰，装饰品

orthodox [ˈɔːθədɒks] *adj*. 传统的，符合社会习俗的

【记】 ortho(正确的) + dox(见解)→正确的想法→传统的

【例】 *Orthodox* Christian churches often have elaborate steeples. 传统的基督教堂都有精致的尖塔。

【同】 conventional, traditional

【反】 unorthodox, heathen

【派】 orthodoxy *n*. 正统观念，正统信仰；正统性

otherwise [ˈʌðəwaɪz] *adv*. 另外，否则；*adj*. 另外的，其他方面的

【记】 other(另外的) + wise(副词词尾，在…方面)→在另外的方面→另外

【例】 1. Seize the chance; *otherwise* you'll regret it. 抓住这个机会，否则你会后悔的。
2. He should have been working, but he was *otherwise* engaged. 他应该在工作，可他却干别的事。

【同】 differently, dissimilarly

【派】 otherwise-minded *adj*. 想法不同的

outbreak [ˈaʊtbreɪk] *n*. (战争的)爆发，(疾病的)发作

【记】 out(向外) + break(打破)→向外打破→(战争)爆发

【例】 The research project fetched up because of the *outbreak* of the war. 由于战争爆发，这个研究计划搁浅了。

【同】 eruption, outburst

outcome [ˈaʊtkʌm] *n*. 结果，后果

【记】 out(出去) + come(出现)→最后出现的事物→结果，后果

【例】 All scientific work of an experimental or exploratory nature starts with some expectation about the *outcome*. 所有实验性或探索性的科学工作，在开始启动的同时，人们都期待着能有所成就。

【同】 consequence, result

outdated [aʊtˈdeɪtɪd] *adj*. 过时的，不流行的

【记】 out(超过) + dat(e)(日期) + ed(加在单词后面构成形容词)→超过期限的→过时的

【例】 The quality is all right, but the style is a bit *outdated*. 质量无问题，只是式样有点过时。

【同】 antique, out-fashioned

【反】 modern, fashionable

【派】 (逆构)outdate *v*. 使过时

outgrow [aʊtˈgrəʊ] *v*. (-grew, -grown)生长速度超过，长得比…快

【记】 out(出去) + grow(长)→长得超过→长得比…快

【例】 By the time he is ten, he has *outgrown* his older brother. 他十岁的时候就已经长得比他哥哥高了。

【同】 overgrow

【派】 outgrowth *n*. 自然的发展，结果

outlay [ˈaʊtleɪ] *n*. (用于某特定目的的)花费，开支

【记】 out(在…之外) + lay(用钱)→在外面花的钱→开支

【例】 The scheme required an initial *outlay* of $3,000,000. 这个计划初步需要三百万美元的经费。

【同】 expense, spending

【反】 saving

outlet ['aʊtlet-lɪt] *n*. 1.(河流、烟等)出口，出路；2.批发商店

【记】 out(出去)+let(让)→让…出去→出口

【例】 1. They found some new *outlets* for their products. 他们为自己的产品找到了一些新的市场。

2. This cosmetics firm has 34 *outlets* in Britain. 这家化妆品公司在英国有34个经销店。

【同】 exit

【反】 inlet

outline ['əʊtlaɪn] *v*. 概述，勾画轮廓；*n*. 要点，大纲

【记】 out(在…之外)+line(线条)→在外面的线条→勾画轮廓

【例】 1. We *outlined* our main objections to the proposal. 我们扼要地说明了反对该建议的意见。

2. He wrote down the *outline* of his lecture. 他写下演讲的提纲。

【同】 abstract, sketch; drawing

outlook ['aʊtlʊk] *n*. 1.观点，看法；2.前景

【记】 out(在…之外)+look(看)→向外看→前景

【例】 1. Whether a joke gives pleasure or pain depends on a person's *outlook*. 一个笑话是会引起愉悦还是痛苦也取决于每个人的见解。

2. The house has a pleasant *outlook* over the valley. 从这所房子可以看到山谷景色优美。

O

【同】 expectation, prospect; view

output ['aʊtpʊt] *n*. 产量，输出量

【记】 out(向外)+put(放置)→放在外面的东西→输出

【例】 The average *output* of the factory is 20 cars a day. 该工厂的平均产量是每天20辆汽车。

【同】 production, yield

【反】 input

outrage ['aʊtreɪdʒ] *n*./*v*. 激怒，引起…义愤

【记】 out(向外)+rage(愤怒)→出离愤怒→激怒

【例】 You can imagine our *outrage* when we heard what he'd done. 你可以想象我们听到他干的事时有多么愤怒。

They were outraged by the announcement of massive price increases. 物价大幅上涨的消息一公布，他们气愤填膺。

【同】 anger, disgust

【派】 outrageous *adj*. 蛮横的，残暴的

outright ['aʊt'raɪt] *adj*./*adv*. 彻底的(地)，完全的(地)，直率的(地)

【记】 out(出去)+right(完全地)→完全出去→彻底的

【例】 1. She was the *outright* winner. 毫无疑问她是优胜者。

2. I told him *outright* what I thought of him. 我坦率地向他说出我对他的想法。

【同】 completely, downright, thoroughly

outskirt [ˈaʊtskɜːt] *n*. 边界，(尤指)市郊

【记】 out(在…之外) + skirt(边缘)→在…的边缘→市郊

【例】 They live on the *outskirts* of Paris. 他们住在巴黎市郊。

【同】 suburb

outstanding [aʊtˈstændɪŋ] *adj*. 杰出的，著名的

【记】 out(出去) + stand(站) + ing(形容词词尾)→站出来的→突出的

【例】 The firm recognized Tom's *outstanding* work by giving him an extra bonus. 公司发给汤姆一笔额外奖金以表彰他工作出色。

【同】 distinguished, prominent, famous

【派】 (逆构)outstand *v*. 凸出，卓然独立

outweigh [aʊtˈweɪ] *v*. 比…重，比…更重要

【记】 out(出去) + weigh(称重)→称重超过→比…重

【例】 On balance, his accomplishments *outweigh* his faults. 权衡起来，他的成就要大于他的过失。

【同】 outbalance, preponderate

oval [ˈəʊvəl] *adj*. 卵形的，椭圆的

【例】 Comets move around the sun like planets, but in long *oval* course. 彗星像行星一样绕太阳运转，然而其轨道呈狭长的椭圆形。

【同】 egg-shaped, ovoid

overall [ˈəʊvərɔːl] *adj*. 全部的，全面的

【记】 over(在…上面) + all(所有)→在所有的上面→全部的

【例】 There's been an *overall* improvement recently. 近来各方面都有所改进。

【同】 total

overcast [ˈəʊvəkɑːst] *adj*. 阴天的，愁闷的 *v*. (-cast, -cast)使阴暗

【记】 over(在…之上) + cast(抛掷)→向上抛东西遮起来→使阴暗

【例】 1. It is a bit *overcast*—it might rain. 天有点阴，可能会下雨。

2. Clouds began to *overcast* the sky. 乌云遮蔽了天空。

【同】 cloudy, gloomy

【反】 sunny, bright

overcome [ˌəʊvəˈkʌm] *v*. (-came, -come)战胜，征服

【记】 over(超过) + come(出现)→超过出现的事物→征服

【例】 We need a spirit of enterprise if we are to *overcome* our difficulties. 如果我们要克服困难，我们就要有进取精神。

【同】 defeat, conquer

【反】 submit, surrender

overdo [ˈəʊvəˈduː] *v*. (-did, -done)做得过分，过分夸张

【记】 over(超过) + do(做)→做的超过了限度→做得过分

【例】 He was trying to be helpful, but he rather *overdid* it. 他想尽力帮忙，但做得有些

过分了.

【同】 exaggerate, magnify

overflow ['əʊvə'fləʊ] *n./v.* 溢出，泛滥

【记】 over(超过)+flow(流动)→水流漫过堤岸→溢出

【例】 The bath is *overflowing*; who left the water running? 浴缸里的水溢出来了，是谁没关水龙头?

【同】 flood, overspill

overhear [ˌəʊvə'hɪə] *v.* (-heard, -heard)无意中听到，偷听

【记】 over(在…之上)+hear(听)→在说话人旁边听→偷听

【例】 I *overheard* him saying he was going to France. 我无意中听到他说要到法国去。

overlap ['əʊvə'læp] *n./v.* (-pped; -pping)复叠起来，与…同时发生

【记】 over(在…之上)+lap(重叠的部分)→在重叠的部分之上→复叠起来

【例】 1. Economics and politics are best studied together as the two subjects *overlap*. 经济学和政治学有部分内容交叉，所以这两门课程最好一起研读。

2. there was no *overlap* between their proposals. 这两种提议没有交迭。

【派】 overlapping *adj.* 重叠，搭接

overload ['əʊvə'ləʊd] *v.* 超载

【记】 over(超过)+load(装载)→超载

【例】 The lights fused because the system was *overloaded* with electrical appliances. 电灯灭了，因线路上用电器超负荷把保险丝烧断了。

【同】 overburden, overcharge

overlook [ˌəʊvə'lʊk] *v.* 1. 忽视，忽略；2. 俯瞰

【记】 over(在…上)+look(看)→在…上看→俯瞰

【例】 1. I will *overlook* your mistake this time. 这次我原谅你的错误。

2. Our garden is *overlooked* by our neighbor's windows. 从邻居的窗口可以看到我家的花园。

【同】 neglect, slight; oversee

overseas ['əʊvə'siːz] *adj.* / *adv.* (亦作 oversea)海外(的)，国外(的)

【记】 over(超越)+sea(海洋)+s→超越整个海洋的→海外的

【例】 The *overseas* trade has become the main project. 海外贸易成为主要的项目。

【同】 abroad, foreign

oversee ['əʊvə'siː] *v.* (-saw, -seen)1. 俯瞰，瞭望；2. 检查，监督

【记】 over(在…之上)+see(看)→从上面看→俯瞰

【例】 1. He happened to *oversee* the burglar leaving the house. 他碰巧看到那盗贼离开房子。

2. You must employ someone to *oversee* the project. 你得雇个人监督这一工程。

【同】 overlook; supervise

【派】 overseer *n.* 监工，工头

overstate ['əʊvə'steɪt] *v.* 夸张的叙述

【记】 over(过度)+state(陈述)→夸大的陈述

【例】 We must neither ignore our problems nor *overstate* them. 我们既不要忽视双方之

间的问题，也不要夸大这些问题。

【同】 exaggerate，magnify

【反】 understate

【派】 overstatement *n*. 大话

overthrow [ˌəuvəˈθrəu] n/*v*. (-threw，-thrown)打倒，颠覆

【记】 over(翻转)＋throw(抛)→把…翻转过来→推翻

【例】 Rebel has *overthrown* the government. 反叛者已经推翻了政府。

【同】 overturn，upset

overt [ˈəuvəːt] *adj*. 明显的，公开的

【例】 The hidden enemies are more deceiving than the *overt* ones，so they are more dangerous. 隐蔽的敌人比公开的敌人具有更大的欺骗性，因而具有更大的危险性。

【同】 bald，obvious，open

【反】 covert

overwhelm [ˈəuvəˈwelm] *v*. 1.淹没；2.制服，压倒

【记】 over(覆盖)＋whelm(淹没)→淹没→压倒

【例】 1. A great mass of water *overwhelmed* the village. 大水淹没了村庄。

2. If I cannot *overwhelm* with my quality，I will overwhelm with my quantity. 如果我不能以质量压倒，我就一定要以数量压倒。

【同】 drown；overmaster，overcome

【派】 overwhelming *adj*. 压倒性的，无法抵抗的

overwrought [ˈəuvəˈrɔːt] *adj*. 过度紧张的，过劳的

【记】 over(过度)＋wrought(古英语 work 的过去式及过去分词，工作)→工作过度的→过度紧张的

【例】 She was in a very *overwrought* state after the accident. 事故发生后她精神十分紧张。

【同】 agitated

owe [əu] *v*. 1.欠；2.把…归功于

【例】 1. He still *owes* us for the goods he received last month. 他上月收到货物，现在还欠着我们钱呢。

2. He *owes* his success more to luck than to ability. 他认为他的成功是靠运气而不是因为自己有能力。

【同】 attribute

【反】 pay

【派】 owing *adj*. 欠债的；应归功于

oxygen [ˈɒksɪdʒən] *n*. 氧，氧气

【记】 oxy(酸)＋gen(产生)→从酸中产生的→氧气

【例】 There was a shortage of *oxygen* at the top of the mountain. 该山顶上缺氧。

【派】 oxygenant *n*. 氧化剂

oxygenic *adj*. 氧的，含氧的

ozone [ˈəuzəun，əuˈz-] *n*. 臭氧

【例】 The pollution had destroyed *ozone* layer and caused many changes in weather. 污染破坏了臭氧层，并引起了许多天气变化。

P

pacific [pəˈsɪfɪk] *adj*. 和平的，平静的；*n*. (the Pacific)太平洋

【记】paci(和平)+fic(做)→使…和平→和平的

【例】1. The night was *pacific*. 黑夜静悄悄的。

2. The spacecraft splashed down in the *Pacific*. 那艘宇宙飞船溅落在太平洋中。

【同】peaceable, peaceful

pacify [ˈpæsɪfaɪ] *v*. 安抚，平息

【记】paci(和平)+fy(动词词尾)→使…和平→使平息→安抚

【例】He tried to *pacify* the protesters with promise of reform. 他试图以改革的承诺安抚抗议者。

【同】appease, mollify, soothe

【反】anger, annoy, irritate

【派】pacification *n*. 讲和，和解，平定

pack [pæk] *n*. 包，盒；*v*. 1. 将某物装入(箱、盒等)；2. 塞满，挤满

【例】1. The traveler took out a bottle of water from the *pack* on his back.
那位旅行者从他的背包中拿出了一瓶水。

2. We leave tomorrow but I haven't begun to *pack* yet! 我们明天动身，但我现在还没开始收拾行李呢！

3. The bus was *packed* with noisy schoolchildren. 这辆公共汽车里挤满了吵吵嚷嚷的小学生。

【同】jam, stuff

【反】unpack

【派】package *n*. 包裹

pact [pækt] *n*. 合同，协定，条约

【例】The two opposition parties made an electoral *pact*. 这两个反对党达成了一项关于在选举中进行合作的协议。

【同】treaty, agreement

painstaking [ˈpeɪnsteɪkɪŋ] *adj*. 辛苦的，辛勤的，艰苦的

【记】pain(痛苦)+s+tak(e)(做)+ing(形容词词尾)→做起来痛苦的→辛苦的

【例】She is not very clever but she is *painstaking*. 她并不很聪明但肯下苦功。

【同】diligent, laborious

palatable [ˈpælətəbl] *adj*. 1. 美味的；2. 愉快的，惬意的

【记】palat(e)(上颚，味觉)+able(形容词词尾)→使味觉好的→美味的

【例】1. Chinese food is quite *palatable*. 中国的食品非常好吃。

2. The truth is not always very *palatable*. 事实真相并非尽如人意。

【同】 delicious，tasty；delectable，pleasing

【反】 unpalatable

pale [peɪl] *adj*. 苍白的，暗淡的

【例】 You are looking rather *pale*, are you ill? 你的脸色有些苍白，你生病了吗？

【同】 dim，faint

【反】 colorful

palm [pɑːm] *n*. 手掌，手心

【例】 European peasants would insert a wooden drill in a round hole and rotate it briskly between their *palms*. 欧洲的农民们会把一根木钻插入一个圆孔里，然后用两个手掌快速的转动木钻。

pamphlet ['pæmflɪt] *n*. 小册子

【记】 pam(= pan，全) + phl(= philos，爱) + et(名词词尾，表示"小")→大家都喜欢的小东西→小册子

【例】 He gave me a *pamphlet* for my call numbers. 他给了我一个小册子记录电话号码。

【同】 booklet，brochure，leaflet

panacea [ˌpænə'sɪə] *n*. 万能药，解决一切问题的方法

【记】 pan(全) + acea(治疗)→全能治疗→万能药

【例】 There's no single *panacea* for the country's economic ills. 国家经济弊病百出，并无万灵药可以医治。

【同】 cure-all

pane [peɪn] *n*. 长方块(窗格)，窗格玻璃

【例】 The *pane* of glass was broken by a football. 一块玻璃被足球打碎了。

【同】 paneling

panel ['pænl] *n*. 1. 仪表板；2. 座谈小组

【记】 pane(长方块) + l→长方块的东西→仪表板

【例】 1. A *panel* of a vehicle is usually under the windshield. 车辆的仪表板一般在挡风玻璃下面。

2. What do the *panel* think? 专题讨论小组有什么意见？

【同】 board；jury

panic ['pænɪk] *n*. 惊慌，恐慌

【记】 pan(希腊神话中人身羊足的神) + ic(形容词词尾转用作名词)→看见 Pan 害怕的→惊慌

【例】 The audience were thrown into a *panic* when the fire started. 一起火观众顿时陷入一片慌乱。

【同】 scare，terror

【派】 panic-stricken *adj*. 受恐慌的，惊慌失措的

panicky *adj*. 恐慌的，惊慌失措的

paperclip ['pepəklɪp] *n*. 回形针

【记】 paper(纸张) + clip(夹子)→夹住纸张的夹子→回形针

【例】 I fastened the pages together with a *paperclip*. 我用一个纸夹把那几页纸夹在

P

一起。

par [pɑː] *n*. 常态，一般状况

【例】 Well, that's about *par* for the course. 那么，那是对于这门课程的一般情况而言。

【同】 average, normal

【反】 abnormal

paradise [ˈpærədaɪz] *n*. 1. 天堂；2. 极乐，至福

【例】 1. Hong Kong is a travellers' *paradise*. 香港是旅游者的乐园。

2. It is sheer *paradise* to relax in a hot bath after a hard day's work. 一天的辛苦工作之后在热水缸里放松一下真是最大的享受。

【同】 heaven

【派】 paradisiacal *adj*. 天堂的，乐园的

paradox [ˈpærədɒks] *n*. 自相矛盾的话，似是而非的矛盾说法

【记】 para(与…相反) + dox(意见)→与一般意见相反的说法→似是而非的矛盾说法

【例】 It is a *paradox* that such a rich country should have so many poor people living in it. 如此富足的国家竟有如此多的穷人，这是个矛盾的现实。

【同】 contradiction

【派】 paradoxical *adj*. 荒谬的

parallel [ˈpærəlel] *adj*. 1. 平行的；2. 类似的，相同的

【记】 para(在旁边) + (a)llel(彼此)→在彼此的旁边→平行的

【例】 1. The railway lines run *parallel* to the road. 铁路线和那条道路平行。

2. My experience in this matter is *parallel* to yours. 在这件事情上，我的经验和你的类似。

【同】 analogue

【反】 oblique

P

paralysis [pəˈrælɪsɪs] *n*. 瘫痪，麻痹

【记】 para(在旁边) + lys(使放松) + e→使放松以分离→瘫痪

【例】 The disease results in creeping *paralysis*. 这种病可发展成脊髓痨.

【派】 paralyze *v*. 使瘫痪，麻痹

paramount [ˈpærəmaʊnt] *adj*. 最重要的，最高权力的

【记】 para(超越) + mount(山)→超越山峰的→最重要的

【例】 The reduction of unemployment should be *paramount*. 降低失业率应是头等大事。

【同】 foremost, predominant, supreme

paraphrase [ˈpærəfreɪz] *v*. 将…释义，改写，意译

【记】 para(旁边) + phrase(说)→用其他的话说→释义，意译

【例】 *Paraphrase* the following obscure passage in modern English. 用现代英语意译下面一段晦涩的文字。

【同】 interpret, rephrase

【派】 paraphrasis *n*. 释义，意译

parasite [ˈpærəsaɪt] *n*. 寄生虫

【记】 para(旁边) + site(食物)→靠近食物旁边→寄生虫

【例】 Don't give money to him; he is a *parasite*. 别给他钱，他是个好吃懒做的人。

【派】 parasitic *adj*. 寄生的

parcel ['pɑːsl] *n*. 小包，包裹；*v*. (-l(l)ed; -l(l)ing)打包

【记】 par(部分) + cel(表示"小"的名词词尾)→分成小的部分→小包

【例】 1. He snipped the string and untied the *parcel*. 他剪断绳子，解开包裹。

2. He *parceled* up the books. 他把书打成了包。

【同】 pack, package

pardon ['pɑːdn] *n*./*v*. 原谅，宽恕

【记】 par(完全) + don(给予)→完全给予→原谅

【例】 1. If I have offended you, I ask your *pardon*. 如有冒犯之处，请多多原谅。

2. *Pardon* my strong language, please. 请原谅我说了激烈的话。

【同】 excuse, forgiveness

【派】 pardonable *adj*. 可以原谅的，难怪的

parliament ['pɑːləmənt] *n*. 议会，国会

【记】 parlia(= parley, 会谈) + ment(名词词尾)→会谈的地方→议会

【例】 Several laws have been passed during the present *Parliament*. 几项新法律已经在本届议会获得通过。

【派】 parliamentary *adj*. 议会的

partial ['pɑːʃəl] *adj*. 1. 部分的；2. 偏袒的，偏爱的

【记】 part(部分) + ial(形容词词尾)→部分的

【例】 1. Our play was only a *partial* success. 我们的剧只能说是差强人意。

2. His *partial* attitude called forth a lot of criticism. 他的偏袒态度招致了不少批评。

【同】 fractional, limited; biased, unfair

【反】 impartial

partner ['pɑːtnə] *n*. 1. 配偶，同组伙伴；2. 合作者，合伙人

【记】 part(部分) + (n)er(表示"人"的名词词尾)→是其中一不分的人→配偶，合伙人

【例】 1. Are you sure you want him to be your *partner*? 你肯定你想要他做你的终身伴侣吗？

2. She is a *partner* in a law firm. 她是法律事务所的一个合伙人。

【同】 mate, spouse; collaborator, cooperator

【派】 *partnership* *n*. 合伙关系；合伙公司，合伙企业

participate [pɑː'tɪsɪpeɪt] *v*. 参与，分担

【记】 parti(部分) + cipate(承担)→承担其中一个部分→参与

【例】 Everyone in the class is expected to *participate* in the discussion. 希望全班同学参加讨论。

【同】 enter, join

【派】 participant *n*. 参加者

participation *n*. 参与，分享

particle ['pɑːtɪkl] *n*. 微粒，点

【记】 parti(部分) + cle(表示"小"的名词词尾)→微小的部分→微粒

【例】 We can see the dust *particles* floating in the sunlight clearly. 我们可以很清楚地看

P

到阳光下的灰尘颗粒。

【同】 mote，particulate

particular [pə'tɪkjʊlə] *adj*. 特殊的，某一的

【记】 parti(部分) + cular(形容词词尾，有…的)→有其中某一部分→特殊的

【例】 Is there any *particular* colour you would prefer? 你有什么特别喜欢的颜色吗？

【同】 exceptional，special

【反】 common，general

【派】 particularly *adv*. 尤其地，特别地

passionate ['pæʃənɪt] *adj*. 热情的，热烈的

【记】 passi(感觉) + (i)on(名词词尾) + ate(形容词词尾)→充满了感情的→热情的

【例】 His *passionate* speech had an effect on our emotions. 他的热情的演讲打动了我们的感情。

【同】 enthusiastic，zealous

【反】 passionless

【派】 (逆构)passion *n*. 激情，热情

passive ['pæsɪv] *adj*. 被动的，消极的

【记】 passi(感觉，忍受) + ve(形容词词尾)→承受的→被动的，消极的

【例】 He played a *passive* role in the marriage. 他在婚姻中扮演了一个被动的角色。

【同】 inactive，negative

【反】 active

【派】 passiveness *n*. 被动，顺从

passport ['pɑːspɔːt] *n*. 护照

【记】 pass(通过) + port(港口)→通过港口的凭证→护照

【例】 You'll also need to bring two *passport* photos with you. 您还需要随身携带两张护照照片。

P

paste [peɪst] *n*. 糊，柔软糊状混合物；*v*. 粘贴

【例】 1. My fingers are beginning to prick after touching that *paste*. 我的手指接触那软膏之后就疼起来了。

2. She *pasted* posters onto the wall. 她把海报粘贴在墙上。

【同】 cement，glue

【派】 paster *n*. 贴纸

paste-up *n*. 东拼西凑的文章

pastime ['pɑːstaɪm] *n*. 消遣，娱乐

【记】 pas(s)(过去) + time(时间)→消磨时间→消遣

【例】 Listening to music is my favorite *pastime*. 听音乐是我最喜欢的消遣。

【同】 recreation，entertainment

pasture ['pɑːstʃə] *n*. 草原，牧草；*v*. 放牧

【例】 1. This *pasture* can no longer carry such a large number of cattle and sheep. 这块草地再也不能供养这么多牛羊了。

2. He's pasturing his cattle on the top meadow. 他正在高处的草地上放牛。

【同】 grassland，meadow

【派】 *pasture*land *n*. 牧场

pat [pæt] *n*./*v*. (-tted; -tting)轻拍

【例】 1. She gave the child a *pat* on the head. 她轻轻拍了一下那孩子的头。

2. She *patted* her hair to make sure it was tidy. 她轻轻地拍拍头发，确保头发整齐。

【同】 rap, tap

patch [pætʃ] *n*. 补缀，碎片；*v*. 修补，补缀

【例】 1. The boy's trousers need a *patch* on the knee. 这孩子的裤子膝盖上需要打个补丁。

2. He *patched* up a couple of old tires. 他补了几条旧车胎。

【同】 mend

patent [ˈpeɪtənt, ˈpætənt] *n*./*v*. (申请)专利；*adj*. 显然的，明白的

【记】 来自拉丁语 patens，公开→专利

【例】 1. The *patent* runs out in three years time. 这项专利期限为3年。

2. It was *patent* to anyone that she disliked the idea. 谁都知道她不喜欢那个主意。

【同】 apparent, manifest

【派】 patency *n*. 明显

patentee *n*. 专利权所有人

paternal [pəˈtɜːnl] *adj*. 父亲的，像父亲的

【记】 pater(父亲)+n+al(形容词词尾)→父亲的

【例】 The employees resented the bosses' *paternal* attitude. 雇员们讨厌老板家长式的管理态度。

【同】 fatherly, fatherlike

【反】 maternal

【派】 paternity *n*. 父权；父系

pathetic [pəˈθetɪk] *adj*. 哀婉动人的，引起怜悯的

【记】 path(痛苦)+etic(形容词词尾)→痛苦的→引起怜悯的

【例】 We saw the *pathetic* sight of starving children. 我们看到挨饿的儿童悲惨可怜的样子。

【同】 miserable, pitiful

patriarch [ˈpeɪtrɑːk] *n*. 家长，族长

【记】 patr(i)(父亲)+arch(统治)→父亲统治→家长，族长

【例】 Her *patriarch* is strict with her. 她的家长对她要求很严。

【派】 patriarchal *adj*. 家长的，族长的

patriotic [ˌpætrɪˈɒtɪk, ˌpeɪtrɪ-] *adj*. 爱国的，有爱国心的

【记】 patri(父亲)+otic(形容词词尾)→爱父亲的→有爱国心的

【例】 His *patriotic* action raised our admiration. 他的爱国行为激起了我们的敬佩。

【同】 loyal

【反】 unpatriotic

【派】 (逆构)patriot *n*. 爱国者

patriotism *n*. 爱国心，爱国精神

P

patronage [ˈpætrənɪdʒ] *n*. 庇护，赞助

【记】 patr(父亲的) + on(名词词尾) + age(名词词尾)→像父亲给予的→庇护

【例】 This orchestra has been established under the *patronage* of the government. 这个交响乐团是在政府赞助下成立的。

【同】 support

【派】 (逆构)patron *n*. 赞助人，资助人

patronal *adj*. 保护的，赞助的

pattern [ˈpætən] *n*. 1. 模式，风格；2. 图案

【记】 pat(父亲的) + tern(= turn，转向)→转向父亲的→与父亲一样的→模式

【例】 1. These sentences all have the same grammatical *pattern*. 这些句子的语法模式都相同。

2. She wore a dress with a *pattern* of roses on it. 她穿了一件带有玫瑰花图案的连衣裙。

【同】 model，example

pause [pɔːz] *n*./*v*. 中止，暂停

【记】 paus(放置) + e→搁置起来→中止

【例】 I'd like to *pause* in my talk. 我想暂时谈到这里。

【同】 hesitate，interruption

【反】 continue

pavement [ˈpeɪvmənt] *n*. 人行道

【记】 pave(铺路) + ment(名词词尾)→铺成的路→人行道

【例】 Several pedestrians had come to slip on the icy *pavement*. 几个行人在结冰的人行道上滑倒了。

【同】 sidewalk

【派】 (逆构)pave *v*. 铺(路、街道等)

peak [piːk] *n*. 顶点，最高峰

【例】 Tourism is at its *peak* in August. 旅游业在八月份达到高峰。

【同】 tip，top，summit

【反】 foot

【派】 peaked *adj*. 尖的

peck [pek] *v*. 啄，啄起

【例】 That bird tried to *peck* the baby. 那只鸟想啄那个小孩。

【派】 peckerwood *n*. 啄木鸟

peculiar [pɪˈkjuːljə] *adj*. 奇特的，罕见的

【记】 pecul(私有财产) + iar(形容词词尾)→独有的→奇特的

【例】 My key has disappeared — this is *peculiar*! 我的钥匙不见了——这可真是太奇怪了。

【同】 odd，particular

【反】 common

【派】 peculiarity *n*. 特性，怪癖

pedagogy [ˈpedəgɪg] *n*. 教育学，教学法

【记】 ped(孩子)+agog(引导)+y(名词词尾)→引导孩子的方法→教育学，教学法

【例】 In the last forty years or so, practically all the efforts to improve the learning of English have gone into *pedagogy*. 40多年来，几乎所有用于提高英语学习效果的努力都集中在教学方法上。

【同】 teaching

【派】 pedagogic(al) *adj*. 教育学的

pedal ['pedl] *n*. 蹬踩，踏板

【记】 ped(脚)+al(名词词尾)→用脚踏的→踏板

【例】 The *pedal* of a cycle is attached to a crank. 自行车的踏板与曲柄相连。

【同】 treadle

peddle ['pedl] *v*. 1. 挑卖，沿街叫卖；2. 传播

【记】 ped(脚)+d+le(动词词尾)→步行(叫卖)→沿街叫卖

【例】 1. He *peddled* small household articles around the town. 他在城里挨家挨户兜售日用百货。

2. I don't know who's been peddling these nasty rumors about me. 我不知道是谁在散播这些针对我的恶毒谣言。

【同】 sell, vend; spread

【派】 *peddler* *n*. 小贩；传播者

pedestrian [pe'destrɪən] *n*. 步行者；*adj*. 徒步的，呆板的

【记】 ped(脚)+estrian(…的人)→走路的人→步行者

【例】 1. Two *pedestrians* and a cyclist were injured when the car skidded. 汽车打滑时伤了两个行人和一个骑自行车的人。

2. Life in the suburbs can be pretty *pedestrian*. 郊区生活有时相当沉闷。

【同】 footer, walker

peel [piːl] *v*. 剥皮，削皮

【例】 They *peeled* off their clothes and jumped into the water. 他们脱去外衣，跳入水中。

【同】 pare, strip

peep [piːp] *n*./*v*. 窥视，偷看

【例】 He took a *peep* at the back of the book to find out the answer to the questions. 他偷偷看了一下书的后面，想找出这些问题的答案。

【同】 glance, glimpse

【派】 peeper *n*. 偷窥者，眼睛

peephole *n*. 窥视孔

peer [pɪə] *n*. 同辈，同等的人；*v*. 凝视，窥视

【例】 1. The opinions of his *peers* are more important to him than his parents' ideas. 在他看来，他同辈人的观点比他父母的观点更为重要。

2. She *peered* through the mist, trying to find the right path. 她透过雾眯着眼看，想找出正确的路。

【同】 compeer; look, gaze

【派】 peerless *adj*. 出类拔萃的，无可匹敌的

penalty ['penltɪ] *n*. 处罚，罚款

【记】pen(处罚) + al(形容词词尾) + ty(名词词尾)→处罚的东西→罚款

【例】1. What is the *penalty* for dangerous driving? 对危险驾车给予什么处罚?

2. Liverpool was given a *penalty* when one of their opponents handled the ball. 利物浦队因对方一队员用手触球而得到一个罚球。

【同】fine，punishment

【反】reward

【派】(逆构)penal *adj*. 刑事的，应受处罚的

penalize *v*. 处罚

penchant ['pɜːŋʃɜːŋ] *n*. (强烈的)倾向，爱好，嗜好

【记】pench(= pens，悬挂) + ant(名词词尾)→悬挂的倾向哪一边→爱好

【例】She has a *penchant* for Indian food. 她爱吃印度食物。

【同】preference，taste

pending ['pendɪŋ] *adj*. 即将发生的，未决的

【记】pend(悬挂) + ing(形容词词尾)→悬着的→即将发生的

【例】A decision on this matter is *pending*. 此事即将作出决定。

【同】forthcoming，imminent

penetrate ['penɪtreɪt] *v*. 穿透，洞察

【记】penetr(里面深处) + ate(动词词尾)→(进入)里面深处→穿透

【例】The headlamps *penetrated* the fog. 车的前灯的光射进雾中。

【同】perceive，pierce

【派】penetrating *adj*. 明察秋毫的，尖锐的

penetration *n*. 穿过，突破

peninsula [pɪ'nɪnsjʊlə] *n*. 半岛

【记】pen(几乎) + insula(岛屿)→几乎成为岛→半岛

【例】Italy is a *peninsula*. 意大利是一个半岛。

pension ['penʃən] *n*. 退休金，养老金

【记】pens(衡量) + ion(名词词尾)→计算(给予金钱)→退休金

【例】He retired on a company *pension*. 他退休时得到公司的退休金。

【同】allowance，subsidy

【派】pensioner *n*. 领养老金(或补助金)的人

pensive ['pensɪv] *adj*. 沉思的，忧愁的

【记】pens(称重，衡量) + ive(形容词词尾)→反复衡量的→沉思的

【例】The woman in this painting has a *pensive* smile. 这幅画上的女人脸上露出忧郁的微笑。

【同】thoughtful，meditative，pondering，sad

pepper ['pepə] *n*. 胡椒粉；*v*. 在…上洒，使布满

【例】1. Ginger，cinnamon，*pepper* and cloves are common spices. 姜、肉桂、胡椒、丁香都是常用的香料。

2. The wall had been *peppered* with bullets. 墙上有密集的子弹痕迹。

【同】capsicum；scatter

perceive [pə'siːv] *v*. 感知，认识到

【记】 per(通过) + ceive(拿取)→凭感觉取得→认识到

【例】 We had already *perceived* how the temperature fluctuated. 我们已注意到温度的波动情形。

【同】 comprehend，realise

【派】 perceivable *adj*. 可知觉的

perception [pə'sepʃən] *n*. 感知，观念

【记】 per(通过) + cept(取) + ion(名词词尾)→通过(感官)获得→感知

【例】 His analysis of the problem showed great *perception*. 他对该问题的分析显示出敏锐的洞察力。

【同】 percept，sensing

【派】 perceptive *adj*. 有理解的

perceptivity *n*. 知觉，知觉力

percussion [pəː'kʌʃən] *n*. 打击乐器

【记】 per(彻底的) + cuss(敲击) + ion(名词词尾)→用力敲击的乐器→打击乐器

【例】 He is a musician who plays *percussion* instruments. 他是一个演奏打击乐器的音乐家。

【同】 drumming

【派】 (逆构)percuss *v*. 轻敲，轻叩

percussionist *n*. 打击乐器乐手

perennial [pə'renjəl] *adj*. 四季不断的，(植物)多年生的

【记】 per(通过) + enn(= ann，一年) + ial(形容词词尾)→经过全年的→四季不断的

【例】 Bamboos are *perennial* grasses that remain in a vegetative state for many years and then suddenly flower，fruit and die. 竹子是多年生草本植物，可以多年保持营养生长状态，然后突然开花、结果，然后死去。

【同】 continual，perpetual

【反】 annual

perfect ['pəːfɪkt，pə'fekt] *adj*. 完美的，正确的；*v*. 使完美，使熟练

【记】 per(彻底的) + fect(做)→做的全面彻底→完美的

【例】 1. The artist's work shows the *perfect* union of craftsmanship and imagination. 这位艺术家的作品表现了技艺和想象力的完美的结合。

2. She needs to *perfect* her Arabic before going to work in Cairo. 她需要把阿拉伯语学好才能到开罗工作。

【同】 flawless，ideal；improve

【反】 imperfect

【派】 perfection *n*. 尽善尽美，完成

perform [pə'fɔːm] *v*. 1. 表演；2. 执行，履行

【记】 per(彻底的) + form(形成)→完全的造型→表演

【例】 1. They are *performing* his piano concerto tonight. 他们今晚演出他的钢琴协奏曲。

2. That notary is authorized to *perform* the certain legal functions. 公证人被授权

执行某些法律职能。

【同】 act; do, execute

【派】 performable *adv*. 可执行的

performance *n*. 表演；履行

perfume ['pɜːfjuːm] *n*. 香味，香水

【记】 per(到处) + fume(烟)→像烟一样到处飘→香味

【例】 The smell of her *perfume* lingered in the empty house. 空屋里仍然飘溢着她的香水味。

【同】 aroma, fragrance

peril ['perɪl] *n*. 危险

【记】 peri(尝试通过) + l→尝试通过→危险

【例】 The ship was in imminent *peril* of being wrecked. 那条船马上就有失事的危险。

【同】 danger, hazard, jeopardy

【反】 safety

【派】 perilous *adj*. 危险的

perimeter [pə'rɪmɪtə] *n*. 周长，周围

【记】 peri(圆的) + meter(测量)→测量圆周围的长度→周长

【例】 The barbed wire fence round the *perimeter* discouraged intruders. 周围有铁丝网阻止了外人闯入。

【同】 border, circumference

period ['pɪərɪəd] *n*. 阶段，周期

【记】 peri(圆的) + od(路途)→绕一周的(时间)→周期

【例】 He was taken on for a three-month trial *period* before being accepted as a permanent member of staff. 在她被接受为固定雇员之前经过了三个月的试用期。

【同】 interval, span

【派】 periodic *adj*. 定期的，周期的

periodical *n*. 期刊，杂志

peripheral [pə'rɪfərəl] *adj*. 外围的，不主要的

【记】 peri(周围) + pher(拿，带) + al(形容词词尾)→传到周围的→外围的

【例】 They are discussing some questions *peripheral* to the main issue. 他们在讨论一些与主要议题无密切关系的问题。

【同】 outer

【反】 central

【派】 periphery *n*. 外围

perish ['perɪʃ] *v*. 死，毁灭

【记】 per(完全，彻底) + ish(动词词尾)→彻底(走)→死

【例】 Almost a hundred people *perished* in the hotel fire last night. 近百人在昨夜旅馆的大火中丧生。

【同】 die, pass away

perjury ['pɜːdʒərɪ] *n*. 伪证，假誓

【记】 per(完全彻底) + jur(发誓) + y(名词词尾)→发誓过头→假誓，假证

【例】 She appeared in court on a *perjury* charge. 她因被指控做了伪证而出庭受审。

【同】 lying

permanent ['pɜːmənənt] *adj*. 长期不变的，永久的

【记】 per(在…期间) + man(存在) + ent(形容词词尾)→一直存在的→永久的

【例】 Nothing can assure *permanent* happiness. 没有什么东西能确保永久的幸福。

【同】 constant，enduring

【反】 impermanent，temporary

【派】 permanence *n*. 永久，持久

permeate ['pɜːmɪeɪt] *v*. 渗透，弥漫

【记】 per(通过) + me(滑行) + ate(动词词尾)→滑行穿过→渗透

【例】 The smell of cooking *permeates* through the flat. 整套房间都弥着漫做菜的气味。

【同】 diffuse，pervade

【派】 permeation *n*. 渗透，透过

permit [pɜː'mɪt，'pəmɪt] *n*. 许可证，执照；*v*. (-tted；-tting)许可，允许

【记】 per(通过) + mit(投，掷)→通过每一关→许可

【例】 1. Students on a visitor visa or work *permit* may study for a maximum of 3 months. 持有访问签证或工作许可的学生可以最多学习 3 个月。

2. I'll come after the meeting if time *permits*. 如果时间许可的话，我开完会就来。

【同】 allow，let

【反】 forbid，prohibit

【派】 permittee *n*. 持证人

permissible *adj*. 可容许的

permission *n*. 许可，允许

permissive *adj*. 许可的，宽容的

pernicious [pɜː'nɪʃəs] *adj*. 有害的，致命的

【记】 per(完全) + nic(杀) + ious(形容词词尾)→完全杀死的→致命的

【例】 Pollution of the water supply reached a level *pernicious* to the health of the population. 水源污染已经达到危及居民健康的程度。

【同】 deadly，fatal，harmful

perpendicular [ˌpɜːpən'dɪkjʊlə] *adj*. 垂直的，直立的

【记】 per(完全) + pend(悬挂) + icu + lar(形容词词尾)→完全悬挂下来的→垂直的

【例】 He'd drunk so much that he found it hard to remain *perpendicular*. 他喝酒太多，简直站都站不直了。

【同】 vertical，upright

【反】 parallel

perpetrate ['pɜːpɪtreɪt] *v*. 犯罪，做坏事

【记】 per(完全) + petr(实现) + ate(动词词尾)→完全实现→做坏事

【例】 Who *perpetrated* that dreadful extension to the front of the building? 谁在那楼房正面加盖了那么一截讨厌的建筑物？

【同】 commit，do

【派】 perpetrator *n*. 凶手，做恶者

perpetual [pə'petʃuəl] *adj*. 永久的，不断的

【记】 per(在…期间)+pet(寻求)+ual(形容词词尾)→一直寻求下去→永久的

【例】 Double agents live in a *perpetual* state of fear. 两面派永远过着提心吊胆的生活。

【同】 constant, permanent

【反】 temporary

【派】 perpetuate *v*. 使(某事物)永久，永存

perpetuation *n*. 永存，不朽

perplex [pə'pleks] *v*. 困惑

【记】 per(彻底的)+plex(折叠)→彻底卷入→困惑

【例】 Faced with that dilemma, he was *perplexed*. 他面对进退两难的局面，不知如何是好。

【同】 puzzle, bewilder

【派】 perplexed *adj*. 困惑的，不知所措的

perplexity *n*. 困惑，混乱

persecute ['pəːsɪkjuːt] *v*. 迫害，困扰

【记】 per(完全，一直)+secut(跟随)+e→穷追不舍→困扰，迫害

【例】 They came to America after being *persecuted* for their religious beliefs. 他们是在因宗教信仰而受到迫害之后来到美洲的。

【同】 oppress

【派】 persecution *n*. 迫害，烦扰

persevere [ˌpəːsɪ'vɪə] *v*. 坚持，坚忍

【记】 per(彻底的)+severe(严格)→彻底的严格→坚持

【例】 You will need to *persevere* if you want the business to succeed. 要想事业成功，就得持之以恒。

【同】 persist

【派】 persevering *adj*. 坚忍的，不屈不挠的

perseverance *n*. 坚定不移

persist [pəː'sɪst] *v*. 固执，持久

【记】 per(一直)+sist(站立)→一直站立着→固执

【例】 They *persisted* in the agricultural reform despite opposition from the famers. 他们不顾农民的反对，执意进行农业改革。

【同】 continue, last

【反】 cease, desist

【派】 persistence *n*. 坚持，持续

persistent *adj*. 持久的，稳固的

personal ['pəːsənl] *adj*. 个人的，私人的

【记】 person(人)+al(形容词词尾)→属于一个人的→私人的

【例】 *Personal* cleanliness is important to health as well as to appearance. 个人清洁对于健康和仪表同样重要。

【同】 individual, private

【反】 impersonal

【派】 personality *n*. 人格，(鲜明的)个性

personnel *n*. 人员，职员

perspective [pə'spektɪv] *n*. 1. 观点，远景；2. 透视图

【记】 per(通过) + spect(看见) + ive(形容词词尾)→通过…看见的→远景，观点

【例】 1. You must get the story in its right *perspectives*. 你必须正确地了解这件事。

2. She drew a row of trees receding into the distance to demonstrate the laws of *perspective*. 她画了一排由近而远高度递减的树以演示透视法的规律。

【同】 position, view

【派】 perspectivity *n*. 透视，明晰度

perspire [pəs'paɪə] *v*. 出汗

【记】 per(完全) + spir(呼吸) + e→(皮肤)呼吸→出汗

【例】 People considered it as an honor to pay strength and *perspire* for it. 大家把为大桥出的一点力，流的一点汗，当做光荣。

【同】 sweat

【派】 perspiration *n*. 汗水；出汗

persuade [pə'sweɪd] *v*. 劝说，说服

【记】 per(彻底的) + suade(劝告)→充分的劝告→说服

【例】 Can you *persuade* her out of her foolish plans? 你能劝她放弃她那些愚蠢的计划吗?

【同】 convince, convict

【反】 dissuade

【派】 persuasion *n*. 说服，说服力

persuasive *n*. 说服者，劝诱

adj. 善说服的

pessimistic [ˌpesɪ'mɪstɪk] *adj*. 悲观的，厌世的

【记】 pessimis(=拉丁语 pessimus，最糟糕的) + tic(形容词词尾)→认为…是最糟糕的→悲观的

【例】 It may be costly to be overly optimistic—but more costly still to be too *pessimistic*. 过度乐观将使我们付出昂贵的代价——但是过度悲观的代价将是更加昂贵的。

【同】 discouraged

【反】 optimistic

【派】 (逆构)pessimism *n*. 悲观，悲观主义

pessimist *n*. 悲观论者，悲观主义者

pertinent ['pɜːtɪnənt] *adj*. 相关的，切题的

【记】 per(完全) + tin(保持) + ent(形容词词尾)→完全保持的→相关的

【例】 The biographer will be seized of all *pertinent* papers and correspondence. 这位传记作者将掌握全部有关文件和信件。

【同】 relevant

pervade [pɜː'veɪd] *v*. 弥漫，渗透

【记】 per(完全) + vade(走)→全部走到→弥漫

【例】 Her work is *pervaded* by nostalgia for a past age. 她的作品充满了怀旧之情。
【同】 diffuse, permeate
【派】 pervasion *n*. 扩散，渗透

pervert [pɜː'vɜːt] *v*. 1. 使堕落，引入歧途；2. 曲解，滥用
【记】 per(完全) + vert(转向)→完全离开(正道)→引入歧途，曲解
【例】 1. Do pornographic books *pervert* those who read them? 看色情书刊能诱人堕落吗？
2. Scientific knowledge was *perverted* to help cause destruction and war. 科学知识被滥用于破坏和战争。
【同】 misdirect; abuse, distort

pest [pest] *n*. 害虫
【例】 Stores of grain are frequently attacked by *pests*. 储存的谷物经常受到害虫的破坏。
【派】 pesticide *n*. 杀虫剂，农药
pest-resistant *adj*. 抗虫的

petition [pɪ'tɪʃən] *n*. 请愿，请求，恳求
【记】 pet(= seek, 寻求) + ition(名词词尾)→寻求→请求
【例】 She filed a *petition* for divorce. 她提出了离婚申请。
【同】 appeal, plea, request

petrol ['petrəl] *n*. 汽油
【例】 Any new source of energy will be welcome, as there is a shortage of *petrol*. 由于石油短缺，任何一种新能源都会受欢迎。
【同】 gasoline, gas
【派】 petroleum *n*. 石油

pharmaceutical [ˌfɑːmə'sjuːtɪkəl] *n*. 药剂，药物；*adj*. 药物的，制药(学)上的
【记】 pharmac(]希腊语 pharmakon, 药物) + eut(名词词尾) + ical(形容词词尾)→药物的
【例】 He works in a large *pharmaceutical* company. 他在一家大的制药公司上班。
【派】 pharmaceutics *n*. 配药学，制药学
pharmaceutist *n*. 药剂师

phase [feɪz] *n*. 时期，局面
【记】 pha(外观) + se(名词词尾)→外面可以看到的东西→局面
【例】 The disease was discovered in an early *phase*. 病在早期已被发现。
【同】 aspect, stage
【派】 phase-in *n*. 逐步采用
phase-out *n*. 逐步淘汰

phenomenon [fɪ'nɒmɪnən] *n*. (复数 -na)现象
【记】 phen(= phan, 出现) + omen(预兆) + on(名词词尾)→出现某种预兆→现象
【例】 International terrorism is not just a recent *phenomenon*. 国际恐怖主义并不是近年才有的现象。
【派】 phenomenal *adj*. 现象的；非凡的，格外的

philosophy [fə'lɒsəfɪ] *n*. 1. 哲学，哲学体系；2. 信念，宗旨

P

【记】 philo(热爱)+soph(智慧)+y(名词词尾)→热爱智慧的学问→哲学

【例】 1. She delivered a talk on *philosophy* to the society. 她给学会作了一次有关哲学的讲话。

2. The *philosophy* of the prisoners during their worst sufferings impressed even their captors. 俘虏们在最困苦时仍处之泰然，连捉住他们的人都深有感触。

【派】 philosophical *adj*. 哲学的

philosopher *n*. 哲学家，哲人

phonetics [fəʊ'netɪks] *n*. 语音学

【记】 phon(声音)+et+ics(名词词尾，表示学科)→研究语音的学科→语音学

【例】 He was popularly regarded as a great authority on *phonetics*. 他被普遍认为是语音学方面的大权威。

【派】 (逆构)phonetic *adj*. 语音的，语音学的

photocopy ['fəʊtəʊˌkɒpɪ] *n*./*v*. 复印，影印

【记】 photo(光)+copy(复制)→利用光来复制→复印

【例】 1. It is a very poor *photocopy* but you should be able to make something of it. 那个照相复制本非常蹩脚，不过你应该能够看懂的。

2. She *photocopied* the contract. 她影印了这份合同。

【同】 copy

【派】 photocopier *n*. 影印机，复印机

photography [fə'tɒgrəfɪ] *n*. 摄影，摄影术

【记】 photo(光)+graph(写，记录)+y(名词词尾)→用光记录下来→摄影

【例】 I've decided to learn *photography* in order that I may better appreciate the beauty of nature. 我决定学摄影以便更能欣赏自然的美。

【派】 photographer *n*. 摄影师

photographic *adj*. 照片的，摄影的

photosynthesis [ˌfəʊtəʊ'sɪnθəsɪs] *n*. 光合作用

【记】 photo(光)+synthesis(合成)→利用光来合成→光合作用

【例】 The rate of *photosynthesis* in a plant can be measured by calculating the rate of its uptake of carbon. 植物光合作用的速度可以通过计算它摄取碳的速度来计算。

【派】 photosynthetic *adj*. 光合的

physical ['fɪzɪkəl] *adj*. 1. 身体的；2. 物质的，自然的，物理的

【记】 physi(cs)(物理的)+cal(形容词词尾)→和物理有关的→物理的

【例】 1. Archaeology, then, is both a *physical* activity out in the field, and an intellectual pursuit in the study or laboratory. 因此，考古学既是在野外的体力活动，又是在书房或实验室的脑力劳动。

2. It's a *physical* impossibility to be in two places at one time. 同时在两地是自然规律上不可能的事。

【同】 bodily

【反】 spiritual; chemical

【派】 (逆构)physics *n*. 物理，物理学

physicist *n*. 物理学者，唯物论者

physician *n*. 医生，内科医生

physiological [ˌfɪzɪəˈlɒdʒɪkəl] *adj*. 生理上的，生理学的

【记】 physi(身体的)+ologi(=ology，…学)+cal(形容词词尾)→关于身体的学问的→生理学的

【例】 The doctors could find no *physiological* cause for his illness. 医生们未能找到他患病的生理学原因。

【派】 (逆构)physiology *n*. 生理学

physiologist *n*. 生理学者

pictorial [pɪkˈtɔːrɪəl] *adj*. 图示的，图画的；*n*. 画报

【记】 pict(o)(图画)+rial(形容词词尾)→用画来解释的→图示的

【例】 1. You can find a *pictorial* record of the event on the Internet. 你可以在网上找到该事件的图片记录。

2. The pretty girl on the cover of the *pictorial* is just a sales gimmick. 画报的封面上印上美女不过是吸引顾客的一种生意眼。

【同】 graphic

picturesque [ˌpɪktʃəˈresk] *adj*. 独特的，如画的

【记】 pictur(图画)+esque(形容词词尾，以…风格)→以图画般的风格→如画的

【例】 He painted the *picturesque* fishing village in the bay. 他画了海湾里一个风景如画的渔村。

【同】 beautiful

pierce [pɪəs] *v*. 1. 刺入，穿孔；2. 深深感动

【记】 pier(]per，通过)+ce(]cer，打击)→打穿→刺入

【例】 1. She had her ears *pierced* so that she could wear ear-rings. 她已经扎了耳朵眼好戴耳环。

2. Her suffering *pierced* their hearts. 她的遭遇让他们深深感动。

【同】 penetrate，thrust

【派】 piercing *adj*. 刺骨的，刺穿的

P

pilferage [ˈpɪlfərɪdʒ] *n*. 行窃，偷盗

【记】 pilfer(偷)+age(名词词尾)→偷窃的行为→行窃，偷盗

【例】 *Pilferage* in the warehouse reduces profitability by about two per cent. 仓库中的失窃使利润损失了2%。

【同】 stealing，theft

【派】 (逆构)pilfer *v*. 行窃，偷盗

pilgrim [ˈpɪlgrɪm]n. 圣地朝拜者，朝圣者

【记】 pil(=per，完全)+grim(国土)→完全走过国土的人→朝圣者

【例】 We met many *pilgrims* on their way to Mecca. 我们遇到许多去麦加朝圣的人。

【同】 palmer

pill [pɪl] *n*. 药丸，丸剂

【例】 The defeat was a bitter *pill* to swallow. 那次失败是一次难以吞咽的苦果。

【同】 tablet

pillar [ˈpɪlə] *n*. 柱，柱子；2. 支持者，栋梁

【记】 pil(l)(堆，墩) + ar(名词词尾)→墩子→柱子

【例】 1. The roof of the church was supported by stone *pillars*. 这座教堂的屋顶由石柱支撑着。

2. He has been a *pillar* of the Church all his life. 他一生都是教会的热心支持者。

【同】 column，mainstay

pilot ['paɪlət] *n*. 飞行员，领航员；*adj*. 示范的，实验性的，试点的

【记】 pil(飞行) + ot(…的人)→飞行的人→飞行员

【例】 1. Mark used to be a *pilot* on the Mississippi River. 马克曾在密西西比河上当过领航员。

2. We are doing a *pilot* study to see if the new product will sell well. 我们正在为这种新产品做试销调查，看它的销路好不好。

【同】 conductor，operator；experimental

pioneer [ˌpaɪə'nɪə] *n*. 开辟者，创始人；*v*. 开辟，发明，创造

【记】 pion(步兵) + eer(名词词尾，…的人)→走在最前面的步兵→开辟者

【例】 1. He was a *pioneer* in the use of X-rays. 他是最早使用 X 光的人。

2. This company *pioneered* the use of the silicon chip. 这家公司开创了使用硅片的方法。

【同】 innovator，forerunner

【派】 pioneering *adj*. 开创性的

pious ['paɪəs] *adj*. (对宗教)虔诚的

【例】 He is a *pious* Christian. 他是一名虔诚的基督教徒。

【同】 devout，dedicated

【反】 impious

【派】 piety *n*. 虔诚

pipe [paɪp] *n*. 管子，导管

【例】 The workers are laying *pipes* under the road. 工人们正在道路下面铺设管道。

【同】 hose，tube

pitch [pɪtʃ] *n*. 1. 球场；2. 音高，高度；3. 沥青，柏油

【例】 1. The crowd invaded the *pitch* at the end of the match. 在比赛结束时，人群涌进了球场。

2. Disagreement reached such a *pitch* that we thought a fight would break out. 分歧达到如此程度，以至于我们以为会发生一场打斗。

3. Touch *pitch*, and you will be defiled. 近朱者赤，近墨者黑。

pivot ['pɪvət] *n*. 枢轴，中心点

【例】 Because her job had been the *pivot* of her life, retirement was very difficult. 因为她的工作一向是她生命的支柱，所以退休后日子很不好过。

【同】 axis

【派】 pivotal *adj*. 枢轴的，关键的

placement ['pleɪsmənt] *n*. 布置，工作安排

【记】 place(地方) + ment(名词词尾)→放在合适的地方→布置

【例】 But remember, you'll have to give me a finder's fee since I am acting as your

P

placement agency. 不过要记着，既然我给你当职业介绍所的介绍人，你要给我职业介绍费。

【同】 arrangement, position

【派】 (逆构)place *n*. 地点；职位，地位；*v*. 放置，任命

plagiarize ['pleɪdʒɪəraɪz] *v*. 剽窃，抄袭

【记】 plagiar(斜的) + ise(动词词尾)→使…变成斜的(书写体是斜的)→抄写→剽窃

【例】 He has *plagiarized* most of the book from earlier studies of the period. 他那本书大部分都是从研究那个时期的著作中剽窃的内容。

【同】 copy

【派】 plagiary *n*. 剽窃

plagiarist *n*. 剽窃者

plagiarism *n*. 剽窃，抄袭

plague [pleɪg] *n*. 瘟疫，灾祸；*v*. 折磨，使苦恼

【例】 1. A great *plague* was then raging in the city. 那时一场大瘟疫正在该城肆虐。

2. She was *plagued* with arthritis. 她患关节炎十分痛苦。

【同】 epidemic, pestilence; afflict, vex

plain [pleɪn] *n*. 平原，草原；*adj*. 简单的，朴素的，清晰的

【例】 1. Such trees can be found in the *plains*. 这种树木可见于平原。

2. The markings along the route are quite *plain*. 路线沿途的标志都十分清楚。

【同】 apparent, obvious

【反】 complicated, fanciful

plaintiff ['pleɪntɪf] *n*. 原告

【记】 pain(捶胸，抱怨) + t + iff(名词词尾)→抱怨的人→原告

【例】 The judge decided for the *plaintiff*. 法官判决原告胜诉。

【同】 complainant

【反】 defendant

P

planet ['plænɪt] *n*. 行星

【记】 来自希腊语的 planan 的被动形式，意思是游走，当时人们认为行星是在天空游走的→行星

【例】 The *planets* of our solar system are Mercury, Venus, Earth, Mars, Jupiter, Saturn, Uranus and Neptune. 我们太阳系的行星有水星、金星、地球、火星、木星、土星、天王星、海王星。

【派】 planetary *n*. 行星的

planetology *n*. 行星学

plastic ['plæstɪk, 'plɑːstɪk] *n*. (塑料)制品；*adj*. 塑胶的，有可塑性的

【记】 plas(模式) + tic(形容词词尾)→可以改变的模式→有可塑性的

【例】 1. *Plastic* is sometimes used instead of leather. 塑胶有时可以替代皮革。

2. There isn't much metal in the bodywork of this new car; it's mainly *plastic*. 这辆新汽车的车身没用多少金属材料，大部分是塑料的。

【同】 flexible

【派】 plasticity *n*. 可塑性

plateau ['plætəʊ, plæ'təʊ] *n*.（复数 -eaus 或 - eaux）1.高原；2.（发展后）稳定状态

【记】 plat（平坦的）+ eau（名词词尾）→平坦的地方→稳定状态

【例】 1. The farmers, living on the Loess *Plateau* about 2200 meters above sea level, have been suffering from a water shortage since the 1970s. 居住在海拔 2200 米的黄土高原上的农民从 20 世纪 70 年代以来就遭受着缺水的痛苦。

2. After a period of rapid inflation, prices have now reached a *plateau*. 经过急剧的通货膨胀之后物价现已趋于平稳。

【同】 tableland

platform ['plætfɔːm] *n*. 月台，平台

【记】 plat（平坦的）+ form（形状）→平坦的东西→月台

【例】 He was walking up and down the station *platform*. 他在火车站的月台上走来走去。

plausible ['plɔːzəbl] *adj*. 似乎可信的，似乎合理的

【记】 plaus（鼓掌）+ ible（形容词词尾）→让人鼓掌的→似乎有理的

【例】 He trotted out a most *plausible* story, but most of us were inclined to doubt the truth of it. 他提出了一个听起来很有道理的说法，但我们大多数人对此都持怀疑态度。

【同】 believable, credible

【反】 actual, genuine

【派】 plausibility *n*. 似乎有理，善辩

platitude ['plætɪtjuːd] *n*. 陈词滥调

【记】 plat（平的）+ itude（名词词尾）→平淡不新奇→陈词滥调

【例】 It's a very uninspiring speech full of *platitudes*. 那是一个充满陈词滥调的平淡的演讲。

【同】 banality, cliche

【派】 platitudious *adj*. 陈词滥调的，陈腐的

playwright ['pleɪraɪt] *n*. 剧作家

【记】 play（戏剧）+ wright（写）→写戏剧的人→剧作家

【例】 The *playwright* Oscar Wilde was noted for his epigrams. 剧作家奥斯卡·王尔德以他的诙谐短诗著称。

【同】 dramatist

plea [pliː] *n*. 请求，恳求

【例】 She made an impassioned *plea* for justice. 她激昂地抗辩，恳求获得公正。

【同】 appeal, supplication, petition

pledge [pledʒ] *n*./*v*. 保证，誓言

【例】 1. Take this ring as a *pledge* of our friendship. 请接受这个戒指作为我们友谊的信物。

2. They *pledged* never to tell the secret. 他们发誓决不泄密。

【同】 guarantee, vow

pliable ['plaɪəbl] *adj*. 柔韧的，柔软的；2.易受影响的，顺从的

【记】 pli（折）+ able（形容词词尾）→可以弯曲的→柔韧的

P

【例】 1. Cane is *pliable* when wet. 藤条潮湿时易弯曲。

2. He's especially *pliable* after a few drinks. 几杯酒下肚之后，他就全无主见了。

【同】 flexible，limber

【反】 rigid

【派】 pliability *n*. 柔韧性

plight [plaɪt] *n*. (恶劣的)情势，困境

【记】 pli(折叠)+ght(名词词尾)→折叠起来→困境

【例】 The poor girl was in a terrible *plight*. 这个可怜的女孩处境极其恶劣。

【同】 predicament，difficulty

plot [plɒt] *n*. 1.小块地；2.(小说的)情节；*v*. (-tted；-tting)密谋，策划

【例】 1. I grow potatoes on my little *plot* of land. 我在那一小块地上种土豆。

2. The *plot* was too complicated for me-I could not follow it. 我觉得情节太复杂——我看不明白。

3. They are *plotting* how to murder him. 他们在密谋如何杀害他。

plug [plʌg] *n*. 1.塞子；2.插头，插销

【例】 1. She pulled the *plug* out of the bathtub and the dirty water ran away. 她把浴缸的塞子拔掉，脏水流走了。

2. I will have to change the *plug* on the hair drier. 我得更换吹风机的插头了。

plum [plʌm] *n*. 1.李子，葡萄干；2.深紫色

【例】 1. Then for dessert there's traditional *plum* pudding or apple pie, plus coffee. 然后就是饭后甜点，有传统的李子布丁、苹果馅饼，还有咖啡。

2. I also want to wear this *plum* satin dress. 我还想穿这件深紫色的绸缎的连衣裙。

plumber ['plʌmbə]*n*. 管子工，铅管工

【记】 plumb(引导)+er(名词词尾)→引导(水)的人→管子工

【例】 We had to call a *plumber* to unblock the drains. 我们得叫管工来通一通下水道。

plump [plʌmp] *adj*. 胖嘟嘟的，丰满的；*v*. 突然放下，重重地坐下

【例】 1. You're getting a bit *plump*—you need to diet! 你有点发胖了——得节食了！

2. All she wanted to do was *plump* down on the sofa and relax. 她想做的就是一屁股倒在沙发上休息。

【同】 fat，round；plunk，plop

plunge [plʌndʒ] *n*./*v*. 跳进，投入

【例】 The car *plunged* off the highway into the sea. 汽车冲出个公路，栽进海里。

【同】 dive，dump

【派】 plunger *n*. 跳进(水中)的人，潜水者

plural ['plʊərəl] *adj*. /*n*. 复数(的)

【记】 plur(许多)+al(形容词词尾)→许多的→复数的

【例】 Most *plural* nouns in English end in "s". 英语的复数名词多以"s"结尾。

【反】 singular

plus [plʌs] *prep*. 加，加上；*adj*. /*n*. 正(号)的，附加的

【例】 1. Two *plus* five is seven. 2加5等于7。

2. The work will cost £10, 000 *plus*. 那幅作品可值一万英镑以上。

【同】 addition, positive

【反】 minus

pneumonia [njuːˈməʊnjə] 肺炎

【记】 pneumon(肺) + ia(拉丁语名词词尾)→肺部出现的问题→肺炎

【例】 He was indebted to her for nursing him through *pneumonia*. 他感激她护理好了他的肺炎。

【派】 pneumonic *adj*. 肺的，肺炎的

poem [ˈpəʊɪm, ˈpəʊem] *n*. 诗，诗体文

【例】 He wrote a *poem* about war. 他写了一首关于战争的诗。

【同】 verse

【反】 prose

poetry [ˈpəʊɪtrɪ, ˈpəʊətrɪ] *n*. (总称)诗，韵文

【记】 poet(诗人) + ry(名词词尾)→诗人写的东西→诗歌

【例】 This dancer has *poetry* in her movements. 这位舞蹈演员的舞姿同诗一般美丽。

【同】 lyric, verse

【反】 prose

【派】 (逆构)poet *n*. 诗人

poetic *adj*. 诗歌的，诗人(一样)的

poise [pɔɪz] *n*. 1. 平衡，均衡；2. 姿势；*v*. 1. (使)平衡；2. 保持…姿势

【例】 1. We admired the graceful *poise* of the dancer. 我们很欣赏那位舞蹈演员的优美舞姿。

2. He *poised* the glass on the edge of the shelf. 他把玻璃杯稳稳的放在架子的边缘上。

3. After years in the wilderness, the term "artificial intelligence" (AI) seems *poised* to make a comeback. 在淡出人们视线多年之后，"人工智能"(AI)这个名词好像又出现准备回归的态势了。

【同】 balance

poison [ˈpɔɪzn] *n*. 毒药，毒物；*v*. 毒害，败坏

【例】 1. These *poisons* can easily enter the food chain, affecting the productivity of fishing and farming. 这些毒药会很容易进入食物链，影响到农业和渔业的生产力。

2. The chemical companies are *poisoning* our rivers with effluent. 这些化学公司排出废水污染着我们的河流。

【派】 poisonous *adj*. 有毒的

polar [ˈpəʊlə] *adj*. 两极的，对立的

【记】 pol(e)(地球的极) + ar(形容词词尾)→两极的，对立的

【例】 The two systems of government are *polar* opposites. 这两种政体正好相反。

【反】 equatorial

【派】 (逆构)pole *n*. 两极；杆，柱

polarize *v*. 使极化，使两极分化

polish [ˈpɒlɪʃ] *v*. 擦亮，使有光泽

【记】 pol(推)+ish(动词词尾)→推来推去→擦去

【例】 I *polished* my buttons with a handkerchief. 我用手帕把钮扣擦亮。

【同】 buff, burnish, shine

【反】 tarnish

poll [pəul] *n*. 民意测验

【例】 The result of the *poll* won't be known until midnight. 投票结果要到半夜才能知道。

【同】 survey

pollution [pə'lu:ʃən, pə'lju:ʃən] *n*. 污染

【记】 pollut(e)(污染)+ion(名词词尾)→污染

【例】 Many young people could not resist the spiritual *pollution*. 很多年轻人不能抵制精神污染。

【同】 contamination

【派】 (逆构)pollute *v*. 污染，弄脏

pollutant *n*. 污染物质，有害物质

ponder ['pɒndə] *v*. 沉思，考虑

【记】 pend(称重，衡量)+er(此处用作动词词尾)→反复衡量→考虑

【例】 He *pondered* for some minutes before giving an answer. 他思考了几分钟才作答复。

【同】 contemplate, deliberate

【派】 ponderous *adj*. 沉重的，笨重的

pool [pu:l] *n*. 水坑，水池；*v*. 合伙，共用

【例】 1. The children ducked each other in the swimming *pool*. 孩子们在游泳池里互相把对方按入水中。

2. If we *pool* our ideas, we may produce a real good plan. 如果我们集思广益，我们能够制定出一个很好的计划。

【同】 pond, puddle; contribute

populace ['pɒpjʊləs] *n*. 平民，大众

【记】 popul(人)+ace(名词词尾)→一般的人→平民

【例】 *Populace* in China live a very happy life now. 中国老百姓现在过着幸福的生活。

【同】 public, citizen

popular ['pɒpjʊlə] *adj*. 1. 流行的，时兴的；2. 受人欢迎的，得人心的

【记】 popul(人)+ar(形容词词尾)→受众人欢迎的→流行的

【例】 1. Do you like *popular* music? 你喜欢流行音乐吗？

2. Her charm of manner made her very *popular*. 她风度优雅，备受欢迎。

【同】 common, prevalent

【反】 unpopular

【派】 popularity *n*. 流行，声望

popularize *v*. 普及

population [ˌpɒpjʊ'leɪʃən] *n*. 人口

【记】 popul(人)+ation(名词词尾)→人的数量→人口

【例】 The main impediment to development is the country's large *population*. 发展的主要障碍是这个国家人口太多。

【同】 people

【派】 (逆构)populate *v*. 居住，使人口聚居于

populational *adj*. 人口的

populous [ˈpɒpjʊləs] *adj*. 人口稠密的，人口多的

【记】 popul(人) + ous(形容词词尾)→人多的→人口稠密的

【例】 We live in a *populous* area near the coast. 我们生活在沿海人口稠密的地区。

【同】 thickly-settled，densely-populated

【反】 sparsely-populated

porcelain [ˈpɔːslɪn，pɔːsleɪn] *n*. 瓷器，瓷

【记】 porc(小猪) + el + ain(名词词尾)→像小猪一样白色的东西→瓷器

【例】 I don't know enough about *porcelain* to be able to price these plates. 我不太懂得瓷器，估计不出这些盘子的价钱。

【同】 china

pore [pɔː，pɒə] *n*. 小孔，气孔，毛孔

【例】 Sweat exudes through the *pores*. 汗从毛孔中渗出。

【派】 porous *adj*. 可渗透的，多孔的

port [pɔːt] *n*. 港口，舱门

【例】 It cost us a lot of money to get the goods from the *port* to our factory. 把货物从港口运到我们工厂花了一大笔钱。

【同】 dock，harbor

portable [ˈpɔːtəbl] *adj*. 便于携带的，手提式的

【记】 port(搬，运) + able(形容词词尾)→可以搬运的→便于携带的

【例】 The documents have been typed into a *portable* computer. 文件已经被输入到一台便携式电脑里了。

【同】 movable，transferable

【反】 stationary

【派】 portability *n*. 可携带，轻便

portion [ˈpɔːʃən] *n*. 一部分，一分

【记】 port(= part，部分) + ion(名词词尾)→其中的一个部分

【例】 The driver must bear a *portion* of the blame for the accident. 司机应该对这场车祸负部分责任。

【同】 part，separation

【反】 whole

portrait [ˈpɔːtrɪt] *n*. 肖像，画像

【记】 por(向前的) + trait(拉拽)→向前拉线，作画→画像

【例】 He finished the *portrait* in a few minutes. 他几分钟就完成了一副肖像画。

【同】 picture，portrayal

【派】 portraitist *n*. 肖像画家

portray [pɔːˈtreɪ] *v*. 描画，描写

P

【记】 por(向前的)+tray(拉拽)→向前拉线→描画

【例】 The book *portrays* the life of an actor. 这本书描述了一个演员的一生。

【同】 depict, picture

【派】 portrayal *n*. 描画，描写

portrayer *n*. 肖像画家

pose [pəuz] *n*. 姿势，姿态；*v*. 1. 装腔作势；2. 引起，造成；3. 提出，陈述

【记】 pos(放置)+e→放置的状态→姿态，姿势

【例】 1. His concern for the poor is only a *pose*. 他对穷人的关心只不过是做做样子罢了。

2. Stop posing and tell us what you really think. 别装蒜啦，告诉我们你的真实想法吧。

3. Heavy traffic *poses* a problem in many old towns. 交通拥挤是许多旧城镇的难题。

4. Allow me to *pose* a question. 请允许我提一个问题。

【同】 posture; pretense; present, set

position [pəˈzɪʃən] *n*. 1. 位置，职位；2. 主张，立场

【记】 pos(放置)+ition(名词词尾)→放置的地方→位置

【例】 1. The house has a very good *position*. 这所房子处于一个很好的位置。

2. Ironically, one major casualty of that extreme *position* has been the environment itself. 具有讽刺意味的是，那种极端主义立场的主要受害者之一竟是环境本身。

【同】 job, location; stand

【派】 positional *adj*. 位置的，地位的

positive [ˈpɒzətɪv] *adj*. 肯定的，积极的

【记】 pos(放置)+(i)tive(形容词词尾)→定下位置的→肯定的

【例】 He was *positive* that he had seen it in the newspaper. 他肯定他已在报纸上看见过。

【同】 convinced, definite, favourable

【反】 negative

【派】 positivity *n*. 积极性

possess [pəˈzes] *v*. 拥有，支配

【记】 pos(能够)+sess(坐着)→能坐在(旁边)的→拥有

【例】 The police asked me if I *possessed* a gun. 警察问我是否有枪。

【同】 hold, occupy

【派】 possession *n*. 拥有，财产

possessive *adj*. 物主的，占有的

possessor *n*. 持有人

post [pəust] *n*. 1. 柱子，标志；2. 岗位，职位；3. 邮件，邮政；*v*. 1. 张贴；2. 邮递

【记】 pos(放置)+t→定下的位置→岗位

【例】 1. The fence was held up by wooden *posts*. 这围栏是用木桩支撑着的。

2. The vacant *post* was advertised in today's paper. 今天报纸上刊登了有关这个空

缺职位的广告。

3. He is dealing with his *post* at the moment. 他此刻正在处理信件。

4. Advertisements have been *posted* up everywhere announcing the new show. 到处贴满了广告宣传这一新节目。

【同】 mark, office, position, mail

【派】 postage *n*. 邮资

postcode *n*. 邮政编码

poster *n*. 海报，招贴

posterity [pɒs'terɪtɪ] *n*. 子孙，后代

【记】 post(在…之后) + er(表示"人") + ity(名词词尾)→后来的人，后继者→子孙，后代

【例】 He left behind an immortal example to all *posterity*. 他给后世留下了不朽的典范。

【同】 descendants, offspring

【反】 ancestors, ascendants

postgraduate ['pəust'grædjuɪt, 'pəust'grædʒuɪt] *n*. 研究生，硕士研究生

【记】 post(在…之后) + graduate(毕业)→(大学)毕业之后→研究生

【例】 The old professor supervises the *postgraduate* students. 这位老教授指导研究生。

postpone [pəust'pəun] *v*. 推迟，拖延

【记】 post(在…之后) + pon(放置) + e→放到后面的→推迟

【例】 The party was *postponed* until 8 o'clock. 晚会推迟到8点举行。

【同】 delay, defer

【反】 hasten, hurry

【派】 postponable *adj*. 可延期的

postponement *n*. 延期，延缓

posture ['pɒstʃə] *n*. 1. 身体的姿势；2. 态度；*v*. 摆姿势，作出姿态

【记】 post(放置) + ure(名词词尾)→放置的状态→姿势

【例】 1. She has very good *posture*. 她举止很优雅。

2. The government adopted an uncompromising *posture* on the issue of independence. 政府在独立的问题上采取了毫不妥协的态度。

3. The negotiators were just posturing when they demanded such high wage increases. 那些谈判代表们提出这么高的加薪要求，只是装装样子罢了。

【同】 position, pose

【派】 postural *adj*. 姿势的，位置的

posturer *n*. 装腔作势的人

potent ['pəutənt] *adj*. 强有力的，有效的

【例】 I was convinced by his *potent* arguments. 他那有力的论据把我说服了。

【同】 mighty, powerful, strong

【反】 impotent

【派】 potence *n*. 力量，权力，能力

potential [pə'tenʃəl] *adj*. 潜在的，可能的；*n*. 潜能

【记】 potent(力量) + ial(形容词词尾)→有力量的→潜能

【例】 1. Education develops *potential* abilities. 教育能开发人的潜能。

2. He hasn't realized his full *potential* yet. 他还没有意识到他的全部潜能。

【同】 possible, promising

【反】 actual

【派】 potentiality *n*. 潜能，潜力

pottery [ˈpɒtərɪ] *n*. 陶器，陶器场

【记】 pot(t)(罐子)+ery(名词词尾)→和罐子一样的东西→陶器

【例】 The archaeologists found gold coins and *pottery* in the lowest level of the site. 考古学家在发掘地最下层找到一些金币和陶器。

【同】 clayware

【派】 potter *n*. 陶工，制陶工人

poultry [ˈpəʊltrɪ] *n*. 家禽

【记】 poult(小鸡)+ry(名词词尾)→(饲养的)小鸡→家禽

【例】 *Poultry* is rather cheap now. 现在的禽肉相当便宜。

【同】 fowl

pound [paʊnd] *n*. 1. 磅；2. 英镑

【例】 1. I lost several *pounds* last month. 我上个月瘦了好几磅。

2. One *pound* coins came into use in Britain in 1985. 英国于1985年开始使用一英镑的硬币。

pour [pɔː, pɒə] *v*. 1. 倾泻，流动；2. 斟，倒(茶)

【例】 1. She *poured* out her worries to the doctor. 她向医生倾诉自己的忧愁。

2. I've *poured* coffee into your cup by mistake. 我错把咖啡倒到你的杯子里了。

【同】 spill, stream

poverty [ˈpɒvətɪ] *n*. 贫穷，缺少

【记】 pover(= poor，贫穷的)+ ty(名词词尾)→贫穷

【例】 The government has pledged itself to wage a war against *poverty* and disease. 政府发誓要进行一场消灭贫穷和疾病的斗争。

【同】 poorness

【反】 treasure, wealth

【派】 poverty-striken *adj*. 极度贫穷的

practical [ˈpræktɪkəl] *adj*. 实际的，现实的，实用性的

【记】 practic(e)(实践)+al(形容词词尾)→实践的→实用的

【例】 The whole scheme began to take on a more *practical* aspect. 整个计划开始具有更切合实际的性质。

【同】 pragmatic, virtual

【反】 impractical, theoretical

【派】 practicality *n*. 实用性

pragmatic [prægˈmætɪk] *adj*. 务实的，实用主义的

【记】 pragm(做，行为)+atic(形容词词尾)→注重行为的→务实的

【例】 I have made a purely *pragmatic* decision to go along with the boss. 我做出了支持老板的决定，纯粹是出于实际的考虑。

【同】 practical

【派】 pragmatical *adj*. 独断的

pragmatist *n*. 实用主义者，从实际出发的人

praise [preɪz] *v*. /*n*. 表扬，称赞

【记】 prais(价格)+e→有价值的→表扬

【例】 Critics *praised* the work as highly original. 评论家们称赞该作品独树一帜。

【同】 value, compliment

【反】 criticize

preach [priːtʃ] *v*. 1.布道; 2.宣扬，鼓吹

【例】 The priest *preached* a sermon on the need of charity. 牧师在布道会上宣讲慈爱的必要。

【同】 sermonize, lecture; advocate

【派】 preacher *n*. 传教士

preachment *n*. 讲道，说教

precaution [prɪˈkɔːʃən] *n*. 预防，警惕

【记】 pre(在…之前)+caution(小心)→提前小心→预防

【例】 I took the *precaution* of locking everything in the safe. 我把一切东西都锁在保险箱里以防万一。

【同】 caution, forewarning

precedent [prɪˈsiːdənt, ˈpresɪdənt] *n*. 先例，前例

【记】 pre(在前的)+ced(去)+ent(形容词词尾)→去前面→在先的→先例

【例】 Imposing a lenient sentence for such a serious crime sets a dangerous *precedent*. 对这样严重的罪行轻判就开了个危险的先例。

【反】 following

【派】 precedence *n*. 优先，居先

precedented *adj*. 有先例的

precise [prɪˈsaɪs] *adj*. /*n*. 精确(的)，准确(的)

【记】 pre(在…之前)+cise(切掉)→预先切好的→精确的

【例】 At the *precise* moment that I put my foot on the step, the bus started. 恰恰就在我登上公共汽车踏板的时候，车子开动了。

【同】 accurate, exact

【反】 incorrect, vague

precious [ˈpreʃəs] *adj*. 宝贵的，贵重的

【记】 preci(价值)+ous(形容词词尾)→有价值的→宝贵的

【例】 Pandas are *precious* creatures. 熊猫是珍贵的动物。

【同】 valuable, treasured

predator [ˈpredətə] *n*. 食肉动物，捕食者

【记】 preda(掠夺)+tor(名词词尾)→掠夺者→捕食者

【例】 Young birds are very vulnerable to *predators*. 幼小的鸟易受食肉动物伤害。

【派】 predatory *adj*. 掠夺性的，损人利己的

predecessor [ˈpriːdɪsesə] *n*. 前任者，被取代之物

【记】 pre(在…之前)+de(离开)+cess(去)+or(…的人)→先前离开的人→前任者

【例】 1. He undid most of the good work of his *predecessor*. 他把前任的大部分业绩毁掉了。

2. Will the new plan be any more acceptable than its *predecessors*? 新计划比原来的计划更能令人满意吗?

【同】 forerunner

【反】 successor

predict [prɪˈdɪkt] *v*. 预知，预言

【记】 pre(在…之前) + dict(说)→事先说→预言

【例】 The economists *predicted* an increase in the rate of inflation. 经济学家预言通货膨胀率将会增长。

【同】 foretell，forecast

【派】 prediction *n*. 预言，预报

predictive *adj*. 成为前兆的

predominant [prɪˈdɒmɪnənt] *adj*. 最显著的，突出的

【记】 pre(在前面) + dom(in)(统治) + ant(形容词词尾)→在前面统治的→突出的

【例】 Honesty is the *predominant* feature of her character. 诚实是她性格的主要特征。

【同】 chief，dominant

【派】 predominance *n*. 优势

predominate [prɪˈdɒmɪneɪt] *v*. 统治，成为主流

【记】 pre(在前面) + dom(in)(统治) + ate(动词词尾)→在前面统治→成为主流

【例】 The views of the left wing have tended to be *predominate* within the party. 左翼的观点趋向于在该党党内占支配地位。

【同】 dominate

【派】 predomination *n*. 卓越，优势

predominator *n*.统治者

P

prefabricated [ˈpriːˈfæbrɪkeɪt] *adj*. 预制的(指装配前已生产好的)

【记】 pre(在…之前) + fabric(构建) + at(e)(动词词尾) + ed(形容词词尾)→提前构建好的→预制的

【例】 He lives in a *prefabricated* hut. 他住在一个用预制构建组装的棚屋。

【同】 ready-made

【派】 (逆构)prefabricate *v*. 预制

prefer [prɪˈfɜː] *v*. (-rred; -rring)更喜欢，宁愿

【记】 pre(在前面) + fer(搬运)→搬运到面前→更喜欢

【例】 He chose Germany, but personally I'd *prefer* to go to Spain. 他选择了德国，而我个人倒更喜欢去西班牙。

【同】 choose，favour

【派】 preference *n*. 偏爱，优先选择，优先权

preferential *adj*. 优先的，特惠的

pregnancy [ˈpregnənsɪ] *n*. 怀孕，怀孕期

【记】 pre(在…之前) + gn(= gen，生产) + ancy(名词词尾)→生产之前的情况→怀孕

【例】 You are advised not to smoke during *pregnancy*. 怀孕期间你最好不要吸烟。
【同】 gestation
【派】 pregnant *adj*. 怀孕的

prejudice ['predʒʊdɪs] *n*. 偏见，成见
【记】 pre(在…之前) + jud(i)(判断) + ce(名词词尾)→事前的判断→偏见
【例】 They accused him of having a *prejudice* against his women employees. 他们指责他歧视女雇员。
【同】 bias, partiality
【派】 prejudiced *adj*. 怀偏见的
prejudicial *adj*. 引起偏见的

preliminary [prɪ'lɪmɪnərɪ] *adj*. 预备的，初步的；*n*. 1.准备工作，初步行动；2.预赛，淘汰赛
【记】 pre(在前面) + limin(门槛) + ary(形容词词尾)→在门槛之前的→预备的
【例】 1. The *preliminary* details had been worked out. 初步的细节已经出来了。
2. There are a lot of *preliminaries* to be gone through before you can visit a foreign country. 在出访外国之前要做好许多准备工作。
3. Our team got beaten in the *preliminaries*. 我们队在预赛中遭淘汰。
【同】 prior

prelude ['prelju:d] *n*. 序幕，前奏
【记】 pre(在…之前) + lude(戏剧)→戏剧前面的部分→前奏
【例】 The bankruptcy of several small firms was the *prelude* to general economic collapse. 几家小商行倒闭了，随之而来的是经济大萧条。
【同】 beginning, overture, prologue
【反】 postlude, epilogue

premier ['premjə, 'premɪə] *adj*. 第一的，首要的；*n*. 总理，首相
【记】 prem(第一) + ier(名词词尾，…的人)→排第一的人→首相，总理
【例】 1. His work on the cause of the diseases is of *premier* importance to the whole world. 他的病理研究工作对全世界至关重要。
2. The *premiers* of the two countries met in Geneva yesterday. 两国首相昨天在日内瓦会晤。
【同】 prime

premise ['premɪs] *n*. 预述，前提
【记】 pre(在…之前) + mise(投掷)→放在前面→前提
【例】 British justice works on the *premise* that an accused person is innocent until he's proved guilty. 英国司法运作的前提是被告在被证明有罪之前是清白的。
【同】 assumption

premium ['prɪmjəm] *n*. 1.额外费用，奖金；2.保险费
【记】 pre(在…之前) + mium(拿)→事先拿的费用→额外费用
【例】 1. During the holiday months hotel rooms are at a *premium*. 在度假的月份，旅馆房间的价钱比平常高。
2. The annual *premium* on my policy is 3000 yuan. 我的保险单每年的保险费是三

P

千元。

【同】 payment

preoccupation [priːˌɒkjʊˈpeɪʃən] *n*. 全神贯注，令人全神贯注的事物

【记】 pre(在…之前)+occup(y)(占据)+ation(名词词尾)→预先占据的→全神贯注

【例】 His main preoccupation at that time was getting enough to eat. 他那时盘算的是如何填饱肚子。

【派】 (逆构)preoccupy *v*. 使全神贯注，迷住

preparation [ˌprepəˈreɪʃən] *n*. 准备，预备

【记】 pre(在…之前)+par(准备)+ation(名词词尾)→事前做准备→预备

【例】 He didn't do any *preparation* for this exam, so he failed. 他考试前没做任何准备，所以不及格。

【同】 provision

【派】 (逆构)prepare *v*. 准备，预备

preparatory *adj*. 预备的

prepared *adj*. 准备好的，有准备的

prerequisite [ˈpriːˈrekwɪzɪt] *n*. 先决条件，前提

【记】 pre(在…之前)+requisite(必备的)→提前必备的东西→先决条件

【例】 A reasonable proficiency in English is a *prerequisite* for/of joining this advanced-course. 掌握适当程度的英语是参加这门高级课程学习的先决条件。

【同】 preconditon

prescribe [prɪsˈkraɪb] *v*. 1. 开药方；2. 规定

【记】 pre(在…之前)+scrib(写)+e→事先写好→开药方

【例】 1. What medicine did the doctor *prescribe* for your illness? 医生开了什么药来治你的病？

2. Army regulations *prescribe* how rifles must be carried. 军规中对持枪方式有明文规定。

【同】 order, recommend

【派】 prescriber *n*. 处方者，建议者

prescription *n*. 处方，药方；指示，规定

present [ˈprezənt] *n*. 1. 赠品，礼物；2. 现在；*adj*. 1. 现在的；2. 出席的，当面的

[prɪˈzent] *v*. 1. 赠送；2. 上演；3. 提出

【记】 pre(在前面)+sent(存在)→就在眼前的→现在的，出席的

【例】 1. This book was a *present* from my brother. 这本书是哥哥送我的礼物。

2. We learn from the past, experience the *present* and hope for success in the future. 我们从过去中学习，体验现在，展望未来的成功。

3. How many people were *present* at the meeting? 有多少人出席会议？

4. He *presented* her with a bunch of flowers. 他献给她一束花。

5. A comedian will *present* a situation followed by an unexpected interpretation that is also apt. 喜剧演员的表演是给出一种情形，并随后给出一个意想不到却很贴切的解释。

6. It *presents* fundamental strategies and approaches in achieving health for all. 为

了实现所有的人的健康，它提出了基本的战略和方法。

【同】 gift; attending; show; deliver

【反】 past; absent

【派】 presence *n*. 出席，到场

presentation *n*. 介绍，陈述

preserve [prɪ'zɜːv] *v*. 保护，保存

【记】 pre(在…之前)+serv(保留)+e→事先保留→保存

【例】 I think these interesting old customs should be *preserved*. 我认为这些有趣的旧习俗应该保存下去。

【同】 conserve, keep

【派】 preservation *n*. 保存

president ['prezədənt,'prezɪdənt] *n*. 总统，校长，总裁

【记】 pre(在前面)+sid(坐)+ent(名词词尾，…的人)→坐在前面的人→总统，院长

【例】 The *president* is strongly desirous that you should attend the meeting. 董事长极希望你能参加会议。

【同】 chairman

【派】 presidency *n*. 任期

presidential *adj*. 总统的

press [pres] *n*. 1.压，按；2.新闻界；*v*. 压，紧抱

【例】 1. Can you have your report ready for the *press* by next week? 你的报告能在下星期赶好付印吗?

2. The power of the *press* is very great. 新闻界的力量非常大。

3. *Press* this button to start the engine. 按这个按钮开动引擎。

【同】 squeeze, stress

【派】 pressing *adj*. 紧迫的，恳切的

pressure *n*. 压力

P

prestige [pres'tiːʒ,pres'tiːdʒ] *n*. 威望，声望

【记】 pre(在…之前)+stige(紧紧抓住)→在做事之前就抓住人心→威望

【例】 The old universities of Oxford and Cambridge still have a lot of *prestige*. 历史悠久的牛津大学和剑桥大学仍然享有很高的声望。

【同】 fame, reputation, renown

【派】 prestigious *adj*. 有名望的，有威信的

presume [prɪ'zjuːm] *v*. 假定，认为

【记】 pre(在…之前)+sume(拿取)→事先拿取→假定

【例】 The law presumes innocence until guilt is proved. 在罪状未证实前，法律假定被告无罪。

【同】 assume, suppose

【派】 presumed *adj*. 假定的，推测的

presumably *adv*. 据推测，大概，可能

presumption *n*. 猜想，想法；专横，傲慢，自行其是

presumptuous [prɪ'zʌmptjuəs] *adj*. 自以为是的，放肆的

【记】 pre(在…之前) + sumptu(拿取) + ous(形容词词尾)→事先拿取的→自以为是的

【例】 I dislike that *presumptuous* young man. 我不喜欢那个自以为是的年轻人。

【同】 arrogant, insolent

pretend [prɪˈtend] *v*. 假装，伪称

【记】 pre(提前) + tend(伸展)→提前伸出→想好借口→伪称

【例】 She *pretends* that she likes them so that she can get their help. 她假装很喜欢他们，借以获得他们的帮助。

【同】 feign, assume

【派】 pretense *n*. 伪装，作假

pretender *n*. 假装者，冒充者

pretension [priːˈtenʃən] *n*. 主张，自负

【记】 pre(提前的) + tens(伸展) + ion(名词词尾)→提前想好的理由→主张

【例】 A woman, having fewer *pretensions*, is far more willing to learn. 一个不是那么自负的女人会更加乐于学习。

【派】 pretentious *adj*. 狂妄的，自命不凡的

prevail [prɪˈveɪl] *v*. 1. 普遍，流行，盛行；2. 胜过，说服

【记】 pre(提前，优先) + vail(强大)→过于强大→流行

【例】 1. Misty weather *prevails* in this part of the country. 该国的这一地区天气多雾。

2. At last justice has *prevailed* and the guilty man has been punished. 正义最终取得了胜利，作恶的人受到了惩罚。

【同】 dominate, triumph

【派】 prevailing *adj*. 流行的，盛行的

prevalence *n*. 流行

prevalent *adj*. 普遍的，流行的

prevent [prɪˈvent] *v*. 防止，预防

P

【记】 pre(在前面) + vent(来到)→(阻挡住)前来的路→防止

【例】 So this does not *prevent* global warming, but merely buys the world six years. 这当然不能阻止全球变暖，只是为地球赢得了仅仅六年的时间。

【同】 hinder, stop, prohibit

【反】 permit

【派】 prevention *n*. 预防，防止

preventative *adj*. 预防性的

preview [ˈpriːˈvjuː] *v*. /*n*. 预展，预演，预习

【记】 pre(在…之前) + view(看见)→事先看→试演

【例】 We attended a sneak *preview* of the winter fashion collection. 我们参观了一次冬季时装预展。

【反】 review

previous [ˈpriːvjəs] *adj*./*adv*. 在前的(地)，早先的(地)

【记】 pre(前面) + vi(道路) + ous(形容词词尾)→前面走过的路→之前的

【例】 *Previous* to the conference we had discussed the matter among ourselves. 在会议之前，我们讨论了这个问题。

【同】 prior, preceding

【反】 following

prey [preɪ] *n*. 被捕食的动物，掠食；*v*. 捕食，掠夺

【例】 1. The lion seized its *prey* and ate it. 狮子抓住猎物，把它吃了。

2. Strong animals *prey* upon weaker ones. 弱肉强食。

【派】 preyer *n*. 猛兽，猛禽

priest [priːst] *n*. 牧师，教士

【例】 The *priest* makes pastoral visits every Thursday afternoon. 牧师每星期四下午对教友进行访问。

【同】 clergyman, pastor

【反】 nun

primal [ˈpraɪməl] *adj*. 1. 最初的，原始的；2. 最基本的，首要的

【记】 prim(第一) + al(形容词词尾)→第一的→首要的

【例】 1. The natural man has only two *primal* passions—to get and to beget. 自然人只有两种最原始的热情：寻找食物与生儿育女。

2. Money was a *primal* necessity to them. 对于他们，钱是主要的需要。

【同】 primeval, primitive, primary

【派】 primality *n*. 原始，首要

primary [ˈpraɪmərɪ] *adj*. 1. 第一位的，首要的；2. 初步的，初级的

【记】 prim(第一) + ary(形容词词尾)→第一位的

【例】 1. Love and hatred are *primary* emotions. 爱和恨是基本的情感。

2. He only accepted the *primary* education off and on in his childhood. 他小时候只断断续续地接受过初等教育。

【同】 principal, prime; elementary

【反】 secondary

prime [praɪm] *n*. 全盛时期，精华；*adj*. 主要的，第一流的

【记】 prim(第一) + e→第一位→精华，主要的

【例】 1. He was about 40 years old, and in the prime of life. 他大约 40 岁，正值盛年。

2. For several years now, tourism has been the prime source of foreign exchange in Nepal and Bhutan. 多年以来，旅游业一直是尼泊尔和不丹最主要的外汇来源。

【同】 perfect; principal, primary

【派】 primer *n*. 初级读本

primitive [ˈprɪmɪtɪv] *adj*. 原始的，初期的

【记】 prim(第一) + itive(形容词词尾)→第一的，最开始的→原始的

【例】 *Primitive* man made himself primitive tools from sharp stones and animal bones. 原始人用尖石块和兽骨为自己制作原始的工具。

【同】 ancient, elementary

【反】 derivative

【派】 primitiveness *n*. 原始

principal [ˈprɪnsəpəl, ˈprɪnsɪpəl] *n*. 负责人，校长；*adj*. 主要的，首要的

【记】 prin(第一) + cip(抓住) + al(形容词词尾)→首先要抓住的→主要的

【例】 1. The *Principal*'s talk will last about fifteen minutes. 校长的讲话大约会持续15分钟。

2. My wages are the *principal* source of my income. 薪金是我收入的主要来源。

【同】 chief, head; dominant, essential

【派】 principalship *n*. 首要的地位，职务

principle ['prɪnsəpl] *n*. 法则，原则

【记】 prin(第一)+cip(抓住)+le(名词词尾)→首先要抓住的东西→法则

【例】 We adhere to the *principle* that everyone should be treated fairly. 我们必须坚持人人都应该被平等对待这一原则。

【同】 precept, rule

【反】 exception

prior ['praɪə] *adj*. 优先的，在前的

【例】 I was unable to attend the meeting because of a *prior* engagement. 我因有约在先，所以未能参加这个会。

【同】 preceding, previous

【反】 following, posterior

【派】 priority *n*. 优先，在前

privilege ['prɪvɪlɪdʒ] *n*. 特权，优惠

【记】 priv(i)(私有的)+leg(法律)+e→一个人的法律→特权

【例】 Education should not be considered to be a *privilege* in a modern society. 在一个现代社会中，受教育不应该被看成是一种特权。

【同】 favour, advantage

【派】 privileged *adj*. 有特权的；荣幸的

probe [prəʊb] *v*. 调查，查究

【例】 The journalist was probing into several financial scandals. 那记者正在调查几起财务丑闻。

【同】 penetrate, examine, investigate

procedure [prə'siːdʒə] *n*. 程序，过程

【记】 pro(向前)+ced(行走)+ure(名词词尾)→在之前走过的路→过程

【例】 What's the *procedure* for opening a bank account? 在银行开办帐户要办什么手续？

【同】 process, routine

proceed [prə'siːd] *v*. 继续前进，继续进行

【记】 pro(向前)+ceed(走)→向前走→继续前进

【例】 He paused to consult his notes, and then *proceeded* with his questions. 他停下来看了看笔记，然后继续提问。

【同】 advance, progress

【反】 recede

【派】 proceeds *n*. 收入，收益

proceeding *n*. 行动，进程

process [prə'ses] *n*. 过程，步骤；*v*. 加工，处理

【记】 pro(向前)+cess(走)→走上前去→过程

【例】 1. Producing a dictionary is a slow *process*. 编成一本字典是一个缓慢的过程。
2. It may take a few weeks for your application to be *processed*. 审查你的申请书也许要等几个星期。

【同】 course, procedure

【派】 procession *n*. 行列，队伍
processive *adj*. 前进的，进行的

proclaim [prə'kleɪm] *v*. 宣告，声明

【记】 pro(在…前面) + claim(大叫)→在众人之前大叫→宣告

【例】 The president *proclaimed* that a new currency would be issued. 总统宣布将发行新货币。

【同】 announce, declare

procrastination [prəuˌkræstɪ'neɪʃən] *n*. 延迟，拖延

【记】 pro(向前) + cras(明天) + tin(转向) + ation(名词词尾)→把…向前转移到明天→拖延

【例】 Two of the key components of the course are time management and overcoming *procrastination*. 这门课程的两个核心组成部分就是时间管理和克服拖拉的习惯。

【同】 cunctation, delay

【派】 (逆构)procrastinate *v*. 延迟，耽搁

procure [prə'kjuə] *v*. 获得，取得

【记】 pro(为了) + cure(关心，照料)→为了…关心→想办法得到→获得

【例】 The book is out of print and difficult to *procure*. 那书已绝版，很难弄到手。

【同】 acquire, get, obtain

【派】 procurement *n*. 获得，取得

prod [prɒd] *v*. 刺激，敦促

【例】 I shall have to *prod* him to pay me what he owes. 我将不得不催促他把欠我的钱还给我。

【同】 poke

prodigal ['prɒdɪgəl] *adj*. 挥霍的，浪费的

【记】 pro(d)(向前) + ig(驱赶) + al(形容词词尾)→向前驱赶的→挥霍的

【例】 I hate the *prodigal* administration. 我痛恨铺张浪费的行政机关。

【同】 extravagant, lavish, wasteful

【反】 frugal

prodigious [prə'dɪdʒəs] *adj*. 巨大的，惊人的

【记】 pro(d)(向前) + ig(驱赶) + ious(形容词词尾)→向前驱赶的→惊人的

【例】 We are all overwhelmed by his *prodigious* memory. 我们都被他那惊人的记忆力折服了。

【同】 colossal, enormous

【反】 small, tiny

【派】 (逆构)prodigy *n*. 天才，惊人的事物

produce [prə'djuːs] *v*. 1. 生产，制造；2. 产生，引起；3. 提出，拿出

【记】 pro(向前) + duce(领导)→向前引导→生产，引起

P

【例】 1. She can *produce* delicious meal from very simple ingredients. 她能用简单配料烹调出美味的饭菜。

2. There is mounting evidence that learning a language *produces* physiological changes in the brain. 越来越多的证据显示，学习一种语言会使大脑产生心理变化。

3. He can *produce* evidence to support his allegations. 他能提出证据以表明他的指控属实。

【同】 create, compose

【反】 consume

【派】 product *n*. 产品，产量；结果，成果

producer *n*. 生产者，制作者

production *n*. 产品，作品

productivity *n*. 生产力，生产率

professional [prəˈfeʃənl] *adj*. 专业的，职业的；*n*. 专业人员，专家

【记】 pro(前面) + fess(说) + ion(名词词尾) + al(形容词词尾)→在前面说的人→在前面讲述的人→专业人员

【例】 1. That doctor has been accused of *professional* misconduct. 那位医生被指控违反医德。

2. She is a real *professional*. 她是个真正的专家。

【同】 occupational, vocational

【反】 amateur

【派】 profession *n*. 职业，专业

professionalism *n*. 专家的地位、特性或方法

proficient [prəˈfɪʃənt] *adj*. 熟练的，精通的

【记】 pro(前面) + fic(做) + ient(形容词词尾)→以前做过的→熟练的

【例】 I'd say I am quite *proficient* at tailoring. 我可以说我对裁缝很在行。

【同】 competent, skilled, skillful

【派】 proficiency *n*. 熟练，精通

profile [ˈprəʊfaɪl] *n*. 侧面，轮廓

【记】 pro(前面) + file(线)→呈现在眼前的线条→轮廓

【例】 I photographed him in *profile*. 我从侧面给他拍照。

profit [ˈprɒfɪt] *n*. 利润，益处；*v*. 获得利润，得益

【记】 pro(向前) + fit(做)→取得进步→利润

【例】 1. There is very little *profit* in selling newspapers at present. 现在卖报纸利润很少。

2. He's getting married again, after two divorces, so he obviously hasn't *profited* by his experiences. 他两次离婚之后又结婚，显然没有吸取以往的教训。

【同】 advantage, benefit

【派】 profitable *adj*. 有用的，有利可图的

profound [prəˈfaʊnd] *adj*. 意义深远的，渊博的

【记】 pro(向前) + found(基础)→把基础一直向前打→深远的

【例】 Our professor is a man of *profound* learning. 我们的教授是一个学识渊博的人。
【同】 deep, intense
【反】 shallow, superficial
【派】 profoundity *n*. 深奥，深刻

program ［'prəugræm］ *n*. 1. 节目，活动；2. 纲要，计划
【记】 pro(在…之前)+gram(书写)→事先书写好的东西→计划
【例】 1. The news *program* overran the allotted time. 新闻节目超出了规定的时间。
2. The hospital building *program* has been delayed by lack of money. 医院建设计划因为缺乏资金而被推迟。
【同】 movement; plan, project
【派】 programmer *n*. 程序师
programming *n*. 规划，设计

progress ［'prəugres］ *n*./*v*. 进步，前进
【记】 pro(向前)+gress(行走)→一直向前行走→前进
【例】 1. The ship made slow *progress* through the rough sea. 船只在汹涌的大海中缓慢前进。
2. Modern medical science is *progressing* rapidly in the countries all over the world. 现代医学在世界各国都进展很快。
【同】 advance, proceed
【反】 regress, retreat
【派】 progression *n*. 前行，进步
progressive *adj*. 前进的，发展的

prohibit ［prə'hɪbɪt］ *v*. 禁止，阻止
【记】 pro(在前面)+hibit(拥有)→在前面压制→禁止
【例】 The law *prohibits* tobacconists from selling cigarettes to children. 法律禁止烟贩向儿童出售香烟。
【同】 ban, forbid, prevent
【反】 permit
【派】 prohibition *n*. 禁止，阻止
prohibitive *adj*. 禁止的，抑制的

project ［'prɒdʒekt］ *n*. 项目，课题；*v*. 1. 投射，放映；2. 预计，推算
【记】 pro(向前)+ject(投掷)→向前投掷→投射
【例】 1. Several members of the Royal Society possessed an interest in language and became engaged in various linguistic *projects*. 皇家社团的几名成员对语言感兴趣，并从事了各种语言学项目。
2. A missile was *projected* into space. 导弹被发射升空。
3. Inflation is *projected* to increase next year. 预计明年通货膨胀率将上升。
【同】 subject; design, plan; show; figure out
【派】 projection *n*. 发射
projectionist *n*. 放映员
projector *n*. 放映机

projectile *n*. 发射物，投掷物

proliferate [prəʊ'lɪfəreɪt] *v*. 增生，繁殖

【记】 proli(后代) + fer(带) + ate(动词词尾)→带来后代→繁殖

【例】 Fish *proliferated* in the warm sees. 鱼在温暖的海域迅速繁殖。

【同】 multiply, manifold

【派】 proliferation *n*. 增殖，扩散

prolific [prə'lɪfɪk] *adj*. 多产的，多结果的，丰富的

【记】 proli(后代) + fic(做，制造)→制造许多后代的→多产的，多结果的

【例】 Last year was a *prolific* period in the composer's life. 去年是作曲家一生中创作丰收的时期。

【同】 fertile, fruitful, productive

prolong [prə'lɒŋ] *v*. 延长，拖延

【记】 pro(向前) + long(长)→向前伸长→延长

【例】 They *prolonged* their visit by a few days. 他们把访问时间延长了几天。

【同】 extend, lengthen

【反】 shorten

【派】 prolonged *adj*. 长时间的，拖延的

prominent ['prɒmɪnənt] *adj*. 卓越的，突出的

【记】 pro(向前) + min(突出) + ent(形容词词尾)→向前突出的→显著的

【例】 Einstein was a *prominent* scientist. 爱因斯坦是一位卓越的科学家。

【同】 notablity

【反】 obscurity

【派】 prominence *n*. 显著，突出物

promise ['prɒmɪs] *n*./*v*. 允诺，答应

【记】 pro(前面) + mise(送)→送在前面的东西→提前说的话→允诺

【例】 1. I don't trust his *promise* to come for a visit. 我不相信他会如约前来访问。

2. I *promise* to return your bicycle on good condition. 我答应一定完好无损地还你的自行车。

【同】 commitment

【派】 promising *adj*. 有希望的，有前途的

promote [prə'məʊt] *v*. 促进，提升

【记】 pro(向前) + mote(移动)→向前移动→促进

【例】 We must *promote* commerce with neighbouring countries. 我们必须促进与邻国的贸易。

【同】 encourage, boost

【反】 degrade

【派】 promotion *n*. 促进，提升

promoter *n*. 发起人，倡导者

prompt [prɒmpt] *v*. 提示，鼓动；*adj*. 敏捷的，即时的

【记】 pro(e)(在前面) + mpt(取，拿)→在前面拿的→即时的

【例】 1. His evasive reply *prompted* me to ask him another question. 他的含糊其词的答

复促使我提出又一个问题。

2. He is always *prompt* in answering letters. 他总是迅速回复来信。

【同】 inspire, remind; quick, immediate

【反】 slow

【派】 promptive *adj*. 推动的，激励的

promulgate ['prɒməlgeɪt] *v*. 1. 颁布(命令、法律)；2. 传播(信念、知识)

【记】 pro(前面) + mulg(= vulg, 人民) + ate(动词词尾)→放公布于人民面前 →颁布

【例】 1. A new law on taxes was *promulgated* yesterday. 昨天颁布了一项新税法。

2. The department joined other organisations to *promulgate* work ethics among young people at work. 该部门与其他机构携手合作，向在职青年推广职业道德。

【同】 declare; spread

【派】 promulgation *n*. 颁布，传播

prone [prəʊn] *adj*. 倾向于…的

【例】 People are more *prone* to make mistakes when they are tired. 人们疲劳时更容易出差错。

【同】 inclined, liable

pronounce [prə'naʊns] *v*. 1. 发音；2. 宣告，断言

【记】 pro(前面) + nounce(报告)→在前面报告→宣告

【例】 1. In the word "knew", the "k" is not *pronouced*. 在"knew"这个词中，"k"是不发音的。

2. The priest said, 'I now *pronouce* you man and wife.' 神父说，"我现在宣布你们两个人成为夫妻。"

【同】 articulate, say

【派】 pronouncement *n*. 声明

pronunciation *n*. 发音，读法

pronounced *adj*. 显著的，明确的

proof [pruːf] *n*. 证据，考验；*adj*. 不能透入的

【例】 1. A soldier's courage is put to the *proof* in battle. 士兵的勇气在战斗中得到考验。

2. The tent is proof against water. 这帐篷是防水的。

【同】 evidence

【派】 proof-read *v*. 校对

propagate ['prɒpəgeɪt] *v*. 1. 繁殖；2. 传播，宣传

【记】 propag(= 拉丁语 propagare, 切割，剪) + ate(动词词尾)→原义为通过剪枝让植物繁殖→繁殖

【例】 1. Plants won't *propagate* in these conditions. 植物在这种条件下不能繁殖。

2. They started a newspaper to *propagate* their ideas. 他们办了一份报纸来宣传他们的主张。

【同】 generate, multiply; broadcast

【派】 propagation *n*. 繁殖；传播

propel [prə'pel] *v*. (-lled; -lling) 推进，驱使

【记】 pro(向前) + pel(推动)→向前推动→推进

P

【例】 His addiction to drugs *propelled* him towards a life of crime. 他吸毒成瘾使他走上了犯罪的道路。

【同】 push, shove, thrust

【派】 propellant *adj*. 推进的

propensity [prə'pensɪtɪ] *n*. 倾向，癖好

【记】 pro(向前)+pens(悬挂)+ity(名词词尾)→悬挂物向前倾的→倾向

【例】 Our grave *propensity* to bureaucracy is inseparable from the current overstaffing of our organizations. 我们严重的官僚主义倾向与现在机构的臃肿是分不开的。

【同】 tendency

proper ['prɒpə] *adj*. 适当的，正确的

【例】 You aren't wearing *proper* clothes for this hot weather. 这么热的天气，你穿的衣服不合适。

【同】 correct, suitable

【反】 improper

【派】 properly *adv*. 适当地，完全地

property ['prɒpətɪ] *n*. 1. 财产，所有物；2. 性质，特性

【记】 proper(自己的)+ty(名词词尾)→属于自己的东西→财产

【例】 1. Please do not move the furniture as this can cause damage both to the furniture and to the *property*. 请您不要挪动家具，因为那样可能会对家具和物品造成损坏。

2. Many plants have medicinal *properties*. 许多植物具有医药性能。

【同】 belongings, possession

proportion [prə'pɔːʃən] *n*. 1. 比例，部分；2. 面积，规模

【记】 pro(向前)+port(分开)+ion(名词词尾)→分成几部分→部分

【例】 1. Her head is out of *proportion* to the size of her body. 她的头部与身体大小不成比例。

2. We are trying to reduce the problem to manageable *proportions*. 我们正努力把问题缩小到可以控制的范围内。

【同】 balance, dimension; area

【反】 disproportion

【派】 proportional *adj*. 成比例的，均衡的

proportionate *adj*. 成比例的

propose [prə'pəuz] *v*. 1. 计划，建议；2. 求婚

【记】 pro(前面)+pose(放置)→放置在前面→计划

【例】 1. I wish to *propose* a toast to our friendship. 我提议为我们的友谊干杯。

2. He was trying to decide whether he should *propose* to her. 他反复思量是否该向她求婚。

【同】 advise, suggest; court

【派】 proposal *n*. 提议，建议

proposition *n*. 观点，命题

proprietor [prə'praɪətə] *n*. 所有者，业主

【记】 propri(拥有的) + etor(名词词尾)→拥有者→业主

【例】 I've written a complaint to the *proprietor* of the hotel. 我向旅馆老板写信投诉。

【同】 owner

【派】 proprietary *adj*. 所有的，私人拥有的

proprietorship *n*. 所有权

propriety [prəˈpraɪətɪ] *n*. (行为、举止等)适当得体

【记】 propri(拥有的) + ety(名词词尾)→拥有的特点→适当

【例】 The way these tourists dress offends local standards of *propriety*.
这些游客的穿着在当地人的眼中简直不成体统。

【同】 correctitude, properness

【反】 impropriety

prose [prəʊz] *n*. 散文

【例】 He writes a very clear simple *prose*. 他写着一手简洁而明快的好散文。

【反】 poetry

【派】 prosaic *adj*. 散文的，散文体的

prosecute [ˈprɒsɪkjuːt] *v*. 对…起诉，告发

【记】 pro(向前) + secu(跟随) + te(动词词尾)→跟着向前→告发

【例】 He vowed that he would *prosecute* them for fraud. 他郑重宣布将起诉他们犯有欺诈罪。

【同】 accuse, charge, sue

【反】 defend

【派】 prosecution *n*. 检举，起诉

prospect [ˈprɒspekt] *n*. 前景，预期

【记】 pro(前面) + spect(看)→看前方→前景

【例】 This experience opened a new *prospect* in his mind. 这一经验为他的思想开阔了新的视野。

【同】 view, expectation

【反】 retrospect

【派】 prospective *adj*. 预期的

prospectus *n*. 章程，简介

prosperous [ˈprɒspərəs] *adj*. 繁荣的，成功的

【记】 pro(向前的) + sper(希望) + ous(形容词词尾)→有希望向前的→繁荣的

【例】 The city at one time must have been *prosperous*, for it enjoyed a high level of civilization. 这座古城在一个时期准是很繁荣的，因为它曾享有高度文明。

【同】 booming, flourishing

【派】 prosperity *n*. 繁荣

protagonist [prəʊˈtægənɪst] *n*. (戏剧，故事，小说中的)主角，领导者

【记】 prot(第一的) + agonist(= actor，演员)→第一位的演员→主角

【例】 The negative *protagonists* in the play inspire hate in me. 该剧中的反面角色激起我心中的仇恨。

【同】 character, leading figure

protest [prə'test,'prəʊtest] *v.* /*n.* 坚决声明，抗议

【记】 pro(在…之前)+test(证据)→在众人面前拿出证据反对→坚决声明

【例】 1. His *protests* on human rights sound hollow. 他就人权问题提出的抗议听来很空洞。

2. He *protested* his innocence. 他声言自己无罪。

【同】 disapprove, object

【反】 approve

prototype ['prəʊtətaɪp] *n.* 原型，典型

【记】 proto(原始的)+type(类型)→原始的类型→原型

【例】 *Prototypes* of medical-diagnosis programs and speech recognition software appeared to be making progress. 医学诊断程序的雏形以及语音识别软件看起来正在不断取得进展。

【同】 archetype, image

【派】 prototypic *adj.* 原型的

protract ['prɒtrækt,prə'trækt] *v.* 延长，拖长

【记】 pro(前面)+tract(拉)→向前拉→延长

【例】 Let's not *protract* the debate any further. 我们不要再继续争论下去了。

【同】 lengthen, extend, prolong

【反】 shorten

proverb ['prɒvɜːb] *n.* 谚语，格言

【记】 pro(前面)+verb(词语)→以前的词语→谚语

【例】 The *proverb* tells us to emulate the industry of the ant. 这格言告诉我们要效法蚂蚁的勤勉。

【同】 adage, byword

【派】 proverbial *adj.* 谚语的，众所周知的

P

provision [prə'vɪʒən] *n.* 1. 供给，准备；2. 规定，条款

【记】 pro(在…之前)+vis(看见)+ion(名词词尾)→提前看到的东西→供给

【例】 1. We set out with enough *provisions*. 我们带上足够的食品出发了。

2. Both sides should act according to the *provisions* of the agreement. 双方都应按协议条款办事。

【同】 preparation, supply; agreement

provisional [prə'vɪʒənl] *adj.* 暂时的，临时的

【记】 provision(准备)+al(形容词词尾)→准备的→临时的

【例】 Then they organized a *provisional* government. 这时他们组织了一个临时政府。

【反】 definitive

【派】 provisionality *n.* 临时性，暂时性

provoke [prə'vəʊk] *v.* 激怒，挑拨

【记】 pro(向前)+voke(呐喊)→冲到前面呼唤→激怒

【例】 His behavior finally *provoked* her into leaving him. 他的行为气得她终于离开了他。

【同】 arouse, evoke

【反】 appease

【派】 provoking *adj*. 气人的，恼人的

prowess [ˈpraʊɪs] *n*. 英勇，杰出的才能

【记】 prow(英勇的) + ess(名词词尾)→英勇

【例】 The soldiers sang a song of victory, describing their *prowess* in battle. 战士们唱起了歌颂他们英勇战斗的凯歌。

【同】 boldness, skill

proximity [prɒkˈsɪmɪtɪ] *n*. 接近，邻近

【记】 proxim(接近) + ty(名词词尾)→临近

【例】 The restaurant benefits from its *proximity* to several cinemas. 那家餐馆位于几家影院附近因而沾光。

【同】 closeness, propinquity

【派】 proximate *adj*. 最接近的

prudent [ˈpruːdənt] *adj*. 审慎的，深谋远虑的

【记】 pr(= pro, 前面) + ud(= vid, 看) + ent(形容词词尾)→提前看的→审慎的

【例】 Young as he was, he was *prudent*. 他虽然如此年轻，却很慎重。

【同】 careful, cautious, discreet

【反】 imprudent

【派】 prudence *n*. 审慎

pseudonym [ˈpsjuːdənɪm]n. 假名，笔名

【记】 pseudo(假的) + nym(名字)→假名

【例】 George Eliot was the *pseudonym* of Mary Ann Evans. 乔治・艾略特是玛丽・安・埃文斯的笔名。

psychiatrist [saɪˈkaɪətrɪst, sɪˈkaɪətrɪst] *n*. 精神病学家

【记】 psych(精神) + iatr(治愈) + ist(名词词尾，…的人)→治愈精神疾病的人→精神病学家

【例】 I was analyzed in Vienna by a famous *psychiatrist*. 在维也纳，一位著名的精神病学家对我进行了精神分析。

【派】 (逆构)psychiatry *n*. 精神病学，精神病治疗法
psychiatrical *adj*. 精神病学的，精神病治疗的

psychology [saɪˈkɒlədʒɪ] *n*. 心理学

【记】 psych(精神，心理) + ology(…学)→关于心理问题的学科→心理学

【例】 Mathematics, *psychology*, and political science-these are my favorite subjects. 数学、心理学和政治学——这些是我所学的课程。

【派】 psychological *adj*. 心理的
psychologist *n*. 心理学家

publication [ˌpʌblɪˈkeɪʃən] *n*. 1. 发表，出版；2. 出版物

【记】 public(公共的) + ation(名词词尾)→使变成公共的东西→出版

【例】 1. The book is ready for *publication*. 这本书已准备好随时出版。
2. The library gets the usual monthly *publications*. 这家图书馆订的是那些常见的月刊。

P

【同】 issue，publishing

publicity [pʌbˈlɪsɪtɪ] *n*. 公开，宣传

【记】 public(公共的)+ity(名词词尾)→让公众知道→公开

【例】 The newspaper gave much *publicity* to the concert. 报纸对这次音乐会进行了充分报道。

【派】 publicize *v*. (公开)宣传，宣扬

publish [ˈpʌblɪʃ] *v*. 出版，公布

【记】 publ(人们)+ish(动词词尾)→放在人们面前→出版

【例】 He has *published* quite a lot of articles. 他发表了不少文章。

【同】 print，release

【派】 publisher *n*. 出版者，发行人

puff [pʌf] *n*. (风的)吹，呼；*v*. 1.喷出；2.喘息

【例】 1. He blew out the candles with a single *puff*. 他一口气吹灭了蜡烛。

2. He often *puffs* cigarette smoke in other's face for fun. 他常常向别人脸上喷烟闹着玩儿。

3. He was *puffing* hard when he reached the station. 他到达车站的时候喘得很厉害。

【同】 blow，whiff

【派】 puffer *n*. 吹嘘者

puffy *adj*. 膨胀的，肿胀的

pulse [pʌls] *n*. 脉搏，脉冲；*v*. 搏动，振动

【例】 1. And the *pulses* would travel over glass fibres, not copper wire. 脉冲将通过玻璃纤维而不是铜线传播。

2. He could feel the blood *pulsing* through his body. 他能感觉到浑身血液在奔腾。

【同】 throb

P

【派】 pulsation *n*. 脉搏，心跳

pump [pʌmp] *n*. 泵，抽水机；*v*. 抽水，抽吸

【例】 1. Can you lend me your bicycle *pump*? 能把你的打气筒借给我吗？

2. The heart *pumps* blood into the veins. 心脏把血液送至血管。

punch [pʌntʃ] *n*. / *v*. 1.用拳猛击；2.打孔

【记】 pun(刺)+ch(动词词尾)→刺出洞→打孔

【例】 1. I'd like to give that man a *punch* on the nose. 我真想对着那个人的鼻子猛击一拳。

2. The ticket-collector *punched* a hole in my ticket. 检票员给我的车票打了孔。

【同】 beat，strike；pierce

【派】 puncher *n*. 打印机

punctual [ˈpʌŋktjʊəl] *adj*. 严守时刻的，准时的

【记】 punct(刺)+ual(形容词词尾)→刺的那一点→准时的

【例】 A *punctual* person always finishes everything ahead of time. 一个守时的人总是把事情提前做好。

【同】 timely，on time

【反】 unpunctual

【派】 punctuality *n*. 准时

puncture [ˈpʌŋktʃə] *n*. 小孔；*v*. 刺破

【记】 punct(刺)＋ure(名词词尾)→刺成的洞→小孔

【例】 1. I've got a *puncture* and my spare is flat too! 我的车胎扎破了，备用的也瘪了！

2. He is in hospital with a *punctured* lung. 他因肺部穿孔而住院。

【同】 puncturing; perforate, pierce

【派】 puncturable *adj*. 可穿孔的，可穿刺的

pungent [ˈpʌndʒənt] *adj*. (指气味、味道)刺激性的，辛辣的

【记】 pung(刺)＋ent(形容词词尾)→刺激的

【例】 He exhaled the *pungent* odor of garlic. 他散发出刺鼻的大蒜味。

【同】 smelling, biting

【派】 pungency *n*. 苦痛，辛辣，刺激

punish [ˈpʌnɪʃ] *v*. 惩罚，处罚

【记】 pun(处罚)＋ish(动词词尾)→处罚

【例】 Dangerous driving should be severely *punished*. 危险驾驶应受严惩。

【同】 penalise

【反】 forgive, reward

【派】 punishment *n*. 惩罚，惩处

puppet [ˈpʌpɪt] *n*. 傀儡，木偶

【记】 pup(p)(小动物)＋et(表示“小”的名词词尾)→像小动物一样的东西→木偶

【例】 Are we the *puppets* of fate? 我们是听任命运摆布的傀儡吗？

【派】 puppetry *n*. 木偶剧演出

purchase [ˈpɜːtʃəs] *n*./*v*. 买，购买

【记】 pur(为了)＋chase(追逐，获得)→为了获得→购买

【例】 1. She made several *purchases* in the dress shop. 她在服装店里买了几样东西。

2. He managed to secure a loan to *purchase* a house. 他设法弄到一笔贷款买了一栋房子。

【同】 buy, shop

【反】 sell

【派】 purchaser *n*. 买方，购买者

purify [ˈpjʊərɪfaɪ] *v*. 使纯洁，净化

【记】 pur(i)(纯洁)＋fy(动词词尾)→使…纯净→净化

【例】 Water is *purified* by passing through the rock. 水在穿透岩石的过程中得到了净化。

【同】 clarify, refine

【派】 purification *n*. 净化

purse [pɜːs] *n*. 1. 钱包，皮包；2. 资金，款项

【例】 1. Her *purse* was stolen when she was on the bus. 她的手袋在公共汽车上被偷了。

2. We have a *purse* of 500, 000 dollars for the winning of a boxing match. 我们筹集了 500, 000 美元的奖金颁发给这次拳击比赛的冠军。

【同】 wallet; fund, money

pursue [pə'sju:] *v*. 1.追赶，追求；2.继续，从事

【记】 pur(= pro，向前) + sue(跟随)→继续向前跟随→追赶

【例】 1. The police *pursued* the stolen vehicle along the motorway. 警察在高速公路上追赶被盗的车辆。

2. It will give them the experience to decide if they wish to *pursue* an interest in this field. 这会让他们有一些体验，然后决定是否有继续从事这一领域的兴趣。

【同】 chase, hunt; engage

【反】 flee

【派】 pursuit *n*. 追击，寻求

pursuer *n*. 追随者

pyramid ['pɪrəmɪd] *n*. 金字塔

【例】 Now let's just refresh our memories by looking at the Healthy Diet *Pyramid*. 现在让我们看一下健康饮食金字塔图，重温一下我们的记忆。

Q

quadruple ['kwɒdrʊpl] *n./adj.* 四倍(的)，四重(的)

【记】 quadru(四倍) + ple(重叠)→重叠四倍→四倍的

【例】 We need *quadruple* the number of players we've got for a full orchestra. 我们要组成完整的管弦乐队，需要有四倍于现有的演奏人员。

【同】 fourfold

quaint [kweɪnt] *adj.* 1.古雅的，古色古香的；2.奇怪的，离奇有趣的

【例】 1. Where are all the old, *quaint* houses like in Amsterdam? 那些像我们在阿姆斯特丹看到的古老雅致的房子都到哪儿去了呢？

2. Sometimes his six-year-old son's saying is *quaint*. 有时，他六岁的儿子说的话很有趣。

【同】 antique; unusual

【反】 modern

qualification [ˌkwɒlɪfɪ'keɪʃən] *n.* 资格(证明)，条件

【记】 quali(品质) + fic(使…化) + ation(名词词尾)→使…应具备的品质→资格

【例】 What sort of *qualifications* do you need for the job? 做这项工作需要什么资格？

【同】 certificate, reservation

【反】 disqualification

【派】 (逆构)qualify *v.* 具有资格，限制

qualified *adj.* 有资格的

quality ['kwɒlɪtɪ] *n.* 质量，品质

【记】 quali(品质) + ty(名词词尾)→质量

【例】 The *quality* of service in this restaurant has improved a lot. 这个饭店的服务质量已经有了很大改善。

【同】 excellence, value

quantitative ['kwɒntɪtətɪv] *adj.* 定量的，数量的

【记】 quant(多少) + it + ative(形容词词尾)→多少的→数量的

【例】 He has made a *quantitative* analysis of social relationships in his newly-published book. 他在自己新出的一本书里对社会关系进行了定量分析。

【反】 qualitative

quantity ['kwɒntɪtɪ] *n.* (巨大的)数目，数量

【记】 quant(多少) + ity(名词词尾)→有多少→数量

【例】 1. It was a bad year for films, in terms of both *quantity* and quality. 今年的电影无论从数量上还是质量上都说不上好。

2. A large quantity of air-conditioners has been sold since the temperature is high. 因为气温很高，有大量空调售出

【同】 amount, mass, quantum

quantum [ˈkwɒntəm] *n*. (复数-ta)1.量，额；2.[物] 量子，量子论

【记】 quant(多少)+um(名词词尾)→多少→量

【例】 1. This discovery marks a *quantum* leap forward in the fight against cancer. 这一发现标志着治疗癌症的一大突破。

2. Einstein made great contribution to the *quantum* theory. 爱因斯坦对量子论做出了巨大的贡献。

【同】 amount, quantity

quarrel [ˈkwɒrəl] *n*./*v*. (-l(l)ed; -l(l)ing)吵架，争论

【记】 quar(抱怨)+rel(动词词尾)→抱怨地说话→吵架

【例】 1. I had a *quarrel* with my flat-mate about who should do the housework. 我和与我同住一单元的人关于谁应做家务事吵了一架。

2. I don't *quarrel* with what you say, but with how you say it. 我并不在意你说了什么，而是不满意你说话的那种方式。

【同】 dispute

【派】 quarreler *n*. 争吵的人，喜欢埋怨的人

quarrelsome *adj*. 爱争吵的，急脾气的

query [ˈkwɪərɪ] *n*./*v*. 疑问，查询

【记】 quer(寻求)+y(动词词尾)→寻求答案→查询

【例】 Your interesting report raises several important *queries*. 你的精彩报告引发出了几个重要问题。

【同】 inquiry, question

quest [kwest] *n*. 寻求，调查研究

【例】 The lawyer was on a *quest* for further evidence. 律师正在到处找寻更多的证据。

【同】 hunt, pursue

Q

questionnaire [ˌkwestɪəˈneə, ˌkwestʃənˈeə] *n*. 调查表，问卷

【记】 quest(追求)+ion(名词词尾)+naire(名词词尾)→追求(问题的)答案→调查表

【例】 Please complete and return the enclosed *questionnaire*. 所附问卷请填妥交回。

【同】 form

queue [kjuː] *n*. 行列，长队；*v*. 排队等待

【记】 que(尾巴)+ue(名词词尾)→像尾巴一样的→长队

【例】 1. There must be at least 50 people in the *queue* — we'll be here till 2 o'clock at this rate. 队伍中至少有50个人——按照这个速度我们一直要在这里待到两点钟。

2. People are queuing to buy tickets. 人们正排队买票。

【同】 line

quit [kwɪt] *v*. (-tted; -tting)离开，辞职

【例】 I've had enough, so I *quit*. 我受够了，所以辞职不干了。

【同】 abandon, cease, stop

【反】 continue, stay

quiver ['kwɪvə] *v*. 振动，颤抖

【记】 quiv(振动)+er(动词词尾，表示动作的重复)→不停地振动→颤抖

【例】 The old man *quivered* with rage. 这位老人气得发抖。

【同】 shake, shiver, tremble

quiz [kwɪz] *n*. 测验，智力竞赛

【例】 We will have a *quiz* tomorrow morning. 我们明天早晨进行一个小测验。

【同】 examine, test

【派】 quizzer *n*. 提问者，测验节目

quota ['kwəʊtə] *n*. 配额，限额

【记】 quot(多大，多少)+a(名词词尾)→多大的量→配额

【例】 The *quota* on import cars has been lifted. 对汽车的进口配额已被取消。

【同】 allotment, number

quotation [kwəʊ'teɪʃən] *n*. 引文，语录；2. 报价单

【记】 quot(中古英语指用数字在书上做记号，引申为引用)+ation(名词词尾)→引用的东西→引文，语录

【例】 1. I found a mistake in this *quotation*. 我在这段引文中发现了一个错误。
2. They gave me a *quotation* for mending the roof. 他们给了我修理屋顶的报价单。

【同】 citation, reference

【派】 (逆构)quote *v*. 引用，引证
quotable *adj*. 可引用的

R

radiant ['reɪdjənt] *adj*.（向四面八方）发光的，光芒四射的

【记】 radi(= ray，光线) + ant(形容词词尾)→有光的→发光的

【例】 Everything looked *radiant* in the morning sun. 在朝阳之下，万物焕然一新。

【同】 beaming，luminous，lustrous，shining

【反】 dim

【派】 radiance *n*. 光辉，闪烁；辐射率

radiation [ˌreɪdɪ'eɪʃən] *n*. 辐射，发散

【记】 radi(光线) + ation(名词词尾)→光线(散发)出去→辐射

【例】 The news of the *radiation* leak caused widespread public alarm. 辐射泄露的消息引起了公众的普遍恐慌。

(逆构)radiate *v*. 放射，传播

radical ['rædɪkəl] *adj*. 1.根本的，基本的；2.激进的

【记】 radi(根) + cal(形容词词尾)→和根有关的→根本的

【例】 1. They called for a *radical* reform of our tax system. 他们要求对税收制度进行根本改革。

2. I don't belong to the school of thought that favors *radical* change. 我不属于激进派。

【同】 extreme，ultra

【反】 conservative

【派】 radicalism *n*. 激进主义

radius ['reɪdjəs] *n*. 半径，范围

【记】 adi(光线) + us(拉丁语名词词尾)→(由中心射出的)光线所到达的范围→半径

【例】 The police searched all the woods within a six-mile *radius*. 警察搜索了在周围六英里以内的树林各处。

raft [rɑːft] *n*. 木排，筏，救生艇

【例】 We found the shipwrecked sailors on a *raft*. 我们在一个木筏子上找到了失事船只的船员。

【派】 rafter *n*. 椽，筏夫

rage [reɪdʒ] *n*. 愤怒，情绪激动

【例】 I was gnashing my teeth with *rage*. 我咬牙切齿愤怒已极。

【同】 anger，fury

ragged ['rægɪd] *adj*. 破烂的，破旧的

【记】 rag(g)(碎屑) + ed(形容词词尾)→像碎屑一样的→破烂的

【例】 His sleeves were *ragged* at the cuffs. 他的袖口磨破了。
【同】 shabby, tattered
【派】 rag *n*. 抹布，碎屑

raise [reɪz] *v*. 1.升起，提高；2.饲养，栽培；3.提出
【例】 1. She *raised* her finger to her lips as a sign for silence. 她举起一根手指放在唇边，示意肃静。
2. I was *raised* by my aunt on a farm. 我是在农场由姨妈抚养大的。
3. I'm glad you *raised* that point. 你能把那一点指出来，我感到很高兴。
【同】 elevate, lift; bring up; put forward
【反】 level, lower
【派】 raised *adj*. 凸起的，浮雕的

rampant ['ræmpənt] *adj*. 蔓生的，猖獗的
【记】 ramp(蔓延) + ant(形容词词尾)→蔓延的→猖獗的
【例】 Sickness was *rampant* in the country. 疾病在这个国家猖獗。
【同】 uncontrolled, unrestrained
【反】 controlled, restrained
【派】 rampancy *n*. 繁茂

random ['rændəm] *n*./*adj*. 任意(的)，任意选取的
【记】 rand(= rush, 匆忙) + om(名词词尾)→匆忙做出来的→任意的
【例】 The librarian took a book at *random* from the shelf. 图书管理员从书架上随便拿了一本书。
【同】 haphazard
【反】 deliberate

range [reɪndʒ] *n*. 1.山脉；2.范围，射程；*v*. 1.排列；2.在…范围
【例】 1. The Appalachian *Range* is 1200 miles long, and consists of the Piedmont Plateau, Appalachian Plateaus and Appalachian *Range*. 阿巴拉契亚山脉全长1200英里，由皮德蒙特高原、阿巴拉契亚高原及阿巴拉契亚山脉组成。
2. Several cars are available within this price *range*. 在这个价格范围内，有好几种汽车可供选购。
3. The children's ages *range* from 8 to 15. 这些孩子们的年龄在8岁到15岁之间。
【同】 compass, scope
【派】 rangetable *n*. 射程表
rangeland *n*. 牧场

rank [ræŋk] *n*. 等级，阶级；*v*. 排列，归类
【例】 1. He is above me in *rank*. 他的级别比我高。
2. I *rank* her among the country's best writers. 我认为她可属全国最优秀作家之列。
【同】 class, categorize

ransom ['rænsəm] *n*./*v*. 赎金，敲诈
【记】 rans(回来) + om(= em, 买)→买回来→赎金
【例】 1. You are our prisoner now and we won't release you until a *ransom* is paid. 你现

R

已遭我们禁锢，要到交出赎金以后，才能放你走。

2. They had to *ransom* the kidnapped diplomat. 他们不得不赎回被绑架的外交官。

【同】 redeem

rapture ['ræptʃə] *n*. 狂喜，极高兴

【记】 rapt(抓，攫取) + ure(名词词尾)→攫取心智→狂喜

【例】 The mother gazed with *rapture* at her new born baby. 母亲着迷地凝视着她刚出生的婴儿。

【同】 ecstasy, delight, joy

【派】 rapturous *adj*. 兴高采烈的，欢天喜地的

rare [reə] *adj*. 稀有的，罕见的

【例】 He's devoted his whole life to the protection of the *rare* animals. 他终生献身于珍稀动物的保护。

【同】 peculiar, scarce

【反】 ordinary

rash [ræʃ] *n*. (不好的事)突然大量出现；*adj*. 鲁莽的，轻率的

【例】 1. Over the following decade the 40-storey Brisbane block suffered a *rash* of failures. 在接下来的10年间，一连串类似的事故发生在这座40层高的布里斯班大楼里。

2. It was *rash* of you to sign the form without reading it. 你看也不看就在表格上签字真太轻率了。

【同】 series; brash, hasty

rate [reɪt] *n*. 1. 比率，速度；2. 价格，费用；*v*. 估价，认为

【例】 1. They drove at a steady *rate*. 他们以平稳的速度开车。

2. What's a reasonable *rate* for the job? 做这件事的合理价格是多少？

3. He is generally *rated* as one of the best modern writers. 他被公认为现代最杰出的作家之一。

【同】 pace; payment, cost; appraise, evaluate

rateable *adj*. 可评价的，按比例的

rating *n*. 等级；收视率

ratify ['rætɪfaɪ] *v*. 批准，认可

【记】 rat(考虑，计算) + ify(动词词尾)→考虑过后→批准

【例】 Over ninety countries *ratify* an agreement to ban the use of these chemicals. 90多个国家批准了一项禁止使用这些化学品的协议。

【同】 approve, confirm

【派】 ratification *n*. 批准

ratio ['reɪʃɪəʊ] *n*. 比，比率

【记】 rat(考虑，推定) + io(名词词尾)→推定的方式→比率

【例】 Men outnumber women here in the *ratio* of three to one. 此地男子数量以三比一超过女子。

【同】 percentage, proportion

ration ['ræʃən] *n*./*v*. 定量，配给

【记】 rat(推定)+(t)ion(名词词尾)→推算出来的份额→定量
【例】 People were *rationed* to one egg a week. 每周配给一个鸡蛋。
【同】 fare, provision

rational [ˈræʃənl] *adj*. 理性的，合理的
【记】 ratio(n)(推理)+al(形容词词尾)→进行推理的→理性的
【例】 No *rational* person would go to work in his pyjamas. 任何神智正常的人都不会穿着睡衣去上班。
【同】 reasonable, sensible
【反】 absurd
【派】 rationality *n*. 合理性，唯理性
rationalistic *adj*. 纯理论的，理性主义的

ravish [ˈrævɪʃ] *v*. 使狂喜，使入迷
【记】 rav(夺取)+ish(动词词尾)→夺取→把…完全征服→使入迷
【例】 He was *ravished* by her beauty. 她的美貌使他倾倒。
【同】 delight, enchant

raw [rɔː] *adj*. 1. 原始的，未加工的；2. 无经验的
【例】 1. The factory is in frequent scarcity of *raw* materials. 这个工厂经常原料不足。
2. His literal style is still rather *raw*. 他的文学风格还很不成熟。
【同】 crude; immature
【反】 ripe

ray [reɪ] *n*. 光线
【例】 He focused the sun's *ray* on a piece of paper with a burning-glass. 他用一面凸透镜把阳光在纸上聚成焦点。
【同】 beam, light

raze [reɪz] *v*. 摧毁，夷为平地
【记】 raz(= ras, 刮，擦)+e→把…刮→摧毁
【例】 The bombs *razed* the building to the ground. 炸弹把那座建筑夷为平地。
【同】 demolish, destroy, flatten

razor [ˈreɪzə] *n*. 剃刀；*v*. 剃
【记】 raz(= ras, 刮，擦)+or(名词词尾)→刮脸用的东西→剃刀
【例】 I shave with an electric *razor*. 我用电动剃须刀刮胡子。
【派】 razor-blade *n*. 剃刀刀片
razor-sharp *adj*. 像剃刀一样锋利的

react [rɪˈækt] *v*. 作出反应，起作用
【记】 re(回应)+act(行动)→做出回应的行动→作出反应
【例】 How did they *react* to your suggestion? 他们对你的建议有什么反应？
【同】 answer, respond
【派】 reaction *n*. 反应，反作用(力)

realize [ˈrɪəlaɪz] *v*. 1. 意识到；2. 实现
【记】 real(真实的)+(i)se(动词词尾)→使成为现实→实现
【例】 1. He could not *realize* his own danger. 他未能意识到自己的危险。

2. My wishes have been *realized*. 我的愿望实现了。

【同】 recognise, understand

【派】 realization *n*. 认识，实现

realistic *adj*. 逼真的，现实主义的

reality *n*. 现实

realm [relm] *n*. 王国，范围

【记】 rea(= reg, 统治) + (l)m(名词词尾)→(国王)统治的地区→王国

【例】 The spy was expelled from the *realm*. 这名间谍被驱逐出境。

【同】 domain, kingdom

rear [rɪə] *n*./*adj*. 1. 后面(的)，背后(的)；*v*. 培养，饲养

【例】 1. It is much like a machine gun mounted on the *rear* of a boat. 它很像是安装在船尾的机关枪。

2. She's *reared* a large family. 她养活一大家人。

【同】 back, posterior

【反】 front

【派】 rearmost *adj*. 最后的

reasonable [ˈriːznəbl] *adj*. 公平的，合理的，适度的

【记】 reason(理智) + able(形容词词尾)→理智的→合理的

【例】 You are fortunate to have such a *reasonable* father. 你有这样一位通情达理的父亲，真是幸运。

【同】 sensible

【反】 absurd, unreasonable

【派】 (逆构)reason *n*. 理由，理智

reasoning *n*. 推理，论证

reassure [riːəˈʃʊə] *v*. 再保证，使放心

【记】 re(再一次) + assure(保证)→再一次保证→使放心

【例】 The manager tried to *reassure* her that she will not lose her job. 经理试图使她解除疑虑，她是不会失去工作。

【同】 assure

【反】 worry

【派】 reassurance *n*. 放心

rebate [ˈriːbeɪt, rɪˈbeɪt] *n*. 回扣，折扣

【记】 re(又，再) + bate(减少)→再次减少→折扣

【例】 He got a tax *rebate* at the end of the year. 他在年底得到了一笔退回的税款。

【同】 discount, refund

rebel [ˈrebəl, rɪˈbel] *v*. (-lled; -lling)反叛，反抗

【记】 re(又，再) + bel(战争)→又引起战争→反叛

【例】 He finally *rebelled* against his strict upbringing. 他终于起来反抗那种严厉管教他的方式。

【同】 revolt, rise

【派】 rebellion *n*. 谋反，反抗

rebellious *adj*. 造反的，反叛的

rebound [rɪˈbaʊnd] *n*./*v*. 弹回，重新跃起

【记】 re(又，再)+bound(跳起)→又一次跳起来→弹回

【例】 The scheme *rebounded* on her in a way she had not expected. 她未曾想到这计谋反倒使她自食其果。

【同】 backlash，bounce

rebuke [rɪˈbjuːk] *v*. 斥责，谴责

【记】 re(又，再)+buke(敲打)→再次敲打→斥责

【例】 She *rebuked* him strongly for his negligence. 她严厉斥责他的疏忽。

【同】 chide，reprimand，scold

【反】 praise

recall [rɪˈkɔːl] *v*. / *n*. 1.回忆，回想；2.收回，召回

【记】 re(回来)+call(呼唤)→呼唤回来→回想

【例】 1. This danger *recalls* him to a sense of duty. 这危险的事唤起了他的责任感。
2. The makers have *recalled* a lot of cars that were unsafe. 制造商已将许多不安全的汽车召回了。

【同】 remember，remind；callback

【反】 forget

reception [rɪˈsepʃən] *n*. 接待处，欢迎会

【记】 re(回来)+cep(t)(取)+tion(名词词尾)→拿回来的地方→接待处

【例】 A *reception* was held in honor of the new director. 举行酒会来欢迎新主任。

【同】 response，entertainment

【派】 receptionist *n*. 前台接待人员

recession [rɪˈseʃən] *n*. 1.撤回；2.(工商业)衰退

【记】 re(回来)+cess(去)+ion(名词词尾)→回到原处→撤回

【例】 1. The slow *recession* of the flood waters created problems for the crews working to restore power to the area. 洪水消退很慢，给工人重新恢复该地区的电力带来了困难。
2. If we can pull through this *recession*, we will be in good shape. 如果我们能渡过这段经济不景气的时间，我们就会好多了。

【同】 receding，withdrawal

【派】 (逆构)recess *n*. 凹进处；(学校等的)短休假；*v*. 使凹进；休息

recipe [ˈresɪpɪ] *n*. 食谱，处方

【记】 re(回来)+cip(取)+e→从(医生处)取回来的东西→处方

【例】 A *recipe* tells you that you need so many eggs, so much milk, etc. 这个食谱上说需要多少鸡蛋、多少牛奶等等.

【同】 prescription

recipient [rɪˈsɪpɪənt] *n*. 接受者，接收者

【记】 re(回来)+cip(i)(取)+ent(名词词尾)→取回的人→接受者

【例】 He was a *recipient* of the Nobel Peace Prize. 他是一个诺贝尔和平奖获得者。

【同】 receiver

reciprocity [ˌrɪsɪˈprɒsɪtɪ] *n*. 互惠，相互关系

【记】 re(回，后) + ci(走) + pro(前) + (c)ity(名词词尾)→向后再向前走→相互关系

【例】 Both sides agreed that they would conduct cooperation and exchanges on the basis of mutual benefits and *reciprocity*. 双方商定，要在双向互利基础上，开展合作和交流。

【同】 mutuality

【派】 reciprocal *adj*. 互惠的，相应的

reciprocate *v*. 互给，互换

recite [rɪˈsaɪt] *v*. 背诵，朗读

【记】 re(再一次) + cite(呼叫)→再一次讲述→背诵

【例】 He *recites* a speech from "Hamlet" to his class. 他向班上的同学背诵"哈姆雷特"中的一段话。

【同】 narrate, recount

【派】 reciter *n*. 朗诵者

recitation *n*. 朗诵，背诵

reckon [ˈrekən] *v*. 1. 计算，总计；2. 估计，猜想

【记】 re(再一次) + ckon(= count，数)→再数一遍→计算

【例】 1. When you did your expenses, did you *reckon* in your taxi fares? 你计算费用时，把计程车费算进去了吗？

2. The news won't worry her, I *reckon*. 我看这消息不会使她不安。

【同】 calculate, count; estimate, suppose

【派】 reckoning *n*. 清算，帐单

reclaim [rɪˈkleɪm] *v*. 1. 改造，开垦；2. 要求收回，要求恢复

【记】 re(回来) + claim(呼唤)→呼喊回来→要求恢复

【例】 1. The usual way to *reclaim* land is to pile sand rock on to the seabed. 通常开拓陆地的方式就是在海床上堆积砂岩。

2. He engaged himself in *reclaiming* young offenders from a life of crime. 他致力于挽救失足少年脱离罪恶的生活。

R

【同】 recover, regain; claim

【派】 reclaimed *adj*. 再生的，回收的

reclamation *n*. 开垦，改造

recognize [ˈrekəgaɪz] *v*. 1. 认可，承认；2. 认出

【记】 re(再一次) + cognis(知道) + e→再一次知道→承认，认出

【例】 1. His thorough knowledge and competence were *recognized*. 他的渊博的学识和工作能力得到了承认。

2. Can you *recognize* her from this picture? 你能从这张照片中认出她吗？

【例】 acknowledge, realize

【派】 recognition *n*. 识别；赞誉，承认

recognized *adj*. 公认的，经过验证的

recommend [rekəˈmend] *v*. 推荐，介绍

【记】 re(再一次) + com(一起) + mend(委托)→经过另一个人委托→推荐

【记】 Can you *recommend* to me a good dictionary? 你能为我推荐一本好字典吗?
【同】 advocate, propose
【派】 recommendatory *adj*. 推荐的,劝告的
recommendation *n*. 推荐,意见

reconcile ['rekənsaɪl] *v*. 和解,调和,调解
【记】 re(再一次)+con(一起)+cile(召集)→再次召集在一起→和解
【例】 We tried to *reconcile* her with her family. 我们试图让她和她的家庭和好。
【同】 conciliate, harmonize
【派】 reconciliation *n*. 和解,调和

recourse [rɪ'kɔːs] *n*. 依靠,求助
【记】 re(回来)+course(流,跑)→流回来→求助
【例】 You'd better have *recourse* to her. 你最好向她求助。
【同】 resort

recover [rɪ'kʌvə] *v*. 恢复,恢复正常
【记】 re(再一次)+cover(掩盖)→再一次掩盖了(问题)→恢复
【例】 He is very ill and unlikely to *recover*. 他病得非常厉害,不大可能恢复健康了。
【同】 regain, retrieve
【同】 recovery *n*. 恢复,防御
recoverable *adj*. 可重获的

recreation [rekrɪ'eɪʃən] *n*. 消遣,娱乐
【记】 re(重新)+cre(创造)+ation(名词词尾)→重新创造活力的行为→娱乐
【例】 His only *recreations* are drinking beer and working in the garden. 他仅有的消遣是喝啤酒和在花园里种花草。
【同】 amusement, entertainment
【派】 (逆构)recreate *v*. 得到休养,(使)得到娱乐
recreational *adj*. 休养的,娱乐的

recruit [rɪ'kruːt] *n*. 新兵,新会员; *v*. 招收,征募
【记】 re(再一次)+cruit(成长)→再一次成长→招募
【例】 1. After the final interview, potential *recruits* were divided into three categories. 在最后一次面试之后,待定的新成员被分为三种类型。
2. We are having difficulties in *recruiting* well-qualified staff. 我们难以招募到素质好的职员。
enlist, enroll
【派】 recruitment *n*. 征募新兵,补充

rectangle ['rektæŋgl] *n*. 长方形
【记】 rect(= right,直的)+angle(角)→四个角都是直的→长方形
【例】 This room is a *rectangle*. 这间屋子是长方形的。
【同】 oblong
【派】 rectangular *adj*. 矩形的,长方形的

rectify ['rektɪfaɪ] *v*. 矫正,调整
【记】 rect(= right,正确的)+ify(动词词尾)→使正确→矫正

R

【例】 I made a mistake that can not be *rectified*. 我犯了一个无法改正的错误。
【同】 amend, correct, remedy
【派】 rectifiable *adj*. 可纠正的，可矫正的
rectification *n*. 纠正，整顿

recycle ['riː'saɪkl] *v*. 反复应用，使再循环
【记】 re(再一次) + cycle(周期，循环)→反复循环→再循环
【例】 The glass from bottles can be *recycled*. 瓶子的玻璃能回收利用。
【例】 reprocess, reuse
【派】 recyclable *adj*. 可再循环的
recycler n 回收站

reduce [rɪ'djuːs] *v*. 减少，缩小
【记】 re(回来) + duc(领导) + e→引导回到原处→减少
【例】 He is trying to *reduce* the family's expenses. 他正尽力减少家庭开支。
【同】 decrease, diminish
【反】 increase
【派】 reduction *n*. 减少，削减
reductive *adj*. 减少的，还原的

redundant [rɪ'dʌndənt] *adj*. 多余的，过剩的
【记】 re(再一次) + (d)und(波动) + ant(形容词词尾)→反复波动的→多余的
【记】 I regret having to make so many staff *redundant*. 我很遗憾不得不裁减这么多职员。
【同】 excess, spare
【同】 deficient, short
【同】 redundancy *n*. 冗余

refectory [rɪ'fektərɪ] *n*. (修道院、学校的)食堂，餐厅
【记】 re(再一次) + fect(做) + ory(名词词尾，…的地方)→反复做(食物)的地方→食堂
【记】 We also request that there be the offices of the Student Counselling Centre, moving this from the *Refectory*. 我们还要求为学生咨询中心设置办公室，把中心从餐厅迁出。
【派】 refection *n*. 便餐，点心

R

refer [rɪ'fɜː] *v*. (-rred; -rring) 1. 提到，涉及；2. 咨询，求助于；3. 参考，引证
【记】 re(回来) + fer(搬运)→搬回原处→参考
【例】 1. Don't *refer* to this matter again, please. 请不要再提这件事了。
2. The dispute was *referred* to the United Nations. 该项争端已提交联合国处理。
3. For further particulars, please *refer* to Chapter Ten. 详情请看第10章。
【同】 concern; direct, consult; relate
【派】 reference *n*. 参照，参考书目；证明书(人)，介绍信(人)

refine [rɪ'faɪn] *v*. 精炼，使文雅高尚
【记】 re(再一次) + fine(完成)→再一次完成→精炼
【例】 After 30 years, the mature author was able to *refine* on the work of his youth. 过去30年，这位作家已经成熟，他可以将年轻时候写的作品修改得更完美了。

【同】 cultivate, polish
【派】 refined *adj*. 精制的；优雅的
refinment *n*.（言谈、举止等的）文雅，精巧；提纯，改良

reflect [rɪ'flekt] *v*. 1. 反射，反映；2. 反省，反思
【记】 re(回来)+flect(弯曲)→使转回来→反射
【例】 1. As their eyes adjusted to the darkness they saw myriad lights *reflecting* off the water. 当眼睛逐渐适应黑暗之后，他们看到了无数的光芒反射在水面上。
2. I'd like to use this tutorial as a feedback session, where you *reflect* on the experience of doing the project. 我想利用这次的辅导课作为一次反馈课，大家可以反思一下自己在做这次项目的时候的经验。
【同】 think, deliberate
reflection *n*. 反映；反思
reflective *adj*. 反射的，沉思的

reflex ['riːfleks] *n*. 反射，反映；*adj*. 反射的，反省的
【记】 re(回来)+flex(弯曲)→使弯曲回来→反射
【例】 1. It's just a dog's *reflex* movement. 这正是狗的反射运动。
2. Sorry I hit you; it was a pure *reflex*. 对不起我撞着你了；这完全是无意的。
【同】 reflection
【派】 reflexible *adj*. 可反射的，反射性的；反省的
reflexion *n*. 反射，反射光

reform [rɪ'fɔːm] *n*./*v*. 改革，改善
【记】 re(再一次)+form(构成)→再一次形成→改革
【例】 It is a plan to *reform* the tax system and make it simpler and fairer. 这是一个旨在改革税务制度，使之更简化和更公平的计划。
【同】 change, improve
【派】 reformer *n*. 改革家，改革运动者

refresh [rɪ'freʃ] *v*. 使恢复，使清新
【记】 re(再一次)+fresh(清新)→使再一次清新→使恢复
【例】 I *refreshed* myself with a cup of coffee. 我喝了一杯咖啡给自己提提神。
【同】 renew, restore
【反】 exhaust
【派】 refreshing *adj*. 提神的，凉爽的
refreshment *n*. 精力恢复；小吃，点心

refuge ['refjuːdʒ] *n*. 庇护，避难所
【记】 re(回来)+fug(逃走)+e→逃回安全地→避难所
【例】 The political dissidents sought *refuge* abroad. 持不同政见者在国外寻求政治避难。
【同】 shelter, haven
【派】 refugee *n*. 难民，流亡者

refund [riː'fʌnd, 'rɪfʌnd] *n*./*v*. 归还，偿还欠款
【记】 re(回来)+fund(资金)→使资金回转→归还

R

【例】 1. I'd like a *refund*. 我想要退款。
2. I'll *refund* you the full cost of your fare. 我来偿付你的全部旅费。
【同】 return, repay
【派】 refundable *adj*. 可退还的，可偿还的
refundment *n*. 退款，退还

refute [rɪ'fjuːt] *v*. 反驳
【记】 re(回来) + fut(流) + e→流回来→反驳
【例】 I was able to *refute* his argument. 我能驳倒他的论点。
【同】 disprove, rebut

regarding [rɪ'gɑːdɪŋ] *prep*. 关于，就…而论
【记】 regard(涉及) + ing(形容词词尾借用为介词词尾)→涉及到…的→就…而论
【例】 I know nothing *regarding* the future. 我对未来一无所知。
【同】 concerning, considering

regenerate [rɪ'dʒenərɪt] *v*. 使新生，革新
【记】 re(再一次) + generate(产生)→使再一次产生→革新
【例】 Their aim is to *regenerate* British industry. 他们的目的是复兴英国的工业。
【同】 renew, reform, revitalize
【反】 unregenerate
【派】 regeneration *n*. 再生，重建
regenerative *adj*. 再生的，更生的

regime [reɪ'ʒiːm] *n*. 政体，政权制度
【记】 reg(i)(统治) + me→统治的模式→政体
【例】 Things will change under the new *regime*. 在新政权下，事情将会发生变化。
【同】 authority, government

region ['riːdʒən] *n*. 地区，区域
【记】 reg(统治) + ion(名词词尾)→统治的地方→地区
【例】 Most of the countries in the *region* have unstable economies. 这个地区大多数国家的经济都不稳定。
【同】 area, district
【派】 regional *adj*. 地方的，地域性的
regionalization *n*. 分成地区，按地区安排

register ['redʒɪstə] *v*. 登记，注册
【记】 re(再一次) + gister(带来)→再一次带来→登记，注册
【例】 The car was *registered* in my name. 汽车是用我的名字登记注册的。
enroll, record
【派】 registration *n*. 注册，报到

regret [rɪ'gret] *n*./*v*. (-tted; -tting) 1. 遗憾，悔恨；2. 抱歉
【记】 re(再一次) + gret(哭泣)→再一次的哭泣→后悔
【例】 1. I have no *regrets* about leaving. 我对离去一事毫不后悔。
2. We *regret* that we are unable to reconsider your case. 我们很遗憾无法再考虑你的情况。

【同】 sorrow; sorry

【反】 content

【派】 regretful *adj*. 后悔的，惋惜的

regretable *adj*. 可叹的，可惜的

regulate ［ˈregjʊleɪt］ *v*. 控制，调节

【记】 reg(u)(统治)＋late(动词词尾)→进行统治→控制

【例】 Your watch is always slow; it needs to be *regulated*. 你的手表总是慢，需要校准一下。

【同】 adjust, rectify

【派】 regulation *n*. 规章，条例

regular *n*. 规则的，经常的

rehabilitate ［ˌriːhəˈbɪlɪteɪt］ *v*. 康复，恢复

【记】 re(再一次)＋ha(＝have, 拥有)＋bili(t)(能力)＋ate(动词词尾)→使再一次具有能力→康复

【例】 The social sevices do their best to *rehabilitate* criminals once they've left prison. 罪犯一旦出狱，社会福利机构就尽最大的努力使他们恢复正常的生活。

【同】 restore, recover

【派】 rehabilitation *n*. 恢复，复原

rehearse ［rɪˈhɜːs］ *v*. 排练，排演

【记】 re(再一次)＋hearse(耙地)→反复耙地→排练

【例】 The actors were *rehearsing* until 2 o'clock in the morning. 演员们一直在排练，直到凌晨两点钟。

【同】 exercise, practice

【派】 rehearsal *n*. 排演，预演

reign ［reɪn］ *v*. 统治

【记】 reign＝reg, 统治

【例】 He *reigned* over the country for forty years. 他统治了这个国家 40 年。

【同】 dominate, rule

【派】 reigning *adj*. 统治的，起支配作用的

reimburse ［ˌriːɪmˈbɜːs］ *v*. 偿还

【记】 re(再一次)＋im(＝in, 在…里面)＋burse(＝bag, 包)→再次放进钱包里→偿还

【例】 We will *reimburse* the customer for any loss or damage. 我们愿赔偿顾客受到的一切损失和损害。

【同】 compensate, refund

reinforce ［ˌriːɪnˈfɔːs］ *v*. 加强，增援

re(再一次)＋in(＝en, 进入)＋force(强壮的)→再一次充满力量→加强

【例】 Our defences must be *reinforced* against attack. 我们必须加强防御设施以抵御进攻。

【同】 fortify, intensify

【反】 weaken

【派】 reinforcement *n*. 增援，加固

reiterate [riːˈɪtəreɪt] *v*. 重申，反复地说

【记】 re(再一次) + iterate(重复地说)→反复地说→重申

【例】 The captain *reiterated* the command to us. 上尉对我们重申了那项命令。

【同】 repeat，restate

【派】 reiteration *n*. 重复，反复

reject [rɪˈdʒekt] *v*. 拒绝，排斥

【记】 re(回来) + ject(丢，掷)→丢回去→拒绝

【例】 He *rejected* their offer of a job. 他拒绝了他们给他的工作。

【同】 decline，refuse

【反】 accept，receive

【派】 rejection *n*. 拒绝

rejective *adj*. 拒绝的，排斥的

rejuvenate [rɪˈdʒuːvɪneɪt] *v*. 使年轻，使恢复

【记】 re(再一次) + juven(年轻) + ate(动词词尾)→使再次年轻→使年轻

【例】 The mountain air will *rejuvenate* you. 山里的空气会使你恢复活力。

【同】 regenerate，revitalize

【派】 rejuvenation *n*. 返老还童，恢复活力

rekindle [ˈriːˈkɪndl] *v*. 再点燃，重新振作

【记】 re(再一次) + kindle(点燃)→重新点燃→重新振作

【例】 Nothing could *rekindle* her extinct passion. 她激情已逝，无从心回意转。

relapse [rɪˈlæps,ˈriːlæps] *v*. 旧病复发，再恶化

【记】 re(回来) + lapse(滑)→滑回去→旧病复发

【例】 He soon *relapsed* into his old bad habits. 他很快就恢复了旧的坏习惯。

【同】 regress，revert，fall back

relate [rɪˈleɪt] *v*. 1.讲述，叙述；2.使联系

【记】 re(回来) + late(带来)→把…带回来→使联系

【例】 1. She *related* to them how it happened. 她向他们讲述了事情发生的经过。

2. It is difficult to *relate* cause and effect in this case. 这个案件中的动机与效果很难联系起来。

【同】 narrate，state；connect

【派】 related *adj*. 有关系的，相关的

relation *n*. 关系，联系

relative [ˈrelətɪv] *n*. 亲戚，亲属；*adj*. 相对的，比较而言

【记】 relat(e)(联系) + ive(形容词词尾转用作名词)→有关系的人→亲戚

【例】 1. The income of your parents，spouse，partner or other *relatives* is not taken into account. 你的父母、配偶、合伙人以及其他亲戚的收入不列入考虑范围。

2. They are now living in *relative* comfort. 他们现在过着比较舒适的生活。

【同】 relation；comparative

【反】 absolute

【派】 relatively *adv*. 比较而言，相对地

relax [rɪˈlæks] *v*. 放松，缓和

R

【记】 re(重新) + lax(松开)→重新松开→放松

【例】 The music will help to *relax* you. 音乐会使你感到轻松。

【同】 loosen, rest

【反】 tighten

【派】 relaxation *n*. 松弛，放松

relaxed *adj*. 不严格的，宽松的

relay [ˈriːleɪ] *v*. /*n*. 1.分程传递，接力赛；2.转播

【记】 re(再一次) + lay(离开)→再次离开，原义是指驿站里替换的马或者打猎时替换的狗→接力赛

【例】 1. Could you *relay* the news to the other teachers? 你能把这个消息传达给其他的老师吗？

2. The pop festival was *relayed* all round the world. 流行音乐会的实况已向全世界转播。

【同】 pass, hand on; deliver, transfer

release [rɪˈliːs] *n*./*v*. 1.释放，让渡；2.(唱片等)发行

【记】 re(再一次) + lease(= lyse, 放松)→再一次放松→释放

【例】 1. The family paid a ransom of 50,000 dollars for the child's *release*. 那家人为了赎回孩子付了5万美元。

2. He was *released* from prison after serving his sentence. 他刑满获释。

3. The new film will be *released* next month. 这部新的电影下个月发行。

【同】 discharge, liberate

【反】 capture

【派】 releasable *adj*. 能释放的，可免除的

relevant [ˈreləvənt] *adj*. 有关的，中肯的

【记】 re(再一次) + lev(升起来) + ant(形容词词尾)→把(问题)再一次提出讨论→有关的

【例】 His nationality isn't *relevant* to whether he's a good teacher. 他的国籍与他是否是位好老师无关。

【同】 connected

【反】 irrelevant

【派】 relevancy *n*. 关联，恰当

reliable [rɪˈlaɪəbl] *adj*. 可靠的，可信赖的

【记】 reli(依靠) + able(形容词词尾)→可以依靠的

【例】 I don't think he is a *reliable* man. 我认为他不是一个可靠的人。

【同】 dependable, trustworthy

【反】 unreliable

【派】 reliability *n*. 可靠性

relieve [rɪˈliːv] *v*. 1.减轻，解除；2.援救，救济

【记】 re(再一次) + liev(= lev, 升起) + e→再次升起来→减轻

【例】 1. The general was *relieved* of his command. 将军被解除了指挥权。

2. The Government acted quickly to *relieve* the widespread distress caused by the

R

earthquake. 地震造成广泛地区的灾难，政府迅速采取行动赈济灾民。

【同】 alleviate, ease; help

【派】 relief *n*. 减轻；援救，救济

relievable *adj*. 可减轻的

religious [rɪ'lɪdʒəs] *adj*. 信奉宗教的，虔诚的

【记】 re(再一次) + lig(绑) + (i)ous(形容词词尾)→再次绑回(神)的身边的→信奉宗教的

【例】 She is very *religious* and goes to church three times a week. 她非常虔诚，每周去教堂三次。

【同】 spiritual, pious

【反】 irreligious

【派】 religion *n*. 宗教，信仰

relinquish [rɪ'lɪŋkwɪʃ] *v*. 放弃，废除

【记】 re(再次) + linqu(= leave, 离开) + ish(动词词尾)→使再次离开→放弃

【例】 I had *relinquished* all hope that she was alive. 我已经放弃了她还活着的一切希望。

【同】 abandon, surrender, waive

【派】 relinquishment *n*. 作罢，让渡

relish ['relɪʃ] *n*./*v*. 喜欢，爱好

【记】 re(再一次) + lish(= lyse, 放松)→使再一次放松的东西→爱好

【例】 1. I tasted the fish my mother cooked with *relish*. 我津津有味地品尝了我妈妈做的鱼。

2. He didn't *relish* the prospect of having to explain his behavior. 他不喜欢对他自己的所作所为作出解释。

【同】 appreciate, enjoy

【反】 loathe

reluctant [rɪ'lʌktənt] *adj*. 不愿意的，勉强的

【记】 re(再一次) + luct(挣扎) + ant(形容词词尾)→反复挣扎的→不愿意的

【例】 They were very *reluctant* to help. 他们不大愿意帮忙。

【同】 unwilling

【反】 willing

【派】 reluctance *n*. 不愿，勉强

remain [rɪ'meɪn] *v*. 继续存在，保持

【记】 re(后来) + main(主要部分)→留下主要的部分→继续存在

【例】 He *remained* poor all his life. 他终生贫穷。

【同】 continue, persist

【反】 destroy, perish

remark [rɪ'mɑːk] *v*. /*n*. 谈论，评论

【记】 re(再一次) + mark(记号)→再次做记号→评论

【例】 1. They made rude *remarks* about her appearance. 他们对她的外表横加粗暴地评论。

2. The editor *remarked* that article was well written. 编者评论说那篇文章写得很好。

【同】 comment, observe

【派】 remarkable *adj*. 非凡的，显著的

remedial [rɪˈmiːdjəl] *adj*. 治疗的，补救的

【记】 re(再次) + med(治疗) + ial(形容词词尾)→再次治疗的→补救的

【例】 He had to do *remedial* exercises for his weak back. 他必须为衰弱的背部做矫正运动。

【同】 curative, therapeutic

【派】 (逆构)remedy *n*./*v*. 治疗(法)，补救

remediable *adj*. 可补救的，可治疗的

remind [rɪˈmaɪnd] *v*. 提醒，使想起

【记】 re(再一次) + mind(想)→使再次想起→提醒

【例】 Can you just *remind* me what the task is exactly? 能请您再提醒我一下任务的内容吗?

【同】 remember, recall

【反】 forget

remit [rɪˈmɪt] *v*. (-tted; -tting) 1. 宽恕，赦免；2. 汇出，汇款

【记】 re(回来) + mit(送)→送回来→宽恕，汇出

【例】 1. The taxes have been *remitted*. 税已豁免。

2. *Remit* the interest to her new address. 将利息寄到她的新地址。

【同】 pardon, forgive; send, pay

remnant [ˈremnənt] *n*./*adj*. 残余(的)，剩余(的)

【记】 remn(= remain，保留) + ant(形容词词尾)→保留的→残余的

【例】 1. The beautiful curtain is made of *remnant* materials. 这个漂亮的窗帘是用零头布做的。

2. I will sell this *remnant* to you, at cost. 我愿将此剩货照成本卖给你。

【同】 leftover, residue

remote [rɪˈməʊt] *adj*. 遥远的，偏僻的

【记】 re(回来) + mot(移动) + e→移到远处→遥远的

【例】 The market for tourism in *remote* areas is booming as never before. 偏远地区旅游业的市场从来没有像今天这样火爆过。

【同】 far, distant

【反】 close, near

remove [rɪˈmuːv] *v*. 1. 移动，迁移；2. 开除，移交

【记】 re(再一次) + move(移动)→再次移动→移动，开除

【例】 1. Our office has *removed* to Shanghai from Beijing. 我们的办公室已从北京迁到上海。

2. That officer must be *removed*. 那位官员必须免职。

【同】 move, take away; transfer, get rid of

【派】 removal *n*、消除，移动

R

removable *adj*. 抽取式的，可移动的

remuneration [rɪˌmjuːnəˈreɪʃən] *n*. 报酬，酬金

【记】re(回来)+muner(给)+ation(名词词尾)→给回来的东西→报酬

【例】He received generous *remuneration* for his services. 他因服务而得到优厚的报酬。

【同】earnings, salary, wage

renaissance [rəˈneɪsəns] *n*. 复兴，新生

【记】re(再一次)+naissance(出生)→再生→复兴

【例】Leonardo da Vinci is a famous artist in the Italian *Renaissance*. 利奥纳多·达·芬奇是意大利文艺复兴时期的一位著名画家。

【同】rebirth, revival

【派】renaissant *adj*. 文艺复兴时期的

render [ˈrendə] *v*. 1. 给予，提供；2. 使得，致使

【记】re(n)(回来)+der(给)→给回来→给予，致使

【例】1. You've *rendered* me a service. 你帮了我的忙。

2. The blow to the head *rendered* him unconscious. 当头一击将他打昏了过去。

【同】give; cause

renew [rɪˈnjuː] *v*. 1. 使更新，恢复；2. 续借

【记】re(再一次)+new(新的)→使再次变新→使更新

【例】1. Spring *renews* the earth. 春天使大地复苏。

2. He *renewed* the book for another two months. 这本书他又续借了两个月。

【同】restore, refresh

【派】renewal *n*. 更新，复兴；续借

renewable *adj*. 可更新的，可恢复的

renounce [rɪˈnaʊns] *v*. 1. 声明放弃；2. 与…断绝关系，否认

【记】re(回)+nounce(说)→把说过的话收回→放弃，否认

【例】1. He *renounced* his claim to the property. 他放弃了财产所有权。

2. He *renounced* his religion and became a Muslim. 他宣布背弃原来的宗教，而成了一个伊斯兰教徒。

【同】abandon, discard; deny

【派】renouncement *n*. 否认，拒绝

renovate [ˈrenəʊveɪt] *vt*. 革新，修复

【记】re(再)+nov(新)+ate(动词词尾)→使再变成新的→革新，修复

【例】The old house is being *renovated*. 这幢老房子正在重新装修。

【同】renew, restitute, restore

【派】renovation *n*. 修复，整修；革新

renown [rɪˈnaʊn] *n*. 名声，传闻；*v*. 使有声望

【记】re(反复的)+nown(=name，名字)→反复出现的名字→名声

【例】1. He won *renown* as a pianist. 他赢得钢琴家的声誉。

2. Edison was *renowned* as an inventor. 爱迪生是位著名的发明家。

【同】celebrity, fame

【派】renowned *adj*. 有名的，有声誉的

R

rent [rent] *v*. 出租，出借；*n*. 租金

【例】 1. She *rents* out rooms to students. 她出租房间给学生住。

2. The lessor can evict the lessee for failure to pay *rent*. 出租人可驱逐不付租金的承租人。

【同】 lease, let

【派】 rental *adj*. 租赁(业)的；*n*. 租费，出租的财产

renunciation [rɪˌnʌnsɪˈeɪʃən] *n*. 放弃，终止

【记】 re(回)+nounci(说)+ation(名词词尾)→把说过的话收回→放弃

【例】 Her ex-husband declared a *renounciation* of the family house. 她前夫宣布放弃对家里的房子的所有权。

【同】 renouncement

repay [riːˈpeɪ] *v*. (-paid, -paid)偿还，报答

【记】 re(回来)+pay(支付)→把钱还回来→偿还

【例】 How can I ever *repay* you for your kindness? 我怎么能报答你的恩惠呢?

【同】 refund, return

【派】 repayable *adj*. 可以偿还的

repayment *n*. 偿还，回报

repel [rɪˈpel] *v*. (-lled; -lling)驱逐，抵制

【记】 re(回来)+pel(驾驶)→让驾驶回去→抵制

【例】 The crew *repelled* the attack. 船员击退了进攻。

【同】 offend, repulse

【反】 attract

【派】 repellent *adj*. 令人厌恶的，排斥的

repetition [ˌrepɪˈtɪʃən] *n*. 重复，循环

【记】 re(再一次)+pet(寻求)+(i)tion(名词词尾)→再一次寻求→重复

【例】 This accident is a *repetition* of the one that happened here three weeks ago. 这起车祸是三星期前在这里发生过的车祸的重演。

【同】 repeat

【派】 (逆构)repeat *n*./*v*. 重复，复述

repetitive *adj*. 重复的，反复性的

replace [riːˈpleɪs] *v*. 代替，接替

【记】 re(重新)+place(地点)→重新放一个地方→代替

【例】 We've *replaced* the old adding machine with a computer. 我们用电脑取代了老式的加法计算器。

【同】 substitute, supplant

【反】 remove

【派】 replaceable *adj*. 可代替的

replacement *n*. 归还，代替品

replenish [rɪˈplenɪʃ] *v*. 再次充满，补充

【记】 re(再一次)+plen(充满)+ish(动词词尾)→再一次装满→补充

【例】 We need to *replenish* our stocks of coal. 我们需要再次补充煤的储备。

【同】 refill, provide
【派】 replenishment *n*. 补给，补充

replicate ['replɪkɪt] *v*. 重复，复制
【记】 re(回来) + plic(折叠) + ate(动词词尾)→折回去，重叠→复制
【例】 These tissue cells *replicate* themselves. 这些组织细胞能自行复制。
【同】 duplicate, repeat
【派】 (逆构)replica *n*. 复制品

represent [ˌriːprɪ'zent] *v*. 1. 表现，描述；2. 代表，象征
【记】 re(再一次) + present(提出)→再次提出→表现
【例】 1. He *represented* himself as an expert. 他把自己说成是专家。
2. The rose *represents* England. 玫瑰花是英格兰的象征。
【同】 depict, describe; symbolize
【派】 representation *n*. 表现，陈述；代表，代理
representative *adj*. /*n*. 代表(性的)，典型(的)

repress [rɪ'pres] *v*. 抑制，镇压
【记】 re(回去) + press(压)→压回去→抑制，镇压
【例】 He *repressed* his natural sexual desires as sinful. 他压抑着本能的性欲，视之为罪恶。
【同】 subdue, suppress
【反】 incite
【派】 repression *n*. 镇压，抑制

reproach [rɪ'prəʊtʃ] *n*./*v*. 责备，谴责
【记】 re(再一次) + proach(接近)→再次接近→责备
【例】 She *reproached* him for forgetting their anniversary. 她责备他竟把他们的结婚周年纪念日忘了。
【同】 accuse, condemn
【反】 praise
【派】 reproachful *adj*. 表示责备的

R

reproduction [ˌriːprə'dʌkʃən] *n*. 繁殖，复制
【记】 re(再一次) + produc(e)(生产) + tion(名词词尾)→再次进行生产→繁殖
【例】 This is not the original; it's only a cheap *reproduction*. 这不是原作，它只不过是廉价的复制品。
【同】 breeding, copy
【派】 (逆构)reproduce *v*. 繁殖，使重现

reptile ['reptaɪl] *n*. 爬行动物
【记】 rept(爬行) + ile(名词词尾)→爬行的动物
【例】 And there's also a *reptile* park in town—that costs more or less the same. 市里还有一个爬行动物公园，价格和这个差不多。
【派】 reptilian *adj*. 爬行动物的，爬虫的

republic [rɪ'pʌblɪk] *n*. 共和国，共和政体
【记】 re(= 拉丁语 res，东西) + publ(人) + ic(名词词尾)→人民的东西→共和国

【例】 The People's *Republic* of China was founded in 1949. 中华人民共和国成立于1949年。

【同】 democracy

【反】 monarchy

【派】 republican *adj*. 共和国的，共和的；*n*. 共和党人

repudiate [rɪˈpjuːdɪeɪt] *v*. 否认，批判，驳斥

【记】 re(回来)+pudi(感到羞耻)+ate(动词词尾)→使感到羞耻→否认

【例】 He *repudiated* the court's decision to offer bail. 他不接受法庭的保释裁决。

【同】 deny, reject, renounce

【派】 repudiation *n*. 批判，驳斥

repulse [rɪˈpʌls] *v*. 击退，拒绝

【记】 re(回去)+puls(驱赶)+e→驱赶回去→击退

【例】 She *repulsed* his proposal. 她拒绝了他的求婚。

【同】 repel, reject

【派】 repulsive *adj*. 令人厌恶的，排斥的

reputation [ˌrepjuːˈteɪʃən] *n*. 名誉，名声

【记】 re(反复)+put(思考)+ation(名词词尾)→让人反复思考的东西，让人反复说的→名声

【例】 He cares nothing about the malicious attack on his *reputation*. 他对别人对他名声的恶毒攻击置之不理。

【同】 honor, respect

【反】 notoriety

【派】 (逆构)repute *n*./*v*. 名誉，认为
reputable *adj*. 著名的，名气好的

request [rɪˈkwest] *v*./*n*. 请求，要求

【记】 re(再一次)+quest(寻求)→再一次寻求→请求

【例】 1. They've made an urgent *request* for international aid. 他们紧急请求国际援助。
2. Your presence is *requested* at the meeting. 请你务必出席会议。

【同】 ask

【反】 grant

require [rɪˈkwaɪə] *v*. 要求，需要

【记】 re(再一次)+quire(寻求)→再一次寻求→要求

【例】 All passengers are *required* to show their tickets. 所有乘客都必须出示车票。

【同】 need, demand

【反】 refuse

【派】 requirement *n*. 需求，必要条件

rescue [ˈreskjuː] *n*./*v*. 援救，营救

【记】 re(再一次)+scue(离开)→使再次离开(不利的境地)→营救

【例】 1. A wealthy sponsor came to our *rescue* with a generous donation. 有个富有的赞助人慷慨捐赠来解救我们。
2. The well-drilled crew managed to *rescue* most of the passengers. 训练有素的机

R

组人员设法营救出了大部分乘客。

【同】 save

【派】 rescuee *n*. 被营救者

resemble [rɪ'zembl] *v*. 像，相似

【记】 re(再一次)+sembl(相似)+e→再(看)也觉得相似→相似

【例】 She *resembles* her sister in appearance but not in character. 她和她姐姐外貌相似，但性格不同。

【派】 resemblant *adj*. 相似的，摹仿的

resemblance *n*. 类同之处

resent [rɪ'zent] *v*. 愤恨，怨恨

【记】 re(再一次)+sent(感觉)→再一次感觉→愤怒

【例】 I bitterly *resent* your criticism. 我对你批评我的话十分反感。

【同】 hate, spite

【派】 resentful *adj*. 愤慨的，怨恨的

resentment *n*. 怨恨，愤恨

reserve [rɪ'zɜːv] *n*. 储备，储藏；*v*. 预订，保留

【记】 re(回来)+serv(保持)+e→保留不拿出来→储备，预定

【例】 1. As I require money quickly I must draw on my *reserve*. 由于我急于用钱，我必须取出存款。

2. Please *reserve* a seat for me. 请为我预定一个座位。

【同】 keep, retain

【派】 reserved *adj*. 保留的，包租的

reservation *n*. 预订；储备

reservoir ['rezəvwɑː] *n*. 水库，蓄水池

【记】 re(回来)+serv(保持)+oir(法语名词词尾)→保留(水)的地方→水库

【例】 This *reservoir* is used to store water for our town. 这个水库是用来为我们小镇储存水的。

residence ['rezɪdəns] *n*. 居住，住所

【记】 re(回来)+sid(坐下)+ence(名词词尾)→回来坐下的地方→住所

【例】 He married an English woman and took up his *residence* in London. 他与一名英国女子结婚并且定居在伦敦。

【同】 dwelling, mansion

【派】 (逆构)reside *v*. 居住

resident *n*. 居民，住户

residential *adj*. 住宅的，居住的

residue ['rezɪdjuː] *n*. 残留物，余留物

【记】 re(回来)+sid(坐下)+ue(名词词尾)→留下的东西→残余物

【例】 The *residue* of estate belongs to his son. 剩余财产属于他的儿子。

【同】 leftover, remnant

【派】 residual *adj*. 残余的，剩下的

resign [rɪ'zaɪn] *v*. 辞去，辞职

【记】 re(再一次) + sign(加上记号)→再一次签署名字→辞职

【例】 She *resigned* her directorship and left the firm. 她放弃了董事职务，离开了公司。

【同】 quit, renounce

【派】 resignation *n*. 辞职(书)，放弃

resigned *adj*. 顺从的，听天由命的

resistance [rɪˈzɪstəns] *n*. 抵抗，阻力

【记】 re(再一次) + sist(站立) + ance(名词词尾)→再次站起来→抵抗

【例】 The aircraft is streamlined to cut down wind *resistance*. 飞机设计成流线型以减少风的阻力。

【同】 opposition, rejection

【反】 obedience

【派】 (逆构)resist *v*. 抵抗，反抗

resistant *adj*. 拒绝的，有阻力的

resolution [ˌrezəˈljuːʃən] *n*. 坚定，决心

【记】 re(回来) + solut(松开，解决) + ion(名词词尾)→返回来解决问题→决心

【例】 She always makes good *resolutions* but never carries them out. 她总是决心很大，却从不见付诸行动。

【同】 determination, resolve

【派】 (逆构)resolute *adj*. 坚决的

resolve [rɪˈzɒlv] *v*. 1. 决心，决定；2. 分解，解决

【记】 re(再一次) + solve(松开)→再一次松开→解决

【例】 1. He *resolved* that nothing should hold him back. 他下决心不让任何事情阻挡他。

2. Intensive efforts are being made to *resolve* the dispute. 现正全力以赴来解决这场纠纷。

【同】 decide, determine

【派】 resolved *adj*. 下定决心的，断然的

resonance [ˈrezənəns] *n*. 共鸣，回声

【记】 re(回来) + son(声音) + ance(名词词尾)→返回来的声音→共鸣

【例】 *Resonance* would occur again, but not so strong as before. 共振会再次发生，但不如先前那么强。

【同】 vibrancy

【派】 (逆构)resonant *adj*. 引起共鸣的

resonate *v*. (使)共鸣，(使)共振

resort [rɪˈzɔːt] *n*. 1. 度假胜地；2. 诉诸，手段；*v*. 求助，采取(措施)

【记】 re(回来) + sort(出现)→经常出现→度假胜地，诉诸(手段)

【例】 1. Hawaii is an excellent tourist *resort*. 夏威夷是极好的旅游胜地。

2. Our only *resort* is to inform the police. 我们唯一的办法就是向警方报案。

3. If negotiations fail we shall have to *resort* to strick action. 假如谈判失败，我们就采取罢工行动。

resounding [rɪˈzaʊndɪŋ] *adj*. 1. 共鸣的；2. 彻底的，十足的

【记】 re(再一次) + sound(声音) + ing(形容词词尾)→再一次发出声音的→共鸣的

【例】 1. They all gave three *resounding* cheers. 他们全部发出了三声响亮的喝彩。
2. The film was a *resounding* success. 那部影片是驰名的成功之作。
【同】 resonant; thorough, great
【派】 (逆构)resound *v*. 回响，赞扬

resource [rɪˈsɔːs] *n*. 1. 资源；2. 机敏，智谋
【记】 re(再一次) + source(站立)→经常出现的东西→资源
【例】 1. *Resources* management is an important business skill. 资源管理是一项重要的经营技能。
2. He is a man of great *resource*. 他是一个足智多谋的男子。
【派】 resourceful *adj*. 资源丰富的；足智多谋的

respect [rɪsˈpekt] *n*. 1. 尊重；2. 着眼点，方面；*v*. 尊敬，尊重
【记】 re(反复的) + spect(看见)→一再注视→着眼点
【例】 1. The new officer soon won the *respect* of his men. 那新来的军官很快博得了士兵的钦敬。
2. In what *respect* do you think the film is biased? 你认为影片在哪一方面失之偏颇？
3. I *respect* you for your honesty. 由于你为人正直，我对你十分敬重。
【同】 adore, esteem
【反】 dishonour
【派】 respectable *adj*. 可敬的，高尚的
respective *adj*. 分别的，各自的
respectively *adv*. 分别地，各自地

respiratory [rɪsˈpaɪərətərɪ] *adj*. 呼吸(作用)的，呼吸器官的
【记】 re(反复的) + spira(呼吸) + tory(形容词词尾)→反复呼吸的过程→呼吸作用
【例】 The lungs are *respiratory* organs. 肺是呼吸器官。
【派】 (逆构)respire *v*. 呼吸
respiration *n*. 呼吸(作用)

respond [rɪsˈpɒnd] *v*. 回答，对…有反应
【记】 re(回来) + spond(承诺)→承诺回去→回答
【例】 I invited her to dinner but she did not *respond*. 我请她吃晚饭，但她未作回答。
【同】 reply, react
【派】 respondency *n*. 响应，一致
respondent *n*. 回答者，被告；*adj*. 回答的，有反应的

response [rɪsˈpɒns] *n*. 反应，响应
【记】 re(回来) + sponse(承诺)→承诺回去→反应
【例】 His idea received an enthusiastic *response*. 他的想法获得热烈的响应。
【同】 reaction, reply

responsible [rɪsˈpɒnsəbl] *adj*. 1. 有责任的，负责的；2. …的原因，应受归咎的
【记】 re(回来) + spons(承诺) + ible(形容词词尾)→承诺过的→有责任的
【例】 1. All pilots are *responsible* for their passengers' safety. 凡是飞机驾驶员均应对乘客的安全负责。

R

2. Smoking is *responsible* for many cases of lung cancer. 吸烟是许多人患肺癌的致病因素。

【同】 liable; accountable

【反】 irresponsible

【派】 responsibility *n*. 责任(感), 职责

restore [rɪs'tɔː] *v*. 恢复, 重建

【记】 re(再一次) + stor(站立) + (a)tion(名词词尾)→再一次站立起来→恢复

【例】 The new manager's job is to *restore* the company to profitability. 新经理的工作是让这家公司能恢复盈利状况。

【同】 renew, return

【派】 restoration *n*. 恢复, 重建

restrain [rɪs'treɪn] *v*. 制止, 抑制

【记】 re(再一次) + strain(拉紧)→重复拉紧→管制

【例】 The police had difficulty in *restraining* the crowd from rushing on to the pitch. 警方难以阻止人群涌入球场。

【同】 confine, restrict

【反】 impel

【派】 restrained *adj*. 受控制的, 节制的

restraint *n*. 遏制, 约束

restrict [rɪs'trɪkt] *v*. 限制, 约束

【记】 re(再一次) + strict(拉紧)→反复的拉紧→限制

【例】 I *restrict* myself to smoking two cigarettes a day. 我限定自己每天只抽两支烟。

【同】 limit, restrain

【反】 derestrict

【派】 restricted *adj*. 受限制的, 有限的

restriction *n*. 限制, 约束

result [rɪ'zʌlt] *n*. 结果, 效果; *v*. 结果, 导致

【记】 re(回来) + sult(跳跃, 弹)→弹回来→结果

【例】 1. These problems are the *result* of years of bad management. 这些问题是由于多年管理不善而造成的。

2. The accident *resulted* in the death of two passengers. 这起事故导致两名乘客丧生。

【同】 consequence, effect

【反】 cause

【派】 resultful *adj*. 富有成效的

resume ['rezjʊ(ː)meɪ] *n*. 概要, 简历; [rɪ'zjuːm] *v*. 重新开始, 继续

【记】 re(再一次) + sume(取得)→再一次获得→重新开始

【例】 1. Please give a *resume* of the evidence. 请给出证言的摘要。

2. She *resumed* her maiden name after the divorce. 她离婚后重新使用娘家的姓。

【同】 continue, restart

【派】 resumption *n*. 重新开始, 恢复

retail ['riːteɪl] *n*. 零售；*v*. 零售

【记】 re(反复的)+tail(切割)→把货品分成小部分出售→零售

【例】 1. Could you tell me the *retail* prices of these shoes? 你能告诉我这些鞋子的零售价吗？

2. These socks *retail* at 1 dollar a pair. 这些袜子零卖一美元一双。

【反】 wholesale

【派】 retailer *n*. 零售商

retailing *n*. 零售业

retain [rɪ'teɪn] *v*. 保持，保留

【记】 re(回来)+tain(拿住)→把东西拿回来→保留

【例】 This village still *retains* its old-world character. 这个村庄仍然保持着古色古香的特色。

【同】 keep, withhold

【反】 abandon

【派】 retainment *n*. 保留，保持

retard [rɪ'tɑːd] *v*. 延迟，阻止

【记】 re(回来)+tard(缓慢的)→慢慢的回来→延迟

【例】 Cold weather *retards* the growth of the crops. 寒冷的天气妨碍了庄稼生长。

【同】 delay, detain

【反】 accelerate

【派】 retardant *adj*. 延缓的，使迟滞的

retardance *n*. 阻滞，迟缓

retire [rɪ'taɪə] *v*. 1. 退休；2. 撤退

【记】 re(回来)+tire(拉，拽)→拉回来→撤退

【例】 1. My father *retired* at the age of 60. 我父亲60岁时退休了。

2. Our forces *retired* to prepared positions. 我们的军队撤退到既设阵地上。

【同】 retreat, withdraw

【派】 retiree *n*. 退休人员

retirement *n*. 退休；撤退

R

retort [rɪ'tɔːt] *v*. 反击，反驳

【记】 re(回来)+tort(扭曲，扭动)→扭转回来→反击

【例】 He *retorted* that it was my fault as much as his. 他反驳说我的错误并不比他的小。

【同】 answer, reply, retaliate

retract [rɪ'trækt] *v*. 缩回，缩进

【记】 re(回来)+tract(拉)→拉回来→缩回

【例】 The undercarriage on light aircraft does not always *retract* in flight. 轻型飞机飞行时起落架不一定缩回。

【同】 shrink, withdraw, pull back

【派】 retractation *n*. 收回

retreat [rɪ'triːt] *n*./*v*. 撤退，退却

【记】 re(回来)+treat(拉拽)→拉回来→撤退

【例】 1. The minister made an undignified *retreat* from his earlier position. 那位部长很不光彩的背离了他原来的立场。

2. The soldiers had to *retreat* when they were beaten in battle. 士兵们在战斗中受挫，不得不撤退。

【同】 withdraw

【反】 advance

retrenchment [rɪˈtrentʃmənt] *n*. 节省，缩减

【记】 re(回来)+trench(切割)+ment(名词词尾)→缩减成原来的程度→删除

【例】 The worsening economic situation has forced the government into a policy of *retrenchment*. 日益恶化的经济状况已迫使政府采取紧缩政策。

【同】 cut，reduction

【反】 increase

【派】 (逆构)retrench *v*. 节约，删减

retrieve [rɪˈtriːv] *v*. 重新找回，取回

【记】 re(回来)+trieve(找到)→找回来→取回

【例】 The company is fighting to *retrieve* its market share. 这个公司正在为恢复其市场份额而奋斗。

【同】 regain，restore，recover

retrospect [ˈretrəuspekt] *n*. 反顾，回顾

【记】 retro(向后)+spect(看)→向后看→回顾

【例】 One's school life seem happier in *retrospect* than in reality. 学校生活回忆起来显得比实际上要快乐。

【同】 review，reflection

【反】 prospect

【派】 retrospective *adj*. 回顾的，怀旧的

reveal [rɪˈviːl] *v*. 泄露，揭开

【记】 re(回来)+veal(=veil，面纱)→取下面纱→揭开

【例】 I promise never to *reveal* his secret. 我答应决不泄漏他的秘密。

【同】 disclose，expose

【反】 conceal

【派】 revelation *n*. 显示，揭露；新发明，启示

revenue [ˈrevɪnjuː] *n*. 收入，国家的税收

【记】 re(回来)+ven(来到)+ue→回来的东西→税收

【例】 The government's *revenue* is made up chiefly of the money we pay in taxes. 政府的收入主要来源是靠我们所交的税。

【同】 income，taxation

revere [rɪˈvɪə] *v*. 尊崇，尊敬

【记】 re(再一次)+vere(害怕)→一再害怕→敬畏→尊崇，尊敬

【例】 People came to the memorial to *revere* the memory of the great leader. 人们来到纪念馆崇敬地纪念这位伟大的领袖。

【同】 admire，adore，esteem，respect

【派】 reverence *n*. 尊敬，尊严，威望

reverent *adj*. 尊敬的，虔诚的

reverse [rɪˈvɜːs] *n*./*v*. 反向，倒转；*adj*. 相反的，倒退的

【记】 re(后面) + verse(转向)→转向后面→倒转

【例】 1. He *reversed* the coin and examined it carefully. 他把硬币倒过来，仔细检查。

2. He did the *reverse* of what we expected. 他所做的和我们预料的正相反。

3. Please read the names on this list in *reverse* order. 请看看这张单子上的名字，从下面往上看。

【同】 regress，overturn；inverse

【反】 obverse

revert [rɪˈvɜːt] *v*. 恢复原状，回到(原来话题)

【记】 re(后面) + vert(转变方向)→转向后面→恢复原状

【例】 He *reverted* to smoking when under stress. 他因受到压力又恢复了吸烟的习惯。

【同】 regress，return

【派】 revertible *adj*. 可回复的，应归还的

review [rɪˈvjuː] *v*./*n*. 回顾，复习

【记】 re(再一次) + view(看)→一再地看→复习

【例】 The airport authorities have promised to *review* their security measurements. 机场当局已答应重新检查他们的安全措施。

【同】 examine，inspect

【派】 reviewal *n*. 校阅，评论

reviewer *n*. 批评家，评论家

revise [rɪˈvaɪz] *v*. 修正，校订

【记】 re(反复的) + vise(看到)→反复的检查→校对

【例】 He *revised* the manuscript of his book before sending it to the publisher. 他对自己那本书的手稿先进行校订，然后才把它交给出版社。

【同】 amend，correct

【派】 reviser *n*. 校订者

revision *n*. 校订，修订本

revive [rɪˈvaɪv] *v*. 使复兴，使重新流行

【记】 re(再一次) + viv(生活) + e→重新活过来→使复兴

【例】 Interest in classic music has *revived* recently. 近来对古典音乐的兴趣又浓厚起来。

【同】 refresh，regenerate

【派】 revival *n*. 复苏，重新流行

revolution [ˌrevəˈluːʃən] *n*. 1. 革命；2. 剧烈的变革

【记】 re(回来) + volut(转变) + ion(名词词尾)→(形势)发生转变→革命

【例】 1. Most countries have had *revolutions* aganist the government. 大多数国家发生过反对政府的革命。

2. Air travel has caused a *revolution* in our way of living. 空中旅行使我们的生活方式完全变了。

【同】 uprising；reform

【派】 revolutionary *adj*. 革命性剧变的，突破性的
revolutionist *n*. 革命家

revolve [rɪˈvɒlv] *v*. 旋转
【记】 re(反复的)+volve(转动)→反复的转动→旋转
【例】 The moon *revolves* around the earth. 月球绕地球运行。
【同】 circle，turn
【反】 fix

revulsion [rɪˈvʌlʃən] *n*. 反感，抽回
【记】 re(回来)+vuls(拉，收缩)+ion(名词词尾)→拉回来→抽回
【例】 She stared at the snake in *revulsion*. 她盯着那条蛇，感到很厌恶。
【同】 repulsion
【派】 (逆构)revulse *v*. 极其厌恶，强烈反感
revulsive *adj*. 诱导的

reward [rɪˈwɔːd] *n*./*v*. 酬劳，奖赏
【记】 re(再一次)+ward(照顾)→再一次的照顾→酬劳
【例】 1. He got a *reward* for helping them. 他因帮助他们而拿到一笔酬金。
2. They *rewarded* the winners with gifts of fruits and flowers. 他们奖给优胜者一些水果和鲜花。
【同】 award，compensate
【反】 punish，punishment
【派】 rewarding *adj*. 报答的，值得的

rhetoric [ˈretərɪk] *n*. 修辞，修辞学
【记】 rhetor(演说家)+ic(名词词尾)→演说家用的东西→修辞，修辞学
【例】 The sentence contains impassioned *rhetoric*. 这个句子含有富有表现力的修辞。

rhythm [ˈrɪðəm，ˈrɪθəm] *n*. 节奏，韵律
【记】 rhy(=flow，流动)+thm→(音乐)流动的样子→节奏
【例】 He is trying to play the same tune in a different *rhythm*. 他正试图用不同节奏演奏同一个曲子。
【同】 beat，tempo
【派】 rhythmic *adj*. 节奏的，合拍的

riddle [ˈrɪdl] *n*. 谜，谜语
【记】 rid(筛)+d+le(名词词尾)→反复筛选→需要猜测的东西→谜
【例】 He could not solve the *riddle*. 他猜不出这个谜。
【同】 enigma，puzzle

ridiculous [rɪˈdɪkjʊləs] *adj*. 荒谬的，可笑的
【记】 ridcu(笑)+lous(形容词词尾)→笑声多的→可笑的
【例】 That fat woman looked *ridiculous* in her tight golden dress. 那位胖妇人穿着金色的紧身礼服，显得滑稽可笑。
【同】 absurd，foolish
【同】 logical，rational
【派】 (逆构)ridicule *n*./*v*. 嘲笑，奚落

R

rift [rɪft] *v*. 开裂，断裂；*n*. 裂缝，长狭谷

【例】 The sun appeared through a *rift* in the clouds. 太阳从云朵的缝隙中露面了。

【同】 breach, split

【派】 rifty *adj*. 裂开的

rigid [ˈrɪdʒɪd] *adj*. 刚硬的，严格的

【记】 rig(= reg, 统治) + id(形容词词尾)→像统治者一样的→刚硬的

【例】 She was *rigid* with fear. 她害怕得全身僵住了。

【同】 hard, stiff

【反】 pliable, yielding

【派】 rigidify *v*. (使)僵化

rigidity *n*. 坚硬，僵化

rigor [ˈrɪgə] *n*. 严酷，严格，严厉

【记】 rig(= reg, 统治) + or(名词词尾)→像统治者的→严酷，严格

【例】 The expedition suffered all the *rigors* of a Canadian winter. 这支探险队饱受了加拿大严冬的折磨。

【同】 hardship, severity

【派】 rigorous *adj*. 严格的，严厉的

rim [rɪm] *n*. 边缘

【例】 She put a flower on the *rim* of the hat. 她在帽子边上放了一朵花。

【同】 edge, fringe

rink [rɪŋk] *n*. 溜冰场，冰球场

【例】 Skating on the skating *rink* is good fun. 在溜冰场溜冰是很有趣的。

【派】 rinker *n*. 溜冰者

riot [ˈraɪət] *n*. 暴乱，骚动

【例】 Research in the United States has shown a relationship between temperature and street *riots*. 美国的一项研究已经表明了气温和街头骚乱两者之间的关系。

【同】 rebel, violence

【反】 peace

【派】 rioter *n*. 聚众闹事者

riotous *adj*. 暴动的，骚乱的

ripen [ˈraɪpən] *v*. (使)成熟

【记】 rip(e)(成熟的) + en(动词词尾)→使成熟

【例】 Long-day plants are adapted for situations that require fertilization by insects, or a long period of seed *ripening*. 长日照植物需要通过昆虫代为授精或需要较长的种子成熟期。

【派】 ripe *adj*. 熟的，成熟的

risk [rɪsk] *n*./*v*. 危险，危害性的事物

【例】 1. Is there any *risk* of the bomb exploding? 这个炸弹有爆炸的危险吗?

2. He *risked* his life when he saved the child from the fire. 他冒着生命危险把孩子从火中救出。

【同】 danger, venture

R

【反】 safety

【派】 risky *adj*. 危险的，有风险的

ritual [ˈrɪtjuəl] *n*. 典礼，(宗教)仪式

【记】 rit(e)(仪式)+ual(形容词词尾转用作名词)→典礼

【例】 *Rituals* are the quintessential religious behavior. 仪式是宗教行为的精髓。

【同】 ceremony

rival [ˈraɪvəl] *n*. 竞争者，对手 *v*. (-l(l)ed; -l(l)ing)竞争，对抗

【记】 riv(流动，跑)+al(名词词尾)→一起跑的人→竞争者

【例】 1. The party leader has been supplanted by his *rival*. 那位政党领导已被他的对手取而代之了。

2. Cricket cannot *rival* football for/in excitement. 板球不如足球有刺激性。

【同】 competitor, match; compete

【派】 rivalry *n*. 竞争；敌对状态

roam [rəum] *v*. /*n*. 漫步，闲逛

【例】 I'm just going to give you a brief account of the history of the museum before letting you *roam* about on your own. 在你们自由参观之前，我先向大家简要介绍一下博物馆的历史。

【同】 ramble, wander

【派】 roamer *n*. 流浪者，漂泊者

roast [rəust] *n*. 烤肉；*v*. 烘，烤

【例】 1. Let's have a nice *roast* for Sunday dinner. 我们星期天晚上好好吃一顿烤肉吧。

2. The beef is *roasting* nicely on the spit. 这块牛肉在烤肉叉上烤得很好。

【同】 barbeque

【派】 roasting *adj*. 极热的，火烫的

robbery [ˈrɒbərɪ] *n*. 抢掠，抢夺

【记】 rob(b)(抢劫)+(e)ry(名词词尾)→抢夺

【例】 He was sent down for ten years for armed *robbery*. 他因持械抢劫被判入狱十年。

【同】 looting

【派】 (逆构)rob *v*. (-bbed; -bbing)抢夺，剥夺

robber *n*. 强盗

robust [rəˈbʌst] *adj*. 强健的，坚定的

【记】 rob(力量)+ust(形容词词尾)→有力量的→强壮的

【例】 The old veteran could lay flat the most *robust* sportsman. 这位沙场老将能把最强壮的运动员拖得筋疲力尽。

【同】 healthy, powerful

【反】 delicate

rot [rɒt] *v*. (-tted; -tting)(使)腐烂，(使)腐败

【例】 The ripe fruit began to *rot* when no one came to pick it. 没有人来摘这些成熟的水果，它们已经开始烂了。

【同】 crumble, decay, disintegrate

【派】 rotten *adj*. 腐烂的

R

rotate [rəʊ'teɪt] *v*. 旋转，(庄稼)轮作

【记】 rot(轮子)+ate(动词词尾)→轮子滚动→旋转

【例】 He *rotates* the handle gently. 他轻轻地转动手柄。

【同】 revolve, turn

【派】 rotatable *adj*. 可旋转的，可转动的

rotation *n*. 旋转，庄稼轮作

rough [rʌf] *adj*. 粗糙的，大致的

【例】 Could you give me a *rough* idea when you'll be back? 你能告诉我你大概什么时候回来吗？

【同】 coarse, crude, approximate

【反】 smooth

【派】 roughly *adv*. 粗略地，大致地

rouse [raʊz] *n*./*v*. 唤醒，激发

【例】 I was *roused* by the sound of the bell this morning. 今天早晨，我被铃声唤醒。

【同】 arouse, awaken

【派】 rousing *adj*. 鼓舞人的，活跃的

route [ruːt] *n*. 路线，路程

【例】 The plane deviated from its usual *route*. 飞机偏离了正常的航线。

【同】 course, path

【派】 routing *n*. 行程安排

routine [ruː'tiːn] *n*. 1. 例行公事，常规；2. 一套动作

【记】 rout(常走的道路)+ine(名词词尾)→经常走的路线→例行公事

【例】 1. They did it as a matter of *routine*. 他们那样做只是例行公事。

2. Physical Fitness instructors prepare *routines* of exercises to suit the individual client's age and level of fitness. 健身中心的指导老师准备不同的练习套路，以适应各个不同年龄和级别的客户。

【同】 arrangement, procedure; set

【派】 routineer *n*. 墨守成规者

royal ['rɔɪəl] *adj*. 王室的，高贵的

【记】 roy(=reg，统治)+al(形容词词尾)→属于统治者的→王室的

【例】 Britain has always had a large navy, called the *Royal* Navy. 英国一直有一支强大的海军，称为皇家海军。

【同】 imperial

【派】 royalty *n*. 皇室，王权

rub [rʌb] *v*. (-bbed; -bbing)摩擦，揩拭

【例】 He *rubbed* his hands to keep them warm. 他揉搓着双手来取暖。

【同】 massage, scrub

【派】 rub-down *n*. 擦洗，磨平

rubstone *n*. 磨(刀)石

rubbish ['rʌbɪʃ] *n*. 垃圾，废物

【记】 rub(b)(擦)+ish(形容词词尾转用作名词)→擦掉的东西→废物

【例】 The dustman comes once a week to collect the *rubbish*. 垃圾工每周来收一次垃圾。

【同】 junk, trash, waste

【派】 rubbishy *adj*. 破烂的，毫无价值的

rudimentary [ruːdɪ'mentərɪ] *adj*. 未成熟的，发育不全的

【记】 rud(i)(= row，粗糙的) + ment(名词词尾) + ary(形容词词尾)→粗糙的东西→未成熟的

【例】 I have only a *rudimentary* grasp of physics. 我对物理学仅有初步的了解。

【同】 fundamental, incomplete

【派】 (逆构)rudiment *n*. 初步，基本原理

ruin [rʊɪn,'ruːɪn] *n*./*v*. 毁灭，丧失

【例】 1. The castle now lies in *ruins*. 那城堡现在已成了一片废墟了。

2. He *ruined* his prospects by carelessness. 他因疏忽大意而断送了前途。

【同】 damage, destroy

【反】 repair, restore

【派】 ruinous *adj*. 带来巨大损失的

rural ['rʊərəl] *adj*. 乡下的，田园的

【记】 rur(乡村) + al(形容词词尾)→乡村里的→田园的

【例】 Where I lived in Ecuador was a very *rural* area. 我在厄瓜多尔居住的地方是一个很有田园风味的地方。

【同】 countrified, rustic

【反】 urban

【派】 rurality *n*. 田园风光

rupture ['rʌptʃər] *v*./*n*. 破裂，裂开

【记】 rupt(断开) + ure(名词词尾)→断开→破裂

【例】 1. He'll *rupture* a muscle if he goes on dancing like that! 他要是继续那样跳舞，会跳得皮开肉裂！

2. It is sad to see the *rupture* of friendly relations between our two countries. 看到我们两国之间的友好关系突然破裂，令人十分痛惜。

【同】 break, crack

rust [rʌst] *n*. 铁锈；*v*. (使)生锈

【例】 1. How can I remove the *rust* from the iron door? 我怎样才能把铁门上的锈除掉呢？

2. The great advantage of this metal is that it doesn't *rust*. 这种金属最大的优点是不生锈。

【派】 rustproof *adj*. 不锈的

S

sack [sæk] *n*. 1.袋子，大包；2.开除，解雇

【例】 1.The *sack* split and the rice poured out. 口袋裂开了，大米撒出来了。

2.If you are late again, the boss will give you the *sack*. 如果你再迟到，老板就会把你解雇。

【同】 bag, pack

sacred [ˈseɪkrɪd] *adj*. 神圣的，不可侵犯的

【记】 sacr(神圣的)+ed(形容词词尾)→神圣的

【例】 Her marriage is *sacred* to her. 她认为自己的婚姻至高无上。

【同】 holy, divine

【反】 profane

sacrifice [ˈsækrɪfaɪs] *n*./*v*. 牺牲，献出

【记】 sacr(神圣的)+fic(做)+e→为神做的东西→牺牲

【例】 1.Success in your job is not worth the *sacrifice* of your health. 以牺牲健康来求得工作上的成功是不值得的。

2.It's the company's policy to *sacrifice* short-term profits for the sake of long-term growth. 为长期发展而牺牲短期利润是公司的方针。

【同】 give

【派】 sacrificial *adj*. 牺牲的，献祭的

safeguard [ˈseɪfˌgɑːd] *n*./*v*. 安全措施，保护

【记】 safe(安全的)+guard(守卫)→守卫…的安全→保护

【例】 1.This cause in the contract is a necessary *safeguard* against our losing money on the deal. 合同中的这项条款是避免我们在买卖中赔钱的重要保障。

2.The Bill of Rights *safeguards* our individual liberties. 权力法案保护我们的个人自由。

【同】 protect, defend

【派】 (逆构)safe *adj*. 安全的，可靠的

safety *n*. 安全，保险

sagacious [səˈgeɪʃəs] *adj*. 有洞察力的，精明的

【记】 sagac(智慧)+ious(形容词词尾)→有智慧的→精明的

【例】 The leader made a *sagacious* decision. 领导做了英明的决定。

【同】 wise, perspicacious

【派】 sagacity *n*. 睿智，聪敏

saint [seɪnt, sənt] *n*. 圣人，道德崇高的人

【记】 sa(i)n(神圣的)+t(名词词尾)→神圣的人→圣人

【例】 You must be a *saint* to be able to stand his temper! 能受得了他的脾气，一定得非常有涵养才行。

【同】 holy

【派】 sainted *adj*. 德高的，成为圣人的

saintly *adj*. 圣洁的

sake [seɪk] *n*. 为…着想，缘故

【例】 She gave him back the money she'd stolen for the *sake* of her conscience. 为了不受良心的谴责，她把从他那偷来的钱还给他了。

【同】 purpose，reason

saline ['seɪlaɪn,sə'laɪn] *adj*. 含盐的，咸的

【记】 sal(盐)+ine(形容词词尾)→含盐的

【例】 The nurse diluted the drug with *saline* water. 护士用生理盐水把药加以稀释。

【同】 salty

【派】 salinity *n*. 盐分，盐浓度

salutary ['sæljʊtərɪ] *adj*. 有益的，有益健康的

【记】 salu(=salv，救助)+t+ary(形容词词尾)→救助的→有益的

【例】 The accident is a *salutary* reminder of the danger of climbing. 这一事故有益的一面是提醒了我们攀登活动是有许多危险的。

【同】 beneficial，healthful，salubrious

【反】 harmful

sample ['sæmpl] *n*. 货样，样本；*v*. 取样，尝试

【记】 s(向外)+ample(拿取)→拿出来→取样

【例】 1. You must send some *sample* to the customer before you go abroad. 在你出国之前，应该先寄给客户一些样品。

2. We *sampled* the stuff and found it satisfactory. 我们抽验了这批材料，认为满意。

【同】 example；try

sanction ['sæŋkʃən] *n*. 批准，同意；2. 制裁，处罚

【记】 sanc(t)(神圣的)+tion(名词词尾)→神圣的裁决→批准，同意

【例】 1. The government gave its *sanction* to what the Minister had done. 政府对这位部长的做法均已认可。

2. Western nations imposed economic *sanctions* on the country. 西方各国对这个国家实行了经济制裁。

【同】 endorsement，permit

sanctuary ['sæŋktjʊərɪ] *n*. 1. 圣所，圣殿；2. 避难所，动物保护区

【记】 sanct(神圣的)+uary(名词词尾)→神圣的地方→圣所，圣殿

【例】 1. It is a classic *sanctuary* in which the rationalist fancy may take refuge. 这是一所古雅的圣殿，理性主义者可以躲在其中。

2. The outlaw was granted *sanctuary* in the church. 这名犯法者获准去教堂避难。

【同】 asylum，haven，refuge

S

sanitation [sænɪˈteɪʃən] *n*. 卫生，卫生设施

【记】 san(i)(健全的)+tation(名词词尾)→(维护身体)健康→卫生，卫生设施

【例】 The people lived in that city can keep *sanitation* clean. 住在那个城市的人们能保持公共卫生设施的清洁。

【派】 sanitary *adj*. 清洁的，保健的

sarcastic [sɑːˈkæstɪk] *adj*. 讽刺的，挖苦的

【记】 sarc(讽刺)+astic(形容词词尾)→讽刺的

【例】 She talked with him with *sarcastic* tones. 她用挖苦的语调和他说话。

【同】 satiric, pungent

【反】 unsarcastic

【派】 sarcasm *n*. 讽刺，挖苦

satiate [ˈseɪʃɪeɪt] *v*. 满足，使过饱

【记】 sati(充满的)+ate(动词词尾)→使充满→满足

【例】 In review a novel, you shall try to titillate rather than *satiate* the reader's interest. 评论一本小说的时候，你应想办法刺激而不是满足读者的兴趣。

【同】 overeat

【派】 satiation *n*. 饱足，饱食，饱满

satire [ˈsætaɪə] *n*. 讽刺文学，讽刺

【记】 sat(充满的)+ire(名词词尾)→充满(各种味道的)→讽刺

【例】 Her novel is a *satire* on social snobbery. 她的小说是描述势利小人的讽刺作品。

【同】 irony

【派】 satiric *adj*. 讽刺的，挖苦的

satisfy [ˈsætɪsfaɪ] *v*. 满足，使满意

【记】 sat(is)(充满的)+fy(动词词尾)→使充满了→满足

【例】 I had to explain the reasons to *satisfy* his curiosity. 我只好解释原因来满足他的好奇心。

【同】 content, gratify

【反】 dissatisfy, discontent

【派】 satisfaction *n*. 满意，满足

satisfactory *adj*. 满意的

satisfying *adj*. 令人满足的，令人满意的

S

saturate [ˈsætʃəreɪt] *v*. 浸透，使湿透

【记】 sat(ur)(充满的)+ate(动词词尾)→使充满→浸透

【例】 We lay on the beach, *saturated* in sunshine. 我们躺在沙滩上，沐浴在阳光里。

【同】 imbue, soak

【派】 saturated *adj*. 渗透的，饱和的

sausage [ˈsɒsɪdʒ] *n*. 香肠，腊肠

【记】 saus(=salted，有盐的)+age(名词词尾)→有盐的东西→香肠

【例】 She loves *sausage* and mash. 她喜欢香肠和土豆泥。

savor [ˈseɪvə] *n*. 滋味，气味

【例】 Life seems to have lost most of its *savor* for him. 对他来说，生活似乎已失去了一

切乐趣。

【同】 flavor，taste

【派】 savory *adj*. 风味极佳的，可口的，味美的

scale [skeɪl] *n*. 1.刻度；2.范围；3.鳞片；*v*. 调节，增，减

【例】 1. This ruler has one *scale* in centimetres and another in inches. 这把尺子上有厘米的刻度和英寸的刻度。

2. We are seeing unemployment on an unprecedented *scale*. 我们现在正经历规模空前的失业现象。

3. Fish have *scales*. 鱼有鱼鳞。

4. The company has begun to *scale* down its operations in Africa. 这家公司已经开始减少在非洲的业务。

【同】 proportion；squama；climb

【派】 scaled *adj*. 有刻度的，成比例的

scamper [ˈskæmpə] *n*./*v*. 蹦蹦跳跳，奔跑

【记】 scamp(匆忙)＋er(表示动作的反复)→匆匆忙忙的→奔跑

【例】 Giggling，the children *scampered* back into the house. 孩子们咯咯笑着，蹦蹦跳跳地跑回屋里。

【同】 scurry，dash

scan [skæn] *n*./*v*. (-nned；-nning)扫描，浏览

【例】 1. The doctors gave him an ultrasonic brain *scan*. 医生给他做了脑部超声波扫描检查。

2. I *scanned* the newspaper when I was waiting for the bus. 等公共汽车的时候，我匆匆浏览了一下报纸。

【同】 skim，glance over

【派】 scanner *n*. 扫描仪

scandal [ˈskændl] *n*. 丑闻，诽谤

【记】 scand(绊倒)＋al(名词词尾)→使绊倒→使出丑→丑闻

【例】 A series of corruption *scandals* led to the fall of the government. 一系列的贪污腐化事件激起民愤，导致政府垮台。

【同】 disgrace，shame

【反】 praise

【派】 scandalous *adj*. 诽谤性的

scarce [skeəs] *adj*. 缺乏的，稀有的

【例】 It was wartime and food was *scarce*. 那时是战争时期，食物短缺。

【同】 rare，deficient

【反】 plentiful，abundant

【派】 scarcity *n*. 缺乏，不足

scarcely *adv*. 几乎不，简直没有

scare [skeə] *n*./*v*. 惊恐，恐慌

【例】 This is a fake video camera which you fix to your wall to *scare* off burglars. 这是一个假的摄像机，你装在墙上，可以吓唬盗贼。

【同】 alarm，frighten

scatter [ˈskætə] *v*. 使分散，散播

【例】 The birds *scattered* at the sound of the gun. 鸟群一听到枪声就四处飞散了。

【同】 disperse，spread

【反】 gather

【派】 scattered *adj*. 离散的，分散的

scattershot *adj*. 漫无目标的，一般的

scenario [sɪˈnɑːrɪəʊ] *n*. 1. 电影剧本，脚本；2. 设想

【记】 scena(stage，舞台)＋rio(名词词尾)→来自意大利语，维舞台写的东西→电影剧本

【例】 1. This is the ultimate nightmare *scenario*. 这是一个极为恐怖、梦魇一般的电影脚本。

2. He outlined several convincing *scenarios* for the outbreak of a nuclear war. 他颇有说服力地概述了核战争爆发时可能出现的几种情况。

【同】 playscript

【派】 scenarist *n*. 剧作家，编剧家

scene [siːn] *n*. (一)场，场景

【例】 And now the *scene* shifts to the warehouse, where the murderer is lying in wait. 现在场景转到仓库，行凶者正埋伏在那里伺机行动。

【同】 setting，stage

【派】 scenic *adj*. 舞台的，风景优美的

scenery [ˈsiːnərɪ] *n*. 风景，景色

【记】 scene(舞台场景)＋ry(名词词尾)→本义是为场景准备的东西→舞台布景→风景

【例】 The *scenery* was as fine as any we saw on the trip. 这里的景色和我们一路上看到的一样美丽。

【同】 landscape

scent [sent] *n*. 气味，香味；*v*. 闻出，嗅

【例】 1. There is a lavender *scent* in the air. 空气中有熏衣草的味道。

2. The dog *scented* a rat. 那狗嗅出有老鼠的气味。

【同】 smell，odor

【反】 stench

【派】 scented *adj*. 洒有香水的，有香味的

schedule [ˈʃedjuːl，ˈskedʒʊl] *n*. 计划(表)，日程安排

【记】 schedu(一张纸)＋le(表示"小"的名词词尾)→一小张纸→日程安排

【例】 He could have finished it on *schedule*, but somehow he fell behind. 他原本能按预定进度做完这件事的，但不知怎地却落后了。

【同】 agenda，timetable

【派】 scheduled *adj*. 预定的，严格按时间表的

scheduling *n*. 行程安排

scheme [skiːm] *n*./*v*. 1. 计划，安排；2. 诡计，阴谋

【例】 1. The manager had worked out a *scheme* for not paying the tax. 这经理想出了一个逃税的诡计。

2. Her enemies are *scheming* her downfall. 她的对头正在策划把她搞垮。

【同】 plan

【派】 schemer *n*. 计划者；阴谋家

scheming *adj*. 计划的；诡计多端的

scholar [ˈskɒlə] *n*. 1. 学者；2. 领有奖学金的学生

【记】 scho(o)l(学校) + ar(名词词尾，…的人)→在学校做研究的人→学者

【例】 1. He ranks high as a *scholar*. 他是第一流的学者。

2. He went abroad to study as a *scholar*. 他作为奖学金获得者赴外学习。

【同】 academician；student

【派】 scholarly *adj*. 学者气质的，学者的

scholarship *n*. 奖学金

scissor [ˈsɪzə] *v*. 剪取，截取；*n*. 剪刀

【例】 She yesterday *scissored* out a poem from a newspaper. 昨天她从报纸上剪下来一首诗。

【同】 cut

【派】 scissor-cut *n*. 剪纸

scold [skəuld] *v*. 责骂，斥责

【例】 If I walk in with muddy boots, Dad always *scolds* me. 如果我穿着有泥的靴子进屋，爸爸就会骂我。

【同】 blame，reproach

【反】 encourage

scoop [skuːp] *n*. 铲子；*v*. 铲取，舀出

【例】 1. There are several *scoops* in my kitchen. 我的厨房里有好几个勺子。

2. *Scoop* out the pulp and serve it with sugar. 把果肉挖出来和糖一起食用。

【派】 scoopful *n*. 满满的一勺子，一勺之量

scope [skəup] *n*. 范围，机会

【例】 Your question is beyond the *scope* of this book. 你所问的问题已超出了这本书的范围。

【同】 extent，range

scorch [skɔːtʃ] *v*. 烤焦，烧焦

【例】 The meat will *scorch* if you don't lower the gas. 如果你不把煤气调小一点，肉就要焦了。

【同】 burn，parch

【派】 scorching *adj*. 灼热的，激烈的

score [skɔː, skɒə] *v*. 得分，计分；*n*. 得分，获得(成功)

【例】 1. Arsenal *scored* in the final minute of the game. 阿森纳队在比赛的最后一分钟进了一球。

2. The *score* was five-nil with five minute left in the game. 比赛离终场还有五分钟时，双方比分为五比零。

【同】 mark

【派】 scoreboard *n*. 记分牌

S

scorn [skɔːn] *n.*/*v.* 轻蔑，嘲笑

【例】 As a professional painter, she *scorns* the efforts of amateurs. 她是专业画家，看不起业余画家的创作。

【同】 contemn, disdain

【反】 respect, appreciate

【派】 scornful *adj.* 轻蔑的

scour [ˈskaʊə] *v.* 冲洗，擦亮

【例】 He *scoured* off the dirt from the floor. 他擦去地板上的污垢。

【同】 scrub, wash

scout [skaʊt] *n.* 侦察员；*v.* 侦察，搜索

【例】 1. Our *scout* choked off the traitor's scream. 我们的侦察兵卡住那个叛徒的脖子使他没有能喊叫出来。

2. I've been *scouting* around town for a better house. 我跑遍了全城想找个好一点的房子。

【同】 pathfinder; search, hunt

scrap [skræp] *n.* 1. 小片，碎屑；2. 废旧材料；*v.* (-pped; -pping)抛弃，拆毁

【例】 1. Only a few *scraps* of news about the disaster have emerged. 那场灾祸的情况只获知了一些零星的消息。

2. The *scrap* merchant has a machine which crushes cars. 那个废品商有个压碎汽车的机器。

3. You ought to *scrap* the old bike and buy a new one. 你应该扔掉这辆旧自行车，买一辆新的。

【同】 chip; waste; discard

【反】 whole

【派】 scrapbook *n.* 剪贴簿

scrappy *adj.* 零散的，片断的

scrape [skreɪp] *n.*/*v.* 刮擦，擦伤

【例】 I must have *scraped* some of the paint off when I was parking the car.
我准是在停放汽车的时候刮掉了一些油漆。

【同】 rub, scratch

【派】 scraper *n.* 刮刀，铲土机

scratch [skrætʃ] *n.*/*v.* 1. 抓挠，划；2. 乱涂，潦草的涂画

【例】 1. I *scratched* the side of the car as I was driving through the gate. 我驾车驶过大门边时把汽车边划破了。

2. He *scratched* his name on the wall with his knife. 他用刀子把自己的名字刻在了墙上。

【同】 rub, scrape

【派】 scratchy *adj.* 潦草的，凌乱的

screen [skriːn] *n.* 1. 屏，银幕；2. 掩蔽物，屏风；*v.* 1. 掩蔽，包庇；2. 筛选，甄别

【例】 1. We sat at the front, very close to the *screen*. 我们坐在前排，非常靠近银幕。

2. There is a beautiful antique *screen* in their living room. 在他们的客厅里有一个

S

漂亮的古董屏风。

3. You can't *screen* your children from the real life forever. 不能总护着孩子，不让他们接触现实生活。

4. A hundred carefully *screened* people were invited to dinner with the President. 经过仔细审查的一百人获邀通总统共进晚餐。

【同】 cover, shelter

【派】 screening *n*. 放映

screenplay *n*. 电影剧本

screw [skruː] *n*. 螺丝钉，螺旋；*v*. 调节，旋动

【例】 She *screwed* the letter into a ball angrily and threw it away. 她生气地把信团成一团，然后扔掉了。

【同】 twist

【派】 screw-cap *n*. 螺旋帽

scribble [ˈskrɪbl] *n*./*v*. 涂鸦，潦草地写

【记】 scrib(写) + (b)le(动词词尾)→(随便地)写→潦草地写

【例】 Do not *scribble* on the wall! 不要在墙上乱涂乱画！

【同】 scratch

scrub [skrʌb] *v*. (-bbed; -bbing)洗擦，擦净

【例】 Although she *scrubbed* the old pot thoroughly, she could not make it look completely clean. 虽然她彻底地用力擦洗那只旧壶，但她无法把它完全洗干净。

【同】 rub

【派】 scrubboard *n*. 洗衣板

scrupulous [ˈskruːpjʊləs] *adj*. 细致的，谨慎小心的

【记】 scrupul(e)(顾虑) + ous(形容词词尾)→有顾虑的→谨慎小心的

【例】 You must take the most *scrupulous* care to keep the wound free from the dirt. 你必须非常小心地护理，以免伤口沾上污物。

【同】 careful, conscientious

【反】 unscrupulous

scrutiny [ˈskruːtɪnɪ] *n*. 详细审查，细阅

【记】 scrut(破烂) + in + y(名词词尾)→原义是指拾荒者在破烂里面仔细寻找→详细审查

【例】 His work looks all right, but it will not bear *scrutiny*. 他的工作似乎很好，但是经不起仔细检查。

【同】 examination, inspection

【反】 neglect

【派】 scrutinize *v*. 细察

scrutinous *adj*. 仔细查看的，好刨根问底的

sculpture [ˈskʌlptʃə] *n*./*v*. 雕刻，雕塑(品)

【记】 sculpt(= carve, 雕刻) + ure(名词词尾)→雕刻出来的东西→雕塑

【例】 1. The water had *sculptured* the rocks into strange shapes. 水把岩石侵袭得奇形怪状。

2. He now has a new commission—a glass *sculpture* for the headquarters building of a pizza company. 他现在有了一项新任务——为一家皮萨公司的总部大楼做一个玻璃雕塑。

【同】 carve; statue

【派】 sculptor *n*. 雕刻家

sculptural *adj*. 雕刻的，雕刻般的

seal [siːl] *n*. 1. 图章，密封；*v*. 封，密封

【例】 1. This document carries the royal *seal*. 这份文件上盖有王室印章。

2. The envelope was firmly *sealed*. 这个信封封得很严实。

【同】 stamp; fasten

【反】 unseal

【派】 sealant *n*. 密封胶，密封剂

sealed *adj*. 未知的，密封的

seclude [sɪˈkluːd] *v*. 使隔离，使孤立

【记】 se(分开)+clude(关闭)→分开关闭→使隔离

【例】 You can't *seclude* yourself from the world. 人不能与世隔绝。

【同】 withdraw, isolate

【派】 seclusion *n*. 独处，隐居

secluded *adj*. 隐退的，隐蔽的

secondary [ˈsekəndərɪ] *adj*. 次要的，中级的

【记】 second(第二)+ary(形容词词尾)→第二位的→次要的

【例】 All other considerations are *secondary* to his safety. 现在首先要考虑的是他的安全，其他事都是次要的。

【同】 subordinate

【反】 primary

secretary [ˈsekrətrɪ] *n*. 秘书，部长

【记】 secret(秘密)+ary(名词词尾)→和秘密相关的人→秘书

【例】 Did you know that Stone ended up marrying his *secretary*? 你知道吗，斯通最终和他的秘书结婚了。

【派】 secretariat *n*. 秘书处，书记处

secretarial *adj*. 秘书的，秘书工作的

S

secrete [sɪˈkriːt] *v*. 1. 分泌；2. 隐秘，隐藏

【记】 se(分开的)+cret(分离)+e→个别隔离→隐藏

【例】 1. Tears are *secreted* by an organ under the upper eyelid. 眼泪由上眼睑下面的器官分泌。

2. The thief found the money *secreted* in the drawer. 小偷发现了藏在抽屉里的钱。

【派】 secretion *n*. 分泌，分泌物

section [ˈsekʃən] *n*. 部分，部门

【记】 sect(切割)+ion(名词词尾)→切割成几个部分→部分

【例】 Signals control each *section* of the railway track. 各种信号控制着铁路轨道的每个部分。

【同】 department, sector

【派】 sectional *adj*. 可组合的

sector ['sektə] *n*. 部分，部门

【记】 sect(切割) + or(名词词尾)→切割成几个部分→部门

【例】 The government made an investigation of the employment in the public and private *sectors*. 政府对国营和私营部门的就业情况作了一次调查。

【同】 section

secure [sɪ'kjʊə] *adj*. 安全的，可靠的；*v*. 1. 保护；2. 获得

【记】 se(远离…的) + cure(注意)→远离忧虑的→安全的

【例】 1. The little boy felt *secure* near his parents. 那小男孩在父母身边感到安心。
2. Can the town be *secured* against attack? 能保护这个市镇不受攻击吗？
3. He *secured* the release of the hostages. 他已经设法使人质获释。

【同】 safe, reliable; protect; acquire, obtain

【派】 security *n*. 安全

sedate [sɪ'deɪt] *adj*. 安静的，镇静的，平静的

【记】 sed(坐) + ate(形容词词尾)→坐着的→安静的

【例】 A lot of old people live in this *sedate* seaside town. 许多老人居住在这个安静的海边小镇。

【同】 calm, peaceful, quiet, tranquil

【反】 lively

sediment ['sedɪmənt] *n*. 沉积物，沉淀物

【记】 sedi(坐) + ment(名词词尾)→坐下来的→沉积下来的东西→沉积物

【例】 You should not drink the wine with a gritty *sediment*. 不要喝有砂粒状沉淀物的葡萄酒。

【同】 deposit

【派】 sedimentary *adj*. 沉积的，沉淀性的

seduce [sɪ'djuːs] *v*. 诱使，勾引

【记】 se(分开) + duce(领导)→带往别处→诱使

【例】 High salaries are *seducing* many teachers into industry. 在高薪利诱之下，许多教师改行进入工业界。

【同】 lure, tempt

【派】 seduction *n*. 诱惑
seductive *adj*. 诱人的

segment ['segmənt] *n*. 部分，片断

【记】 seg(切割) + ment(名词词尾)→切成几部分→片断

【例】 The company dominates this *segment* of the market. 这家公司控制了这一部分市场。

【同】 division, section

【派】 segmental *adj*. 部分的
segmentation *n*. 分割

segregate ['segrɪeɪt] *v*. 分开，隔离

S

【记】 se(分开)+gregat(收集)+e→离开集体→隔离

【例】 The two groups of fans must be *segregated* in the stadium. 必须把体育场中这两部分球迷隔开。

【同】 isolate, disconnect

【反】 mix

【派】 segregated *adj*. 被隔离的，种族隔离的

segregation *n*. 种族隔离

seize [siːz] *v*. 抓住，夺取

【例】 Don't hesitate; *seize* the first opportunity that comes along! 别再犹豫了，一有机会就抓住它!

【同】 grasp, snatch

【反】 release, loose

【派】 seizure *n*. 抓，夺取

select [sɪˈlekt] *v*. 选择，挑选

【记】 se(分开的)+lect(选择)→挑选出来→选择

【例】 She *selected* a diamond ring from the collection. 她从收藏品中挑选了一枚钻石戒指。

【同】 choose, pick

【派】 selection *n*. 选择，挑选

selective *adj*. 选择的，选择性的

self-evident [ˈselfˈevɪdənt] *adj*. 不言而喻的

【记】 self(自我)+evident(显然的)→自己显示出来的→不言而喻的

【例】 Her sincerity is *self-evident*. 她是真心实意，这是显而易见的。

【同】 obvious

【派】 self-evidence *n*. 显然，不证自明

semantic [sɪˈmæntɪk] *adj*. 语义的

【记】 seman(=sign，符号)+tic(形容词词尾)→与符号有关的→语义的

【例】 And it isn't a mere *semantic* nicety. 它不只是语义上的细微差别。

【派】 semantics *n*. 语义学，符号学

semanticist *n*. 语义学者

semester [sɪˈmestə] *n*. (尤指美国大专院校的)学期

【例】 This last *semester*, if it has done nothing else, has given me confidence in myself. 最后这个学期，即使没有给我其他的任何东西，也给了我自信。

【同】 term

semiconductor [ˈsemɪkənˈdʌktə] *n*. 半导体

【记】 semi(一半)+conductor(导体)→不完全的导体→半导体

【例】 *Semiconductor* is a kind of various solid crystalline substances, such as germanium or silicon. 半导体是一种固态结晶物质，如锗或硅。

【反】 conductor

seminar [ˈsemɪnɑː] *n*. 讨论会，研究会

【记】 semin(种子)+ar(名词词尾)→孕育种子之处→研究会

【例】 The old professor had presided over a *seminar* for theoretical physicists. 老教授主持了一次理论物理学家的研讨会。

【同】 conference，workshop(专题学术讨论会)

senate ['senɪt] *n*. 参议院，上院

【记】 sen(年长的)+ate(名词词尾)→由有权威的人组成的地方→参议院

【例】 The *senate* has voted to support the president's defence plans. 参议院已投票支持总统的防务计划。

【派】 senator *n*. 参议员，评议员

senatorial *adj*. 参议院的，参议员的

senior ['siːnjə] *adj*. 资格较老的，地位较高的；*n*. 更年长的人，四年级生

【记】 sen(年长的)+ior(表示比较级)→更年长的→资格较老的，高年级生

【例】 1. He is *senior* to me，though he is younger. 他地位比我高，虽然他比我年轻。

2. He is my *senior* by two years. 他比我大两岁。

【同】 elder，older

【反】 junior

【派】 seniority *n*. 资历

sensational [sen'seɪʃənəl] *adj*. 令人兴奋的，轰动性的

【记】 sens(感觉)+ation(名词词尾)+al(形容词词尾)→让人有感觉的→令人兴奋的

【例】 The newspapers played up *sensational* social news. 各报大肆渲染耸人听闻的社会新闻。

【同】 exciting，marvelous

【派】 (逆构)sensation *n*. 感觉，感情

sensible ['sensəbl] *adj*. 1.明智的，合理的；2.可感觉到的，明显的

【记】 sens(感觉)+ible(形容词词尾)→能感觉到的→明显的

【例】 1. Saving your presence，I don't think the suggestion is very *sensible*. 请恕我直言，我认为这个建议不太合情理。

2. Are you *sensible* of the dangers of your position? 你觉察出你处境中的危险了吗？

【同】 reasonable，thoughtful，wise

【反】 insensible

【派】 sensibility *n*. 敏感性，感性；识别力

sensitive ['sensɪtɪv] *adj*. 1.敏感的，灵敏的；2.易受伤害的，易怒的

【记】 sens(感觉)+ive(形容词词尾)→感觉到的→敏感的

【例】 1. This is such an *sensitive* issue that perhaps the press should not be told. 这是一个非常敏感的问题，恐怕不应该告诉新闻界。

2. Don't be so *sensitive*—I was not criticizing you. 别那么神经过敏，我不是在批评你。

【同】 responsive，reactive；tender，touchy

【反】 insensitive

【派】 sensitivity *n*. 敏感

sensory ['sensərɪ] *adj*. 感觉的，感官的

【记】 sens(感觉)+ory(形容词词尾)→感觉的

【例】 His *sensory* organs can't function well after the accident. 那次事故后，他的感觉器官出了问题。

【同】 sensorial

【反】 extrasensory

sentiment ['sentɪmənt] *n*. 情感，多愁善感

【记】 sent(i)(感觉)+ment(名词词尾)→感觉丰富→情感

【例】 There is no room for *sentiment* in business. 做生意不能婆婆妈妈的感情用事。

【同】 affection, emotion

【派】 sentimental *adj*. 感伤性的，感情脆弱的

sentimentalism *n*. 感情主义，感情用事

separate ['sepəreɪt] *adj*. 分开的，个别的；*v*. 分开，隔离

【记】 se(分开的)+par(a)(准备)+te(动词词尾)→准备分开的→分开

【例】 1. This word has three *separate* meanings. 这个词有三个不同的意思。

2. The war *separated* many families. 战争使许多家庭妻离子散。

【同】 individual; divide, part

【反】 joint, unite

【派】 separation *n*. 分离，分开

sequence ['siːkwəns] *n*. 次序，顺序

【记】 sequ(跟随)+ence(名词词尾)→一个跟随一个的→次序

【例】 We will deal with events in historical *sequence*. 我们将按照历史上的先后顺序研究这些事件。

【同】 series, succession

【派】 sequent *adj*. 接续而来的

sequential *adj*. 连续的，相续的

serene [sɪ'riːn] *adj*. 宁静的，平静的

【例】 His *serene* smile calmed all of us down. 他脸上安详的微笑使我们都冷静下来。

【同】 calm, pacific, peaceful, tranquil

【反】 furious

【派】 serenity *n*. 平静，安宁

S

serial ['sɪərɪəl] *adj*. 一系列的，连载的；*n*. 连载小说(图画、广播、电视等)

【记】 seri(结合)+al(形容词词尾)→结合在一起的→一系列的

【例】 1. Currency notes bear *serial* numbers. 钞票上有连续的号码。

2. 'The Archers' is a British radio *serial* that has been heard every day for many years. "阿彻斯"是多年来每天都能听到的英国广播连续剧。

【同】 consecutive, sequential

【派】 (逆构)series *n*. 连续剧，丛书

serious ['sɪərɪəs] *adj*. 1. 严肃的，认真的；2. 严重的，重大的

【例】 1. Playing is a *serious* business. 玩是一件严肃的事情。

2. This company was in *serious* financial difficulties. 这家公司陷入严重的财政困难。

【同】 earnest, solemn; grave, severe
【反】 frivolous
【派】 seriousness *n*. 严肃，认真

sermon [ˈsɜːmən] *n*. 说教，布道
【例】 The priest preached a *sermon* on the need of charity. 牧师在布道会上宣讲慈爱的必要。
【同】 lecture, speech

session [ˈseʃən] *n*. 1. 会议，会期；2.(从事某一活动的)一段时间
【记】 sess(坐)+ion(名词词尾)→坐在位子上→会议
【例】 1. Several bills were enacted at the end of this *session* of Parliament. 这届国会结束时，好几个议案制定成为法律。
2. After several *sessions* at the gym, I feel a lot fitter. 我在健身房锻炼了几次以后，觉得身体好多了。
【同】 conference, meeting

setback [ˈsetbæk] *n*. 挫折，退步
【记】 set(放置)+back(向后的)→放在后面的→退步
【例】 This is a major *setback* to our hopes of reaching an agreement. 这是对我们达成协议的希望的严重挫折。
【同】 frustration, reversal
【反】 advancement, progressing

settle [ˈsetl] *v*. 1. 安家，定居；2. 解决，决定
【记】 set(固定)+tle(动词词尾)→固定在某个位置→安家，决定
【例】 1. After years of travel we decided to *settle* here. 经过数年的旅行之后，我们决定在这里定居。
2. The two companies *settled* out of court. 两家公司在法院外了结了争端。
【同】 inhabit; resolve
【派】 settled *adj*. 固定的，确立的
settlement *n*. 解决；小居民点

severe [sɪˈvɪə] *adj*. 严厉的，剧烈的
【记】 se(分开)+ver(友好的)+e→把友好的分开→严厉的
【例】 She received *severe* head injuries in the accident. 她在事故中头部受了重伤。
【同】 serious, strict
【反】 lenient, mild
【派】 severance *n*. 断绝
severity *n*. 严肃，严重

sewer [ˈsjʊə] *n*. 下水道，阴沟
【例】 The *sewer* in the toilet was blocked. 卫生间的下水道堵住了。
【派】 sewage *n*. (下水道里的)污物
sewerage *n*. 排水设备，污水

shabby [ˈʃæbɪ] *adj*. 破旧的，不光彩的
【记】 shab(b)(=scab, 疤，痂)+y(形容词词尾)→像疤一样的→破烂的

S

【例】 You look rather *shabby* in those clothes. 你穿着那种衣服显得很寒酸。
【同】 worn
【反】 decent
【派】 shabby-genteel *adj*. 穷要面子的

shackle [ˈʃækl] *n*. 手铐，脚镣，桎梏；*v*. 加桎梏，束缚
【例】 1. Nowadays, people have shaken off the *shackles* of some conventions. 今天，人们已经摆脱了一些习俗的束缚。
2. He's too young to *shackle* himself with the responsibilities of a family. 他还太年轻，不能用家庭责任来束缚自己。
【同】 chain, manacle, fetter

shade [ʃeɪd] *n*. 1. 阴暗，荫凉；2. 轻微的区别，不同的程度
【例】 1. There are no trees or bushes to give *shade*. 没有树木或灌木丛可以遮荫。
2. I think it's a *shade* warmer today. 我觉得今天暖和一点儿。
【同】 shadow; subtlety
【反】 sunshine
【派】 shady *adj*. 多荫的，可疑的

shadow [ˈʃædəʊ] *n*. 阴影，隐蔽处；*v*. 遮蔽，使朦胧
【记】 shad(e)(阴凉) + ow(名词词尾)→有阴凉的地方→阴影
【例】 1. He walked along in the *shadows* hoping no one would recognize him. 他走在暗处，希望没有人认出他来。
2. He felt he was being *shadowed*, but he couldn't see anyone behind him. 他感觉到有人在跟踪他，但他看不见身后的人。
【同】 shade
【反】 sunshine
【派】 shadowy *adj*. 有阴影的，阴凉的

shallow [ˈʃæləʊ] *adj*. 浅的，浅薄的
【例】 She has a rather *shallow* personality. 她的个性相当浅薄。
【同】 superficial
【反】 deep
【派】 shallow-brained *adj*. 头脑简单的

S

shame [ʃeɪm] *n*. 羞愧，羞耻
【例】 To my *shame* I never thanked him for his kindness. 我感到羞愧的是，对他的好意我从未表示过感谢。
【同】 disgrace, dishonour
【反】 esteem, honour
【派】 shameful *adj*. 不体面的，丢脸的
shameless *adj*. 不知羞耻的

sharp [ʃɑːp] *adj*. 尖锐的，锋利的
【例】 I cut my finger on a *sharp* stone. 我的手指被一块锋利的石头划破了。
【同】 keen, severe
【反】 dull, flat

【派】 sharpen *v*. 削尖，磨尖
sharp-eyed *adj*. 目光敏锐的

shatter [ˈʃætə] *v*. 1.粉碎，破坏；2.使心烦意乱，使震惊

【例】 1. My dreams have been *shattered*. 我的梦想已经破灭了。
2. We were *shattered* by the news. 这一消息震动了我们。

【同】 destroy，smash

【派】 shattery *adj*. 易粉碎的
shattering *adj*. 令人极度不安的，令人震惊的

shave [ʃeɪv] *v*. (shave，shaved 或 shaven)剃，刮；*n*. 刮胡须，修面

【例】 1. The lorry *shaved* the barrier，scraping its side. 那辆卡车掠过路障，刮坏了车身。
2. He had a *shave* and a bath. 他刮了脸，又洗了澡。

【同】 razor

【派】 shaver *n*. 剃须刀

shear [ʃɪə] *n*. (一般用复数 shears)(剪羊毛、修树篱等用的)大剪刀；*v*. (sheared，sheared 或 shorn)修剪，剪切

【例】 1. With a few quick snips of the *shears* he pruned the bush. 他用大剪刀几下子就把灌木给修剪好了。
2. *Shorn* of all the real power by the new laws，the deputy president soon became obsolete. 所有的实权被新的法律剥夺殆尽，副总统的职务很快被架空了。

【同】 clip，fleece

sheer [ʃɪə] *adj*. 全然的，纯粹的

【例】 I met her by *sheer* chance. 我完全出于偶然遇见了她。

【同】 pure

shell [ʃel] *n*. 1.贝壳，壳；2.炮弹

【例】 1. All that remained of the building after the fire was an empty *shell*.
一场大火过后，这座建筑剩下的只是一个空壳。
2. The building was destroyed by an artillery *shell*. 这座建筑物被炮弹炸毁了。

【派】 shelly *adj*. 有壳的，多壳的
shellproof *adj*. 防弹的

shelter [ˈʃeltə] *n*. 庇护，遮蔽物；*v*. 庇护，保护

【记】 shel(l)(外壳)+ter(名词词尾)→有外壳保护的→遮蔽物

【例】 1. They befriended the young girl，providing her with food and *shelter*. 他们热心照顾这个年轻的姑娘，给她吃的，给她住处。
2. These plants must be *sheltered* from direct sunlight. 这种植物必须遮起来，免受阳光直射。

【同】 protect，shield

【派】 sheltery *adj*. 遮蔽的，庇护的

shepherd [ˈʃepəd] *n*. 牧羊人；*v*. 看管，带领

【记】 she(e)p(绵羊)+herd(管理家畜的人)→管理绵羊的人→牧羊人

【例】 The teacher was *shepherding* the group of children into the bus. 老师照管着一群

S

孩子上公共汽车。

shield [ʃiːld] *n*. 盾，防护物；*v*. 保护，遮蔽

【例】 He raised his arm to *shield* himself from the blow. 他举起手臂挡住了向他打来的一拳。

【同】 defend, preserve

shift [ʃɪft] *n*./*v*. 转换，转移

【例】 1. A sudden *shift* in the wind warned of the coming storm. 风向的突然转变预示着暴风雨即将来临。

2. His eyes *shifted* to the telephone. 他的眼光转向了电话机。

【同】 change, alter

【派】 shifter *n*. 开关

shifty *adj*. 变化的，不可靠的

shine [ʃaɪn] *v*. (shone, shone 或 shined)照耀，发光；*n*. 光泽，光亮

【例】 1. The clouds parted and the sun *shone* (out). 云开了，太阳出来了。

2. Would you put a good *shine* on these boots? 你把这些靴子好好擦一下好吗？

【同】 burnish, polish

【派】 shining *adj*. 光亮的，华丽的

shiny *adj*. 有光泽的，晴朗的

shipment [ˈʃɪpmənt] *n*. 装船，出货

【记】 ship(船只) + ment(名词词尾)→放到船上去→装船

【例】 Finally the honey is poured into barrels for *shipment*. 最后蜂蜜被倒在桶里，准备装船。

【同】 freight, load

shiver [ˈʃɪvə] *n*./*v*. 颤抖，发抖

【例】 Having to make a speech always gives me the *shivers*. 让我演讲我就吓得直哆嗦。

【同】 quiver, tremble

【派】 shivering *adj*. 颤抖的

shivery *adj*. 颤抖的，令人悚然的

shortcoming [ˈʃɔːtkʌmɪŋ] *n*. 缺点，短处

【记】 short(缺少的) + coming(来到)→目前所缺少的东西→缺点

【例】 She was quick to list all his *shortcomings*. 她很快把他的缺点全都列举了出来。

【同】 defect, weakness

【反】 merit, virtue

shortsighted [ʃɔːtˈsaɪtɪd, ˈʃɔːtsaɪtɪd] *adj*. 近视的，目光短浅的

【记】 short(短的) + sight(视力) + ed(形容词词尾)→视力短的→目光短浅的

【例】 It is very *shortsighted* not to spend money on repairing your house. 不想花钱修理你的房子，这是没有远见。

【反】 longsighted, foresighted

shoulder [ˈʃəuldə] *n*. 肩膀，肩部；*v*. 肩负，承当

【例】 1. She burrowed her head into my *shoulder*. 她把头紧靠在我的肩膀上。

2. She won't *shoulder* all the blame for the mistake. 她不承担该过失的全部责任。

【同】 bear，undertake

【派】 shouldermark *n*. 肩章

shove [ʃʌv] *v*. 推挤，猛推

【例】 He dragged her out of the door and *shoved* her into the street. 他把她拖到门口，猛地把她推到马路上。

【同】 jostle，push，thrust

shower [ˈʃauə] *n*. 1. 阵雨；2. 淋浴；*v*. 下阵雨，阵雨般地落下

【例】 1. Jack's shoes were caked with mud in a country road after a *shower*. 阵雨过后走在乡村小路上，杰克的鞋子上沾了些泥块。

2. She is taking a *shower*. 她正在洗淋浴。

3. It has started to *shower*，you had better take your umbrella. 天开始下阵雨了你最好带着伞。

【同】 rain

shrewd [ʃruːd] *adj*. 精明的，敏锐的

【记】 shrew(一种像老鼠一样的小动物) + d→像老鼠一样狡猾的→精明的

【例】 His skill in negotiating earned him a reputation as a *shrewd* tactician. 他的谈判技巧使他赢得了精明战略家的名声。

【同】 smart，sharp

【反】 dull

【派】 shrewd-brained *adj*. 头脑精明的

shrewdness *n*. 机灵

shrink [ʃrɪŋk] *v*. (shrank 或 shrunk，shrunk 或 shrunken)变小，收缩

【例】 Will this woolen sweater *shrink* when washed? 这件羊毛衫洗后会缩水吗?

【同】 contract

【反】 expand，stretch

【派】 shrinkable *adj*. 会收缩的

shrinkage *n*. 收缩

shrub [ʃrʌb] *n*. 灌木，灌木丛

【例】 The naughty boy hid the books in the *shrub*. 这个淘气的孩子把书藏在了灌木丛里。

【同】 bush

【派】 shrubbery *n*. 灌木，灌木林

shudder [ˈʃʌdə] *n*./*v*. 颤抖，战栗

【记】 shudd(= shake，颤抖) + er(表示动作的重复)→不停地颤抖→战栗

【例】 She *shuddered* at the sight of the dead body. 她一看到死尸就战栗起来。

【同】 quiver，tremble

shuffle [ˈʃʌfl] *n*./*v*. 1. 洗纸牌，重新组合；2. 拖着脚走

【例】 1. Who is going to *shuffle*? 该谁洗牌了?

2. The old lady *shuffled* across the room. 那位老妇人拖着脚步走过了房间。

shuttle [ˈʃʌtl] *n*. 1. 梭子；2. 往返汽车，航天飞机；*v*. 穿梭，往返

【记】 shutt(= shoot，射) + le(名词词尾)→投射的东西→织布用的梭子→穿梭

【例】 1. There is a *shuttle* service between the town center and the station. 在市中心和火车站之间有短程往返的穿梭运行班车。

2. We *shuttled* the passengers to the city center by helicopter. 我们来来回回地用直升机把旅客运送到市中心。

【派】 shuttlecraft *n*. 航天飞机

shuttlecock *n*. 羽毛球

sickness ['sɪknɪs] *n*. 疾病，呕吐

【记】 sick(生病的)+ness(名词词尾)→疾病

【例】 Some people develop altitude *sickness* when climbing high mountains. 有些人在爬高山时会发生高山反应。

【同】 disease, illness

【反】 health

【派】 (逆构)sick *adj*. 不舒服，有病的

siege [siːdʒ] *n*. 包围，围攻

【例】 The Greeks laid *siege* to Troy. 希腊人开始围攻特洛伊城。

【同】 blockade, encirclement, besieging

sigh [saɪ] *v*./*n*. 叹息，叹气

【例】 1. With a hopeless *sigh*, he turned away. 他发出一声绝望的叹息，转身走开了。

2. She looked out of the window, *sighing* for her lost youth. 她看着窗外，为她失去的青春而惋惜。

sight [saɪt] *n*. 1. 视力，看见；2. 名胜，风景

【例】 1. We laughed at the *sight* of his strange clothes. 一看到他古怪的穿着，我们就笑了。

2. Come and see the *sights* of London. 来看看伦敦的名胜。

【同】 look, vision; spectacle

【派】 sighted *adj*. 看得见的，有视力

sightsee ['saɪtsiː] *v*. (-saw, -seen; -seeing)观光，游览

【记】 sight(风景)+see(看)→看风景→观光

【例】 Some people like to lie on the beach, but I prefer to go *sightseeing*. 有些人喜欢在海滩上躺着，但是我宁愿去游览。

S

【同】 travel

【派】 sightseer *n*. 游览者，观光者

sign [saɪn] *n*. 标记，征兆；*v*. 签名，署名

【例】 1. Dark clouds are a *sign* of rain or snow. 乌云是雨或雪将至的预兆。

2. The documents are ready to be *signed*. 这些文件已准备好，可以签字了。

【同】 mark; endorse

【派】 signal *n*. 信号

signpost ['saɪnpəʊst] *n*./*v*. 路标

【记】 sign(标志)+post(柱子)→标志性的柱子→路标

【例】 1. The *signpost* indicates the right way to go. 路标标示正确的前进路线。

2. These country roads aren't very well *signposted*. 这些乡村公路没有设置明显的

路标。

【同】 guidepost

signature [ˈsɪgnɪtʃə] *n*. 签名，署名

【记】 sign(a)(记号) + ture(名词词尾)→签上属于自己的记号→签名，署名

【例】 Her *signature* is almost illegible. 她的签字很难辨认。

【派】 signatory *n*. 签名人，签字者，签约国

significance [sɪgˈnɪfɪkəns] *n*. 意义，重要性

【记】 sign(记号) + ifi(= ify，做) + cance(名词词尾)→作出明显的标记→重要性

【例】 This new discovery of oil is of great *significance* to this area's economy. 这次新发现的石油对这个地区的经济有着重大的意义。

【同】 importance，consequence

【反】 insignificance

【派】 significant *adj*. 有意义的，重大的，重要的

signify [ˈsɪgnɪfaɪ] *v*. 表示，预示

【记】 sign(记号) + ify(动词词尾，做)→作出记号→表示

【例】 Do dark clouds *signify* rain? 有乌云是否显示要下雨？

【同】 mean，indicate

【派】 signification *n*. 含意，表明

silt [sɪlt] *n*. 淤泥，泥沙；*v*. 淤塞，塞满

【例】 1. The harbor is being up with *silt*. 那海港被淤泥阻塞了。
2. The old harbor *silted* up years ago. 旧港在多年前已积满淤泥。

【派】 siltation *n*. 沉积作用，淤积

similar [ˈsɪmɪlə] *adj*. (to)相似的，类似的

【记】 simil(相似) + ar(形容词词尾)→相似的

【例】 I sympathize with you; I've had a *similar* unhappy experience myself. 我很同情你，我自己也有过类似的不幸遭遇。

【同】 alike，like

【反】 dissimilar

【派】 similarity *n*. 类似，类似之处

simplicity [sɪmˈplɪsɪtɪ] *n*. 简单，朴素

【记】 sim(一个) + pli(倍，重) + city(名词词尾)→只有一层→简单

【例】 The monastic community generally lives a life of *simplicity*. 僧侣界通常过着简朴生活。

【同】 plainness

【反】 complexity

【派】 (逆构)simple *adj*. 简单的，朴素的
simplistic *adj*. 简单化的

simplify [ˈsɪmplɪfaɪ] *v*. 单一化，简单化

【记】 simpl(e)(简单的) + ify(动词词尾)→使变得简单→简单化

【例】 She *simplified* the instructions so that the children could understand them. 她简化了指令以便于儿童理解。

【反】 complicate

【派】 simplification *n*. 简化

simulate [ˈsɪmjʊleɪt] *v*. 模拟，冒充

【记】 simul(类似)+ate(动词词尾)→使类似→仿真

【例】 He shook a sheet of metal to *simulate* the noise of thunder. 他摇动一块金属薄片来模拟雷声。

【同】 imitate, pretend

【派】 simulation *n*. 仿真，假装

simulative *adj*. 模拟的，假装的

simultaneous [ˌsɪməlˈteɪnjəs] *adj*. 同时的，同时发生的

【记】 simul(相似的)+taneous(形容词词尾)→相似的时间→同时的

【例】 The *simultaneous* demonstrations are held in London and New York. 在伦敦和纽约同时举行示威游行。

【同】 coincident

【派】 simultaneity *n*. 同时发生，同时

sin [sɪn] *n*. 罪过，过失

【例】 The Bible says adultery is a *sin*. 圣经上说通奸是罪恶。

【同】 wickedness, evil, crime

【派】 sinful *adj*. 有罪的，罪孽深重的

singe [sɪndʒ] *v*. 微烧，烫焦

【例】 I'm afraid I've *singed* your shirt with the hot iron. 我恐怕是用热熨斗把你的衬衫烫焦了。

【同】 scorch, sear

singular [ˈsɪŋgjʊlə] *n*. 单数；*adj*. 1. 单独的；2. 非凡的

【例】 1. The noun "mouse" is *singular*; it is the *singular* form of "mice". 名词"mouse"是单数，它是"mice"的单数形式。

2. He is a person of *singular* courage and honesty. 他是一个极为勇敢和诚实的人。

【同】 unique

【反】 plural

【派】 singularity *n*. 单一；奇异，非凡

S

sinister [ˈsɪnɪstə] *adj*. 不吉的，不祥的

【记】 sin(i)(罪恶)+(s)ter(形容词词尾)→有罪的→不吉利的

【例】 She had a *sinister* foreboding that the plane would crash. 她有个不祥的预感，飞机要失事。

【同】 evil, ominous

【反】 good, virtuous

sink [sɪŋk] *v*. (sank, sunk)沉浸，使沉没

【例】 My feet *sank* into the mud. 我的双脚陷到泥里去了。

【同】 decline, fall

【反】 float, rise

【派】 sinkable *adj*. 易下沉的

sinkage *n*. 下沉

site [saɪt] *n*. 场所，地点

【例】 Rescue workers rushed to the *site* of the plane crash. 抢救人员冲向飞机坠毁的现场。

【同】 location, position

situate [ˈsɪtjʊeɪt] *v*. 使位于，使处于

【记】 situ(=site, 地点) + ate(动词词尾)→使处于…地点→使位于

【例】 The company wants to *situate* its headquarters in the north. 公司想把总部设在北方。

【同】 locate, place

situation [ˌsɪtjʊˈeɪʃən] *n*. 1. 地点，位置；2. 情况，形势

【记】 situat(e)(使位于) + ion(名词词尾)→使处于…位置或状态→地点，情况

【例】 1. The *situation* of the house gives it magnificent views of in three directions. 房子所处的地点使之三面均可眺望壮丽的风景。

2. He doesn't seem to understand the gravity of the *situation*. 他似乎没有意识到形势的严重性。

【同】 case, condition

skeleton [ˈskelɪtən] *n*. 1. 骨骼，骨架；2. 基干，纲要

【例】 1. A long illness made a *skeleton* out of him. 长期的卧病使他骨瘦如柴。

2. I've written the *skeleton* of my report, but I have to fill in the details. 我已写出报告的梗概，但我必须补充细节。

【同】 bones; sketch, frame

【派】 skeletal *adj*. 骨骼的，骸骨的

skeptical [ˈskeptɪkəl] *adj*. 怀疑论的，怀疑的

【记】 scept(考虑) + ical(形容词词尾)→要考虑的→怀疑的

【例】 The leader had the gift of being able to infuse enthusiasm into the most *skeptical* member of the group. 那位领导人很有天赋，能使团体中最持怀疑态度的人都充满热情。

【同】 disbelieving, doubting

【派】 skeptic *n*. 怀疑论者

skepticism *n*. 怀疑论，怀疑主义

sketch [sketʃ] *n*. 1. 草图，概略；2. 短剧，独幕剧

【例】 1. On the back of the book, there is a brief biographical *sketch* of the author. 书后有作者生平的简介。

2. In his most recent satirical *sketch* Heywood sent up fashionable young women who worked for charitable causes. 海伍德在最近的一篇讽刺小品里讽刺了那些为慈善事业工作的时髦女郎。

【同】 outline

【派】 sketchy *adj*. 粗略的

skillful [ˈskɪlfʊl] *adj*. 熟练的，显示技术的

【记】 skill(技巧) + ful(形容词词尾)→有技巧的→熟练的

S

【例】 He is a *skillful* football player. 他足球踢得很好。

【同】 apt, proficient

【反】 unskillful

【派】 (逆构)skill *n*. 技能,熟练

skilled *adj*. 熟练的

skim [skɪm] *v*. (-mmed; -mming)撇去,(从表面)轻轻掠过

【例】 My approach is to *skim* the book first to see what's important and what isn't. 我的方法是首先浏览一下这本书,确定什么是重要的,什么是不重要的。

【同】 brush, scan

skip [skɪp] *v*. (-pped; -pping)1.跳;2.逃过,遗漏

【例】 1. The little girl *skipped* along at her mother's side. 这小女孩在她妈妈身边蹦蹦跳跳地往前走。

2. She *skipped* the boring bits of text and just looked at the pictures. 她把课文中沉闷的地方略过,只看图画。

【同】 jump, leap; omit, pass over

skyrocket [skaɪˈrɒkɪt,ˈskaɪrɒkɪt] *v*. 猛涨,突增

【记】 sky(天空)+rocket(火箭)→像火箭升空一样→猛涨

【例】 House prices are *skyrocketing*. 房价飞涨。

【同】 rocket, soar

skyscraper [ˈskaɪskreɪpər] *n*. 摩天大厦

【记】 sky(天空)+scrap(e)(刮,擦)+er(名词词尾)→擦到天空的东西→摩天大厦

【例】 As construction techniques improved, the *skyscraper* became a reality. 随着建筑技术的进步,摩天大楼成为现实。

【同】 building

【派】 skyscraping *adj*. 极高的,高耸的

slack [slæk] *n*. 松弛,静止; *adj*. 松弛的,疏忽的

【例】 1. The tractor took up the *slack* and pulled the trailer out of the mud. 拖拉机拉紧拖缆,把拖车从泥中拉了出来。

2. Winter is the *slack* season at most hotels. 冬天是大多数旅馆的淡季。

【同】 loose

【反】 tight

【派】 slacken *v*. 松弛,减弱

slander [ˈslɑːndə] *n*./*v*. 诽谤,说…的坏话

【记】 sland(绊倒)+er(名词词尾)→使绊倒→使出丑→诽谤

【例】 Her company is suing her for *slander* because of her remarks about their safety record. 由于她发表了关于公司安全记录的言论,该公司正以诽谤罪起诉她。

【同】 aspersion, defamation

【反】 eulogize

slang [slæŋ] *n*. 俚语,行话

【例】 Don't use *slangs* in your essays. 不要在论文中使用俚语。

【同】 jargon

slant [slɑːnt] *n*. 斜面，倾向；*v*. 使倾斜，歪向

【例】 1. Has your roof a sharp *slant*? 你的屋顶是否有一个陡峭的斜面？

2. Most handwriting *slants* to the right. 大多数手写体都向右斜。

【同】 slope，tilt

slap [slæp] *n*./*v*. (-pped；-pping)掌击，拍击

【例】 1. He gave her a *slap* on the cheek and she began to cry. 他打了她一耳光，她就哭起来了。

2. The doctor *slapped* the hysterical child to make him calmer. 医生拍了拍那个歇斯底里发作的孩子，使他安静下来。

【同】 hit，smack

slash [slæʃ] *n*./*v*. 1. 猛砍，鞭打；2. 大量削减

【例】 1. He is *slashing* wildly at his opponent with a sword. 他正用剑疯狂地朝对手乱砍。

2. The new president *slashed* the defence budget by almost 30%. 新总统大幅度削减了约 30%的国防预算。

【同】 cut

【派】 slashing *adj*. 尖锐的，苛刻的

slaughter [ˈslɔːtə] *n*./*v*. 屠宰，残杀

【例】 Thousands of people are needlessly *slaughtered* each year in road accidents. 每年有成千上万的人在交通事故中枉死。

【同】 kill

【派】 slaughterhouse *n*. 屠宰场

slaughterous *adj*. 好杀戮的

slay [sleɪ] *v*. (slew，slain)杀，杀死，杀害

【例】 The slaves *slew* their masters with swords. 奴隶们用刀杀死了主人。

【同】 kill，murder

【派】 slayer *n*. 杀人者，凶手

sledge [sledʒ] *n*. 雪橇

【例】 Supplies were brought to us on large *sledges* from a ship fifteen kilometres away at the ice edge. 供给品在一艘位于冰的边缘、大约 15 千米处的船上，用大雪橇运送给我们。

【同】 sled，sleigh

slender [ˈslendə] *adj*. 苗条的，微弱的

【例】 The spider hung suspended on its *slender* thread. 蜘蛛悬吊在它的细长的丝上。

【同】 slim，thin

【反】 stout

slice [slaɪs] *n*. 薄片，片段

【例】 1. Give me a *slice* of bread please. 请给我一片面包。

2. I'm only putting money into this scheme if I get a *slice* of the action. 我若能分一杯羹，才出钱参与这一计划。

【同】 piece

slide [slaɪd] *v*. (slid, slid)滑动，滑行 *n*. 1.滑，滑动；2.幻灯片

【例】 1. The book *slid* off my knee. 书从我膝上滑落。

2. The children were taking turns on the *slides* in the playground. 孩子们在操场上轮流滑滑梯。

3. They showed us some color *slides* of their holiday. 他们为我们放映了他们度假时拍的一些彩色幻灯片。

【同】 glide

slight [slaɪt] *adj*. 轻微的，纤弱的

【例】 1. I haven't the *slightest* idea what you are talking about. 我一点也不明白你在说些什么。

2. Her *slight* frame was shaken by bouts of coughing. 她纤弱的身躯因阵阵咳嗽而发颤。

【同】 slender，delicate

【派】 slightly *adv*. 轻微地，有一点

slip [slɪp] *n*. 1.滑倒，事故；2.纸片；*v*. (-pped; -pping)滑动，滑倒，

【例】 1. Write your name and address on this pink *slip*. 在这张粉红色纸条上写下你的姓名和地址。

2. It was icy, and people were *slipping* and sliding all along the street. 路上结着冰，街上的行人纷纷滑倒在地。

【同】 slide

【派】 slipper *n*. 拖鞋

slippery *adj*. 滑的，光滑的

slogan [ˈsləugən] *n*. 标语，口号

【记】 slo(军队) + gan(喊叫)→原义为(苏格兰高地和爱尔兰氏族)战斗的呐喊→口号

【例】 I wish the exclamation mark had not been painted out, it would have made the *slogan* more forceful. 我想那个惊叹号要是没有被涂掉就好了，它会使标语更加有力。

【同】 catchword，motto

slope [sləup] *n*. 斜坡，倾斜

【例】 His cottage is on the gentle *slope* of the hill. 他的小屋在山的缓坡上。

【同】 incline，tilt

【派】 slopy *adj*. 倾斜的

sluggish [ˈslʌgɪʃ] *adj*. 行动迟缓的，缓慢的

【记】 slug(g)(偷懒) + ish(形容词词尾)→偷懒的→行动迟缓的

【例】 These tablets make me feel rather *sluggish*. 我吃了这些药片感到困倦无力。

【同】 dull，slow

【反】 fast，quick

slumber [ˈslʌmbə] *n*./*v*. 睡眠，微睡

【例】 1. He awoke from his *slumber*. 他睡醒了。

2. The volcano had *slumbered* for years. 这火山已经很多年不活动了。

【同】 doze，drowse

【反】 wake
【派】 slumberous *adj*. 昏昏欲睡的，催眠的

slump [slʌmp] *v*. 猛然落下，跌落
【例】 What caused share values to *slump*? 股价暴跌是什么原因？
【同】 drop，sink，plunge

smart [smaːt] *adj*. 1.帅气的，衣着讲究的；2.灵巧的，聪明的
【例】 1. Make yourself *smart* before my parents arrive. 趁我的父母还没到，你快去打扮一下。
2. It was *smart* of you to bring a map. 你很聪明，能想到带张地图。
【同】 stylish；clever，intelligent
【反】 silly，stupid
【派】 smartness *n*. 机灵，敏捷
smarty *n*. 自作聪明的人

smash [smæʃ] *n*./*v*. 打碎，撞击
【例】 The lock was rusty，so we had to *smash* the door open. 锁锈住了，我们得把门砸开。
【同】 shatter，crash
【派】 smashing *adj*. 粉碎性的，猛烈的

smelt [smelt] *v*. 熔炼(矿石、金属)
【例】 The ore is *smelted* in this large factory. 这个大型工厂里熔炼矿石。
【同】 fuse，melt
【派】 smeltery *n*. 冶炼厂

smooth [smuːð] *adj*. 光滑的，平稳的
【例】 Her skin is as *smooth* as silk. 她的皮肤像丝绸一样光滑。
【同】 glossy，polished
【反】 rough，uneven
【派】 smoothen *v*. 使平滑，使平和
smooth-tongued *adj*. 油嘴滑舌的，花言巧语的

smother [ˈsmʌðə] *v*. 厚厚地覆盖，使窒息
【例】 He *smothered* the baby with a pillow. 他用枕头把婴儿闷死了。
【同】 choke，stifle
【派】 smothery *adj*. 令人透不过气的

smuggle [ˈsmʌgl] *v*. 走私
【记】 smug(蹑手蹑脚)+g+le(动词词尾)→蹑手蹑脚地走→偷偷地→走私
【例】 He was caught *smuggling* cameras into the country. 他向这个国家走私照像机被抓住。
【派】 smuggler *n*. 走私者，走私犯

snack [snæk] *n*. 快餐，点心
【例】 We were in a hurry so we had to make do with a quick *snack*. 我们时间很紧，只好胡乱吃了顿小吃。
【同】 nosh，refection

【派】 snackery *n*.（和 snackerie 通用）快餐部，快餐厅

snap [snæp] *v*.（-pped；-pping）突然折断，突然断裂

【例】 The violin string *snapped* because it was fastened too tight. 小提琴的弦上得太紧，突然断了。

【同】 burst，crack

【派】 snapshot *n*. 快照，简单的印象

sneak [sniːk] *v*. 鬼鬼祟祟而行，潜行

【例】 The cat ate the food and *sneaked* off. 猫吃完食物就偷偷跑了。

【同】 creep，slink

【派】 sneaker *n*. 鬼鬼祟祟的人；运动鞋

sneer [snɪə] *v*. 讥笑，嘲笑

【例】 He's always *sneering* at my suggestions. 他总是对我提出的建议嗤之以鼻。

【同】 jeer，mock，scoff

snobbish [ˈsnɒbɪʃ] *adj*. 势利眼的，谄上傲下的

【记】 snob(势利的人) + b + ish(形容词词尾)→势利眼的

【例】 Jane feels she can never compete with these *snobbish* people. 简·爱感到她永远无法同这些势利的人们竞争。

【同】 disdainful，haughty

【派】 snob *n*. 势利的人；假内行

soak [səʊk] *n*./*v*. 浸泡，浸透

【例】 Don't stand out there：you'll get *soaked* through. 你别站在外边，要不全身都要湿透了。

【同】 drench，pluck

【反】 dry

【派】 soakage *n*. 浸润，浸透

sober [ˈsəʊbə] *adj*. 1.清醒的，未喝醉的；2.审慎的，严肃的

【例】 1. He is perfectly *sober*. 他根本没喝醉。

2. Make a *sober* estimate of what is possible. 审慎地估计可能发生的情况。

【同】 calm，clear-headed；serious，sensible

【反】 drunken，intoxicated；irrational

S

social [ˈsəʊʃəl] *adj*. 1.社会的；2.社交的，交际的

【记】 soci(结交) + al(形容词词尾)→与人结交的→交际的

【例】 1. Her research is centred on the *social* effects of unemployment. 她的研究课题是失业对社会的影响。

2. A little *social* drinking does no harm，but be aware of drinking alone. 为应酬喝少量的酒并没有什么害处，但切忌一个人喝闷酒。

【同】 sociable

【反】 unsocial

【派】 socialize *v*. 使社会化，使社会主义化

solar [ˈsəʊlə] *adj*. 太阳的，日光的

【记】 sol(太阳) + ar(形容词词尾)→与太阳有关的→太阳的

【例】 The *solar* cell can convert the energy of sunlight into electric energy. 太阳能电池能把阳光的能量转化为电能。

【反】 lunar

solely ['səʊllɪ] *adv*. 仅仅，只单独地

【记】 sol(e)(唯一的)+ly(副词词尾)→唯一地→仅仅

【例】 Our quality is based *solely* on our sales samples. 我们的质量完全以货样为准。

【同】 only, entirely

【派】 (逆构)sole *adj*. 单独的，唯一的

solemn ['sɒləm] *adj*. 庄严的，隆重的

【记】 sol(e)(唯一的)+emn(一年)→一年一度的(宗教仪式)→庄严的

【例】 Do you give me your *solemn* pledge that you won't go there? 你能向我严肃的保证你不会去那里吗?

【同】 serious

【反】 frivolous

【派】 solemnity *n*. 严肃，一本正经

solicit [sə'lɪsɪt] *v*. 恳求，乞求

【记】 soli(完全)+cit(召唤)→完全召唤人心→恳求

【例】 May I *solicit* your advice on a matter of some importance? 我有一件要事可以请教你吗?

【同】 appeal, ask, beg

【派】 solicitous *adj*. 热切期望的；关心的

solicitant *adj*. 请求的，乞求的

solicitor [sə'lɪsɪtə] *n*. 律师，法律顾问

【记】 soli(整个的)+cit(e)(呼叫)+or(名词词尾)→完全唤起人心的人→律师

【例】 The *solicitor* is preparing a case in the court tomorrow. 这位律师正在为明天法庭审理的案件做准备。

【同】 attorney, lawyer

solid ['sɒlɪd] *n*. 固体，立体；*adj*. 1. 固体的，坚固的；2. 可靠的，一致的

【记】 sol(e)(唯一的)+id(名词词尾)→完全成为一个整体的→固体

【例】 1. Cheese is a *solid*; milk is a liquid. 奶酪是固体，奶是液体。

2. Water becomes *solid* when it freezes. 水结冰时便变成固体。

3. The miners were *solid* on this issue. 矿工们在这件事上是一条心的。

【同】 firm, rigid

【反】 fluid

【派】 solidify *v*. (使)凝固，巩固

solidarity *n*. 团结，一致

solitary ['sɒlɪtərɪ] *adj*. 孤独的，独居的

【记】 sol(唯一，单独)+it+ary(形容词词尾)→唯一的，单独的→孤独的

【例】 His childhood was repressed and *solitary*. 他的童年是压抑而孤独的。

【同】 alone, lonely

【派】 solitude *n*. 孤独，独处，与世隔绝

soluble ['sɒljʊbl] *adj*. 可溶的，可溶解的

【记】solu(松开) + (a)ble(形容词词尾)→可以在水中松开的→可溶解的

【例】This substance is *soluble* in alcohol. 这种物质能够溶解在酒精中。

【同】dissolvable

【反】insoluble

【派】solubilize *v*. 使溶解

solution [sə'lju:ʃən] *n*. 解答，解决办法

【记】solu(松开) + tion(名词词尾)→(使问题)松开→解答

【例】We haven't found the *solution* yet, but I'm sure we're on the right track. 我们还没有找到解决办法，但我肯定我们的思路是对的。

【同】resolution

solve [sɒlv] *v*. 解决，解答

【记】solv(松开) + e→松开→解答

【例】The greatest scholar cannot *solve* this difficult problem. 再伟大的学者也没有办法解答这个难题吧。

【同】answer, resolve

【派】solvable *adj*. 可以解的，可以解决的

somewhat ['sʌmhwɒt] *adv*. 多少有点，稍微

【记】some(一些) + what(什么)→在某种程度上有一些→稍微

【例】The price was *somewhat* higher than I'd expected. 这价格比我预料的稍高一些。

【同】slightly

soothe [su:ð] *vt*. 1. 使(某人)平静，安慰；2. 使(痛苦，疼痛)缓和或减轻

【例】1. A nice cup of tea will *soothe* your nerves. 一杯好茶可以使你的心绪平静下来。

2. A bit of embrocation will *soothe* your bruised knee. 用一点搽剂可使你那青肿的膝部消肿。

【同】comfort, console, solace

【反】irritate

sophisticated [sə'fɪstɪkeɪtɪd] *adj*. 1. 久经世故的，高雅时髦的；2. 高度发展的，精密复杂的

【记】soph(聪明的) + ist(名词词尾，…的人) + i)at(e)(动词词尾) + ed(形容词词尾)→聪明的人所拥有的→久经世故的

【例】1. She always wears *sophisticated* clothes. 她经常穿着考究的衣服。

2. As far as defense is concerned, we need to buy more *sophisticated* weapons. 就防御的观点来说，我们需要购买更多精密的武器。

【同】worldly; advanced

【反】naive

【派】(逆构)sophisticate *n*. 久经世故的人；*v*. 篡改，使变得世故

sophistication *n*. 强词夺理，诡辩

soporific [ˌsəʊpə'rɪfɪk] *adj*. 催眠的，想睡的

【记】sopor(深睡) + if(= ify，做，使) + ic(形容词词尾)→使深睡的→催眠的

【例】I dozed off during the *soporific* speech. 我听着那催人入睡的讲话，不知不觉打起盹来了。

S

【同】 somnific, sleep-inducing
【反】 lively, stimulating

sour [ˈsauə] *adj*. 酸的
【例】 Most green fruits are *sour*. 大多数未熟的水果都是酸的。
【同】 acid, vinegary
【反】 sweet

source [sɔːs] *n*. 来源，消息来源，
【记】 sour(站起来) + ce(名词词尾)→涌上来的地方→来源
【例】 For several years now, tourism has been the prime *source* of foreign exchange in Nepal and Bhutan. 多年以来，旅游业一直是尼泊尔和不丹最重要的外汇来源。
【同】 derivation, origin

sovereign [ˈsɒvrɪn] *n*. 君主，统治 *adj*. 至高无上的，君主的
【记】 sover(= super, 在…之上的) + eign(王朝)→至高无上的王权→君主
【例】 1. No earthly *sovereign* can do what he pleases. 没有一个世间君王可以为所欲为。
2. *Sovereign* power must lie with the people. 最高权力必须属于人民。
【派】 sovereignty *n*. 君主，主权

span [spæn] *n*. 跨度，一段时间
【例】 Modern medicine has increased man's life *span*. 现代医学延长了人的寿命。
【同】 interval
【派】 spanless *adj*. 不可测量的

spare [speə] *adj*. 多余的，剩下的；*v*. 节约，节省
【例】 1. What do you like doing in your *spare* time? 你在闲暇时喜欢做什么？
2. No trouble was *spared* to ensure our comfort. 为了确保我们的舒适，已经竭尽全力。
【同】 excessive, extra; save
【反】 waste
【派】 sparetime *adj*. 业余的，闲暇的

spark [spɑːk] *n*. 火花，火星；*v*. 闪烁，鼓舞
【例】 1. There was a wild *spark* in his eyes. 他的两眼炯炯发光。
2. His comment *sparked* off a quarrel between them. 他提的意见引起了他们之间的争吵。
【同】 flash, glimmer
【派】 sparkly *adj*. 闪耀的

sparse [spɑːs] *adj*. 稀少的，稀疏的
【例】 The television coverage of the event was rather *sparse*. 电视上对这件事报道很少。
【同】 scanty, scarce
【反】 dense
【派】 sparsity *n*. 稀少

spawn [spɔːn] *v*. 1. 产卵，大量生育；2. 使大量出现
【例】 1. Salmon swim upriver to their birthplaces in order to *spawn*. 大马哈鱼游至河流

S

上游的出生地去产卵。

2. The computer industry has *spawned* a lot of new companies. 由于电脑工业的发展，许多新公司纷纷成立。

【同】 breed, reproduce

specialize ['speʃəˌlaɪz] *v*. 专门从事，专攻

【记】 special(专门的) + ize(动词词尾)→使…专门化→专门从事

【例】 He *specializes* in oriental history. 他专门研究东方史。

【反】 diversify, generalize

【派】 specialization *n*. 特殊化，专门化

species ['spiːʃɪz] *n*. (复数同)种，种类

【记】 spec(看见) + ies(名词词尾)→外观相同的事物→种类

【例】 This rare bird has become an endangered *species*. 这种珍禽已成为濒临灭绝的物种。

【同】 kind, sort

【派】 specimen *n*. 范例，标本

specify ['spesɪfaɪ] *v*. 明确说明，详细指明

【记】 spec(看见) + ify(动词词尾)→使…看起来(不同)→明确说明

【例】 Please *specify* when you will be at home tomorrow. 请确切说明你明天何时会在家。

【同】 define

【反】 generalise

【派】 specific *adj*. 详细而精确的，明确的

specification *n*. 详述，说明书

specimen ['spesɪmɪn, 'spesɪmən] *n*. 标本，样品

【记】 spec(i)(看) + men(名词词尾)→让人看的东西→样品

【例】 The museum displays the *specimen* of ancient Chinese porcelain. 这个博物馆展出中国古瓷器标本。

【同】 example, sample

spectacular [spek'tækjʊlə] *adj*. 引人入胜的，壮观的

【记】 spec(t)(看见) + acular(形容词词尾，…的)→让人一直看着的→引人入胜的

【例】 The goalkeeper made a *spectacular* dive to save the goal. 守门员做了一个精彩的鱼跃动作救回一球。

【同】 dramatic, prominent

【派】 spectacle *n*. 观览物，奇观

spectacularity *n*. 壮观，引人注目

spectator [spek'teɪtə] *n*. 参观者，观众

【记】 spect(看) + at(e)(动词词尾) + or(名词词尾)→观看的人→观众

【例】 The big match attracted 25, 000 *spectators*. 这场大赛吸引了25000名观众。

【同】 observer, watcher, onlooker

spectrum ['spektrəm] *n*. (复数-tra)1.光谱，频谱；2.系列，范围

【记】 spect(看见) + rum(名词词尾)→看得见的范围→光谱

【例】 1. *Spectrum* refers to the distribution of a characteristic of a physical system or phenomenon. 频谱指的是物理体系或现象特征的分布。
2. There's a wide *spectrum* of opinions on this problem. 对这个问题的说法众说纷纭，莫衷一是。
【派】 spectrometer *n*. 光谱仪，谱仪

speculate [ˈspekjʊˌleɪt] *v*. 1. 推测，猜测；2. 做投机买卖
【记】 spec(u)(看见) + late(动词词尾)→(用心)来看→推测
【例】 1. I wouldn't like to *speculate* on the reasons for her resignation. 我不愿意猜测她辞职的原因。
2. She *speculates* in oil shares. 她做石油股票的投机买卖。
【同】 suppose, guess; venture
【派】 speculation *n*. 思考，推测；投机买卖
speculator *n*. 投机者，投机商

sphere [sfɪə] *n*. 1. 球，球体；2. 范围，领域
【例】 1. The earth is not a perfect *sphere*. 地球并不是一个完全的球体。
2. Government is expanding its *sphere* of influence to cover all parts of our lives. 政府正在扩大它的影响范围，以把我们的生活的各个方面都管起来。
【同】 ball, globe; field
【派】 spherical *adj*. 球的，球形的
hemisphere *n*. 半球

spicy [ˈspaɪsɪ] *adj*. 加香料的，辛辣的
【记】 spic(e)(香料) + y(形容词词尾)→加香料的
【例】 Generally speaking, I don't like *spicy* food. 我一般不爱吃辛辣的食物。
【同】 hot
【派】 (逆构)spice *n*. 香料，调味品

spill [spɪl] *n*./*v*. (spilt, spilt; 或-ed, -ed)溢出，散落
【例】 Put the cap back on the bottle, otherwise the juice will *spill*. 把瓶盖儿盖好，要不汁液就洒出来了。
【同】 overflow
【派】 spillage *n*. 溢出，溢出量

spin [spɪn] *n*./*v*. (spun, spun; spinning)旋转
【例】 1. The pitcher gave a *spin* to the ball. 投手使球旋转。
2. The motorcycles were *spinning* along at full speed. 摩托车正全速疾驰。
【同】 turn, rotate

spine [spaɪn] *n*. 脊椎，地面隆起地带
【记】 spin(刺) + e→骨骼→脊椎
【例】 He got an injury to his *spine* when he fell off his horse. 他从马上摔下来，伤了脊梁骨。
【同】 backbone
【派】 spinal *adj*. 脊骨的，脊髓的

spiral [ˈspaɪərəl] *n*. 螺旋；*v*. (-l(l)ed; -l(l)ing)盘旋

S

【记】 spir(a)(线圈)+al(名词词尾)→用线圈做的的东西→螺旋

【例】 1. A snail's shell is *spiral* in form. 蜗牛壳是螺旋形的。

2. The smoke *spiraled* upwards. 那股烟袅袅上升。

【同】 coil, whorl

【派】 spirality *n*. 螺旋形

spiritual ['spɪrɪtjʊəl] *adj*. 精神的,灵魂的

【记】 spir(呼吸)+it(名词词尾)+ual(形容词词尾)→和呼吸有关的→精神的

【例】 I care more about the *spiritual* life than the substantial life. 和物质生活相比,我更注重精神生活。

【同】 immaterial, unworldly

【反】 material, physical

【派】 (逆构)spirit *n*. 精神,灵魂

spiritualism *n*. 唯心论,灵性

spiritualist *n*. 唯心论者,巫师

spirituality *n*. 精神性,灵性

splash [splæʃ] *n*./*v*. 飞溅,溅落

【例】 The children love *splashing* water over each other. 孩子们喜欢互相泼水。

【同】 sprinkle

【派】 splashy *adj*. 易溅的,泼溅的

splendor ['splendə] *n*. 光彩,显赫

【记】 splend(发光)+or(名词词尾)→发出的光→光彩

【例】 The court of King Solomon was noted for its *splendor*. 所罗门国王的宫廷以其华丽著称。

【同】 brilliance, glory

【派】 splendid *adj*. 壮丽的,辉煌的

split [splɪt] *n*./*v*. (split, split; splitting)劈开,分裂

【例】 She was *splitting* logs with an axe. 她正用斧子劈木头。

【同】 crack, divide

【反】 unite

【派】 splitting *adj*. 爆裂似的,极快的

spoil [spɔɪl] *v*. (spoilt, spoilt 或-ed, -ed)1. 破坏,扰乱;2. 宠坏,溺爱

【例】 1. The new road has completely *spoiled* the character of the village. 新建的公路彻底毁掉了那个村庄的特色。

2. That little girl is terribly *spoilt*—her parents give her everything she asks for. 那个小女孩真被惯得不像话——父母对她是有求必应。

【同】 damage, destroy; pamper

sponsor ['spɒnsə] *n*. 赞助人;*v*. 发起,赞助

【记】 spons(约定)+or(名词词尾,…的人)→约定给予保证的人→赞助人,发起人

【例】 I am doing a *sponsored* swim on Saturday. Will you sponsor me? 星期六我要参加慈善游泳,您要出钱赞助吗?

【同】 promoter, supporter

【派】 sponsion *n*. 担保

sponsorial *adj*. 保证人的，主办者的

spontaneous [spɒnˈteɪnjəs-nɪəs] *adj*. 自然发生的，不由自主的

【记】 sponta(拉丁文，自己的意愿)+neous(形容词词尾)→出自自己意愿的→不由自主的

【例】 Her successful jump brought a *spontaneous* cheer from the crowd. 她成功地跳过横杆后，观众即时爆发出一阵欢呼声。

【同】 natural, impulsive

【反】 induced

【派】 spontaneity *n*. 自然，自发

sporadic [spəˈrædɪk] *adj*. 不定时发生的，零星的

【记】 spor(e)(孢子)+ad+ic(形容词词尾)→像孢子一样四处散布的→零星的

【例】 Despite the *sporadic* disturbances, the dictator was still riding high. 虽不时有骚动事件，该独裁者仍能控制局势。

【同】 scattered, irregular

【反】 continual

spot [spɒt] *n*. 1. 场所，现场；2. 斑点，污点；*v*. 1. 发现，看出；2. 沾污，弄脏

【例】 1. Spain is our favorite holiday *spot*. 西班牙是我们喜欢的度假地点。

2. Which has *spots*? The leopard or the lion? 豹和虎身上哪一个有斑点？

3. They were *spotted* by police as they were entering the bank. 他们走进银行时被警察认出来了。

【同】 location, place; blot

【派】 spotlight *n*. 聚光灯

spotty *adj*. 多斑点的，多污点的，

spouse [spaʊz] *n*. 配偶(指夫或妻)

【例】 Job is available for *spouse* on campus and in the community. 校园里和社区里有配偶可做的工作。

【同】 mate

sprawl [sprɔːl] *v*. 伸开四肢躺坐，不规则的扩展

【例】 He was *sprawling* in the sofa in front of the TV. 他伸开手脚坐在电视机前的沙发上。

【同】 expand, stretch

spray [spreɪ] *n*./*v*. 喷射，喷溅

【例】 1. We parked the car by the sea and it got covered with *spray*. 我们把汽车停在海边，结果车上全是水沫。

2. The gangsters sprayed the car with machinegun bullets. 匪徒们用机枪狂扫汽车。

【同】 splash, sprinkle

【派】 sprayer *n*. 喷雾，喷雾器

sprint [sprɪnt] *n*./*v*. 短跑，全速冲刺

【例】 He *sprinted* past the other runners just before reaching the tape. 他在到达终点之

S

前全速冲刺，超越了其他赛跑者。

【同】 dash

【派】 sprinter *n*. 短跑选手，短跑运动员

sprout [spraʊt] *v*. 长出，萌芽

【例】 Leaves began to *sprout* from the trees. 树上开始长叶子了。

【同】 bud, grow, shoot up

spur [spɜː] *n*. 踢马刺，刺激；*v*. (-rred; -rring)鞭策，刺激

【例】 1. She went to London on the *spur* of the moment. 她一时兴起就到伦敦去了。
2. What *spurred* her to do that? 是什么促使她那么干的?

【同】 prod, prick

spurt [spɜːt] *v*. 喷出，涌出

【例】 Blood *spurted* out from the wound. 血从伤口涌出。

【同】 flow, gush, squirt

squabble [ˈskwɒbl] *v*. /*n*. 口角，争论

【例】 I hate to *squabble* with my wife about money. 我厌恶为钱的事与太太争吵。

【同】 dispute, quarrel

square [skweə] *adj*. 四方形的，方的，平方的；*n*. 正方形，广场

【例】 1. The road turned *square* to the left. 这条路成直角向左转去。
2. The little girl drew a *square* on the paper. 小女孩在纸上画了一个正方形。

【反】 round

squash [skwɒʃ] *n*. 1. 挤压，压扁；2. 壁球

【记】 s(ex, 出去) + quash(打碎)→把…打碎→挤压

【例】 1. Five people in this car is a bit of *squash*, but we will manage. 五个人坐在这辆小汽车里是有点挤，但是我们可以应付过去。
2. Do you play *squash*? 你会打壁球吗?

【同】 crush, mash

【派】 squashy *adj*. 易压碎的，熟透的

squeeze [skwiːz] *n*./*v*. 挤压，压榨

【记】 s(ex, 出去) + queeze(= quease, 压)→压出去→挤压

【例】 The children *squeezed* together to make room for me to sit down. 孩子们挤在一起，以便腾出空来让我坐下。

【同】 crush, press

stability [stəˈbɪlɪtɪ] *n*. 稳定性，稳定度

【记】 sta(站立) + bil + ity(名词词尾)→站立的状态→稳定性

【例】 The government has taken a measure to maintain the *stability* of prices. 政府已经采取了措施以确保物价稳定。

【同】 constancy, stableness

【反】 instability

【派】 (逆构)stable *adj*. 稳定的，牢固的

stabilize [ˈsteɪbɪlaɪz] *v*. 稳定，坚固

【记】 sta(站立) + bil + ize(动词词尾)→使站好→稳定

【例】 His condition has now *stabilized*. 他的情况稳定下来了。
【同】 balance
【反】 alter，change
【派】 stabilization *n*. 稳定性

stack [stæk] *n*. 堆，一堆；*v*. 堆叠
【例】 1. There is a *stack* of dishes to be washed in the kitchen. 厨房里还有一大堆盘子要洗。
2. The floor was *stacked* up with books. 地板上堆满了书。
【同】 heap，pile

stadium [ˈsteɪdɪəm] *n*. (复数-diums 或 - dia)体育场，运动场
【记】 stad(长度，跑道) + ium(名词词尾)→有跑道的地方→体育场
【例】 The fans poured out of the *stadium* cheering wildly. 球迷们欣喜若狂地从体育场中蜂涌而出。
【同】 arena

staff [stɑːf] *n*. 1. 棍，拐杖；2. 全体职员，全体雇员
【例】 1. The old man leant on a long wooden *staff*. 老人拄着一根长长的木手杖。
2. If the fire-alarm goes，*staff* should assemble outside the building. 火警警报响时，全体人员应到楼外集合。
【同】 crutch；faculty
【派】 staffman *n*. 职员(尤指编辑或记者)
staffwork *n*. 参谋工作，管理工作

stagger [ˈstægə] *v*. 蹒跚，摇晃
【记】 stag(推) + g + er(动词词尾)→一直往前推→站不稳，蹒跚
【例】 The drunk man *staggered* across the room. 那个醉汉摇摇晃晃地穿过房间。
【同】 flounder，stumble，sway
【派】 staggering *adj*. 巨大的，惊人的

stagnant [ˈstægnənt] *adj*. 不流动的，呆滞的
【记】 stagn(站立) + ant(形容词词尾)→站立不动的→不流动的
【例】 Due to low investment，our industrial output has remained *stagnant*. 由于投资少，我们的工业生产一直停滞不前。
【同】 inactive，sluggish
【反】 active
【派】 stagnancy *n*. 停滞，迟钝

stainless [ˈsteɪnlɪs] *adj*. 不锈的，无瑕疵的
【记】 stain(污点) + less(没有)→没有污点的→不锈的
【例】 It's made of *stainless* steel which is guaranteed for 20 years. 它是由不锈钢制成的，质保 20 年。
【同】 unstained，taintless
【反】 stained，tainted
【派】 (逆构)stain *n*. 污点，瑕疵；*v*. 染污，沾污

stale [steɪl] *adj*. 1. 不新鲜的，走味的；2. 无趣味的，陈腐的

【例】 1. They had nothing to eat but *stale* bread. 除了陈面包外，他们没有别的东西可吃。

2. Her performance has become *stale*. 她的表演没有新意了。

【反】 fresh

stall [stɔːl] *v*. 停留，迟延；*n*. 摊，摊位

【记】 sta(站立)+ll→站立不动→停留

【例】 1. If you try to start off in top gear you'll *stall*. 要是刚一发动就用最高挡，那就会熄火。

2. Never buy food from a market *stall*. 千万别在小摊上买食物。

【同】 delay；booth

【派】 stallman *n*. 摊贩

stammer ['stæmə] *n*./*v*. 口吃，结巴着说出

【例】 1. The boy dare not answer the questions because of his *stammer*. 这个小男孩因为结巴不敢回答老师的问题。

2. He *stammers* when he feels nervous. 他一紧张就结巴。

【同】 stutter

【派】 stammerer *n*. 口吃的人

standard ['stændəd] *adj*. 标准的，规范的；*n*. 标准，规范

【记】 stand(站)+ard(=ort，地点)→站立的地点→标准

【例】 1. Searching handluggage at airports is now *standard* procedure. 在机场检查手提行李现在已成例行程序。

2. There is no absolute *standard* for beauty. 美是没有绝对的标准的。

【同】 received；criterion，norm

【派】 standardize *v*. 使符合标准，使标准化

stare [steər] *v*. 凝视，盯着看

【例】 She was *staring* into the distance. 她凝视着远方。

【同】 look，gaze

starve [stɑːv] *v*. 挨饿，饿死

【例】 They tried to *starve* him into submission. 他们试图用饥饿来使他就范。

【同】 hunger

【反】 feed，satiate

【派】 starvation *n*. 饥饿，饿死

statement ['steɪtmənt] *n*. 陈述，声明

【记】 state(陈述)+ment(名词)→陈述

【例】 She refused to make a *statement* to the police in case she incriminated herself. 她拒绝向警方作陈述以免受连累。

【同】 account，declaration

static ['stætɪk] *adj*. 静止的，静态的

【记】 sta(站立)+tic(形容词)→一直站立的→静止的

【例】 House prices，which have been *static* for several months，are now rising again. 房价稳定了几个月，现在又上涨了。

【同】 still，inactive

【反】 active，dynamic

stationary ['steɪʃənərɪ] *adj*. 稳定的，不变的

【记】 sta(站立)+tion(名词)+ary(形容词)→站立不动的→稳定的

【例】 An astronaut will attempt to leave the *stationary* spaceship and then return to it. 一名宇航员试着离开静止不动的宇宙飞船，然后再返回。

【同】 fixed，steady

【反】 flexible

stationery ['steɪʃənərɪ] *n*. 文具，信笺

【记】 sta(站立)+tion(名词)+er(人)+y(名词)→固定在一个地方卖东西的人(区别于游走的小商贩)所卖的东西→文具

【例】 He's been helping himself to my *stationery*. 他未经许可一直用我的文具。

【派】 (逆构)stationer *n*. 文具商，文具店

statue ['stætjuː] *n*. 雕像，塑像

【记】 sta(站立)+tue(名词词尾)→站立的东西→雕像

【例】 The *Statue* of Liberty was presented to the United States of America in the nineteenth century by the people of France. 自由女神雕像是法国人民在19世纪送给美国的。

【同】 figure，sculpture

status ['steɪtəs] *n*. 1.地位，身份；2.情形，状况

【记】 stat(站立)+us(名词词尾)→站立的状态→状况

【例】 1. He is a person of important social *status*. 他是一个有重要社会地位的人。
2. Please state your name，age and marital *status*. 请说出你的姓名、年龄以及婚姻状况。

【同】 station，position；condition

steadfast ['stedfəst] *adj*. 坚定的，坚信的

【记】 stead(=stand，站)+fast(牢固地)→牢牢地站在那里→坚定的

【例】 He is *steadfast* in his faith. 他坚守自己的信念。

【同】 firm，steady，unwavering

steady ['stedɪ] *adj*. 稳定的，坚定不移的

【记】 st(e)a(站立)+(d)y(形容词词尾)→站立不动的→稳定的

【例】 I know she is *steady* in her purpose. 我知道她意志坚定。

【同】 constant，firm

【反】 unsteady

steak [steɪk] *n*. 牛排，鱼片

【例】 How do you like your *steak* done，sir? Rare. 先生，你喜欢你的牛排烧到几成熟？生一点。

【派】 steakhouse *n*. 牛排餐厅

steep [stiːp] *adj*. 1.险峻的，陡峭的；2.急剧上下的

【例】 1. They climbed the *steep* mountain inch by inch. 他们一点一点地攀上那座陡峭的山。

S

2. There is a *steep* rise in prices. 物价飞涨。

【同】 abrupt, sharp

【反】 gradual

steer [stɪə] *v*. 驾驶，掌舵

【例】 He *steered* the car skillfully through the narrow streets. 他熟练地驾驶着汽车穿过狭窄的街道。

【同】 control, direct, drive, guide

【派】 steering *n*. 操纵，掌舵

stem [stem] *n*. 茎，干，柄；*v*. (-mmed; -mming)滋生，起源于

【例】 1. She bought some roses with long *stems*. 她买了一些枝干很长的玫瑰花。

2. The predent difficulties *stem* from our failure to deal with the problem when it first arose. 目前的困难是由于我们没有能在问题一出现时就加以处理。

【同】 stalk, trunk; originate

【派】 stemlike *adj*. 茎状的，柄状的

stereo ['stɪərɪəʊ] *n*. 立体声；*adj*. 立体的，立体声的

【例】 I've got a fridge and a *stereo* system which I've just bought from a friend. 我刚弄到一个冰箱和一套立体音响，是从一个朋友那里买的。

【派】 stereotype *n*. 铅版；陈腔滥调，老套

sterilize ['sterɪləɪz] *v*. 杀菌，消毒

【记】 steril(e)(不能生育的) + ize(动词词尾，使…)→使(细菌)不能繁殖→杀菌

【例】 Have these instruments been *sterilized*, nurse? 护士，这些器具消过毒了吗?

【同】 disinfect, sanitise

【派】 sterilization *n*. 杀菌，消毒

stern [stɜːn] *adj*. 苛刻的，严厉的

【例】 He received a *stern* rebuke from his superior. 他受到上司的严厉斥责。

【同】 severe, strict, stringent

【反】 gentle, lenient

stick [stɪk] *n*. 棍，棒，杖；*v*. (stuck, stuck)粘贴

【例】 1. The old man could not walk without a *stick*. 这老人没有手杖就走不了路。

2. The paint was still wet and the door handle *stuck* to my hand. 油漆还没有干，门把手粘住了我的手。

【派】 sticker *n*. 不屈不挠的人，滞销物

sticky *adj*. 粘的

S

stiff [stɪf]] *adj*. 僵硬的，拘谨的

【例】 Her rather *stiff* manner puts people off. 她那相当生硬的态度使人们都不敢来。

【同】 firm, rigid

【反】 flexible

【派】 stiff-necked *adj*. 顽固的

stiffen *v*. 使硬，使僵硬

stifle ['staɪfl] *v*. 1. 使窒息，使透不过气来；2. 扼杀，抑制

【例】 1. I'm *stifling* in here; open a window, someone! 这里太闷，我受不了啦，谁来打

开一下窗子！

2. I was so sleepy that I could scarecely *stifle* a yarn. 我困极了，简直忍不住要打呵欠。

【同】 choke，smother；curb，suppress

【反】 stimulate

stigma ['stɪgmə] *n*. 耻辱，污名

【记】 stig(刺) + ma(名词词尾)→刺上的记号(以前指在奴隶身上刺的记号)→耻辱

【例】 Living in sin is no longer the social *stigma* it once was. 现在同居不再像过去那样被认为是一种社会的耻辱行为。

【同】 disgrace，shame，stain

【反】 honor

stimulate ['stɪmjʊleɪt] *v*. 激励，刺激

【记】 stimul(= stimulus，赶牛用的棒子) + ate(动词词尾)→用棒子赶→激励

【例】 I hoped my warning would *stimulate* her to greater efforts. 我希望我的告诫会促使她作出更大的努力。

【同】 motivate，rouse

【反】 deaden

【派】 stimulation *n*. 兴奋(作用)，刺激

stimulus *n*. (复数-li)刺激(物)，促进

stimulant *n*. 刺激物，兴奋剂

sting [stɪŋ] *n*./*v*. (stung，stung)刺，刺痛

【例】 1. Does a bee die when it loses its *sting*? 蜜蜂失去螫针会死吗?

2. She was *stung* on the arm by a bee. 她的手臂被蜜蜂螫了一下。

【同】 bite，prick

stipend ['staɪpend] *n*. 津贴，奖学金

【记】 stip(原指发给士兵的钱) + (p)end(称量)→经常性的发的钱→津贴

【例】 I am writing to you to apply for a fellowship with a *stipend* in your university. 我写信是想来贵校进修，并盼能给予助学金。

【同】 payment

stipulate ['stɪpjʊleɪt] *v*. 约定，规定

【记】 stipul(讨价还价) + ate(动词词尾)→讨价还价，谈条件→约定

【例】 The company fails to pay on the date *stipulated* in the contract. 该公司没有按合同中规定的日期付款。

【同】 specify

【派】 stipulation *n*. 规定，条款

stir [stɜː] *n*. 轰动，搅动；*v*. (-rred；-rring)摇动，搅和

【例】 A gentle breeze *stirred* the leaves. 微风吹动了树叶。

【同】 mingle，mix

【反】 still

【派】 stirring *adj*. 激动人心的，活跃的

stitch [stɪtʃ] *v*. 缝，缝合；*n*. 一针，缝针

【记】 stitch = stinct，刺→缝

【例】 1. Will you *stitch* a button on this shirt? 请你在这件衬衫上钉一颗钮扣好吗？

2. The doctor put three stitches in my head. 医生在我头上缝了三针。

【同】 sew

stock [stɒk] *n*. 1. 贮存，库存；2. 股票，股份；*v*. 储存

【例】 1. Have you any grey pullovers in *stock*? 你们有灰色套头毛衣的现货吗？

2. The New York *stock* exchange crashed in 1929. 纽约股票交易所于 1929 年大崩溃。

3. That shop *stocks* all types of shoes. 那家商店备有各种类型的鞋子。

【同】 store；share

【派】 stockmarket *n*. 证券市场

stockbroker *n*. 股票经纪人

stomach [ˈstʌmək] *n*. 胃，腹部

【例】 Don't swim on an empty *stomach*. 不要空腹时游泳。

【同】 abdomen，belly

【派】 stomachache *n*. 胃痛，肚子疼

storage [ˈstɒrɪdʒ] *n*. 贮藏，保管

【记】 stor(e)(贮存) + age(名词词尾)→贮藏，保管

【例】 His furniture is in *storage* while he finds a new house. 他在找新房子时把家具存放在仓库里。

【例】 stock

【派】 (逆构)store *v*. 贮藏，存储；*n*. 商店，店铺

stout [staʊt] *adj*. 粗胖的，结实的

【例】 She became rather *stout* as she grew older. 随着年龄增大，她有点发胖。

【同】 strong，sturdy

【反】 feeble

【派】 stout-hearted *adj*. 勇敢的，刚毅的

straight [streɪt] *adj*. 直的，诚实的；*adv*. 直接，一直

【记】 strai(拉直) + ght→完全拉紧→直的

【例】 1. He drew a *straight* line on the paper. 他在纸上画了一条直线。

2. Come *straight* away after school. 放学后直接回家。

【同】 upright，honest

【反】 bent

【派】 straighten *v*. 弄直，伸直

straightforward *adj*. 正直的，坦率的

strain [streɪn] *n*. 过度的疲劳，张力；*v*. 拉紧，扭伤

【例】 1. A *strain* or a blow to a limb, though painful at the time, generally resolves itself. 四肢拉伤或者遭到击打，尽管当时很疼，一般很快自己就会恢复。

2. Too heavy a load will *strain* the rope to its breaking point. 负载过重会把绳子拉紧到崩断的地步。

【同】 tense, extend

【反】 relax

strait [streɪt] *adj*. 艰难的，因狭窄而难以通过的；*n*. 地峡，海峡

【记】 stai(拉紧) + t→拉紧→狭窄的

【例】 1. The door is rather *strait*. 这门相当窄。

2. The *strait* was named after its discoverer. 这个海峡是以它的发现者命名的。

【同】 narrow

【反】 broad

strategy [ˈstrætɪdʒɪ] *n*. 战略，策略

【例】 I think we should work out a *strategy* to deal with this situation. 我想我们应该制订出一项行动计划，用来对付这种情况。

【同】 scheme, tactics

【派】 strategic *adj*. 战略的，战略上的

strategics *n*. 兵法

stray [streɪ] *v*. 1. 迷路，走失；2. 离题，远离；*adj*. 迷失的，流浪的

【例】 1. Some of the sheep have *strayed* from the flock. 一些羊离开了羊群。

2. He constantly *strayed* from the main point of his talk. 他不断偏离他的话题。

3. The *stray* cat was picked up by a kind girl. 走失的猫被一个善良的姑娘收留了。

strength [streŋθ] *n*. 力量，强度

【记】 streng(= strong, 强壮的) + th(名词词尾)→力量

【例】 I have hardly enough *strength* left to move my feet. 我连移动双脚的力气都几乎没有了。

【同】 force, power

【反】 weakness

【派】 strengthen *v*. 加强，巩固

stress [stress] *n*. 压力，重压；*v*. 强调，重读

【例】 1. I can't bear the *stresses* and strains of modern life. 我不能忍受现代生活的压力和紧张。

2. I must *stress* that what I say is confidential. 我要强调我说的话是保密的。

【同】 pressure, emphasis

【派】 stressful *adj*. 有压力的

stretch [stretʃ] *n*./*v*. 伸展，舒展(身体)

【记】 stre(ss)(拉紧) + tch(名词词尾)→向(各个方向)拉紧→伸展

【例】 1. I got out of the bed and had a good *stretch*. 我起床后舒服地伸了个懒腰。

2. The desert *stretched* away into the distance. 沙漠一直延伸到远方。

【同】 extend, spread

【反】 shrink

【派】 stretchy *adj*. 有弹性的

stride [straɪd] *v*. (strode, stridden)大步走过，跨过；*n*. 大步，阔步

【例】 1. She *strode* purposefully up to the door and knocked loudly. 她故意大步走到门前，并大声地敲门。

2. In a few *strides* he crossed the room. 他几大步就穿过了房间。

【同】 pace, step

strife [straɪf] *n*. 斗争，冲突

【例】 These firms are at *strife*. 这几家商行彼此不和。

【同】 conflict, dispute

strike [straɪk] *v*./*n*. (struck, struck)1. 冲击，打击；2. 罢工

【例】 1. The bombers made a sudden *strike* on the harbor. 轰炸机对这港口进行了一次突然袭击。

2. It was not long before tragedy struck again. 没多久，灾难又再次降临。

3. The union *struck* for better work conditions. 工会为争取更好的工作条件而罢工。

【同】 hit; walkout

【派】 striking *adj*. 显著的，惊人的

string [strɪŋ] *n*. 细绳，一串，一行；*v*. (strung, strung)排成一列

【例】 1. Puppets are worked by *strings*. 木偶是用线来操纵的。

2. She *strung* the beads with a fine nylon. 她用细尼龙线把珠子串了起来。

【同】 thread; line

stringent ['strɪndʒənt] *adj*. 严厉的，迫切的

【记】 string(拉紧)+ent(形容词词尾)→态度紧张的→严厉的

【例】 *Stringent* measures have been taken to deal with street crime. 为对付街头犯罪已采取严厉措施。

【同】 pressing, tight

【派】 stringency *n*. 严格，紧迫

strip [strɪp] *n*. 条，带；*v*. (-pped; -pping)剥，剥去

【例】 1. Our football players have a red and white *strip*. 我们队的足球队员们穿着红白两色的队服。

2. They *stripped* off and jumped into the pool. 他们脱掉衣服，跳进了池子。

【同】 bare, deprive

stripe [straɪp] *n*. 斑纹，条纹

【例】 Tigers have orange fur with black *stripes*. 老虎的皮毛是橘黄色的，带有黑色条纹。

【同】 mark

strive [straɪv] *v*. (strove, striven)努力，奋斗

【例】 They are *striving* hard to make greater progress. 他们正在努力争取更大的进步。

【同】 endeavor, struggle

stroke [strəʊk] *n*. 1. 击，敲，报时的钟声；2. (网球等)一击，(划船，游泳等)一划，(绘画等)一笔

【例】 1. She arrived on the *stroke* of 12. 她在钟敲12点的时候到了。

2. I can't swim yet, but I've made a few *strokes* with my arms. 我还不会游泳，但我用胳膊划了几下。

【同】 hit, blow

S

structure ['strʌktʃə] *n*. 结构，建筑物；*v*. 建筑，构成

【记】struct(建筑)+ure(名词词尾)→建筑

【例】1. Can you analyze the *structure* of the sentence for me? 你能给我分析一下这个句子的结构吗？

2. You need to *structure* your arguments more carefully. 你需要更为仔细地组织自己的论点。

【同】building, configuration; organize

【派】structural *adj*. 结构的，建筑的

structurism *n*. 结构主义

struggle ['strʌgl] *n*./*v*. 斗争，努力

【记】strugg(=strut, 昂首走路)+le(名词词尾)→在(困难中)昂首走路→斗争

【例】1. Several people were hurt in the *struggle*. 在打斗中，有几个人受伤。

2. He *struggled* with his assailants and eventually drove them off. 他同攻击他的人进行搏斗，最后把他们赶走了。

【同】conflict, fight

【派】struggling *adj*. 奋斗的，努力的

stubborn ['stʌbən] *adj*. 顽固的，固执的

【例】You might as well talk to a stone as try to argue with a *stubborn* woman. 你与其跟一个倔女人争吵，还不如对一块石头说话。

【同】headstrong, inflexible, unyielding

【反】docile

studio ['stjuːdɪəʊ] *n*. 画室，工作室，录音室

【例】He is working in his photographic *studio*. 他正在摄影室工作。

【同】workroom

stuff [stʌf] *n*. 原料，素材；*v*. 塞满，填充

【例】1. A kind of plastic *stuff* is used to make the plates. 这些盘子是用一种塑料制造的。

2. His pocket was *stuffed* full of dirty hankerchiefs. 他的口袋里塞满了脏手绢。

【同】material; fill

【派】stuffy *adj*. 乏味的

stunning ['stʌnɪŋ] *adj*. 令人吃惊的，震惊的

【记】stun(n)(使惊吓)+ing(形容词词尾)→让人吃惊的，震惊的

【例】His plays are distinguished only by their *stunning* mediocrity. 他的戏剧与众不同之处就是平凡得出奇。

【同】amazing, astonishing

【派】(逆构)stun *n*./*v*. (-nned; -nning)晕倒，晕眩

subject ['sʌbdʒɪkt] *n*. 题目，主题；*adj*. 未独立的，受…影响的；[səb'dʒekt] *v*. 使屈从于，隶属

【记】sub(在下面)+ject(投掷)→投身于…之下→隶属

【例】1. How many *subjects* are you studying this semester? 这学期你选了几门课程？

2. In all cases, mining is *subject* to stringent controls and approvals processes. 在任

S

何情况下，采矿都要有严格的控制以及审核过程。

3. The weaker tribes were *subjected* by another warlike race. 各较为弱小的部落被另一个好战的民族所征服。

【同】 theme，topic；dependent；submit

【反】 object

【派】 subjection *n*. 征服，隶属

subjective *adj*. 主观的，个人的

sublimate [ˈsʌblɪmeɪt] *v*. 使升华，纯化

【记】 sub(在下面)+lim(门槛)+ate(动词词尾)→使在门槛下，达到→使升华

【例】 Once he settled down，he *sublimated* his desires for women into a daily regimen of exercise. 他安定下来以后，把自己对女人的欲望转化为每日按时的锻炼。

【同】 purify，refine

【派】 sublimation *n*. 升华；高尚化

sublime [səˈblaɪm] *adj*. 庄严的，崇高的

【记】 sub(在下面)+lim(门槛)+e→使在门槛下，达到→崇高的

【例】 There is but one step from the *sublime* to the ridiculous. 从崇高到荒谬只有一步之遥。

【同】 grand，noble，prominent

subliminal [sʌbˈlɪmɪnl] *adj*. 潜意识的，意识下的

【记】 sub(在下面)+limin(门槛)+al(形容词词尾)→在门槛下，在局限之下→潜意识的

【例】 *Subliminal* advertising on TV has been banned. 电视上的潜意识广告(指仅瞬间出现于屏幕上的广告)已遭禁播。

【同】 subconscious

submerge [səbˈmɜːdʒ] *v*. 使沉没，淹没

【记】 sub(在下面)+merge(浸)→浸在下面→淹没

【例】 At the first sign of danger the submarine will *submerge*. 一有危险迹象，潜艇就会潜入水中。

【同】 immerse，sink

submit [səbˈmɪt] *v*. (-tted；-tting)1. 提交，呈递；2. 顺从，屈服

【记】 sub(在下面)+mit(传递)→从下面传递→提交

【例】 1. We should *submit* our plans to the council for approval. 我们应该向理事会提交计划以求批准。

2. He was losing the fight，but he would not *submit*. 他在拳击中正节节败退，但是他并不服输。

【同】 present；surrender，yield

【反】 resist

【派】 submission *n*. 屈服，服从

submissive *adj*. 顺从的

subordinate [səˈbɔːdɪnɪt] *n*. 部属，下级；*adj*. 次要的，从属的

【记】 sub(在下面)+ordi(n)(顺序)+ate(形容词词尾)→次序在下面的→次要的

【例】 1. He was always friendly to his *subordinates*. 他对下级一向和蔼可亲。

2. All the other issues are *subordinate* to this one. 所有问题都要从属于这一问题。
【同】 follower; dependent, inferior
【派】 subordination *n*. 部属，次要

subscribe [səbˈskraɪb] *v*. 1. 捐款，捐赠；2. 订阅，签署(文件)
【记】 sub(在下面) + scrib(写) + e→写在下面→签署(文件)
【例】 1. How much do you *subscribe* to the disaster fund? 你向赈灾基金捐了多少钱？
2. The magazine is trying to get more readers to *subscribe*. 该杂志正在大力发展新订户。
【同】 contribute; sign
【派】 subscriber *n*. 捐献者；订户，签署者
subscription *n*. 捐献；订阅，签署

subsequent [ˈsʌbsɪkwənt] *adj*. 后来的，随后的
【记】 sub(在后面) + sequ(跟随) + ent(形容词词尾)→在后面跟随的→后来的
【例】 He confessed to other crimes *subsequent* to the bank robbery. 他供认抢劫银行案后，又坦白了其他罪行。
【同】 following, next
【反】 previous
【派】 subsequence *n*. 后继，随后
subsequential *adj*. 后来的，并发的

subsidiary [səbˈsɪdjərɪ] *adj*. 辅助的，附属的；*n*. 子公司
【记】 (在后面) + sid(坐) + iary(形容词词尾)→坐在后面的，次要的→附属的
【例】 1. Can I ask a *subsidiary* question? 我可以问一个附带的问题吗？
2. Most of the group profit is contributed by the *subsidiary* in the far east. 集团的大部分利润是由远东的子公司缴纳。
【同】 accessory, auxiliary; subordinate

subsidize [ˈsʌbsɪdaɪz] *v*. 给…补助，资助
【记】 sub(在后面) + sid(坐) + ize(动词词尾)→坐在后面(给予支持)→资助
【例】 Farming is partly *subsidized* by the government. 农业得到政府的部分补贴。
【同】 assistance
【派】 subsidization *n*. 补助，津贴
subsidy *n*. 补助金，津贴

subsist [səbˈsɪst] *v*. 活下去，生存
【记】 sub(在下面) + sist(站)→站在下面→存在，生存
【例】 How do they manage to *subsist* on such a low wage? 他们这点工资怎么糊口？
【同】 exist, live, survive
【派】 subsistencen. 生存，生计

substance [ˈsʌbstəns] *n*. 物质，实质
【记】 sub(在下面) + stan(站立) + ce(名词词尾)→站在(表象)之下的东西→实质
【例】 There is not anything of real *substance* in their book. 他们的书中没有什么实质性的内容。
【同】 essence, matter

S

substantial [səb'stænʃəl] *adj*. 1. 物质的，实质的；2. 相当数目的，可观的

【记】 sub(在…之下的)＋stan(站立)＋tial(形容词词尾)→位于(表象)之下的→实质的

【例】 1. The architecture of this house is very *substantial*. 这座房子的结构很牢固。

2. By careful strategy she negotiated a *substantial* pay rise. 她精心策画后，谈妥了大幅增加工资的事。

【同】 essential, material; significant

【反】 insubstantial

substantiate [sʌbs'tænʃɪeɪt] *v*. 证实，加强

【记】 sub(在下面)＋stant(站)＋i＋ate(动词词尾)→使站在下面→把事实摆出来→证实

【例】 Can you *substantiate* your accusations against him? 你指责他，能提出事实根据吗?

【同】 confirm

【派】 substantive *adj*. 真正的，实际的，有实质的

substitute ['sʌbstɪtjuːt] *n*. 代用品，代替者；*v*. 代替，替换

【记】 sub(在下面)＋stitute(站立)→站在下面的→代用品

【例】 1. Water is not a proper *substitute* for wine. 水不是酒的适当代用品。

2. Can you *substitute* for me at the meeting? 你代我去开会好吗?

【同】 replace

【派】 substitution *n*. 代替，代用

subtle ['sʌtl] *adj*. 微妙的，精致的

【记】 sub(下面)＋tle(织)→继续向下织→精致的

【例】 He is a man of *subtle* and refined sensibility. 他是个感情细腻的男子。

【同】 clever, delicate

【反】 simple

【派】 subtlety *n*. 微妙，精明

subtraction [səb'trækʃən]n. 减少，减法

【记】 sub(下面)＋tract(拉)＋ion(名词词尾)→向下拉→减少

【例】 Two from five is a simple *subtraction*. 5减2是简单的减法。

【同】 deduction, minus

【反】 addition

【派】 subtractive *adj*. 减去的；负的

subtropical ['sʌb'trɒpɪkəl] *adj*. 副热带的，亚热带的

【记】 sub(在下面)＋tropic(热带)＋al(形容词词尾)→在热带之下的→亚热带的

【例】 This country has a *subtropical* climate. 这个国家属于亚热带气候。

【同】 semitropical

【派】 subtropics *n*. 亚热带地方

suburb ['sʌbɜːb] *n*. 郊区

【记】 sub(在…附近)＋urb(城市)→在城市附近的→郊区

【例】 Living in the *suburbs* you may suffer a little discomfort. 住在乡下，你会感到有些不方便。

【同】 outskirt

【派】 suburban *adj*. 郊外的，偏远的

S

suburbaniten. 郊区居民

subvert [səb'vɜːt] *v*. 颠覆，暗中破坏

【记】 sub(下面)+vert(转移)→从下面翻转过来→颠覆

【例】 Instead of cooperating, he worked to *subvert* her authority. 他并不合作，反而暗中破坏她的威信。

【同】 overthrow, undermine, weaken

【反】 uphold

【派】 subversive*adj*. 颠覆性的，破坏性的

successive [sək'sesɪv] *adj*. 连续的，继承的

【记】 suc(=sub，在后面)+cess(行进)+ive(形容词词尾)→从后面不断前行的→连续的

【例】 It happened on two *successive* days. 这种情况连续发生了两天。

【同】 sequent, consecutive

【反】 discontiguous, inconsecutive

【派】 succession *n*. 连续，继承

successional *adj*. 接连的，连续性的

succinct [sək'sɪŋkt] *adj*. 简明的，简洁的

【记】 suc(=sub，在下面)+cinct(绑，束缚)→在下面收缩→简洁的

【例】 But I do love your four-word proverbs and idioms. They are so *succinct* and expressive. 不过，我确实喜欢你们的四字成语，简练而生动。

【同】 compact, concise

succumb [sə'kʌm] *v*. 屈服，屈从

【记】 suc(=sub，在下面)+cumb(躺)→躺在下面→屈服

【例】 The city *succumbed* after only a short siege. 该城受围困仅很短时间就不再抵抗了。

【同】 surrender, yield, give way

【反】 survive

suck [sʌk] *v*. 吸吮，吸取

【例】 Don't *suck* your thumb; it's so dirty. 别舔手指头，太脏了。

【同】 absorb, draw

【派】 sucking *adj*. 吸奶的，乳臭未干的

suckling *adj*. 哺乳的，未断奶的

sue [sjuː,suː] *v*. 1.向…请求，请愿；2.提出诉讼，控告

【例】 1. The other side realize they are beaten, and are *suing* for peace. 另一方知道自己输了，因而要求讲和。

2. He was *sued* for breach of contract. 他因毁约而被起诉。

【同】 ask; litigate, prosecute

suffer ['sʌfə] *v*. 遭受，忍受

【记】 suf(=sub，在下面)+fer(忍受)→在下面忍耐→忍受

【例】 They *suffered* huge losses in the financial crisis. 他们在经济危机时遭受了巨大的损失。

【同】 bear, endure

【反】 enjoy

【派】 sufferance *n*. 忍耐

suffering *n*./*adj*. 苦楚(的)，受难(的)

sufficient [sə'fɪʃənt] *adj*. 足够的，充足的

【记】 suf(= sub，在下面) + fic(制作) + (i)ent(形容词词尾)→在下面制作的→足够的

【例】 There wasn't much food，but it was *sufficient* for our needs. 食物不多，但能满足我们的需要。

【同】 enough，adequate

【反】 insufficient

【派】 (逆构)suffice *v*. 足够，有能力

sufficiency *n*. 充足，自满

suffrage ['sʌfrɪdʒ] *n*. 选举权，投票

【记】 suf(= sub，在下面) + frag(碎片) + e→在下面用碎片表决(原来投票用的是陶瓷碎片)→投票

【例】 When was universal *suffrage* introduced in your country? 贵国是什么时候实行普选权的？

【同】 ballot，vote

【派】 suffragette *n*. 主张妇女参政权的女子

suffragist *n*. 妇女政权论者

suffuse [sə'fjuːz] *v*. 弥漫，充满

【记】 suf(= sub，下面) + fuse(流)→向下流→弥漫，充满

【例】 The evening sky was *suffused* with crimson. 黄昏时分天空红霞灿灿。

【同】 flush，perfuse

【派】 suffusive *adj*. 充满的，洋溢的，弥漫的

suffusion *n*. 充满，弥漫

suicide ['sjʊɪsaɪd] *n*. 自杀，自毁

【记】 su(i)(自己) + cid(e)(切割)→切割自己→自杀

【例】 She tried to commit *suicide*, but we saved her life by chance. 她试图自杀，但我们碰巧救了她。

【同】 killing，self-destruction

S

【派】 suicidal *adj*. 自杀的，自取灭亡的

suit [sjuːt] *v*. 合适，相配；*n*. 一套衣服

【记】 su(跟随) + it(动词词尾)→继续做下去→符合

【例】 1. I've found a job that *suits* me down to the ground. 我找到了一份工作，对我再合适不过了。

2. He bought a pin-stripe lounge *suit* yesterday afternoon. 他昨天下午买了一套细条纹西装。

【同】 adapt，fit

【反】 disarrange，misfit

【派】 suitable *adj*. 合适的，适当的

suitability *n*. 合适，相配

suitcase *n*. 手提箱，衣箱

sum [sʌm] *n*. 总数，金额；*v*.（-mmed；-mming）概括，总结

【例】 1. I had to spend a large *sum* of money to get it back. 我得花一大笔钱才能把它弄回来。

2. The last section *sums* up all the arguments on either side. 最后一段总结了双方的全部论点。

【同】 amount，quantity；total

【反】 part，portion

【派】 sum-up *n*. 总结

summarize [sʌməraɪz] *v*. 概述，摘要

【记】 summ(总数)+(a)rise(动词词尾)→归纳为一个总体→概述

【例】 She *summaried* the aims of the new party in a couple of sentences. 她用几句话概况了新政党的宗旨。

【同】 brief，outline

【派】 summary *n*. 摘要，概要

summit ['sʌmɪt] *n*. 1. 山峰，顶点；2.（政府首脑的）最高级会议

【记】 summ(总数，最高的)+it(名词词尾)→最高点→顶点

【例】 1. The Hungarian view is magnificent from the *summit* of the mountains. 从群山之颠看到的匈牙利景色非常壮丽。

2. The president attended a *summit* in Washington. 总统出席了在华盛顿召开的最高级会议。

【同】 peak，climax

【反】 bottom

summon ['sʌmən] *v*. 召唤，传唤，召集

【记】 sum(=sub，下面)+mon(提醒)→向下面的提醒→召唤

【例】 The shareholders were *summoned* to a general meeting. 那些股东被召集去参加股东大会。

【同】 assemble，call

sumptuous ['sʌmptjʊəs] *adj*. 奢侈的，华丽的

【记】 sumpt(拿，取)+uous(形容词词尾)→取很多的→奢侈的

【例】 The poor girl was astonished by the *sumptuous* furnishings of the mansion. 这个贫穷的女孩被大厦里的豪华的陈设惊呆了。

【同】 luxurious，imposing，opulent

【反】 mean

superb [sjuː'pɜːb] *adj*. 极好的，华丽的

【记】 super(在…之上的)+b→比其它都要好的→极好的

【例】 The sports facilities are *superb* in this city. 这个城市的运动设施是一流的。

【同】 brilliant，magnificent

superficial [sjuːpə'fɪʃəl] *adj*. 浅薄的，肤浅的

【记】 super(在上面)+fic(做)+ial(形容词词尾)→在表面上做的→肤浅的

【例】 He is too *superficial* to appreciate great literature like this. 他太肤浅，无法欣赏

S

这类文学巨著。

【同】 shallow

【反】 deep, profound

【派】 superficiality *n*. 表面性的事物，浅薄

superintend [ˌsjuːpərɪnˈtend] *v*. 主管，管理，监督

【记】 super(在上面) + in(朝着) + tend(伸展，延伸)→在上面延伸(影响→管理，监督

【例】 The manager is *superintending* the staff's work. 经理正在监督工人的工作。

【同】 administrate, oversee, supervise

【派】 superintendent *n*. 主管，负责人；主日学校校长

superior [sjuːˈpɪərɪə] *adj*. 1. 上级的；2. 质量或价值更好的，出众的

【记】 super(在上面) + ior(表示比较级)→在更高处的→上级的

【例】 1. I'll report you to your *superior* officer! 我要把你的情况报告给你的上司！
2. This western restaurant is *superior* to the one we went to last week. 这家西餐馆比我们上星期去的那一家好。

【同】 greater, higher

【反】 inferior

【派】 superiority *n*. 优越，高傲

supernatural [ˌsjuːpəˈnætʃərəl] *adj*. 超自然的，神奇的

【记】 super(在上面) + natur(e)(自然) + al(形容词词尾)→超出自然的

【例】 A common theme in horror stories is of a monstrous creature raised by *supernatural* power from the dead. 恐怖故事中的一个共同主题是关于一个由超自然的力量使之从死亡中复活过来的怪物。

【同】 mysterious

【反】 natural

【派】 (逆构)supernature *n*. 超自然界

supersede [ˌsjuːpəˈsiːd] *v*. 代替，淘汰

【记】 super(在上面) + sede(坐)→坐在…的上面→代替

【例】 Motorways have largely *superseded* ordinary roads for long-distance travel. 高速公路多已取代了普通公路。

【同】 replace, supplant

S

superstitious [ˌsjuːpəˈstɪʃəs] *adj*. 迷信的

【记】 super(在上面，超越) + sti(站立) + tious(形容词词尾)→超越站立的地方的→迷信的

【例】 It is a common *superstitious* viewpoint that black cats are unlucky. 认为黑猫不祥是一种很普遍的迷信观点。

【同】 fetishistic

【派】 superstition *n*. 迷信

supervise [ˈsjuːpəvaɪz] *v*. 监督，管理

【记】 super(在上面) + vise(看见)→在上面看→监督

【例】 The chief clerk *supervises* the work of the department. 文书组长负责监督该部门的工作。

【同】 manage, oversee

【派】 supervision *n*. 监督，指导

supervisor *n*. 管理人，督学

supplant [sə'plɑːnt] *v*. 排挤，取代

【记】 sup(在下面) + plant(种植)→种在下面→取代

【例】 Oil has *supplanted* coffee as our main export. 原油已经取代咖啡成为我们的主要出口货物。

【同】 replace, supersede

supple ['sʌpl] *adj*. 柔软的，灵活的，柔顺的

【记】 sup(在下面) + ple(填充)→能在下面填充的→柔软的

【例】 Exercise keeps you *supple*. 经常锻炼可使身体灵活。

【同】 flexible, limber, pliable

【反】 stiff

supplement ['sʌplɪmənt] *n*. 补充，附录，增刊；*v*. 补充

【记】 sup(在下面) + ple(填充) + ment(名词词尾)→填充在下面的→补充

【例】 1. The money I got was a useful *supplement* to my ordinary income. 我得到的那笔钱是很管用的外快。

2. She *supplements* her diet with vitamin tablets. 她服用维生素片剂以补充规定食谱中的营养。

【同】 appendant, complete

【派】 supplementary *n*. 增补者，增补物；*adj*. 增补的，补充的

supplementation *n*. 增补，补充

supply [sə'plaɪ] *n*. 补给，供应品；*v*. 补给，供给

【记】 sup(在下面) + ply(填充)→填充在下面→补给

【例】 1. The brain needs a continuous *supply* of blood. 大脑需要不断地供血。

2. The merchant *supplies* goods to them. 商人向他们供应货物。

【同】 furnish, provide

【反】 demand

【派】 supplier *n*. 供应者，供应厂商

suppose [sə'pəʊz] *v*. 认为，猜想

【记】 sup(在下面) + pose(放置)→把想法放在下面→猜想

【例】 We *suppose* that the situation will improve. 我们认为形势会好转。

【同】 imagine, think

【派】 supposal *n*. 想象，推测

supposing conj. 何不，万一

supposedly *adv*. 按说，应该

suppress [sə'pres] *v*. 压制，压抑

【记】 sup(在下面) + press(压)→用力向下压→压制

【例】 The revolt was *suppressed* in a matter of hours. 叛乱在几小时之内就镇压下去了。

【同】 repress, restrain

【派】 suppression *n*. 镇压，抑制

S

supreme [sjuː'priːm] *adj*. 极度的，至高的

【记】 supr(在…之上)+eme(最高级)→在最上面的→极度的

【例】 *Supreme* authority resides in the President. 最高权力属于总统。

【同】 extreme, utmost

【派】 supremacy *n*. 地位最高的人，霸权

surface ['sɜːfɪs] *n*. 地面，表面

【记】 sur(在…之上)+face(正面)→在物体正面上→表面

【例】 Beneath that apparently calm *surface* is a man of fierce temper. 文静的外表掩盖着的是一个火暴脾气的人

【同】 exterior, face

【反】 interior

【派】 surficial *adj*. 地表的，地面的

surf ['sɜːf] *n*./*v*. 冲浪

【例】 If the waves are big enough, we'll go *surfing*. 如果浪够大的话，我们就去冲浪。

【派】 surfer *n*. 冲浪运动员

surge [sɜːdʒ] *n*./*v*. (浪涛)汹涌，奔腾

【例】 1. A *surge* of demonstrators broke through the fence. 汹涌而来的示威者冲破了围栏。

2. Anger *surged* up within him. 怒火在他心中燃烧。

【同】 billow, wave

【派】 surgent *adj*. 澎湃的，汹涌的

surging *adj*. 汹涌的，活动猛烈的

surgery ['sɜːdʒərɪ] *n*. 外科手术，诊所

【例】 He underwent open-heart *surgery*. 他接受了体外循环心脏手术。

【同】 operation

【派】 surgical *adj*. 外科的，手术上的

surgeon *n*. 外科医生

surmise [sə'maɪz] *n*./*v*. 推测，猜测

【记】 sur(在…上面)+mise(送，放)→把(心思)放上→猜测

【例】 1. Your first *surmise* was right. 你第一次猜的对。

2. We *surmised* that the delay was caused by some accident. 我们推测迟延是由某种事故所致。

【同】 guess, presume, suspect

surmount [sɜː'maʊnt] *v*. 登上，克服，越过

【记】 sur(在…上面)+mount(攀登)→攀登到…之上→登上，克服

【例】 I think most of these obstacles can be *surmounted*. 我认为这些障碍大多数都是可以克服的。

【同】 overcome

【派】 surmountable *adj*. 可战胜的，可克服的

insurmountable *adj*. 不能克服的，不能超越的

surname ['sɜːneɪm] *n*. 姓氏

【记】 sur(在…上面)+name(名字)→加在名字之上的→姓氏

【例】 Just call me by my *surname*, cut out the Mr. 就叫我的姓吧，去掉先生二字。

surpass [səː'pɑːs] *v*. 超越，胜过

【记】 sur(在…上面)+pass(通过)→在…之上通过→胜过

【例】 Men *surpass* women in strength. 男人比女人力气大。

【同】 exceed，excel

surplus ['səːpləs] *n*. 盈余，余款；*adj*. 过剩的，剩余的

【记】 sur(在…之上的)+plus(更多的)→比需要的更多→盈余的

【例】 1. A time of great *surplus* is followed by a time of shortage. 物资大量过剩时期之后，就是随之而来的物资短缺时期。

2. We are giving away all our *surplus* apples. 我们准备把多余的苹果全部送人。

【同】 excess，extra

【反】 deficit

surrender [sə'rendə] *v*. 放弃，投降

【记】 sur(在上面)+render(给予)→把东西放在上面→放弃

【例】 We would rather die than *surrender*. 我们宁死而不投降。

【同】 abandon，submit

【反】 resist

surrounding [sə'raʊndɪŋ] *n*. 周围的事物，环境

【记】 sur(在上面)+round(环绕)+ing→环绕在…上面的→周围的

【例】 Animals in zoos are not in their natural *surroundings*. 动物园中的动物没有自然环境。

【同】 circumstance，setting

【派】 (逆构)surround *v*. 包围，环境

surveillance [sə'veɪləns] *n*. 监视，监督

【记】 sur(在上面)+veil(l)(看)+ance(名词词尾)→在上面看→监视

【例】 Detectives kept the quarry under *surveillance* for weeks. 侦探们监测那个目标已有好几个星期了。

【同】 watch

survey ['səːveɪ] *n*. 调查，概括；[sə'veɪ] *v*. 调直，概括

【记】 sur(在…之上)+vey(看)→从上面往下看→调查

【例】 1. Follow-up *survey* shows that the reoccurrence rate is only 5%. 跟踪调查表明复发率仅为5%。

2. In this book, the author *surveys* recent developments in linguistics. 作者在本书中概述了语言学目前的发展情况。

【同】 view

【派】 surveyable *adj*. 可观察的，一目了然的

surveyor *n*. 测量员，检察员

survive [sə'vaɪv] *v*. 活下来，幸存

【记】 sur(在…之上)+vive(生活)→经过…还活着→幸存

【例】 You need to be tough to *survive* in the jungle. 要在丛林中活下来就要有坚忍不拔

的意志。

【派】 survival *n*. 生存，幸存

survivor *n*. 幸存者，生还者

suspect [səsˈpekt] *v*. 怀疑，推测；*n*. 嫌疑犯，犯罪嫌疑人

【记】 sus(在…下面)+(s)pect(看见)→看见(表面)之下的东西→推测

【例】 1. He seems poor, but I *suspect* that he has quite a lot of money. 他看上去很穷，可是我怀疑他很有钱。

2. The police have taken the *suspect* to the police station. 警察把这个嫌疑犯送到了警察局。

【同】 distrust, doubt

【反】 trust

【派】 suspectable *adj*. 可疑的，有嫌疑的

suspicious *adj*. 疑心的，怀疑的

suspicion *n*. 猜疑，怀疑

suspend [səsˈpend] *v*. 吊起，悬挂，暂停

【记】 sus(在…下面)+pend(悬挂)→悬挂

【例】 She was *suspended* from school for stealing. 她因有偷窃行为遭勒令停学处分。

【同】 hang, interrupt

【派】 suspension *n*. 悬挂，暂停

suspense *n*. 悬念，情节

sustain [səsˈteɪn] *v*. 保持，支撑

【记】 sus(在…下面)+tain(保持)→在下面支持→支撑

【例】 The foundations were not strong enough to *sustain* the weight of the house. 这地基不够牢固，无法承受房屋的重量。

【同】 support, uphold

【派】 sustainable *adj*. 可持续的，足可支撑的

sustained *adj*. 持续不变的，相同的

sustenance [ˈsʌstɪnəns] *n*. 食物，生计，营养物

【记】 sus(在…下面)+ten(支持)+ance(名词词尾)→在下面支持的东西→食物，营养

【例】 He gave money for the *sustenance* of a poor family. 他把钱给一穷人家维持生活。

【同】 aliment, nourishment

swallow [ˈswɒləʊ] *n*. 1. 燕子；2. 吞咽；*v*. 咽，吞没

【例】 1. One *swallow* does not make a summer. 一燕不成夏。(仅有的一次幸运或好事并不意味着一切都好。)

2. Taking pills is easy; just put them in your mouth and *swallow*. 服用药片很容易，只要放在口中咽下即可。

【同】 devour, eat

【派】 swallower *n*. 吞咽者

swallowtail *n*. 燕尾服

swamp [swɒmp] *n*. 沼泽，湿地

【例】 The heavy rain has turned the small garden into a *swamp*. 大雨使这小花园变成了

一块沼泽地。

【同】 bog, marsh

【派】 swampy *adj*. 沼泽的，湿地的

swarm [swɔːm] *n*. 蜂群，一大群；*v*. 挤满，密集

【例】 1. The locust *swarm* has destroyed all the crops and vegetables. 蝗虫群毁坏了所有的庄稼和蔬菜。

2. The crowd *swarmed* out of the cinema after the film ended. 电影结束后，人们从电影院蜂拥而出。

【同】 crowd, throng

sway [sweɪ] *v*. 摇摆，摇动

【例】 The trees were *swaying* gently in the wind. 树在风中轻轻摇曳。

【同】 swing

swear [sweə] *v*. (swore, sworn)宣誓，发誓

【例】 They *swore* an oath to carry out their duties faithfully. 他们发誓要忠实履行自己的职责。

【同】 vow

sweep [swiːp] *v*. (swept, swept)打扫，席卷

【例】 She *swept* the floor clean. 她把地板打扫干净。

【同】 brush, clean

swift [swɪft] *adj*. 迅速的，敏捷的

【例】 They've been very *swift* to deny these rumors. 他们在辟谣方面反应迅速。

【同】 fast, rapid

【反】 slow

swing [swɪŋ] *n*. 秋千，摆动；*v*. (swung, swung)摇摆，回转

【例】 1. The children are playing on the *swings* in the park. 孩子们在公园里荡秋千。

2. This will *swing* public opinions against the government. 这将使公共舆论转而反对政府。

【同】 dangle, sway

【派】 swinging *adj*. 愉快活跃的，多姿多彩的

switch [swɪtʃ] *n*. 开关，转换；*v*. 转换，转变

【例】 1. Polls showed a *switch* to Labour. 民意测验表明形势转而对工党有利。

2. He *switched* the conversation from one subject to another. 他转变话题。

【同】 shift, turn

syllabus [ˈsɪləbəs] *n*. (复数-buses或-bi)课程提纲，大纲

【记】 syl(一起的) + lab(取) + us(名词词尾)→需要一起获取的东西→需要掌握的东西→大纲

【例】 "Hamlet" is on this year's English literature *syllabus*.《哈姆雷特》是本学年英语文学教学大纲中规定的作品。

【同】 program

symbol [ˈsɪmbəl] *n*. 象征，符号

【记】 sym(= syn，一起) + bol(投掷)→和…一起投掷→象征

S

【例】 The dove is the *symbol* of peace. 鸽子是和平的象征。

【同】 sign, representation

【派】 symbolic *adj*. 象征性的，作为象征的

symbolism *n*. 象征作用，象征意义

symbolize *v*. 象征，用符号表现

symbology *n*. 象征学

symmetry [ˈsɪmɪtrɪ] *n*. 对称性，匀称

【记】 sym(一起，同) + metry(-measure，测量，尺寸)→相同的尺寸→对称

【例】 We admired the perfect *symmetry* of the building's design. 我们很欣赏这建筑设计的对称之美。

【同】 balance

【反】 asymmetry

【派】 symmetrical *adj*. 对称的

sympathetic [ˌsɪmpəˈθetɪk] *adj*. 支持的，同情的

【记】 sym(一起的) + path(e)(感觉) + tic(形容词词尾)→有一样的感觉的→同情的

【例】 We asked for her support in the election, but she wasn't *sympathetic*. 我们请求她在选举中给予支持，但她无动于衷。

【同】 pitiful

【派】 sympathize *v*. 同情，共鸣

sympathy *n*. 同情，同情心

symphony [ˈsɪmfənɪ] *n*. 交响乐，交响曲

【记】 sym(一起) + phon(声音) + y(名词词尾)→一同响起→交响乐

【例】 The first movement of the *symphony* is beautiful. 这部交响乐的第一乐章是很优美的。

【派】 symphonic *adj*. 交响乐的

symphonist *n*. 交响乐作曲家

symptom [ˈsɪmptəm] *n*. 症状，征兆

【记】 sym(一起) + ptom(降临)→和(病)一起降临的东西→症状

【例】 The lower production levels are a *symptom* of widespread dissatisfaction among the workforce. 生产水平低下是工人普遍存在不满情绪的征兆。

S

【同】 indication, omen, sign

【派】 symptomatic *adj*. 症状的，征兆的

synchronize [ˈsɪŋkrənaɪz] *v*. 同步，同时发生

【记】 syn(一起) + chron(时间) + ize(动词词尾)→使时间一起→同时发生

【例】 The sound on a film must *synchronize* with the action. 影片中的声音必须与动作配合一致。

【同】 contemporize

【反】 desynchronize

synonym [ˈsɪnənɪm] *n*. 同义字(词)

【记】 syn(一起，同) + nym(= name，名字)→相同的名字→同义词

【例】 Don't mix up this pair of *synonyms*. 别把这两个同义词混淆了。

【反】 antonym

【派】 synonymous *adj*. 同义的

synopsis [sɪ'nɒpsɪs] *n*. (复数-ses)大纲，梗概

【记】 syn(一起)+ops(=opt，看)+is(名词词尾)→一起看的东西→大纲

【例】 This is a *synopsis* of the plot of a movie. 这是一个电影情节的梗概。

【同】 abstract，outline，summary

synthesis ['sɪnθɪsɪs] *n*. (复数-ses)综合物，合成

【记】 syn(一起)+thes(放置)+(s)is(条件)→放在一样的条件下→合成

【例】 Her novels are an odd *synthesis* of English reserve and Welsh emotionalism. 她的小说把英格兰人的拘谨和威尔士人的情感外露很独特地结合在一起。

【反】 analysis

【派】 synthesize *v*. 综合，合成

synthetic *adj*. 合成的，人造的

syrup ['sɪrəp] *n*. 糖浆，果汁

【例】 She dosed up the children with cough *syrup*. 她把止咳糖浆给孩子们吃了。

【同】 sirup

【派】 syrupy *adj*. 糖浆似的，像糖浆的

system ['sɪstəm] *n*. 系统，体系，体制

【记】 sy(s)(=syn，一起)+tem(站立)→站立在一起的→系统

【例】 Do you know how to log in to the *system*? 你知道怎么登录进入这个系统吗?

【同】 arrangement，organisation

【派】 systematic(al) *adj*. 组织性的，系统的

systematize *v*. 使系统化

S

T

tablet [ˈtæblɪt] *n*. 1.碑，牌匾；2.药片

【记】 tabl(e)(工作台) + et(表示"小"的名词词尾)→小而平的东西→牌匾，药片

【例】 1. Her memorial is carved on that stone *tablet* on the wall. 纪念她的铭文刻在墙面上的石牌子上。

2. He explains that it is sold in capsules, *tablets* and mixed with herbs. 他解释说这种混合药草的药物以胶囊、药片的形式出售。

【同】 capsule, pill

taboo [təˈbuː] *n*./*v*. 禁忌，避讳

【例】 There is a *taboo* on smoking in this office. 在这个办公室里一向都是不吸烟的。

【同】 forbid, prohibit

tacit [ˈtæsɪt] *adj*. 心照不宣的，默许的

【记】 tac(安静的) + it(形容词词尾)→安静的→心照不宣的

【例】 It is believed the management and the unions have reached a *tacit* agreement on the matter. 据说资方和工会在这件事上已经达成了默契。

【同】 implied, silent

tackle [ˈtækl] *v*. 处理，解决

【记】 tack(钉) + le(动词词尾)→钉住…→处理，解决

【例】 What's the best way to *tackle* this problem? 什么是解决这个问题的最好方法?

【同】 handle, undertake

tactic [ˈtæktɪk] *n*. (常用复数)战术，策略

【记】 tact(接触) + ic(名词词尾)→和人接触的智慧→战术

【例】 These *tactics* are unlikely to help you. 这种方法对你未必有用。

【同】 strategy, maneuver

【派】 tactical *adj*. 战术的

tactician *n*. 战术家

tag [tæg] *n*. 标签，附属物；*v*. (-gged; -gging) 1.加标签于；2.紧随

【例】 1. Each coat in the store has a *tag* with the price on it. 店里的每一件上衣都有标签标出价格。

2. *Tag* the bottles now or we will forget which one is which. 现在就给这些瓶子贴上标签吧，否则我们就会弄不清哪一个瓶子是那种东西了。

3. If you are going to the cinema, do you mind if I *tag* along with you? 你要是去看电影，我也跟你一起去行吗?

【同】 label; trail

talent [ˈtælənt] *n*. 天才，才干

【例】 What they need most is managerial *talent*. 他们最需要的是管理人才。

【同】 ability, genius

【反】 inability, incapability

【派】 talented *adj*. 有天才的，有才干的

talentless *adj*. 无能的

tally [ˈtælɪ] *n*./*v*. 一致，符合

【记】 tall(= tail, 剪切) + y(名词词尾)→剪切以符合→一致，符合

【例】 1. Don't forget to keep a careful *tally* of what you spend. 别忘了仔细记下你的开支账目。

2. Your figures don't *tally* with mine. 你的数字和我的不符。

【同】 correspond, match

tame [teɪm] *adj*. 温顺的，驯服的

【例】 The pigeons are so *tame* that they will sit on your shoulder. 这些鸽子不怕人，能落在人的肩膀上。

【同】 mild, obedient

【反】 wild

【派】 tameless *adj*. 难驯服的，野性的

tamper [ˈtæmpə] *v*. 干预，篡改

【例】 The records of the meeting had been *tampered* with. 会议记录已被人擅自改动。

【同】 meddle, interfere

tangible [ˈtændʒəbl] *adj*. 可触摸的，确实的

【记】 tang(接触) + ible(形容词词尾)→可以接触到的→确实的

【例】 The police need *tangible* proof of his guilt before they charge him. 警方需要有他犯罪的确凿证据，然后才控告他。

【同】 concrete, touchable

【反】 intangible

tantalize [ˈtæntəlaɪz] *v*. 招惹，挑逗

【记】 tantal(来自 Tantalus，是希腊神话中主神宙斯(Zeus)的儿子。他因泄露天机被罚站于有果树的水中，水深及下巴，口渴想喝水时水即减退，腹饥想吃果实时，树枝即升高，不得饮食。) + ize(动词词尾)→像 Tantalus 一样地被戏弄→挑逗

【例】 He was *tantalized* by visions of power and wealth. 他追求不到可望而不可即的权力和财富，受尽了折磨。

【同】 tease, taunt

【派】 tantalizing *adj*. 非常着急的

tap [tæp] *n*. 1. 轻敲；2. 水龙头；*v*. 1. (-pped; -pping)轻扣，轻拍；2. 开发，利用

【例】 1. Don't leave the *taps* running. 要记得关上水龙头。

2. That girl *tapped* her fingers on the desk impatiently. 那个女孩不耐烦地用手指轻扣桌面。

3. Since man is able to *tap* such resources as oil and metals, why can't he develop and harness other energy resources? 既然人类能利用石油和金属这样的能源，为

什么不能开发和利用其他能源呢?

【同】 knock; faucet; develop, exploit

【派】 tap-dance *n*. 踢踏舞

tap-water *n*. 自来水

untapped *adj*. 未使用的

taper [ˈteɪpə] *v*. 1.逐渐变窄,变细;2.逐渐减少

【记】 tap(带子)+er(表示动作的重复的动词词尾)→把…变成带子→逐渐变窄

【例】 1. She has long *tapering* fingers. 她十指纤纤。

2. Financial aids generally *taper* off after the first year of college. 助学金通常在大学一年级之后逐渐减少。

【同】 narrow, sharpen

tardy [ˈtɑːdɪ] *adj*. 延迟的,缓慢的

【记】 tard(慢)+y(形容词词尾)→缓慢的

【例】 His boss was dissatisfied with his *tardy* progress. 老板对他缓慢的进度不满意。

【同】 belated, late, overdue

target [ˈtɑːgɪt] *n*. 目标; *v*. 以…为目标

【记】 targ(e)(盾牌)+et(表示"小"的名词词尾)→小的盾牌→攻击的目标→目标

【例】 1. The embassy is an obvious *target* for terrorist attacks. 大使馆是恐怖分子攻击的明显目标。

2. Welfare spending is being cut, so it should be *targeted* on the people who need it most. 福利开支正在削减,所以它只应该用于最需要它的那部分人。

【同】 aim, object

tariff [ˈtærɪf] *n*. 关税,进出口货物

【例】 The government will raise the *tariff* barriers against foreign goods. 政府将对进口商品提高关税壁垒。

【同】 duty

tarnish [ˈtɑːnɪʃ] *v*. 1.使失去光泽,使晦暗;2.玷污,败坏

【记】 tarn(=dull,暗的)+ish(动词词尾)→使变暗→使失去光泽

【例】 1. Silver, copper, and brass need to be polished frequently to prevent them from *tarnishing*. 银器、铜器和黄铜器需要经常擦拭才不会失去光泽。

2. The firm's good name was badly *tarnished* by the scandal. 这件丑事玷污了公司的好名声。

T

【同】 discolor, stain

taste [teɪst] *n*. 1.味道,味觉;2.爱好,品味

【例】 1. I've got a cold, so I have lost my sense of *taste*. 我感冒了,尝不出味道。

2. Modern art is not to everyone's *taste*. 现代艺术不见得合所有人的口味。

【同】 savor; sense

【反】 distaste

【派】 tasteful *adj*. 有鉴赏力的

tasty *adj*. 美味的,可口的

taxation [tækˈseɪʃən] *n*. 征税,纳税

【记】 tax(税)+ation(名词词尾)→征税

【例】 The government obtains revenue through direct *taxation* and indirect *taxation*. 政府通过直接征税和间接征税而获得岁入。

【同】 revenue

【派】 (逆构)tax *n*. 收税，税款；*v*. 对…征税

tease [tiːz] *v*. /*n*. 戏弄，嘲笑

【例】 At school, the other children always *teased* me because I was fat. 在学校，其他的孩子总是取笑我，因为我长得胖。

【同】 joke, mock

【派】 teasy *adj*. 爱戏弄人的，令人恼火的

technique [tek'niːk] *n*. 技术，工艺

【记】 techn(技术，技艺)+ique(名词词尾)→技术，工艺

【例】 He displayed a flawless *technique* in the competition. 他在竞赛中显示出了精湛的技艺。

【同】 technics

tedious ['tiːdɪəs] *adj*. 单调乏味的，沉闷的

【记】 ted(厌倦)+ious(形容词词尾)→令人厌倦的→乏味的，沉闷的

【例】 We had to sit through several *tedious* speeches. 我们只得坐在那里听着几个乏味的讲演。

【同】 tiresome, boring

【反】 exciting, interesting

【派】 tedium *n*. 厌倦，乏味

teenager ['tiːnˌeɪdʒə] *n*. (13岁到19岁的)青少年

【记】 teen ag(e)(十几岁的)+er(表示"人"的名词词尾)→十几岁的人→少年

【例】 It is not easy to educate *teenagers*. 教育青少年不是件容易的事。

【同】 adolescent

【反】 adult

【派】 (逆构)teenage *adj*. 十几岁的

telecommunication ['telɪkəmjuːnɪ'keɪʃən] *n*. 无线电通讯，电信学

【记】 tele(遥远的)+communicat(e)(交流)+ion(名词词尾)→从远处交流→电子通讯

【例】 We've looked in general at the *telecommunication* market in the UK over the last few sessions. 在过去的几个会议里，我们从总体上了解了英国的电讯市场。

telescope ['telɪskəʊp] *n*. 望远镜

【记】 tele(遥远的)+scope(看)→从远处看→望远镜

【例】 I saw them through *telescopes* from the top of the building. 我从大楼的顶端用望远镜看到了他们。

【派】 telescopic *adj*. 远视的，伸缩的

temper ['tempə] *n*. 1. 性情，脾气；2. 韧性，硬度；*v*. 变坚韧，变硬

【例】 1. It is generally believed that *tempers* grow shorter in hot, muggy weather. 人们普遍认为在闷热、潮湿的天气里人的脾气会变得比平常急躁。

2. Steel is *tempered* by heating it and then putting it into cold water. 钢是通过加

热再放进冷水里回火炼成的。

【同】 feeling，mood；toughness

【派】 temperament *n*. 气质，性情

bad-tempered *adj*. 坏脾气的

good-tempered *adj*. 好脾气的

temperate ['tempərɪt] *adj*. 1.有节制的，适度的；2.温带的，温和的

【记】 temper(调节)+ate(形容词词尾)→进行调节的→有节制的

【例】 1.Please be more *temperate* in your language. 在言语上请再克制一些。

2.Ninety per cent of the country lies in the *temperate* zone. 这个国家90%的地方都是温带。

【同】 moderate，mild

【反】 intemperate

【派】 temperance *n*. 节制，自制；戒酒；禁酒

temperature *n*. 温度

tempo ['tempəʊ] *n*. (复数-pos或-pi)(音乐的)速度，拍子

【记】 temp(时间)+o(…的状态)→按时间快慢→速度，节拍

【例】 Your *tempo* is too slow. 你演奏的速度太慢了。

【同】 pace

temporary ['tempərərɪ] *adj*. 暂时的，临时的

【记】 tempor(时间)+(a)ry(形容词词尾)→时间不长的→暂时的

【例】 Students often find *temporary* jobs during their summer holidays. 学生们常常在暑假做临时工。

【同】 impermanent，temporal

【反】 permanent

【派】 temporarily *adv*. 暂时地，临时地

tempt [tempt] *v*. 吸引，诱惑

【例】 They tried to *tempt* her into staying with offers of promotion. 他们提出给她晋级来劝说她留下。

【同】 lure，seduce

【派】 temptation *n*. 诱惑，诱惑物

temping *adj*. 诱惑人的

T

tenable ['tenəbl] *adj*. 合理的，可维持的

【记】 ten(保持)+able(形容词词尾)→可以保持的→合理的

【例】 The view that the earth is flat is no longer *tenable*. 认为地球是平的这一观点站不住脚了。

【同】 reasonable

【派】 tenability *n*. 可保持的状态

tenant ['tenənt] *n*. 承租人，房客

【记】 ten(保持)+ant(名词词尾，…的人)→保持房子的人→房客

【例】 Do you own your house or are you a *tenant*? 你的房子是自己的还是租的？

【同】 resident，renter

【反】 landlord

【派】 tenancy *n*. 租佃，租赁

tend [tend] *v*. 1.倾向于；2.照看，照料

【例】 1. Women *tend* to live longer than men. 女人多比男人长寿。

2. She *tended* her husband lovingly during his long illness. 在丈夫长期卧病期间，她一直温柔体贴地服侍他。

【同】 incline；attend

【反】 disincline

【派】 tendency *n*. 趋势，倾向

tendentious *adj*. 有倾向的，有偏见的

tender [ˈtendə] *adj*. 脆弱的，温柔的；*v*. 正式提供或提出某事

【记】 tend(张开)+er(形容词词尾)→易于伸展的→温柔的

【例】 1. He recovered soon under his wife's *tender* loving care. 在妻子体贴入微的关怀下，他很快就痊愈了。

2. He *tendered* his resignation to the Prime Minister. 他向首相递了辞呈。

【同】 gentle，sensitive；offer

【反】 cruel，tough

【派】 tender-hearted *adj*. 心肠软的，慈善的

tense [tens] *adj*. 紧张的，拉紧的

【记】 tens(张开)+e→张开的→变为紧张

【例】 It is difficult to be natural when one is *tense*. 人在紧张的时候很难泰然自若。

【同】 strained，tight

【反】 flabby，loose

【派】 tension *n*. 紧张，不安

tensile [ˈtensaɪl] *adj*. 可拉长的，拉力的

【记】 tens(张开)+ile(形容词词尾)→能够张开的→可拉长的

【例】 The *tensile* strength of a rope is the amount of weight it can hold without breaking. 一根绳子的抗张强度是它在不会断裂的限度内所能承受的重量。

【同】 ductile，tractile

【派】 tensility *n*. 伸力，伸长性

tentative [ˈtentətɪv] *adj*. 试验性的，尝试的

【记】 tent(尝试)+ative(形容词词尾)→进行尝试的→试验性的

【例】 We have made *tentative* plans for a holiday but haven't dedcided anything certain yet. 我们已经考虑了好几个度假的初步计划，但是还没有做出任何决定。

【同】 experimental，temporary

【反】 final

【派】 tentation *n*. 假设，试验

term [təːm] *n*. 1.学期，期限；2.专门名词，术语；3.条款

【例】 1. Are there any exams at the end of this *term*? 这个学期期末有考试吗？

2. The generic *term* for wine，spirits and beer is alcoholic beverages. 葡萄酒、烈性酒、啤酒的通称是酒类饮料。

3. The *terms* of the treaty were clear. 条约的条款明白无误。

【同】 semaster, period; terminology

terminate ['tɜːmɪneɪt] *v*. 停止，终结

【记】 term(边界) + in + nate(动词词尾)→到达边界→终结

【例】 The meeting *terminated* in disorder. 会议在混乱中结束。

【同】 conclude, end

【反】 begin, commence

【派】 terminal *n*. 终点站，终端；*adj*. 末期，每期的

termination *n*. 终止

terminus *n*. 火车、汽车的终点站

terrace ['terɪs] *n*. 梯田，平台

【记】 terr(土地) + (a)ce(名词词尾)→高而平坦的地方→梯田，平台

【例】 In China hill farmers grow rice on *terraces*. 在中国，山区农民在梯田上种水稻。

terrain [tə'reɪn] *n*. 地带，地形

【记】 terr(土地) + ain(名词词尾)→地的形态→地形

【例】 A jeep is ideal for driving over rough *terrain*. 吉普车很适合在高低不平的路面上行驶。

terrestrial [tɪ'restrɪəl] *adj*. 陆地的，陆生的

【记】 terr(土地) + estr(东西) + ial(形容词词尾)→在土地上的→陆地的

【例】 Although they can swim, the polar bears are *terrestrial* animals. 北极熊虽然会游泳，但也是陆栖动物。

【同】 mundane

【反】 celestial

terrify ['terɪfaɪ] *v*. 使害怕，使恐惧

【记】 terr(惊吓) + ify(表示"做"的动词词尾)→使…受到惊吓→使害怕

【例】 The little girl was *terrified* out of her wits. 这个小女孩吓得魂不附体。

【同】 frighten, horrify

【派】 terrific *adj*. 令人恐怖的；(口语)棒极了

terrified *adj*. 恐惧的，受惊吓的

territory ['terɪtərɪ] *n*. 领土，版图

【记】 terr(土地) + itory(场所，范围)→在地面上的范围→领土

T 【例】 Our representatives travel over a large *territory*. 我们的推销员活动地区很广。

【同】 land, realm

【派】 territorial *adj*. 领土的

territorialism *n*. 地方主义

terror ['terə] *n*. 害怕，恐怖

【记】 terr(使惊吓) + or(名词词尾)→使…被惊吓→恐怖

【例】 The people ran from the enemy in *terror*. 人们惊恐的躲避着敌人。

【同】 fear, horror

【派】 terrorism *n*. 恐怖主义，恐怖行动

terroristic *adj*. 恐怖主义的

tertiary [ˈtɜːʃərɪ] *adj*. 第三的，第三等的

【记】 tertia(=拉丁语 tertius，第三) + ry(名词词尾)→第三的

【例】 It will help the *tertiary* industry of Hongkong to enter the mainland market. 这将帮助发展香港的第三产业进入内地市场。

testify [ˈtestɪfaɪ] *v*. (to)证明，证实

【记】 test(证据) + ify(表示"做"的动词词尾)→作证→证明

【例】 Two witnesses *testified* against her and one in her favor. 有两个证人的证词对她不利，而另一个人的对她有利。

【同】 prove, verify

【派】 testifier *n*. 证人，证明者

testimony *n*. 证明，证言

textile [ˈtekstaɪl] *n*. 纺织品

【记】 text(编织) + ile(…的东西)→编织出来的东西→纺织品

【例】 Their main exports are *textiles*, especially silk and cotton. 他们的主要出口货物是纺织品，特别是丝绸和棉布。

【同】 cloth, fabric

texture [ˈtekstʃə] *n*. 质地，肌理，结构

【记】 text(编织) + ure(名词词尾)→编织的结构→质地

【例】 This kind of cloth has a close *texture*. 这种布质地很紧密。

【同】 composition, structure

【派】 textural *adj*. 组织上，构造上

textured adj 质地粗糙的，有织纹的

theme [θiːm] *n*. 题目，主题

【例】 The *theme* of our discussion was 'Europe in the 1980s'. 我们讨论的主题是"20 世纪 80 年代的欧洲"。

【同】 subject

【派】 thematic *adj*. 主题的，论题的

theoretical [θɪəˈretɪkəl] *adj*. 理论上的，纯理论的

【记】 theor(e)(理论) + tical(形容词词尾)→关于理论的→理论上的

【例】 This book is too *theoretical*; I need a practical one. 这本书理论性太强，我需要一本实用的。

【同】 abstract, theoretic

【反】 empirical

【派】 (逆构)theory *n*. 理论，原理

theorist *n*. 理论家

therapy [ˈθerəpɪ] *n*. 治疗，疗法

【记】 therap(服务) + y(名词词尾)→为…服务的→治疗

【例】 Self-help is an important element in *therapy* for the handicapped. 伤残人士在治疗中，自助自立是个重要因素。

【同】 treatment

【派】 therapist *n*. 治疗专家

T

therapeutic *adj*. 治疗的，治疗学的

therefore [ˈðeəfɔː] *adv*. 因此，所以

【例】 We have a growing population and *therefore* we need more food. 我们的人口在增长，因此我们需要更多的食物。

【同】 hence, consequently

thermal [ˈθɜːməl] *adj*. 热的，热量的

【记】 therm(热) + al(形容词词尾)→热的，热量的

【例】 It is a kind of *thermal* insulation designed to prevent the loss of body heat. 这是一种为防止身体热量散失而设计的热绝缘材料。

【同】 caloric, thermic

【派】 thermometer *n*. 温度计

thermostat *n*. (建筑物、烤箱中的)恒温器

thesis [ˈθiːsɪs] *n*. (复数-ses)论题，论文

【记】 thes(放置) + (s)is(名词词尾)→把意见放进去→论文

【例】 He is writing his doctoral *thesis*. 他正在写博士论文。

【同】 dissertation, topic

thief [θiːf] *n*. (复数 thieves)小偷，贼

【例】 The *thief* slipped away down a side street. 小偷悄悄从一条小马路溜走了。

【同】 pilferer

【派】 thievery *n*. 偷窃

theft *n*. 偷，行窃，偷窃行为

thigh [θaɪ] *n*. 大腿，股

【例】 I walked the last six miles in water up to my *thighs*. 我在深及大腿的水中走完了最后 6 英里。

thorough [ˈθʌrə] *adj*. 彻底的，详尽的

【例】 They've promised a *thorough* inquiry into the plane crash. 他们答应对这次飞机失事进行彻底的调查。

【同】 complete, exhaustive

【派】 thoroughgoing *adj*. 全面的，细致的

thread [θred] *n*. 线，线状物；*v*. 将线穿过

【例】 1. He passed me a coil of *thread*. 他递给我一卷线。

2. The little girl *threaded* the shells together and wore them round her neck. 小女孩把贝壳穿成一串，戴在脖子上。

【同】 string

【派】 threadlike *adj*. 线状的

threadbare *adj*. 磨薄的，磨旧的

threaten [ˈθretn] *v*. 威胁，恐吓

【记】 threat(威胁) + en(动词词尾)→威胁

【例】 The strikers were *threatened* with dismissal if they did not return to work. 罢工者受到威胁说，如果他们不复工，就会被解雇。

【同】 menace, peril

【派】 threat *n*. 恐吓，威胁

threatening *adj*. 胁迫的，危险的

threshold [ˈθreʃhəʊld] *n*. 1.门槛，起点；2.极限

【记】 thresh(捶打谷子等脱粒)+old(旧的)→被捶打得很旧的→被践踏的→门槛

【例】 1. He was on the *threshold* of his career. 他的事业刚刚起步。

2. As you all know, the normal noise *threshold* for private housing is 55 decibels. 大家都知道，私人住宅能接受的正常的噪音极限是55分贝。

【同】 doorway, gateway

thrift [θrɪft] *n*. 节俭，节约

【记】 thrif(繁荣)+t(名词词尾)→繁荣的根本→节俭

【例】 To practice *thrift* is a virtue. 节俭是美德。

【同】 saving, austerity

【反】 waste

【派】 thriftless *adj*. 浪费的，无价值的

thrifty *adj*. 节约的

thrill [θrɪl] *n*./*v*. 发抖，激动

【例】 She was *thrilled* when the handsome filmstar kissed her. 当那位英俊的电影明星吻她的时候，她欣喜若狂。

【同】 excite, shiver

【派】 thrilling *adj*. 毛骨悚然的，使人感动的；

thrive [θraɪv] *v*. (-ed, -ed 或 throve, thriven)兴旺，茁壮成长

【例】 A business cannot *thrive* without good management. 没有良好的经营管理，事业就不会兴旺发达。

【同】 flourish, prosper

【反】 decline

throng [θrɒŋ] *n*. 群，人群；*v*. 蜂拥，群集

【例】 1. A patient *throng* was waiting in silence. 一大群人耐心地静候着。

2. Passengers *thronged* the station waiting for their trains. 乘客们拥挤在车站里等候火车。

【同】 crowd, gather

thunder [ˈθʌndə] *n*. 雷声，隆隆声；*v*. 打雷

【例】 The train *thundered* through the station. 火车隆隆地驶过车站。

【派】 thunderous *adj*. 打雷的，声音极大的

thundershower *n*. 雷阵雨

tide [taɪd] *n*. 潮，潮汐；2.潮流，趋势

【例】 1. A crab was left stranded on the beach when the *tide* ebbed. 退潮时，一只蟹被困留在沙滩上。

2. The *tide* of public opinion seems to be turning against the government. 公众舆论的趋向看来是转向不利于政府的方向。

【同】 surge

tighten [ˈtaɪtən] *v*. 变紧，拉紧

【记】 tight(紧的)+en(动词词尾)→使…变紧→拉紧

【例】 Will you *tighten* this screw; it's very loose. 你把这个螺丝拧紧好吗，它太松了。

【同】 fasten

【反】 loosen

【派】 (逆构)tight *adj*. 紧的，紧密的

tilt [tɪlt] *v*. (使)倾斜，翘起

【例】 The table top suddenly *tilted* and all the plates and glasses crashed onto the floor. 桌面突然翘起，所有的杯盘全部滑落在地板上打碎了。

【同】 incline, lean

【派】 tilted *adj*. 倾斜的，翘起的

timber [ˈtɪmbə] *n*. 木材，木料

【例】 We must safeguard forest *timber*. 我们必须保护森林。

【同】 lumber, wood

【派】 timbering *n*. 木材，建筑用材

timid [ˈtɪmɪd] *adj*. 胆小的，羞怯的

【记】 tim(害怕)+id(形容词词尾)→容易害怕的→胆小的

【例】 These problems call for bold, not *timid*, responses. 这些问题需要勇敢而不是怯懦去面对。

【同】 afraid, shy

【反】 bold, courageous

【派】 timidity *n*. 胆怯

tint [tɪnt] *v*. 给…着色，染

【例】 The sunset has *tinted* the sky with pink. 落日把天空染成了粉红色。

【同】 color, dye

tip [tɪp] *n*. 1. 顶，尖端；2. 小费；3. 秘密消息，建议；*v*. (-pped; -pping)置于顶端

【例】 1. The dinners gave bigger *tips* when the sun was shining and smaller *tips* when it wasn't. 阳光灿烂的时候，就餐的客人给很多小费，相反就给较少的小费。

2. This manual is full of useful *tips*. 这本小册子里有很多实用的小建议。

3. The legs of the table were *tipped* with rubber. 桌子腿上装上了橡皮头。

【同】 top, point; money; suggestion

tissue [ˈtɪsjuː] *n*. 1. 薄纱，薄纸；2. 组织

【记】 tis(s)(编织)+ue→编织出来的东西→组织

【例】 1. She used paper *tissues* to blow her nose. 她用棉纸擤鼻子。

2. The *tissues* have been destroyed and a scar has formed. 那些组织受到破坏，形成一道疤痕。

titanic [taɪˈtænɪk] *adj*. 巨大的

【记】 titan(希腊神话中的巨人)+ic(形容词词尾)→像巨人一样的→巨大的

【例】 *Titanic* waves beat aginst the shore during the hurricane. 飓风到来的时候，巨浪敲击着海岸。

【同】 large, huge

title [ˈtaɪtl] *n*. 1. 头衔，标题；2. 冠军；*v*. 加标题于，(电视或电影的)附加字幕

【例】 1. The *title* just won't come to mind. 那个标题就是想不起来。

2. They're fighting for the world *title* tonight. 他们今晚争夺世界冠军。

3, What will you *title* your book? 你给你的书起什么书名?

【同】 caption, headline; championship; entitle

【反】 deprive

【派】 titled *adj*. 有头衔的，有官衔的

title-holder *n*. 冠军

toast [təust] *n*./*v*. 1. 烤面包; 2. 干杯

【例】 1. He spread some strawberry jam on his *toast*. 他把草莓酱涂在烤面包片上。

2. Ladies and gentlemen, I'd like to propose a *toast* to the bride and bridegroom. 女士们，先生们，我提议为新娘和新郎干杯。

【同】 bake; drink

【派】 toaster *n*. 举杯祝贺者

toasty *adj*. 祝酒的

toe [təʊ] *n*. 趾，脚趾，足尖

【例】 He was wet from top to *toe*. 他从头到脚都湿透了。

【同】 digit

toil [tɔɪl] *n*./*v*. 苦干，辛勤劳动

【例】 The slaves *toiled* up the hill pulling the heavy blocks. 那些奴隶艰难地把沉重的石块拖上山。

【同】 work, labour

【反】 rest

【派】 toiler *n*. 辛苦工作的人

toilful *adj*. 费力的，辛苦的

token ['təukən] *n*./*adj*. 象征(的)，记号(的)

【例】 My husband gave me a ring as a *token* of our first meeting. 我的丈夫送我一枚戒指，以纪念我们的初次见面。

【同】 sign, mark

tolerate ['tɒləreɪt] *v*. 忍受，容忍

【记】 toler(容忍) + ate(动词词尾)→忍受

【例】 I won't *tolerate* your bad manners any longer. 我再也不能忍受你那种恶劣的态度了。

【同】 bear, endure, stand

【派】 tolerable *adj*. 可容忍的

tolerant *adj*. 容忍的，宽容的

tolerance *n*. 宽容，忍受

toll [təul] *n*. 1. 通行税，费; 2. 代价，损失; *v*. 1. 征收; 2. 敲钟

【例】 1. Electronically *tolled* highways might be used to ensure that drivers pay charges geared to actual road use. 电子收费的公路可以用来确定司机交的费用和实际走过的里程相符。

2. The government tried to keep the death *toll* at a lower level. 政府力图将死亡人

数控制在较低标准。

3. The church bell *tolled* the hour. 教堂鸣钟报时。

【同】 charge, fare, fee

【派】 tollbooth *n*. 收费亭，收费处

tone [təʊn] *n*. 音调，语调

【记】 ton(音调) + e→语调，音质

【例】 The speaker urged us in rising *tones* to support his cause. 演讲者以激昂的语气要求我们支持他的事业。

【同】 intonation, sound

【派】 toneless *adj*. 缺乏声调的，沉闷的

tongue [tʌŋ] *n*. 1. 舌头；2. 语言，方言

【例】 1. Their scandalous affair has really set *tongues* wagging. 他们的风流事可招来了不少闲话。

2. English is her mother *tongue*. 英语是她的母语。

【同】 language, speech

topography [təˈpɒgrəfɪ] *n*. 地形(学)，地势

【记】 topo(地方) + graph(书写) + y(名词词尾)→对地点的描述→地形学，地势

【例】 Eruptions have rifted continents, raised mountain chains, constructed islands and shaped the *topography* of the earth. 火山爆发使大陆断裂，使山脉长高，使小岛形成，使地貌定型。

【同】 terrain

【派】 topographer *n*. 地形学者

topographic *adj*. 地形学的

torment [ˈtɔːment] *n*./*v*. 痛苦，折磨

【记】 tor(= tort, 扭曲) + ment(名词词尾)→使扭曲→折磨

【例】 1. That child is a *torment* to his parents. 这孩子对他的父母是一种折磨。

2. She *torments* everyone with silly questions. 她用无聊的问题来烦扰大家。

【同】 agony, pain, torture

【反】 comfort

torpid [ˈtɔːpɪd] *adj*. 懒散的，死气沉沉的，不活泼的

【记】 torp(麻木) + id(形容词词尾)→麻木的→迟钝的

【例】 The heat and humidity made us *topid*. 炎热和潮湿的天气使我们感到浑身无力。

【同】 sluggish

【派】 torpidity *n*. 麻痹

torpor *n*. 迟钝，不活泼

torrent [ˈtɒrənt] *n*. 急流，洪流

【记】 tor(r)(沸腾) + ent(名词词尾)→像沸腾了一样的东西→急流

【例】 A *torrent* of water swept down the valley. 急流自山谷奔腾而下。

【同】 deluge, flood

【派】 torrential *adj*. 奔流的

torture [ˈtɔːtʃə] *n*./*v*. 折磨，拷问

【记】 tor(t)(扭曲)+ture(名词词尾)→使人处于扭曲的状态→折磨

【例】 The people accused the regime of *torturing* its political opponents. 人民谴责该政权迫害政敌。

【同】 distress, torment

【反】 comfort

【派】 torturous *adj*. 拷问的，痛苦的

tough [tʌf] *adj*. 硬的，艰苦的

【例】 We won the contract, but only through a lot of *tough* negotiating. 我们赢得了合同，但是却经过了多次不屈不挠的谈判才达到目的。

【同】 hardy, strong

【反】 tender, weak

【派】 toughen *v*. (使)变坚韧，变顽固

toughminded *adj*. 意志坚强的

tournament [ˈtʊənəmənt] *n*. 锦标赛，联赛

【记】 tour(n)(转动)+a+ment(名词词尾)→马儿转动方向→(中世纪)马上比试大会→锦标赛

【例】 The *tournament* is open to amateurs as well as professionals. 这次比赛不仅职业运动员可以参加，而且业余运动员也可以参加。

【同】 contest, championship

tow [təʊ] *v*. 拖引，牵引

【例】 We have to *tow* that car to the nearest garage. 我们不得不把汽车拖到最近的修车厂。

【同】 drag, draw, haul, pull

toxic [ˈtɒksɪk] *adj*. 有毒的，中毒的

【记】 tox(毒)+ic(形容词词尾)→有毒的

【例】 The factory has been sending out *toxic* wastes. 这家工厂一直在排放有毒的废物。

【同】 poisonous, venomous

【派】 toxicity *n*. 毒性

trace [treɪs] *v*. 追溯，追踪；*n*. 1.踪迹，痕迹；2.微量，少许

【记】 trac(拉拽)+e→托拽出来的痕迹→踪迹

【例】 1. The family can *trace* its history to the 17th century. 这个家族的历史可以追溯到17世纪。

2. Did the police find any *trace* of the murderer? 警方发现凶手的行踪了吗？

3. They found *traces* of poison in the dead man's blood. 他们发现死者的血液里有微量的毒素。

【同】 track; bit

track [træk] *n*. 轨迹，足迹；*v*. 追踪

【记】 trac(拉拽)+k→东西拽过留下的痕迹→轨迹，足迹

【例】 1. We reached the temple through an unfrequented mountain *track*. 我们沿着一条人迹罕至的小径到达了寺庙。

2. They *tracked* the criminal to his hiding-place. 他们跟踪那名罪犯直到他的藏身

T

之处。

【同】 trail，trace

【派】 tracker *n*. 追踪者，追踪系统

tractable [ˈtræktəbl] *adj*. 1. 易处理的，易加工的；2. 温顺的，易于驾驭的

【记】 trac(t)(拉拽)＋able(形容词词尾)→容易拉拽的→易处理的

【例】 1. Gold and silver are *tractable* metals. 金和银是容易加工的金属。

2. He is a *tractable* boy. 他是个听话的孩子。

【同】 manipulable；obedient，docile

【反】 intractable

tradition [trəˈdɪʃən] *n*. 传统，惯例

【记】 tra(对面)＋dit(给予)＋ion(名词词尾)→给予对面→往下传→传统

【例】 It is a *tradition* that the young look after the old in their family. 在他们家，年轻的照顾年长的是一个传统。

【同】 custom，convention

【派】 traditional *adj*. 传统的

traditionist *n*. 传统主义者

tragic [ˈtrædʒɪk] *adj*. 悲惨的，可悲的

【例】 Her *tragic* story touched us all deeply. 她的经历很悲惨，我们都深受感动。

【同】 catastrophic，disastrous

【反】 comic

【派】 tragedy *n*. 悲剧，惨案

tragicomic *adj*. 悲喜剧的

trail [treɪl] *n*. 踪迹，痕迹；*v*. 跟踪，追踪

【记】 tra(c)(拉拽)＋il→拖出来的痕迹→踪迹

【例】 1. The wounded animal left a *trail* of blood behind it. 受伤的动物在身后留下一道血迹。

2. The dog *trailed* him constantly. 这条狗总跟在他的后面。

【同】 trace，track

【派】 trail-car *n*. 拖车

trait [treɪt] *n*. 特征，特性

【记】 tra(c)(拉拽)＋it(行走)→被…拉着走的→特别的东西→特征

【例】 Anne's generosity is one of her most pleasing *traits*. 安妮的为人慷慨是她最受人喜欢的个性之一。

【同】 characteristic，feature

tramp [træmp] *v*. 重步走，踏

【例】 Who's been *tramping* all over this carpet in muddy shoes? 谁穿着带泥的鞋子在地毯上到处踩？

【同】 walk

【派】 tramper *n*. 流浪者

trample [ˈtræmpl] *v*. 踩踏，蹂躏

【记】 tramp(重步走)＋le(动词词尾，表示动作的重复)→一直重步走→践踏

T

【例】 Don't *trample* on the grass. 请勿践踏草地。

【同】 tramp, tread

tranquil [ˈtræŋkwɪl] *adj*. 安静的

【记】 trans(在…之上)+quil(休息)→静止于其上的→安静的

【例】 He leads a *tranquil* life in the country. 他在乡间过着宁静的生活。

【同】 calm, quiet

【反】 noisy

【派】 tranquility *n*. 宁静

transaction [trænˈzækʃən] *n*. 交易，处理

【记】 trans(穿越)+act(推进)+ion(名词词尾)→不断推进事物→交易，处理

【例】 They told me the compute system was temporarily down, so they couldn't do any *transactions*. 他们告诉我说计算机系统暂时坏了，所以他们不能做任何交易。

【同】 dealing

【派】 (逆构)transact *v*. 办理，交易
transactor *n*. 处理者，办理人

transcend [trænˈsend] *v*. 超越，胜过

【记】 tran(s)(在…之上)+scend(攀登)→向上攀登→超越

【例】 Such matters *transcend* man's knowledge. 这些问题人类是无法了解的。

【同】 exceed, surpass

【派】 transcendence *n*. 卓越，出类拔萃
transcendent *adj*. 卓越的，出众的
transcendental *adj*. 先验的，超越的
transcendentalism *n*. 先验论，超验主义

transcribe [trænsˈkraɪb] *v*. 抄写，誊写

【记】 tran(s)(转移)+scribe(写)→写在其它地方→抄写

【例】 She jotted down a few notes, and later *transcribed* them into an exercise book. 她草草做了些笔记，然后誊写在练习本上。

【同】 rewrite

【派】 transcript *n*. 手稿，抄本，(根据录音的)文字记录
transcription *n*. 抄写，抄本

transfer [ˈtrænsfɜː] *n*. / *v*. (-rred; -rring)移动，迁移

【记】 trans(转移)+fer(搬运)→搬运到其它地方→迁移

【例】 His employer *transferred* him to another office. 老板把他调到了另一个办公室。

【同】 move, shift

【派】 transferable *adj*. 可转移的，可转换的
transference *n*. 移动，转让

transfix [trænsˈfɪks] *v*. 1. 刺穿；2. 使吓呆，使发愣

【记】 trans(穿过)+fix(固定)→穿过…而固定→刺穿

【例】 1. The fox was *transfixed* by an arrow. 那只狐狸被箭射穿。
2. She stood *transfixed* with horror. 她吓呆了。

【同】 pierce, empale

transform [træns'fɔːm] *v*. 转换，改变

【记】 trans(转移)+form(形式)→改变形式→转换

【例】 Success and wealth *transformed* his character. 成功和财富改变了他的性格。

【同】 convert，transmute

【反】 retain

【派】 transformable *adj*. 可以变化的

transformation *n*. 变化，转化

transient ['trænzɪənt] *adj*. 短暂的，暂时的

【记】 trans(转移)+i(t)(行走)+ent(形容词词尾)→很快就走的→暂时的

【例】 Her feeling of depression was *transient*. 她那抑郁的心情一会儿就过去了。

【同】 momentary，temporary

【反】 permanent，eternal

【派】 transiency *n*. 顷刻，无常

transitory *adj*. 短暂的

transit ['trænzɪt] *n*. 经过，通行，运输

【记】 tran(s)(穿过)+it(走)→走着穿过→经过

【例】 It is unrealistic to expect people to give up private cars in favor of mass *transit*. 寄希望于人们放弃私家车而热爱公共交通工具是不切实际的。

【派】 transition *n*. 转变，过渡

transmit [trænz'mɪt] *v*. (-tted；-tting)传输，传达

【记】 trans(穿过)+mit(发送)→使穿过…而发送→传输

【例】 After about 300 hours of training they are generally sufficiently fluent to *transmit* the language to the next generation. 经过300个小时的培训，他们基本上能说一口流利的当地语，足以把这种语言传给下一代。

【同】 carry，convey

【派】 transmission *n*. 发射，传输

transmitter *n*. 传送者，发射台

transparent [træns'peərənt] *adj*. 1.透明的；2.显然的，明晰的

【记】 trans(穿过)+parent(出现)→穿过…而出现→透明的

【例】 1. Plain glass is *transparent*. 普通的白玻璃是透明的。

2. The meaning of this passage seems quite *transparent*. 这一段的意思看来是相当清楚的。

【同】 clear，obvious

【派】 transparency *n*. 透明，透明度

transpire [træns'paɪə] *v*. 1.泄露；2.发生；3.发散，排出

【记】 trans(通过)+spire(呼吸)→通过…呼吸→发散，排出

【例】 1. It later *transpired* that he hadn't been telling the truth. 他当时没有说真话，这在后来显露出来了。

2. What *transpired* later next is not known exactly. 接下来发生了什么并不十分清楚。

【同】 disclose；happen；exude

【派】 transpiration *n*. 蒸发(物)，散发；泄露秘密，透露

transplant ['trænsplɑːnt] *n*./[træns'plɑːnt] *v*. 移居，移植

【记】 trans(转移) + plant(种植)→换一个地方种植→移植

【例】 1. He hated being trasplanted from his home in the country to the noise and bustle of life in the city. 他很不喜欢从乡间的居所迁居到了喧闹的城市里。

2. She had a bone-marrow *transplant*. 她接受了骨髓移植手术。

【同】 reset，shift，transfer

【派】 transplantate *n*. 移植器官

transplantation *n*. 迁移，移植

transport [træns'pɔːt] *v*. /*n*. 运输，运送

【记】 trans(穿过) + port(搬运)→搬着穿过→运输

【例】 1. The goods were *transported* by train. 货物是用火车来运输的。

2. The *transport* of goods by air is very expensive. 空运货物费用十分昂贵。

【同】 carry，transfer

【派】 transportation *n*. 运输，运送

trap [træp] *n*. 圈套，诡计；*v*. (-pped；-pping)诱捕，设陷阱

【例】 1. The police set a *trap* to catch the thief. 警察设下了捉拿窃贼的圈套。

2. By clever questioning they *trapped* him into making a confession. 他们用巧妙的提问诱使他招认了。

【同】 catch，trick

trash [træʃ] *n*. 无价值之物，垃圾

【例】 Sue was troubled to see *trash* everywhere. 苏看到到处是垃圾很苦恼。

【同】 junk，rubbish

【派】 trashery *n*. 废物，垃圾

trashman *n*. 垃圾清理工

tray [treɪ] *n*. 碟子，盘子

【例】 He put the toast on the breakfast *tray*. 他把烤面包片放到早餐托盘里。

【派】 trayful *n*. 满盘，一盘之量

treason ['triːzn] *n*. 叛逆，叛国

【记】 treas(= trad，传递) + on(名词词尾)→把(秘密)传递出去→叛国

【例】 He was executed for *treason*. 他因叛国罪已处死。

【同】 betrayal

【派】 treasonable *adj*. 背叛的，叛国的

treasure ['treʒə] *n*. 财富，珍品；*v*. 珍爱，珍藏

【记】 treas(储藏) + ure(名词词尾)→储藏起来的东西→财富

【例】 1. This museum has many art *treasures*. 这家博物馆收藏了许多艺术珍品。

2. Such a lesson should be *treasured* in our memories. 这样的宝贵教训应该铭记在心。

【同】 forturn，wealth；cherish

【派】 treasury *n*. 宝藏，宝库；[ðreasʊry]英国财政部

treasurer *n*. 财务员，出纳员

T

treatise ['triːtɪz] *n*. 论文，论述

【记】 treat(处理，研究) + (i)se(动词词尾转用作名词)→研究的成果→论文

【例】 The professor asked him to write a *treatise* on the subject. 教授要求他就这个课题写篇论文。

【同】 thesis，dissertation

treaty ['triːtɪ] *n*. 条约，谈判

【记】 treat(处理) + y(名词词尾)→处理的结果→条约，谈判

【例】 The conference drew up the terms of the peace *treaty*. 大会草拟了和平条约的条款。

【同】 agreement，convention

tremble ['trembl] *n*./*v*. 战栗，颤抖

【例】 The bridge *trembled* as the train sped across it. 火车过桥时速度很快，震得桥身直颤。

【同】 quiver，shake

tremendous [trɪ'mendəs] *adj*. 巨大的，极大的

【记】 trem(颤抖) + en + (d)ous(形容词词尾)→让人颤抖的→巨大的

【例】 There are *tremendous* advantages to involving parents or guardians in the program. 让家长和监护人参与到项目中来会带来巨大的好处。

【同】 huge，enormous

【反】 small，minute

【派】 tremendously *adv*. 可怕地，非常地

trenchant ['trentʃənt] *adj*. 一针见血的，精辟的

【记】 trench(切割) + ant(形容词词尾)→被切割看得很清楚→精辟的

【例】 He made a hard hitting speech with some *trenchant* comments about the government's failures. 他作了一次用词激烈的演讲，对政府的失误作了一针见血的批评。

【同】 hard-hitting，sharp，intelligent

trend [trend] *n*./*v*. 倾向，趋势

【例】 1. The prices of houses are *trending* upwards. 房价趋于上涨。

2. The youth like to follow the latest *trends* in fashion. 年轻人喜好追求最新的流行款式。

【同】 tendency，drift

【派】 trendy *adj*. 流行的；*n*. 穿着时髦的人

trial ['traɪəl] *n*. 1. 审讯，审判；2. 试验，考验

【记】 tri(= try，尝试，审讯) + al(名词词尾)→试验，审讯

【例】 1. The defendant claimed that he had not had a fair *trial*. 被告声称未获公正审讯。

2. The new drug has undergone extensive medical *trials*. 这种新药已作了大量的医学试验。

【同】 experiment，test

【派】 (逆构)try *v*. 试图，努力；审讯

triangle [ˈtraɪæŋgl] *n*. 三角形(物体)

【记】 tri(三个)+angle(角)→有三个角的→三角形

【例】 The angles of a *triangle* total 180. 三角形的三角之和等于180°。

【派】 triangular *adj*. 三角形的，三人间的

tribal [ˈtraɪbəl] *adj*. 部落的

【记】 trib(e)(部落)+al(形容词词尾)→部落的

【例】 In Africa they were used for *tribal* ceremonial dress. 在非洲，它们被用来作为部落庆典的服装。

【派】 (逆构)tribe *n*. 部落

tribute [ˈtrɪbjuːt] *n*. 礼物，颂词

【记】 tribut(赠予)+e→赠予的东西→礼物

【例】 The musician gave full *tribute* to his former teacher. 这位音乐家盛赞了他过去的老师。

【同】 compliment，contribution

trick [trɪk] *n*. 1. 窍门，技艺；2. 诡计，骗局；*v*. 欺骗，哄骗

【例】 1. He played some clever magic *tricks*. 他表演了一些巧妙的魔术。

2. These children loved playing *tricks* on their teacher. 孩子们喜欢捉弄老师。

3. The police *tricked* him into making a confession. 警察哄骗他作了招认。

【同】 magic，antic；deception；deceive，delude

【派】 tricker *n*. 欺骗者，恶作剧者

tricky *adj*. 狡猾的，机警的；微妙的

trickle [ˈtrɪkl] *n*. 细流；*v*. 滴，细流

【记】 trick(敲打)+le(动词词尾，表示动作的重复)→不停地敲打→不停地滴落→细流

【例】 1. The stream is reduced to a mere *trickle* in summer. 夏天那条小河的水量减少，成了涓涓溪流。

2. Blood *trickled* from the wound. 血从伤口一滴一滴流出来。

【同】 drip，dribble

trifle [ˈtraɪfl] *n*. 琐事，少量

【记】 tri(三个)+fle(名词词尾)→到处都有的东西→琐事

【例】 He spends all his time on crosswords and other *trifles*. 他把所有的时间都用在做纵横填字游戏和其他无聊的活动上。

【派】 trifler *n*. 不务正业的人

trifling *adj*. 不重要的

trigger [ˈtrɪgə] *n*. (枪的)板机，触发；*v*. 引起，触发

【记】 trig(拉)+(g)er(名词词尾)→拉的东西→扳机

【例】 1. The climatic *trigger* for this flowering cycle is not yet known, but the adaptive significance is clear. 这种轮回的气候诱因现在尚不得知，但是它的适应性意义却很清楚。

2. Careless political action can *trigger* off a war. 不慎重的政治行动能引发一场战争。

【同】 begin，start

trim [trɪm] *adj*. 整齐的，整洁的；*v*. (-mmed；-mming)整理，装饰

【例】 1. The house is very well maintained, with fruit trees and *trim* garden. 房子维护得很好，还有果树和修剪整齐的花园。

2. I'll have my hair *trimmed* tomorrow. 明天我要修剪头发。

【同】 neat, tidy; clip, cut

【反】 untidy

triumph [ˈtraɪəmf] *n*./*v*. 胜利，成功

【记】 来自古拉丁语 triumpe(罗马教士举行宗教仪式时唱的圣歌)→庆祝胜利

【例】 1. The story of her *triumph* over cancer is very moving. 她战胜癌症的故事非常感人。

2. The Allies *triumphed* over the Axis. 协约国战胜了轴心国。

【同】 success, victory

【反】 defeat, failure

【派】 triumphal *adj*. 胜利的，凯旋的

triumphant *adj*. 胜利的，狂欢的

trivial [ˈtrɪvɪəl] *adj*. 不重要的，琐碎的

【记】 tri(三个) + vi(a)(道路) + al(形容词词尾)→各处都有的→不重要的

【例】 Don't be angry over such *trivial* matters. 别为这些琐事生气。

【同】 trifling

【反】 important

【派】 (逆构)trivia *n*. 琐事

tropic [ˈtrɒpɪk] *n*. 热带，回归线

【记】 trop(转) + ic(形容词词尾转用作名词)→太阳到此往回转→回归线

【例】 This plant only grows in the *tropics*. 这种植物只生长在热带地区。

【派】 tropical *adj*. 热带的，热情的

troupe [truːp] *n*. 团，队(尤指马戏团、芭蕾舞团)

【例】 When the *troupe* walks up out of the water, you get this amazing feeling. 当马戏团从水中走出来的时候，你会感到十分惊讶。

【同】 band, company

【派】 trouper *n*. 演员，戏团演员，

trudge [trʌdʒ] *v*. 跋涉，吃力地走

【记】 trudge = trude 推→推着走→吃力地走

【例】 The old man *trudged* home through the deep snow. 老人踩着积雪，步履艰难地往家走。

【同】 plod

trunk [trʌŋk] *n*. 树干，躯干

【例】 Some birds can hollow out a nest in the tree *trunk*. 一些鸟可以在树干上凿洞筑巢。

【同】 bole, stem

【反】 branch

tube [ˈtjuːb] *n*. 管，管子

【例】 Our television *tube* has broken. 我们的电视机显像管坏了。

【同】 pipe

tuition [tjuːˈɪʃən] *n*. 讲授，学费

【记】 tuit(保护) + ion(名词词尾)→受保护的费用→受教育的费用→学费

【例】 Students' grants cover their *tuition* fees. 学生补助金包括学费在内。

【同】 education, schooling

【派】 tuitional *adj*. 讲授的，学费的

tune [tjuːn] *n*. 曲调，和谐；*v*. 调整，调谐

【例】 1. The violin is not quite in *tune* with the piano. 这小提琴跟钢琴的调子不太和谐。
2. Stay *tuned* to us for the latest sports results. 请继续收听我们播放的最新比赛结果。

【同】 harmony, melody; adjust, set

【反】 untune

【派】 tuneful *adj*. 和谐的，音调优美的

tunnel [ˈtʌnl] *n*. 隧道，地道；*v*. (-l(l)ed; -l(l)ing)掘，挖(隧道等)

【记】 tunn(管道) + el(名词词尾)→地下的管道→地道

【例】 1. Moles make underground *tunnels*. 鼹鼠常打地洞。
2. The prisoners *tunnelled* their way to freedom. 囚徒们挖地道逃跑，重获自由。

【同】 burrow, cave

turbid [ˈtɜːbɪd] *adj*. 浑浊的，污浊的

【记】 turb(扰乱) + id(形容词词尾)→扰乱的→浑浊的

【例】 Several different spacies of fish inhabit these *turbid* shallow waters. 有几种不同的鱼生活在这片混浊的浅水中。

【同】 cloudy, murky

【反】 clear

【派】 turbidity *n*. 混浊，混乱

turbulent [ˈtɜːbjʊlənt] *adj*. 吵闹的，骚动的；2. 狂暴的，汹涌的

【记】 turb(搅拌，扰乱) + ulent(形容词词尾)→搅动的→骚动的

【例】 1. This has been a *turbulent* week for the government. 对于政府来说，这是动荡的一周。
2. The sea is too *turbulent* for sailing. 海浪太大，不宜航行。

【同】 riotous, tumultuous

【反】 calm, peaceful

【派】 turbulence *n*. 骚乱，动荡

turmoil [ˈtɜːmɔɪl] *n*. 骚动，混乱

【记】 turm(= turb, 搅拌) + oil(名词词尾)→被搅动→混乱

【例】 The London Stock Exchange is in *turmoil* today. 今天伦敦证交所一片混乱。

【同】 commotion, disturbance, turbulence

tutor [ˈtjuːtə] *n*. 导师，辅导教师；*v*. 指导

【记】 tu(t)(照顾) + or(名词词尾表示"…的人")→照顾的人→导师

【例】 1. A relationship of mutual respect is encouraged between students and *tutors*. 提

T

倡学生和导师之间的互相尊重。

2. He *tutored* the child in physics. 他给这小孩辅导物理。

【同】 instruct, teacher

【派】 tutorial *n*. 指南；个人辅导

tutorship *n*. 家庭教师，辅导

twilight [ˈtwaɪlaɪt] *n*. 黎明，暮色

【记】 twi(两者) + light(光芒)→两者之间的光→黎明，黄昏

【例】 I could not see their faces clearly in the *twilight*. 暮色朦胧中我看不清他们的脸。

【同】 dawn, dusk

【派】 twilit *adj*. 沉浸在柔和的微光中的

twinkle [ˈtwɪŋkl] *n*./*v*. 闪烁，闪光

【记】 twink(眨眼) + le(动词词尾，表示动作的反复)→反复眨眼→闪烁

【例】 Her eyes *twinkled* with mischief. 她的眼睛里闪着调皮的光辉。

【同】 glimmer, sparkle

【派】 twinkling *adj*. 闪烁的，发光的

twist [twɪst] *v*. 扭绞，歪曲

【记】 twi(两者) + st(站)→两者站在一起→两者绞缠在一起→扭绞

【例】 The metal frame tends to *twist* under pressure. 这种金属框受压后容易变形。

【同】 distort

【派】 twisty *adj*. 扭曲的，狡猾的

tycoon [taɪˈkuːn] *n*. 大企业家，大亨

【记】 来自日语 shogun，是幕府时代对将军的称谓

【例】 In the book, a *tycoon* unaccountably becomes the hero's friend. 在这本书中，一个大亨莫名其妙地成为了主人公的朋友。

【同】 big businessman

typical [ˈtɪpɪkəl] *adj*. 典型的，象征性的

【记】 typ(类型) + cal(形容词词尾)→属于特别的类型→典型的

【例】 This paiting is fairly *typical* of his early work. 这幅画是他早期作品相当典型的代表作。

【同】 distinctive, representative

【派】 typicality *n*. 典型性，特征

tyranny [ˈtɪrənɪ] *n*. 暴政，专治

【记】 tyran(t)(暴君) + n + y(名词词尾)→暴君的统治→暴政

【例】 The world has experienced many *tyrannies*. 这个世界已经经历过许多个专政政权。

【同】 dictatorship, monocracy

【派】 tyrannical *adj*. 暴虐的，残暴的

U

ultimate ['ʌltɪmɪt] *adj*. 最后的，最终的

【记】 ultim(最后的) + ate(形容词词尾)→最后的

【例】 For early explorers, it was *ultimate* survival contest. 对于早期的拓荒者来说，它是最后的生存竞争。

【同】 terminal, final

【反】 proximate

【派】 ultimately *adj*. 最终地，最后地

ultramodern [ˌʌltrə'mɒdən] *adj*. 超现代化的，超时髦的

【记】 ultra(超越) + modern(现代的)→超越现代的→超现代化的

【例】 But not all the glass technology that touches our lives is *ultramodern*. 但是不是所有我们在生活中接触到的玻璃工艺都是超现代化的。

【派】 ultramodernism *n*. 超现代主义

ultrasonic ['ʌltrə'sɒnɪk] *n*./*adj*. 超声波(的)

【记】 ultra(超越) + son(声音) + ic(形容词词尾)→在声音之上的→超声波的

【例】 The doctor gave him an *ultrasonic* brain scan. 医生给他做了脑部超声波扫描检查。

【同】 supersonic

【派】 ultrasonics *n*. 超声波学

ultraviolet ['ʌltrə'vaɪəlɪt] *n*./*adj*. 紫外线(的)，紫外(的)

【记】 ultra(超越) + violet(紫色)→超越紫色之外的→紫外线

【例】 They use *ultraviolet* lamp to kill pests. 他们使用紫外线灯杀死害虫。

unanimous [juː'nænɪməs] *adj*. 意见一致的，无异议的

【记】 un(= uni 一个) + anim(意志) + ous(形容词词尾)→一个意志的→意见一致的

【例】 The villagers are *unanimous* in their opposition to the building of a bypass. 村民一致反对修建旁道。

【同】 agreed, concurrent

【派】 unanimity *n*. 全体一致，一致同意

unbiased ['ʌn'baɪəst] *adj*. 无偏见的，公正的

【记】 un(没有) + bias(偏见) + ed(形容词词尾)→无偏见的

【例】 A corpus enables the linguist to make *unbiased* statements about frequency of usage, and it provides accessible data for the use of different researchers. 语料库使语言学家能够对语言的使用频率提出公正的说法，并且为不同研究者的使用提供可获得的资料。

【同】 impartial, fair

【反】 biased

uncanny [ʌn'kænɪ] *adj*. 离奇的，不可思议的

【记】 un(没有) + canny(谨慎的)→不能以谨慎的方式去理解→离奇的

【例】 I had an *uncanny* feeling of being watched. 我有一种奇怪的感觉，好像有人监视我。

【同】 mysterious, weird

unconscious [ʌn'kɒnʃəs] *adj*. 1.不省人事的，无意识的；2.未意识到的，未觉察的

【记】 un(不，无) + conscious(有意识的)→无意识的

【例】 1. This wounded soldier was *unconscious* from his loss of blood. 这名伤员由于失血过多而昏迷不醒。

2. He was *unconscious* of his mistake. 他没意识到自己犯了错误。

【同】 insensible, senseless; oblivious, absent-minded

【反】 conscious

uncover [ʌn'kʌvə] *v*. 揭开，揭露

【记】 un(没有) + cover(覆盖)→没有覆盖的→揭开

【例】 Agents have *uncovered* a plot against the President. 特工人员发现了一个反对总统的阴谋。

【同】 disclose, expose

【反】 cover

underestimate ['ʌndər'estɪmeɪt] *n*./*v*. 评价过低，低估

【记】 under(在…之下) + estimate(估计)→在估计之下的→低估

【例】 Never *underestimate* your opponent. 千万不要低估对手。

【同】 underrate, undervalue

【反】 overestimate

【派】 underestimation *n*. 低估

undergo [ˌʌndə'gəʊ] *v*. (-went, -gone)经历，遭受

【记】 under(在…之下) + go(行走)→行走于(苦难)之下→遭受

【例】 According to the writer, left-handed people have *undergone* hardship for years. 根据作者所说的，左撇子的人们多年来饱尝艰辛。

【同】 encounter, experience

undergraduate [ˌʌndə'grædjʊɪt] *n*. (尚未取得学位的)大学生；*adj*. 大学生的

【记】 under(在…之下的) + graduate(毕业)→还未从学校毕业的(学生)→大学生

【例】 1. He is a Harvard *undergraduate*. 他是哈佛大学的学生。

2. The four years of *undergraduate* study there was fruitful. 四年的大学本科学习收获很大。

【同】 collegian

【反】 graduate

underground ['ʌndəraʊnd] *adj*. 地下的，秘密的；*n*. (英)地铁

【记】 under(在…下面) + ground(地面)→在地下的→地下的，地铁

【例】 1. The action takes place in *underground* cities where the environment is controlled by computers. 这次行动发生在地下城，这里的环境是由计算机控制的。

2. We went on the *Underground*. 我们乘地铁去的。

【同】 belowground, secret; subway

underlie [ˌʌndəˈlaɪ] *v*. (-lay, -lain; -lying)位于…之下，成为…的基础

【记】 under(在…之下) + lie(位于)→位于…之下→成为…的基础

【例】 I think a lack of confidence *underlies* his aggressive manner. 我认为他表现出咄咄逼人的态度是因为他缺乏信心。

【派】 underlying *adj*. 根本的，潜在的

undermine [ˌʌndəˈmaɪn] *v*. 逐渐削弱，暗中破坏

【记】 under(在下面) + mine(开采)→在下面挖掘→暗中破坏

【例】 They will do anything to *undermine* their adversary's reputation. 他们会不择手段地去损害对手的名誉。

【同】 destroy, sabotage, weaken

undertake [ˌʌndəˈteɪk] *v*. (-took, -taken)承担，许诺

【记】 under(在下面) + take(拿起)→从下面拿起→承担

【例】 She *undertook* responsibility for the changes. 她承担了作出这些改变的责任。

【同】 engage, promise

【派】 undertaker *n*. 承办者，承担者

undertaking *n*. 事业，承诺

undo [ˈʌnˈduː] *v*. (-did, -done)解开，取消

【记】 un(不，非) + do(做)→把做好的东西变成相反的→取消

【例】 He *undid* most of the good work of his predecessor. 他把前任大部分的业绩毁掉了。

【同】 open, unmake

【反】 do, make

【派】 undone *adj*. 解开的，拆开的

undue [ˈʌnˈdjuː] *adj*. 不当的，过度的

【记】 un(不，非) + due(适当的)→不适当的

【例】 He tried to exercise an *undue* influence upon his colleagues. 他想对他的同事施加不适当的影响。

【同】 excessive, unreasonable

【反】 due

unfold [ʌnˈfəʊld] *v*. 展开，显露

【记】 un(不，非) + fold(折叠)→把折叠的变成相反的→展开

【例】 The story *unfolds* as the film goes on. 随着影片的放映，故事情节展开了。

extend, spread

【同】 fold

【派】 unfolded *adj*. 展开的，解开的

uniform [ˈjuːnɪfɔːm] *adj*. 统一标准的，一贯的；*n*. 制服(式样)

【记】 uni(一个) + form(形式)→一个形式的→统一的

【例】 1. The rows of houses are *uniform* in appearance. 这一排排的房子外观相同。

U

2. The students are wearing school *uniforms*. 学生们穿着校服。

【同】 consistent, unvarying

【反】 multiform, various

【派】 uniformity *n*. 统一(性), 一致(性)

unify [ˈjuːnɪfaɪ] *v*. 统一, 一体

【记】 uni(一个) + fy(动词词尾)→使成为一个整体→统一

【例】 Is it possible to *unify* such scattered islands into a nation? 有可能把这样一些散落在大海上的岛屿统一成一个国家吗?

【同】 combine, unite

【反】 disunify

【派】 unification *n*. 统一, 一致

uninhabited [ˈʌnɪnˈhæbɪtɪd] *adj*. 无人居住的

【记】 un(没有) + habit(居住) + ed(形容词词尾)→没有人居住的

【例】 Tonight I'm going to talk to you about that remarkable continent-Antarctica-remote and at present *uninhabited* on a permanent basis. 今晚我要向大家讲述那个不同寻常的大陆, 南极洲——那里遥远, 而且还没有人在那里永久居住。

【同】 deserted, unoccupied

【反】 inhabited

unique [juːˈniːk] *adj*. 独特的, 唯一的

【记】 uni(一个) + que(形容词词尾)→只有一个的→唯一的

【例】 He's caught the *unique* opportunity. 他抓住了那唯一的机会。

【同】 only, single, unusual

【派】 uniqueness *n*. 唯一性, 独特性

unite [juːˈnaɪt] *v*. 联合, 团结

【记】 uni(一个) + te(动词词尾)→变成一个→联合

【例】 The two governments have *united* to combat terrorism. 两国政府联合起来打击恐怖主义。

【同】 combine, unify

【反】 disunite, divide

【派】 union *n*. 联合, 合并
united *adj*. 团结的, 一致的
unity *n*. 结合, 一致

U

unparalleled [ʌnˈpærəleld] *adj*. 空前的, 独一无二的

【记】 un(没有) + parallel(平行) + ed(形容词词尾)→没有平行的→独一无二的

【例】 This is a tremendous change *unparalleled* in the history of China and of the world. 这是一个巨大的变化, 这是自有世界历史和中国历史以来无可比拟的大变化。

【同】 unequalled, unique

unprecedented [ʌnˈpresɪdəntɪd] *adj*. 空前的, 史无前例的

【记】 un(不, 无) + precedent(先例) + ed(形容词词尾)→没有先例的→空前的

【例】 Some economists showed their anxiety on *unprecedented* level of unemployment.

一些经济学家对失业率达到前所未有的程度表示忧虑。

【同】 extraordinary, unduplicated

universe ['juːnɪvɜːs] *n*. 宇宙，世界

【记】 uni(一个) + vers(转变) + e→转变成一个整体→宇宙

【例】 The Earth is only one of the numerous planets in the *universe*. 地球只是宇宙中众多星体中的一个。

【同】 cosmos, world

【派】 universal *adj*. 普遍的，全体的

unravel [ʌn'rævəl] *v*. (-l(l)ed; -l(l)ing) 1. 解开，散开；2. 弄清楚

【记】 un(不，非) + ravel(纠缠，混乱)→把纠缠在一起的打开→拆开，弄清楚

【例】 1. The sweater has started to *unravel*. 这件毛线衫开始脱线了。

2. The mystery was slow to *unravel*. 那个迷花了很长时间才解开。

【同】 undo, disintegrate

【反】 ravel

unveil [ʌn'veɪl] *v*. 使公诸于众，揭开

【记】 un(不，非) + veil(面纱)→除去面纱→揭开

【例】 The queen today *unveiled* a plaque to open the new hospital. 女王今天为一家新医院的开张揭了幕。

【同】 expose, reveal

【反】 veil

update [ʌp'deɪt] *v*./*n*. 使现代化，更新

【记】 up(向上) + date(日期)→跟上日期→跟上时代→使现代化

【例】 The CD-ROMS contain exactly the same information as the reference books as the two are *updated* together. 这种CD光驱精确的包含了和参考书同样的信息，因为两者是同时更新的。

【同】 modernize

【派】 updated *adj*. 最新的，现代化的

upgrade ['ʌp'gdeɪt] *v*. 升级，更新

【记】 up(向上) + grade(级别)→等级上升→升级

【例】 The consulate was *upgraded* to embassy status. 该领事馆已经被升级为大使馆。

【同】 advance, promote

【反】 downgrade

【派】 upgrading *n*. 改进，升级

uphold [ʌp'həʊld] *v*. (-held, -held) 支持，维护

【记】 up(向上) + hold(抓，握)→向上举起→支持

【例】 It is up to the government to *uphold* the rights of individual citizens. 政府有责任维护各个公民的权利。

【同】 support, sustain

【反】 subvert

【派】 upholder *n*. 支持者，支撑物

upright ['ʌp'raɪt] *adj*./*adv*. 垂直的，直立的

【记】 up(向上)+right(恰当的)→恰恰向上的→垂直的

【例】 Several columns among the ruins still stood *upright*. 在废墟中依然挺立着几根柱子。

【同】 erect, vertical

【反】 horizontal

upset [ʌp'set] *n*./*v*. (-set, -set; -setting)颠倒，混乱

【记】 up(向上)+set(放置)→置于上方→倾覆

【例】 1. Last-minute changes caused a great deal of *upset*. 出现的临时变动造成一片混乱。

2. If they develop these new weapons, it will *upset* the balance of power. 如果他们研制这些新武器，那么力量的平衡就会被打破。

【同】 disconcert, disorder

【派】 upsetting *adj*. 令人心烦的，令人苦恼的

uptake ['ʌpteɪk] *n*. 摄取，领会

【记】 up(向上)+take(拿)→向上拿取→摄取，领会

【例】 The rate of photosynthesis in a plant can be measured by calculating the rate of its *uptake* of carbon. 光合作用的速度可以通过计算它摄取碳的速度来衡量。

【同】 consumption, ingestion

urban ['ɜːbən] *adj*. 城市的，居住在城市的

【记】 urb(城市)+an(形容词词尾)→城市的

【例】 You can find out many advantages in *urban* life. 你会发现都市生活中有许多便利之处。

【反】 rural

【派】 urbanism *n*. 都市生活，都市化

urbanite *n*. 都市人

urbanization *n*. 城市化

urge [ɜːdʒ] *v*. 催促，力劝；*n*. 强烈欲望，迫切要求

【例】 1. They *urged* us to give our support. 他们敦促我们给予支持。

2. I had a sudden *urge* to tell the boss what I thought of him. 我突然非常想告诉老板我对他的看法。

【同】 impulse, push

【反】 limit, restrain

【派】 urgent *adj*. 急迫的，紧要的

urgency *n*. 紧急，紧急的事

usurp [juː'zɜːp] *v*. 篡夺，篡位

【记】 usu(用)+rp(=rape，强夺)→为了使用强夺→篡夺

【例】 Henry IV *usurped* the throne of England. 亨利四世篡夺了英国的王位。

【同】 assume, seize, take over

【派】 usurpation *n*. 篡夺

utensil [juː'tensl] *n*. 器具，器皿

【记】 ut(使用)+ens+il(名词词尾)→使用的东西→器具

【例】 I have to buy some kitchen *utensils* before starting cooking. 开始做饭前，我还得去买些厨房用具。

【同】 appliance, device, implement, tool

utilitarian [ˌjuːtɪlɪˈteərɪən] *adj*. 功利的，实利的；*n*. 功利论者

【记】 utilit(y)(使用) + arian(名词词尾，表示"…的人")→注重实用性的人→功利论者

【例】 What are *utilitarian* objects to a Westerner may be prized objects in other cultures. 对于西方人来说是功利主义的东西，在其他文化背景中却可能是珍藏品。

【同】 useful

【派】 (逆构)utility *n*. 效用，有用

utilize *v*. 利用，使用

utilization *n*. 利用

utmost [ˈʌtməʊst] *adj*. 最远的，极度的

【记】 ut(在外面) + most(最高级)→在最外面的→最远的

【例】 With the *utmost* respect, I think you are wrong. 尽管对您极其尊重，我仍然认为您是错误的。

【同】 extreme, farthest

utter [ˈʌtə] *v*. 发出，做声；*adj*. 完全的，彻底的

【例】 1. The wounded man *uttered* a groan. 那受伤的人发出痛苦的呻吟。

2. It was an *utter* waste of time. 这完全是浪费时间。

【同】 express, speak; complete, pure

【派】 utterance *n*. 发声，说话方式

U

V

vacancy [ˈveɪkənsɪ] *n*. 空白，清闲

【记】 vac(空的)+ancy(名词词尾)→空白

【例】 We have *vacancies* in the typing pool. 我们打字组缺少人手。

【同】 emptiness

【反】 fullness

【派】 vacant *adj*. 空白的，神情茫然的

vacation [vəˈkeɪʃən] *n*./*v*. 度假，休假

【记】 vac(空的)+ation(名词词尾)→空的时间→度假

【例】 I was on *vacation* last week and didn't receive your fax. 上星期我正在度假，没收到你们的传真。

【同】 holiday

vaccine [ˈvæksiːn] *n*. 疫苗

【记】 vacc(=vacca，cow，牛)+ine(名词词尾)→牛痘→疫苗

【例】 This *vaccine* will give you immunity for two years. 接种这种疫苗可有两年免疫力。

【派】 vaccinate *v*. 进行预防接种

vacuum [ˈvækjuəm] *n*. (复数-cuums或-cua)真空

【记】 vac(空的)+uum(名词词尾)→空的状态→真空

【例】 Some pumps and all *vacuum* cleaners work by suction. 有些泵和所有真空吸尘器都是借吸力工作的。

【同】 vacuity

【派】 vacuum-packed *adj*. 真空包装的

vague [vegɪ] *adj*. 含糊的，不清楚的

【记】 vag(漫游)+ue→(思想)漫游的→含糊的

【例】 I have the *vaguest* notion what you mean. 我一点都不明白你在说什么。

【同】 ambiguous，obscure

【反】 clear，distinct

vain [veɪn] *adj*. 徒然的，虚荣的

【例】 We tried in *vain* to make him change his mind. 我们想使他改变主意，结果是白费心机。

【同】 ineffectual，boastful

【反】 effective，modest

valiant [ˈvæljənt] *adj*. 勇敢的，英勇的

【记】 val(强壮的)+iant(形容词词尾)→强壮的→勇敢的

【例】 She made a *valiant* attempt to laugh. 她放大了胆笑了起来。

【同】 brave, courageous, fearless

【反】 timid

valid ['vælɪd] *adj*. 有效的，正当的

【记】 val(价值)+id(形容词词尾)→有价值的→正当的

【例】 A credit card is not a *valid* proof of identity. 银行卡不是有效的身份证明文件。

【同】 effective, lawful

【反】 invalid

【派】 validate *v*. 使有效，确认

validity *n*. 有效性，合法性

vanish ['vænɪʃ] *v*. 逐渐消散，消灭

【记】 van(空的)+ish(动词词尾)→变成空的→逐渐消失

【例】 Half the world's 6,800 languages are likely to *vanish* within two generations. 世界上的6800种语言中，有一半将会在两代时间之内消失。

【同】 disappear, fade

【反】 appear

vanity ['vænɪtɪ] *n*. 空虚，虚荣

【记】 van(i)(空的)+ty(名词词尾)→空的东西→空虚

【例】 She married the rich man out of *vanity*. 她出于虚荣心而嫁给了那个富人。

【同】 conceit, pride

【反】 reality

vanquish ['væŋkwɪʃ] *v*. 征服，击败

【记】 vanqu(克服)+ish(动词词尾)→克服→征服

【例】 They *vanquished* their enemy in battle. 他们在战斗中打败了敌人。

【同】 beat, conquer, overcome

【派】 vanquisher *n*. 征服者，胜利者

vapor ['veɪpə] *n*. 蒸汽，烟雾

【例】 More than 90% of this gas is water *vapor* from the deep earth. 这种气体中的90%是来自地球深处的水蒸气。

【派】 vaporous *adj*. 蒸汽多的，冒出蒸汽的

vaporization *n*. 蒸发

variable ['veərɪəbl] *adj*. 易变的，可变的；*n*. 变数，变量

【记】 vari(变化)+able(形容词)→变化的→易变的

【例】 1. The quality of the hotel food is distinctly *variable*. 这个旅馆的饭菜有时很好有时很差。

2. The temperature was a *variable* in the experiment. 在该实验中温度是个变量。

【同】 diverse

【反】 constant, invariable

【派】 variability *n*. 可变性

variety [və'raɪətɪ] *n*. 变化，多样性

【记】 vari(变化)+ety(名词词尾)→变化→多样性

【例】 The hotel offers its guests a wide *variety* of amusements. 这个旅馆为住客提供了各种各样的娱乐活动。
【同】 diversity
【反】 monotony
various [ˈveərɪəs] *adj*. 不同的，各种各样的
【记】 var(i)(变化)+ious(形容词词尾)→变化的→不同的
【例】 For *various* reasons I'd prefer not to meet him. 由于各种原因，我不愿见他。
【同】 different，diverse
varnish [ˈvɑːnɪʃ] *n*. 清漆，光泽面；*v*. 1. 涂清漆；2. 掩饰，粉饰
【例】 1. Hot plates may spoil the *varnish* on the table. 滚烫的盘子会损坏桌面的光泽。
2. The table has been *varnished*. 桌子上已经涂过清漆了。
3. They have tried every means to *varnish* the truth. 他们想尽办法，掩饰真相。
【同】 lacquer，paint
vary [ˈveərɪ] *v*. 改变，变化
【例】 The price *varies* according to the season. 价格随季节变化。
【同】 alter，change，diverge
【派】 variant *n*. 变体，变形
variation *n*. 变化
vast [vɑːst] *adj*. 1. 广泛的，广阔的；2. 大量的，巨额的
【例】 1. The *vast* plains stretch for hundreds of miles. 辽阔的平原绵延数百英里。
2. Species are becoming extinct in *vast* numbers, and the planet's air and water are becoming ever more polluted. 物种正在大量的灭绝，而地球上的水和空气受到越来越严重的污染。
【同】 huge，immense，large
【反】 narrow
【派】 vastitude *n*. 广度
vegetarian [ˌvedʒɪˈteərɪən] *adj*. 素食的；*n*. 素食者，食草动物
【记】 vegeta(= vegetable，蔬菜)+rian(表示"人"的名词词尾)→吃蔬菜的人→素食者
【例】 1. And we'd better make sure there's good *vegetarian* food. 而我们最好保证会有好的素食。
2. Not a few of my friends are *vegetarian*. 我朋友中不少人吃素。
【反】 carnassial
vehement [ˈviːɪmənt] *adj*. 猛烈的，激烈的
【记】 vehe(运送)+ment(= mind，思想感情)→传达感情的→激烈的
【例】 She made a *vehement* attack on the government's policies. 她强烈谴责政府的政策。
【同】 ardent，fierce，furious，violent
【派】 vehemence *n*. 热切，激烈，激情
vehicle [ˈviːɪkl] *n*. 1. 交通工具；2. 媒介物，传播手段
【记】 vehi(搬运)+cle(名词词尾)→搬运物→交通工具
【例】 1. A bumper is a part of a motor *vehicle*. 保险杆是机动车辆的一部分。

2. Television has become an important *vehicle* for spreading political ideas. 电视已成为传播政治思想的重要媒介。

【同】 carriage, conveyance; medium

【派】 vehicular *adj*. 车的，用车运载的；作为媒介的

veil [veɪl] *n*. 面纱，掩饰物；*v*. 戴面纱，隐藏

【例】 1. Most Moslem women wear *veils* in public places. 大多数穆斯林妇女在公共场所都戴着面纱。

2. He tried to *veil* his contempt at my ignorance. 他试图掩饰对我的无知的蔑视。

【同】 mask

【反】 unveil

vein [veɪn] *n*. 1. 血管，静脉；2. 情趣，特色，风格

【例】 1. Royal blood runs in his *veins*. 他有皇家血统。

2. There is a *vein* of melancholy in his character. 他的性格中有少许忧郁的气质。

【反】 artery

veneration [venəreɪʃən] *n*. 尊敬，崇拜

【记】 vener(爱，渴望) + ation(名词词尾)→对…充满爱→尊敬，崇拜

【例】 The Chinese people hold their ancestors in great *veneration*. 中国人非常尊敬祖先。

【同】 respect, reverence

【派】 (逆构)venerate *v*. 尊敬，崇拜

venerable *adj*. 值得尊敬的，庄严的

vengeance ['vendʒəns] *n*. 复仇，报仇

【记】 venge(复仇) + ance(名词词尾)→复仇

【例】 He swore to take *vengeance* on the people who had killed his sister. 他发誓要报复杀死他妹妹的人。

【同】 revenge

【派】 (逆构)venge *v*. 为…报仇，替…复仇

vengeful *adj*. 复仇心重的，报复的

ventilation [ventɪ'leɪʃən] *n*. 通风，流通空气

【记】 venti(风) + lat(带来) + ion(名词词尾)→把风带来→通风

【例】 In the noisiest areas mechanical *ventilation* will have to be installed in the exterior walls. 在最喧闹的地区，机械通风设备要被装在外面的墙上。

【同】 air

【派】 (逆构)ventilate *v*. 使通风，装通风设备

venture ['ventʃə] *n*./*v*. 冒险，投机

【记】 vent(来) + ure(名词词尾)→(带着风险)前来→冒险

【例】 1. All our hopes rested upon this *venture*. 我们所有的希望都寄托在这次冒险上了。

2. He *ventured* his life to save a little girl from drowning. 他冒生命危险救起了一个小女孩，使她免于淹死。

【同】 adventure, risk

【派】 venturer *n*. 冒险者

V

venturous *adj*. 好冒险的，大胆的
venturesome *adj*. 好冒险的，行为冒险的

venue ['venjuː] *n*. (事件的)发生地点，举行场所
【记】 venu(来)+e→来到的地方→发生的地点
【例】 The Grand Hotel, *venue* of this week's talks, is packed out. 作为本周会谈场所的格兰德大酒店已经客满。
【同】 spot

verbal ['vɜːbəl] *adj*. 口头的，语言的
【记】 verb(字，词)+al(形容词词尾)→用词的→口头的
【例】 The teacher teaches us the *verbal* skills. 老师告诉我们使用言辞的技巧。
【同】 oral, spoken
【反】 written

verdict ['vɜːdɪkt] *n*. 判断，(法律)裁决
【记】 ver(真实的)+dict(说话)→真实的话语→法律裁决
【例】 The jury brought in a *verdict* of guilty. 陪审团作出有罪的裁决。
【同】 decision, judgment, sentence

verify ['verɪfaɪ] *v*. 检验，查证
【记】 ver(i)(真实的)+fy(动词词尾)→确认是否真实→检验
【例】 The computer *verified* whether the data was loaded correctly. 计算机已查实数据输入是否正确。
【同】 certify, confirm
【派】 verifiable *adj*. 能作证的，能证实的
verification *n*. 确认，查证

vernacular [və'nækjulə] *n*. 本地话，方言；*adj*. 本国的，本地的
【记】 vernacul(家里的奴隶)+ar(名词词尾)→奴隶说的话→土话，方言
【例】 1. He speaks an incomprehensible *vernacular*. 他说的是一种无法听得懂的方言。
2. The Roman Catholic Church now uses *vernacular* services instead of Latin ones. 罗马天主教现在举行宗教仪式时都用本国语言而不用拉丁语。
【同】 jargon, dialect

versatile ['vɜːsətaɪl] *adj*. 通用的，多才多艺的
【记】 versa(改变)+(t)ile(形容词词尾)→可以改变的→通用的
【例】 He's a very *versatile* performer; he can act, sing, dance, and play the piano. 他是个多才多艺的演员，会演戏，唱歌，跳舞，还会弹钢琴。
【同】 adaptable, talented
【派】 versatility *n*. 多功能性

V

verse [vɜːs] *n*. 韵文，诗篇
【记】 ver(改变)+se(名词词尾)→改变为新的格式→韵文
【例】 Most of the scene is written in *verse*, but some is in prose. 这场戏大部分内容是用韵文写成的，但也有一些是散文形式的。
【同】 poetry, rhyme
【反】 prose

version ['vɜːʃən] *n*. 1.版本，变化形式；2.翻译

【记】 ver(改变)+sion(名词词尾)→转换成别国的语言→翻译

【例】 1. The two newspapers gave different *versions* of what happened. 两家报纸对发生的事说法不一。

2. These books are English *versions* of Aristotle. 这些书籍是亚里士多德作品的英文译本。

【同】 adaptation, description; translation

versus ['vɜːsəs] *prep*. (缩写为 v. 或 vs.)与…相对，反对

【记】 vers(转向)+us(拉丁语词尾)→转到另外一个方向→与…相对

【例】 The search so far has focused on the effectiveness of "traditional" *versus* "modern" teaching techniques. 迄今为止，研究活动一直聚焦于探讨"传统"与"现代"教育技巧的有效性上。

【同】 against

vertical ['vɜːtɪkəl] *adj*. 垂直的，直立的；*n*. 垂直线(面)

【记】 vert(i)(转向)+cal(形容词词尾)→转向(下)的→下垂的东西→垂直的

【例】 The northern face of the mountain is almost *vertical*. 这座山向北的一面几乎是垂直的。

【同】 erect, upright

【反】 horizontal

vessel ['vesl] *n*. 1.船，容器；2.血管，导管

【记】 ves(s)(瓶子)+el(表示"小"的名词词尾)→小的瓶子→容器

【例】 1. There are some fishing *vessels* in the harbor. 港湾里有许多渔船。

2. A blood *vessel* is an elastic tubular channel, such as an artery, a vein and so on. 血管是一种有弹性的管道，例如动脉、静脉等等。

【同】 boat, container; vein

vest [vest] *n*. 汗衫，内衣；*v*. 1.穿衣服；2.授予，归属

【例】 1. The police survived because of his bulletproof *vest*. 这位警察因为穿了防弹背心才得以生还。

2. The constitution *vests* the president with the power to declare war. 宪法授予总统宣战权。

vet [vet] *n*. 兽医；*v*. (-tted; -tting)1.诊疗，作兽医；2.检查

【例】 1. I took my dog to the *vet*'s. 我带我的狗去兽医所看病。

2. The recruits were thoroughly *vetted* before they were allowed into the secret service. 情报机关招募的新成员要经过严格的审查才能录用。

【派】 veterinary *n*./*adj*. 兽医(的)

veteran ['vetərən] *n*. 老兵，富有经验的人；*adj*. 老兵的，经验丰富的

【记】 veter(老的)+an(名词词尾表示"…的人")→(年纪./资历)老的人→老兵，老手

【例】 My grandfather is a *veteran* of the Second World War. 我的祖父是第二次世界大战时的老兵。

【同】 experienced, practiced

veto ['viːtəʊ] *n*. (复数-toes)否决，否决权；*v*. 否决，禁止

【例】 Permanent members of the United Nations Security Council have a *veto* over any proposal. 联合国安全理事会常任理事国对一切提案均有否决权。

【同】 deny, refuse

vex [veks] *v*. 使烦恼，恼怒

【例】 His silly chatter would *vex* a saint. 他说的话很无聊，多有涵养的人也会气的发火。

【同】 annoy, irritate, provoke

【反】 please

【派】 vexation *n*. 恼怒，苦恼的原因

via [ˈvaɪə, ˈviːə] *prep*. 通过，取道

【例】 Inter-library loans are available locally and nationally *via* the British Library. 通过英国图书馆可以在当地和全国范围内进行馆际借阅。

viable [ˈvaɪəbl] *adj*. 1. 能养活的，能生育的；2. 可通行的，可实施的

【记】 vi(路) + able(形容词词尾)→能够走得通的→可以实施的

【例】 1. There is a continuing debate about the age at which a human fetus can be considered *viable*. 关于人类胚胎在怀孕几个月的时候能够养活，仍然众说不一。
2. The scheme is not economically *viable*. 这个计划从经济效益来看是不可行的。

【同】 feasible, practicable

【派】 viability *n*. 生存能力，发育能力

vibrant [ˈvaɪbrənt] *adj*. 鲜明的，生气勃勃的

【记】 vibr(a)(颤动) + ant(形容词词尾)→颤动的→生气勃勃的

【例】 The hope is that this area will develop into a *vibrant* commercial center. 希望该地区能发展成一个充满活力的商业中心。

【同】 spirited

【派】 vibrancy *n*. 振动，活跃

vibrate [vaɪˈbreɪt] *v*. 颤动，震动

【记】 vibr(a)(颤动) + ate(动词词尾)→颤动

【例】 The bus *vibrated* when the driver started the engine. 当司机发动了发动机时，公共汽车颤动着。

【同】 quake, quiver, shake, oscillate

【派】 vibration *n*. 振动，颤动

vicinity [vɪˈsɪnɪtɪ] *n*. 邻近，接近

【记】 vicin(邻近) + ity(名词词尾)→邻近

【例】 All the ships in the *vicinity* of the crash joined in the search for survivors. 撞船事故发生附近地区的所有船只都参加了搜寻幸存者的工作。

【同】 nearness, neighborhood

【派】 vicinal *adj*. 邻近的

vicious [ˈvɪʃəs] *adj*. 不道德的，恶意的

【记】 vic(罪恶) + ious(形容词词尾)→罪恶的→恶意的

【例】 I have many women patients who say they have completely given up exercise because the pain makes them so miserable, but of course that starts up a *vicious* circle. 我有很多女病人，她们说她们已经完全放弃了锻炼，因为疼痛让她们痛苦不堪，但是显然这样做开始了一个恶性的循环。

【同】 sinful，wicked

【反】 virtuous

【派】 (逆构)vice *n*. 恶行，罪恶

victim ['vɪktɪm] *n*. 牺牲者，受害者

【例】 She was the *victim* of a road accident. 她是一场交通事故的受害者。

【同】 prey，sufferer

【反】 beneficiary

victory ['vɪktərɪ] *n*. 胜利，克服

【记】 vict(征服)+(o)ry(名词词尾)→征服→胜利

【例】 Labor did not have a easy election *victory* in East Oxford Dictionary. 工党在牛津东区的选举中的胜利来之不易。

【同】 conquest，triumph

【反】 defeat

【派】 victor *n*. 胜利者

victorious *adj*. 获胜的，胜利的

vigilant ['vɪdʒɪlənt] *adj*. 警觉的，警惕的

【记】 vigil(醒着的)+ant(形容词词尾)→醒着的→警觉的

【例】 The police said that the public should remain *vigilant*. 警方说公众应保持警惕。

【同】 alert，cautious，watchful，wide-awake

【派】 vigilance *n*. 警戒，警惕；敏感

vigorous ['vɪgərəs] *adj*. 精力旺盛的，有力的

【记】 vig(有生气的)+or(名词词尾)+ous(形容词词尾)→有生气的状态→精力旺盛的

【例】 He never ceased to chase after his dream in his *vigorous* youth. 在精力充沛的年轻时代他从未停止过追求自己的梦想。

【同】 active，energetic，robust

【派】 (逆构)vigor *n*. 精力，活力

vindicate ['vɪndɪkeɪt] *v*. 证明…正确，证明…无辜

【记】 vin(力)+dic(说)+ate(动词词尾)→竭力的说→辩解，证明…正确

【例】 Subsequent events *vindicatedhis* suspicions. 后来的事实表明他的怀疑有道理。

【同】 justify

【派】 vindicative *adj*. 辩护的，辩明的

vindication *n*. 辩护，辩明

violate ['vaɪəleɪt] *v*. 违反，妨碍

【记】 viol(冒犯)+ate(动词词尾)→冒犯某事物→违反

【例】 These findings appear to *violate* the laws of physics. 这些研究结果似乎有违物理定律。

【同】 break，offend

【反】 abide，conform，obey

【派】 violation *n*. 违反，妨碍

violence ['vaɪələns] *n*. 暴力(行为)

【记】 viol(冒犯)+ence(名词词尾)→冒犯某事物的行为→暴力行为

【例】 The young man was charged with robbery with *violence*. 这个年轻人被控暴力抢劫。

【同】 force

【派】 violent *adj*. 猛烈的，暴力的

viral ['vaɪrəl] *adj*. 病毒引起的，滤过性毒菌的

【记】 vir(=virus，病毒)+al(形容词词尾)→病毒引起的

【例】 It can also make you more vulnerable to *viral* and bacterial infections. 它还会使我们对病毒和细菌感染的免疫能力下降。

virgin ['vɜːdʒɪn] *n*. 处女；*adj*. 纯洁的，原始的

【记】 virg(少女)+in(=on，名词词尾)→(未婚)少女→处女

【例】 1. She remained a *virgin* all her life. 她终生未婚。

2. This is the *virgin* voyage of the ship. 这是这艘船的处女航。

【同】 pure，original，fresh

【派】 virginity *n*. 童贞，(未婚女子的)独身生活

virtual ['vɜːtjuəl] *adj*. 实际上的，事实上的

【记】 virtu(e)(美德)+al(形容词词尾)→美德的→实际上的

【例】 Our deputy manager is the *virtual* head of the business. 我们的副经理是公司的实际负责人。

【同】 real，actual

【派】 virtually *adv*. 事实上，实质上

virtue ['vɜːtjuː] *n*. 美德，优点

【例】 He said his plan had the *virtue* of being the easiest to implement. 他说他的计划的优点是最简单易行。

【同】 merit，morality

【反】 vice

【派】 virtuous *adj*. 善良的，贞洁的

virus ['vaɪərəs] *n*. 病毒，毒害

【例】 Today fibre optics are used to obtain a clearer image of smaller and smaller objects than ever before—even bacterial *viruses*. 今天，人们使用纤维光学来更清楚地认识比从前越来越微观的事物，——甚至是细菌病毒。

【同】 poison，toxin

visa ['viːzə] *n*./*v*. 签证

【记】 vis(看见)+a(名词词尾)→给人看的(证件)→签证

【例】 Students on a visitor *visa* or work permit may study for a maximum of 3 months. 持有访问签证或工作许可的学生可以最多学习三个月。

viscous ['vɪskəs] *adj*. 黏性的

【例】 They cannot revert to their original *viscous* state, and their shape is thus fixed forever. 它们不能够恢复到原始的黏性状态，而它们的形状也会永远固定。

【同】 sticky，viscid

vision [ˈvɪʒən] *n*. 1. 视力，视觉；2. 幻象，景象
【记】 vis(看见)＋ion(名词词尾)→眼睛能看到的→视力
【例】 1. If any of the following occur，discontinue taking the medicine and contact your doctor：dizziness，vomiting，blurred *vision*. 如果有下列任何情况发生，请停止服药，并向您的医生咨询：头晕、呕吐、视力模糊。
2. I had a *vision* of the end of the world. 我在梦幻中见到了世界末日。
【同】 sight；fantasy，illusion
【派】 visible *adj*. 看得见的，明显的
visual *adj*. 视觉的，直观的

vital [ˈvaɪtl] *adj*. 生死攸关的，重大的
【记】 vit(生存的)＋al(形容词词尾)→和生存相关的→生死攸关的
【例】 This point is *vital* to my argument. 这一点对我的论据极为重要。
【同】 fatal，crucial
【反】 dispensable
【派】 vitality *n*. 活力，生命力
vitalize *v*. 激发

vivid [ˈvɪvɪd] *adj*. 生动的，逼真的
【记】 viv(生活)＋id(形容词词尾)→有生气的→生动逼真的
【例】 The girl gave a *vivid* description of the event. 那女孩对这件事作了一番生动的描述。
【同】 bright，lively
【反】 dull

vocabulary [vəˈkæbjʊlərɪ] *n*. 词汇(表)，词汇量
【记】 vocabul(＝vocable，词)＋ary(表示"整体"的名词词尾)→词的整体→词汇表
【例】 You can look up this word in the *vocabulary*. 你可以在词汇表里查这个词。
【同】 lexicon

vocal [ˈvəʊkl] *adj*. 发声的，歌唱的
【记】 voc(声音)＋al(形容词词尾)→和声音有关的→发声的
【例】 The tongue is one of the *vocal* organs. 舌头是发声器官之一。
【同】 spoken，voiced

vocational [vəʊˈkeɪʃənəl] *adj*. 天职的，职业的
【记】 vocation(职业)＋al(形容词词尾)→职业的
【例】 We will have some *vocational* training before graduation. 毕业前，我们会接受一些职业训练。
【同】 occupational，professional
【派】 (逆构)vocation *n*. 职业，天职

vogue [vəʊg] *n*. 时尚，流行；*adj*. 流行的，时髦的
【例】 His novels had a great *vogue* ten years ago. 他的小说十年前风靡一时。
【同】 fashion，popularity
【派】 voguish *adj*. 时髦的，一度流行的

void [vɔɪd] *n*. 空旷，空虚；*adj*. 空的，无效的

【例】 1. The child's death left a painful *void* in his parents' lives. 孩子的死给父母的生活留下了痛苦的空虚。
2. That part of the town is completely *void* of interest for visitors. 游客对城镇的那个地段完全不感兴趣。
【同】 emptiness; vacant, null
【反】 full, valid

volatile ['vɒlətaɪl] *adj*. 挥发性的，可变的
【记】 volat(飞) + ile(形容词词尾，表示"…的")→可以飞起来的→挥发性的
【例】 He has a highly *volatile* personality. 他有着反复无常的个性。
【同】 inconstant
【反】 nonvolatile
【派】 volatility *n*. 挥发性
volatilize *v*. 挥发

volcano [vɒl'keɪnəʊ] *n*. 火山
【记】 volcan(= Vulcan，罗马神话中的火神) + o(表示"人或物")→和火有关的东西→火山
【例】 An active *volcano* may erupt at any time. 活火山随时可能喷发。
【派】 volcanic *adj*. 火山(性)的

volume ['vɒljuːm, 'vɒljəm] *n*. 1. 卷，册；2. 量，大量
【记】 volu(卷，滚) + me(名词词尾)→卷起来的东西→卷，册
【例】 1. You'll find the article in *volume* 9 of the encyclopedia. 你可以在大百科全书的第九卷找到这篇文章。
2. The television is too loud; turn the *volume* down. 电视声音太响了，把音量调低点儿。
【同】 book; capacity, mass
【派】 voluminous *adj*. 卷数多的，长篇的；容积大的

vomit ['vɒmɪt] *n*./*v*. 呕吐，呕吐物
【例】 He *vomited* up all he had eaten. 他把吃下的东西全吐了出来。
【同】 puke, retch

vote [vəʊt] *v*. /*n*. 投票，表决
【例】 1. At the end of the meeting, a *vote* was taken on the motion. 会议结束前对该项提议进行了表决。
2. Parliament *voted* the bill through without a debate. 国会未经辩论就投票通过了这项法案。
【同】 suffrage, election
【派】 voter *n*. 投票者，选举人

voucher ['vaʊtʃər] *n*. 代金券，优惠购物券
【记】 vouch(担保) + er(名词词尾)→被担保的凭证→代金券
【例】 Some firms give their workers luncheon *vouchers*. 一些公司发给员工午餐券。
【同】 coupon
【派】 (逆构)vouch *v*. 担保，证明

vow [vaʊ] *n*./*v*. 誓约，宣誓

【例】 Nuns are under *vows* of poverty, chastity and obedience. 修女必须立誓保持清贫、贞节、顺从。

【同】 promise, swear

voyage [ˈvɔɪɪdʒ] *v*./*n*. 旅行，航程

【记】 voy(路) + age(名词词尾)→走过的路→航程

【例】 1. The ship will start its maiden *voyage* next Monday. 这艘船将于下周一开始它的处女航。

2. They planned to *voyage* across the Pacific Ocean. 他们计划做穿越太平洋的旅行。

【同】 navigate, sail

vulgar [ˈvʌlgə] *adj*. 庸俗的，粗鲁的

【记】 vulg(平民) + ar(形容词词尾)→属于平民阶层的→庸俗的

【例】 She dressed in cheap and *vulgar* finery. 她穿着廉价而庸俗的华丽衣服。

【同】 coarse, indecent

【反】 decent, elegant

【派】 vulgarian *n*. 俗物，俗人

vulnerable [ˈvʌlnərəbəl] *adj*. 易受攻击的，脆弱的

【记】 vulnera(vulnerate, 受伤) + ble(形容词词尾)→易受伤害的→脆弱的

【例】 Your arguments are rather *vulnerable* to criticism. 你的论据有漏洞，经不起人家的批评。

【同】 defenseless, unprotected

【反】 defensive

【派】 vulnerability *n*. 弱点，攻击

W

wag [wæg] *v*./*n*.(-gged; -gging)摇摆，摇动

【例】 Dogs *wag* their tails when they are pleased. 狗一高兴就摇尾巴。

【同】 swing, wave, waggle

wagon ['wægən] *n*.(也可作 waggon)四轮马车，货车

【例】 The *wagon* jogged along on the rough road. 马车沿着崎岖不平的道路颠簸前行。

【同】 carriage, van

waist [weɪst] *n*. 腰部，腰

【例】 She wears a ribbon belt round her *waist*. 她在腰部束了一条缎带。

wander ['wɒndə] *v*. 漫步，徘徊

【例】 The river *wanders* through some very beautiful country. 这条河流曲折蜿蜒的流经一些风景秀丽的乡村。

【同】 ramble, roam

wane [weɪn] *v*. 1.(月)呈下弦，亏缺；2.减少，衰落

【例】 1. The moon waxes and *wanes* every month. 月亮每个月都有盈亏。

2. His influence had *waned* in the company. 他在公司的影响力减弱了。

【同】 decline, recede

【反】 wax

ward [wɔːd] *n*. 1.守卫，保护；2.牢房，病房；*v*. 守护，躲开

【例】 1. The patient now has moved into the isolation *ward*. 病人现在已经搬进了隔离病房。

2. Brushing your teeth regularly helps to *ward* off teeth decay. 经常刷牙可以防止龋齿。

【同】 guard, protect; cellblock

【派】 warder *n*. 看守人，门卫

warehouse ['weəhaus] *n*. 仓库，货栈

【记】 ware(器皿) + house(房屋)→存放器皿的房屋→仓库

【例】 They stored their goods in a *warehouse*. 他们把货物储存在一个仓库里。

【同】 depot, storehouse

【派】 (逆构)ware *n*. 陶器，器皿

warfare ['wɔːfeə] *n*. 战争，竞争

【记】 war(战争) + fare(走，进行)→进行战争→战争

【例】 There is open *warfare* between the opponents of the plan and its supporters. 支持与反对这项计划的人已经公开论战。

【同】 war
【反】 peace
【派】 (逆构)war *n.*/*v.* 战争，作战
wartime *n.* 战时

warrant ['wɒrənt] *n.* 授权，正当理由；*v.* 1.使有正当理由；2.保证，批准
【例】 1. You shouldn't arrest him without *warrant*. 你不能毫无根据地逮捕他。
2. This tiny crowd doesn't *warrant* such a large police presence. 没有理由出动这么多的警察来对付这么一小群人。
3. The law *warrants* this procedure. 这一程序是法律批准的。
【同】 certificate, justify, guarantee
【派】 warrantor *n.* 保证人，担保人
warranty *n.* (正当)理由，授权
warrantable *adj.* 可证明为正确的，可证实的；可担保的

wary ['weərɪ] *adj.* 机警的，警惕的
【记】 war(e)(当心，留意) + y(形容词词尾)→一直留意的→机警的
【例】 She was *wary* of strangers. 她很警惕陌生人。
【同】 watchful, cautious
【派】 wariness *n.* 谨慎，小心

waterproof ['wɔːtəpruːf] *adj.* 防水的，不透水的
【记】 water(水) + proof(防…的)→防水的
【例】 I bought a *waterproof* watch. 我买了一块防水表。
【同】 rainproof, watertight

waver ['weɪvə] *n.*/*v.* 动摇，颤抖
【记】 wav(e)(波动) + er(表示动作的反复)→一直在波动→动摇
【例】 While we were *wavering*, somebody else bought the house. 当我们还犹豫不决的时候，别人把那所房子买下了。
【同】 hesitate, quiver
【派】 wavering *adj.* 摇摆的，犹豫不决的

wavy ['weɪvɪ] *adj.* 波状的，摇摆的
【记】 wav(e)(波动) + y(形容词词尾)→波动的→波状的
【例】 Her *wavy* hair fell in loose wisps and loops upon her shoulders. 她那一头波浪般的长发一簇簇一圈圈地散垂在肩上。
【同】 rippled, wavelike
【派】 (逆构)wave *n.*/*v.* 波动；致意

wax [wæks] *n.* 1.蜡，蜡状物；2.月亮由亏转盈；*v.* 变大，月亮渐满
【例】 1. He lit up a *wax* candle. 他点燃了一支蜡烛。
2. Throughout history empires have *waxed* and waned. 历史上各个帝国的革故鼎新均有兴衰。
【同】 grow, rise
【反】 wane

weapon ['wepən] *n.* 武器，兵器

【例】 The fisher used a spear as his *weapon*. 渔夫用矛作为武器。
【同】 arm, munition

weary ['wɪərɪ] *adj*. 疲倦的，厌烦的
【例】 I feel *weary* after such a long journey. 经过这么长时间的旅行后，我觉得很累。
【同】 tired, exhausted
【反】 vigorous, energetic
【派】 weariness *n*. 厌烦，疲劳
wearisome *adj*. 令人疲倦的，厌烦的

weather ['weðə] *n*. 天气，气候；*v*. 使受风吹雨打，使风化
【例】 1. What is the *weather* like today? 今天天气情况怎样？
2. The rock *weathered* through the centuries. 岩石经历了上百年的风雨侵蚀。
【同】 climate; endure
【派】 weathercast *n*. 气象预报
weathering *n*. 侵蚀，风化

weave [wiːv] *n*. 编织法，编织；*v*. 1. 编织；2. 使迂回前进
【例】 1. She has been taught to *weave* as a child. 她从小就学会织布了。
2. The road *weaves* through the range of hills. 这条公路在群山中绕来绕去。
【同】 braid, intertwine
【反】 unweave
【派】 weaver *n*. 织布者，织工
weaving *n*. 编织

wedding ['wedɪŋ] *n*. 婚宴，结婚典礼
【记】 wed(结婚) + d + ing(形容词词尾转用为名词词尾)→结婚的场合→结婚典礼
【例】 The royal *wedding* was an occasion of great festivity. 皇室婚礼是喜庆的盛事。
【同】 marriage
【派】 (逆构)wed *v*. (-dded; -dding)娶，嫁，结婚
wedded *adj*. 已结婚的，结合的

weep [wiːp] *n*./*v*. (wept, wept)哭泣，哀悼
【例】 When he heard the news he broke down and *wept*. 当他听到这个消息时控制不住感情，哭了起来。
【同】 cry, mourn
【反】 laugh, smile
【派】 weeping *n*. 流泪的；树枝下垂的
weepy *adj*. 要哭的，催人泪下的

weird [wɪəd] *adj*. 怪诞的，奇异的
【例】 He looks like nothing on earth in those *weird* clothes. 他穿着奇装异服难看极了。
【同】 strange, uncanny, odd
【反】 natural

welfare ['welfeə] *n*. 幸福，福利
【记】 wel(好) + fare(进行)→情况进行得很好→幸福，福利
【例】 The government decided to promote public *welfare*. 政府决定发展公共福利。

【同】 benefit, prosperity

【反】 misery

【派】 welfarism *n*. 社会福利制度,

wheel [wiːl,hwiːl] *n*. 轮,车轮,(汽车的)方向盘; *v*. 推动,转动

【例】 1. I'm rather tired; will you take the *wheel*? 我累了,你来驾驶好吗?

2. The mother *wheeled* the baby round the park. 母亲用小车推着婴儿在公园游玩。

【派】 wheelchair *n*. 轮椅

whirl [hwɜːl] *v*. /*n*. 旋转,急走

【例】 1. He can't adjust himself to the *whirl* of modern life in this big city. 他无法适应这个大都市的现代生活的忙碌。

2. The wind *whirled* the dead leaves about. 风吹得枯叶在四处回旋。

【同】 rotate, twirl

whisper [ˈwɪspə,ˈhwɪspə] *n*. /*v*. 耳语,密谈

【例】 Don't you know it's rude to *whisper*? 你难道不知道窃窃私语是不礼貌的吗?

【同】 mumble, murmur

【反】 shout

【派】 whisperer *n*. 拨弄是非的人,告密者

whispery *adj*. 轻声的

whistle [hwɪsl] *n*. /*v*. (吹)口哨,(鸣)汽笛

【记】 whist(= whiz, 飕飕的声音) + le(名词词尾)→发出飕飕声的→口哨

【例】 1. He gave a loud *whistle* of gladness. 他吹了一声响亮的口号表示高兴。

2. The referee *whistled* and the game began. 裁判哨子一响,比赛开始了。

【派】 whistler *n*. 吹口哨的人

wholesale [ˈhəulseɪl] *adj*. 批发的,大规模的

【记】 whole(整个的) + sale(出售)→整个的出售,大批的出售→批发的

【例】 The *wholesale* prices of these shirts are 45 dollars. 这些衬衫的批发价是45美元。

【反】 retail

【派】 wholesaler *n*. 批发商

wholesome [ˈhəulsəm] *adj*. 卫生的,有益健康的

【记】 whole(完全的) + some(形容词词尾,表示"有…倾向")→完全(正常)的样子→卫生的

【例】 In order to maintain physical well being, a person should eat *wholesome* food and get sufficient exercise. 为了维持身体健康,一个人应该吃有益健康的食品,并经常锻炼身体。

【同】 healthy, beneficial

【反】 unwholesome, harmful

wicked [ˈwɪkɪd] *adj*. 邪恶的,缺德的

【记】 wick(坏) + ed(形容词词尾)→坏的→邪恶的

【例】 That was very *wicked* of you. 你干的事可真缺德。

【同】 bad, evil

【反】 upright，virtuous

【派】 wickedness *n*. 邪恶，不道德

wig [wɪg] *n*. 假发

【例】 The actress wore a black *wig* over her blond hair. 这个女演员在她的金发上套上黑色的假发。

【同】 hairpiece，toupee

【派】 wigged *adj*. 戴假发的

wink [wɪŋk] *n*./*v*. 眨眼，使眼色，闪烁

【例】 He *winked* at me to show that he was playing a joke on the others. 他向我眨了眨一只眼，意思是他正在开别人的玩笑。

【同】 blink，twinkle

wisdom ['wɪzdəm] *n*. 智慧，学识

【记】 wis(e)(聪明的) + dom(名词词尾)→聪明→智慧

【例】 His father's *wisdom* was hardly handed down to him. 他父亲的智慧几乎没有传到他身上。

【同】 intelligence，wit

【反】 folly，stupidity

【派】 (逆构)wise *adj*. 英明的，狡猾的

wistful ['wɪstfʊl] *adj*. 渴望的，想往的

【记】 wist(意图) + ful(形容词词尾)→有意图的→想往的

【例】 The boy looks with *wistful* eyes at the toy on display. 那男孩看着展出的玩具，眼中流露出渴望的神情。

【同】 desirous，longing，yearning

wit [wɪt] *n*. 智力，智慧

【例】 It is surely not beyond the *wit* of the government to solve this simple problem. 政府的确不应该没有能力解决这个简单的问题。

【同】 wisdom，intelligence

【反】 folly，stupidity

【派】 witty *adj*. 机智的，诙谐的

withdraw [wɪð'drɔː] *v*. (-drew，-drawn)取消，撤回

【记】 with(向相反的方向) + draw(拉引)→向相反的方向拉→撤回

【例】 The troops have been *withdrawn* from the danger area. 部队已经撤出危险地带。

【同】 remove，retreat

【反】 deposit

【派】 withdrawal *n*. 收回，取消

withdrawn *adj*. 性格内向的；偏僻的

W

wither ['wɪðə] *v*. 凋谢，消亡

【例】 The flowers will *wither* if you don't put them in water. 如果你不把这些花放在水里，它们就会凋谢。

【同】 fade，shrivel

【派】 withered *adj*. 枯萎的，干瘪的

withhold [wɪð'həʊld] *v*. (-held, -held)保留，抑制

【记】 with(向相反的方向)+hold(持有)→抓住不让向另外的方向→抑制

【例】 The board has decided to *withhold* part of their grant money from certain students. 委员会决定不发给某些学生的部分助学金。

【同】 keep, retain

withstand [wɪð'stænd] *v*. (-stood, -stood)抵挡，经受住

【记】 with(相反的方向)+stand(站立)→对着…站着→抵挡

【例】 She had a pair of shoes that will *withstand* hard wear. 她有一双非常耐穿的鞋。

【同】 endure, resist

witness ['wɪtnɪs] *n*. 证人，证据；*v*. 目击，作证

【记】 wit(知道)+ness(名词词尾)→知道的人→证人

【例】 1. Police have appealed for *witnesses* to come forward. 警方呼吁目击者挺身而出。

2. Did anyone *witness* the traffic accident? 有谁目击了这场交通事故？

【同】 see, observe, testify

workforce [wɜːkfɔːs] *n*. 劳动力，工人总数

【记】 work(工作)+force(力量)→参与工作的力量→劳动力

【例】 The whole *workforce* is out on strike. 全体劳工都在罢工。

【同】 manpower

workshop ['wɜːkʃɒp] *n*. 1. 车间；2. 研习会

【记】 work(工作)+shop(店铺)→工作的店铺→工作的地方→车间

【例】 1. There are more than fifty workers in this *workshop*. 这个车间里有五十多个工人。

2. We'll have a poetry *workshop*. 我们将开个诗歌研习会。

worship ['wɜːʃɪp] *n*. 崇拜，礼拜；*v*. (-p(p)ed; -p(p)ing)崇拜，尊敬

【记】 wor(th)(价值)+ship(名词词尾，"…的样子")→把价值有形化→崇拜

【例】 1. She was blind to the silent *worship* in his eyes. 她没有发觉他眼里流露出的无声的敬慕之情。

2. She *worshipped* him and refused to receive his critics. 她很崇拜他，听不进别人对他的批评。

【同】 esteem, honor

【反】 contempt, scorn

【派】 worshiper *n*. 参加礼拜者，崇拜者

worshipful *adj*. 崇拜的，可贵的

wrap [ræp] *n*. 外套，包裹；*v*. (-pped; -pping)包装，缠绕

【例】 1. The plans for the new space mission are still under *wraps*. 新的太空宇航计划仍未公开。

2. I *wrapped* the rug around the sick man's legs to keep him warm. 我用毯子把病人的腿包了起来，让他暖和一点儿。

【同】 enclose, envelop

【反】 unwrap, loosen

wreath [riːθ] *n*. 花圈，花冠

【例】 They laid *wreaths* at the war memorial. 他们向阵亡将士纪念碑献花圈。
【同】 garland
【派】 wreathe *v*. 缠绕，围着

wreck [rek] *n*. 失事船(飞机等的)残骸，失事；*v*. 破坏，拆毁
【例】 1. Have they found the *wreck* of the ship? 他们找到那艘船的残骸了吗?
2. The ship was *wrecked* on the rock. 船在岩石上撞毁了。
【同】 crash，destroy
【派】 wreckage *n*. 遭难，失事

wrinkle [ˈrɪŋkl] *n*./*v*. (使生)皱纹
【记】 wrink(扭曲)＋le(名词词尾)→(脸)扭曲了的→起皱纹的
【例】 She is beginning to get *wrinkles* around her eyes. 她眼角上开始出现皱纹了。
【同】 crease，crinkle
【派】 wrinkly *adj*. 有皱纹的，易生皱纹的

Y

yacht [jɒt] *n*. 游艇，快艇，帆船

【记】 yacht 本义是"追击"，原来是用做追击海盗的船→快艇

【例】 The *yacht* hit a rock and damaged her bows. 游艇碰上了礁石，撞坏了船头。

【同】 boat

yearn [jɜːn] *v*. 渴望，怀念

【例】 He *yearned* for his home and family. 他怀念故国家园。

【同】 long, desire

【派】 yearning *n*. 向往，渴望

yield [jiːld] *v*. 1. 出产，生产；2. 屈服，屈从；*n*. 产量，收益

【例】 1. His business *yields* big profits. 他的生意带来巨大的利润。

2. Despite all our attempts to break it open, the lock would not *yield*. 尽管我们想方设法要把锁弄断，它却仍然纹丝不动。

3. These trees gave a high *yield* of fruit this year. 这些果树今年获得了大丰收。

【同】 produce; concede; output

【反】 stand

yolk [jəʊk] *n*. 蛋黄，卵黄

【例】 The *yolk* is the yellow part in an egg. 蛋黄是鸡蛋中的黄色部分。

【派】 yolky *adj*. 蛋黄的，似蛋黄的

Z

zeal [ziːl] *n*. 热心，热诚

【例】 She works with great *zeal*. 她热情洋溢地工作。

【同】 ardor, passion, enthusiasm

【反】 apathy, indifference

【派】 zealous *adj*. 热心的

zigzag [ˈzɪgzæg] *adj*. 曲折的，之字形的；*v*. 曲折行进

【记】 zig(转弯) + zag(急转)→转来转去→曲折的

【例】 1. There is a *zigzag* path in the garden. 花园里有一条之字形的小道。

2. The path *zigzags* up the hill. 这条小道向山顶蜿蜒而上。

【同】 bendy; twist

附录:分类词汇表

1 Philosophy 哲学

Logic 逻辑学

universal *adj*. 全称的;*n*. 全称命题
concept *n*. 概念
gist *n*. 要义
term *n*. 项
middle *n*. 中项
proposition *n*. 命题
premise *n*. 前提
antecedent *adj*.前提的,前件的;*n*.前提,前件
hypothesis *n*. 假设,前提
contingent *adj*. 或有的,不是逻辑上必然的
implication *n*. 蕴涵
connotation *n*. 内涵,含义
denotation *n*. 外延,指称
association *n*. 联想,联合
analogy *n*. 类比
conjecture *n*./*v*. 假设
reasoning *n*. 推理,推论
demonstrate *v*. 证明
statement *n*. 陈述,综述
counterargument *n*. 驳论,抗辩
incompatible *adj*. 不能同时成立的(两个以上的命题)
inconsistency *n*. 矛盾,不相容性
contradiction *n*. 矛盾,矛盾命题
undistributed *adj*. 不周延的
conclusion *n*. (三段论的)性质判断
fallacy *n*. 谬误,谬论
dichotomy *n*. 二分法
syllogism *n*. 三段论法
induction *n*. 归纳(法)
deduction *n*. 演绎(法)
dialectic(s) *n*. 逻辑论证,辩证法

Psychology 心理学

hang-up *n*. (尤指精神或感情上摆脱不掉的)烦恼,焦虑
drive *n*. 内驱力
stimulus *n*. 刺激
resistance *n*. 抵抗,阻抗
attribute *n*. 属性,性质
pattern *n*. 模式
intention *n*. 意图,意念
identity *n*. 同一性,一致
feedback *n*. 反馈
abnegation *n*. 放弃
egocentrism *n*. 自我中心主义
egoism *n*. 自我主义
altruism *n*. 利他主义
extrovert *n*. 性格外向者
introvert *n*. 性格内向的人
affirmative *adj*. 肯定的
caution *n*. 小心,谨慎,警告

Philosophies 哲学

stoicism *n*. 斯多葛哲学
sophism *n*. 诡辩
sophist *n*. 诡辩家,诡辩者
skepticism *n*. 怀疑论
skeptic *n*. 怀疑论者
empiricism *n*. 经验主义,经验论
epistemology *n*. 认识论
hedonics *n*. 享乐(主义)论
ontology *n*. 存在论
theism *n*. 有神论
pantheism *n*. 泛神论
parallelism *n*. 心身平行论
determinism *n*. 决定论
idealism *n*. 唯心主义,唯心论
materialism *n*. 唯物主义,唯物论
utilitarianism *n*. 功利主义
humanism *n*. 人本主义理论
humanitarianism *n*. 人道主义
pessimism *n*. 悲观,悲观主义
positivism *n*. 实证论,实证主义
structuralism *n*. 构造主义

一般哲学用词

ideology *n*. 意识形态
substance *n*. 性质
awareness *n*. 觉知

paradigm *n*. 范式
principle *n*. 原则
disciple *n*. 信徒，弟子
erudite *adj*. 博学的
oncoming *adj*. 即将来临的，接近的；*adj*. 基础的，基本的
fundamental *n*. 基本原则，基本原理
adamant *adj*. 固执的
specific *adj*. 特殊的
perceive *v*. 感知，察觉
simplify *v*. 单一化，简单化

2 Religion 宗教

Theology 神学

theology *n*. 神学
salvation *n*. 灵魂得救，超度
redemption *n*. 救赎，赎罪
mission *n*. 传道，传道权
missionary *n*. 传教士
pilgrim *n*. 圣地朝拜者，朝圣者
eschatology *n*. 末世学，来世论
Adventism *n*. 耶稣复临论
Advent *n*. 基督降临，降临节
atheism *n*. 无神论
monotheism *n*. 一神论，一神教
polytheism *n*. 多神教，多神论
satanism *n*. 恶魔崇拜，恶魔主义
diabolism *n*. 魔法，妖术

Christianity 基督教

Christianity *n*. 基督教
Catholicism *n*. 天主教
Protestantism *n*. 新教
Baptist Church *n*. 浸礼会教堂
Quakers *n*. 教友派信徒，贵格教徒
denomination *n*. 教派
orthodox *adj*. 正统的，东正教的
heterodox *adj*. 异端的，异教的
pagan *n*. 异教徒
infidel *n*. 无信仰者，异教徒
convert *v*. 使…改变信仰
Providence *vt*. 天意，上帝的保佑；神，上帝
Province *n*. 大教区
parish *n*. 教区
chapel *n*. 小礼拜堂
worship *v*. 礼拜，拜神
Mass *n*. 弥撒
benediction *n*. 礼拜末尾的祝祷，（餐前餐后的）谢恩祷
hymn *n*. 赞美诗，圣歌
sermon *n*. 布道，说教
intone *v*. 唱或吟咏（圣歌）
New(Old) Testament 新（旧）约全书
apocalypse *n*. 启示录
devil *n*. 魔鬼
omnipotence *n*. （全能的）上帝
lord *n*. 上帝
crucify *v*. 把…钉在十字架上
apostle *n*. 使徒（指耶稣十二使徒）
doom *n*. 末日审判
doomsday *n*. 最后审判日
resurrection *n*. 人类的复活
Easter *n*. 复活节
clergyman *n*. 牧师，教士
archbishop *n*. 大主教
cardinal *n*. 枢机主教，红衣主教
minister *n*. 牧师，（某些教派的）教长
persecution *n*. 迫害时期
martyrdom *n*. 殉难，殉道
martyr *n*. 殉道者，殉教者

Other Religions 其它宗教

Islam *n*. 伊斯兰教
Muslim *n*. 穆斯林，伊斯兰教徒
mosque *n*. 清真寺
Hinduism *n*. 印度教
Hindi *n*. 北印度语，印地语
Hindu temple 印度庙宇
sutra *n*. 佛经
Judaism *n*. 犹太教
rabbi *n*. 拉比（犹太人的学者），犹太传教士
synagogue *n*. 犹太人集会，犹太教会堂
Buddhism *n*. 佛教
Buddhist *n*. 佛教徒
meditation *n*. （尤指宗教的）默想
nirvana *n*. （佛教）涅，极乐世界
karma *n*. 因果报应，羯磨
Samsara (transmigration) *n*. 轮回
reincarnation *n*. 再投胎，再生
Confucianism *n*. 孔教，儒教

一般宗教用词

religious dispute 宗教冲突
religious cult 宗教崇拜
primitive religion 原始宗教
ritual *n*. (宗教)仪式
foresight *n*. 预见
deification *n*. 神格化，奉若神明
spell *n*. 符咒
circumcision *n*. 割礼
immolation *n*. 祭物
fabulous *adj*. 神话般的，奇异的
pious *adj*. 虔诚的
sacred *adj*. 神的，神圣的
sanctity *n*. 圣洁
spirit *n*. 灵魂，幽灵
incorporeal *adj*. 灵魂的
secular *adj*. 尘世的，世俗的
profane *adj*. 亵渎的
blasphemy *n*. 亵渎(的言行)
malediction *n*. 诅咒

3 Economics 经济学

Economy 经济

GNP(Gross National Product) 国民生产总值
trade cycle 贸易循环，商业周期
financial crisis 金融危机
panic *n*. 惊慌，恐慌
moratorium *n*. 延期偿付
recession *n*. (经济)衰退，不景气
stagnation *n*. 停滞
depression *n*. 萧条，不景气
inflation *n*. 通货膨胀
stagflation *n*. 通货滞胀，不景气状况下之物价上涨
deflation *n*. 通货紧缩
depreciation *n*. 贬值
devaluation *n*. 贬值
revaluation *n*. 升值
price fluctuation 物价波动
slump *n*./*v*. 衰退，(物价)暴跌
skyrocket *v*. 使...迅速上升，飞涨
rapid growth 迅速增长
boom *n*./*v*. 繁荣
expansionary policy 经济扩张政策
buoyant *adj*. (价格等)有上涨倾向的；(国家收入等)趋向增长的

Finances 金融

fiscal year 财政年度
fiscal *adj*. 财政的，国库的
national treasury 国库
budget *n*./*v*. 预算
bottom line *n*. 底线
fund *n*. 资金，基金
subsidy *n*. 补助金，津贴
annuity *n*. 年金
tariff *n*. 关税
preferential *adj*. 优先的，特惠的
declare *v*. 申报(纳税品等)
revenue *n*. 收入，税收
defraud the revenue
Value Added Tax 增值税
levy *n*./*v*. 征收，征税
assess *v*. 确定(税款等)的数额；征收(税款等)

monetary circulation 货币流通

monetary system 货币体系
fiat money 不兑现纸币
paper note 纸币
counterfeit *n*. 假币；*adj*. 假冒的，假装的；*v*. 仿造，伪造
principal *n*. 资本，本金
interest *n*. 利息
passbook *n*. 存款簿，银行存折
installment *n*. 分期付款
stock *n*. 股票
bond *n*. 公债，债券
stocks and bonds 股票和债券
blue chip 执行股票，蓝筹股
bill *n*. 纸币，钞票
bill of debt 债票
bill of dishonor 拒付汇票
clearing house 票据交换所
endorse *v*. 在(票据)背面签名，签署
pecuniary *adj*. 金钱的，金钱上的
due *n*. 应得物；[复]应付款；*adj*. 应得的；应付的，到期的

business 商业

small and medium-sized enterprises 中小企业
incorporation *n*. 合并，组成公司；公司

consolidation *n*. 巩固，合并
mergers & acquisitions 收购兼并，并购
audit *n*./ *v*. 审计，稽核
output *n*. 产量
increment *n*. 增加;盈余，利润
gains *n*. 利润，获利
surplus *n*. 剩余，盈余；*adj*. 过剩的
the black-ink balance 贷方余额
deficit *n*. 赤字
futility *n*. 无益，无用
shutdown *n*. 关门，停工
bankruptcy *n*. 破产
bust *n*. 萧条，破产
liquidate *v*. 清算
proprietary name *n*. 注册商标，专利商品名
tycoon *n*. 企业界大亨
recruit *n*. 新兵，新人；*v*. 招募，招聘

transaction 交易

transaction *n*. 办理，交易
monopoly *n*. 垄断
oligopoly *n*. 寡头垄断
monopoly and oligopoly 垄断与寡头垄断
proprietary *adj*. 专利的，有专利权的；*n*. 所有者，所有权
retail *n*./*v*. 零售;*adj*. 零售的
wholesale *n*./*v*. 批发;*adj*. 批发的
rush *n*. 匆促，抢购热潮
glut *n*./*v*. 充斥，供过于求
bargain *n*. 交易，成交商品;便宜货;*v*. 议价
commodity *n*. 日用品
line *n*. 运输公司
inventory *n*. 详细目录，存货清册；*v*. 盘存，盘点
stocktaking *n*. 存货盘点
current price 现价，时价
appraise *v*. 评价，估价
barter *n*./*v*. 物品交换，实物交易
swap *v*./*n*. 交换，作交易
advance *n*./*v*. 预付(款)
voucher *n*. 凭证，凭单;<美>优惠购货券
waive *v*. 搁置，延期进行
cession *n*. 让与(他人)债权
gratuitous conveyance 免费转让
gratuitous *adj*. 免费的(free)
stipulate *v*. (在协议、条约或契约上)规定
covenant *n*./*v*. (缔结)盟约，契约
subcontract *n*. 转包合同
mortgage *n*./*v*. 抵押
security *n*. 安全
reimbursement *n*. 偿还，补偿;报销

一般经济学用词

check and balance 制约平衡，制衡原则
the trade imbalance 贸易不平衡
equilibrium *n*. 平衡，均衡
outlay *n*. 费用
profligacy *n*. 极度的浪费，恣意的挥霍
extravagance *n*. 奢侈，铺张
avocation *n*. (个人)副业，业余爱好
auction *n*./*v*. 拍卖
bidding *n*. 投标，出价
competitive bidding 竞标，竞争出价
tender *v*. (～for)投标
appropriation *n*. 拨款
smuggle *n*./*v*. 走私
speculate *v*. 做投机买卖
detriment *n*. 损害，有害物
fiasco *n*. 惨败，大失败

4 Law 法律

Crime 犯罪

criminal *n*.罪犯,犯罪者 *adj*.犯罪的,犯法的
principal *n*. 主犯
suspect *n*. 嫌疑犯
accessory *n*. 从犯，同谋者;*adj*. 同谋的
outlaw *n*. 歹徒，逃犯
ex-convict *n*. 从前曾被判刑的人
delinquency *n*. 行为不良，错失
misdemeanor *n*. 轻罪
felony *n*. 重罪
arson *n*. 纵火，纵火罪
homicide *n*. 杀人
robbery *n*. 抢掠，抢劫
rape *n*. 强奸
sexual harassment 性骚扰
larceny *n*. 盗窃罪

fraud *n*. 欺骗，欺诈罪
blackmail *n*./*v*. 敲诈，勒索
perjury *n*. 伪誓，伪证
embezzle *v*. 盗用，挪用
manipulate *v*. 篡改(账目等)
bug *v*. 装置窃听器，窃听
commit *v*. 犯(法)，干(坏事)
violate *v*. 违犯，侵犯
conspiracy *n*. 共谋，阴谋
illegal *adj*. 违法的
iniquity *n*. 不公正
injustice *n*. 不公平
contingency *n*. 意外事故，偶然错误
lucre *n*. 钱财，利益

Lawsuit 诉讼

lawsuit *n*. 诉讼
criminal suit 刑事诉讼
procedure *n*. 程序，手续
sue *v*. 控告，提出诉讼
indict *v*. 起诉，控告
accuse *v*. 控告
appeal *n*. 上诉
lose a suit(case) 败诉
withdraw(drop) a suit 撤诉
prosecution *n*. 起诉，诉讼;原告，控方
complaint *n*. 申诉，控告
petition *n*. 申请书，上诉状
warrant of attorney (给诉讼代理人或律师的)委托书
warrant of arrest(arrest warrant) 逮捕证，拘票
search warrant 搜查证
writ *n*. 文书，正式文件
plaintiff *n*. 起诉人，原告
arbitrator *n*. 仲裁人，公断者
defendant *n*. 被告
suspicion *n*. 猜疑，怀疑
summon *v*. 传唤，传唤到庭
alleged *adj*. 声称的，有嫌疑的
false charge 编造的罪名
invalidity *n*. 无效力
autopsy *n*.(为查明死因而做的)尸体解剖，验尸

Trial 审判

courtroom *n*. 法庭，审判室
hearing *n*. 听证，听证会
default *n*./*v*. 缺席
jury *n*. 陪审团，陪审员
judge *n*. 法官，审判员
prosecutor *n*. 原告，起诉人，公诉人
lawyer *n*. 律师
defense *n*. 辩护词;辩护律师
testimony *n*. 证词(尤指在法庭所作的)
testify *v*. 证明，作证
witness *n*. 证人，证词;*v*. 作证
cross-examine *v*. 诘问(对方证人)，反复询问
interrogation *n*. 审问
take the fifth *v*. 以美国宪法第五条修正案为庇护(避而不答)
mute *n*. 拒不答辩的被告
plea *n*. 辩解，抗辩
verdict *n*. (陪审团的)裁决，判决
sentence *n*./*v*. 判决，宣判
jeopardy *n*. 有罪受刑的可能性，刑事案件中被告的处境
conviction *n*. 定罪，宣告有罪
guilt *n*. 罪行
precedent *n*. 先例

Punishment 处罚

capital punishment 死刑
execution *n*. 执行法庭决议;处死，死刑
life imprisonment 无期徒刑
imprisonment *n*. 关押
custody *n*. 拘留，监禁
monetary penalty 罚款处分
suspended sentence *n*. 缓刑
probation *n*. 缓刑
bail *n*./*v*. 保释

一般法律用词

constitution *n*. 宪法
criminal law 刑法
penal *adj*. 刑事的，刑法上的
judicial *adj*. 司法的，法院的
judicature *n*. 司法
act *n*. 法案，法令
agreement *n*. 契约，协议
code *n*.法典，法规，章程
bylaw *n*. 次要法规
due process 法定诉讼程序
amnesty *n*. (尤指对反政府政治犯的)特赦
implication *n*. 牵连
double jeopardy 一罪不受两次审理原则，双重危境

feasible *adj*. 可行的，切实可行的

enforce *v*. 推行，实施(法律等)

5 Politics 政治

Election 选举

by-election 递补选举
campaign *n*. 活动，竞选运动
canvass *v*. 游说，拉选票
address *n*./*v*. 演讲，演说
debate *n*./*v*. 争论，辩论
candidate *n*. 候选人
aide *n*. 助手，副官
delegate *n*. 代表；*v*. 委派…为代表
demagogue *n*. 煽动政治家
referendum *n*. 公民投票
ballot box 投票箱
suffrage *n*. 投票，选举权
vote *n*./*v*. 投票，选票
abstention *n*. 弃权
poll *n*. 选举之投票
plurality *n*. (选举中获得的)相对多数，相对多数票
unanimous *adj*. 意见一致的，无异议的

Government 政府

authorities *n*. 当局，官方
sovereignty *n*. 主权，主权国家
autonomy *n*. 自治
inaugurate *v*. 举行就职典礼
inaugural *adj*. 就职的，开始的；*n*. 就职演说
summit conference(talk) 峰会
protocol *n*. 草案，协议
ratify *v*. 批准，认可
publicize *v*. 宣扬，宣传
autarchy *n*. 独裁，专制
appointment *n*. 任命，选派；职位，职务
cabinet *n*. 内阁
bicameral *adj*. 两院制的
the House 议院
senator *n*. 议员
Congress *n*. (美国)国会
Parliament *n*. (英国)议会
independent *n*. 中立派，无党派议员
opposition party 反对党
secession *n*. 脱离，分裂主义
hard-liner *n*. 不妥协者
official *n*. 官员，公务员；*adj*. 官方的，正式的
consul *n*. 领事
deputy *n*. 议员，下院议员
rehabilitation *n*. 复职，复位
subvert *v*. 颠覆，策反

一般政治学用词

bureaucracy *n*. 官僚，官僚作风，官僚机构
democracy *n*. 民主政治，民主主义
communism *n*. 共产主义
totalitarianism *n*. 极权主义
hegemony *n*. 霸权
abolition *n*. 废除，废除奴隶制度
petition *n*. 请愿，请愿书
frontier *n*. 国境，边境
airspace *n*. 空域，领空
subject peoples
minority *n*. 少数，少数民族
racialism *n*. 种族主义，种族歧视
oppression *n*. 压迫，镇压
ouster *n*. 驱逐，剥夺
riot *n*. 暴乱，骚动
turmoil *n*. 骚动，混乱
political impasse 政治僵局
impasse *n*. 僵局
stalemate *n*. 僵持，僵局
status quo 现状
stopgap *n*. 临时替代的人或物，权宜之计
intransigent *adj*. 不妥协的，难和解的
anonymous *adj*. 匿名的

6 Sociology 社会学

Family Relationship 家庭关系

kinship *n*. 血族关系
lineage *n*. 血统，世系
consort *v*. 配偶(特指在位君主的夫或妻)
spouse *n*. 配偶(指夫或妻)

offspring *n*. (单复数同形)子孙，后代
sibling *n*. 兄弟姐妹，同胞
half brothers 同母异父(或同父异母)兄弟
illegitimate *adj*. 私生的
pedigree *n*. 血统，家谱
bastard *n*. 私生子
adoption *n*. 收养
testament *n*. 遗嘱
engagement *n*. 婚约
fiancé *n*. 〈法〉未婚夫
fiancée *n*. 〈法〉未婚妻
go-between *n*. 媒介者，中间人(middleman)
separation *n*. 分开，夫妻法定分居
alimony *n*. (离婚或分居后在诉讼期间男方给女方的)赡养费，生活费
divorce *n*./*v*. 离婚
break up 破坏，解体
infancy *n*. 婴儿期，幼年时代
juvenile *adj*. 青少年的；*n*. 青少年
adolescence *n*. 青春期
climacteric *n*. 更年期
senile *adj*. 老年的，高龄的
senescent *adj*. 老了的，衰老了的
precocious *adj*. 早熟的，发育过早的

Social Issue 社会问题

social integration 社会融合，社会整体化
walkout *n*. 罢工
disorder *n*. 混乱，无秩序状态
uproar *n*. 喧嚣，骚动
delinquency *n*. 行为不良，错失
juvenile delinquency 青少年犯罪
alienation *n*. 疏远，异化
minority *n*. 少数
bystander *n*. 旁观者
cultural bias 文化偏见
population density 人口密度
overpopulation *n*. 人口过剩
underpopulated *adj*. 人口稀少的
exodus *n*. 大批的离去
congestion *n*. (交通的)拥挤；(人口)稠密
pollution *n*. 污染
skyscraper *n*. 摩天大楼
metropolitan *adj*. 大城市的，大都会的
satellite *n*. 人造卫星
outer city 市郊

Social Welfare 社会福利

social security *n*. 社会保障
institution *n*. 公共机构，协会
infrastructure *n*. 基础建设
public facilities 市政设施
public utilities(works) 公用事业
prosperity *n*. 繁荣
charity *n*. 慈善，慈善团体
life annuity *n*. 终身年金
average life expectancy 平均寿命预期值
longevity *n*. 长命，寿命
community *n*. 社区，团体

一般社会学用词

throng *n*. 人群；*v*. 群集
peer group 同年龄组，同年龄群体
gregarious *adj*. 社交的
altruism *n*. 利他主义
egoism *n*. 自我主义，利己主义
contrariety *n*. 矛盾，相反物
consensus *n*. 多数人的意见，舆论
culminate *v*. 达到顶点
heyday *n*. 全盛期，年富力强时期
denomination *n*. 命名
alias *n*. 别名，化名
pseudonym *n*. 假名，笔名
paradigm *n*. 范例，典范
demography *n*. 人口统计学
census *n*. 人口普查

7 Anthropology 人类学

Cultural Anthropology 文化人类学

philology *n*. 语言学，文献学
mythology *n*. 神话
legend *n*. 传说
epic *n*. 史诗
folk story 民间故事
speculation *n*. 思索；做投机买卖
animism *n*. 万物有灵论
primitive religion 原始宗教
religious cult 宗教崇拜
sanctuary *n*. 圣所，圣殿；避难所
worship *n*./*v*. 崇拜，礼拜

aboriginal *adj*. 土著的，原来的；*n*. 土著居民
indigenous *adj*. 本土的
funerary *adj*. 葬礼的，埋葬的
nomadic *adj*. 游牧的
acquired *adj*. 已获得的，已成习惯的；习得的
antiquity *n*. 古代
forebear *n*. 祖先，祖宗
descendant *n*. 子孙，后裔
descend *v*. 下来，遗传
custom *n*. 习惯，风俗
dwelling *n*. 住处
implement *n*. 工具，器具
weaver *n*. 织布者，织工
loom *n*. 织布机，织机
erect *v*. 使竖立，树立
flourish *n*./*v*. 繁荣，茂盛
restoration *n*. 恢复，重建
pillar *n*. 柱子
watercourse *n*. 水道，河道

Social Anthropology 社会人类学

community *n*. 社区，团体
clan *n*. 部落，氏族
lineage *n*. 血统，世系
tribe *n*. 部落，部族
chieftain *n*. 酋长，首领
regime *n*. 政权，政权制度
legitimism *n*. 正统主义
monogamous *adj*. 一夫一妻的
matrilineal *adj*. 母系的
matriarchy *n*. 女家长制，女族长制
patriarchy *n*. 家长统治，父权制
monarchy *n*. 君主政体，君主政治
hereditary *adj*. 世袭的，遗传的
hierarchy *n*. 等级制度
class *n*. 阶级，社会等级
status *n*. 身份，地位
aristocrat *n*. 贵族
patrician *n*. 贵族；*adj*. 贵族的
plebeian *n*. 平民，庶民；*adj*. 平民的
turmoil *n*. 骚动，混乱
depredation *n*. 掠夺；毁坏
retaliation *n*. 报复，报仇
ups and downs 盛衰，沉浮(rise and fall)

一般人类学用词

biological anthropology 生物人类学
pluralism *n*. 多数状态；多重性
enigma *n*. 谜
juxtaposition *n*. 并置，并列
labyrinth *n*. 迷宫，难解的事物
phenomenon *n*. 现象
adjustment *n*. 调整，调节
adaptive *adj*. 适应的
radical *adj*. 基本的，激进的；*n*. 激进分子
inchoate *adj*. 初步的，早期的
ominous *adj*. 恶兆的，不吉利的
medieval *adj*. 中世纪的
elapse *v*. (时间)过去，消逝
persist *v*. 坚持，持续
testify *v*. 证明，证实

8 Education 教育

Campus Life 校园生活

academic adviser 学业导师
associate professor 副教授
faculty *n*. 全体教员；(大学的)系，学院
dean *n*. (大学)院长，系主任
chancellor *n*. 大学校长
freshman *n*. 新生，大学一年级学生
sophomore *n*. 大学二年级学生
junior *n*. 大学三年级学生
senior *n*. 大学四年级学生
dean's list (大学中定期公布的)优秀学生名单
repeater *n*. (不及格)重考者，重修(某课程)者
undergraduate *n*. 在校大学生
varsity *n*. 大学；大学运动代表队
alumnus *n*. (pl. alumni) 男毕业生，男校友
alumna *n*. (pl. alumnae) 女毕业生，女校友
scholarship *n*. 奖学金
grant *n*. 补助金，助学金
government aid 政府救济
student loan 助学贷款
sign up for 签约从事
extracurricular activities 课外活动
quote *v*. 引用，引证
submit *v*. 提交，递交
assignment *n*. 任务，作业

plagiarism *n*. 剽窃
bibliography *n*. 书目，参考书目
reference book 参考书
reserved book 保留图书
handout *n*. 分发的印刷品，散页
roll *n*. 名单
signboard *n*. 布告板

Academic Affairs Management 学校事务管理

curriculum *n*. 课程
syllabus *n*. 课程提纲
semester *n*. 学期
term paper *n*. 学期报告
credit *n*. 学分
absolute evaluation 绝对评价
relative evaluation 相对评价
scale *n*. 刻度，范围;阶梯
preliminary *adj*. 预备的,初步的;*n*.预考,预赛
grade *n*. 等级，级别;*v*. 评分，评级
GPA(Grade Point Average) 平均成绩点数
academic performance 学业成绩
academic probation 试读，见习
withdraw *v*. (从学校)领回
flunk *n*./*v*. 失败，考试不及格
drop-out *n*. 中途退学的人
skip *v*. 跳，跳读
transfer *n*. 转移，转学
application form 申请书，申请表
enrollment *n*. 登记，注册
matriculate *v*. 被录取入学;*n*. 被录取者
commencement *n*. 毕业典礼，学位授予典礼
dissertation *n*. (学位)论文
monograph *n*. 专论
diploma *n*. 文凭，毕业证书
bachelor's degree 学士学位
master's degree 硕士学位
doctor's degree 博士学位
certificate *n*. 证书，证明书
transcript(academic) *n*. 成绩单
report (card) *n*. 成绩单
recommendation *n*. 推荐(信)

Subject 科目

major subject 主要科目
liberal arts 文科
required/mandatory subject 必修课
optional subject 选修课
pedagogy *n*. 教育学
ethics *n*. 伦理学
pharmacy *n*. 药剂学
medicine *n*. 药，医学
earth science 地球学
geography *n*. 地理学
social studies(social science) 社会科学
economics *n*. 经济学
politics *n*. 政治，政治学
history *n*. 历史，历史学
world history 世界历史
language arts 语言艺术学科
fine arts 美术
physical education 体育

Educational Institution 教育机构

community *n*. 团体，社团，界
college *n*.(综合大学中的)学院,(独立的)学院
university *n*. (综合)大学
graduate school 研究生院
administration office 行政办公室
auditorium *n*. 会堂，礼堂
gymnasium *n*. 健身房，体育馆
dormitory *n*. 宿舍
sorority *n*. 女学生联谊会
fraternity *n*. 兄弟互助会，兄弟会

一般教育用词

primary education 小学教育，初等教育
secondary education 中等教育(指初、高中)
lecture-based education 以授课为基础的教育
audiovisual education 视听教育
distance education 远程教育
lifelong education 终身教育
alternative education 选择性教育

9 Literature 文学

Genres of Literature 文学体裁

genre *n*. 类型，流派
epic *n*. 史诗
lyric *n*. 抒情诗
ode *n*. 颂诗，颂歌

elegy *n*. 挽歌
sonnet *n*. 十四行诗
anthology *n*. 诗选，文选
verse *n*. 韵文，诗
prose *n*. 散文
biography *n*. 传记
autobiography *n*. 自传
chronicle *n*. 编年史
fiction *n*. 小说
narrative *n*. 记叙文，记叙体
folklore *n*. 民间传说
fairy tale 童话
anecdote *n*. 轶事，奇闻
fable *n*. 寓言
allegory *n*. 寓言
satire *n*. 讽刺文学
epigram *n*. 警句，讽刺短诗
innuendo *n*. 暗讽，影射
parody *n*. 歪改，(模仿他人文体所做的)游戏诗文
setting *n*. 背景
protagonist *n*. 主角
denouement *n*. 结局

Rhetoric 修辞学

rhetoric *n*. 修辞学
metaphor *n*. 隐喻，暗喻
allusion *n*. 隐喻，暗示
irony *n*. 反话，讽刺
paradox *n*. 自相矛盾的话
ellipsis *n*. 省略，省略符号
alliteration *n*. 头韵
rhyme *n*. 韵，押韵
style *n*. 文体
stylist *n*. 文体学家
terse *adj*. 简洁的，精练的
flowery *adj*. 绚丽的，华丽的
archaic *adj*. 古老的，古体的
colloquial *adj*. 口语的，通俗的
civilized *adj*. 文雅的
dialect *n*. 方言，土语
cliché *n*. 陈词滥调
stereotype *n*. 陈腔滥调，老套
archetype *n*. 原型
wit *n*. 妙语，趣语

Writing 写作

version *n*. 译本，版本
installment *n*. 连载;连续剧
orthography *n*. 正确拼字，正字法
gloss *v*./*n*. 作注释，评注
annotation(footnote, comment) *n*. 注解，评注
commentator *n*. 注释者，评论员
bibliography *n*. 书目，参考书目
synopsis *n*. 提纲，情节摘要
compendium *n*. 纲要，概略
epitome *n*. 摘要
draft *n*. 草稿，草案
abridge *v*. 删节，精简
punctuate *v*. 加标点于
paraphrase *v*. 解释
proofread *v*. 校正，校对
revise *v*. 修订，修改

Copyright 版权

copyright *n*. 版权，著作权
pirate *n*. 盗印者，盗版者
piracy *n*. 侵犯版权，非法翻印
royalty *n*. 版税，特许权使用费
posthumous *adj*. 死后的，作者死后出版的
anonymous *adj*. 匿名的
pseudonym *n*. 笔名
authenticity *n*. 确实性，真实性
authorship *n*. 原创作者
censorship *n*. 审查制度
crib *v*. 抄袭
plagiarize *v*. 剽窃
excerpt *v*. 摘录，引用

一般文学用词

catharsis *n*. 净化;宣泄
metaphysical *adj*. 形而上学的，超自然的
cynicism *n*. 犬儒主义，愤世嫉俗
deconstruction *n*. 解构
libel *n*. 以文字损害名誉，诽谤
eulogy *n*. 赞词，颂词
literacy *n*. 有文化，有读写能力
phonetics *n*. 语音学
scoop *n*. 内幕消息，独家新闻
subscribe *v*. 订阅
recite *v*. 背诵，朗读

10 Art History 艺术史

Artistic Movements 艺术运动

School *n*. 画派
manner *n*. 风格，手法
Gothic *n*. 哥特式
Rococo *n*. 罗可可艺术
Impressionism *n*. 印象派
Pointillism *n*. (印象派画家的)点画法
Post-Impressionism *n*. 后期印象派
Symbolism *n*. 象征派
Art Nouveau 新艺术派
Avant-Garde *n*. 先锋派
Abstractionism *n*. 抽象派
Fauvism *n*. 野兽派
Cubism *n*. 立体派
Dadaism *n*. 达达派
Surrealism *n*. 超现实主义
Expressionism *n*. 表现主义
Futurism *n*. 未来派
Art Deco *n*. 装饰艺术
Postmodernism 后现代主义
Pop Art *n*. 流行艺术
Performance Art 表演艺术
Environmental Art 环境艺术
Op Art 光效应绘画艺术，欧普艺术

Painting 绘画

watercolor painting 水彩画
oil painting 油画
mural painting 壁画
figure painting 人物画
still-life painting 静物画
landscape painting 风景画
portrait *n*. 肖像，人像
hue *n*. 色调(tint)，颜色(color)
pigment *n*. 色素，颜料
chromatic *adj*. 彩色的
monochrome *n*. 单色
motley *adj*. 五颜六色的，杂色的
azure *n*. 天蓝色
chiaroscuro *n*. (绘画中的)明暗对照法
transparent colors 透明色
limpid *adj*. 清澈的，透明的
translucent *adj*. 半透明的
opaque *adj*. 不透明的
obscure *adj*. 暗的，朦胧的
luminous *adj*. 明亮的
lucent *adj*. 光亮的，透明的
luster *n*. 光彩，光泽
brushstroke *n*. 一笔，一画，绘画的技巧
fresco *n*. 壁画
tempera *n*. 蛋彩画

Sculpture 雕塑

sculpture *n*. 雕刻，雕塑
sculptor *n*. 雕刻家，雕塑家
mason *n*. 泥瓦匠，石匠
three dimensional artwork 三维艺术品
statue *n*. 雕像
carve *v*. 雕刻
wood carving 木雕刻品，木刻
woodprint *n*. 木版画
marble *n*. 大理石雕刻品
lithograph *n*. 石版画，平版画
copperplate print 铜板画
etching *n*. 蚀刻版画，蚀刻术
engraving *n*. 雕刻术，雕版
emboss *v*. 饰以浮饰，使浮雕出来
plaster cast 石膏模型
bust *n*. 半身像，胸像
symmetry *n*. 对称，匀称

Architecture 建筑

architecture *n*. 建筑，建筑学
architect *n*. 建筑师
layout *n*. 规划，设计
floor plan 建筑的平面图
profile *n*. 剖面，侧面
vertical *n*. 垂直线，垂直面
ornate *adj*. 装饰的，华丽的
stately *adj*. 庄严的，宏伟的
structural *adj*. 结构的，建筑的
ratio *n*. 比，比率
decoration *n*. 装饰，装饰品
exterior *adj*. 外用的
style *n*. 风格
order *n*. 次序，顺序
feature *n*. 特色，特征
support *n*. 支撑，支柱
column *n*. 圆柱

base *n*. 底部，基座
shaft *n*. 轴，杆状物
capital *n*. 柱头，柱顶
scroll *n*. 卷轴，涡管
grave *n*. 墓穴，坟墓
Doric *n*./*adj*. 多立克式(的)
Ionic *n*./ *adj*. 爱奥尼亚式(的)
Corinthian *n*./*adj*. 科林斯式(的)

一般艺术用词

fine arts 美术
formative arts 造型艺术
appreciation *n*. 欣赏，鉴赏
connoisseur *n*. 鉴赏家，鉴定家
vandal *n*. 汪达尔人，摧残文化艺术者
reproduction *n*. 复制(品)，仿制(品)
gallery *n*. 美术陈列室，画廊
aesthetic *adj*. 美学的，审美的
vantage point *n*. 有利位置，优越地位
composition *n*. 结构，构图
deformation *n*. 在绘画中由于明暗、色调不准而歪曲了原来的形象
rendering *n*. (艺术品的)复制图;(建筑物等)透视图，示意图
lurid *adj*. 过分渲染的，(画的颜色等)刺目的
decadence *n*. 颓废
lambent *adj*. 闪烁的
blur *v*. 涂污，弄得模糊不清
symbolize *v*. 象征
illustrate *v*. 图解，加插图于
caricature *n*. 讽刺画，漫画
retouch *v*. 修饰，润色

11 Music 音乐

Composition 乐曲

composition *n*. 乐曲
compose *v*. 作曲
arrange *v*. 改编，编曲配器
masterpiece *n*. 杰作
movement *n*. 乐章
note *n*. 音符
musical notation 音符
clef *n*. 音部记号
scale *n*. 音阶，音列
major (scale) *n*.大音阶
minor (scale) *n*.小音阶
chromatic (scale) *n*.半音阶
tune *n*. 曲调，调子
beat *n*. 拍子
upbeat *n*. 弱拍
refrain *n*. 叠句，副歌
word *n*. 词

Playing 演奏

execution *n*. 演奏，(演奏)技巧
improvisation *n*. 即席演奏
variation *n*. 变奏，变调
accompaniment *n*. 伴奏
undertone *n*. 低音
andantino *n*. 小行板
chord *n*. 弦，和音
cacophony *n*. 不协和音，杂音
harmonious *adj*. 和谐的，协调的
bow *n*. 乐弓
pluck *v*. 弹，拨
strike *v*. 击打，弹奏
fingering *n*. 用指弹奏，指法
instrument *n*. 乐器
percussion (instrument) 打击乐器
string *n*. (弓，乐器的)弦
string quartet 弦乐四重奏曲
fiddle *n*. 小提琴
recorder *n*. 八孔长笛
harpsichord *n*. 大键琴
conductor *n*. (乐队)指挥
philharmonic *n*. 交响乐团

Western Music 西方音乐

polyphony *n*. 复调音乐，对位法
orchestra music 管弦乐
symphonic *adj*. 交响乐的，和声的
concerto *n*. 协奏曲
chamber music 室内乐
opera *n*. 歌剧
march *n*. 进行曲
national anthem *n*. 国歌
overture *n*. 序曲，前奏曲

一般音乐用词

musical literature 音乐文献
conservatory *n*. 音乐学校

contemporary *adj*. 当(现)代的
radical *adj*. 根音的
solemn *adj*. 庄严的，隆重的
threnody *n*. 悲歌，哀歌
tone *n*. 音调
tone-deaf *adj*. 音盲的
marine band 海军乐队
inventiveness *n*. 原创，独创性
enthusiasm *n*. 热情，狂热

12 Film 电影

Film Industry 电影行业

filmmaker *n*. 电影摄制者，制片人
film/movie director *n*. 电影导演
blockbuster *n*. 消耗巨资拍摄的影片，大片
box office 票房，票房收入
preview *v*. 预演，试映
running/show time 放映时间
rating *n*. 等级，级别
restricted *adj*. 受限制的，R级的
exclusive *adj*. 独家享有的，专有的
distribute *v*. 发行
release *v*. 发行
first-run theater 首映式
ticket agency 售票代理处
usher *n*. (电影院，戏院等公共场所的)招待员，引座员
horror *n*. 恐怖片
independent film 独立短片
documentary film 纪录片，文献片
monochrome film 黑白影片
continuity *n*. (电影、广播、电视节目的)连续
dramatist *n*. 剧本作者
adaptation *n*. 改编，改写本
casting *n*. 挑选演员，扮演
cinematic *adj*. 电影的，影片的

Technique 技艺

technique *n*. 方法，技艺
computer graphics 电脑图形图像
stop-action *adj*. 瞬时摄影的，连续摄影的
special effects 特技，特效
visual effects 视觉效果
optical illusion *n*. 幻觉，错觉
close-up *n*. 特写镜头
double-exposure shot 两次曝光拍摄
shot *v*. 拍摄
montage *n*. 蒙太奇，文学音乐或美术的组合体
dissolve *v*. 使(电影，电视画面)渐隐
fade *v*. (电影或广播中画面和声音的)渐变
echo *n*. 回声，回音
prop *n*. 道具
scenery *n*. 风景;舞台布景
score *n*. 配乐
subtitle *n*. 字幕
sound track 声轨，音轨

一般电影用词

motion picture 电影
nouvelle vague(法)新浪潮
criticism *n*. 评论，评论性文章
commentary *n*. 按语，评论
critical *adj*. 批评性的，评论性的
sentimental *adj*. 感伤性的，情感的
macabre *adj*. 恐怖的，令人毛骨悚然的
outdated *adj*. 过时的，不流行的
malfunction *n*. 故障，失灵
jam *n*. 堵塞
latest *adj*. 最近的，最新的
alteration *n*. 变更，改造
innovation *n*. 改革，创新

13 Archaeology 考古学

Excavation 出土文物

excavate *v*. 挖掘，挖出
digging *n*. 挖掘
site *n*. 地点，遗址
relics *n*. 遗物，遗迹
artifact *n*. 人造物品
mound *n*. 土墩，护堤
dolmen *n*. 巨石墓，史前墓石牌坊
mummy *n*. 木乃伊
skeletal *adj*. 骨骼的，骸骨的

authentic *adj*. 可信的
sampling *n*. 取样;样品
specimen *n*. 样品,样本
fragment *n*. 碎片,断片
shard *n*. (玻璃或陶瓷器皿的)碎片
pottery *n*. 陶器
haft *n*. 柄,把手
scraper *n*. 刮器,刮刀

Paleontology 古生物学

paleontology *n*. 古生物学
fossil *n*. 化石
progenitor *n*. 祖先,始祖
progeny *n*. 后裔
Homo Erectus 直立人
hominoid *n*. 人科之动物,类人猿
ape *n*. 猿
trilobite *n*. 三叶虫
ammonite *n*. 菊石
mammoth *n*. 猛犸,长毛象
tusk *n*. 长牙,獠牙
stratum *n*. 地层,岩层
stratigraphy *n*. 地层学
anachronism *n*. 时代错误
date *n*. 年代,时期
decipher *v*. 译解(密码等)
archive *n*. 档案文件
hieroglyph *n*. 象形文字,图画文字
cuneiform *n*. 楔形文字;*adj*. 楔形的,楔形文字的
geometric pattern 几何图样

Age 时代

prehistoric *adj*. 史前的
primeval *adj*. 原始的
pristine *adj*. 原始的,早期的
Ice Age 冰河时代
glacial epoch *n*. 冰川时期
Pleistocene Epoch 更新世
Stone Age *n*. 石器时代
Paleolithic *adj*. 旧石器时代的
Mesolithic *adj*. 中石器时代的
Neolithic *adj*. 新石器时代的
Bronze Age 青铜器时代
Iron Age 铁器时代
chronology *n*. 年代学,年表

一般考古学用词

origin *n*. 起源,由来
sculpture *n*. 雕刻,雕塑
scythian *n*. 斯基台人
unprecedented *adj*. 空前的
extant *adj*. 现存的,尚存的
prevalent *adj*. 普遍的,盛行的
die out 灭绝
engrave *v*. 雕刻,铭刻
depict *v*. 描述,描写
polish *n*./*v*. 磨光,擦亮
deform *v*. (使)变形
attest *v*. 证明,证实

14 U.S. History 美国历史

Government 政府

Federal government 联邦政府
American Revolution 美国独立战争
the Declaration of Independence 独立宣言
Independence Day 美国独立日
federalism *n*. 联邦政治,联邦制度
feudalism *n*. 封建制度
monarchy *n*. 君主政体,君主政治
imperialism *n*. 帝国主义,帝制
colonization *n*. 殖民地化,殖民
Capitol *n*. 国会大厦,州议会大厦
Representative *n*. 众议院议员
framer *n*. 组成者,筹划者

Law 法律

the Bill of Rights《人权法案》
provision *n*. 规定,条款
convention *n*. 条约,协议,契约
privilege *n*. 特权,特别待遇;基本公民权力
women's suffrage 妇女投票权
Supreme Court 最高法院
circuit court 巡回法庭
patent *n*. 专利,专利权
Prohibition 禁酒令
Bootlegging *n*. 非法制造、运送、销售(酒类等)
unconstitutional *adj*. 违反宪法的
ratify *v*. 批准,认可
consolidate *v*. 统一,合并

promulgate *v*. 发布，公布

The Civil War 美国内战

American Civil War 美国内战(南北战争)
Emancipation Proclamation《解放黑人奴隶宣言》
the Union 联邦
the Confederacy 南部邦联
thrall *n*. 奴隶，束缚
slavery *n*. 奴隶身份，奴隶制度
persecute *v*. 迫害
suppression *n*. 镇压
segregation *n*. 种族隔离
racial discrimination 种族歧视
integration *n*. 取消种族隔离
armed conflicts 武装冲突
class warfare 阶级斗争
carnage *n*. (尤指在战场上的)残杀，大屠杀
massacre *n*. 残杀，大屠杀
casualty *n*. 伤亡，伤亡人员
captive *n*. 俘虏
armistice *n*. 停战，休战
cavalry *n*. 骑兵
artillery *n*. 炮，炮兵
rifle *n*. 来复枪，步枪
musket *n*. 步枪
sweeping *adj*. 扫荡的
tactic *n*. 策略，战略
disarmament *n*. 裁军，裁减军备
dismemberment *n*. 分割，瓜分(国土等)

Society 社会

Pilgrim Fathers 清教徒前辈移民
Puritan *n*. 清教徒
Quaker *n*. 基督教教友派成员，贵格会教徒
early settlers 早期定居者
covered wagon 有篷大马车;篷车
wagon train 马车队
migrate *v*. 移动，移往
blaze a trail 开辟道路，作先导
famine *n*. 饥荒
hardship *n*. 困苦，艰难
ranch *n*. 大农场
pasture *n*. 草原，牧场
plantation *n*. 种植园，大农场
public domain (美国政府的)公有土地
agrarian *adj*. 有关土地的，耕地的
arid *adj*. 干旱的，贫瘠的(土地等)
Sutter's Mill 苏特矿场
bonanza *n*. 富矿带
locomotive *n*. 机车，火车头
Roaring Twenties 兴旺的 20 年代
crusade *n*. 十字军东侵，宗教战争
Great Depression 大萧条
regrate *v*. 囤积(粮食，商品等)，倒卖
flowering *adj*. 开花的;*n*. 成熟
(the)Dust Bowl 风沙浸蚀区
greenback *n*. 美钞
hierarchy *n*. 等级制度
peer *n*. 贵族(指公、侯、伯、子、男中的任一爵位)
baron *n*. 男爵(英国世袭的最低级的贵族爵位)
commoner *n*. 平民，无爵位的人
redemptioner *n*. 出卖劳力来抵偿船资之移民
itinerant preacher 巡回牧师，巡回传教士
upheaval *n*. 动乱，剧变
uprising *n*. 起义

关于美国的一般情况用词

Indian reservation 印第安人保留地
minority *n*. 少数，少数民族
philanthropist *n*. 慈善家
benefactor *n*. 捐助者，赠送者
Pulitzer Prize 普利策奖
steel magnate 钢铁大亨
deity *n*. 神，神性
muckraker *n*. 搜集并揭发丑事的人
anomaly *n*. 不规则，异常的人或物
doctrine *n*. 教条，学说
trial and error *n*. 反复试验

15 Mathematics 数学

Algebra 代数学

algebra *n*. 代数学
equation *n*. 方程式，等式
par *n*. 同等，同位，同价
variable *n*. 变数，变量
square *n*. 平方
cube *n*. 立方

arithmetic *n*. 算术，算法
addition *n*. 加，加法
subtraction *n*. 减，减法
multiplication *n*. 乘法
division *n*. 除法
plus *prep*. 加，加上；*n*. 加号，正号
minus *prep*. 减去；*n*. 减号，负号
times *prep*. 乘，乘以
calculation *n*. 计算
reckon *v*. 计算，总计

Number Theory 数论

real number 实数
imaginary number 虚数
odd number 奇数
even number 偶数
fraction *n*. 分数
decimal *adj*. 十进的，小数的
decimal system 十进制
dozen *n*. 一打，12 个

Geometry 几何学

geometry *n*. 几何学
triangle *n*. 三角形
quadrangle *n*. 四角形，四边形
trapezoid *n*. 梯形，不等边四边形
parallelogram *n*. 平行四边形
rhombus *n*. 菱形，斜方形(diamond)
rectangle *n*. 长方形，矩形
square *n*. 正方形
pentagon *n*. 五角形，五边形
hexagon *n*. 六角形，六边形
heptagon *n*. 七角形，七边形
octagon *n*. 八边形，八角形
parallel *adj*. 平行的，相同的；*n*. 平行线
circle *n*. 圆周
circumference *n*. 圆周
arc *n*. 弧，弓形
periphery *n*. 圆柱(体)表面，外围
diameter *n*. 直径
radius *n*. 半径
sector *n*. 扇形
sphere *n*. 球，球体
cylinder *n*. 圆柱体
cone *n*. 锥形物，圆锥体
prism *n*. 棱柱
pyramid *n*. 角锥，棱椎
central angle 圆心角
degree *n*. 度数，度
grade *n*. 等级，级别
level *n*. 水平线，水平面；*adj*. 水平的
vertical *adj*. 垂直的；*n*. 垂直线，垂直面
perpendicular *adj*. 垂直的，正交的；*n*. 垂线
convergent *adj*. 会集于一点的，会聚性的
diagonal (line) 对角线
parabola *n*. 抛物线
ellipse *n*. 椭圆，椭圆形
width *n*. 宽，宽度

一般数学用词

algorithm *n*. 运算法则
calculus *n*. 微积分学
function *n*. 函数
set *n*. 集合
matrix *n*. 矩阵
probability *n*. 概率
statistics *n*. 统计学，统计表

16 Physics 物理学

Electric Current 电流

ammeter *n*. 电表
alternating current 交流电
direct current 直流电
electrode *n*. 电极
anode *n*. 阳极，正极
cathode *n*. 阴极
terminal *n*. 终端，接线端
charge *n*. 负荷，电荷
voltage *n*. 电压，伏特数
voltmeter *n*. 伏特计
electromagnetic wave 电磁波
magnetic field 磁场
magnetism *n*. 磁，磁力
generator *n*. 发电机，发生器
conductor *n*. 导体，导线
semiconductor *n*. 半导体
insulation *n*. 绝缘

Dynamics 动力学

dynamics *n*. 动力学

mechanics *n*. 机械学,力学
force *n*. 力，力量
universal gravitation 万有引力
free fall 自由降落
theory of relativity 相对论
strain *n*. 拉力，张力
torsion *n*. 扭(力)矩，转(力)矩
hydrodynamics *n*. 流体力学，水动力学
fluid *n*. 液体，流质;*adj*. 液体的，流体的
buoyancy *n*. 浮力
vacuum *n*. 真空
sound wave 声波，音波
wavelength *n*. 波长
resonance *n*. 共鸣，回声;谐振，共振
vibration *n*. 振动，颤动
amplitude of vibration 振幅
pendulum *n*. 摆，钟摆
symmetrize *v*. 使对称，使均衡
proton *n*. 质子
neutron *n*. 中子
particle *n*. 粒子；质点
electron *n*. 电子
meson *n*. 介子
quantum *n*. 量子，量子论
quark *n*. 夸克
fission *n*. 裂开，裂变
fusion *n*. (核)聚变，核合成
critical mass 临界物质

Law of Motion 运动定律

inertia *n*. 惯性，惯量
mass *n*. 质量
friction *n*. 摩擦，摩擦力
velocity *n*. 速度，速率
accelerated velocity 加速度
centrifugal force 地心引力
centripetal force 向心力
elasticity *n*. 弹力，弹性
kinetic energy 动能
potential energy 势能
radiant energy 辐射能
mechanical energy 机械能

Optics 光学

visible rays 可视光线
ultraviolet rays 紫外线
infrared rays 红外线
disperse *v*. 使(光线)分散，使弥散
deviation *n*. 背离
radiation *n*. 放射，辐射；辐射线
reflection *n*. 反映，反射；映像
refraction *n*. 折光，折射
anaclastic *adj*. 屈折的，由折射引起的
concave lens 凹透镜
convex lens 凸透镜
diameter *n*. 直径
radius *n*. 半径，半径范围

一般物理学用词

specific gravity 比重
volume *n*. 体积;量
density *n*. 密度
pressure *n*. 压，压力
capillarity *n*. 毛细管作用，毛细管现象
surface tension 表面张力
cohesive *adj*. 凝聚性的，内聚性的
virtual *adj*. 虚的
impulsive *adj*. 瞬动的，冲击的
spatial *adj*. 空间的，立体的，三维的
static *adj*. 静态的，静力的
application *n*. 施加力，荷载
annihilation *n*. 湮灭
malleability *n*. 有延展性，柔韧性
flexibility *n*. 弹性,挠性
fluctuation *n*. 波动，起伏
lever *n*. 杆，杠杆
foundation *n*. 基础;基本原理

17 Chemistry 化学

Periodic Table (元素)周期表

periodic table (元素)周期表
element *n*. 元素
oxygen *n*. 氧
hydrogen *n*. 氢
nitrogen *n*. 氮
carbon *n*. 碳
silicon *n*. 硅
chlorine *n*. 氯
helium *n*. 氦
zinc *n*. 锌
tin *n*. 锡

manganese *n*. 锰
lead *n*. 铅
uranium *n*. 铀
cadmium *n*. 镉
aluminum *n*. 铝
isotope *n*. 同位素
sulfuric acid 硫磺酸
hydrochloric acid 盐酸
phosphate *n*. 磷酸盐

Chemical Reaction 化学反应

chemical action 化学反应
chemical symbol 化学符号
chemical equation 化学反应方程式
replacement 移位，置换
ingredient *n*. 成分;拼份，拼料
content *n*. 含量，容积(量)
solution *n*. 溶液
solvent *adj*. 溶解的，有溶解力的;*n*. 溶媒，溶剂
solute *n*. 溶解物，溶质
insoluble *adj*. 不能溶解的
stable *adj*. 稳定的
molecular *adj*. 分子的，由分子组成的
saturation *n*. 饱和(状态)，饱和度
concentration *n*. 浓缩，浓度
osmosis *n*. 渗透(作用)，渗透性
diffusion *n*. 扩散；渗滤
dilution *n*. 稀释；稀释法
combustion *n*. 燃烧
composition *n*. 合成物，混合物
decomposition *n*. 分解
enzyme *n*. 酶
catalyst *n*. 催化剂
reactant *n*. 反应物
acceptor *n*. 接收器
acid *n*. 酸
alkalinity *n*. 碱度
compound *n*. 混合物，化合物
inorganic compounds 无机化合物
oxide *n*. 氧化物
oxidize *v*. (使)氧化
neutralize *v*. 中和
corrode *v*. 腐蚀，侵蚀
reagent *n*. 反应物，试剂
oxidizing agent 氧化剂
reducing agent 还原剂
additive *n*. 添加剂
coolant *n*. 冷冻剂，冷却液
brine *n*. 盐水

Matter 物质

gas *n*. 气体
liquid *n*. 液体
solid *n*. 固体
freezing point 冰点，凝固点
melting point 熔点
boiling point 沸点
steam *n*. 蒸汽，水汽
evaporation *n*. 蒸发(作用)
vaporization *n*. 汽化器，蒸馏器
liquefaction *n*. 液化
solidification *n*. 凝固
sublimation *n*. 升华，升华物
colloid *n*. 胶质，胶体
filter *n*. 过滤器，滤纸
deposit *n*. 沉淀物;*v*. 沉淀
condense *v*. 浓缩

一般化学用词

alchemy *n*. 炼金术
alloy *n*. 合金
plate *n*. 镀金或镀银器皿;*v*. 镀(金，银等)，电镀
inject *v*. 注射，注入
purify *v*. 使纯净，净化
crude *adj*. 天然的，未加工的;*n*. 原(生)材料，天然物质
viscous *adj*. 粘性的，粘滞的
exothermic *adj*. 发热的，放出热量的
incandescent *adj*. 遇热发光的，白炽的
explosive *adj*. 爆炸(性)的;*n*. 爆炸物，炸药
toxic *adj*. 有毒的
venomous *adj*. 有毒的，分泌毒液的
moldy *adj*. 发霉的，腐臭的
lukewarm *adj*. (指液体)微温的
thermometer *n*. 温度计
outcome *n*. 结果
crystal *adj*. 结晶状的;*n*. 结晶，晶体
property *n*. 性质，特性
texture *n*. 结构，组织
amylum *n*. 淀粉
protein *n*. 蛋白质
carbohydrate *n*. 碳水化合物
mineral *n*. 矿物

18 Astronomy 天文学

Celestial Body 天体

Mercury 水星
Venus 金星
Earth 地球
Mars 火星
Jupiter 木星
Saturn 土星
Uranus 天王星
Neptune 海王星
Pluto 冥王星
planet *n*. 行星
asteroid *n*. 小游星，小行星
comet *n*. 彗星
meteor *n*. 流星
meteorite *n*. 陨星，陨石
heavenly bodies 天体
celestial sphere 天球(一个想象假设的无限大球体)
ecliptic *n*. 黄道；*adj*. 黄道的，日(或月)食的，
solar system 太阳系
galaxy *n*. 星系，银河系
nebular *adj*. 星云的
cluster *n*. 串，丛
constellation *n*. 星群，星座
Polaris *n*. 北极星
variable star 变星
rotation *n*. 旋转
revolution *n*. 绕转，旋转
solar eclipse 日食
lunar eclipse 月食

Astrophysics 天体物理学

antimatter *n*. 反物质
interstellar matter 星际物质
stellar *adj*. 恒星的
proton *n*. 质子
sunspot *n*. 太阳黑子
pulsar *n*. 脉冲星
magnetic storm 磁暴
supergiant star 超巨星
supernova *n*. 超新星
white dwarf star 白矮星
red giant star 红巨星
inactivity *n*. 静止，不活泼，休止状态
air resistance 空气阻力
friction *n*. 摩擦，摩擦力
repulsion *n*. 推斥，排斥
gravitational *adj*. 重力的
weightlessness *n*. 无重状态
Van Allen Radiation Belt 范艾伦辐射带
apogee *n*. 远地点
perigee *n*. 近地点

Astronautics 太空航空学

aerospace *n*. 航空宇宙
astronaut *n*. 太空人，宇航员
astronautics *n*. 太空航空学
vessel *n*. 船，舰；飞船
carrier rocket 运载火箭
booster rocket 助推火箭
combustion chamber 燃烧室
blast off *v*. 点火起飞
circumlunar flight 环月飞行
blackout *n*. 中断
telemetry *n*. 遥感勘测
HST = High-Speed Tester 高速试验机
balloon satellite 气球卫星
application satellite 应用卫星
broadcasting satellite 广播卫星

一般天文学用词

eccentricity *n*. 偏心率(度)；偏心距
axis *n*. 轴
orbit *n*. 轨道；*v*. 绕…轨道而行，进入轨道
track *n*. 轨迹；*v*. 追踪
observatory *n*. 天文台，气象台
observe *v*. 观察，观测
detect *v*. 侦查，探测
luminous *adj*. 发光的，明亮的
stationary *adj*. 静止的，不动的
transparency *n*. 透明，透明度
naked eye 肉眼
concentration *n*. 集中，集合
condense *v*. (使)浓缩
congeal *v*. (使)冻结，(使)凝结
astrology *n*. 占星术，占星学
leap year 闰年

19 Geography 地理学

Topography 地形学

topography *n*. 地形学
rugged *adj*. 高低不平的，崎岖的
highland *n*. 高地，丘陵地带
plateau *n*. 高地，高原
canyon *n*. 峡谷，溪谷
waterfall *n*. 瀑布
gorge *n*. 山峡，峡谷
ridge *n*. 山脊，山脉
pass *n*. 关口
cliff *n*. 悬崖，绝壁
bluff *n*. 断崖，绝壁
basin *n*. 盆地
plain *n*. 平原，草原
flood plain 河漫滩，洪泛区
delta *n*. 三角州
coast *n*. 海岸
sand dune *n*. 沙丘
cape *n*. 海角，岬
peninsula *n*. 半岛
archipelago *n*. 群岛
inland river 内河
watershed *n*. 分水岭
meander *n*. 曲流；*v*. 蜿蜒而流
tributary *adj*. 支流的；*n*. 支流
estuary *n*. 河口，江口
lagoon *n*. 泻湖，礁湖，盐水湖
eutrophic lake 富营养湖，滋养湖
freshwater lake 淡水湖
swamp *n*. 沼泽，湿
hot spring 温泉
geyser *n*. 间歇泉

Location 位置

geographical *adj*. 地理学的，地理的
GPS (Global Position System)全球定位系统
compass *n*. 罗盘，指南针
latitude *n*. 纬度
longitude *n*. 经度，经线
altitude *n*. (尤指海拔)高度
rotational axis 旋转轴
the North Pole 北极
true north *n*. 真北(非地磁北)
magnetic north *n*. 磁北
Northern Hemisphere 北半球

一般地质学用词

erosion *n*. 腐蚀，侵蚀
corrosion *n*. 侵蚀，腐蚀状态
weather *v*. 侵蚀，使风化
landmass *n*. 大陆
cavern *n*. 巨洞，洞窟
colliery *n*. 煤矿
canal *n*. 运河

20 Meteorology 气象学

Weather Forecast 天气预报

Weather Bureau 气象局
temperature *n*. 温度
wind chill(factor)风寒
below freezing 零下
Celsius *n*. 摄氏度
Fahrenheit *n*. 华氏度
precipitation *n*. 降雨量，降水(量)
downfall *n*. 暴雨，大雪
humidity *n*. 湿气，湿度
cold front *n*. 冷锋，冷面
warm front *n*. 暖锋
trough *n*. 低压槽；槽形低压
anticyclone *n*. 反气旋，高气压
wind velocity 风速
wind direction 风向
westerlies *n*. 西风带
trade wind *n*. 信风
typhoon *n*. 台风
hurricane *n*. 飓风，狂风
cyclone *n*. 旋风，暴风
gale *n*. 大风
blast *n*. 一阵(风)，一股(气流)
squall *n*. 暴风，暴风雪
frost *n*. 霜，霜冻
sleet *n*. 冰雨，雨夹雪，霰

blizzard *n*. 暴风雪
hail *n*. 冰雹
hailstorm *n*. 雹暴
tempest *n*. 暴风雨
heavy snow 大雪
sprinkle *n*. 小雨，间断雨
drizzle *n*. 细雨，毛毛雨
shower *n*. 阵雨
downpour *n*. 倾盆大雨
torrential rain 暴雨
cloudburst *n*. 倾盆大雨
thunderstorm *n*. 雷暴
haze *n*. 薄雾，阴霾
mist *n*. 薄雾
fog *n*. 雾
dew *n*. 露

Weather 天气

inclement weather
inclement *adj*. 险恶的，严酷的
frigid *adj*. 寒冷的
bleak *adj*. 寒冷的，阴冷的
dreary *adj*. 沉闷的
chilly *adj*. 寒冷的
torrid *adj*. 很热的，炽热的
scorching *adj*. 灼热的
sweltering *adj*. 闷热的，酷热的
stuffy *adj*. 闷热的，不通气的
sultry *adj*. 闷热的，酷热的
heat wave 热浪
serene *adj*. 平静的，晴朗的
halcyon *adj*. 太平的，平静的
overcast *adj*. 阴天的，阴暗的
dense *adj*. 密集的，浓厚的
arid *adj*. 干旱的，干燥的
damp *n*. 湿气；*adj*. 潮湿的

Climate 气候

continental climate 大陆性气候
oceanic climate 海洋性气候
desert climate 沙漠气候
subtropical climate 亚热带气候
tropical climate 热带气候
temperate climate 温带气候
monsoon climate 季风气候
highland climate 高原气候
subarctic climate 副极带气候
polar climate 极地气候

一般气象学用词

equinox *n*. 昼夜平分点，春分或秋分
spring equinox 春分
autumnal equinox 秋分
summer solstice 夏至
winter solstice 冬至
air current 气流
air mass 气团
atmosphere *n*. 大气，空气
atmospheric pressure 大气压力
barometric *adj*. 气压的
lightning rod 避雷针
fallout *n*. 辐射微尘，原子尘
avalanche *n*. 雪崩
drought *n*. 干旱
deluge *n*. 洪水，大水灾
flood *n*. 洪水，水灾
inundation *n*. 洪水
geyser *n*. 天然喷泉，间歇泉
glacial epoch 冰川时期
glacier *n*. 冰河
icecap *n*. 常积不消的冰，冰盖
moisture *n*. 潮湿，湿气
droplet *n*. 小滴
soaked *adj*. 湿透的
parched *adj*. 炎热的
evaporate *v*. 蒸发，消失
shiver *v*. 颤抖，打冷战

21 Oceanography 海洋学

Tide 潮汐

tidal energy 潮汐能
tidal wave 潮汐波，浪潮
tsunami *n*. 海啸
wave *n*. 波，波浪
gyre *n*./*v*. 旋回，旋转
whirlpool *n*. 漩涡，涡流
current *n*. 水流，气流
downwelling *n*. （海洋在地壳板块压力下的）下降
upwelling *n*. 上涌，上升流（指海水由较深层上升到较浅层的过程）

circulation *n*. 循环，环流
counterclockwise *adj*./ad*v*. 反时针方向的（地）
drift *n*./*v*. 漂流

Submarine Topography 海底地形

submarine *adj*. 水下的，海底的
topography *n*. 地形，地形学
ocean floor 洋底，海底
continental shelf *n*. 大陆架
submarine valley 海底谷
strait *n*. 地峡，海峡
seamount *n*. 海山
trench *n*. 溪谷，峡谷

一般海洋学用词

Pacific Ocean 太平洋
Atlantic Ocean 大西洋
Indian Ocean 印度洋
Antarctic Ocean 南冰洋，南极海
saliferous *adj*. （岩层等）含盐的
salinity *n*. 盐分，盐度
plankton *n*. 浮游生物
mooring *n*. 停泊处
peak *n*. （物体的）尖端，隆起部分；山顶
submerge *v*. 淹没
submersible *adj*. 可潜入水中的；*n*. 潜水艇，潜水器

22 Geology 地质学

Rock 岩石

igneous rock 火成岩
plutonic rock *n*. 火成论
metamorphic rock 变质岩
sedimentary rock 水成岩
limestone *n*. 石灰石
granite *n*. 花岗岩
extrusive *adj*. 挤出的，喷出的
molten *v*. 熔化；*adj*. 熔铸的
alluvial *adj*. 冲积的，淤积的
eject *v*. 逐出，撵出；喷射
crystallize *v*. 使结晶，晶化
deposit *n*. 堆积物，沉淀物；*v*. 沉淀
debris *n*. 碎片，残骸
metamorphosis *n*. 变形
stalactite *n*. 钟乳石
stalagmite *n*. 石笋
accumulation *n*. 积聚，堆积物
sediment *n*. 沉淀物，沉积
lithification *n*. 岩化

Tectonics 筑造学

tectonics *n*. 筑造学
tectonic plate （地球表面的）构造板块
continental drift theory 大陆漂移说
supercontinent *n*. 超大陆
plate *n*. （形成地壳的）板块
plate tectonics 板块构造论
earthquake *n*. 地震
earth's axis *n*. 地轴
seismic *adj*. 地震的
seismic intensity 地震强度，地震烈度
seismic wave 地震波
epicenter *n*. 震中，中心
Richter scale *n*. 里氏震级
tremor *n*./*v*. 震动，颤动
tsunami *n*. 海啸
crust *n*. 外壳，硬壳
mantle *n*. 地幔
magma *n*. （有机物或矿物的）稀糊，岩浆
volcanic eruption 火山爆发
volcanic zone 火山带
crater *n*. 火山口
lava *n*. 熔岩，火山岩
liquefy *v*. （使）溶解，（使）液化
drift *n*. 冲洗，漂流物；*v*. （使）漂流

Stratigraphy 地层学

stratigraphy *n*. 地层学
law of superposition 地层层序律
terrane *n*. 岩层
rift *n*. 裂缝，裂口
correlation *n*. 相互关系，相关（性）
stratify *v*. （使）成层
stratum *n*. 地层
unconformity *n*. 不整合，不整合面
specimen *n*. 标本，样品，样本
chronological *adj*. 按年代顺序排列的
subterranean *adj*. 地下的

一般地质学用词

chasm *n*. 深坑，裂口
upheaval *n*. 隆起

bulge *n*. 凸出部分；*v*. 凸出，膨胀
aurora *n*. 北极光
transformation *n*. 变化，转化
mechanics *n*. (用作单数)机械学，力学
wear away/down/off/out 磨损
weather *v*. 风化，侵蚀
meander *n*./*v*. 蜿蜒而流

23 Biology 生物学

Classifying Living Things 生物的分类

taxonomy *n*. 分类法，分类学
categorize *v*. 加以类别，分类
species *n*. 种类
genus *n*. 属
family *n*. 科
order *n*. 目
class *n*. 纲
phylum *n*. 门
kingdom *n*. 领域，界

Heredity & Evolution 遗传和进化

heredity *n*. 遗传
trait *n*. 显著的特点，特性
genetic *adj*. 遗传的，起源的
gene pool 基因库
DNA (deoxyribonucleic acid) 脱氧核糖核酸(遗传物质)
chromosome *n*. 染色体
dominant *adj*. 显性的
recessive *adj*. 隐性的；*n*. 隐性性状
distribute *v*. 散布，分布
atavism *n*. 隔代遗传，返祖现象
variety *n*. 变化；品种；变种
mutation *n*. 变化；(生物物种的)突变
hybrid *n*. 杂种，混血儿；*adj*. 混合的，杂种的
offspring *n*. (单复数同形)子孙，后代
evolution *n*. 演变，进化
adaptation *n*. 适应性的改变；感官适应性调节
survival of the fittest 适者生存
natural selection *n*. 自然选择，物竞天择说
naturalist *n*. 自然主义者，博物学者

Cell 细胞

cytology *n*. 细胞学
specimen *n*. 样品，样本
building block 构件
tissue *n*. 组织
protoplasm *n*. 原生质
metaplasm *n*. 后成质
cytoplasm *n*. 细胞质
membrane *n*. 膜，隔膜
nucleus *n*. 细胞核
nucleic acid *n*. 核酸
vacuole *n*. 空泡，液泡

Biochemistry 生物化学

biochemistry *n*. 生物化学
organism *n*. 生物体，有机体
microbe *n*. 微生物，细菌
microscopic *adj*. 用显微镜可见的；极小的
metabolism *n*. 新陈代谢
aerobic *adj*. 依靠氧气的，与需氧菌有关的
anaerobic *adj*. 没有空气而能生活的，厌氧性的
anabolism *n*. 合成代谢
catabolism *n*. 异化作用，分解代谢
photosynthesis *n*. 光合作用
respiration *n*. 呼吸，呼吸作用
secretion *n*. 分泌，分泌物(液)
osmotic pressure 渗透压
amino acid *n*. 氨基酸
enzyme *n*. 酶
yeast *n*. 酵母，发酵粉
ferment *n*. 酵素，发酵
gland *n*. 腺
mineral *n*. 矿物；无机物
protein *n*. 蛋白质；*adj*. 蛋白质的

一般生物学用词

biologist *n*. 生物学家
fauna *n*. 动物群；动物志
flora *n*. 植物群；植物志
symbiotic *adj*. 共生的
parasitic *adj*. 寄生的
communicable *adj*. 传染的，可传染的
mammary *adj*. 乳房的，乳腺的
population *n*. 虫口；种群(量)
natural enemy 天敌
enmity *n*. 敌意
host *n*. 寄主，宿主

circulation *n*. 循环
nervous system 神经系统
conjugation *n*. (两个生殖细胞的)接合(作用)
culture *n*./*v*. 培育;培植
nest *n*. 巢，窝
niche *n*. 小生境
natural death 正常死亡
feature *n*. 特征，特色
crust *n*. 外壳，硬壳;表层，外皮
sucker *n*. (寄生植物的)吸枝，腋芽;吸盘
fin *n*. 鳍，鱼翅
beak *n*. 鸟嘴，喙
bill *n*. (水禽等细长而扁平的)嘴
agility *n*. (动作)敏捷，轻快
homeostasis *n*. (社会群体的)自我平衡，原状稳定
uniformity *n*. 同样，一致;均匀性
intake *n*. 吸入，摄取;吸收之量
larva *n*. 幼虫，幼体(pl. larvae)
ornithology *n*. 鸟类学，禽学
sense *n*. 感官，官能
infest *v*. 大批滋生
piscatorial *adj*. 渔业的，渔民的
angle *v*. 用钩和钓钓鱼
hobble *v*. 蹒跚，跛行
lacerate *v*. 撕碎，撕裂;*adj*. (叶子等)撕裂状的
annihilate *v*. 消灭，摧毁
endangered *adj*. 有危险的，将要绝种的
defunct *adj*. 死了的
exterminate *v*. 消灭，根除
extinction *n*. 消灭;(生物等的)灭绝
terminate *v*. 终止，结束

24 Botany 植物学

Plant Parts 植物各部分

vein *n*. 叶脉;翅脉
foliage *n*. 树叶，植物
stoma *n*. (植物)气孔
bough *n*. 大树枝，主枝
stem *n*. 茎，干，柄，梗
trunk *n*. 树干
taproot *n*. 主根，直根
fibrous roots 须根

Photosynthesis 光合作用

photosynthesis *n*. 光合作用
chlorophyll *n*. 叶绿素
carbon dioxide *n*. 二氧化碳
oxygen *n*. 氧
glucose *n*. 葡萄糖
cellulose *n*. 纤维素
starch *n*. 淀粉
absorb *v*. 吸收

Reproduction 繁殖

fertilization *n*. 受精作用(现象)
pollination *n*. 授粉
alternation of generations 世代交替
hermaphrodite *n*. 两性体;*adj*. 雌雄同体的
sprout *n*. 苗芽;*v*. 萌芽
burgeon *n*. 嫩芽;*v*. 萌芽
kernel *n*. (硬壳果)仁，核
germinate *v*. 发芽，发育
spore *n*. 孢子
proliferous *adj*. 繁殖的

Parts of a Flower 花的各部分

bloom *n*. 花;*v*. 开花
petal *n*. 花瓣
corolla *n*. 花冠
pollen *n*. 花粉
sap *n*. 树液，汁液
nectar *n*. 花蜜
stamen *n*. 雄蕊，雄性花蕊
anther *n*. 花粉囊
carpel *n*. 心皮
ovary *n*.(植物)子房
stigma *n*. (植物)柱头
sepal *n*. 萼片

Characteristics 特征

transpiration *n*. 蒸发
respiration *n*. 呼吸，呼吸作用
parasite *n*. 寄生植物
perennial *adj*. 四季不断的，(植物)多年生的
nocturnal *adj*. 夜晚的，夜间活动的
brittle *adj*. 易碎的
airborne *adj*. 空气传播的
juicy *adj*. 多汁的
feral *adj*. 野生的

indigenous *adj*. 土产的，本地的
rampant *adj*. 蔓生的，繁茂的
lush *adj*. 茂盛的，青葱的
densely ad*v*. 浓密地
seasonally *adj*. 季节性的
tropism *n*. 向性，向性运动
gravitropism *n*. 向重力性
hydrotropism *n*. 向水性
phototropism *n*. 趋光性，向光性
extract *n*. 精，汁，榨出物
take hold 抓住
flourish *n*./*v*. 茂盛，兴旺
prune *v*. 剪除，修剪
shed *v*. 脱落
wilt *v*./*n*. 枯萎，畏缩

一般植物学用词

vegetation *n*. 植被，(总称)植物
conifer *n*. 松类，针叶树
evergreen tree *n*. 冬青树，常青树
deciduous tree 落叶树
lumber *n*. 木材
underbrush *n*. 树林下的草丛，下层林丛
thorn *n*. 刺，棘，荆棘
sapling *n*. 树苗，小树
seedling *n*. 秧苗，树苗
turf *n*. 草根土，草皮
weed *n*. 野草，杂草
fern *n*. 蕨类植物
lichen *n*. 青苔，地衣，苔藓
fungus *n*. 菌类，蘑菇
context *n*. 菌肉层
maize *n*. 玉米
cob *n*. 玉米棒子
roost *n*. 栖木
annul ring 年轮
resin *n*. 树脂
stubble *n*. 断株，茬
bark *n*. 树皮
husk *n*. (果类或谷物的)外壳
tentacle *n*. (植物)腺毛
pigment *n*. 色素，颜料
auxin *n*. 茁长素，植物激素
graft *n*. 嫁接，(接技用的)嫩枝
devastating *adj*. 破坏性的，毁灭性的
dire *adj*. 可怕的
formidable *adj*. 可怕的，令人生畏的
emerge *v*. 显现，暴露;形成
invade *v*. 侵袭
disperse *v*. (使)分散，(使)散开
conserve *v*. 保存，保藏
habitat *n*. (动植物的)生活环境，产地、栖息地
marshland *n*. 沼泽地
meadow *n*. 草地，牧场

25 Zoology 动物学

Animal Kingdom 动物界

chordate *adj*. 有脊索的，脊索动物的;*n*. 脊索动物
invertebrate *adj*. 无脊椎的;*n*. 无脊椎动物
sponge *n*. 海绵，海绵状物；寄生虫
mollusk *n*. 软体动物
echinoderm *n*. 棘皮类动物
coelenterate *n*. 腔肠动物;*adj*. 腔肠动物的
arthropod *n*. 节肢动物;*adj*. 节肢动物的
arachnid *n*. 蜘蛛类动物;蜘蛛纲
crustacea *n*. 甲壳纲动物
bug *n*. 小虫，臭虫
vertebrate *n*. 脊椎动物;*adj*. 有椎骨的，有脊椎的
fish *n*. 鱼，鱼类
amphibian *adj*. 两栖类的;*n*. 两栖动物
reptile *n*. 爬虫动物;*adj*. 爬行的，爬虫类的
bird *n*. 鸟，禽
mammal *n*. 哺乳动物
cyclostomata *n*. 环口目
primate *n*. 灵长类的动物
rodent *adj*. 咬的，啮齿目的;*n*. 啮齿动物
livestock *n*. 家畜，牲畜
finch *n*. 雀科鸣禽(如燕雀，金翅雀等)
ruminant *adj*. 反刍动物的;*n*. 反刍动物
parasite *n*. 寄生虫
herbivore *n*. 草食动物
carnivore *n*. 食肉动物
omnivore *n*. 杂食动物
biped *n*. 两足动物
quadruped *n*. 四足动物
scavenger *n*. 食腐动物

predator *n*. 食肉动物，捕食其他动物的动物
carrion *n*. 死肉，腐肉；*adj*. 腐肉的，吃腐肉的
prey *n*. 被捕食的动物
game *n*. 猎物
moose *n*. 驼鹿
antelope *n*. 羚羊
sperm *n*. 鲸油
killer whale *n*. 逆戟鲸，虎鲸
serpent *n*. 蛇(尤指大蛇或毒蛇)
raptor *n*. 猛禽，肉食鸟
dinosaur *n*. 恐龙
tadpole *n*. 蝌蚪

Reproduction 繁殖

reproduction *n*. 繁殖
sexual reproduction 有性生殖
asexual reproduction 无性生殖
egg cell 卵细胞
sperm *n*. 精液，精子
fertilization *n*. 授精；受孕(受精)作用
female *n*. 女性，雌兽；*adj*. 女性的，雌的
hermaphrodite *n*. 具有两性者，两性体；*adj*. 雌雄同体的
breed *v*. 生育，繁殖
mate *n*. 配偶；*v*. 交配
bear *v*. 生(孩子)
hatch *n*./*v*. 孵，孵化
lay *v*. 产(卵)，下蛋
descend *v*. 遗传

Characteristics 特征

precocial *adj*. 早熟性的，生下就有很高程度独立活动能力的
altricial *adj*. 孵出后需母鸟照顾一段时期的，晚成雏的
nocturnal *adj*. 夜出的，夜间活动的
rampant *adj*. (兽类)跳起的，用后腿直立的
ferocious *adj*. 残忍的，凶猛的
aggressive *adj*. 好斗的，攻击性的
cold-blooded *adj*. 冷血的
ambidextrous *adj*. 两只手都很灵巧的
torpid *adj*. 麻痹的，迟钝的；蛰伏的
dormant *adj*. 睡眠状态的，蛰伏的，休眠的
hibernate *v*. 冬眠
aestivate *v*. 夏眠
live off *v*. 靠…为生
inhabit *v*. 居住于，栖息
migrate *v*. 移动，(鸟类的)迁徙
burrow *n*. 洞穴；*v*. 挖地洞
camouflage *v*./*n*. 伪装
capture *v*./*n*. 捕获，捕捉
procure *v*. 获得
swoop *n*./*v*. 突然下降，猛扑
fend *v*. 保护，避开
pant *n*./*v*. 喘气，喘息
claw *n*. 爪，脚爪
paw *n*. 手掌；(动物的)爪子，脚爪
spine *n*. 脊柱，脊椎骨；棘状突起，刺
mane *n*. 鬃毛
proboscis *n*. 鼻子，长鼻
shell *n*. 贝壳，壳
tentacle *n*. (动物)触须，触角
leathery *adj*. 似皮革的，坚韧的
chambered *adj*. 隔成房间的

一般动物学用词

flock *n*. 羊群，(禽、畜等的)群，大量
herd *n*. 兽群，牛群，牧群
lair *n*. 野兽的巢穴，躲藏处
den *n*. 兽穴，洞穴
habitat *n*. (动植物的)生活环境，栖息地
scrap
behavioral *adj*. 动作的，行为的
transparent *adj*. 透明的，透光的
hollow *n*. 洞，窟窿；*adj*. 空的，凹的
pervasive *adj*. 弥漫的，遍布的
bare *adj*. 赤裸的，无遮蔽的
mature *adj*. 成熟的；*v*. 成熟

26 Entomology 昆虫学

Insect 昆虫

termite *n*. 白蚁
leaf-cutter ant 切叶蚁
wasp *n*. 黄蜂
bumblebee *n*. 大黄蜂
honeybee *n*. 蜜蜂
moth *n*. 蛾，蛀虫
tiger moth *n*. 虎蛾，灯蛾
cicada *n*. 蝉
treehopper *n*. 角蝉

mosquito *n*. 蚊子
fly *n*. 苍蝇，两翼昆虫
firefly *n*. 萤火虫
mayfly *n*. 蜉蝣类，飞蝼蛄
dragonfly *n*. 蜻蜓
butterfly *n*. 蝴蝶
grasshopper *n*. 蚱蜢，蝗虫
locust *n*. 蝗虫，蚱蜢
ladybug *n*. 瓢虫
thornbug *n*. 刺椿象
cockroach *n*. 蟑螂
flea *n*. 跳蚤
mite *n*. 小虫，(乳酪上的)蛆；螨类
spider *n*. 蜘蛛
worm *n*. 虫，蠕虫，蚯蚓
centipede *n*. 蜈蚣
beetle *n*. 甲虫

Structure 结构

exoskeleton *n*. 外骨骼
endoskeleton *n*. 内骨骼
shell *n*. 贝壳，壳
sensor *n*. 传感器
compound eye(昆虫的)复眼
antenna *n*. 触角，触须
mandible *n*. 下颚，下颚骨
proboscis *n*. 鼻子，长鼻
abdomen *n*. 腹，腹部
spiracle *n*. (昆虫的)气门
sac *n*. 囊，液囊
gland *n*. 腺
spinneret *n*. (蜘蛛、蚕等的)吐丝器
rear *n*. 屁股

Attack and Defense 攻击和防御

assault *n*./*v*. 攻击，袭击
threat *n*. 威胁，凶兆
destructor *n*. 破坏者
victim *n*. 牺牲者，牺牲品
infestation *n*. (害虫等)群袭，出没
adaptation *n*. 适应
protection *n*. 保护
camouflage *n*./*v*. 伪装
avoidance *n*. 避免
coloration *n*. 染色，着色
warning color 警告(颜)色
sonar *n*. 声纳，声波定位仪
scale *n*. 尺度，刻度；规模，大小
nocturnal *adj*. 夜间发生的，夜间活动的
toxic *adj*. 有毒的，中毒的
inedible *adj*. 不适于食用的，不能吃的
scare off 吓跑，吓退
startle *v*. 震惊
swathe *v*. 绑，裹，包围
shield *v*. 遮蔽；保护，防护
anchor *n*. 锚；*v*. 抛锚，锚定
ensnare *v*. 诱捕
encapsulate *v*. 装入胶囊，压缩

Characteristics 特征

elasticity *n*. 弹力，弹性
viscosity *n*. 粘质，粘性
spiral *adj*. 螺旋形的；*n*. 螺旋
resilient *adj*. 弹回的，有回弹力的
flagelliform *adj*. 鞭状的，细长而柔软的
insectivorous *adj*. 食虫的，食虫动植物的
multiply *v*. 繁殖，增加
mate *n*. 配偶，对手；*v*. 交配
excrete *v*. 排泄，分泌
suck *v*. 吸，吮
feed on *v*. 以…为食

Life Cycle 生活周期

egg *n*. 蛋，鸡蛋，卵
larva *n*. 幼虫
caterpillar *n*. 毛虫
chrysalis *n*. 蛹，茧
pupa *n*. 蛹
pupate *v*. 化蛹
imago *n*. 成虫期，成虫

一般昆虫学用词

colony *n*. 集群，群体
hive *n*. 蜂房，蜂箱
population *n*. 虫口
metamorphosis *n*. 变形
deformed *adj*. 不成形的，丑陋的
misshapen *adj*. 奇形怪状的，畸形的
hollow *n*. 洞；*adj*. 空的
sturdy *adj*. 强健的；*n*. 家畜晕倒病
versatile *adj*. 多方面的，多种的
dwindle *v*. 缩小，减少
eradicate *v*. 根除
degradation *n*. 降级，退化
insecticide *n*. 杀虫剂
parasite *n*. 寄生虫
pest *n*. 害虫，有害动物

segment *n*. 段，节
diameter *n*. 直径
vibration *n*. 振动，摇动
yield *v*. 出产，生产

27 Ecology 生态学

Ecosystem 生态系统

ecological system 生态系统
ecological efficiency 生态效应
biomass *n*.（单位面积或体积内）生物的数量
biodiversity *n*. 生物品种
biosphere *n*. 生物圈
biome *n*.（生态）生物群系
fauna *n*. 动物群，动物志
flora *n*. 植物群，植物志
organism *n*. 生物体，有机体
species *n*. 种类，（原）核素
community *n*.（生物）群落
natural enemy 天敌
habitat *n*.（动植物的）生活环境，产地、栖息地
rain forest *n*. 雨林
permafrost *n*. 永久冻结带
wetland *n*. 潮湿的土壤，沼泽地
watershed *n*. 分水岭
aquatic *adj*. 水的，水生的，水栖的
terrestrial *adj*. 陆地的
woodland *n*. 森林地，林地
alpine *adj*. 高山的，阿尔卑斯山的
valley *n*.（山）谷，流域
endangered *adj*. 有危险的，有灭绝危险的
extinct *adj*. 灭绝的
wildlife *n*. 野生动植物
nekton *n*. 自游生物
omnivore *n*. 不偏食的人
carnivore *n*. 食肉动物，食虫植物
herbivore *n*. 草食动物
vegetation *n*. 植被，（总称）植物
section *n*. 部分，断片，节
span *n*. 跨度，范围
poach *v*. 偷猎
jeopardize *v*. 危害
perish *v*. 毁灭，死亡

Cycle of Material 物质循环

cycle of matetial 物质循环
energy flow 能流
food chain 食物链
food web 食物网
ecological niche 生态龛位，生态位
producer *n*. 生产者
consumer *n*. 消费者
decomposer *n*. 分解体
accumulate *v*. 积聚，堆积
decay *v*. 腐朽，腐烂

一般生态学用词

chemosynthesis *n*. 化学合成
tract *n*.（土地等）的一大片
hectare *n*. 公顷
elevation *n*. 上升，海拔
reservoir *n*. 水库，蓄水池
timber *n*. 木材，木料
deforestation *n*. 采伐森林，森林开伐
desertification *n*. 荒漠化，沙漠化
climatic *adj*. 气候上的
isolated *adj*. 隔离的，孤立的
evolutionary *adj*. 进化的
aboriginal *adj*. 土著的，原来的；*n*. 土著居民
abundant *adj*. 丰富的，充裕的
emerge *v*. 显现，浮现，暴露
advance into 进入到…
intrude *v*. 闯入，侵入
recede *v*. 后退
tarnish *v*. 失去光泽，锈蚀
erode *v*. 侵蚀，腐蚀
enforce *v*. 强迫，加强

28 Engineering 工程学

Electrical Engineering 电气工程

galvanic cell 原电池，自发电池
grounding *n*. 接地
superconductor *n*. 超导（电）体
semiconductor *n*. 半导体

conductor *n*. 导体，导线
conduit *n*. 导线管，(电缆)管道
integrated circuit(IC) 集成电路
leakage *n*. 漏，渗漏
tuning *n*. 调谐
transistor *n*. 晶体管
scramble *v*. 扰频，改变频率
radio *n*. 无线电广播
reception *n*. 接收(力)
transmission *n*. 播送，传输
teleprinter *n*. 电传打字机
insulation *n*. 绝缘
tensile *adj*. 张力的，拉力的
propulsion *n*. 推进，推进力

Chemical Engineering 化学工程

polymer chemistry 高聚物化学
polymer *n*. 聚合体
resin *n*. 树脂
thermosetting resin 热固树胶
rubber *n*. 橡胶
vulcanization *n*. (橡胶的)硫化(过程)
cure *n*. 硫化，固化
accelerator *n*. 加速器
elastic *adj*. 弹性的
pneumatic *adj*. 空气的，气体的
compression *n*. 浓缩，压缩
mold *n*. 结晶器，坩埚
solder *n*. 焊料；*v*. 焊接
laminate *v*. 碾压

一般工程学用词

factory automation (FA) 工厂自动化
abrasion *n*. 磨损
corrosion *n*. 侵蚀，腐蚀状态
obsolete *adj*. 废弃的；过时的
obsolete equipment 陈旧设备
pilot 排障器；操纵器
prototype *n*. 原型
pathfinder *n*. 探险者，开创者
breakthrough *n*. 突破

29 Computer 计算机

Hardware 硬件

CPU(central processing unit) 中央处理器
microprocessor *n*. 微处理器
peripheral device 外围设备
memory unit 存储单元，存储装置
access time *n*. 存取时间
optical memory 光存储器
memory chip 存储器片
mouse *n*. 鼠标
terminal *n*. 终端，接线端
laptop computer 膝上型计算机

Software 软件

freeware *n*. 免费软件
configuration *n*. 构造，配置
operating system 操作系统
retrieval system 检索系统
assembler *n*. 汇编程序
code *n*. 代码，编码
binary code 二进制码
runtime *n*. 运行时间

一般计算机用词

algorithm *n*. 运算法则
volatile *adj*. 易失的(电源切断后信息消失)
compatible *adj*. 一致的，兼容的
realtime 实时
interactive *adj*. 交互式的
portable *adj*. 手提(式)的，便携式的
equivalent *adj*. 相等的，等价的
office automation 办公自动化
throughput *n*. 吞吐量
capacity *n*. 容量，负载量
store up 贮存
microchip *n*. 微芯片
wetware *n*. 湿件

30 Transportation 交通运输

Traffic 交通

public transportation 公共交通
round *n*. 环形路；*v*. 绕弯，绕行
traffic congestion 交通拥堵

traffic jam 交通阻塞
traffic light 红绿灯
isolation *n*. 封锁交通
pedestrian *n*. 步行者；*adj*. 徒步的
traverse *v*. 横越，横向乱走
jaywalk *v*. 擅自穿越马路
derail *v*. 出轨
license plates 牌照
turn signal *n*. (车辆的)转向灯
spare tire *n*. 备用轮胎
puncture *n*. 穿孔，车胎穿孔
maintenance *n*. 维护，保养

Road 公路

thoroughfare *n*. 通路，大道
highway *n*. 高速公路，大路
freeway *n*. 高速公路
expressway *n*. 高速公路
toll road 收费公路
bypass *n*. 旁路
overpass *n*. 天桥，立交桥
underpass *n*. 地下道，高架桥下通道
sidewalk *n*. 人行道
crosswalk *n*. 人行横道
lane *n*. (乡间)小路；航线
alley *n*. 小路，小径
back road 支路，乡间的道路
shortcut *n*. 捷径
detour *n*. 便道，绕路；*v*. 绕路而行
devious *adj*. 偏僻的，曲折的

一般交通用词

carriage *n*. 四轮马车，(铁路)客车厢
wagon *n*. 四轮马车，货车
raft *n*. 筏，救生艇，橡皮船
liner *n*. 班机
charter *v*. 租，包(船、车等)
embark *v*. 上船，上飞机
embargo *n*./ *v*. 禁止出入港口，禁运
manifest *n*. 载货单，旅客名单
freight *n*. 货运；运费
manned *adj*. 有人驾驶的，有人操纵的
convoy *v*. 护航，护送

31 Energy 能源

Energy 能源

alternative energy 代用能源
clean energy 清洁能源
renewable energy 可再生能源
solar energy 太阳能
energy-efficient *adj*. 节约能源的
energy conservation 能源节约
energy consumption 能量消耗
energy resources 能源资源
natural resources 天然资源
electricity *n*. 电，电力
generator *n*. 发电机
nuclear power 核能
power supply 电源，电力供应
power plant (station) 发电厂，发电站
tidal power plant 潮水发电厂
hydroelectric power station 水电站
thermal power station 热电站，火力发电站
thermal *adj*. 热的，热量的
renewable *adj*. 可更新的，可再生的
sustainable *adj*. 足可支撑的，可持续的
enrich *v*. 使丰富，富集化

Fuel 燃料

synthetic fuel 合成燃料
fossil fuel 矿物燃料，化石燃料
gas station 加油站
gaseous *adj*. 气体的，气态的
LPG (Liquefid Petroleum Gas) 液化石油气体
LNG(Liquefied Natural Gas)液化天然气
gasoline *n*. 汽油
diesel *n*. 柴油机，内燃机
petroleum *n*. 石油
kerosene *n*. 煤油
crude oil 原油
oil drilling 石油钻探
oil field 油田
oil refinery 炼油厂
oil-producing country 石油生产国
oil-tanker *n*. 油船，油轮
pipeline *n*. 管道，管线
reserve *n*. 储备(物)，储藏量
reserve power 备用功率，备用动力
reservoir *n*. 水库，蓄水池

一般能源用词

harness *v*. 利用(河流、瀑布等)产生动力(尤指电力)
power *n*. 动力;*v*. 供以动力
drive *n*. 推进力，动力;*v*. 推动、发动(机器等)
exploit *v*. 开发，开采;使用
extract *v*. 提取，榨出
mine *n*. 矿，矿山，矿井;*v*. 开矿，开采
submerge *v*. 浸没，淹没
compress *v*. 压缩，浓缩
deplete *v*. 耗尽，使衰竭
immense *adj*. 广大的，巨大的
formidable *adj*. 强大的，强有力的
inherent *adj*. 固有的，内在的
substantial *adj*. 坚固的，实质的
site-specific 特定地点
unspoiled *adj*. 未损坏的
vulnerable *adj*. 脆弱的，易受损害的
daylight saving time 夏令时
blackout *n*. 灯火管制
chamber *n*. 燃烧室
combustion *n*. 燃烧
internal combustion engine 内燃机
swell *v*. 使膨胀，使增长
maintenance *n*. 维护，维修，保养
quest *n*./*v*. 探索，寻找
byproduct *n*. 副产品
drawback *n*. 困难，障碍

32 Environment 环境

Water Pollution 水污染

BOD(Biochemical Oxygen Demand) 生化需氧量
COD(Chemical Oxygen Ded mand) 化学需氧量
oil spill 漏油
seep *v*. 渗出，渗漏
discharge *v*./*n*. 排出(气体、液体等)，流出
abound in 富于
heavy metal 重金属
lead poisoning 铅中毒
fresh water 淡水
groundwater *n*. 地下水
wastewater *n*. 废水
sewage *n*. 下水道，污水
bleacher *n*. 漂白剂
detergent *n*. 清洁剂，去垢剂
water-soluble 可溶于水的
noxious *adj*. 有害的
untreated *adj*. 未处理的，未加工的
aquatic *adj*. 水的，水生的，水栖的

Air Pollution 空气污染

greenhouse effect 温室效用
global warming 全球气候变暖
ozone hole 臭氧层空洞
emission *n*. 排出物，排放
exhaust *v*./*n*. 排气，排气装置
release *v*./*n*. 释放，放出
diffuse *v*. 漫射，扩散;*adj*. 散开的，弥漫的
photochemical smog 光化烟雾
acid rain 酸雨
aerial *adj*. 生活在空气中的，空气的

Soil Pollution 土壤污染

fertilizer *n*. 肥料(尤指化学肥料)
herbicide *n*. 除草剂
pesticide *n*. 杀虫剂
pest *n*. 害虫
landfill *n*. 垃圾掩埋
garbage *n*. 垃圾，废物
plastic bag 塑料袋
disposable *adj*. 一次性的，用后即可丢弃的
waste disposal 废物处理
toxic waste 有毒废物
industrial waste 工业废弃物
radioactive waste 放射性废物
discard *v*. 丢弃，抛弃;*n*. 废品(物)，废料
absorb *v*. 吸收
ruin *n*. 废墟，遗迹

Pollution 污染

contaminate *v*. 污染
public hazards 公害
pollutant *n*. 污染物质

PCB 多氯联苯
biphenyl *n*. 联苯
biochemical *adj*. 生物化学的
carcinogenic *adj*. 致癌物(质)的
catastrophic *adj*. 悲惨的，灾难的
lethal *adj*. 致命的
detrimental *adj*. 有害的
sick house syndrome 致病建筑综合症

Environmental Protection 环境保护

environmentally-friendly *adj*. 环保的，环保型的
environmental watchdog 环境监察机构
environmentalist *n*. 环境保护论者，环境论者
advocate *n*. 提倡者，拥护者；*v*. 提倡，拥护
conservationist *n*. (天然资源的)保护管理论者
conserve *v*. 保存，保藏
shield *n*. 护罩，盾；*v*. 保护，防护
purify *v*. 使纯净，净化
rescue *v*./*n*. 援救，救助
rebuild *v*. 重建，改造
repair *n*./*v*. 修理，修补，补救
replant *v*. 再植，移植
reprocess *v*. 再加工
recycle *v*./*n*. 再循环，重复利用
recycled paper 再生环保纸
salvage *v*./*n*. 废品回收
reclamation *n*. 改造，(废料等的)收回
reserve *n*./*v*. 储备，保存；保护区
bulwark *n*. 防波堤
reproductive *adj*. 再生的
sustainable *adj*. 可持续的
shortsighted *adj*. 近视的，眼光短浅的
superficial *adj*. 表面的
countermeasure *n*. 对策

一般环境用词

environment *n*. 环境
underpinning *n*. 基础，基础材料
consequence *n*. 结果，后果
depletion *n*. 损耗
peril *n*. 危险
plight *n*. 情况，困境
outbreak *n*. 爆发
vulnerable *adj*. 易受攻击的，脆弱的
inadvertent *adj*. 疏忽的，因疏忽所致的
endangered *adj*. 有危险的
shallow *adj*. 浅的，浅薄的
profound *adj*. 深刻的，意义深远的
tranquil *adj*. 安静的
rooted *adj*. 根深蒂固的
flourishing *adj*. 繁茂的，繁荣的
fertile *adj*. 肥沃的，富饶的

33 Medicine 医学

Body Organs 人体器官

respiratory organ 呼吸器官
circulatory organ 循环器官
cerebrum *n*. 大脑
cerebellum *n*. 小脑
cranium *n*. 头盖，头盖骨
marrow *n*. 髓，骨髓
spinal cord *n*. 脊髓
nostril *n*. 鼻孔
esophagus *n*. 食道
bronchus *n*. 支气管
breast *n*. 胸部，乳房
abdomen *n*. 腹，腹部
aorta *n*. 大动脉
artery *n*. 动脉
pancreas *n*. 胰腺
intestine *n*. 肠
liver *n*. 肝脏
kidney *n*. 肾
ovary *n*. (生物)卵巢
limb *n*. (四)肢，手足
joint *n*. 关节
epidermis *n*. 表皮，上皮
chromosome *n*. 染色体
nerve *n*. 神经
tissue *n*. 组织
membrane *n*. 膜，隔膜

Disease 疾病

germ *n*. 细菌
carrier *n*. 带菌者
immunity *n*. 免疫性
HIV (Human Immunodeficiency Virus) 艾滋病病毒
antibody *n*. 抗体

acute *adj*. 急性的
lethal *adj*. 致命的
progressive *adj*. 进行性的
hereditary *adj*. 遗传的
contagious *adj*. 传染性的，会感染的
epidemic *adj*. 流行的，传染的；*n*. 时疫，流行病
latency period 潜伏期
stroke *n*. (疾病)突然发作，中风
paralysis *n*. 瘫痪，麻痹
dementia *n*. 痴呆
cardiac *n*. 强心剂
heart attack 心脏病发作
high blood pressure 高血压(症)
influenza *n*. 流行性感冒
sore throat *n*. 喉咙痛
sore *adj*. 疼痛的
asthma *n*. 哮喘
tuberculosis *n*. 肺结核
pneumonia *n*. 肺炎
leukemia *n*. 白血病
breast cancer *n*. 乳癌
diabetes *n*. 糖尿病，多尿症
gastric ulcer *n*. 胃溃疡
hepatitis *n*. 肝炎
arthritis *n*. 关节炎
neuralgia *n*. 神经痛
bruise *n*. 瘀伤，擦伤
measles *n*. 麻疹，风疹
smallpox *n*. 天花
polio *n*. 脑灰质炎，小儿麻痹症
cataract *n*. 白内障
hyperopia *n*. 远视
athlete's foot *n*. 脚癣，脚气
intoxication .n 中毒
drug addiction 吸毒成瘾，药瘾
hallucination *n*. 幻觉，幻想
hypnosis *n*. 催眠状态，催眠
mental illness 精神病
trauma *n*. 外伤，损伤；精神创伤
amnesia *n*. 健忘症
insomnia *n*. 失眠，失眠症
phobia *n*. 恐怖病，恐惧症
obsession *n*. 强迫症
neurosis *n*. 神经症，神经衰弱症
anorexia *n*. 食欲减退，厌食
bulimia *n*. 易饿病
depression *n*. 抑郁症
manic depression 躁郁症

Symptom 症状

onset *n*. 发作
fit *n*. 突然发作，痉挛
anemia *n*. 贫血，贫血症
vertigo *n*. 眩晕
dizzy *adj*. 晕眩的
syncope *n*. 昏厥
nausea *n*. 反胃，恶心
dyspepsia *n*. 消化不良
constipation *n*. 便秘
diarrhea *n*. 痢疾，腹泻
excrement *n*. 排泄物，大便
sperm *n*. 精液，精子
saliva *n*. 口水，唾液
sputum *n*. 唾液，痰
sneeze *n*. 喷嚏；*v*. 打喷嚏
choke *v*. 窒息，哽住
side effect (药物等的)副作用
aftereffect *n*. 副作用

Treatment 治疗

remedy *n*. 药物；治疗法
heal *v*. 治愈，医治
recuperate *v*. 复原
panacea *n*. 万能药
inoculate *v*. 预防注射，接种疫苗
vaccination *n*. 接种疫苗，种痘
alleviate *v*. 使(痛苦等)减轻
palliate *v*. 减轻，缓和(疾病、痛苦等)
soothe *v*. 使(痛苦，疼痛)缓和或减轻
pain reliever 镇痛药
tranquilizer *n*. 镇定剂
disinfect *v*. 消毒
antiseptic *adj*. 杀菌的，消过毒的；*n*. 杀菌剂
toxic *adj*. 有毒的，中毒的
antidote *n*. 解毒剂
administer *v*. 给药，用药
ointment *n*. 药膏
antibiotic *n*. 抗生素
antioxidant *n*. 抗氧化剂
prescription *n*. 处方，药方
dose *n*. 剂量，(一)剂，(一)服
pharmaceutical *n*. 药物；*adj*. 制药(学)上的

Hospital 医院

surgeon *n*. 外科医生

physician *n*. 医师，内科医师
nursing staff 护理人员
ward *n*. 病房
stethoscope *n*. 听诊器
diagnose *v*. 诊断
medical certificate *n*. 健康证明；诊断书
endoscopy *n*. 内窥镜检查法
early detection of cancer 癌症的早期发现
recurrence *n*. 复发
surgical instruments 外科器械
bleeding *n*. 出血，流血
coagulation *n*. 凝结，血凝固
transfusion *n*. 输血，输液
transplantation *n*. 移植(术)
anesthesia *n*. 麻醉
coma *n*. 昏迷
vegetable *n*. 植物人
cerebral death 脑死亡
euthanasia *n*. 安乐死

一般医学和健康用词

internal medicine 内科医学
surgery *n*. 外科，外科学；手术室
plastic surgery 整形手术，整形外科
orthopedics *n*. 矫形术
dermatology *n*. 皮肤医学，皮肤病学
ophthalmology *n*. 眼科学
otolaryngology *n*. 耳鼻喉学
obstetrics and *n*. 妇产科
gynecology *n*. 妇科医学
pediatrics *n*. 小儿科
psychiatry *n*. 精神病学，精神病治疗法
anatomy *n*. 解剖学
hygiene *n*. 卫生，卫生学
sanitary *adj*. (有关)卫生的
corporal *adj*. 肉体的，身体的
feeble *adj*. 虚弱的，无力的
meager *adj*. 瘦的(人体部分)
malnutrition *n*. 营养不良
obesity *n*. 肥胖
regimen *n*. 食物疗法；养生法
diet therapy 饮食疗法
vegetarian *n*. 素食者
strain *n*. 过度的疲劳，紧张；(身体的)扭伤，拉伤
barren *adj*. 不生育的，不孕的
pregnancy *n*. 怀孕
miscarriage *n*. 流产
delivery *n*. 分娩
sterilization operation 节育手术
contraceptive (pill) *n*. 避孕药
complexion *n*. 面色，气色
afflict *v*. 使痛苦，折磨
exacerbate *v*. 恶化
incapacitate *v*. 使无能力，使不能